de Gruyter Studies in Organization 17

Organization Theory and Class Analysis

de Gruyter Studies in Organization

An international series by internationally known authors presenting current fields of resarch in organization.

Organizing and organizations are substantial pre-requisites for the viability and future developments of society. Their study and comprehension are indispensable to the quality of human life. Therefore, the series aim to:

– offer to the specialist work material in form of the most important and current problems, methods and results;
– give interested readers access to different subject areas;
– provide aids for decisions on contemporary problems and stimulate ideas.

The series includes monographs, collections of contributed papers, and handbooks.

Organization Theory and Class Analysis

New Approaches and New Issues

Editor: Stewart R. Clegg

Walter de Gruyter · Berlin · New York 1990

Editor
Stewart R. Clegg
Professor of Sociology
Head of the Dept. of Sociology
The University of New England
Armidale N.S.W. 2351
Australia

Library of Congress Cataloging - in - Publication Data

> Organization theory and class analysis : new approaches and new issues /
> editor, Stewart R. Clegg.
>   p. cm. -- (De Gruyter studies in organization ; 17)
>   "In July 1987 the contributions represented in this volume were the focus of
> discussion in a session of the EGOS (European Group for Organizational
> Studies) colloquium" -- Pref.
>   Includes bibliographical references.
>   ISBN 0-89925-567-1 (U.S. : alk. paper)
>   1. Industrial sociology--Congresses. 2. Division of labor--Congresses. 3. Or-
> ganization--Congresses. 4. Social classes--Congresses. 5. Socialism--Congres-
> ses. I. Clegg, Stewart. II. European Group for Organizational Studies.
> III. Series.
> HD6952.O74 1989
> 306.3'6--dc20   89-23778
>   CIP

Deutsche Bibliothek Cataloging in Publication Data

> **Organization theory and class analysis** : new approaches and new issues / ed.:
> Stewart R. Clegg. – Berlin ; New York : de Gruyter, 1989
>   (De Gruyter studies in organization ; 17)
>   ISBN 3-11-012003-8
> NE: Clegg, Stewart R. [Hrsg.]; GT

♾ Printed on acid free paper.

Typesetting and Printing: Buch- und Offsetdruckerei Wagner GmbH, Nördlingen
Binding: Lüderitz & Bauer Buchgewerbe GmbH, Berlin
Cover Design: Johannes Rother, Berlin

Preface

In July 1987 the contributions represented in this volume were the focus of discussion in a session of the EGOS (European Group for Organization Studies) Colloquim on 'Technology as the Two-Edged Sword of Technical Chance.' As will be evident from the contributions, most participants in the session responded rather more to the sessional theme of 'Theoretical and Empirical Linkages Between Organization Theory and Class Theory' than they did to the issue of technological change.

It seemed at the time of the colloquim that the papers presented achieved a degree of thematic continuity which was well developed. This is even more evident from the edited and revised papers included here. It is for this reason that in the introduction to the volume. 'Organization Theory and Class Analysis' above all, I have tried to tell the story that each chapter has to offer, to introduce the themes and issues of each chapter, and to point to the continuities and discontinuities which exist between them, so that the readers will be able to infer for themselves from the introduction whether a particular chapter addresses their interests.

I would like to take the opportunity to use this preface to make some acknowledgements. In particular, I must acknowledge the responsiveness of the contributors to the volume to the many communications which issued from Armidale at frequent interals. Without the efficient support of Trish Marshall this appearance of rational planning and efficiency would have been impossible to sustain. The Department of Sociology at the University of New England offered material support which facilitated the difficult task of organizing a northern hemisphere conference from the southern hemisphere and I would like to acknowledge that help. More generally, Janet Batchler of the Faculty of Arts has done a cheerful and efficient job of translating my 2B pencilled strokes into neat word processed copy, as have Trish Marshall and Rosyln Mortimer. In West Yorkshire, David Hickson, Lawrence and Alma Bowker were, as ever, considerate and facilitative. In Antwerp, Albert Mok, Kristine De Decker, Mia Phillips and Luc Peters made everything run smoothly. Lynne and Jonathon helped everywhere, as William has more recently. Finally, Bianka Ralle, the editor-in-chief of Walter de Gruyter with whom I have dealt, has been one of the most efficient publishers with whom one could wish to deal. Responsibility for the volume remains with myself and the contributors alone: none of these good people or institutions are responsible for anything to do with the book other than their help in seeing it this far. From now, the responsibility rests here.

Armidale, August 1989   Stewart Clegg

Contents

Between Rational Choice and Durkheimian Solidarity
Frans Kerstholt

"New" Social Inequalities and the Renewal of the Theory of Social Inequalities
Reinhard Kreckel

Classes, Collectivities and Corporate Actors
Barry Hindess

II. Management in Class and Organization Structures

Ownership and Management Strategy
Glen Morgan

International Management and the Class Structure
Jane Marceau

Managers and Social Classes
Harri Melin

Technical Workers: A Class and Organisational Analysis
Chris Smith

III. Class Restructuring and Organizations

Disorganised Capitalism and Social Class
John Urry

Managing the Multinationals: The Emerging Theory of the Multinational
Enterprise and Its Implications for Labour Resistance
Harvie Ramsay and Nigel Haworth

Work Organization Under Technological Change: Sources of Differentiation and the Reproduction of Social Inequality in Processes of Change
Wolfgang Littek and Ulrich Heisig

The New Rise of Self-Employment and Industrial Structure
Timo Toivonen

IV. The Labour Process, Class Structure and Gender

Exploring the Class and Organisational Implications of the UK Financial
Services
David Knights and Hugh Willmott

Organization and Class: Burawoy in Birmingham
Dennis Smith

The Class/Gender/Organization Nexus
Rosemary Crompton

Masculine/Feminine Organization: Class versus
Gender in Swedish Unions
Alison E. Woodward and Håkon Leiulfsrud

Contents XIII

V. Classless Organizations?

Between Class Analysis and Organization Theory: Mental Labour
Guglielmo Carchedi

Against the Current: Organizational Sociology and Socialism
Stewart R. Clegg and Winton Higgins

Political Domination and Reproduction of Classless Organizations
Amir Ben-Porat

Socialised Industry: Social Ownership or Shareholding Democracy?
Tom Clarke

Sociologies of Class and Organization

Stewart R. Clegg

1. Introduction

In the European traditions of sociology which centre on the classical forebears of Marx, Weber and Durkheim, issues of social class could not be avoided: for each theorist, one of the most significant features of modernity which required address was the structural transformation that emergent forms of modern organization were wreaking to the more settled communities and economies of pre-industrial society. Of course, each theorist had different concerns and conceptions associated with these changes, but the important thing is that for each of them social relations in and of production were central to their concern with "organization" as a keynote of modernity.

When the modern sociology of organizations began to establish itself, initially around the work of theorists of management (Pugh, Hickson and Hinings 1964) and subsequently around the concerns with "bureaucracy" of Merton and his colleagues at Columbia in the period after the Second World War, it was primarily through the Weberian corpus that obeisance was made to the classical tradition. Oddly, however, perhaps under the assumption that issues of class in Weber were easily dissociated from his concerns with the sociology of bureaucracy and of economic life in general (which contemporary interpretations such as those of Turner (1981) would caution against), the issues of class analysis came increasingly to be a separate enterprise to those of organizational analysis. Indeed, class analysis itself seemed perilously near to extinction at the hands of a more general and multi-dimensional concern with stratification rather than class. In organizational analysis, residual concerns with issues of stratification or class were more often than not to be left primarily to specialists in industrial sociology or industrial relations. Although a schematic representation, this picture would be familiar to those people who came to organization theory in the 1960s.

The picture changed rapidly. The re-appraisal of Marx and Marxian themes which exploded in the late 1960s in sociology seemed destined to create ripples in almost every substantive sociological field, and the sociology of organizations was no exception. By the late 1970s and early 1980s there was a plethora of work in the field looking at issues such as "class and control" or "the organization and control of the labour process" (Clegg and Dunkerly (1980) comes to mind). Despite the strenuous objections of some defenders of a more orthodox conception of Organization Theory (Donaldson 1985) from which the classical sociological concern with social relations in/of production has been largely expunged in favour of a focus on "organizational design," the stem of organizational sociology had delivered a great many distinct strains to the more general field of organization analysis. Included in these are those who still persist in the concern with class relations and organization control or design as the inextricable core of any analysis of central features of modernity: the increasingly complex organizations which contain work and social life more generally.

A large part of the impetus to recognize the importance of class analysis was clearly politically driven. In Europe a number of Marxist intellectuals in the 1960s and 1970s were constructing a systematic structural analysis of class to both remedy a crucial lacuna in Marx's own work and to provide some pointers for Marxist political action. The work of Poulantzas (1975), in particular, belongs to this tendency, as do the analyses of Carchedi (1977) (whose recent work is represented in this volume).

The highly theoretical and abstract work by European Marxists such as Poulantzas and Carchedi was concerned primarily to update the categories and logic of class analysis to deal with the far more complex organizational world of the late twentieth century, compared to the rather simple small family factories of the mid-nineteenth century. For such a world as prevailed then, a basically binary characterization of organizational relations as either property owning and controlling or ownerless and controlled, might have seemed sufficient for most eventualities of description, particularly where a rhetorical purpose could be discerned. However, such a "simple abstract model" was in fact hardly adequate, even in the mid-nineteenth century, as Marx recognized (see the account of his "three models" in Clegg, Boreham and Dow 1986, chapter two). It increasingly became less so as the nature of changing organization relations undercut all its assumptions: the development of public as well as private ownership; the separation of financial property ownership from effective financial control; the separation of financial control from actual control of day-to-day organization, and, as organizations outgrew the unity of personal surveillance and direct control, the development of both more abstract, impersonal and routinized controls as well as more personal incentives. Thus, given the renaissance of Marxist analysis in the social sciences in the 1960s and 1970s, the crucial task which writers like Carchedi and Poulantzas posed for themselves was to develop a more complex, abstract model for doing class analysis, one which was still recognizably Marxian but which was also capable of addressing contemporary organization reality (see Johnson 1975, for a sympathetic critique of how the task was approached).

One point should be observed at this stage in the introduction. It has been suggested thus far that the concerns of class analysis were largely evacuated from the arena of organization analysis, as this had developed by the early 1970s. To be even-handed it is just as important to note that in the renaissance of class analysis which occurred with Poulantzas' (1975) and Carchedi's (1977) initial contributions, the very important inputs that should have been derived from the sociology of organizations concerning the empirical delineation of this changed organization reality were equally absent. Two fields of class and organization analysis, which had been as one in Marx's and Weber's concerns, respectively with the labour process and the sociology of economic life, had become professionally and intellectually differentiated to a very large degree.

Rapprôchment between class and organization analysis has not been entirely absent. Both Carchedi (1977) and Wright (1978) drew upon Braverman's (1974) return to Marx's (1976) focus on the labour process and the "labour process debate" is by now well established. However, the majority of recent labour process studies have been conducted as case studies, recalling an earlier industrial anthropology in method, while the case study has for some years now hardly been the most favoured method of organization analysis. Indeed, there is considerable formal similarity between some of the leading studies in empirical organization analysis, such as the structural work of the Aston school, and the structural and empirical class analysis of Wright (1985) and the projects associated with his enterprise. Both work on empirically delineating dimensions of structure initially grounded, in rationalist terms, in a less empirical, sometimes more prescriptive, and certainly more wide-ranging literature. Both produce structural "maps" of the presumed "real" structures of class and organizations, and both use modern multivariate methods to do so. Moreover, both collect data on organization and work design, decision making, centralization of authority, autonomy and control. Yet there has been little effective interchange between the projects on class structure and those on organization structure.

The reasons for this lack of interchange are complex, but one is apparent; due to the differentiation and specialization of knowledge in substantive fields of sociology (let alone between it and young pretenders such as organization analysis and class analysis), there existed little objective opportunity for intellectual traffic. The conduits did not exist, or if they did, they were rarely used. While the density of traffic may be an intellectual market judgement, it may also reflect trained incapacity and indifference bread from the bliss of highly specialized training, as well as the "knowledge interests" of the respective fields.

The chapters represented in this volume were commissioned by way of a response, in the form of preparatory bridge-work, to reconnecting these by now differentiated sub-specialisms. As a strategy, of course, it has an evident weakness: if the situation is differentiated to the extent suggested, and there are many independent labourers commissioned to design a bridge, more than one crossing, of more than one design, is likely to eventuate. As the reader of this volume will discover, this is in fact the case. However, rather than viewing the fertility of the exercise as a weakness one might be tempted to regard it as a strength: in a situation of competitive marketing of similar but differentiated intellectual products, both Lakatos (1970) and neo-classical economics more generally suggest that only the strong seed, sewn in the most fertile ground, will survive. Such a volume as this may well serve as a ground-preparing exercise.

2. Classes, Structures and Actors

General theories of class and class structure are a mainstay of sociology (for example, Carchedi 1977; Carchedi 1987; Giddens 1973; Parkin 1979; Poulantzas 1975; Wright 1978; Wright 1985). Typically, they have been dichotomously generated around either a Marxist or Weberian axis. Few attempts at such general theory have tried to systematically link class structures with organization structures and the actors who comprise them. While some exceptions exist, they have not gone in for systematic empirical explanation couched in these terms, but have tended to more macro-levels of theorizing (for example, Clegg and Dunkerley 1980; Clegg et al. 1986).

Broad paradigmatic differences between Marxist and Weberian approaches to class are identified by Val Burris' chapter "Classes in Contemporary Capitalist Society: Recent Marxist and Weberian Perspectives." Marxist approaches to what he takes to be the central issue in recent debate, the problem of conceptualizing salaried intermediate classes, are, he suggests, characterized by an emphasis on objective structures of social positions, production relations, on fundamental class conflict occasioned by a struggle over economic exploitation, and by a prioritization of class as the major social cleavage. Weberians, by contrast, he suggests, regard class as an effect of social action, as a market phenomena, as an asymmetry of power and authority and as just one of several potential bases of social cleavage. Despite these different emphases, an increasing isomorphism between Marxist and Weberian accounts is detected by Burris. Consequently, it is important to identify those debates that transcend the paradigmatic emphases and which preoccupy both Marxist and Weberian proponents.

The central debate transcending "paradigmatic boundaries" is that over the identity and analysis of those intermediate class positions between "labour" and "capital". Burris identifies five basic strategies available for addressing this central debate from proponents of both camps: intermediate class positions may be differentiated from working class positions on the basis of the following: manual vs. non-manual occupations (Giddens and Poulantzas); supervisors vs. non-supervisors (Dahrendorf and Carchedi); productive vs. unproductive labour (Collins and Poulantzas); professionals and managers vs. routine employees (Goldthorpe and the Ehrenreich's); credentialled vs. uncredentialled workers (Parkin vs. Wright). As Burris demonstrates by critically constrasting the first named Weberian position with the second named Marxist position, there are more or less coherent arguments for adopting one position or the other in these five debates.

When confronted by contrasting coherence in intellectually debated and diametrically opposed positions, the exposure of these positions more or less implicit hypotheses to the available data on which they may be tested is advisable. Burris does this by looking at the extent to which the different theories of class structure correspond to cleavages in the pattern of political opinion, as this is displayed in readily available survey material. Given that a preponderant interest in class structure has always been concerned with the extent to which various models of it can better predict dependent variables such as income or attitudes, then this procedure is a sound one to follow. Using a technique known as "dichotomous cluster analysis," Burris demonstrates that from the five strategies identified, three seem to be consistently more useful for empirical analysis of this kind. These are models that distinguish on the basis of supervision vs. non-supervision; credentials vs. non-credentials; and the distinction between professionals and managers contrasted with routine employees. Burris' chapter concludes with a discussion of the strengths of each of these models as predictors of various dependent variables surveyed, and with a plea for future work to explicitly transcend the Weberian/Marxist divide by strategically theorizing the interaction between production relations and market relations. I would add the observation that to do this adequately would also mean attrempting to break down the divide between organization and class analysis, by re-situating the analytical enterprise as an investigation of social relations within labour, capital and product markets as these intersect within concrete organizations, rather than dealing with the abstraction of these involved in national household surveys and the aggregation of individual (rather than organizational) data which this entails.

With the development of recent approaches to "analytical Marxism," which explicitly attempt to ground class analysis in actors' rational choices, it has seemed to some empirically yet Marxist minded sociologists that a nexus between class structure, questions of organizational asset or resource control, and actors' rational choices is capable of resolving some vexed issues of the central sociological concern with class. The prime mover in this regard is the major comparative research effort associated with the "Comparative Project on Class Structure and Class Consciousness," a project developed by Erik Olin Wright.

In their contribution "Analytical Marxism and Class Theory," Raimo Blom and Markku Kivinen, who are members of the Finnish research team engaged in the "comparative class project," introduce us to much of the terrain of recent Marxist debate in the decade since Poulantzas, Braverman and Carchedi first reinvigorated it. Chief amongst the protagonists in moving this debate forward has been the work of Wright (particularly his 1985 book, *Classes*). In their contribution to this volume Blom and Kivinen engage the suppositions of this "analytical Marxism," and in so doing provide a guide to some of the central issues which have structured recent debate in class analysis, concerning the "problem of the middle class" – those organizational agents whose structural position is most ambiguous for Marxist analysis.

It was Wright who popularized the phrase "contradictory class locations" to describe the structural location of certain "middle" class positions within organizational relations concerned with control and supervision of labour power and resource allocation. On the conventional binary criteria of ownership and control opposed to non-ownership and non-control, deployed as a conceptual mechanism for identifying class location, these positions were inexplicable; they occupied a void, a space unmapped by such elegantly simple abstractions. In his earlier work Wright (1978) offered one resolution of this absence; in his subsequent study of *Classes* (1985) he was to offer both a critique of this earlier solution to the problem of the middle classes and a fresh resolution of it.

Wrights earlier solution was to regard middle class positions as located in the grip of contradictory "real interests"; those of both the bourgeoisie and the working class. In his revised version he is still prepared to concede that managers may have relational properties of both non-ownership and controlling locations in the constitutions of their own positions. However, the position of managers as non-owners who exercise control hardly exhausts the range of class positions which are neither unambiguously bourgeois nor ineradicably proletarian. On the one hand, there are petty-bourgeois positions, which Wright regarded as "survivors" of earlier modes of production (a conception which hardly does the range of petty-bourgeois enterprise full justice: see Clegg et al. 1986, chapter four). On the other hand, there are those "semi-autonomous" employees who are subject to little or no direct-control, control no one themselves, but are still employees. Part of the problem with the categorization of semi-autonomous employees is too great a conceptual coupling of control to personal surveillance as its effective mechanism, a problem which is evident in Braverman's (1974) work. Wright (1985) extends this point further by noting that his earlier work (Wright 1978) centred not, as he believes a Marxist should, on exploitation but on domination. It is this "error" which his "Wright Mark II" commitment to analytical Marxism is designed to address.

The resources for resolving the exploitation problem are found by Wright (1985) in the economist John Roemer's (1982) work, in which he formulates hypothetical games which organization members might participate in under the conditions of different modes of production. Exploitation will occur in games constructed on the basis of unequal resource distribution of productive assets; those who would be worse off if they withdrew from the game are exploiting, because economically oppressing, those whose interests would not be diminished by withdrawal.

By using the notion of there being assets in not only means of production, but also in organization control and in the possession of scarce skills, Wright (1985) extends the binary map of classes formed on simple property owning control to a complex set of twelve class locations, in which various kinds of managers, supervisors and experts are defined in the places previously occupied by contradictory class locations.

Blom and Kivinen take issue with Wright's (1985) "twelve-class" model by noting how it loses the historical dimension of his earlier work (1978), and how that earlier work itself represented a better response, by their criteria, to certain problems inherent in Braverman's (1974) labour process approach, than the parallel European debates which centred on German contributions to the "capital logic" school (see Holloway and Piccioto 1978). While Wright (1985) rejects the labour process approach to conceptualizing classes, they argue, he has implicitly adopted a "distributional" rather than "production" centred view of exploitation. In the Marxist lexicon this is a case of "one step forward, two steps back." Like Carchedi (1977; 1987), they would insist on a view of classes grounded in actual relations of and in production, the organization and control of the labour process, relations centred on a dialectic of autonomy and control.

Consideration of concrete instances of organization and control of the labour process clearly signals that there are additional forms of autonomy to those simply predicated on a zero sum game of capital control and labour resistance. Of particular importance are those connected with the employment of professionals in organizations and the way in which claims to "tacit knowledge" and "indetermination," based on professionalization, function to construct the "new middle classes" (see Boreham 1983; Clegg et al. 1986). However, professional employment in complex organizations is not the only source of organizational autonomy claims, as Blom and Kivinen outline. Moreover, some of these sources of autonomy are not so much premised on resistance to capital, but are "capital adequate": that is they are not contradictory but are indeed "given" as part of managerial strategy.

On the basis of this more complex conceptualization of autonomy they are able to define various sorts of mental labour on the basis of particular power resources which enter into the structuration of class situation and class consciousness, which they test on Finnish data. Mental labour based on capital, professional, scientific-technical and managerial autonomies are what they regard as the *équipage* of the core of the new middle class; twenty-five per cent of employees in Finland would enter into this category, which they propose is a more coherent construction than that which can be arrived at via either of Wright's analyses. Against his core conceptual mechanism of "given interests" they propose that interests can only be defined on the basis of different collective power resources and strategies, which must in part be organizationally located, having reference to both organization, labour, capital and product market conditions. (This aspect remains underdeveloped but implicit in their chapter.) These will change as the historical processes of the capitalist mode of production change, a historical dimension lacking in Wright's (1985) revised "analytical Marxism." Consequently, they argue, there is no theory of capitalism in analytical Marxism, nor, given the methodological individualism of its premises, they suggest, is there room for one. In this respect, as their excursus on Weber suggests, the latter is in a better position to grasp the relationship between class action and social change than are the analytical Marxists. The theoretical way forward, they suggest, is to return to the revised version of labour process theory which they propose, with its multiple and complex notion of autonomy.

Certainly, in terms of building bridges between organization and class analysis, there is much to recommend this revised route from Wright's (1978) earlier work. Different types of organizations will differ in the autonomous niche-space opportunities that they present for skilful members to turn to their advantage. Moreover, these opportunities for autonomy will have to be seen in terms broader than individual organizations, because of the role that extra-organizational resources can play in entering into class action within specific organizations. However, these theories remain to be explored elsewhere than in this complex critique of one of the most influential strands of contemporary social science analysis.

Most of the running in recent debates concering class analysis has been made by arguments with clear Weberian or Marxian lineage, to such an extent that the previously dominant status-attainment model of functionalist sociology has been virtually eclipsed in its pure "status" form, as researchers have had increasing recourse to "class" variables as well as those of "status attainment". (Robinson and Kelley 1979). The same renaissance of "class" based explanation is also evident in studies of social mobility (Goldthorpe, Llewellyn and Payne 1980).

The important issue in class analysis, as we have already seen, is the question of which variety of Marxian or Weberian theory is embraced by a given theorist and which is most useful for particular empirical exercises in explanation. Frans Kerstholt, in his chapter "Between Rational Choice and Durkheimian Solidarity," proposes that Weberian class theory is best regarded as an improved Marxist theory, improved because it is stripped of the "metaphysics" of Marxism's commitment to the labour theory of value and the economic determinism which in the past has so often characterized Marxist work. Its claims to be "Marxist" theory are seemingly more empirical than theoretical: research by Weberians such as Goldthorpe consistently demonstrates the applicability of some Marxist precepts but through non-Marxist presuppositions.

Amongst the most important of recent Weberian contributions has been Parkin's (1979) defence of "bourgeois" theory. Kerstholt notes how Parkin's position, with its stress on the social organization of collective strategic action, connects with the concerns of "analytical" or "rational choice" Marxism. In addition, some interpretations of Weber (Ingham 1970) also reformulate his approach in terms which can be explicitly united with rational choice theory.

While Wright (1985) has regarded his earlier theory (Wright 1978) as implicitly more Weberian than Marxian, when comparison is made in terms of the theoretical relative weight of "domination" (a Weberian theme) or "exploitation" (a Marxian theme), Kerstholt would argue that in fact the rational choice Marxism of the later work is closer to a Weberian theory of social inequality, as this would be specified from the "new" interpretation of Weber which rational choice theory provided. This new rational choice theory remains too methodologically individualist, however. It offers no purchase on the organization and formation of collective action. Consequently, it requires supplementation with an explicit focus on both "the logic of collective action" and the Durkheimian theory of the formation of solidary groups through rituals. From these perspectives, he maintains, the micro-foundations of collective and organization properties can be generated. Rationally operating collective actors will arise through at least two mechanisms: those of Durkheimian ritual solidarity and those of rational solutions to the "prisoners" dilemma as it has been posed by Olson (1965).

While the contributions by Burris, Blom and Kivinen and Kerstholt all propose new ways of breathing life back into the classical corpus of sociology's concerns with class, the remaining papers in Part One are altogether more sceptical about the wisdom of such an exercise. As Kreckel begins his contribution "'New' Social Inequalities and the Renewal of the Theory of Social Inequalities,' his "opening assumption [. . .] is that classical theories of social inequality have lost a good deal of their explanatory power, as well as of their political relevancy and plausibility in everyday discourse." Such classical theories, he suggests, are no longer in tune with the changed circumstances of the present. The historical conditions which initially sustained them have been transformed. This is true, he argues, for not only Marxist but also non- and anti-Marxist perspectives, because of their common framework of assumptions, of which three are singled out. These are an assumption, first, of "vertical" inequality; second, that these hierarchical inequalities occur within specific "solitary" societies; third, that the social relations of work or production should be conceived as the basis of social inequality.

Assumptions of the essential nature of "work society" are necessarily based on the reality of only a minority of a given population: all categories of officially defined economically inactive persons are omitted. Consequently, theorists such as Gorz (1982) would redefine the central conflict as occurring not within relations of production, but between those who are already contained within these relations and those who are only marginally, peripherally involved, or excluded altogether from paid work. On the one hand, this produces a process in which employment in organizations, whose conditions and contracts of employment mediate between the capital market and the labour market, becomes more important for analysis. The reason for this is that nearly all paid work has become organizationally located and these organizations are now, in Giddens' (1973) terms, the major loci of "proximate" structuration of social inequalities within and between categories of labour and capital. On the other hand, to the extent that elements of the costs of social reproduction have been re-located into the public sphere, then an additional major source of distributive inequalities emerges with the formation of more or less stable "welfare classes", dependent on political dictate, collective provision and organizational delivery of various "public" goods and services.

Traditionally, the costs of social reproduction have been loated in households, carried by women. This is subvention both to male labour and for capital, inasmuch as some of the reproduction costs of the present and next generation of workers are privatized. It is no longer the case that sociology can ignore this massive area of unseen, unpaid domestic work, with its inequalities marking not only those women who do not participate in the "formal" economy but also those who do. The women's liberation movement has highlighted one important aspect of the "informal" economy; other components of participants in this "unofficial" world of work should also be counted amongst those marginalized by a classical conception of class relations or social inequality.

Consideration of informal economic actors and of non-formal economic actors must be made, suggests Kreckel, alongside other sources of inequality not rooted in production relations. Amongst these are inequalities arising from citizenship and non-citizenship rights, from disparate identities sustained in civil society, form regional disparities. All these, taken together, weaken the notion that inequalities are necessarily and most importantly vertical. They may be far more pluralistic than this model allows: sexual and ethnic discrimination, for instance, is organized and experienced not only through work, but also through leisure, housing access and so on. Regional inequalities not only occur within nations; they also occur between them. Consequently, Kreckel maintains, it may be insufficient to take a single administrative entity, the nation state, as a focus for analysis. The "new international division of labour" requires consideration of the role of "external hinterlands" of labour for core nation states in the world economy; these states have relations of inequality between them at a global, structural level.

The vertical image of social inequality is historically well embedded, as much because forms of hierarchical organization in the shape of bureaucracies are so constitutive of our experience of what social reality is. Metaphorically, this dominance has been the reason why non-vertical forms of social inequality have evaded adequate conceptualization in terms which are also cognizant of "vertical" sources of stratification, but which do not theoretically prioritize or privilege these vis-à-vis other, implicitly, more residual categories. As candidate for such an alternate metaporical role he proposes the notions of centre-periphery.

Images of centre and perpiphery are able to contain the central idea that social inequality is always rooted in relations which constitute asymmetrically structured fields of power. Power relations and forces are more concentrated towards the centre and more dispersed at the periphery, by definition. Such a model, it is proposed by Kreckel, has the scope to be more multi-dimensional than the single vertical axis allows. At the least it should entail an end to those practices whereby male nationals, who are employed within a given administrative entity, form the only social reality in which inequalities occur. Instead, research strategies should, as a matter of theoretical orientation, focus on "peripheral situations," those settings and locations of structural disadvantage in which the disorganization of both action and consciousness will tend to be maximized because the available power resources are largely elsewhere. Of course, any specific centre-periphery relations form a dynamic and shifting field of force when viewed globally: the centre and the periphery will be such in terms which are always relative, both to issues of spatial and social location.

Kreckel's analysis would admit a complex plurality of social actors to the conceptual arena: men and women having religious, ethnic, sexual, national identities; occupying positions in fields of force constituted by spatial relations, production relations, welfare relations and so on. It is not clear that these actors would be "classes," however, as in the Marxist tradition of vertical analysis. Kreckel affords such putative actors no special place. Nor should they be provided such privilege, according to Hindess' argument.

The central message of Barry Hindess' chapter on "Classes, Collectivitieses and Corporate Actors" is that classes are not nor can be social actors, despite the conception of them as such which has been institutionalized in both Marxian and Weberian influenced varieties of social analysis. His argument is not made from the auspices of "theoretical humanism," auspices which propose the reduction of all actors to their individual human constituents. Classes are not ruled out of court because they are comprised of people, poeple who should take analytical precedence as the real social actors. Hindess is prepared to envisage an array of non-inivdual actors, where an actor is conceptualized as a locus of decision and action. On these criteria, he argues, phenomena such as churches, corporations or courts may unproblematically be considered to be social actors. Classes may not.

As a collectivity, Hindess argues, classes have no identifiable means of formulating decisions nor of acting on them. They lack any organizational mechanisms. In the absence of these they cannot be considered as entities which can act. If they cannot exist as actors then they cannot be said to do the things which have typically been central to the concept of class in Marxism: they cannot struggle, make history, enjoy conflict, have hegemony, develop consciousness, fail to realize their "real interests" and so on.

Classes are not collective actors, he maintains, because there is no locus of decision and calculation which can act as a class: they lack any identifiable means of taking decision. Thus, he would argue, to talk of them as if they were conceptual mechanisms capable of explaining anything is "a kind of fantasy." From this perspective classes could only be viewed as either discursively constituted but polemical entities or as purely categorical phenomena, distributionally differentiated strata of variable outcomes, to be explained by social actors proper, but which in themselves explain nothing. They might function as shorthand descriptions and glosses of more or less arbitrarily distinct distributions of certain social goods such as health, education, credentials, mortality rates and so on. However, a description of how these outcomes are distributed should not be confused with an explanation of them. For that, one must have recourse to some conception of a social actor.

One way of circumventing these objections is to argue that there are in fact objective and structurally given "real interests" which belong to classes, where the notion of class is less a distributional outcome but more an analytical abstraction to which individuals – or, bearing in mind Kreckel's objections, a limited range of formally recognized economically active ones – can be related. Whether or not individual actors then do things or display attitudes consonant with what one would anticipate they would, given the assumptions of the abstraction, become an object of investigation, in which various inter-mediating social actors, that do have agency and organization form, can function as either conduits or barriers to the expression of these "real interests." Thus political parties, trade unions, employers associations and such become "stand-ins" for the abstractions of class, and their social actions come to be regarded as symptomatic signs of class action. However, the relation between the abstraction and the real through the link of "real interests" (which, confusingly, are usually not realized in any sense that would make them empirically real) ends up being an explanation of nothing – a range of things that do not happen as they ought to happen if the abstraction were to be realized. Hindess regards the idea of objective interests that are real but not reconized as an imaginary problem. Posed in these terms it is easy to see how and why one might agree with him.

A further consequence of this position is resistance to explaining the real actions of actual social actors such as corporate or trade union organizations in terms of the putative underlying abstraction – that of the class struggle. To do this would assume not only an unwarrantable clarity of interest realization in the abstracted entities but also an unsustainable assumption about the homogeneity of interests involved in the social action of their putatively expressive forms.

Hindess concludes his contribution by reference to a recent work by Clegg, Boreham and Dow (1986), *Class, Politics and the Economy*. The arguments of this text are interpreted to support the view that comparative analysis can demonstrate that the development of social policy in the advanced capitalist economies can be understood in terms of a struggle between classes. Such a view is "uninformative," asserts Hindess, noting that from this perspective, what is to be done to improve the provision of policy is left unspecified. Perhaps. This introduction is not the place in which to conduct personal point-scoring, a less than edifying spectacle at the best of times. Suffice to say that on the coherent assumptions of Hindess' definition of a social actor, then his argument follows.

How realistic are the coherent assumptions that Hindess articulates? The assumptions are that *an* actor is *a locus* of decision and action. Thus a corporation or a political party may be a social actor, because they can be said to so act. But can they? Are not such organizational entities rather more arena constituted by diverse locales, in which struggles to command policy outcomes take place, between "natural persons" and other social actors such as factions or departments? If so, then the outcomes themselves – the loci of decision/calculation – are somewhat uninformative if we do not know how they got to be there, what was excluded and how. Moreover, there are many instances of failure to achieve implementation in the literature, because of organizational contestation over concrete decision and calculation. The view of a social actor as a locus of calculation/decision is overly rationalistic and underplays the ambiguity, plurality, contradiction and differential interests endemic to processes of decision and calculation. There are typically many loci, not a locus. Consequently, unless one is to banish abstraction totally from scientific discourse (which would be a devastatingly inconoclastic move), one may discern a policy drift in such decision and calculation as occurs in terms of some relatively coherent abstraction of what polar types of such policy might look like. Conventionally, such abstractions are expressed in terms of classes whose effects can be displayed structurally in empirical terms of given differential distributional outcomes. Unless one operates with an ultra-empiricism governing the real, immediately apparent nature of phenomena (such as would rule out of court any abstract scientific mechanisms such as germs or atoms), together with some phenomenological dictate that only those things that actors think real are real, one could invoke classes as phenomena just as one might invoke germs or viruses. To deny the scientific usefulness of those would be a peculiar practice. They have been most decisive actors at stages in human history (the 14th century "Black Death" which wiped out a quarter of Europe's population and altered the balance of power within feudal relations between key classes of actors), although they can function neither as loci of decision nor of calculation. Do we thus deny their social effects, visible in distributional outcomes such as mortality? No more than we should classes on the same criteria, one might say. As a heuristic claim and principle class may have its uses, if we can demonstrate that there is a pattern of coherence to the outcomes associated with diverse social actors' calculations and decisions, in families, firms, courts etc. If, in addition, we can demonstrate that politics pursued on this assumption of a putatively class pattern of coherence do have determinate effects which are demonstrable through comparative empirical analysis, and which are different to the effects of other forms of what we might call class politics, then can not the abstraction remain in use?

3. Management, Calculation and Control

The implications of Hindess' argument are immediately apparent from considering the first chapter in Part Two of this volume, Glenn Morgan's "Ownership and Management Strategy." If it is problematic to pose entities called classes as the type of phenomena which have "interests," Morgan suggests that it is hardly easier to establish what organization interests are, other than through close study of the discursive politics which surround their constitution as such.

In discursive conceptions of politics, as has been argued elsewhere, "Politically strategic action consists of coupling calculations, beneficial claims, and discursive categories in such a way that traffic in these has to pass through the network constructed by the representations of the interests thus secured" (Emmison, Boreham and Clegg 1988: 138). The empirical backdrop to such politics is the interpretation of the ways in which managers, those archetypal new middle class personnel, are influenced and constrained by ownership relations. Morgan's chapter is thus situated at the nub of the organization/class analysis nexus: the interpretation of "interests" is made in an organizational mode, as the outcome of a discursive politics waged over the ownership and control of the corporation. In this chapter the argument proceeds empirically on the basis of a case study of a British tobacco-based group, the Imperial Group, from the mid-1970s to the point at which it was taken over by the Hanson Trust in 1986.

Morgan's point of entry into the linkage between class and organization analysis is through revisiting the ownership and control debate which was initiated by Berle and Means (1932). This debate has been centred on what Morgan refers to as a "dualism" in which ownership and management are regarded as two radically separated phenomena, rather than something unified in the person of a capitalist owner-manager.

Morgan regards this dualism critically, particularly as it has led to the neglect of the interrelationship between ownership and management. Berle and Means' notion of owners directly controlling managers on a day-to-day basis should be replaced with one of influence exerted through institutional, rather than personal, ownership and share dealing on the stock exchange. Such influence is mediated through the rational choices firms as actors must make to secure working capital from other markets in the form of loans, and which other firms make about under-valued takeover targets; under-valued in terms of their share prices relative to their asset values. Consequently, management's interests are at hostage to the day by day judgements of owners as to the share values of the firms they manage. Within this context, different types of management will have different types of interest.

Management types are differentiated by Morgan on the basis of a notion of "circuits of capital," an abstraction used to distinguish financial circuits, where property is produced through the manipulation of profit *per se,* from industrial circuits, where profit derives from valorization – the increase in value achieved by manufacturing activity. Both circuits exit within the same organization setting, maintains Morgan. In some countries these are in tension, due to the nature of institutional arrangements, while in others they are less so. Analysts agree that the tensions are greater in the UK, USA and Australia than they are in Japan, West Germany or Sweden, for example (Armstrong 1984; Higgins and Clegg 1988). At the heart of these different institutional arrangements are variations in national financial, accounting and stock exchange conventions. Where these encourage management to choose to promote high share values, as in the UK, in order to satisfy short-term requirements by institutional investors, then financial manipulation becomes the rational strategy for achieving these objectives. A consequence of this is to reduce opportunities for management to make long-term investments in manufacturing, with its uncertain and long-term horizons. It is from these rational choices, constructed under conditions in which environmental influence is appreciated, that the tensions between the financial and industrial circuit managers derive. Such tensions are evidenced in the case study of the Imperial Group.

The case study is complex and there is little point in summarizing it here. The point of Morgan's analysis is to show that the rational choices constituting organization interests are the result of a constant interplay between ownership, control and managerial strategy. What have earlier been referred to as patterns of coherence can be seen in these strategies. Distinct "modes of rationality" (Higgins and Clegg 1988) are at work in the distinct circuits. Ownership does constrain management, not in a static manner but in the way in which the large institutional chareholders frame the rational choices which the managers can make.

Morgan's chapter is a sophisticated example of a complex class analysis, drawing on Marxist political economy in its analysis of circuits of capital, but one which displays an appreciation, from organization analysis, of the complex nature of the organization *qua* social actor. Consequently, it is not so much an analysis of class struggle between managers and workers, as a more orthodox labour process approach might be. Rather, it is an analysis of the different interests that diverse managerial stake-holders can construct an organization as having, which links the level of abstraction – circuits of capital – to the actual locus of calculation and decision which defines an organization as a social actor.

Morgan's contribution deals implicitly with managers as an international class; Jane Marceau does so explicitly. From her perspective on "International Management and the Class Structure," complex organizations may be seen as being composed of elite occupational positions and associated opportunities for resource control. These positions are open for possession by individuals. While all individuals may appear to be born equal, they are clearly not to be regarded as such by virtue of the probability that their occupational and organization destinations will be vertically stratified. Marceau's research demonstrates that elite positions in elite firms are disproportionately open to capture and colonization by the sons of traditional bourgeois families in the nations of Western Europe. Consequently, one can speak of an "international business class" emerging, one which links the national bourgeoisie of Europe through a network initially comprised of nodal points occupied by elite Business Schools, and which is subsequently reproduced through internationally active business organizations. The new organization structures of these firms become conduits for the reproduction of national capitalists. At the apex of these international firms are managers drawn from the ranks of male off-spring of national bourgeoisie. Ownership and control re-merge through these bourgeois sons, who use their organizational positions as a means of reproducing family fortunes based on earlier forms of enterprise, under the conditions of contemporary capitalism. Family fortunes thus can become "portfolioized." Moreover, they become aggregated through conscious marriage strategies followed by these bourgeois families, as part of the overall "reconversion strategies" that entail the reproduction of bourgeois class advantage.

The decline of national firms and the rise of divisionalized international conglomerates has not spelt the end to the bourgeois dominance that the scions of these smaller, older and more traditional national firms had once enjoyed in their respective national arena. International firms merely provided altered frameworks for such aggregate class action, in which, due to the fact that the families of origin no longer own the firms, the pursuit of profit must be more single-minded. In pursuit of this, the cushion against adversity which family capital affords presents such bourgeois sons with certain comparative advantages.

Comparative advantage takes a visible form in the restricted range of disciplines and institutions in which the international business management class has been educated in Europe. Pathways were clearly marked through traditionally prestigious disciplines of engineering, law, economics, supplemented by some commercial studies, which channelled into elite business schools such as INSEAD. From these locales, fast-track, job-hopping circuitous career paths were the route to success. Family background served not only in financial terms; it also provided an example in which the attitudes, values and expectations appropriate to entrepreneurial action were well understood. Family networks of support and advice also helped in this, not least in securing prestigious positions in the first place. In addition, spatial elements entered into consideration: exposure in and to the elite recreational sites in Europe ensures not only that one can be seen to be a "chap," someone whose social connections and behaviour are impeccable, but also that one can move easily and freely from one such site to another, through the media of familial households maintained there.

Overall, from Marceau's research there emerges a picture of a series of strategic locales occupied by actors who share and are comfortable in a milieu of privilege, a milieu which has a complex but subtle role to play in shaping a recognizably coherent pattern among the members of the "international class structure of business." Although this structure is international, it is nonetheless characterized by precisely those rituals of collective solidarity which Kersholt identifies: in this sense it emerged from a distinct stratum of status, where that intrinsic element is buttressed by other more extrinsic criteria such as credentials and a fast-track. The achievement of the latter is displayed through choices of sector, function and type of company and place of work, which enables these actors to thrive as profit-making managers. It is this entrepreneurialism which leads them either to re-unify ownership and control at the peak of international firms, or, if thwarted, to take over or found new, smaller firms.

The international managers whom Marceau studied are clearly the elite of that heterogeneous category of workers known as management. In fact, in strictly class terms they should rather be thought of as property owners in addition to being strategic managers, a combination which would conventionally lead one to think of them as capitalists, as members of a "corporate ruling class" (Clegg et al. 1986). Management owes some of its heterogeneity as a category to the process of its genesis as a specific set of functions, as Harri Melin outlines in the introduction to his contribution, "Managers and Social Classes." In recent years two major lines of enquiry have intersected in the study of managers. First, a concern with "managerial strategies" of control and resistance, which has developed out of the "labour process" debate, with the realization that "management" could not be regarded as a simple extension of "capital." Indeed, neither of these simple categories is conceptually very useful, and an acquaintance with debates in organization theory about management, its resources, strategies and power (Mintzberg 1983) is sufficient to remedy recourse to such grand abstractions. Clearly they require further deconstruction, as both Melin and Marceau demonstrate. The second distinct emphasis in studies of management has been carried by a trajectory developing in empirical studies of the "new middle classes," in the wake of earlier theoretical contributions from writers such as Poulantzas, Carchedi and Wright, all of whom sought to accomodate this class within a Marxist model of the class structure of contemporary advanced industrial capitalist societies. Melin's contribution to the book represents work done at the point of intersection of these two trajectories, enabling him in the second section of the paper, "Control of the Labour Process," to raise a number of sound objections to much of the debate that has taken place: it conflates the importance of the labour process; pays insufficient attention to contrasting comparative labour markets, particularly with respect to consideration of union density and power; has generalized from a limited number of primarily US case studies; neglects the role of product markets (and, one might add, capital markets); and has, with a few exceptions, paid insufficient attention to the fact that the conditions of control have been different at the different stages of development (Clegg 1981 was an attempt to do this).

In defining managers, different approaches to the issue of demarcating the new middle class will generate different depictions of which positions are to be regarded as management. Melin systematically reviews the criteria deployed in a number of studies in both Western and Eastern Europe, before concentrating on the major contributions by Wright (1978; 1985). In particular, the focus is on Wright's (1985) most recent attempt to develop a perspective within "analytical Marxism" with which to replace his earlier conceptualization of middle class managers as the occupants of "contradictory locations" in the class structure, subject to attraction from the polar opposites of "labour" and "capital."

The importance of Wright's work cannot be underestimated, if only because of the breadth of the international comparative research effort it has generated. Consequently, research teams involved in this effort have a particular interest in clarifying their own theoretical position and research strategy with respect to Wright's (1978; 1985) changing position. The Finnish team, in particular, as their contributions to this volume indicate, have enjoyed a lively debate, which in research terms has focused on the conceptual importance of "autonomy" (this has also been at the focus of the Australian project's conceptualization of class: see Clegg and Matheson 1987), as well as that of supervisory authority and decision-making power. It is to gradations in autonomy, authority and decision making that an adequate conceptualization of management should look.

When the composition of managers in the class structure is systematically compared on the same criteria across a number of companies, it becomes apparent that there are consistent variations in the pattern of work organization across advanced capitalist countries. Managers are a higher proportion of the class structure, and thus one would infer of work organizations generally, in the United States than elsewhere. In all countries, however, there is a clear male bias in the gender composition of managers, and in the greater cluster of power (autonomy, authority and decision making) which is available to these male managers. Beyond these patterns, there are many differences between managers' tasks, responsibilities and powers in the six nations surveyed. (The countries reported on are the United States, United Kingdom, Sweden, Norway, Finland and Canada.) Two patterns of organization decision making present themselves: a Nordic pattern and an American pattern, marked in the former by a more extensive participation in decision making while in the latter it is more restricted. The differences are particularly marked with respect to budgetary control. While Nordic managers tend to have greater organizational authority, Anglo-American managers tend to have greater supervisory authority.

Melin's research differentiates between top managers, task managers and nominal or lower managers. It was found that the proportion of top managers was highest in the Nordic countries, while the proportion of lower or nominal managers was highest in North America, pointing to a far more centralized pattern of work organization in the Nordic countries and one which is much lower in the North American cases. As a well-supported finding of the Aston school is that centralization tends to increase as the size of organization increases, this would lead one to hypothesize that the differences can be attributed to industry-structure variations in the size of organizations across the countries (see Pugh and Hickson 1976 for the original Aston studies).

A number of other contrasts emerge which one might be tempted to attribute to major comparative variations in what has been termed the "class politics" (Clegg et al. 1986) of the respective countries. These have to do with the class backgrounds and ambitions of the managers: these are far more homogeneously middle class in the North American pattern, than they are in the Nordic countries, as "class politics" hypotheses would lead one to expect. Countries with strong social democratic parties, which have enjoyed political hegemony and governance, and which are supported by a dense base of union organization, produce a different type of worker, even in the managerial ranks, than emerges from more politically and economically "liberal" conjectures ("liberal" in contrast to "social democratic," it should be clear). Not only are Nordic managers

more likely to have a wage earner background; they are more likely to be unionized.

The heterogenity of managers is even more evident from this study than it was
before, because it adds the important dimension of cross national variation.
Management and managers in the United States cannot be thought to be typical
for the rest of the advanced capitalist societies, a caution it is well to consider in
view of the great weight of United States' teaching, research and case material.
The differences that occur can be attributed, in part, it has been argued, to
distinct national profiles of "class politics" (see Clegg et al. 1986, chapter 9).

It has been a convention in sociological studis of both class and organizations to
differentiate organization positions and their occupants on a "blue-collar"/
"white-collar" basis (a convention which Carchedi's contribution to this volume
will be seen to question). One consequence of this axial principle is the fact that
there has been a steady growth in the advanced societies of white-collar positions
and predominantly white-collar organizations. What this means has been a matter for some debate. As on most things to do with class there are broadly Weberian and Marxian positions. The contribution by Chris Smith to this volume on
"Technical Workers: A Class and Organizational Analysis" opens with a consideration of this debate as a means of focusing on the theoretical approaches which
have been developed for the analysis of one type of white-collar worker – those
who do "technical labour."

The Weberian explanation of the growth of white-collar workers stresses
changes in power and market relations, attendant upon the increasing bureauc-
ratization of the modern world. The focus is seen to be on market capacities as
the criteria for distinguishing class positions, an approach whose outcome, suggests Smith, is conceptual fragmentation. What is being fragmented must be an
opposed conceptualization: in this case the determinate and simple (if less realistic) lines of cleavage which result from older binary models such as the "simple
descriptive model" found in the "Communist Manifesto" (see Clegg et al. 1986,
chapter two, for a consideration of Marx's class models).

More recent attempts at Marxist theorizing have had to abandon any such
binary assumptions in the interest of an appreciation of the contemporary complexity of organizational reality, in particular the role of "technical workers".
Smith identifies two main traditions in this more recent trend. One is the conceptualization of technical workers as members of the "new working class" developed in France by Gorz (1976) and Mallet (1975).

The second tradition centres around the contributions of more global approaches to the conceptualization of the class structure associated with Braverman (1974), Poulantzas (1975) and Carchedi (1977). For these writers technical
workers were to be seen not as "new" members of the working class but as a
fraction of an expanding "new middle class". Each of these positions is subject to
careful scrutiny by Smith. The tradition of Gorz (1976) and Mallet (1975) over-
states the democratizing, collectivizing impact of technology on collective labour

and consequently understates the possibilities for dilution and fragmentation of the attendant skill formation. It is the latter emphasis which is paramount in Braverman (1974), who regards technical workers as an intermediate stratum in an organization hierarchy designed by corporate management to divide and fragment workers. Whether these workers are more or less inclined to the capital or the labour camp will, Braverman (1974) suggests, depend on the extent to which they monopolize technical knowledge of production, or have been excluded from it. Smith suggests that Braverman's analysis is too rigid in its insistence on the downward flow of, and exclusion from, knowledge.

Poulantzas (1975) and Carchedi (1977) are characterized by Smith as "structural Marxists" – writers who concentrate on the conceptualization of class in terms of structural models. In these models, explanatory focus is given neither to the conditions of work (as in Gorz and Mallet) nor the "skill structure" and "positive ideological qualities" which Braverman stresses. Instead, the focus is on the functional location of positions as agents of either capital or labour.

Although Poulantzas (1975) regards technical labourers as productive labour, because they create "surplus value," he does not regard them as members of the working class because of their function of supervision and control of other manual workers. Thus, whether they know it or not, Poulantzas would argue that such workers fulfil the function of capital, not of labour. Consequently, they are on the "mental" labour side of a mental/manual labour divide by virtue not of their economic but their political and ideological functions within organizations, according to Poulantzas. Problems abound with this analysis, as has been argued in detail elsewhere (Clegg et al. 1986, chapter 6). Smith concentrates on two particular problems. One is the fact that Poulantzas generalizes a formal model from the particularities of the French industrial scene, while the other is that it ignores completely the situational conditions within diverse organizational settings. It theorizes by fiat. Consequently, the facts of specific national or organizational conditions fail to fit the general model.

Carchedi's (1977) analysis is the original locus of a conceptualization of the new middle class as occupants of simultaneously contradictory class locations. They are defined as agents who perform both the "global functions of capital" concerned with surveillance and control of the "collective labourers" as well as the "collective labour functions" which define the proletariat. Technical workers will thus be functionally defined as new middle class workers where they supervise and control the "collective labourers." The problem that Smith sees with this analysis is the lack of any contextual reference to specific conditions of organization culture which constitute the meaningful context in which these functional relationships occur. Once more the problem is one of the articulation between a formal model and the specific conditions within which the model is to be applied. Where the model does not correspond to the meaningful grasp of the situation enjoyed by those whose relations it formally expresses, does this mean that the vagaries and particularities of time and place, expressed through case studies, should be used to invalidate the model or should the model be used to "invalidate" the contextual meaning? As Hindess observed in his earlier chapter, there is indeed a strong tradition of the latter in Marxism's emphasis on "false" consciousness. On the other hand, if we do not "privilege" a model but instead grant priority to the privilege of others' interpretations of reality, is there not the danger of letting mundane forms of (mis)understanding over-rule analysis?

Smith resolves such issues by coming down in favour of an approach in which, with due regard to the comparative and historical context, the "cultural legacy" which constitutes workers' identities is understood in terms of the processes of training, skill formation, organizational locale and work which have generated the predominant understandings. It is these contingent factors, Smith maintains, which will determine the resolution of their contradictory class location by technical workers. Thus, he follows Carchedi (1977) to the extent that he regards his conceptualization of the class structure to be a realist depiction of generative tendencies for class formation. However, he would want to refer to organizational particulars in order to see to what extent, how and why these tendencies for class formation have been realized.

What technical work is will vary nationally, depending on national variations in the institutional frameworks in which such skills are constructed. National variation as well as organizational contingencies thus enter into the process of class formation, so that distinctly British, French and American models of "technical work" are identified. General models of capitalism have to be seen in the variable context of institutionally distinct capitalist nations, within whose specific organizations structural tendencies which are inherent in the nature of capitalism will be mediated by particular managerial strategies. Whereas Marxist analyses have overstated the determinants of the general model of class structure in capitalism, Weberian approaches, suggests Smith, have understated these while focusing far too much on the micro-organizational particulars, a tendency which in studies of technical workers he identifies with Whalley's (1986) work. The outcome of this approach is a social constructionist or phenomenological-view of class, one with which Smith takes issue.

The remainder of the chapter proceeds through a detailed critique of Whalley's work to an empirical analysis of technical workers at the confectionery division of the Cadbury-Schweppes corporation, based in the Bournville factory in Birmingham, England. The occasion for the research was a re-organization of technical work under a major capital investment programme. Through an analysis of the processes involved in this re-structuring Smith develops a framework for locating class in an organizational context. Corporate management strategies are at the focus of his analysis. Such strategies may be related to internal controls over technical workers as well as being designed to externalize transaction costs by replacing the hierarchical organizational relationship between management and technical workers with one mediated by market, sub-contracting relationships. The changes eventuating from the implementation of managerial strategies changed not only the nature of technical work but also the technical workers' ideological disposition toward it and the other social relations within the organization. Technical workers lost some of their autonomy, not through processes of de-skilling, but as a result of their central functions becoming subject to market exposure. Consequently, technical workers were subject to a process in which their "contradictory class location" was resolved in terms of their managerial agency.

By contrast, with the move to managerial agency which was occasioned by changing internal controls, the strategy of externalization redefined technical workers as petty bourgeoisie. In the past the predominant organization method for securing technical work was to employ technical workers. However, Smith suggests that increasingly this work will be "bought in" from outside, independent, sub-contracting agencies. These small businesses would redefine the owners as technical petty bourgeoisie rather than workers. Again one would anticipate a quite different set of ideological dispositions to characterize this type of technical work.

With this contribution Chris Smith does achieve a real *rapprôchment* between organization and class analysis. The organization analysis stresses the institutional structuring of organization contexts, and within these fosters an approach which combines a realist view of class as a structure of underlying tendencies with a consideration of the role that knowledgeable agents and rational action can play in realizing these tendencies in one form or another. In this way the extremes of either de-contextual general formal theory or non-formal, specific and contextual reportage may be avoided.

4. Class Restructuring and Organization

Class restructuring through organizational development is, as Smith suggests, an ongoing feature of capitalism as a dynamic economic system. While proletarianization may have seemed a dominant tendency in the 1960s, by the 1970s it was class decomposition which preoccupied the structural Marxists as they sought to conceptualize the rapidly changing reality in terms which preserved the ordered totality of Marxist analysis. In the 1980s Smith identifies new organization tendencies, which we might call "marketization," which are currently re-structuring class relations. As Marx and Engels said in that memorable phrase, re-called in the introduction to John Urry's discussion of "Disorganized Capitalism and Social Class," under capitalism "All that is solid melts into air..." Indeed. The dynamism of capitalism on a world scale is such that class relations never stand still. Even as the form of the relation appears recurrent in its opposition of labour and capital, its expression is subject to changing tensions. As we have seen already in the contributions to this volume, these tensions form the infrastructure upon which organization and class analysis construct their accounts. Examples of this have been the "managerial revolution" of the 1930s, the "proletarianization" of white-collar workers in the 1960s, the "deskilling hypothesis" of the 1970s.

Capitalism as the harbinger of modernity, the permanent vehicle of transformation and change: this is the theme for John Urry's contribution to this volume. Marx and Engels outlined the form of this modern epoch in the "Manifesto," in a development which Urry terms "organized capitalism" (also see Lash and Urry 1987; Offe 1987). Against the conventional views of both Marxists and Weberians, however, Urry does not argue that this is an epoch whose ethos of organization is still increasingly evident in the ascendancy of monopoly capitalism or the rationalization of the world. On the contrary. Since the end of the Second World War, Urry argues, the advanced societies have become increasingly host to an era of "disorganized capitalism."

Academic consensus has it that the era of organized capitalism began in the late nineteenth century. Its features are familiar: we know them as increasing centralization and control both organizationally and in the economy; the rise of cartels; finance capitals' dominance; the rapid rise of a bureaucratized intelligentsia and its allied occupations; the rapid development of interest organizations such as unions and employers associations; an increased role for the state in mediating with peak organizations of these bodies; forms of "imperialism" and economic "neo-imperialism"; an increase in what the French call "plannification" in the state sphere, together with an increasing technocratization generally; increasing sectoral and national concentration of industrial capitalism; increasing dominance of extractive/manufacturing industry employment; regionalization of national economies based on these industries; increasing plant size in employment; increasing dominance of very large industrial sites over particular regions through the provision of centralized services (especially commercial and financial).

Together these form an interactive matrix within which capitalism in various countries becomes increasingly organized. Three factors, suggests Urry, determine the timing and extent of national variations within the matrix: the "take-off" point – the earlier it is, the less organized capitalism will be because of the costs of late development; the survival rate of pre-capitalist organizations into the capitalist period – the more of these survive, the greater the degree of organization; the size of country – smaller countries, in order for their industries to compete internationally, it is hypothesized, had to become more organized. On this basis Urry accounts for the distinct patterns of capitalist organization which developed in Germany, Britain and the United States. It is a bold and imaginative sketch of a theory of modernity whose lynchpin is the central concept of organization.

The corollary of this theory of modernity is an equally dramatic sketch of postmodernity whose *leitmotif* is disorganization. It is manifested, suggests Urry, through de-concentration of capital; increasing relative importance of a "service" or "new middle" class compared with the diminishing de-instrustrialized working class and an allied rise in "new social movements" as its members increasingly forsake the politics of class for those of civil society; a decline in centralized collective bargaining in favour of company and plant-level negotiation; a series of structural gaps and "crises" opening up between state and capital: – multinationals vs. nation states; fiscal crises; the crisis of the welfare state; the crisis of neo-corporatism; the internationalization of organized capitalism into the Third World and of some of the latters surplus population into the First World; a decline of class politics in favour of aggregative "catch-all" parties; the "post-modernization" of culture; increasing national and sectoral participation in capitalism; diminishing importance of manufacturing/extractive sectors and increasing importance of service industry; declining regionalization; "downsizing" in plants and a shift of labour intensive activities through a new international division of labour to Third World sites; the decline of industrial city dominance.

The factorial lists are somewhat overwhelming, but they do relate to widely perceived structural changes within the advanced societies. Urry's hypothesis is that, *ceteris paribus,* "the greater the extent to which a nation's capitalism was organized, the more slowly and hesitantly its capitalism will disorganize." On this basis, he sees disorganization occurring in Britain and the USA from the 1960s, France from the late 1960s/early 1970s, Germany from the 1970s and Sweden from the late 1970s/early 1980s. The hypothesis is then argued for each of the three main classes of contemporary capitalism: the capitalist class, the "service" or "middle" class and the working class. With this elaboration the argument is expounded at greater length and in greater detail.

Without entering into too many points of discussion of this provocative and bold argument, one may note the following in passing. First, the perspective developed is one which is remarkably centred on Britain, certain European countries and the United States. Notably absent is any discussion of East Asian capitalism in Japan, Hong Kong, Singapore, Taiwan and South Korea, for example. A number of striking counterfactuals to the broad sweep of the argument could be located in the relative "disorganization" of Hong Kong and Taiwan and the relative "organization" of South Korea and Singapore. All are "late developers" of diverse size and have a strong element of survival of pre-capitalism. This introduction will not enter into these debates in any detail, as the editor has done so elsewhere (see Clegg, Dunphy and Redding 1986; Clegg and Redding 1989). Suffice to say that there are important matters of the interpretation of East Asian capitalism which require consideration for such a broad synthesis to be sustainable.

A second point of controversy is the temporal articulation of the organization/disorganization hypothesis. Recently, in respect to theories of modernity and post-modernity (with which the hypotheses advanced by Urry have considerable elective affinity), Bauman (1987) has argued that these tendencies (towards modernity and post-modernity) are less to be considered as temporally successive and more as co-present. Organization and disorganization may thus be similarly co-present tendencies, polar opposites around which some countries will tend to cluster while others will display contradictory tendencies which might resolve either way or merely muddle through, despite the price to be paid, economically, for doing so. (This is an argument I have developed at length elsewhere and it would not be appropriate to re-iterate it in this introduction. However, interested readers may wish to consult Clegg, Higgins and Spybey (1989) for an argument which proposes such an interpretation in the context of a consideration of not only Western but also Asian capitalism.)

If the interpretation of organization/disorganization were to be sustained as one of co-present tendencies, then this would necessarily make specific national outcomes an object of political calculation and struggle, particularly of those countries least coherently articulated on either pole. As Urry acknowledges, major actors in such struggles would have to be states, multinational enterprises and labour unions, irrespective of other interested actors. In approaches to the literature on multi-national enterprises, as Harvie Ramsay and Nigel Haworth outline at the outset of their argument in "Managing the Multinationals: The Emerging Theory of the Multinational Enterprise and its Implications for Labour Resistance," there has been a tendency to regard multinationals as social actors easily able to defeat other protagonists such as national states and labour unions.

It is possible that the importance of multinational corporations (MNCs) has of late been underemphasized in the literature, suggest Ramsay and Haworth, in contrast to the often exaggerated fears and anticipations of the earlier literature from the 1950s to mid-1970s. (The work of Wheelwright (e.g. 1978) represents a typical version of this response in which MNCs were cast as the villains of late capitalism, an analysis which was of considerable influence in the labour movement in Australia at this time: see AMWSU (1977) *Australia Ripped-Off*, for an example.) Developments in MNCs since the mid-1970s suggest that there are still good, if less exaggeratedly extrapolatory, reasons for concern over their role in the world economy: the volume of world trade within and between MNCs, their increasing dominance of the service sector as well as of manufacturing and extractive industry; the development of "marketization" strategies for organizing relationships, sometimes referred to as "Japanization" (see Wilkinson and Oliver 1988 for a British overview). Ramsay and Haworth see these developments as important reasons why MNCs should not disappear from analytical focus, nor simply be castigated as the villains of an abstract drama between "capital" and "labour", one in which their rationality is assumed to be all-conquering. By contrast, they argue, MNCs may sometimes be seen as sites of uncertainty and contradictory decision making, an insight better sustained by management theorists than by radical analysts of a Marxist persuasion.

MNCs have problems reconciling three types of factors, it is suggested. These are: location-specific factors; ownership-specific factors, and internal manage-

ment perceptions and interests. In contrast to the views of either functionalist
Marxists or functionalist organizational theorists, organizational design is hardly
such a well-developed "science" as some of its promoters would have (Donaldson 1985) that problems of co-ordination, communication and control within
international organizations are able to be relegated to the status of easily man-
ageable contingencies. As Mintzberg (1983) would instead insist, power and
conflict are more the norm in and around organizations.

What comes through strongly from Ramsay and Haworth's contribution is that
MNCs are a complex of arena and locales in which diverse social actors, with
different stakes and interests in the corporation, are involved in political as well
as rational organization. In particular, they identify local or functional managers
as a political interest group who are in a position in MNC information circuits to
be able to strongly represent their views. Outside agencies, from the consulting
networks of Business Schools and Management Consultants, are also an influential group who have ample opportunity to wreak political mischief with their
organizational fads. A central issue in the political organization of MNCs is the
structuring of their operations as more or less centralized, an issue of considerable complexity and uncertainty, given the diverse nature of subsidiaries, divisions and host countries with which MNCs may have to deal, and the issues these
pose for a rational business strategy. A highly centralized strategy can easily
come to grief in the context of local particularities, as Ramsay and Haworth
outline in their example.

National governments are not simply passive bystanders or obedient lap-dogs of
MNC strategy. Within the indeterminancy of political calculation within their own
arenas, they may well seek to constrain MNCs' strategies with respect to their
national economies, both in terms of existing companies and in terms of procuring
further national investment. Centralized, overly globally rational strategies on the
part of the MNC may not be the best way to face this indeterminancy.

Ramsay and Haworth argue that this more realistic appreciation of MNCs'
indeterminate organization around the uncertainty principle of politics opens
points of potential leverage for strategists representing the labour movement,
particularly to the extent that they are able to coerce, coopt or otherwise use
aspects of state power in pursuit of their objectives. A key point of leverage is the
general area of Human Resource Management, where the employment of labour
will always pose a potential for resistance which may be inimical to the best
strategic analyses derived from elsewhere in the global corporation. Overall, the
thrust of Ramsay and Haworth's conclusion is to ensure that analytical fatalism
does not overawe a realistic assessment of the opportunities for engagement and
leverage on the part of labour strategists. However limited these points of
pressure may be, they will never be entirely absent, except in the fantasies of
radical pessimists on the left or radical idealists on the right. This chapter stands
as a counter to the attribution of "superagency" which such rationalist ex-
travagances presume.

The response of structuralist Marxists to the organizational consequences of class restructuring was typically that represented by Braverman (1974). It was anticipated that there would be a widespread de-skilling and degradation of working conditions as capitalist relations of production were consolidated at ever higher levels of efficiency. In particular, such theses ought to apply to workers in those positions most exposed to "proletarianization" tendencies, the intermediate strata of "white-collar workers". Moreover, in a country such as West Germany, which has been at the forefront of efficient capitalist restructuring, these effects should be particularly visible. The contribution to this volume by Wolfgang Littek and Ulrich Heisig suggests that one should be sceptical about such structuralist Marxist hypotheses.

"Work Organization Under Technological Change: Sources of Differentiation and the Reproduction of Social Inequality in Processes of Change" reports on empirical research conducted by Littek and Heisig into the impact of restructuring on male white-collar professional workers in the early 1980s, in three industrial firms in West Germany.

Weaker versions of labour process theory than Braverman's (1974) have spoken not of tendencies to de-proletarianization so much as of a "dialectic of resistance and control" (Littler and Salaman 1982). However, not even this version, with its stress on resistance to re-structuring, was corroborated in the responses of the white-collar workers who were studied. (However, we do not know to what extent this sample was typical of such workers. In the context of the detailed theoretical argument which follows this is not a major concern. The contribution that the chapter makes is not simply to hypothetical disconfirmation but the generation of new theory and hypotheses for explaining the discrepant finding – discrepant in terms of received labour process theory, that is.)

White-collar workers, rather than resisting re-structuring, seemed to welcome and support it. Opportunities for strengthening, rather than weakening, their occupational position within the micro-politics of organization life were the reason for this reception. White-collar workers perceived restructuring in such favourably opportunistic terms as a result of the managerial strategies employed to hasten the restructuring attendant on technological changes within these organizations. Consequent to these strategies, rather than white-collar workers being levelled down to the conditions which prevailed for blue-collar workers, the structural gap between these groups of workers was deepend further. The high trust relations which characterized the work context of white-collar workers were supported rather than undercut by the technical changes underway. In the "terrain of struggles" which is the organization, white-collar resources, coalitions and game strategies prevailed over those of blue-collar workers, within the strategic game which management action initiated.

Littek and Heisig's argument is developed within the framework of a segmentation perspective, one which implicitly draws on a framework developed by the British industrial relations writer, Alan Fox (1974), in the same year that Braverman's (1974) much better known but far less insightful model was published. Segmentation contributes to the overall social stability of the organization by recasting opportunities for hierarchical conflicts into a competitive lateral game of struggle between different groups in which advantaged groups seek to reproduce their advantage and in which weaker groups are obliged to participate, if only not to lose further organization ground.

Differences in work games and their outcomes are attributable to the degree to which the qualifications claimed by the various work groups are grounded in knowledge or skill. (Knowledge equates with prerequisites to perform more or less complex work in which personal decisions and flexibility are required, while skill may be seen in the ability to carry out more or less complex prescribed work.) The latter is the preserve of blue-collar workers far more than it is of white-collars: knowledge characterizes the base of their relationship with management to a much greater extent, propose Littek and Heisig. Management consequently depends to a great extent on the personal commitment and cooperation of knowledge workers to an extent to which it does not for skill workers.

Within each bloc of white- and blue-collar workers internal stratification occurs. Within each group these articulate around formal qualifications and relationships to "arena of uncertainty". Within the knowledge workers group of white-collar workers, marginal increments to personal resource control may be achieved on the basis of small group or individual control of uncertainty (see Crozier 1964 for the classic formulation; Hickson et al. 1971 for its systematization into an intraorganizational theory of power; Clegg 1975 for some critical comments on this exercise). For blue-collar workers, leverage over control of uncertainty can only be achieved by collective action. Such an explanation relies not only on differences between the labour market conditions of the two groups distinguished but also on the nature of the trust relations which constitute these. This key distinction is outlined in a series of schemata in the chapter which elaborate how the trust/uncertainty relations intersect and overlap with the credentialling process that generates types of skill and knowledge.

Consent is the desired by-product of high trust organization interrelations, as far as management is concerned, while for knowledge workers it is traded for control over working conditions and social exchange relations which will deliver prestige, status and influence. Cooperation and participation are thus strategies of self-interest for knowledge workers as much as defensive behaviour, resistance and insubordination are for skill workers. Marginal white-collar workers are caught between the two strategies. They will tend to be excluded from intimate followship by self-interest on the part of core knowledge holders in not diluting their knowledge base, while, in their own interest, they will tend to be reluctant to define their own *declassé* fate by seeking solidaristic fraternity. Hence the intimate fellowship of management and high trust workers tends to exclude and marginalize not only blue-collar workers but also less credentialled white-collar workers.

Recessionary conditions of restructuring serve to strengthen the knowledge class/management ties, because the more competitive conditions of such times place a greater premium on creative, positive and adaptive abilities, and their efficient use by management. This is not true across the board in organizations: it does not apply to relations with low trust blue-collar workers who become more rather than less dispensable in these conditions, argue Littek and Heisig. Any analysis which extrapolates only one aspect of these changes, either increasing high trust or tightening low trust relations, into a tendency, will miss the overall picture, conclude Littek and Heisig.

If increases in the proportions of knowledge workers, or new class employees, is one aspect of the global tendencies identified by Urry as capitalist disorganization, the other class which it is predicted will swell with these processes of restructuring is that of the petty bourgeoisie: those own account and small employers whom Marx and Engels in the "Manifesto" had confidently expected to wither away. It is this class (carefully defined in terms of available data) which is the focus of Timo Toivonen's "The New Rise of Self-Employment and Industrial Structure", a study of non-agricultural self-employment in nine OECD countries.

The comparative data since 1970 suggests that there is a strong U-curve relationship in the proportion of self-employed to total employment outside agriculture, with the decline halting or stagnating during the mid-1970s. The function fits best for Belgium, Finland, France, Germany, Italy, the Netherlands, Norway, Sweden, the United Kingdom and the USA, with Denmark and Japan being exceptions. The percentages of self-employment vary markedly. Within Japan and Italy the percentages are over 20%, whereas in the three Nordic countries they are only 5–7%.

A comparison was made for all those countries for which data was adequate (which excluded Belgium, Italy and the United Kingdom) to contrast the lowest year of self-employment with the subsequent highest year of self-employment. During the same broad period changes in industrial structure were also studied. What changes occurred were small, but all in the same direction: an increase in the services sector and a decrease in the manufacturing sector, as Urry had noted earlier. Large differences in self-employment are found between different industries and different countries, with, in general, the highest concentration in trade, construction and services, while the smallest is generally in mining and energy production. Japan and Italy have the highest percentage of self-employment, while the USA; Finland and Sweden had the smallest, the range being from around 2–3% to almost 13%.

Using an analytic technique known as shift-share analysis, it is possible to determine to what extent the changes in percentages of self-employment are attributable to changes in the distribution of employment across economic sectors, or to compositional changes within industries. In every case except France, change can be more readily attributed to internal shifts of a compositional kind within industries than to structural shifts across sectors. Why should these changes have occurred?

One hypothesis for the changing composition of self-employment argues that the push factor of increasing unemployment in a national economy is likely to increase self-employment, as the latter becomes a rational choice for people who would otherwise be unemployed. Against this, however, it has been proposed that the generally stagnatory conditions attendant upon recession will serve to decrease small business. Toivonen does not consider that the available evidence supports the push hypothesis, although a more mediated "anticipatory economic climate" variable might be more plausible.

Another factor to consider in the rise of the self-employed class and their organizations is government policy. On the assumption that conservative governments will be more facilitative of small business and self-employment, an index of right influence on government over the period in question may have a significant correlation with the rise of self-employment and thus contribute to an explanation.

The data supports the assumption that unemployment rise, and a rise in self-employment, are connected positively, while of course it can say nothing about why this happens, and what the meaningful connections in the correlation are. Little in the way of strong support can be adduced for the government policy variable, expressed in terms of conservatism, at least in the simple correlation coefficients. Nor do regression equations shed much more light. What might some of the other influencing variables be? Toivonen considers that a number of organization level variables may be the causal factors at work, such as the growth in sub-contracting (which both Urry and "Japanization" writers have seized on as symptomatic of contemporary capitalist restructuring), growth in franchising and the opportunities opened up by new technology. For the latter, at least, there is indirect, if limited, support in Toivonen's comparative data.

The conclusions that he reaches are, of necessity, tentative. In fact, they are more in the way of big questions for future research, particularly in terms of their implications. As he concludes, "If unemployment, public sector employment, and self-employment all continue to grow, will we then in the next century be in a situation where a remarkable portion of people of working-age is either outside employment, employed in the public sector, or self-employed? Have traditional theories about classes and organizations gone totally astray?" The question may be somewhat audacious in speculating from a set of tendencies, but it does focus for us the way in which so many of our ideas both about class structure and organization structure are dependent on a set of assumptions about the nature of employment relations. Changes in these may well be radically revising the landscape so familiar to both Marxian and Weberian scholars, with their implicit context of large-scale organizations as the envelope for economic action and activity. One does not expect the disappearance of a Fortune 500, but some of the contractual relations which constitute it may well change, as "Japanization" hypotheses suggest (see Wilkinson and Oliver 1988).

5. The Labour Process, Class Structure and Gender

The focus of the chapter on "Exploring the Class and Organisational Implications of the UK in Financial Services" by David Knights and Hugh Willmott is upon the organization of financial services in the context of changing relations of political and economic power. Prompted by a concern to appreciate the wider significance of an intensive field study of management control within Pensco, a medium-sized UK life insurance and pensions company, the chapter explores the relevance of Marxian insights for understanding the nature of this sector. The relevance and limits of Marxian-inspired debates on ownership and control, the commodity form and the distinction between productive and unproductive labour are considered and addressed in terms of their significance for analysing "class" and "organization" in financial services.

The perspecitve on "class" and "organization" developed in this chapter is one which focuses upon the reproduction and/or transformation of capitalist relations of production. In particular, it is necessary to emphasize that the term "organization" is not being used to describe an entity. Nor is "class" used to describe a common position or strata within the social structure. Rather, for the purposes of this chapter, organization is considered as a *process* and class as a principle which *structures* this process. In the context of contemporary U.K. society, the authors regard the *dynamic* nature of the capital-labour *relation* as the most significant expression of class. This relation is regarded as one which is articulated in a variety of sites in which it selectively exploits and reforms (and is reformed by) other kinds of power relation and their associated struggles, such as those of gender, age and race. This historical process involves a continuing struggle as individuals, often, though not necessarily, acting collectively, strive to facilitate or resist the dynamics of change – dynamics which are most adequately interpreted through Marxian frames of reference.

Following Marx, the chapter argues that a concentration upon the capital-labour relation provides a most appropriate means of interpreting contemporary UK society in general, and the processes of management control within Pensco in particular. However, the authors are anxious not to subscribe to Marxist analyses which sustain either a "productivist" philosophical anthropology or which fail to appreciate critical interdependencies within the capital-labour relation. In combination, these flaws within Marx's theory are seen as being responsible for a lack of analytic concern with the importance of other struggles (e.g. gender, race) and for an economistic conception of (objective) class boundaries and (subjective) class formation. In this chapter, the focus is less on various struggles and more upon the broader significance and impact of financial services for understanding continuity and change in capitalist (i.e. class) society.

The chapter is organized as follows. First, the study is situated vis-à-vis a brief synopsis of relevant developments in organizational theory. During the past two decades orthodox organization analysis, now centred upon contingency theory and population ecology theory, has been challenged and/or complemented by varieties of phenomenology and radical structuralism. In particular, left-radical organization theorists (e.g. Clegg and Dunkerley 1980) have drawn upon both neo-Marxist and neo-Weberian analyses to explore how class and power relations are reproduced through work organization. Accordingly, a brief sketch is made of the key differences between Weberian and Marxian conceptions of the central institutions of capitalist society, concluding in favour of an emphasis upon the latter on the grounds that Marx provides a more effective framework for understanding the role of financial services in the reproduction of capitalist (i.e. class) institutions and organizations. Then, in the following section, a critical review of Marx's understanding of the dynamics of capitalist development is provided in which it is argued his neglect of that interdependence within the structure of the capital-labour relation is reflected in an almost exclusive attention on the contradictory and polarizing features of those relations.

Some aspects of Marx's analysis have particular relevance for the study of financial services. Three questions are raised. First, can the products of insurance and pensions companies be analysed as commodities? Second, is the Marxian formulation of the separation of ownership and control convincing? Third, does Marx's philosophical anthropology provide an adequate basis for analysing the organization and control of the labour process in capitalist society? Briefly, in respect of the ownership and control debate, it is suggested that the contemporary significance of insurance and pensions companies resides not only in their role as mobilizers of diffuse sources of capital. It also resides in their effect upon the constitution of the subjectivity of those who, through their payment of premiums, transform diffuse forms of income into capital through the medium of these companies. These more micro effects are as important as the impact of financial capital upon the structure of ownership and its implications for the autonomy of corporate management.

Financial services are commodities that involve similar processes in their production and consumption as those goods which have been seen by traditional Marxists as central to the commodification of social relations. Within the analysis of management control within the labour process debate, an emphasis upon the antagonism of interests between capital and labour has tended to deflect attention from the existential as well as economic value of workers' investments in existing forms of control. It is argued that the progressive individualization and anonymization of subjectivity in advanced capitalist societies, and especially in work organizations, is inadequately recognized within labour process theory. More specifically, there is a failure to appreciate the historical pressures in contemporary society to privilege the struggle for individual security (e.g. by investing the self in, or seeking to distance it from, existing organizational practices) over and against collective action which is designed to attain politico-economic emancipation.

In the final section, Marx's philosophical anthropology is applied to an interpretation of changes in management control at Pensco, a medium-sized insurance company. The argument reflects the contention that both structuralist (antihumanist) and voluntarist (humanist) variants of Marxist analysis tend either to minimize or misrepresent the significance of subjectivity in the reproduction of the mode of production. In its structuralist mode, actors are reduced to passive bearers of class interests. And in its voluntarist guise, actors are represented as more or less conscious of their class interests. The basic limitation of both formulations concerns their common privileging of class identity and interests. This leads them to assume the relationship between the structure of production relations and the constitution of actors' identity and interests is free of contradiction. Overlooked is the possibility that the constitution of subjectivity in advanced capitalist society may not, in fact, lead them to identify "interest" primarily with "class."

Overall, the concern of this chapter is to develop a form of organizational analysis which draws from and develops the insights of Marx without becoming blinded or desensitized to other forms of analysis. More specifically, the complexity of organizational practices is appreciated whilst simultaneously their conditions and consequences in the dynamic development of the capital-labour relation are also grasped.

This chapter offers a welcome fusion of what have frequently been quite distinct approaches, particularly with the work of writers influenced by labour process theorists. It is not only in this chapter that this body of work is addressed. It is also the focus of the following chapter.

A number of landmark books have helped to define the "labour process" perspective, such as Braverman (1974). More recently the work of Michael Burawoy (1979; 1985) has received considerable attention, some of which is contained in this volume, in Dennis Smith's chapter on "Organization and Class: Burawoy in Birmingham."

Dennis Smith's focus in this chapter is on Burawoy's (1985) more recent book on *The Politics of Production: Factory Regimes under Capitalism and Socialism*. His interest in this work is in applying aspects of Burawoy's argument about "factory regimes" to the analysis of two quite distinct regions within the same historical place and time, nineteenth and early twentieth century Birmingham and Sheffield (building implicitly, it would seem, on the method used by Foster 1974). The second aspect of his consideration of Burawoy's (1985) adequacy is to make the analytic focus even more specific by concentrating on two distinct and important organizations in the context of Birmingham: the Cadbury chocolate factory at Bournville and the Austin motor works at Longbridge.

Burawoy (1985) develops a global theory of "factory regimes" – the modes whereby production is organized – as situated in the institutional relationship between the ideological and political practices of the factory and state, and the ways in which the state intervenes in the factory regime. The context for considering these relations must also include a number of other variables. Amongst these are the extent to which the workforce is separated from the means of subsistence, market structure aspects and the nature of subordination in the labour process, considered in Marxist terms of the degree of formal or informal subordination. Three sets of intervention assume a causal power in his account of these relationships: the intervention of the state within the factory regime; the intervention of the factory regime in its impact on the reproduction of labour power; also the intervention of the state on this reproduction of labour power. On this basis he identifies three distinct types of regime which Smith considers relevant for the British case: despotic, hegemonic and hegemonically despotic regimes. In the despotic type the state does not intervene at all directly within the factory regime or upon reproduction; the hegemonic type is characterized by increased state intervention in both spheres. Hegemonic despotism appears to combine strategies of marketization of reproduction by the state, strategies for a "new international division of labour" by capitalists; and a changed balance of power internal to the "factory" in the favour of capital, achieved through a more "flexible" workforce.

Smith notes that Burawoy's theoretical ambition is not modest. It will, Burawoy maintains, explain both English working class reformism and a revolutionary movement in Russia. Comparisons are drawn by Smith with what might be called Barrington Moore's (1969) theory of "agricultural regimes", in less than favourable terms, contrasting the context of their respective global theorizing, rich comparative and historical detail, and dynamics of analysis. In particular, suggests Smith, those factors which are external to the factory are relatively neglected in Burawoy's account.

Problems which an unduly restricted account of a "factory regime" present for historical analysis of organization case studies are evident in Smith's consideration of Birmingham in the early and mid-nineteenth century. In place of "factory regime" the concept of "workplace regime" is proposed as an expanded focus capable of incorporating the linkages which existed between the few factories and the extensive domestic and workshop production which characterized both Birmingham and Sheffield for much of the nineteenth century (and which survived in an attenuated but still significant form in Birmingham into the mid-twentieth century). Economic historians such as Pollard (1959) and Mathias (1983) have stressed how Sheffield and Birmingham enjoyed a number of similarities in their class formation at the workplace level during the nineteenth century, making the comparison one which is aptly chosen.

On Burawoy's hypothesis, similar factory regimes should produce similar outcomes with respect to the ways in which the working class participates in society and politics. The cases of Birmingham and Sheffield prove to be a counterfactual to the claim. Sheffield developed a strong syndicalist tradition in its labour movement and, with the advent of the steelworks, a highly segmented "housing class" structure, one split between middle class suburbs and a large urban working class core which, from an early period, regularly returned Labour candidates in elections. This was not the case in Birmingham which never developed the syndicalist traditions so evident in Sheffield, nor the same degree of class polarization.

Smith maintains that the Sheffield/Birmingham difference is not attributable solely to the explanatory factors stressed in the "factory regime" acount. Smith stresses not only the factory regime but wishes to view it within a broader framework which incorporates reference to men and women not only as actors within a certain social class, but as also having identities and attributes formed in a wider civil society and which find expression in other social movements, in addition to those of labour. This expression takes place within the overall context of class structure, its formation, decomposition and change and the alliances struck between the major actors who define this broader framework.

Application of this framework sketches a tale of two quite distinct cities. A more geographically isolated Sheffield is depicted in which there was a more divided working class with less linkages and alliances in the civil sphere with local bourgeois society. Bourgeois society at its peak was more globally networked into British capitalism than it was locally embedded. By the 1920s the sphere of civic politics had become solidly Labour. Birmingham, by contrast, was dominated by conservative politics and alliances which incorporated the working class; cooptation by "civic liberalism" rather than opposition by "civic socialism" characterized the scene in Birmingham. Smith demonstrates how the working class strategy in each city could be seen to be rational in terms of the different class context of each of the cities. The implication of this, as in the work of earlier writers such as Foster (1974), is that no singular, overall logic of class formation can be demonstrated. As has been argued at length elsewhere, class politics can not be read off from class structure but must be seen as embedded within the complex articulation of civil society (Clegg et al. 1986; Emmison et al. 1988).

In his argument thus far Dennis Smith has established that at a general level of community organization, two similar cities can give rise to quite different political organization. However, this is not yet a sustained critique of Burawoy's position. For that one would have to show, with more specificity, that two similar organizations at the factory level need not respond similarly to the impact of "external" factors on factory regimes. Burawoy's hypothesis would then be undercut in two ways: in the argument from workplace regimes to political organization and in the argument from external factors to factory regime. The latter would be a more providential critique, if only because the notion of workplace regime (while making a useful point about the extent to which organization may be achieved by market relations as well as hierarchical relations) ist not, strictly speaking, the concept that Burawoy uses.

In the remainder of his contribution Dennis Smith compares the two factories of Cadbury's and Austin's in the Birmingham suburbs of Bournville and Longbridge. Although they produced, respectively, chocolates and automobiles, there were a number of similarities in their organization, as well as major differences.

Both adopted mass production techniques as the basic method of production organized around the moving assembly line. Kin networks embedded recruitment practices in their respective local communities; in each firm workers built on this communal embeddedness with widespread participation in clubs, both sporting and social.

The differences were acute and manifested themselves in the attitudes of the workers to the management and the works, and vice versa. Where paternalist provision of facilities was the rule at Cadbury, at Austin the regime was far more despotic: works police rather more than works council. Such differences are amenable to an explanation, insists Smith, in which the role of those external factors glossed in Burawoy's account are emphasized. Whereas Cadbury's sought to make working for them a morally rewarding as well as well-paid experience for their employees, at Austin the relationship was constituted far more explicitly in terms of the cash nexus. These differences are not simply between "market despotism" and "paternalism", organizing a "hegemonic" regime. As Smith argues, in fact, the "paternalism", that one might suppose characterized hegemonic managerial strategies, had by the late 1970s become a source of labour's legitimacy rather than that of management, as the latter sought to reconstruct employee relations in the changed conditions that prevailed after a corporate takeover of the old Cadbury's by Schweppes, a multi-divisional food and beverage conglomerate, during the changed economic environment of the late 1970s. In these circumstances, says Smith; "hegemony" becomes a resource for resistance rather than control. In the terms in which he depicts the Longbridge works, the account seems closer to Burawoy's terms.

Smith draws four conclusions from this careful consideration of Burawoy's model against the details of his cases. Each of these serve to reiterate the importance of considering what Burawoy terms "factory regimes" within the indeterminate triangulatory containment of organization relations by not only those of *class structure,* but also of *the state* and the particulars of locally lived and expressed *civil society.*

One of the most evident aspects of any comparison between the Bournville and Longbridge social relations, which Smith does not focus on, are the gender relations which characterized each factory organization. The Bournville factory production line was staffed almost entirely by female production workers in white overall coats, caps and hair nets, while the blue-collar workers at Longbridge were all male. If differential strategies of relatively tougher and more tender management developed at each site, then one might anticipate that an account which stressed the role played by gender relations would be important. It is unfortunate that this element is not only downplayed in Burawoy but also absent from Smith's critique.

In the next paper in this section Rosemary Crompton begins to redress this oversight, one which is by no means a rare occurrence, in her contribution "The Class/Gender/Organization Nexus." At the outset she notes that "organizations," as a field of enquiry, is an interdisciplinary focus for the majority of its practitioners (although some, to be sure, would probably find offence in this lack of boundedness (e.g. Donaldson 1985) allowing intrusion to the concerns represented in this volume). While conceding that recent enthusiasms for "radical critique" or "critical organization theory" have done something to enrich the multi-paradigmatic flavour of organization analysis, Crompton wants to develop it further by elaborating the proposition that work organizations are significantly structured by gender as well as class relations.

As a proposition, she notes, it is not entirely novel, having been explored most frequently by adherents of what Burrell and Morgan (1979) have termed the "radical humanist" paradigm, contributors to which have explored issues of sexuality (e.g. Hearn and Parkin 1987) and gender (e.g. Collinson and Knights 1986) within organizations. Prior to a consideration of the class/gender/organization nexus within a specific type of organization – building societies – Crompton iterates some recent sociological approaches to "theorizing gender."

Early attempts at this theorization derived from not only role theory but also Marxist perspectives. Both of these tended to be over-deterministic and allowed insufficient specificity to the gender relations they sought to theorize. Instead, the latter were seen as a reflex of action deriving from structures which were conceptually elsewhere, in classically functionalist exogenous accounts of change.

Theories of patriarchy have been developed which seek to articulate the assumption that men, as a category, oppress the opposing category of women. Such crude and biological essentialism deserves short shrift from sociology, as Crompton suggests. However, with forms of functionalism on the one hand, and essentialism on the other, the theorization of gender might be thought to have reached an impasse. A way out of this was proffered by "dual systems" theory, in which an element of each of functionalism and essentialism was combined: capitalism constructs "empty" class positions; patriarchy determines who fills them. Consequently, organizations would be the product of not only capitalistic but also patriarchal structures. However, the essentialist problem of assuming what is to be explained as an outcome, patriarchy, as if it were an explanation, still remains.

In an effort to circumvent these problems but still retain the acknowledgement that patriarchal outcomes invariably occur in fields such as the structuring of organization relations, some writers have sought to develop a "reality" theory of patriarchy, paralleling, as is noted, similar attempts at realism in the sociology of organizations. (For such an attempt see Clegg 1983.) The object of such an exercise is to specify the structural, generative underlying mechanisms which constitute the phenomenal appeareance of the world of apparent reality; to go beneath the surface, as it were. Crompton cites Walby's (1986) study of male exclusionary practices in textiles, engineering and clerical work from 1800 to after the Second World War as an attempt at a realist account of patriarchy.

While Crompton would admit of a formal realism to categories of class such as "bourgeois" and "proletarian" (which other contributions to the debate would deny, such as Hindess' chapter in this volume), she notes that gender relations depend for their reality on the personal interaction of individuals in a way in which class does not. Gender relations simultaneously constitute and are constituted by lived experience. (In this, according to "structurational" sociologists, they may be no different from many other "social" phenomena: e.g. Giddens 1984.) Consequently, to research gender relations, just as one might research organization relations more generally, theoretically informed case studies are required which can tap into this lived experience that connects personal lives and social structure, history and biography.

In what is an apt sociological pun, Crompton proceeds to a case study of "Building Societies." First she outlines the way in which the building society industry is organized, before developing an analysis of gender relations, labour market practices and their interconnection within the context of changing industry structure, state policy towards feminist issues and the changing credential basis of the knowledge used in the industry. The initial focus is on "cashier clerks," the fastest growing occupation in the industry, and one which is almost entirely female, but was once "a job" predominantly done by men; however, when it was a male preserve it was hardly the same job, argues Crompton. As the workforce was feminized, so was the job.

The underlying mechanism which transformed both the nature of the work and the workforce was organization restructuring contingent upon the adoption of computer technology. It was this which enabled the development of retail outlets in which efficient machine operators could handle financial advice, using terminals connected to a central computing facility at a location remote from the branch. Women were recruited to fill these new cashiering jobs; the work was created and filled as "women's work," to provision the financial services being marketed to working class customers who had hitherto not been recruited as a market by the major financial institutions. On this market basis the industry grew rapidly in the 1960s and 1970s, recruiting many women, for none of whom would promotion to managerial levels, a male preserve, have normally been a career expectation. Management was instead entered via Management Traineeships, where, unlike cashiering, both men and women now compete in the same labour market, as a result of changed state regulation through Equal Opportunities Legislation.

Part of the changed regulatory environment consisted of an Equal Opportunities Commission (EOC), a body equipped to investigate possible breaches of the legislation: i.e. exclusionary male strategies. Ample evidence of these are documented with respect to the building society industry. Of more interest is the way in which the archive assembled by the EOC demonstrated that formally rational criteria, which appeared to be the very essence of that universalism so admired in bureaucracy by many liberal observers (e.g. Perrow 1986, in the introductory chapter to his *Complex Organizations: A Critical Essay*), could in practice be constituted in such a way that desired outcomes (i.e. female exclusion from managerial ranks) were still achieved, but with more difficulty, as Crompton makes clear. Universalistic criteria may not serve to eradicate particularistic prejudice in organizational recruitment and selection, but they do make it much more difficult to legitimate.

A number of conclusions can be drawn from this account, suggests Crompton. First, organization structuring of occupational relations is the major mechanism of the gendering of jobs, seen in the context of specific labour market conditions. Second, in the same way, accountability of this structuring to an outside body charged with legislating specific social policy for equal employment opportunity can, in the context of another but equally specific set of labour market conditions, serve to undermine exclusionary practices by challenging their outcome.

The project reported here has to be seen in the context of other research conducted by the author (Crompton and Jones 1984). When it is, Crompton argues, it becomes possible to see the way in which the impact of de-skilling and work fragmentation attendant on the restructuring of organization relations in white-collar bureaucracies has been "buffered" by female recruitment to the new jobs and the reproduction of an internal labour market for men.

Crompton concludes on an optimistic note, by noting the resistance of women to their exclusion from senior white-collar grades within the industry, in the context of the EOC. However, a caution may be necessary. To the extent that credentialled women may now compete more equally with credentialled men, this may tell us a great deal about changes in the organization/gender nexus. However, it tells us nothing of how this interacts with the class nexus, unless we entertain some notion of a perfect market in "intelligence," untrammelled by class processes and practices, being translated without distortion into credentials. As Crompton has argued elsewhere (Crompton and Gubbay 1977), and as education sociologists have frequently researched (e.g. Halsey et al. 1980), such assumptions would be profoundly unrealistic. Delimitation of gender inequality in the context of "knowledge" labour markets will not effect the reproduction of class and gender inequality in what Littek and Heisig (in this volume) have characterized as those labour markets constructed around notions of "skill" rather than knowledge. Data coming out of the comparative project on class structure and class consciousness suggests that, in fact, the working class across the advanced societies seems to be disproportionately female (see Wright 1985 for the Swedish and US data).

If there were one type of organization in which one might expect structured inequality to be minimized, it would be trade unions, particularly in that most social democratic of countries, Sweden, which, according to some accounts at least, offers an indication of what a more equal and a transformative "class politics" might be (e.g. Clegg et al. 1986). However, as Alison E. Woodward and Hakon Leiulfsrud observe in the final contribution to this section, in a chapter titled "Masculine/Feminine Organization: Class versus Gender in Swedish Unions," this would be to ignore what they term the "male nexus" of politics and production in which unions are situated. (Notwithstanding this, however, it is the case that almost 90% of the Swedish labour force is unionized, so women in the workforce will hardly be excluded from formal membership.)

In writing of unions as a "male nexus," Woodward and Leiulfsrud are contrasting them to the motion of the family as a "female nexus": the contrast which feminist writing has noted between the masculine, public world and the private, feminized domestic sphere. However, rather than dichotomizing the sphere of reproduction and the sphere of production, they propose to link them in order to analyse female strategies in each. In doing so, as they observe, female union activity has to be seen as actively shaped by a highly integrated set of factors involving labour market structure, "female" job categories and their working conditions as well as the nature of female life in the family. Thus, in seeking to connect consideration of households and workplaces, families and organizations, with employment and union organization, Woodward and Leiulfsrud are involved in a sociological analysis of organizations not as self-contained, bounded and self-evident entities, but as sites in which the interpenetration of life-worlds will be evident.

The chapter begins with a consideration of recent research on gender and union activity and moves on to empirical data on Sweden, drawn from the Swedish project results in the comparative project on class structure and class consciousness. In particular, the interest is in how family organization interacts with union activity in the shaping of political attitudes.

Woodward and Leiulfsrud note that until very recently there has been an academic preconception of the passive working woman. This can no longer be held. Research suggests instead that women's activity, just as men's, is situationally dependent on work sectors, work histories and so on. Women and men in similar situations will probably develop similar attitudes; however, as Crompton's case study suggests, the gendered nature of job construction will frequently ensure that women will rarely be in precisely the same jobs as men. To some extent, that women have appeared to be less active than men in union affairs is in part because the nature of this activity has been defined in ways which align with typically male points of view, or because of the way these points of view have constructed available accounts. To some extent, there may be direct male repression and exclusion of females. It is important to note that this is decreasingly the case: in comparable industries, internationally, female and male unionism rates are of similar frequency, with women providing much of the new membership in newly unionizing sectors. Women's demands for union activity differ from men's: not only do they want equal pay but also better working and welfare conditions, linked to family and community. For married women, participation may be restricted to working hours and contexts spatially close to home, because of family ties and the overwhelming share of domestic labour which is still done by women, despite the fact that the two income family, in which both wage earners' contributions are vital, has become a norm in countries such as Sweden. Consequently, the organizational frequency and activity rate of men and women in Swedish unions is virtually identical.

The nature of male and female organizational issues for union activity differs noticeably. Female dominated unions are more likely to raise local welfare state rather than national wage-level issues, and to concentrate on health, personal relations at work and issues of sexual equality, in appraising new technology, for example. Female dominance raises new, previously "non"-issues, on to the agenda.

Women in Sweden are themselves, within the middle class at least, as likely to be involved in union organization as working class men, and the higher up the class structure one goes, the less evident the gender differences are. Unions, as formal organizations, are arenas in which male and non-working class people, with more surplus time for participation, are able to involve themselves more effectively.

Woodward and Leiulfsrud demonstrate that, interpreting the Swedish data, social class is more powerful than gender in predicting union acitivity. There is an interaction between family situation, class position and gender which can be seen by comparing "class homogeneous" with "class heterogeneous" families. (That is to contrast families in which each partner is of the same class with families in which they are not.) Most frequently, non-working class males are married to working class females; less frequently is the non-working class wife married to a working class husband. Class homogeneous husbands and wives experience the world differently from class heterogeneous partners. The class position of oneself as a woman worker is of greater moment in fixing womens' identity than being the spouse of a particular class of man. Thus men and women in full-time employment in the same class positions will have about the same degree of union activity as each other. As they have less time at work, they will participate less. Women are the major part-time workers, but they participate less not because they are women but because they are employed part-time. The more that women participate in union organization, the more their class congruent attitudes increase, consciousness being raised through struggle. This relationship is strengthened by being in a class homogeneous family, and weakened by being in a class heterogeneous one.

Union organization, socialist party preference and support for the welfare state are linked, with the organizational location *qua* class situation being more determinate for working class women married to middle class men, than is their spouse's class. Involvement in organization seems to over-determine involvement in marriage.

The organization life-worlds of spouses of the same class position present similar structural locations and issues, even if the particulars of specific workplaces differ greatly. For cross class families there is no such continuity and one might anticipate greater contradiction between the worlds of work and the home for at least one partner. To test this out Woodward and Leiulfsrud carried out an intensive investigation of 30 cross class families, 15 with a working class husband, 15 with a working class wife. A range of strategies for dealing with not only home-life, but also organization life revealed themselves in their qualitative data, suggesting that any focus on organizational activity and participation which did not include variables related to family situation would be missing an important source of variation in membership attributes and dispositions. Correlatively, the organizational work-place is not the only arena of struggle for women workers. Union modes of organization and issue representation can assist struggle in both spheres.

6. Classless Organizations?

As has been argued in detail elsewhere in *Class, Politics and the Economy*, the earliest conceptions of class structure, in an explicit sense, derived from political economy in its classical form in the eighteenth century. Formally, Smith and Ricardo signalled the emergence of a new moral and economic order, premised not on a tradition to be learnt, but on the rationalizing instrument of mastery over production methods. Their vision, as Marx demonstrated, was implicitly teleological: the emergent relations of production between bourgeois masters and proletarian workers formed the horizon of their thought. It was this horizon which Marx sought to project into a possible future in which, with the overcoming of class relations, there might be a dawning of real human history. Such a vision had the benefits of being more explicitly teleological than either Smith or Ricardo's. However, its teleology posed the problem for those who adopted Marx's convictions, of how to get from the here-and-now of classes to the future-perfect, redemptory state of classlessness? Marx's answer, that immanent structural tendencies inherent to the development of capitalism would offer ample opportunities for appropriate political action to secure the desired outcome, became the orthodoxy of Marxists after Marx, in the Second International, an orthodoxy from which a number of heretics resiled.

On the one hand, analytical social scientists of Weber's ilk, while they were convinced of the reality of social classes (albeit in terms somewhat, but not markedly, dissimilar to the main thrust of Marx's approach: see Clegg et al. 1986), remained altogether more sceptical about the immanent transcendence of this reality in the Soviet Union or elsewhere: other teleologies of an altogether more this-worldly disposition preoccupied them: the future looked only more bleak and uncomprehendingly rationalized to the cultural perspective in which Weber and his heirs were constituted. On the other hand, within debates in the Second International in the early years of the twentieth century, two distinct lines emerged. One of these was an orthodox view, associated with Eduard Bernstein's dominant faction in the German social democratic party. Marxists need do nothing other than wait for the inevitable crisis of capitalism. The immanent tendencies would simplify the class structure in time for the coming crisis. The other line, associated with Rosa Luxemburg and Anton Pannekoek, was altogether more activist and concerned ideas of prefigurational socialism: designing and constructing organizations in the here-and-now which would anticipate the post-revolutionary future. Each of these views has distant echoes in contemporary academic debates around "radical organization theory."

One echo emerges in the debates over the structural location of the "middle strata" – those people who in seemingly expanding numbers during the twentieth century occupied positions between "labour" and "capital", positions which were an acute embarrassment to orthodox Marxism. In posing as his theme "the degradation of work in the twentieth century", Braverman (1974) initiated a renewed academic debate on some well-trodden political ground. One of the major contributors to the renewal of debate on the nature and definition of the "middle class", within the more general renaissance of class analysis which his work helped to occasion, was Guglielmo Carchedi. A series of papers published in the journal *Economy and Society* during the mid-1970s, as well as a book *On The Economic Identification of Social Classes* (1977) marked his contribution as an original formal resolution of some of the central issues that were posed for Marxist analysis by the twentieth century development of capitalism in the advanced societies. These contributions have not been without critics (e.g. Clegg et al. 1986; Johnson 1977) but they have, nonetheless, been the basis for what has been seen to be a significant *rapprôchment* between class and organization analysis (Clegg and Dunkerley 1980), as well as being a topic for many of the contributors to this volume.

"Between Class Analysis and Organization Theory: Mental Labour" is the title of Carchedi's contribution to this volume, in which he continues the project launched in the earlier work of developing an adequate conceptualization of class structure, one whose adequacy may be judged both in terms of the aims of the Marxist theoretical project and the analysis of contemporary conditions. The starting point for such an analysis is Braverman's (1974) *Labour and Monopoly Capital*. Three lacunae are established in this work: an absence of a dialectical method of social research; a failure to distinguish labour from non-labour; and a lack of conceptual specificity with respect to the distinction of "mental labour" from other forms of labour. As lacunae they have a well-established pedigree: Carchedi locates the same problems in the historic debates in the Second International on the notion of "socialist organization." Carchedi's chapter is a re-joining of that debate in order to achieve a resolution of it markedly different to that which prevailed at the time. The resolution went in Lenin's favour, and thus produced a situation in which issues of socialist organization as a collectively reasoned enterprise were to be marginalized in favour of an authoritarianism in which the "party," both theoretically and practically, would manage and resolve contradictions. Consequently, in "official Marxism" as it developed from the Second International, little attention was given to conceptualizing what might be an alternative form of organization to that of the hierarchical and authoritarian forms of both the party and the capitalist enterprise, a situation of some embarrassment to Western Marxist critics of capitalist organization.

An alternative position to that of Lenin's was developed in the Second International by Rosa Luxemburg and Anton Pannekoek. From their perspective, unlike that of orthodox Marxism, a distinctive form of socialist organization, unlike that of either the party or the capitalist firm, was possible. Its core principles were those of collectivism, developed to the furthest extent in Pannekoek's notion of "council communism," a conception which Carchedi regards as having been eliminated or at best marginalized from more recent debate. Thus the collective memory of debate on organizational forms has been obliterated, even by most Marxists, of potentially the most radical contributions: those which challenged the roots of present-day pervasive organizational forms. (It is significant, for example, that in the most authoritative academic work on collectivist organizations in recent years, Rothschild and Whitt's (1986) *The Cooperative Workplace,* neither Luxemburg's nor Pannekoek's contributions are considered.) Carchedi develops from these neglected voices a conception of what "socialist organization" entails. Briefly, one can enumerate these as follows:

(1) Organizational development premised on the reciprocal rather than restrictive development of each member.
(2) Co-operation not discipline as the major mechanism of intra-organizational relations.
(3) Job design premised on the expansion of human capacities rather than their restriction.
(4) Task allocation such that all tasks enjoy work which not only transforms natural and social reality but also develops opportunities for new knowledge.
(5) A division of labour functional for the all round, rather than one-sided, development of the individual.

On this basis Carchedi develops an argument which attempts to break the deadlock on imagination that he regards as having been the heritage of the Second International. He does so by re-addressing a dichotomy which has been at the centre of both Poulantzas' and Braverman's conceptualization of the distinction between the working class and the new middle class (Poulantzas called them, rather confusingly, "new petty bourgeoisie"). The dichotomy is that posed between "mental" and "manual" labour, a distinction which has been at the core of the de-skilling debate in labour process theory (Wood 1982). If it is the relation between mental and manual labour, between conception and execution, which is at the heart of the distinctions between workers and middle class managers, then questions raised by organization analysis must be central to class analysis. It will be the specific practices of organization design which will calibrate this relationship. Carchedi's purpose is thus three-fold: to reconsider the mental/manual labour cleavage; to demonstrate how a more adequate understanding of this can contribute to a clarification of the class content of mental labour; and third, to articulate the relationship between a particular type of mental labour, computer work and the possibility of socialist organization.

At the outset Carchedi rejects the mental/manual cleavage. No work is, nor can be, entirely thoughtless, as this nomenclature implies. The correct distinction must be between mental and material labour, where the latter transforms material objects and the former transforms knowledge. These notions of material and mental transformations are Carchedi's building-blocks for discussing the notion of labour. What follows is an incisive discussion of the formal processes involved in the labour process of material and mental transformations, transformations which, he argues, have a necessary dialectical relationship in which one or the other of the two types of transformation will be dominant. Which of these it will be is determined by whether the product of the labour process in question is exchanged primarily because of its material qualities or because of its knowledge content, a matter determined, says Carchedi, in the moment of exchange (where that exchange is a social rather than individual phenomenon).

Posing and resolving the previous issues is preparatory to Carchedi resolving the question "What is material and mental labour?" to which the answer is dependent on "whether the determinant transformations are material or mental." Ordinarily these issues have to be posed within the context of a collective organization of the labour process of many people. Within this collective labour process material labourers will be those who in their work are primarily involved in material transformations, while mental labourers are primarily involved in the transformation of knowledge. From this perspective, what may appear on the surface to be objectively similar work, such as typing, takes on a markedly different character depending on the type of material transformation in which it is done. (Carchedi uses the comparison of a copy typist with a journalist.)

On the basis of the distinctions elaborated between mental and material labour one can now reconceptualize a central problem of socialist organization: that is, how to fuse the two in one complex labour process rather than radically separate them to different classes of people. As Carchedi observes, from this perspective, categories such as "mental" vs. "manual labour" or "blue-collar" vs. "white-collar" workers function as sociologically quite inadequate distinctions with which to represent the cleavages within modern complex organization. Moreover, where one side of these distinctions is allied with "productive" labour, with exploitation, and the other with "unproductive" labour and being the "exploiter," it produces an equally inadequate basis for discriminating organization relations on the basis of social relations of production. (As an original author of the "contradictory class locations" analysis derived from such distinctions, Carchedi is here making a subtle auto-critique.)

Finally Carchedi considers the implications for the mental labour process of the widespread adoption of computer technology, in an argument which is at once provocative and insightful. It is provocative because it argues that computers are by virtue of the formalized mechanical reasoning embedded in them, a capitalist tool, inimical to a more dialectical organization, contra to many who see the increasing use of computers as a source of liberation from dull compulsion in work. Insightful, because he draws on an understanding of the sociology of music to make his point. What is clear from Carchedi's conclusions are that one cannot expect, against the arguments of some engineers, that computerization will democratize work. Arguments that propose that this will be so suggest it is because computer adoption will necessarily lead to less strict regulation and more autonomy in work, in order that the computer may be reflexively monitored. Nothing could be further from Carchedi's conclusions. It is to the central organization of material and mental labour that any project for democratic, socialist organization should turn, rather than technological fetishism.

If Carchedi's contribution to this volume represents a working out of the Luxemburg/Pannekoek position, the chapter by Stewart Clegg and Winton Higgins, "Against the Current: Organizational Sociology and Socialism," derives from a unique critique of Bernstein's position developed in Sweden by the great theoretician of the Swedish social democratic party, Ernst Wigforss, by way of some recent debates in organizational theory. The contrast with Carchedi's position is evident. For Carchedi the position advanced by Clegg and Higgins would be an example of that pragmatic revisionism opposed by his argument. Clegg and Higgins, by contrast, would seem to argue implicitly that Carchedi's position is too utopian for application to other than quite small-scale organizations. In essence, their argument seeks to accept some of the criticisms which have been made of the lack of concern in radical criticism with some central issues for organization theory of organization design. This relative neglect is attributed by them to some inherently utopian aspects of the Marxist legacy, ones which surface in a pessimistic and fatalistic vein in some contemporary work. (Some of Harvie Ramsay and Nigel Haworth's (1984) earlier work is a target. In fact, in their contribution here the criticism that Clegg and Higgins make (originally in *Organization Studies,* 1987) appears to be implicitly acknowledged by Ramsay and Haworth.) Like Carchedi, Clegg and Higgins point to the centrality of those debates which occurred around the Second International. Unlike Carchedi, they resolve them not in Luxemburg/Pannekoek's favour, nor do they follow Lenin. Instead, they highlight the subsequent debate which produced Wigforss' critique of Bernstein's contribution. Finally, they sketch a "provisional utopia" centred on a model of reconstructed property relations and social relations quite different to those which prevail in most contemporary organization designs.

Clegg and Higgins specify some aspects for the design of organizations which are to be constructed outside the property and social relations which prevail in most contemporary organizations. Amir Ben-Porat, in his contribution to this section, deals with the "Political Domination and Reproduction of Classless Organizations." The type of "classless organization" which is focused on is the kibbutz, as it developed in the Jewish community in pre-war Palestine and in the post-war State of Israel. To analyse the kibbutz's place in what is an evidently capitalist as well as Zionist state, he uses the "articulation of modes of production" approach. The kibbutz is to be seen as a subordinate mode of production, with distinct patterns of articulation with the dominant capitalist mode of production, within the social formation which is today the State of Israel.

What marks the kibbutz off as a distinct organizational form corresponding to a specific mode of production, is its collectivist design and functioning, and the correlative absence of class divisions premised on unequal relations of ownership and control. The kibbutz does not contain these; therefore, maintains Ben-Porat, it is, in the terms of formal Marxist theory, a classless organization. The chapter traces the historical development of this form within the context of the British mandate over Palestine and the subsequent creation of the post-war Israeli state. Central to its development as a specific organization form has been a very strong sense of politically and ideologically religious agency, oriented to fundamental economic problems of unemployment. With the kibbutz's consolidation, latterly, as increasingly an industrial as well as an agricultural form of production, the expansion of industry has undermined its collectivist form. In 1987 about 25% of kibbutz employees were non-kibbutzim; rather than members they were hired wage labour. Moreover, the kibbutz have become decreasingly an enclave of socialism, holding the surrounding traffic of capitalism at arm's length through either a basically subsistence or self-reproducing local economy. The kibbutz have become increasingly involved in exchange relations with the surrounding capitalist economy, and with a state which Ben-Porat, in Poulantzian fashion, regards as the organizational apparatus which ensures a degree or factor of cohesion between the different modes of production contained in its social formation. It is because of the dominance of the "political instance" in the reproduction of these modes of production, that the kibbutz mode has survived, so that now, in the absence since 1977 of the strong state support it once enjoyed, it is self-reproductive.

One common lesson can be drawn from both Clegg and Higgins' and Ben-Porat's contributions. This is the central role that the policies and practices of the state play in contributing the framework of "rules of the game" within which various forms of organization may be constituted and reproduced. Further support is given to this point by Tom Clarke in the final contribution to this volume: "Socialized Industry: Social Ownership or Shareholding Democracy?"

In an extremely well-documented paper, drawing on a wealth of data, Clarke addresses what have been seen by many commentators to be the fundamental transformations in both organization reality and class relations in the United Kingdom which have occurred under the Conservative Party government of Mrs. Thatcher. Privatization of state owned organizations has been a major plank of the policy of this government. Explicit to this has been a programme not just for changing formal ownership relations of production, but also class relations more generally. The target has been to further undermine trade unionism in Britain by making property owning a more salient social relation than that of being an employee. For empirical reasons which Clarke elaborates, concerning the nature of this share-holding revolution, it is unlikely that these ambitions of class transformation will be realized. In fact, he is drawn to the conclusion that although undoubted changes have occured in the relations of ownership, these may have less to do with visions of a new democracy or efficiency than with the ideological role of these.

In conclusion, let me observe only that the contributions to the volume represent an important and underdeveloped conjuncture in contemporary social science scholarship. Not all the contributions will prove productive, obviously. Nor is there any singular or essential similarity to the contributors' grasp of the relations between organizations and classes. Indeed, as I hope that this introduction has indicated, they are a variable range of papers and concerns. Sufficiently so, that for readers concerned to develop their understanding of the organization/ class nexus there should be something of relevance here for their own work.

References

AMWSU, (Amalgamated Metalworkers and Shipwrights Union) *Australia Ripped-Off*. Sydney: AMWSU. 1977

Armstrong, P., Competition Between the Organizational Profession and the Evaluation of Management Control Systems, in: K. Thompson (Ed.) *Work, Employment and Unemployment*. London: Open University Press. 1984

Bauman, Z., *Legislators and Interpreters*. Cambridge: Polity Press. 1987

Berle, A. A. and G. C. Means, *The Modern Corporation and Private Property*. New York: Macmillan. 1932

Boreham, P., Indetermination: Professional Knowledge, Organization and Control, *Sociological Review* 31, 4, 693–718. 1983

Braverman, H., *Labour and Monopoly Capital: The Degradation of Work in the Twentieth Century*. New York: Monthly Review. 1974

Burawoy, M., *Manufacturing Consent*. Chicago: University of Chicago Press. 1979

Burawoy, M., *The Politics of Production. Factory Regimes under Capitalism and Socialism*. London: Verso. 1985

Burrell, G. and G. Morgan, *Sociological Paradigms and Organizational Analysis*. London: Heinemann. 1979

Carchedi, G., *On the Economic Identification of Social Classes*. London: Routledge and Kegan Paul. 1977

Carchedi, G., *Class Analysis and Social Research*. Oxford: Blackwell. 1987

Clegg, S., *Power, Rule and Domination*. London: Routledge and Kegan Paul. 1975

Clegg, S., Organization and Control, *Administrative Science Quarterly* 26, 4: 545–62. 1981

Clegg, S., Phenomenology and Formal Organizations: A Realist Critique, in:

S. B. Bacharach (ed.), *Research in the Sociology of Organizations: A Research Annual.* Greenwich, Conn: JAI. Press, 102–152. 1983

Clegg, S., P. Boreham and G. Dow, *Class, Politics and the Economy.* London: Routledge and Kegan Paul. 1986

Clegg, S. and D. Dunkerley, *Organization, Class and Control.* London: Routledge and Kegan Paul 1980

Clegg, S. R., D. Dunphy and S. G. Redding (eds), *The Enterprise and Management in East Asia.* Centre of Asian Studies: University of Hong Kong. 1986

Clegg, S. R. W. Higgins and T. Spybey, "Post-Confucianism," Social Democracy and Economic Culture, in: S. R. Clegg and S. G. Redding (eds.), *Capitlism in Contrasting Cultures,* Berlin: De Gruyter. 1989

Clegg, S. R. and G. Matheson, The Social Organization of Class, unpublished paper, the Department of Sociology. University of New England, Armidale. 1987

Clegg, S. R. and S. G. Redding, *Capitalism in Contrasting Cultures.* Berlin: De Gruyter. 1989

Collinson, D. and D. Knights, "Men Only": Theories and Practices of Job Segregation in Insurance, in: D. Knights and D. Collinson (eds.), *Gender and the Labour Process.* London: Macmillan. 1986

Crompton, R. and J. Gubbay, *Economy and Class Structure.* London: Macmillan. 1977

Crompton, R. and G. Jones, *White-Collar Proletariat: De-Skilling and Gender in the Clerical Labour Process.* London: Macmillan. 1984

Crozier, M., *The Bureaucratic Phenomenon.* London: Tavistock. 1964.

Donaldson, L., *In Defence of Organization Theory: A Response to the Critics.* Cambridge: Cambridge University Press. 1985

Emmison, M., P. Boreham and S. Clegg, Against Antinomies: For a Post-Marxist Politics, *Thesis Eleven* 18: 124–142. 1988

Foster, J., *Class Struggle and the Industrial Revolution: Early Industrial Capitalism in Three English Towns.* London: Methuen. 1974

Fox, A., *Beyond Contract: Work, Power and Trust Relations.* London: Faber. 1974

Giddens, A., *The Class Structure of the Advanced Societies.* London: Hutchinson. 1973

Giddens, A., *The Constitution of Society.* Cambridge: Polity Press. 1984

Goldthorpe, J. H., C. Llewellyn and C. Payne, *Social Mobility and Class Structure in Modern Britain.* Oxford: Clarendon Press. 1980

Gorz, A. (ed.), *The Division of Labour: The Labour Process and Class Struggle in Modern Capitalism.* Brighton: Harvester. 1976

Gorz, A., *Farewell to the Working Class: An Essay on Post-Industrial Socialism.* Boston: South End Press. 1982

Halsey, A. H., A. F. Heath and J. M. Ridge, *Origins and Destinations: Family, Class and Education in Modern Britain.* Oxford: Clarendon Press. 1980

Hearn, J. and W. Parkin, *"Sex" at "Work": the Power and Paradox of Organization Sexuality.* Brigthon: Wheatsheaf. 1987

Hickson, D. J., C. R. Hinings, C. A. Lee, R. E. Schneck and J. M. Pennings, A Strategic Contingencies Theory of Intra-Organizational Power, *Administrative Science Quarterly* 16: 216–29. 1971

Higgins, W. and S. R. Clegg, Enterprise Calculation and Manufacturing Decline, *Organization Studies* 9, 1: 69–90. 1988

Holloway, J. and S. Piccioto (eds.), *State and Capital: A Marxist Debate*. London: Edward Arnold. 1978

Ingham, G., Social Stratification: Individual Attributes and Social Relationships, *Sociology* 4: 105–113. 1970.

Johnson, T., "What is to be Known?" The Structural Determination of Social "Class", *Economy and Society* 7: 194–233. 1977

Lakatos, I., Falsification and the Methodology of Scientific Research Programmes, in: I. Lakatos and A. Musgrave (eds.), *Criticism and the Growth of Knowledge*. Cambridge: Cambridge University Press, pp. 91–195. 1970

Lash, S. and J. Urry, *The End of Organized Capitalism*. Cambridge: Polity Press. 1987

Littler, C. and G. Salaman, Bravermania and Beyond: Recent Theories of the Labour Process, *Sociology* 16: 251–69. 1982

Mallet, S., *The New Working Class*. Nottingham: Spokesman Boots. 1975

Marx, K., *Capital, vol. 1*. Harmondsworth, Penguin. 1976

Mathias, P., *The First Industrial Nation*. London: Methuen. 1983

Mintzberg, H., *Power In and Around Organizations*. Englewood Cliffs, NJ: Prentice Hall. 1983

Moore, B., *The Social Origins of Dictatorship and Democracy*. Harmondsworth: Penguin. 1969

Offe, C., *Disorganized Capitalism*. Cambridge: Polity Press. 1987

Olson, M., *The Logic of Collective Action*. Cambridge: University Press. 1965

Parkin, F., *Marxism and Class Theory: A Bourgeoise Critique*. London: Tavistock 1979

Perrow, C., *Complex Organizations: A Critical Essay*. New York: Random House. 1986

Pollard, S. J., *A History of Labour in Sheffield*. Liverpool: Liverpool University Press. 1959

Poulantzas, N., *Classes in Contemporary Capitalism*. London: New Left Books. 1975

Pugh, D. S., D. J. Hickson and C. R. Hinings, *Writers on Organizations*. London: Lyon Grand and Green. 1964

Pugh, D. S., D. J. Hickson, *Organizational Structure in its context: The Aston Programme*, 1. Farnborough: Saxon House. 1976

Ramsay, H. and N. Haworth, Worker Capitalists? Profit-Sharing, Capital-Sharing and Juridicial Forms of Socialism, *Economic and Industrial Democracy: An International Journal* 5/3: 259–324. 1984

Robinson, V. and J. Kelley, Class as Conceived by Marx and Dahrendorf: Effects on Income Inequality and Politics in the United States and Great Britain, *American Sociological Review* 44, 1: 38–57. 1979

Roemer, J., *A General Theory of Exploitation and Class*. Cambridge: Cambridge University Press. 1982

Rothschild, J. and J. A. Whitt, *The Cooperative Workplace: Potentials and Dilemmas of Organizational Democracy and Participation*. Cambridge: Cambridge University Press. 1986

Turner, B. S., *For Weber*. London: Routledge and Kegan Paul. 1981

Walby, S., *Patriarchy at Work*. Cambridge: Polity Press. 1986

Whalley, P., *The Social Production of Technical Work*. London: Macmillan. 1986

Wheelwright, E. L., *Capitalism, Socialism or Barbarism? The Australian Predicament.* Sydney: ANZ Press. 1978

Wilkonson, B. and N. Oliver (eds.), Special issue on "Japanisation", *Industrial Relations Journal* 19, 1. 1988

Wood, S. (ed.), *The Degradation of Work? The De-skilling controversy.* London: Hutchinson. 1982

Wright, E. O., *Class, Crisis and the State.* London: New Left Books. 1978

Wright, E. O., *Classes.* London: Verso. 1985.

I. Classes, Structures and Actors

Classes in Contemporary Capitalist Society: Recent Marxist and Weberian Perspectives

Val Burris

1. Introduction

The class structure of contemporary capitalist society has been a subject of considerable interest and controversy in recent years. The main focus of this controversy has been the class position of salaried intermediaries and their role in the class struggle. With few exceptions, most of the participants in this debate agree that there are significant numbers of persons in contemporary capitalist society who cannot be classified as part of the working class, even though they work for a salary or wage. Various names have been applied to this group – "new middle class," "new petty bourgeoisie," "service class," or "professional-managerial class" – and competing theories have been advanced to explain the nature and significance of these positions within the class structure.

Two issues have been central to this debate. First is the question of specifying the boundaries between classes – especially that which separates intermediate class positions from the working class. Second is the question of predicting the alignment of these intermediate positions in the political struggle between capital and labor. These two questions are related in the sense that the choice of particular criteria to define the boundary between classes typically implies a conception of the interests around which classes are likely to mobilize within the political arena. Conversely, evidence on political behavior has often been used to support or criticize particular definitions of class boundaries.

Marxian and Weberian theorists take somewhat different approaches to the analysis of salaried intermediate classes. Generally speaking, Marxists conceptualize class as an objective structure of social positions, while Weberians treat class as an effect of social action. Marxists define classes in terms of the social relations of production, while Weberians focus on the distributional relations of the market. Marxists view class conflict as fundamentally a struggle over economic exploitation, while Weberians place greater emphasis on conflicts that are rooted in asymmetries of power and authority. Finally, Marxists tend to stress the primacy of class over other bases of social cleavage, while Weberians treat class as merely one of several potential bases of political association and struggle.

Despite these broad paradigmatic differences, Marxist and Weberian theorists have covered very similar terrain in their analyses of the class structure and arrived at surprisingly similar criteria for defining salaried intermediate classes.

As I have argued elsewhere, there has been a notable trend in recent years toward the convergence of Marxist and Weberian perspectives in the area of class analysis (Burris 1987). Marxists have drawn heavily upon Weberian concepts in their attempt to adapt classical Marxism to the conditions of contemporary capitalist society. At the same time, there has been a parallel movement among Weberian theorists to reinterpret Weber's sociology in a manner that renders it more compatible with the premises of Marxism (Collins 1980; Turner 1981). An adequate survey of contemporary theories of class structure must therefore address not only the theoretical differences between Marxist and Weberian approaches, but also the substantive debates that cut across this paradigmatic boundary and are reproduced within both the Marxist and Weberian camps.

In this paper I examine the debate over the nature of the class structure from both a theoretical and an empirical direction. The first part of the paper presents a critical overview of five basic strategies that have been proposed for identifying and analyzing intermediate class positions. The first interprets the boundary between working class and middle class positions as a division between manual and nonmanual occupations. The second views this boundary as a division between supervisory and nonsupervisory workers. The third stresses the distinction between productive and unproductive labor. The fourth distinguishes between professionals and managers on the one side and routine employees on the other. The fifth emphasizes the division between credentialled and uncredentialled workers. Marxist and Weberian variants of each of these five strategies are discussed and attention is given to the relative merits of each.

The second part of the paper presents an empirical analysis of the relationship between class position and political ideology. The aim of this analysis is to determine which of the various models of class structure is most consistent with the alignment of individuals on key political issues. Survey data for the United States is used to estimate the political distance between proletarian and intermediate class positions and to compare the different models of class structure in terms of their correspondence or noncorrespondence with empirical cleavages in political opinion. The results of this empirical analysis reinforce some of the theoretical conclusions regarding the strengths and weaknesses of different models of class structure and direct our attention to several issues for further research.

2. Manual versus Nonmanual Occupations

One of the most widely accepted boundaries for distinguishing proletarian and nonproletarian class positions is the division between manual and nonmanual occupations. This criterion is particularly favoured among Weberian theorists, but is also central to certain Marxist theories of class structure. Among Weberians, Anthony Giddens' *The Class Structure of the Advanced Societies* is the most systematic recent attempt to elaborate a theory of intermediate class positions in terms of the distinction between manual and nonmanual occupations. Following Weber, Giddens defines classes in terms of their differential access to market rewards. In contemporary capitalism, Giddens argues, there are three general types of "market capacity" that are important in the structuring of classes: ownership of property in the means of production; possession of educational or technical qualifications; and possession of manual labour power. These provide the foundation for three basic classes in capitalist society: an "upper," "middle," and "lower" or "working" class. One of the problems with defining classes from the standpoint of the market, Giddens recognizes, is that differences in market capacity generate an indeterminate plurality of class locations, rather than a finite number of discrete and bounded classes. To remedy this problem. Giddens proposes that the strength and location of class boundaries is determined by the manner in which differences in market capacity are reinforced or crystallized by what he calls mechanisms of class "structuration." Four such mechanisms are identified by Giddens: (1) the closure of mobility opportunities within and between generations; (2) differences in the technical conditions of labour; (3) differences in authority; and (4) differences in patterns of consumption. On each of these dimensions, Giddens argues, the division between manual and nonmanual occupations provides the most appropriate boundary for distinguishing between working class and middle class positions. Empirically, Giddens maintains, nonmanual occupations receive higher market rewards than manual occupations; they are relatively resistant to upward mobility from manual ranks; they are physically and socially isolated within the technical organization of labour; they participate more fully in the authority structure of the enterprise; and they tend to cluster into distinctive status or residential communities.

The chief difficulty with this conception of class structure is that the manual/ nonmanual division is a purely *nominal* boundary between classes. It functions merely as a conventional reference point around which, Giddens argues, a variety of social processes have converged to produce a qualitative break in the continuum of market capacities. There is nothing *inherent* in the nature of manual or nonmanual labour that confers distinctive class interests upon those who engage in such labour. Hence, the model yields little insight into the material bases of political alignment or opposition between classes. Moreover, insofar as Giddens defense of the manual/nonmanual boundary is primarily empirical, it is also subject to empirical challenge. Most notably, in the case of lower nonmanual employees there is considerable question as to whether these positions have more in common with higher nonmanual employees than they do with manual workers. Many of these jobs have become degraded and deskilled; their income advantage has eroded; their exercise of authority is negligible; and their claims to status are increasingly tenuous (Braverman 1974). Does this mean that lower nonmanual workers should be classified as working class, or that the more privileged manual workers should be classified as middle class? Either of these interpretations would be more consistent with the rigorous application of Giddens' criteria than his own adherence to the manual/nonmanual dichotomy.

Marxist theorists have tended to view the manual/nonmanual dichotomy somewhat differently. Generally speaking, they have denied that nonmanual workers as a group should be classified as "middle class," and argued that the class interests of routine nonmanual workers are not fundamentally different from those of the proletariat. An exception to this tendency is found in the work of Nicos Poulantzas (1975). In Poulantzas' theory, classes are defined by a combination of three criteria: economic, political and ideological. The principle factor in defining social classes, according to Poulantzas, is the distinction between those who produce and those who appropriate surplus value (more on this later). This relationship of economic exploitation is reinforced, however, by political and ideological relations that are also part of the determination of classes. At the political level this is accomplished through the relations of supervision and authority within the capitalist enterprise. According to Poulantzas, the work of management and supervision under capitalism entails not only the technical coordination of the labour process, but also the enforcement of capitalist domination over the working class. This places salaried managers and supervisors in an antagonistic relation to the working class. At the ideological level Poulantzas identifies the basic class relation as the division between mental and manual labour. Poulantzas argues that this division also reproduces the subordination of the working class by excluding them from the "secret knowledge" of the production process and thereby reinforcing their dependence upon capital. For this reason, professionals, technicians, and even routine office workers are seen by Poulantzas as occupying positions antagonistic to the working class.

Compared with Giddens' defence of the manual/nonmanual dichotomy, Poulantzas' theory has the advantage of ascribing this class boundary an *intrinsic,* and not merely nominal, significance. Manual and nonmanual workers are viewed by Poulantzas as occupying two poles of an antagonistic relation, rather than merely two points on a scale. This allows him to develop a more coherent analysis of the class interests upon which political conflicts are likely to be based. Nevertheless, it is still possible to question the empirical appropriateness of this location of class boundaries. Even if we accept Poulantzas' argument that the monopolization of productive knowledge is a form of class domination, and that those who monopolize such knowledge are in an antagonistic relation to the working class, it does not follow that *all* mental workers, including routine clerical and sales employees, should be placed in this category. The labour processes in many offices and commercial enterprises are arguably just as rationalized, as despotically controlled, and as mechanized as those of industry. Poulantzas' claim that routine mental workers participate in certain "rituals" and "cultural practices" that symbolize their ideological distance from manual workers does not demonstrate their domination over those workers, particularly when they themselves are no less separated from the knowledge necessary for the direction of the production process.

3. Supervisors versus Nonsupervisors

A second model of class structure emphasizes the relation between supervisors and nonsupervisors as the basic class division among salaried employees. Within their respective theoretical camps, Ralf Dahrendorf and Guglielmo Carchedi present two variants of this approach. Following Weber, Dahrendorf rejects the Marxist thesis of the primacy of economic relations over authority relations. Turning Marx on his head, Dahrendorf ascribes a dominant role to authority relations in the structuring of social conflict. According to Dahrendorf, classes are not primarily economic groupings. "Classes are social conflict groups the determinant [. . .] of which can be found in the participation in or exclusion from the exercise of authority" (Dahrendorf 1959: 138). During an earlier stage of capitalism, class relations assumed the *appearance* of property relations, insofar as the exercise of authority largely corresponded to the distribution of property. With the separation of ownership from control within the modern corporation, however, Dahrendorf argues that class relations have been severed from their linkage to property ownership. The major line of political cleavage in contemporary capitalist society is not between property owners and nonowners. Neither is it between manual and nonmanual workers. According to Dahrendorf, it is the division between those employees who exercise supervisory authority and those who are excluded from such authority.

The chief problem with this theory is its failure to explain the connection between authority and class interests. Dahrendorf's assumption that the exercise of authority *in itself* generates an opposition of interests between those in authority and those who are subject to authority is highly questionable. Whether or not authority entails an opposition of interests depends upon the mode in which it is exercised (with consent or coercion) and the ends to which it is directed. No such conditions are specified by Dahrendorf. Having severed authority relations from any linkage with property interests, he provides no alternative explanation for the antagonistic nature of authority relations in contemporary capitalism.

A very different conception of supervisory authority is suggested by Marxist theorists. As already noted, Poulantzas interprets supervision within the capitalist enterprise as one of several forms of domination that reinforce the exploitation of labour. This perspective is developed more fully by Carchedi (1977), who views the distinction between supervisors and nonsupervisors as the main class division among salaried employees. Like Dahrendorf, Carchedi notes the tendency toward the separation of property ownership and supervisory authority within the modern capitalist enterprise. Rather than interpreting this as a displacement of property interests, however, Carchedi views the emergence of a class of salaried managers as a process of the delegation of authority functions that remain grounded in and subordinate to the interests of property ownership.

In this fashion, Carchedi provides what is lacking in Dahrendorf's theory – an explanation of the antagonistic nature of authority relations. The exercise of supervisory authority, for Carchedi, is a form of control and surveillance, the purpose of which is to enforce the expropriation of surplus labour from nonsupervisory workers. It is for this reason that the class interests of salaried managers (the "new middle class" in Carchedi's terminology) are opposed to those of workers under their supervision. Carchedi accounts for the antagonistic nature of the supervisor/nonsupervisor relation, however, only by raising questions about its adequacy as a boundary between classes. If one accepts the logic of Carchedi's argument, the question arises as to why he restricts the delegated functions of capital to those of supervision alone. Certainly there are other forms of domination (e.g., those described by Poulantzas as the monopolization of productive knowledge) that are also integral to the expropriation of surplus labour. Recognizing this fact, many of those who have built upon the foundation of Carchedi's model have sought to expand his notion of the functions of capital to encompass a wider range of professional and technical occupations (Carter 1985; Clegg, Boreham and Dow 1986).

4. Productive versus Unproductive Labour

A third conception of class boundaries emphasizes the distinction between productive and unproductive labour. This distinction is most often encountered within Marxist theory, although similar notions have been proposed by some Weberian theorists. Among Marxists, the most influential defender of the productive labour/unproductive labour dichotomy is Nicos Poulantzas. Poulantzas (1975) defines productive labour as labour which is hired by capital and which produces material commodities (and thereby also surplus value for the capitalist). State employees, office workers, sales workers, and service workers are excluded from the working class because they engage in unproductive labour. They belong instead to what Poulantzas calls the "new petty bourgeoisie." In Poulantzas' view, such unproductive workers stand outside of the dominant capitalist relation of exploitation. Their interests are antagonistic to the working class in the sense that their subsistence ultimately derives from the surplus that is extracted from productive workers.

Numerous objections have been raised against this conception of salaried intermediate class positions (Hunt 1977; Wright 1976). Some have criticized the arbitrariness of Poulantzas' restriction of productive labour to those who produce surplus value in *material* goods production only. Others have noted that many positions within the social division of labour combine a mix of productive and unproductive activities. Most important, however, is the question of whether or not Poulantzas' distinction between productive and unproductive labour corresponds to any fundamental differences in worker interests or experience. While it is true that *some* unproductive workers are exempt from exploitation, many unproductive workers are exploited no less than productive workers; only the mechanism of their exploitation differs. According to Marx (1967: 300), the labour of productive workers is expropriated in the form of surplus value; that of unproductive workers is expropriated in the form of unpaid labour time which reduces the cost to the capitalist of appropriating part of the surplus value produced elsewhere. For most routine commercial and clerical workers the concrete experience of exploitation is essentially identical to that of productive workers. In both cases workers are engaged in an antagonistic relation with employers over the rate of exploitation and control of the labour process. If class boundaries are supposed to illuminate fundamental differences of interest and experience, it is doubtful whether unproductive labour should be treated as a sufficient condition for exclusion from the proletariat.

Because they reject Marx's conception of class as a relationship based on the expropriation of surplus labour, Weberians have shown little interest in the distinction between productive and unproductive labour. Rather than defining class as a relationship of exploitation in production, they have privileged relations of market competition and/or differences in bureaucratic authority. A partial exception can be found in the writings of Randall Collins. Collins (1979) broadens the Marxist concept of exploitation to encompass a variety of social practices by which one group enhances its rewards by closing off opportunities to others. Within this framework, he distinguishes between productive labour and what he calls "political labour". Productive labour is labour that produces material wealth, while political labour is labour that determines the appropriation of wealth – e.g., by shaping the entry requirements, career channels, responsibilities, and rewards of occupational positions. "This distinction separates the two major social classes: the working class engaged in productive labour, and the dominant class engaged in political labour. Both classes expend energy, but it is the subordinated class that produces wealth, whereas the dominant class determines its distribution" (Collins 1979: 52). The dominant class accomplishes this goal, according to Collins, through the employment of cultural resources that enable it to build alliances and to impose a self-serving definition of reality upon subordinate classes.

A major difficulty with this approach is that most occupations involve a combination of productive and political labour. It is not clear where, or even *whether*, any qualitative boundaries between classes can be identified on the basis of this model. Collins' distinction between "working class" and "dominant class" is not really a distinction between discrete classes; it merely designates two "aspects" of jobs that combine in different ways to produce an indeterminate number of occupational interest groups (Collins 1979: 53). A further problem with Collins' theory concerns his conception of the causes of class inequality. Collins attributes the unequal distribution of wealth to the imposition of extraeconomic (political or cultural) restraints on the free operation of the market. "A perfect market tends to produce perfect equality of incomes; hence, it is the *restraints* on the market that account for inequality in wealth" (Collins 1975: 421). Notably absent from this view is any recognition of the manner in which market competition, even in the absence of restraints, promotes inequality by accelerating the concentration of property (Murphy 1984: 553–554). Questions can also be raised about the role that Collins attributes to cultural practices in maintaining class inequality. Collins is primarilly concerned to debunk the meritocratic view that differential rewards are merely a return to differences in productivity. One may reject that view, however, without accepting Collins' alternative claim that privileges of dominant classes are based on nothing more substantial than their ability to mystify others into accepting the necessity of existing economic arrangements.

5. Professionals and Managers versus Routine Employees

If there is any movement toward a consensus on the question of class boundaries, it is probably toward the view that professionals and managers should be classified as salaried intermediaries, while manual and routine nonmanual employees belong to the working class. My own view is that this model provides the most adequate conception of the class structure of contemporary capitalism, although the theoretical basis of this model is still in need of further development. Among Marxists, this model of class structure is usually grounded in an analysis of the place that professionals and managers occupy within the relations of production, while Weberians are more likely to focus on the market situation of these two occupational groups. Not all Marxists and Weberians can be so neatly classified, however. In this section I discuss those theories that analyze professionals and managers from the standpoint of production relations, while the next section examines analogous theories that are constructed from the standpoint of the market.

Within the Marxist camp, Barbara and John Ehrenreich's theory of the professional-managerial class is one of the most influential attempts to conceptualize professionals and managers as a salaried intermediate class. The Ehrenreichs argue that, in the course of capitalist development, a distinctive new class has emerged, which they call the "professional-managerial class" (PMC for short). The PMC is defined as "consisting of salaried mental workers who do not own the means of production and whose major function in the social division of labour may be described broadly as the reproduction of capitalist culture and class relations" (Ehrenreich and Ehrenreich 1977: 13). This includes both those who carry out this reproduction function in their roles as agents of social control or as producers and propagators of ideology (teachers, social workers, psychologists, journalists, etc.) and those who do so through their performance of administrative and technical roles which perpetuate capitalist relations of production (managers, engineers, technicians, etc.). Despite the wide range of occupations included within this category and the somewhat fuzzy boundaries separating it from the ruling class above and the working class below, the Ehrenreichs maintain that the PMC nevertheless constitutes a single, coherent class. Its members share not only a common economic function, but also a common cultural existence, characterized by distinctive patterns of family life (emphasizing individual achievement), their own forms of self-organization (professional associations), their own specific ideology (technocratic liberalism), and their own institutions of class reproduction and socialization (colleges and universities).

Historically, the Ehrenreichs argue, the PMC emerged with the rise of monopoly capitalism as part of a broader transformation of capitalist class relations. The formation of the PMC depended upon the coexistence of two conditions which were only met during the early part of the twentieth century: (1) the expansion of the social surplus to a point sufficient to sustain a new unproductive class; and (2) the development of the class struggle to the point that a class specializing in the reproduction of capitalist class relations became a necessity to the bourgeoisie. The expansion of professional and managerial positions satisfied this need by extending capitalist control over the production process, creating mass institutions of social control, and reorganizing working-class life within a framework of mass consumer culture. Forged out of the heat of class struggle between the proletariat and the bourgeoisie, the PMC is enmeshed in a complex web of partly complementary, partly antagonistic class relations. As an agent of bourgeois cultural and technological hegemony, the PMC occupies an objectively antagonistic position in relation to the working class. However, as salaried employees, members of the PMC also conflict with the bourgeoisie, which they confront as a limit to their professional autonomy and an obstacle to their vision of a technocratic society. The PMC is therefore, according to the Ehrenreichs, a "reservoir of anti-capitalist sentiment", albeit of an elitist and reformist variety.

From a more Weberian perspective, John Goldthorpe presents a different argument for viewing professionals and managers as a salaried intermediate class. Whereas the Ehrenreichs ascribe a class unity to professional and managerial employees on the basis of their common function in the reproduction of capitalism, Goldthorpe (1982) stresses the similarity of their employment situation within the modern bureaucratic enterprise. Building upon Weber's classic account of the position of the bureaucratic official, Goldthorpe argues that professional and managerial employees are alike in the sense that both exercise responsibilities that presuppose an element of *trust* in the relation between employer and employee. "These employees, in being typically engaged in the exercise of delegated authority or in the application of specialist knowledge and expertise, operate in their work tasks and roles with a distinctive degree of autonomy and discretion; and in direct consequence of the element of trust that is thus necessarily involved in their relationship with their employing organization, they are accorded conditions of employment which are also distinctive in both the level and kind of rewards that are involved" (Goldthorpe 1982: 169). Goldthorpe uses the term "service class" to describe this distinctive employment situation and argues that the objective conditions of this class lead to the conclusion that it will play an essentially conservative role in modern society. Whatever radical tendencies currently exist within this class, Goldthorpe attributes to the heterogeneity of class backgrounds of those who have been recruited into this class during its recent expansion and the fact that it has not yet achieved a stable demographic or cultural identity.

The chief question to be asked about these models of class structure is whether they provide a convincing argument for the *distinctiveness* and *unity* of professional and managerial occupations from the standpoint of class interests. In this regard, Goldthorpe's theory has some advantages over that of the Ehrenreichs. As other critics have noted, the Ehrenreichs' notion of the "reproduction of capitalist class relations" is a rather elusive criterion for distinguishing class positions (Noble 1979; Wright 1980). Strictly speaking, reproduction is not a separate task restricted to professional and managerial positions; it is an effect of the production process in general. Even members of the working class function to reproduce capitalist class relations simply by their participation in the capitalist production process.

By comparison, Goldthorpe's notion of the autonomy that some occupations exercise over key areas of responsibility, and the privileges they reap from employers' need to secure their loyalty, does a better job of specifying what is distinctive about professional and managerial employment. One may still question, however, whether this commonality is sufficient to yield an *identity* of class interests. Consider, for example, the difference between corporate managers and professionals in the cultural, scientific and educational fields. The former are hired directly by capitalists, granted delegated authority over the production process, and rewarded primarily for their role in the appropriation of surplus. The latter are often employed outside of capitalist organizations, derive their authority from the state or their claim to specialized knowledge, and exercise responsibilities that are more tangential to the appropriation of surplus. Both groups are privileged, but only the former would seem to have a direct stake in capitalism as a mode of production. The latter group, according to many studies, has been much more receptive to anti-capitalist ideologies (Brint 1984; Ladd 1979; McAdams 1987). The fact that these political differences are aligned with differences in employment situation raises doubts over Goldthorpe's claim that they are merely the temporary result of an underdevelopment of class identity.

6. Credentialled versus Uncredentialled Workers

An alternative argument for excluding salaried managers and professionals from the working class is the market advantages they derive from the possession of educational credentials. This thesis is most commonly developed within a Weberian framework, although Marxist variants can also be found. Among Weberians, Frank Parkin (1979) presents one of the more interesting versions of this argument. Parkin is a strong advocate of the Weberian premise that classes must be analyzed from the standpoint of social *action*. In his theory, classes are conceptualized neither as the occupants of structural positions, nor the embodiment of systemic forces, but as concrete collectivities, distinguished by their particular mode of social *closure*. Two generic types of social closure are identified by Parkin. "Exclusionary closure" refers to the actions by which privileged groups utilize some group attribute as the basis for monopolizing opportunities that are denied to outsiders. "Usurpationary closure" describes the countervailing efforts of subordinate groups to win a greater share of resources. The chief difference between these two types of closure is the direction in which power is exercised: exclusionary closure entails a downward use of power; usurpationary closure entails the use of power in an upward direction.

The familiar distinction between bourgeoisie and proletariat is then reconceptualized by Parkin as "an expression of conflict between classes defined not specifically in relation to their place in the productive process but in relation to their prevalent modes of closure, exclusion and usurpation, respectively [...]. For definitional purposes, the dominant class in a society can be said to consist of those social groups whose share of resources is attained *primarily* by exclusionary means; whereas the subordinate class consists of social groups whose *primary* strategy is one of usurpation" (Parkin 1979: 46, 93). According to Parkin, property ownership is only one of several forms of exclusionary closure used by the dominant class. Equally important is the use of educational credentials as a means of restricting entry into privileged occupations. By this criterion, Parkin places managers and professionals in the dominant class, and routine (uncredentialled) employees, both manual and nonmanual, in the subordinate class.

Two problems with this approach can be noted. First is the circular nature of Parkin's definition of class (Barbalet 1982). The dominant class is defined as those who use exclusionary closure, while exclusionary closure is defined merely as power that is exercised in a downward direction, i.e., by a dominant class. The subordinate class is defined as those who use usurpationary closure, while usurpationary closure is defined merely as power that is exercised in an upward direction, i.e., by a subordinate class. Within the circle of this tautology the meaning of "dominant" and "subordinate" classes evaporates. More important, Parkin fails to specify any basis for the power that is utilized to achieve closure other than the resources that are themselves the object of closure efforts. He rejects any inherent structural basis to class (such as property relations, bureaucratic authority, or the division of labour), and seeks to ground classes purely in social action. This leads to an entirely circular form of argument in which class relations are seen as providing the bases of power that are mobilized in exclusionary actions, which in turn produce social classes.

A more specific problem with Parkin's theory is the equivalence he ascribes to property and credentials in defining the dominant class. Whatever the appropriateness of using credentials to exclude salaried managers and professionals from the working class, it stretches credulity to place these positions in the same class as capitalist property owners. In capitalist society, the power and resources accruing to those with educational credentials is hardly commensurate with those accruing to property ownership, nor are the processes by which these forms of closure are sustained necessarily identical. Recognizing this problem, advocates of Parkin's perspective have proposed a distinction between "principle" and "derivative" forms of exclusionary closure to capture the primacy of property ownership in capitalist society and to theorize the relationship between property and such secondary forms of exclusion as credentials (Murphy 1984).

A very different argument for the importance of market relations in defining intermediate classes is presented by Erik Olin Wright. Wright is relatively distinct among Marxists in arguing that market relations are fundamental in the determination of classes. In his book *Classes,* Wright begins with the traditional Marxist premise that class is basically a relationship of exploitation (the transfer of labour from one class to another); but he rejects the usual Marxist view that exploitation depends mainly on the relations of production – e.g., the institution of wage labour and capitalists' domination over workers at the point of production. Following Roemer (1982), Wright argues that given an unequal distribution of property in the means of production, market exchange will yield an exploitative transfer of labour from the property poor to the property rich regardless of the nature of production relations. From this he concludes that production relations are incidental to the functioning of exploitation and the definition of classes in capitalist society. What matters is the institution of market exchange and the unequal distribution of different forms of property.

In Wright's view, the dominant form of exploitation in capitalist society is that based on the private ownership of the means of production, but there are also subsidiary forms of exploitation that derive from the unequal distribution of other productive assets. One such asset Wright calls "organization assets", by which he means control over the conditions for the coordination of labour. According to Wright, organization is itself a source of productivity; by controlling this asset, managers are able to exploit the labour of nonmanagers. A second such asset is skills – especially those whose supply is artificially restricted through credentials. By monopolizing this productive asset, Wright argues, credentialled workers (e.g., professionals) are able to exploit the labour of less skilled workers. Salaried managers and professionals are thus distinguished from the working class by their ownership of skills (credentials) or organization assets. According to Wright, their disproportionate share of these assets enables them to exploit the labour of other workers, even as they themselves are exploited by capitalists.

Wright's concept of "organization assets" has not been well received by other Marxist theorists (Carchedi 1986, Meiksins 1988). With this notion, Wright attempts to reconceptualize supervision (an authority relation) as a form of property ownership (a basis of exploitation). It is not clear, however, in what sense organization can be treated as an "asset" akin to property or skills. It cannot be owned or exchanged on the market in the same way as property or skills; it has no existence apart from the positions within which it is exercised and cannot be transferred by its "owner" from one use to another. Neither can control over organization be clearly separated from control over the material means of production. If the exercise of supervisory authority is judged important in defining social classes, the basic choices for conceptualizing this relation would seem to be those proposed by Dahrendorf and Carchedi. Either authority *per se* is the basis upon which classes are constituted, or else supervision must be viewed as a delegated function that is ultimately based on control over the material means of production. In my opinion, the latter view provides a more appropriate standpoint for conceptualizing the class position of salaried managers.

Wright's concept of credential-based exploitation is more plausible, although problems can be noted here also. According to Wright, the rewards accruing to credentialled employees reflect the greater share of productive assets with which they enter the market. This raises two questions: Are credentialled workers genuinely more productive? And is it the market that determines their rewards or the relations of production? On the first point, no one would deny that credentials are sometimes a mechanism for restricting and certifying genuinely productive skills. Wright's wholesale acceptance of this view, however, ignores a wealth of empirical evidence demonstrating the tenuousness of the relationship between credentials and productivity and between productivity and market rewards (Bowles and Gintis 1976; Collins 1979). As Collins points out, the skills of professionals are often more "political" than productive. On the question of the relationship between credentials and productivity, the more cynical outlook of those Weberians like Parkin and Collins, who see credentials as an essentially arbitrary political/cultural mechanism for restricting opportunities, while one-sided in its own way, nevertheless captures a truth that is missing in Wright's analysis.

On the second point, Wright's argument that it is the market that determines the rewards of credentialled employees is also open to question. Again, there is certainly a partial truth to this proposition. Within a pure market model, restrictions on the supply of skilled labour will tend to drive up its value. The lifetime rewards of most credentialled workers, however, are determined at least as much by hierarchically structured "internal labour markets" as they are by open market forces. Goldthorpe's notion of the autonomy that professionals exercise over key decisions, and the dividends that they receive to ensure their loyalty to organizational goals, captures this aspect of professional privilege more adequately than Wright's account.

7. An Empirical Comparison of Class Models

In the conclusion of this paper I shall return to the theoretical problems involved in the identification of intermediate classes. First, I want to examine briefly the empirical question of the degree to which these different theories of class structure correspond (or fail to correspond) to actual cleavages in the pattern of political opinion. Certainly one of the objectives of a theory of class structure is to be able to predict the alignment of groups on key political issues. This does not mean that we can simply "test" the validity of different theories of class structure – at least not on the basis of political opinion data. Used in a theoretically informed fashion, however, evidence on the political alignment of individual class positions should be of value in assessing the competing arguments of different theories of class structure.

The data used to compare these theories of class structure are taken from the 1977–78 NORC General Social Survey. The NORC survey includes detailed information on the occupation and industry of workers, their educational attainment, whether they are salaried or self-employed, and whether they supervise other workers. This information was used to classify employees according to each of the five class dichotomies discussed above. After excluding all self-employed workers, the five criteria of intermediate class position were operationalized as follows: (1) *Nonmanual workers* were defined as employees in managerial, professional, technical, clerical, and sales occupations. (2) *Supervisors* were defined as employees who indicate that they supervise the work of others, excluding teachers (who supervise mainly students, not other workers), and workers in lower manual occupation (who were assumed to perform mainly functions of coordination, rather than control and surveillance). (3) *Unproductive labour* was defined as consisting of all nonmanual and supervisory employees (as defined in above), plus manual workers in trade, finance, insurance, real estate, public administration and service industries. (4) *Professionals and managers* were defined as employees in professional and higher technical occupations, plus supervisors (as defined above). (5) *Credentialled workers* were defined as employees with a bachelor's (4-year college) degree or higher.

Seven political opinion and attitude items were chosen as dependent variables. These included political party preference (as measured by one's vote in the 1976 presidential election), political alienation (a seven-item scale), support for income redistribution, support for state welfare spending, confidence in corporations, confidence in unions, and subjective class identification (dichotomized as working class/middle class). An eighth dependent variable, personal income, was added as a rough measure of economic privilege and because of its use in previous studies of class structure (Robinson and Kelley 1979; Wright 1985; Wright and Perrone 1977).

The different models of class structure were then evaluated using a dichotomous cluster analysis. Respondents were grouped dichotomously into proletarian and intermediate class positions as defined by each model and measurements were made of the mean distance between these two clusters on each dependent variable (see O'Brien and Burris 1983 for an elaboration and justification of this method of comparing class models). These scores enable us to compare the degree of correspondence between the class boundaries specified by each model and empirical differences in the political and economic characteristics of individuals.

For all five of the models examined, the positions defined as salaried intermediaries are more likely to call themselves "middle class", more likely to vote Republican, less politically alienated, less supportive of income redistribution and state welfare spending, have more positive view of corporations, a more negative view of unions, and a higher personal income than those defined as working class. As shown in Table 1, however, the five models differ considerably in their degree of polarization on these variables. Shown here for each model of class structure are the mean differences between proletarian and intermediate classes (in standard deviations) on each dependent variable. The larger this difference, the greater the correspondence between the class model in question and empirical cleavages on the dependent variable. A double asterisk indicates the class model that most closely corresponds to the distribution of responses on each dependent variable. A single asterisk indicates the model with the second highest degree of correspondence.

The findings in this table can be summarized as follows. First, there is comparatively little correspondence between either the manual/nonmanual dichotomy or the productive/unproductive dichotomy and empirical cleavages in income or political opinion. In no instance do either of these dichotomies provide the best classification of workers with respect to political attitudes. In general, the supervisory/nonsupervisory dichotomy, the credentialled/uncredentialled dichotomy, ans the distinction between professionals/managers and routine employees are the most consistent with the pattern of political opinion. The distinction between supervisors and nonsupervisors corresponds most closely to the

Table 1. Class Differences in Income and Political Attitudes Among Salaried Workers According to Alternative Models of Class Structure

	Mean Difference Between Classes in Standard Deviations				
	Manual versus non-manual	Productive versus unproductive	Supervisors versus non-supervisors	Professional-managerial versus routine	Credentialled versus uncredentialled
Political party preference	0.41*	0.27	0.47**	0.37	0.35
Political alienation	0.44	0.34	0.37	0.47*	0.57**
Support for income redistribution	0.39	0.28	0.52**	0.40	0.47*
Support for welfare spending	0.21	0.00	0.25**	0.23*	0.12
Confidence in corporations	0.18	0.10	0.48**	0.23	0.29*
Confidence in unions	0.39	0.34	0.28	0.40*	0.78**
Subjective class identification	0.50	0.45	0.64	0.66*	0.83**
Personal income	0.37	0.15	1.16**	0.91*	0.72

Note: N is approximately 1200; the number varies slightly because of the different number of missing values.

*/** The greatest difference between class means on each dependent variable (indicating the class model that most closely corresponds to the pattern of empirical cleavages on that dependent variable) is indicated by a double asterisk (**). The second greatest difference between class means on each dependent variable is indicated by a single asterisk (*).

distribution of responses on the income variable, political party preference, support for income redistribution, support for welfare spending, and confidence in corporations. The distinction between credentialled and uncredentialled workers provides the best fit with political alienation, confidence in unions, and subjective class identification. The division between professionals/managers and routine employees provides the second best fit with five of the eight dependent variables.

These findings are open to different interpretations. One conclusion, however, is inescapable. However we conceptualize it – in terms of supervisory authority, professional autonomy, or educational credentials – the most significant political and economic cleavage among salaried employees is one that cuts through the middle of the white-collar ranks. In terms of income and political opinion, the basic cleavage among salaried employees is thus one that places manual workers (both productive and unproductive) and routine nonmanual workers on one side and some combination of supervisory, professional, and/or credentialled employees on the other. This conclusion is also reinforced by prior research on intergenerational mobility, friendship networks, and residential patterns (Vanneman 1977).

8. Conclusion

Drawing upon these empirical findings, as well as the theoretical points raised earlier in the chapter, I shall summarize by presenting some tentative conclusions about the class structure of contemporary capitalist society. This will be done by addressing, in turn, each of the basic divisions that has been proposed as a boundary between the proletariat and intermediate class positions.

First, I would argue that there is no justification, empirical or theoretical, for viewing the distinction between productive and unproductive labour as a criterion of class position. It is true that many salaried intermediate positions are largely unproductive. The expansion of unproductive labour is therefore an important factor in explaining the historical growth of intermediate class positions. From the standpoint of class interests and experience, however, the majority of unproductive workers occupy positions that are indistinguishable from those of productive workers.

For similar reasons, I would reject the division between manual and non-manual labour as a boundary between proletarian and intermediate class positions. There may have been a time, early in the 20th century, when the manual/nonmanual division did approximate a boundary between classes (see Burris [1986] for a discussion of this issue). The expansion and rationalization of clerical and sales occupations, however, has long since altered the class position of routine white-collar employees. At the present time, the manual/nonmanual division is better understood as an fractional division within the working class than as a boundary between classes.

The division between supervisory and nonsupervisory employees is more appropriate as a criterion for excluding positions from the working class. The clearest justification for this exclusion is provided by Carchedi who conceptualizes supervision as a delegated capitalist function of enforcing the expropriation of surplus labour through the control and surveillance of the labour process. Empirically, this class divison is confirmed by the consistency with which managers and supervisors occupy opposing positions to other salaried employees on a wide range of political issues.

Whether nonsupervisory professionals should also be excluded from the working class is a more difficult question. The various theorists surveyed propose a number of criteria by which such positions might be differentiated from the working class. The Ehrenreichs argue that they reproduce the subordination of other workers in their roles as agents of social control and purveyors of bourgeois ideology. Goldthorpe argues that they reap special benefits from their employers because of the discretion they exercise over key organizational functions. Parkin argues that they monopolize economic opportunities through their successful efforts at exclusionary closure. Wright argues that they exploit other workers through their disproportionate ownership of skill assets. Each of these criteria captures a partial truth about the nature of intermediate class positions, although none of them is without problems. At the root of many of these problems are the inherent limitations of seeking to conceptualize class as exclusively a market *or* a production relation.

Attempts to conceptualize the class position of salaried intermediaries from the standpoint of market relations (credentials) tend to downplay those aspects of class inequality and class conflict that are inherent in the structure of production relations. Some of the interests and privileges of salaried intermediate positions exist for reasons that are independent of the market characteristics of the individual agents who come to occupy those positions. In an earlier era, for example, the assistants and overseers hired by capitalist entrepreneurs derived significant benefits from their exercise of delegated authority, even though they possessed little in the way of specialized skills or credentials. With or without credentialist restrictions on the supply of skilled labour, employees who exercise strategic functions that are crucial to the interests of the dominant class (especially when those functions are not easily monitored in a direct and detailed fashion) can be expected to reap rewards that encourage their loyalty to that class. Exclusive focus on the market characteristics of salaried intermediaries also ignores some of the most important issues of class conflict between salaried intermediaries and capitalist employers – e.g., conflicts over autonomy, deskilling, and other factors relating to the "proletarianization" of professional occupations (Derber 1982). Finally, ascribing a class identity to salaried intermediaries on the basis of their possession of credentials gives insufficient weight to oppositions of interest that exist between different situses of professional and managerial employment – e.g., between corporate managers and professionals in the cultural, scientific, and educational fields.

On the other hand, attempts to conceptualize the class position of salaried intermediaries exclusively from the standpoint of production relations can deflect attention from processes of class formation that occur primarily through acquisition and intergenerational transmission of market advantage. Classes are not merely "empty places" within the structure of production relations; they are concrete collectivities with some degree of intergenerational continuity and a tendency toward the formation of a common culture. From the latter perspective, the closure of market opportunities plays an important and partly autonomous role. Market relations can function to reconcile opposing positions within the social relations of production – e.g., through the density of intergenerational mobility between different situses of professional and managerial employment. They also provide an autonomous focus of struggle, within and between classes, that is irreducible to conflict inherent in the structure of production relations.

The challenge for contemporary class analysis is to develop appropriate ways of theorizing the *interaction* between production relations and market relations in the determination of social classes. For Weberians this means giving greater attention to structural antagonisms that are inherent in the relations of production. For Marxists it means abandoning the view that market relations are a purely secondary or derivative aspect of class formation. If we are to further our understanding of the complex (and sometimes contradictory) factors that shape the political alignment of salaried intermediaries, neither of these dimensions of class formation can be ignored.

References

Barbalet, J. M., Social Closure in Class Analysis: A Critique of Parkin, *Sociology* 16/4: 484–497. 1982
Bowles, Samuel and Herbert Gintis, *Schooling in Capitalist America.* New York: Basic. 1976
Braverman, Harry, *Labor and Monopoly Capital.* New York: Monthly Review. 1974
Brint, Steven, New Class and Cumulative Trend Explanations of the Liberal Political Attitudes of Professionals, *American Journal of Sociology* 90/1: 30–7. 1984
Burris, Val, The Discovery of the New Middle Class, *Theory and Society* 15/3: 317–349. 1986
Burris, Val, The Neo-Marxist Synthesis of Marx and Weber on Class, in *The Marx Weber Debate.* N. Wiley (ed.), pp. 67–90. Newbury Park, Ca.: Sage. 1987
Carchedi, Guglielmo, *On the Economic Identification of Social Classes.* London: Routledge & Kegan Paul. 1977
Carchedi, Guglielmo, Two Models of Class Analysis, *Capital and Class* 29: 195–215. 1986
Carter, Bob, *Capitalism, Class Conflict and the New Middle Class.* London: Routledge & Kegan Paul. 1985
Clegg, Stewart, P. Boreham, and G. Dow, *Class, Politics and the Economy.* London: Routledge & Kegan Paul. 1986
Collins, Randall, *Conflict Sociology.* New York: Academic. 1975
Collins, Randall, *The Credential Society.* New York: Academic. 1979
Collins, Randall, Weber's Last Theory of Capitalism: A Systematization, *American Sociological Review* 45: 925–942. 1980
Dahrendorf, Ralf, *Class and Class Conflict in Industrial Society.* Stanford, Ca.: Stanford University Press. 1959
Derber, Charles, *Professionals as Workers: Mental Labor in Advanced Capitalism.* Boston: Hall. 1982
Ehrenreich, Barbara and John Ehrenreich, The Professional-Managerial Class, *Radical America* 11/2: 7–32. 1977
Giddens, Anthony, *The Class Structure of the Advanced Societies.* New York: Harper & Row. 1973
Goldthorpe, John, On the Service Class, its Formation and Future, in *Social Classes and the Division of Labor.* A. Giddens and G. Mackenzie (eds.), pp. 162–185. New York: Cambridge University Press. 1982
Hunt, Alan, Theory and Politics in the Identification of the Working Class, in *Class and Class Structure.* Alan Hunt (ed.), pp. 81–112. London: Lawrence & Wishart. 1977

Ladd, Everett C., Jr., Pursuing the New Class: Social Theory and Survery Data, in
    The New Class. B. Bruce-Briggs (ed.), pp. 101–122. New Brunswick, N. J.: Trans-
    action. 1979
Marx, Karl, *Capital,* Volume 3. New York: International. 1967
McAdams, John, Testing the Theory of the New Class, *Sociological Quarterly* 28/1:
    23–49. 1987
Meiksins, Peter, A Critique of Wright's Theory of Contradictory Class Locations,
    Critical Sociology 15/1 73–82. 1988
Murphy, Raymond, The Structure of Closure: A Critique and Development of the
    Theories of Weber, Collins, and Parkin, *British Journal of Sociology* 35/4: 547–556.
    1984
Noble, David, The PMC: A Critique, in: *Between Labor and Capital.* Pat Walker
    (ed.), pp. 121–142. Boston: South End. 1979
O'Brien, Robert M. and Val Burris, Comparing Models of Class Structure, *Social
    Science Quarterly* 64/3: 445–459. 1983
Parkin, Frank, *Marxism and Class Theory: A Bourgeois Critique.* New York: Colum-
    bia University Press. 1979
Poulantzas, Nicos, *Classes in Contemporary Capitalism.* London: New Left Books.
    1975
Robinson, Robert V. and Jonathan Kelley, Class as Conceived by Marx and Dahren-
    dorf, *American Sociological Review* 82/4: 38–58. 1979
Roemer, John, *A General Theory of Exploitation and Class.* Cambridge, Ma: Har-
    vard University-Press. 1982
Turner, Bryan S., *For Weber.* London: Routledge & Kegan Paul. 1981
Vanneman, Reeve, The Occupational Composition of American Classes, *American
    Journal of Sociology* 44/1: 783–807. 1977
Wright, Erik Olin, Class Boundaries in Advanced Capitalist Societies, *New Left
    Review* 98: 3–42. 1976
Wright, Erik Olin, Varieties of Marxist Conceptions of Class Structure, *Politics and
    Society* 9/3: 323–370. 1980
Wright, Erik Olin, *Classes.* London: New Left Books. 1985
Wright, Erik Olin and Luca Perrone, Marxist Class Categories and Income Inequal-
    ity, *American Sociological Review* 42/1: 32–55. 1977

Analytical Marxism and Class Theory*

Raimo Blom and Markku Kivinen

Abstract

Analytical Marxism represents an important turning-point in Western Marxism. It is an attempt to tackle the classical problems using new theoretical tools, primarily the state-of-the-art methods of analytical philosophy and "positivist" social science. This article attempts to assess this new trend within the field of class research.

Analytical Marxists like to stress the point that they are unorthodox, but in fact their starting-points are in many respects very traditional. For analytical Marxism, Marx is above all a theorist of history. This means that the tradition fails to take into account the most important results of the "capital-logical" research of the 1970s, according to which traditional Marxism – which evolved after Marx's death within the Second International – seriously deforms Marx's thought. The hard core of Marx's theorizing, which is contained in *Capital* and various preliminary works, is largely ignored. Although the article highlights these shortcomings, it is not a defence of capital-logical class theory. Rather, it is argued that an adequate elaboration of class theory must be aware of the unsolved problems of both analytical Marxism and capital-logical Marxism. On this basis the article proposes new starting-points for class analysis in general and for the theory of the new middle classes in particular.

1. Introduction: Marxism and "analytical Marxism"

Analytical Marxism represents an important turning-point in Western Marxism: it is an attempt to tackle the classical problems using new theoretical tools. The critical Western intellectual is once again trying on a new pair of glasses. The intention is to take a fresh look at the old subject which has become familiar and fallen into oblivion many times over: Marx and Marxism. Despite the novelty of it all, there is also a certain continuity from Althusser, who emphasized the importance of a careful reading of Marx using the tools of modern science and philosophy. But whereas for Althusser these tools were French epistemology, structuralist linguistics, and psychoanalysis, the new school is primarily inspired by the state-of-the-art methods of analytical philosophy and "positivist" social science.

The new trend started with Gerald Cohen's study entitled *Karl Marx's Theory of History: A Defence* (1978). Today, there are number of influential theorists who may be counted among the representatives of the school: John E. Roemer

(1981; 1982 a; 1986), Jon Elster (1985 a; 1985 b), Erik Olin Wright (1985 a; 1986), Allen W. Wood (1981), Robert Brenner (1986), Adam Przeworski (1985), etc. The subjects discussed by these writers range from the theory of history through Marx's theory of value, classes and development theory to the concept of critique in Marx's theory. Two of the theorists have dealt with the problematics of class at the level of class structure: Roemer and Wright. Additionally, Elster has attempted to problematize the role of class actors. In the case of value theory, the reassessment has implied a rejection or thorough revision of the labour theory of value (see Cohen 1979; Hodgson 1980; 1982; cf. Roemer 1986; also Bohman 1986; Hunt 1986).

Analytical Marxists like to stress the point that they are unorthodox. The point at which they seem to break most radically with earlier Marxist trends is in their analysis of the constitution of society. Alan Carling (1986), for example, has pointed out that the whole tradition could be regarded as a Marxism of rational choice. A common starting-point of the school lies in the view that societies are composed of human individuals who, being endowed with resources of various kinds, attempt to choose rationally between various courses of action. On the other hand, this does not mean accepting a structureless agency as a basic premise: structures are intentional and non-intentional outcomes of the rational choices made by agents.

However in many respects the starting-points of analytical Marxism are very traditional and orthodox. The problems are most evident in the case of Marx's theory of capitalism. For analytical Marxism, Marx is above all a theorist of history. This means that the tradition fails to take into account the most important result of the "capital-logical" research of the 1970s according to which traditional Marxism – which evolved after Marx's death within the Second International – seriously deforms Marx's thought. Much in the same way as the Second International, analytical Marxism hinges on those stages of Marx's thinking in which he was least critical of Ricardo: in other words, on the materialist concept of history as presented in the "German Ideology" and on Marx's theory of capitalism, which he developed in the late 1840s and early 1850s. The hard core of Marx's theorizing which is contained in *Capital* and various preliminary works – the critique of political economy – is largely ignored.

In this paper it is our intention to describe the consequences of this one-sided reading of Marx for the class theory presented by analytical Marxists. By pointing to these shortcomings we do not want to defend the capital-logical class theory. Rather, the main conclusion we shall present is that an adequate elaboration of class theory must be aware of the unsolved problems of both analytical Marxism and capital-logical Marxism. We start with an assessment and critique of Erik Olin Wright's class theory; in this context we can see the relevance of the more general problems of analytical Marxism. On the other hand, some of the starting-points and ideas presented by Wright can be regarded as important steps forward within Marxist class theory. In the third section, we move on to propose our own alternative solution to the middle-class problem. Finally, we discuss in more general terms the relationship between analytical Marxism and the problem of the constitution of society and class analysis in general.

2. Wright's Theory and Some Critical Comments

2.1 Contradictory Locations Within Class Relations – First Version

Wright's fundamental conceptual innovation was to insist that not all positions within a class structure need be uniquely situated within a given class; certain positions can be regarded as having a multiple class character. Rather than eradicating these positions by artificially classifying them into one class or another, they should be studied in their own right (Wright 1978: 61–83). The concept of contradictory class locations within class relations does not imply pigeon-holing people within an abstract typology. Instead, it refers to objective contradictions among the real processes of class relations.

To fully grasp the nature of the class structure of capitalist societies, therefore, we need first to understand the various processes which constitute class relations, analyse their historical transformation in the course of capitalist development, and then examine the ways in which the differentiation of these various processes has generated a number of contradictory class locations within the class structure of advanced capitalist societies (Wright 1978: 62).

Wright identifies three central processes of class relations:
- the progressive loss of control over the labour process by the direct producers;
- the elaboration of complex authority hierarchies within capitalist enterprises and bureaucracies;
- the differentiation of the functions originally embodied in the entrepreneurial capitalist (Wright 1978: 64–74).

In his analysis of the elaboration of complex authority hierarchies, Wright differentiates three central processes underlying the basic capital-labour relation; control over labour power, control over investments and resource allocation. He adopts Poulantzas's categories of economic ownership and possession to characterize these dimensions. While the third is essentially the same as economic ownership, the first two comprise possession.

The capitalist and working classes are polarized on each of the three dimensions. The capitalists control the accumulation process, decide how the physical means of production are to be used, and exercise control over authority relations. The workers are excluded from all forms of control.

Wright makes a distinction between two levels of abstraction in terms of the conceptual differentiation between mode of production and "social formation". At the level of the pure capitalist mode of production, capitalists and workers represent the only class positions. However, when one moves to the level of social formation, there also appear other classes. The petty bourgeoisie represents the simple commodity mode of production. At this level the non-coincidence of the three dimensions of class relations defines certain positions as occupying contradictory locations between the basic classes (Wright 1978: 73–74).

Thus, according to Wright there are three clusters of positions within the social division of labour which can be characterized as contradictory locations within class relations:

(1) managers and supervisors who lack economic ownership but who do control financial resources, physical means of production, and the labour power of other wage workers to varying degrees;

(2) semi-autonomous employees who retain relatively high levels of control over their immediate labour process and thus find themselves in a contradictory location between the working class and the petty bourgeoisie;

(3) small employers who occupy a contradictory location between the bourgeoisie and the petty bourgeoisie.

2.2 Wright's Autocritique

While wishing to remain faithful to the general idea that certain positions may have a multiple class character, Wright modifies the characterization of the basic class relations in a very fundamental way (Wright 1985 a: 19–63). According to Wright, the rationale of seeing positions which are simultaneously bourgeois and proletarian as contradictory is based on the concept of contradictory interests. The basic class relation of capitalism generates objectively contradictory interests for workers and capitalists. Contradictory locations exist on both sides of these inherently contradictory interests.

As far as the managerial positions are concerned, this makes sense as long as they can be characterized as combining relational properties of proletarian and bourgeois class locations, because this implies a systematic inconsistency of their interests.

But why in the world should semi-autonomous employees be viewed as having internally inconsistent interests? To say that semi-autonomous employees have contradictory (rather than simply heterogeneous) interests is to imply that the proletarian pole of their class location generates interests that contradict those generated by the petty-bourgeois pole of their location. Presumably this petty-bourgeois pole defines interests in the preservation of autonomy within the labour process. By virtue of what does autonomy in the labour process define objective interests that contradict working class interests? The only answer I could provide was to say that workers had interests in the *collective* control over the labour process – collective autonomy if you will – which was opposed to the individualized autonomy of semi-autonomous employees. This, however, was unsatisfactory since collective control over the labour process is not necessarily opposed to significant spheres of individual control over one's own work (Wright 1985 a: 52).

Wright concludes that semi-autonomous employees as well as small employers might be called heterogeneous or dual locations, but there is nothing inherently contradictory in their positions. However, to regard autonomy within the labour process as a class criterion is problematic in an even more general sense. Wright raises three issues (Wright 1985 a: 52–55).

The argument that autonomy is a "petty-bourgeois" characteristic of class relations rests heavily on what may be a rather romantic image of the petty bourgeoisie as independent direct producers characterized by a unity of "mental and manual" labour or "conception and execution". This can be problematized in terms of both historical and structural objections.

Structurally, it is worth noting that self-employed petty-bourgeois producers may actually have little choice over how they produce and sometimes even over what they produce. Their autonomy is restricted first of all by the markets, by credit institutions, and by long-term contracts with capitalist firms. Wright's general idea of autonomy as a class criterion was based on Braverman's idealized conception of the precapitalist relations of production and of the nineteenth-century craft tradition in particular. In his autocritique Wright (1985 a) considers this to be highly problematic.

Historically, Wright argues, the semi-autonomous employee category contains two quite different sorts of positions: highly autonomous craftsmen and "professional-technical" wage-earners. These distinct types of autonomy may be related to simple commodity production in different ways. In fact the latter types of autonomy, which occur within contemporary bureaucratically organized institutions, cannot be treated as remnants of "simple commodity production."

Semi-autonomy as a class criterion is also problematic because of its seemingly contingent character based on a particular work setting. And finally, a number of counterintuitive results have emerged in the course of the empirical specification of autonomy:

For example, if autonomy is defined in terms of control over what one produces and how one produces it, then many janitors in schools who also perform a variety of "handyman" tasks will end up being more autonomous than airline pilots (Wright 1985 a: 55).

Rejection of the category of semi-autonomous employees represents merely one step in Wright's new effort to systemize class theory. The most fundamental modification is the shift in emphasis from domination to exploitation in the concept of class (Wright 1985 a: 56–57). According to Wright, the concept of contradictory class locations within class relations has rested almost exclusively on relations of domination. The relationship between class and exploitation was expressed only as a rhetorical reference and not as a constitutive element of the analysis of class structures. So, the shift to an exploitation-centred concept of class strengthens the link between the analysis of class locations and the analysis of objective interests.

The previous use of domination instead of exploitation also implied the difficulty that the conceptual framework did not contain adequate criteria for a systematic understanding of post-capitalist class structures. There were no elements which could give any specificity to the class structures of "actually existing socialist societies." Since Wright believes that statist – as he puts it – societies are not really capitalist, this kind of abstraction points to the theoretical underdevelopment of concepts.

The foundations for Wright's new endeavours are provided by John E. Roemer's (1981, 1982 a) theory. Wright modifies and elaborates Roemer's notions about exploitation to produce a more rigorous basis for the concept of contradictory class locations.

2.3 Class Relations and Forms of Exploitation

Two main lines of argumentation can be distinguished in Roemer's theory of exploitation. The first develops the neo-Ricardian theory of unequal exchange, while the other, trying to solve the anomalies of the first, approaches the concept of exploitation from the game theory angle. The crucially important aspect of this approach is the formation of hypothetical alternative games.

In Roemer's view exploitation can be defined as a particular kind of causal relationship between the incomes of different actors. If it can be established that the welfare of the rich is related to the deprivation of the poor in a causal way, then it can be argued that the rich exploit the poor. The game theory approach treats the organization of production as a game and means it is possible to compare different sorts of exploitation systems.

A particular coalition of players (S) can be said to exploited if the following conditions hold:

(1) There is an alternative, which we may conceive as hypothetically feasible, in which S would be better off than in its present situation.
(2) Under this alternative, the complement of S, the coalition S', would be worse off than at present (Roemer 1982a: 194–195).

Different forms of exploitation can be defined on the basis of specific rules of withdrawal, which would tend to favour a certain coalition of agents. According to Roemer, the material basis for exploitation is the unequal distribution of productive assets. Roemer defines four types of exploitation, three of which are

related to traditional Marxist concepts of modes of production: capitalist exploitation, feudal exploitation, and socialist exploitation. The fourth type he refers to
as status exploitation.

The definition of alternative games for each mode of production represents an
essential condition for conceptualization. Under capitalism workers own no
"physical assets" (means of production) and they must sell their labour power to
the capitalist for a wage. In game theory, workers are exploited in so far as it can
be demonstrated that there exists an alternative to capitalism in which both
conditions hold (Roemer 1982 a: 202–211). Roemer and Wright argue that in
such a game each worker would receive his/her per capita share of the total
productive assets of society. Within this kind of alternative game the workers
would be better off, and the capitalist worse off.

In the case of feudalism the withdrawal rule might be that the player leaves the
game with his personal assets rather than with his per capita share of the total
assets (Roemer 1982 a: 199–210). The peasants would therefore be better off
when freed from all obligations of personal bondage; conversely, the feudal lords
would be worse off. This kind of withdrawal rule cannot be applied to capitalism
because the workers would be worse off if they withdrew from the game with only
their personal assets.

Wright's and Roemer's conceptualizations of the withdrawal rule for feudalism
are in fact different. Roemer considers only two kinds of assets: physical or
alienable assets and skill or inalienable assets. Wright also includes labour power
as a productive asset. Wright therefore wishes to remove Roemer's withdrawal
rule (freedom from obligations of personal bondage) and replace it with a more
materialist one (leaving the game with one's labour power).

In the alternative game for socialist exploitation (Roemer emphasizes that he is
mainly concerned in his theorizing with social inequality in socialist societies),
each player would receive his per capita share of inalienable assets (Roemer
1982 a: 238–263). A certain coalition of players would be characterized as
socialistically exploited if it could improve its position by withdrawing from the
game with its per capita skills, leaving its complement worse off. Skill-based
inequalities should be seen as a basis for exploitative relations if people with
scarce skills receive an income in excess of the cost of producing those skills. The
highly skilled therefore have a vested interest in maintaining skill differentials.

Wright argues, however, that these categories do not help us to understand
existing socialist societies, which are apparently not ruled by an elite of experts
and where skill inequalities do not constitute a pivot around which society re-
volves. Roemer has attempted to confront this problem by using the concept of
status exploitation. The exploitation exercised by those in bureaucratic positions
is based on the fact that "there is some extra remuneration to holders of these
positions which accrues solely by the virtue of the position and not by the virtue
of the skill necessary to carry out the tasks associated with it" (Roemer 1982 a:
243).

Wright is critical of Roemer's failure to base his theory of status exploitation on any particular type of asset. Status is not in any way related to the material conditions of production. According to Wright, the asset which is lacking in Roemer's analysis can be referred to as "organization". Obviously there is an interdependence between organization and other assets but "organization – the conditions of coordinated production among producers in complex division of labour – is a productive resource of its own right" (Wright 1985 a: 79).

In capitalist societies managers control the organization assets within companies under constraints imposed by capitalists through their ownership of capital assets. The anarchy prevailing in capitalist markets means there is no coordination of productive activities across labour processes. In "statist" societies organization assets play a far more important role, because this kind of coordination becomes a societal task which is centrally organized. Control over organization assets is no longer limited to the level of the company, but extends to the central planning organs within the state. In this sense it can be said that this control – bureaucratic power – defines the material basis for class relations and exploitation. Authority was fundamental to Wright's previous theory, but now it is not regarded as an asset: "organization is the asset which is controlled through a hierarchy of authority" (Wright 1985 a: 80).

If control over organization assets is a basis for exploitation, then non-managers would be better off if they were to withdraw with their per capita share of organization assets, leaving managers (or bureaucrats) worse off. This would be equivalent to the democratization of organizational control.

Wright insists that the crucial factor in exploitation is the control of the surplus, not the actual income of managers and bureaucrats.

The claim that managers or bureaucrats would be "worse off" under conditions of a redistribution of organization assets refers to the amount of income they effectively control, and which is therefore potentially available for personal appropriation, not simply the amount they actually personally consume (Wright 1985 a: 102).

Although Wright employs the concept of surplus, he does not accept the traditional Marxist idea of surplus value. Throughout his work he refers to surplus product which is meant to be independent of the tenets of the labour theory of value. According to Roemer the labour theory of value provides a misleading basis for a theoretical understanding of exchange and is unnecessary for an understanding of capitalist exploitation. Roemer rejects all labour-transfer views of exploitation, Wright is more on the lines of traditional Marxism. According to Wright, it is possible to restore the central thrust of the traditional Marxian concept of exploitation by marking a distinction between what can be called "economic oppression" and exploitation. "The critical addition is the idea that in the case of exploitation the welfare of the exploiting class depends upon the work of the exploited class" (Wright 1985 a: 75). In the case of simple economic oppression, the oppressing class only has interests in protecting its own property rights; in the case of exploitation, it also has interests in the productive activity of the exploited. Thus, for Wright, exploitation is combination of economic oppression and appropriation.

Since concrete societies are always characterized by complex patterns of exploitation relations, the definition of a given society as capitalist, socialist, state socialist, or feudal depends on the dominant form of exploitation.

The theory of contradictory class locations must be redefined on the basis of relations of exploitation. Wright distinguishes two different kinds of non-polarized class relations:

(1) There will tend to be class positions that are neither exploited nor exploiters. For example a self employed petty-bourgeois with average capital stock would be neither exploiter nor exploited under capitalism. He/she is a person who has exactly the per capita level of the relevant asset.

(2) There will also be some positions which are at the same time exploiting along one dimension of exploitation and exploited on another. "Highly skilled wage-earners (e.g. professionals) in capitalism are a good example: they are capitalistically exploited because they lack assets in capital and yet are skill exploiters. Such positions are what are typically referred to as the 'new middle class' of a given class system" (Wright 1985 a: 87).

Based on Wright's new scheme, Table 1 and 2 presents the criteria for and a typology of wage earner's class positions in capitalism. In addition to exploitation based on the ownership of capital assets, we can also distinguish two subordinate relations of exploitation. Wright attempts to distinguish a whole field of class locations which are distinct from the polarized classes: expert managers, non-managerial experts, expert supervisors, etc.

Wright also suggests that, depending upon the particular combinations of exploitation relations in a given society, it is always possible to find different forms of contradictory class locations. In feudalism the most important contradictory location is constituted by the bourgeoisie. Managers and state bureaucrats should be regarded as representing a critical contradictory location within capitalism, whereas in state socialism the crucial contradictory location is constituted by the intelligentsia or experts (Wright 1985 a: 89).

There are three broad strategies available to contradictory class locations (Wright 1985 a: 124). First, they can use their position as exploiters to gain individual entry into the dominant exploiting class; for instance, under capitalism managers can use their personal assets to buy capital, property, stocks, etc.

Second, they can attempt to forge an alliance on the basis of the hegemonic strategy of the dominant class. Finally, they can form an alliance with the principal exploited class:

This does not mean, however, that class alliances between workers and some segments of contradictory locations are impossible. Particularly under conditions where contradictory locations are being subjected to a process of "degradation" – deskilling, proletarianization, routinization of authority etc. – it might be quite possible for people in those contradictory locations which are clearly net-exploited to see the balance of their interests as being more in line with the working class than with the capitalist class (Wright 1985 a: 125).

Table 1. Criteria for Operationalization of Exploitation-Asset Concept of Class Structure 1)

I.	Assets in means of production			
		Entrepreneurs		Amount of workers
	1. Bourgeoisie	yes		10 or more
	2. Small employers	yes		2–10
	3. Small bourgeoisie	yes		0–1
	4. Wage worker	no		
II.	Assets in organization control			
		Directly involved in making policy decisions for the organization		Supervisor with real authority over subordinates
	1. Managers	yes		yes
	2. Supervisors	no		yes
	3. Non-management	no		no
III.	Assets in scarce skills/talent			
		Occupation	Education credential	Job autonomy
	1. Expert	Professionals		
		Professors		
		Managers	B. A. or more	
		Technicians	B. A. or more (in Sweden and Finland a high school degree or more)	
	2. Marginal	School teachers		autonomous
		Craftworkers		autonomous
		Managers	less than B. A.	
		Technicians	less than B. A.	
		Sales	B. A. or more	
		Clerical	B. A. or more	
	3. Uncredentialled	Sales	less than B. A. or non-autonomous	
		Clerical	less than B. A. or non-autonomous	
		Manual noncrafts		

Note to Table 1:
The International Project on Class Structure and Class Consciousness uses the following coding system for autonomy:
Level of Conceptual Autonomy
1. High, unambiguous   4. Medium, probable
2. High, probable   5. Low
3. Medium, unambiguous   6. None

To classify as semi-autonomous, the respondent must have autonomy at least on the "Medium," "unambiguous" level. High conceptual autonomy indicates that the respondent has to plan or design important aspects of the final product or service. On the level of medium autonomy, the respondent has to be able to plan important aspects of the work procedure: how he/she does his work – but not the final product or service. Because in some services it is difficult to make a distinction between the product and the procedure, Wright adds the dimension of problem solving: non-routine problem solving as an essential aspect of work implies high conceptual autonomy whereas routine problem solving implies autonomy on the medium level.

Table 2. Distribution of the Labour Force in the Class Matrix Using the Exploitation-Centred Concept of Class

Assets in the means of production				
Owners	Non-owners			
1. Bourgeoisie	4. Expert managers	7. Semi-creden-tialled managers	10. Uncredential-led managers	+
U.S. 1.8%	U.S. 3.9%	U.S. 6.2%	U.S. 2.3%	
Sweden 0.7%	Sweden 4.4%	Sweden 4.0%	Sweden 2.5%	
Finland 0.7%	Finland 3.8%	Finland 6.1%	Finland 3.3%	Organi-zation assets
2. Small employers	5. Expert superv.	8. Semi-creden-tialled super-visors	11. Uncredential-led supervisors	
U.S. 6.0%	U.S. 3.7%	U.S. 6.8%	U.S. 6.9%	> 0
Sweden 4.8%	Sweden 3.8%	Sweden 3.2%	Sweden 3.1%	
Finland 2.5%	Finland 0.8%	Finland 1.4%	Finland 2.8%	
3. Petty bourgeoisie	6. Expert non-managers	9. Semi-creden-tialled workers	12. Proletarians	
U.S. 6.9%	U.S. 3.4%	U.S. 12.2%	U.S. 39.9%	–
Sweden 5.4%	Sweden 6.8%	Sweden 17.8%	Sweden 43.5%	
Finland 18.4%	Finland 3.5%	Finland 17.4%	Finland 41.0%	

+ > 0 –

Skill/credential assets

United States: N = 1487
Sweden: N = 1179
Finland: N = 1435

2.4 Classes and the Labour Process – Some Critical Remarks

There is no doubt that Wright's views are heuristically inspiring. His class theory is based on broad historical visions of successive modes of production. He believes he can even ascertain the direction of historical transformations and probable forms of the state and ideology for each form of exploitation.

In this paper we do not intend to discuss the far-reaching implications of Wright's theory of class, but restrict ourselves to commenting on the fundamental conceptual starting-points of the theory itself. Our basic argument is that Wright's reformulated theory is a step backwards when compared with the previous one. On the other hand, we are also suggesting a theoretical alternative to the previous conception, which, we believe, avoids some of the most crucial anomalies of Wright's theory.

Wright's new theory has already attracted several critical remarks:
(1) Doubts have been raised as to whether Wright's ideas actually differ from Weber or neo-Weberian concepts of the middle class (Giddens 1985).
(2) Claus Offe has emphasized the particular legal mediations and mystifications which are connected with the relationship between capital and labour (Offe 1985: 83–88).
(3) Gordon Marshall and David Rose, two British researchers in Wright's international project, have criticized his vague operationalization of skill assets on the basis of job traits. For example, they show that the application of different occupational coding systems tend to change the picture of class structures (Marshall and Rose 1986: 450–454).
(4) According to Guglielmo Carchedi (1986), there is a fundamental difference between Marx's and Wright's concepts of abstraction.

To the best of our knowledge, no one has so far paid any attention to Wright's relation to the labour process debate.

Let us repeat that our critique is primarily concerned with certain basic conceptual solutions of Wright's theory. We fully agree that an exact definition of class criteria is essential for any class analysis, but at the same time it is important to note that this effort must form an integral part of class analysis; we shall expand on this view later. Also, we want to dissociate ourselves from the kind of trivial critique which rejects the use of the survey method in class research: at different levels of class analysis it is both useful and necessary to apply different kinds of methods. For example, the survey method is particularly well-suited for purposes of describing the class structure and for analysing the basic structures of class situation, but in the case of class consciousness it is obviously a far too restrictive tool (Finnish Class Project 1985: 42–49). An abstract critique of methods evades all substantial theoretical and empirical problems.

Our main criticisms of Wright's exploitation-based concept of class are concerned with three interrelated issues:
(1) The significance of the concept of mode of production as the basis for class

theory, that is the relationship between Marx's critique of political economy and historical materialism;

(2) The idea that classes should be analysed from the production point of view and not on the basis of relations of appropriation;

(3) The reasons that Wright gives for rejecting his old theory of autonomy as a class criterion.

(1) Wright claims that his new theory of contradictory class locations is applicable not only to capitalist society; his theory of classes draws on a more general theory of history. However, this kind of reasoning is very problematic. Wright seems to avoid the problems arising from the relationship between Marx's theories of history and capitalism by restricting his theorizing to the level of historical materialism.

Wright's version of Marxism, no matter how it is modified, will always remain fundamentally a theory of history in the spirit of the Second International (on this point, see Jukka Gronow (1986); Finn Damm Rasmussen (1985) has also drawn attention to Wright's connection with the Marxism of the Second International, but he fails to see the crucial differences). In this sense Wright's new concepts of exploitation offer nothing really new. He still insists that the starting-point for theories of class should be anchored in different modes of production. Throughout his work Wright neglects Marx's theory of capitalism, its method and fundamental concepts. It is not only dogmatism to assert that Marx's main tenets are contained in his critique of political economy. For Marx, historical materialism was a methodological guide; he never considered it a systematic theory. He made systematical efforts to conceptualize capitalism as a particular mode of production specifically in the critique of political economy. The concept of class should be linked to the other concepts contained in the theory of capitalism. Any attempt to combine classes within capitalism directly to the concept of mode of production is doomed to lead to confusion.

This is clearly visible in Wright's first theory, where he attempted to combine concepts of real appropriation and ownership with concepts for capitalism (Wright 1978: 72–73). The background to this line of argumentation, both the theoretical intention and the specific concepts, can be traced back to Etienne Balibar. However, this kind of reasoning always leads to reductionism, as for example when autonomy (or secret knowledge about the labour process, as Poulantzas puts it) is identified with "minimal ownership" of the means of production.

But how, then, should class they be linked up with the concepts of Marx's theory of capitalism? The importance of Marx's critique of political economy for the analysis of classes was first highlighted during the 1970s by Projekt Klassenanalyse (PKA) (1973) in the FRG. PKA was a Marxist research group which was active both in the field of class (especially 1973) and the theory of the state (1974). The project became known for its emphasis of Marx's critique of political economy as a system (see Bischoff 1973; for a more general introduction and evaluation of PKA's theory, see Blom and Kivinen 1987). PKA's theory may be regarded as perhaps the most consistent effort to build a class theory on the basis of Marx's conceptual apparatus, but it still lies open to many criticisms. A comparison of Wright's theory with PKA's also points to the potentially developable elements in the former. In PKA's conceptual apparatus, which follows the capital-logical tradition, classes are primarily determined on a form-genetic basis, and distinctions are also made between different methods obliging the actual producer to yield his surplus labour. Class criteria are taken to be economic form-determinants such as "productive work" (internal differentiation within the working class) and "derivative forms of incomes" (differentiation of the middle class, which consists mainly of state employees from the working class). There is no conceptual link between these notions and Wright's theories on different forms of exploitation.

However, this claim does not do justice to Wright's analysis, at least as far as his first version of class theory is concerned. The fact is that capital logic was lacking in many important aspects of class theory and Wright's links to Braverman seem to open perspectives to class analysis from those blind spots of that theoretical tradition.

One of the main criticisms against PKA relate to the view of capitalism as a closed system. Norbert Kostede was one of the writers who criticized PKA because it abstracted from the relations of domination and mental work (Kostede 1976: 119–132). This is no doubt true: managerial hierarchies can be found both in private and in state companies; in both situations there is some differentiation between mental and manual labour; and last but not least, forms of control vary from simple control by the capitalist to bureaucratic control by complex managerial hierarchies.

Braverman's ideas on class analysis are not based on the concepts of traditional historical materialism, nor does he attempt to produce class criteria by way of conceptual derivation. While PKA emphasizes the unambiguous nature of the class criteria deduced, Braverman sees classes in terms of more relative and historical concepts. Referring to the difficulties that confronted the German debate before World War I with the attempt to "define" the class position of clerical employees, Braverman argues that today similar difficulties must be faced when seeking to define the intermediate strata. He writes:

These difficulties arise, in the last analysis, from the fact that classes, the class structure, the social structure as a whole, are not fixed entities but rather ongoing processes, rich in change, transition, variation, and incapable of being encapsulated in formulas, no matter how analytically proper such formulas may be (Braverman 1974: 409).

The analysis of this process (or processes) requires an understanding of the internal relations and connections which provide its motive power; only this way can we hope to explain its direction as a process. The problem of defining the place of particular elements in the process is a secondary one and does not require the definition of unambiguous class criteria. The "new middle class" therefore occupies its intermediate position because it takes its characteristics from both sides of the polar class structure: it receives its petty share in the prerogatives and rewards of capital and also bears some marks of the proletarian condition.

Wright's idea of contradictory class locations and fundamental processes of class relations can be seen as an effort to develop Braverman's view towards a systematic class map of capitalist society. In three instances Wright's concept seems to fare better than that of PKA. First, it is not blind to the historical development of work control. Secondly, it does not stick to the economic form determinations of labour but attempts to define class criteria on the basis of a conceptual differentiation within the labour content (domination and autonomy). And third, Wright takes into account the possibility of dual class criteria.

Whereas the treatment of historical processes of class relations was no doubt one of the greatest merits of Wright's first class theory, in the second it seems to have become lost. When assets are defined on the basis of different modes of production, they cannot be theorized within the historical processes of the capitalist mode of production. Organizational assets are not derived from the historical processes in which the functions of capital are differentiated and complex managerial hierarchies are developed. Nor is the problem of skill thematized in the context of the development of control within capitalist enterprises.

(2) It is not only the historical aspect of class theory which is lost in Wright's new version; the idea of the importance of work content has also disappeared. Roemer has confronted this problem by making a distinction between exploitation and alienation (Roemer 1982 c: 267). According to Roemer, the relations of ownership determine the characteristics of exploitation, while forms of work organization define the quality of alienation. Thus, he says, classes cannot be conceptualized from the point of view of the labour process. However, as Guglielmo Carchedi has shown, this kind of reasoning leads to absurd implications. In order to conceptualize the new notion of exploitation, Wright and Roemer shift their analysis from the level of production to that of distribution.

Suppose that the capitalist would give back to the labourers the surplus they appropriated. This is an absurd example which I use only for didactical purpose, not to build a theory on it, as game theorists do. In this case there would be no exploitation, in terms of distribution. Yet, at the level of production there would have been no change. The labourers might not be exploited any more in a distributional sense. But the nature of the exploitative relations at the level of production, the fact that the workers would still have no say as to what to produce, for whom to produce it, would not have changed. Both the distribution and the production aspects of exploitation are necessary (Carchedi 1986: 198–199).

This kind of criticism certainly hits the target. However, from the point of view of the capital-logical tradition, it would be more adequate to say that both exploitation and repression (or alienation) should be taken into account in formulating class criteria (see Schanz 1977). We shall return to the problems of this kind of "fundamental critique" later. But how could class analysis start from an analysis of the relations of production? Carchedi (1977) offers the concepts of the functions of global capital and the collective worker. According to his class theory, those who carry out the functions of the collective worker can be defined as working class, while those who belong to the bourgeoisie carry out exclusively the functions of global capital. Characteristic of the new middle class, Carchedi maintains, is that it does not own the means of production but participates in the functions of both global capital and the collective worker. Obviously, Carchedi is also trying to formulate Braverman's ideas into a more systematic class theory.

But how should contributions like this be assessed in the light of the criticism which has been levelled against Braverman in the labour process debate? (For evaluations of Braverman, see Burawoy 1978, 1979 and 1983; Cutler 1978; Edwards 1979; Elger 1982; Finnish Class Project 1985; Friedman 1977; Littler 1982; Stark 1980; Wood 1987). To answer this question, we must take a closer look at the anomalies involved in Wright's idea of job autonomy as a class criterion.

(3) First of all, we must recognize that Wright's new version, in which skill replaces autonomy as a class criterion, is not particularly fruitful. The theory of the degradation of work within capitalism is replaced by the conception of socialist exploitation. However, the attempt to build a theory of the development of skill within capitalism obviously leads us back to the same problems as we encountered with the concept of autonomy; that is, problems related to the organization of work and strategies of organization within capitalist enterprises. From the very same process, Wright now adopts another aspect as a class criterion. It is evident that the precise theoretical meaning of skill is just as problematic as that of autonomy. For instance, according to Littler (1982: 7–11) at least three definitions of skill can be found in different traditions:
– one approach is to regard it as an objective characteristic of work routines and job knowledge;
– another widespread conception is to define skill as job autonomy;
– third, there is "socially constructed" skill.

To make the subject even more controversial, it can also be argued that in the German research concerning the labour process the main concern has been with the very concept of skill and qualification, whereas the concept of control has been more fully elaborated in the Anglo-American discussion (see Lappe 1986).

Problems with coding cause Wright to throw overboard the whole theoretical concept of autonomy; however he fails to show that the new concept can avoid similar problems. We argue that it would have been more worthwhile to examine the theoretical anomalies that are linked to this concept of autonomy and to relate them to the empirical problems.

Criticisms of Braverman in the context of the labour process debate also apply to Wright's conceptual starting-points in three essential respects.

(a) Braverman has an idealized picture of precapitalist relations of production. When dealing with the degradation of work, Braverman persistently uses an idealized artisan as a referent. Wright also draws an idealized picture of the unity of the producer's mental and manual work in simple commodity production. But the conceptual link between simple commodity production and autonomy in the capitalist labour processes seems to be very obscure; only a minor part of the autonomy found in capitalistically organized labour processes can be traced back to the work of an artisan.

Wright's autocritique takes into account not only this kind of anomaly, but also the existence of two different kinds of autonomy. However, he fails to elaborate this point, and the problem of the non-coincidence of the theoretical conception and empirical content of autonomy remains unsolved. In fact, other types of autonomy can also be identified in addition to the two types described by Wright.

(b) When Braverman explains that one managerial strategy – Taylorism – can once and for all solve the problems of control of living labour within capitalism, he seems to neglect both the possibility of alternative managerial strategies and the influence of worker resistance. Without committing ourselves to any particular conceptualization of various managerial strategies, it is certainly justified to argue that the separation of the conception from execution by scientific management is not necessarily the best strategy for capital and management in the organization of the labour process. Other strategies can be more useful because, for instance, they are less expensive than total Taylorization or because they can reduce worker resistance. This has become clear in the many analyses of the different strategies of managerial control.

(c) If autonomy is determined by different forms of resistance (power resources) and strategies, then the theory of job autonomy should be based on an analysis of the "politics of production" in the sense that Michael Burawoy uses the term.

Burawoy wishes to clarify the conceptual foundations of Marxian theory of the labour process by making a distinction between relations of production and "relations in production" (Burawoy 1979: 13–30). Burawoy argues that the essence of the capitalist labour process consists in the simultaneous obscuring and securing of surplus value. This implies that the reproduction of relations in production should also be assured. That is, the political and ideological aspects of the labour process should also be taken into account. "This implies that there are two essential forms of politics: that linked to the relations in production – the politics of production – and that linked to the relations *of* production – global politics" (Burawoy 1979: 220).

Braverman's attempt to analyse the control of the labour processes in exclusively "objectice" terms – at the level of class-in-itself (Klasse an sich) but not at the level of class-for-itself (Klasse für sich) – cannot hope to succeed (see also Burawoy 1983 and Burawoy 1985). This also means that the one-sided logic of Wright's class theory which deduces class struggle from class structure (but never vice versa) (Cohen 1982) is called into question. If one wants to use class criteria which are connected to work content (domination and autonomy in certain senses of the terms), it is important that we investigate class struggle at the level of the politics of production.

3. New Middle Classes and Autonomy – An Alternative Solution

As far as the investigation of the new middle classes is concerned, it is essential to avoid the postulation of the ideological and political aspects of the "relations in production" only on the basis of the antagonism between two class subjects. In addition to the two kinds of autonomy based on the logic of capital and on worker resistance respectively, there are also other types, because there are power resources which cannot be reduced to these fundamental classes. A paradigmatic example of these is provided by the power resources and strategies which are connected to professionalization. Only when these are taken into account can the autonomy and mental labour of the new middle classes be conceptualized in an adequate theoretical context.

In this perspective it is not possible to reduce the fundamental processes of class relations to the three mentioned by Wright in his development of the concept of contradictory class relations. The following processes, at least, should be investigated if the aim is to explain various types of job autonomy:
– professionalization (professional autonomy);
– development of complex managerial hierarchies (capital-adequate autonomy);
– the development of new scientific and technical trades and professions (scientific-technical autonomy);
– the differentiation between clerical and managerial work and the changing nature of the latter (clerical autonomy);
– the inclusion of caring work in the sphere of wage labour and its hierarchization and professionalization (autonomy of caring and reproduction);
– the changing nature of craftsmen's skills and qualifications (craftsman's autonomy);
– particular control strategies in small firms (autonomy in small enterprises).
   (On the theoretical foundations of different types of autonomy, see Kivinen 1987a: 51–58 and Kivinen 1987b).

The concept of capital-adequate autonomy was formulated to refer to the fact that autonomy is not necessarily contradictory with the logic of capital. As a matter of fact we can identify two sorts of capital-adequate autonomy: managerial and supervisory functions on the one hand, and several functions which are related to capital reproduction on the other. The conceptual distinction between professional and capital-adequate autonomy is based on the argument that "a radical distinction must be drawn between those circumstances in which, on the other hand, "professionalism" may be viewed as a privilege *bestowed* by the employer, and on the other, where "professionalism" is a measure of the autonomy *achieved* by an occupational group" (Crompton and Jones 1984: 234). Nor should capital-adequate autonomy be identified with the scientific-technical intelligentsia. The former means taking care of the inter-organization of the valorization process, while the latter is concentrated on the technological aspects of the work process.

In the Finnish Class Project the type of autonomy was coded by researchers on the basis of several questions concerning:
– occupation;
– description of work tasks;
– autonomy (respondents were asked to give an example of the possibility of planning and designing their work);
– restrictions of autonomy;
– size of work organization.

Occupation was not the only criterion because an engineer, for example, may represent either capital-adequate or scientific-technical autonomy. Therefore, types of autonomy were coded according to the job description. If they were mainly related to financial aspects, they were regarded as representing capital-adequate autonomy, and if they were related to technological aspects, they were coded as scientific-technical autonomy.

This conceptualization of autonomy has important implications for the analysis of class criteria. Wright adopts autonomy as a class criterion only for those wage labourers who do not have any decision-making authority as far as investment, physical capital and other people's labour are concerned. When autonomy is thematized more thoroughly, it is possible that the combination of domination and autonomy as class criteria cannot be theorized in such a straightforward manner. Instead of defining domination as a primary criterion, one should first conceptualize the various forms of mental labour (type of autonomy).

The definition of types of autonomy as particular sorts of mental labour implies a divergence from many previous efforts to conceptualize the distinction between mental and manual labour. At least five different kinds of definitions have been suggested.

(1) David Lockwood makes the distinction on the basis of empiricist criteria: dirty hands and white hands (Lockwood 1958)

(2) In the capital-logical tradition there have been many controversial efforts to define mental labour using Marx's categories of complex and simple labour (see Järvelä 1978).

(3) French theorists, such as Poulantzas (1975) and Bourdieu (1980), define mental labour on the basis of particular symbols and rituals.

(4) Barbara and John Ehrenreich (1979: 12) formulate a functionalist defini-

tion for mental labour. According to them, it is the function of mental wage labourers to "reproduce capitalist culture and class relations."

(5) Wright identifies job autonomy with mental labour.

We attempt to modify and elaborate this idea by defining various sorts of mental labour on the basis of particular power resources. It should be emphasized that mental labour or power resources cannot be defined at the level of the general division of labour, as Barbara and John Ehrenreich do. Also, autonomy and power resources cannot be reduced to symbolic dimensions.

Nicholas Abercrombie and John Urry (1983: 128–153) have also called for conceptualizations of various forms of mental labour. However, they wish to link these to the problematics of production and the realization of surplus value. If this can be taken to mean that power resources and processes of class relations should be connected with theorizing of particular accumulation regimes such as Fordism or post-Fordism, we could accept that (see e.g. Aglietta 1982, Hirsch 1985). But we would be more skeptical about the adoption of such categories as productive and unproductive labour as class criteria. The deficiences of such an effort can be convincingly shown with reference to the capital-logical tradition.

The adoption of the processes of class relations as a starting-point also leads to another significant difference in relation to Wright's ideas. From a theoretical definition of class criteria, we cannot proceed directly to arguments concerning the composition of class groups or the concrete contents of class criteria in a certain country at a certain moment in time. In the first place it is obvious that the position of qualitatively different kinds of mental labour within the class structure cannot be determined ahistorically, without giving due attention to the stage of development of the related processes. Second, it is also important to note that the significance of various processes of class relations may differ considerably between different countries. Not only are there differences in the class structures of different countries, but class criteria are also historically specific.

Markku Kivinen has performed this kind of analysis of the structuration of class situation and class consciousness in Finland. The most fundamental results are presented in the following thesis:

The core of the new middle classes is composed of those who represent professional, capital-adequate and scientific-technical types of autonomy, irrespective of their managerial functions, and those who have managerial functions in office work.

Those in performance-level office work with some degree of autonomy, as well as craftsmen, careworkers and workers in small enterprises who do have autonomy, form a group of contradictory class locations which fall in the middle ground between the core of the new middle classes and the working class. In the class situation of these groups, we can detect features which are characteristic of both the core of the new middle classes and the working class. Finally, within these types of autonomy, those in managerial positions come closer to the core of the new middle class (Figure 1).

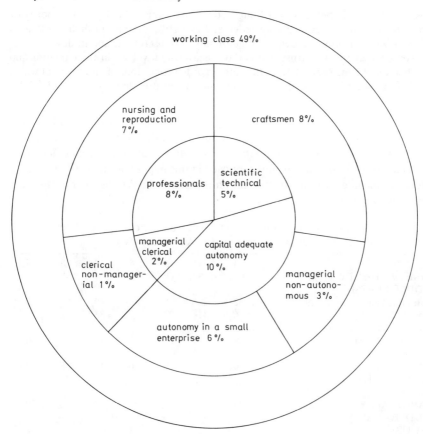

Figure 1. Class Positions of Finnish Wage Workers

The inner circle describes the core of the new middle classes, representing 25% of all wage workers; the second circle includes the marginal groups, who also account for 25%.

This theory also implies that there is no single unambiguous class position for wage labourers. At the same time, it is important to realize that no particular content of mental labour nor any class situation connected with different types of autonomy can be analysed as combinations of the determinants of the bourgeoisie or the working class. Also, there are no privileges which characterize mental labour in general; different forms of mental labour have their own dynamics and processes of determination.

This kind of conception seems to come rather close to the theory of the "service class." The derivation of class criteria is however rather different. John Goldthorpe asserts:

Raimo Blom and Markku Kivinen

These employees, in being typically engaged in the exercise of delegated authority or in the application of specialist knowledge and expertise, operate in their work tasks and roles with a distinctive degree of autonomy and discretion; and in direct consequence of the element of trust that is thus necessarily involved in their relationship with their employing organisation, they are accorded conditions of employment which are also distinctive in both the level and kind of rewards that are involved (Goldthorpe 1982: 169).

Instead of postulating a general element of trust class theory should explain various processes that bring about positions with a distinctive degree of autonomy. Table 3 shows the differentiation of Wright's contradictory class locations according to the basic class groups proposed in this paper and the various types of autonomy included within them. Certain anomalies in Wright's conception are immediately visible.

Table 3. The Distribution of Wright's Redefined Contradictory Class Location According to Class Groups Based on Types of Autonomy (%)

	1	2	3	4	5	6	7	8	9
CORE OF THE NEW MIDDLE CLASSES	78	50	68	78	69	30	61	48	1
Professional autonomy	19	38	32	22	8	18	0	0	0
Capital adequate autonomy	35	13	6	41	23	7	35	32	1
Scientific-technical autonomy	8	0	29	7	38	5	16	8	0
Autonomy of office work/managerial positions	16	0	0	7	0	0	10	8	0
MARGINALLY MIDDLE CLASS GROUPS	22	50	23	22	31	32	39	48	20
Autonomy of care and reproduction	14	13	23	5	0	0	10	8	7
Craftsman's autonomy	3	0	0	9	15	22	10	12	3
Autonomy of office work	0	0	0	0	0	1	0	0	2
Autonomy of a small enterprise	0	0	0	3	8	8	13	0	6
Managerial positions without autonomy	5	38	0	5	8	1	6	28	1
WORKING CLASS	0	0	10	0	0	40	0	4	79
N	37	8	31	58	13	158	31	25	379
Total	100	100	101	100	100	102	100	100	100

1 = Expert managers   2 = Expert supervisors
3 = Expert non-managers   4 = Semi-credentialled managers
5 = Semi-credentialled supervisors   6 = Semi-credentialled workers
7 = Uncredentialled managers   8 = Uncredentialled supervisors
9 = Proletarians

It is important to note that there are some rather clear differences between the two theories. In all of Wright's class groups, there are both those who belong to the core of the middle classes and those who are only marginally middle class, if class position is defined on the basis of types of autonomy. Similarly, in the categories which Wright defines as marginally middle class (uncredentialled supervisors and semi-credentialled workers), there are many who belong to the core of the middle class.

As Wright does not regard type of mental labour as crucial for the definition of class criteria, his class groups include people in different class situations. For example, his "expert manager" category also includes many careworkers, since some of these participate in decision-making and have advanced qualifications. However, Wright neglects the fact that the power resources available to careworkers for exercising the strategy of professionalization are rather limited (Larson 1977: 196). In fact their class situation is also characterized by certain markedly proletarian features. Their wage is no better than that of the working class, their work is both physically and mentally demanding, they often have to work shifts, and they have no career prospects. The large class group of semi-credentialled workers, which according to Wright should be close to the working class, also seems to be extremely heterogenous; it includes people representing the core of the new middle classes as well as those from marginally middle class and working class groups. There are many professionals whose middle class situation is based on a successful profesional strategy. On the other hand, there are many craftsmen whose power resources derive from the "secrets of the craft," but whose situation is actually very proletarian in terms of income, qualifications and workload.

To summarize, Wright's new theory is in fact even more anomalous than his first one. Wright started his critique against his own category of semi-autonomous employees by stating that it does not explain the nature of any particular interests. We would argue that his new theory does so to an even lesser extent. This is because interests can only be defined on the basis of an analysis of qualitatively different power resources and class situations.

The basis for the different interests of autonomous and non-autonomous wage workers is not constituted by the individual vis-à-vis collective autonomy; rather, different collective power resources constitute the basis for strategies which bring about a privileged class situation for some wage workers. Neither autonomy nor skill can therefore be taken *in abstracto* as class criteria without consideration of qualitatively different processes of class relations.

4. The Class Theory of Analytical Marxism: Its Theoretical Nature

4.1 Fundamental Critique and the Levels of Class Theory

In our critique of the class theory of analytical Marxism, we proceed from the problem of class basis within capitalism to that of class action, which represent discrete levels of class analysis. An adequate theory of social classes under capitalism must be based upon a theory of capitalism; we cannot start directly from the classes themselves. At this first level of analysis, there are also certain important methodological problems. In the case of analytical Marxism, a central problem relates to the adoption of methodological individualism as a basis for a theory of capitalist society. As regards the criteria for defining social classes, the main problem is related to the concept of exploitation. We shall first briefly describe the limits and levels of class theory, and then discuss the limitations of the concept of class action as applied by analytical Marxism. Finally, we shall attempt to clarify our position by a comparison of Weber's work on classes and the theory of analytical Marxism.

In his introduction to a collection of articles on analytical Marxism, Roemer (1986: 14) notes that in the class concept of analytical Marxism "class- and exploitation status are not taken to be defining characteristics of agents, but emerge of more basic information". In this sense the class theory of analytical Marxism is based not only on game theory's concept of exploitation, but it also includes in its presentation the underlying theory of the constitution of society. Therefore, from this point of view, its basic intentions are analogous to those of Marxist class theories which are based on *Capital*. Also, this is the starting-point from which fundamentalist Marxist critiques have attacked the class theory of Erik Olin Wright and, at the same time, the class theory of analytical Marxism more generally. Sharp criticism has also been directed against methodological individualism and the problems of empirical validity.

In a sense it is quite surprising that analytical Marxism has departed from the school of Marxism which hinges on the critique of political economy. After all, Marx himself was concerned to give a full scientific account of the law of motion of capitalist society and its economic anatomy on the basis of a system of categories. The aim of this account was to describe the form assumed by social relations, including the relations of appropriation, in capitalist society. It abstracts from what in historical terms is governed by mere chance, from temporary and occasional phenomena. In contrast to this, Roemer, for example, is trying to develop a general theory of exploitation with which he could explain the class struggle (1982 a: 274). Further, in defending methodological individualism, he argues that "class analysis must have individualist foundations" (1982 b: 513).

Roemer adopts a method whereby he advances, along the paths indicated by game theory, from differences in ownership to the concept of exploitation and further to the class division of society. Przeworski (1985: 225) names these transitions as "the wealth-class correspondence theory" and "the class-exploitation correspondence theory".

Discussing the method of political economy in the introduction to *Grundrisse,* Marx writes:

the population is an abstraction if I leave out, for example, the classes of which it is composed. These classes in turn are an empty phrase if I am not familiar with the elements on which they rest. E.g. wage labour, capital, etc. These latter in turn presuppose exchange, division of labor, prices, etc. (Marx 1973: 100).

In the same context, Marx argues that the method of rising from the abstract to the concrete is the only proper method where "the concrete is concrete because it is the concentration of many determinations, hence unity of the diverse" (Marx 1973: 101). It is clear from this general methodical description that concepts such as class or exploitation can only be defined within the total context of the theory of capitalism, at a particular stage of presentation. Therefore these concepts already presuppose certain categories which characterize capitalism. In a similar way, in spite of the methodological differences, we can locate the place of Weber's class concept in the totality of his sociological analysis of the economy. His presentation advances from the definition of market position to class situations and further to the definition of social classes (and unfolding further still into analyses of classes' market action, exchange and competition and market struggles) (see Ritsert 1987: 31).

For Marx, exploitation involves the appropriation of surplus value, which is a form of surplus-labour according to the labour theory of value. Marx's concept of exploitation does have its preconditions: there must be private ownership of the means of production (a premise also accepted by Roemer) and wage labour, i.e. the separation of the workers from the means of production and the need to sell his labour power to the capitalist. Exploitation is not (unlike for Roemer) voluntary, but based on coercion. How the appropriation of surplus-value is legitimized in capitalism and whether or not the wage worker is aware of this, are questions which belong to a different level. Without a presentation of the "anatomy" of capitalism, it would be impossible to conceptualize the economic necessities which make exploitation possible. Capitalist exploitation is connected with coercion in another way, too. The production process and the worker are always controlled in one way or another. In order to understand the dynamics of capitalism, it is important to gain an understanding of the structural changes – including everything from variations in unemployment to the methods used in producing surplus-value and changes in the forms of organizing and controlling labour – in both necessities. In this respect too, Roemer thinks differently: he understands exploitation as a market event, as a manifestation of unequal distribution. For Marx, production holds a central position in the process of exploitation.

Marx's presentation of the critique of political economy is also a presentation of the inversion of social relations in capitalism. He proceeds from simple circulation to an analysis of capital production and the process of accumulation, and finally to an analysis of the surface relations, presented in the form of the trinity formula. Marx's account is thus also a presentation of the *structural relations* which prevent awareness of exploitation. Roemer, due to his methodological choices, does not include this aspect in his analysis.

According to Roemer's "ethical materialism," "the aduced decomposition of society into exploiters and exploited corresponds to the class struggle of capitalism" (Roemer 1982 a: 275). When we know who the exploiters are and who the exploited are, we also know what is happening in the class struggle. This is giving a very simplified form to the question of consciousness and the complex nature of class struggle and other struggles in society. It has also been argued (Przeworski 1985: 227) that Roemer's model presupposes a static equilibrium and does not allow for the possibility of the working class to improve its position under capitalism, nor does it take into account the fact that when the amount of social riches remains constant, a change would merely lead to an inversion of the present setting: the workers become the exploiters and the capitalists the exploited. In other words, Roemer does not have any explanation or theory for a change in the system itself or in its structural principles, including the principles concerning the direction of production and distribution.

Fundamentalist critique (see Carchedi 1986; Rasmussen 1985) has one point in common with the capital-logical class theories which are based on reconstructions of Marx (see Mauke 1970; Beckenbach et al. 1973; the studies of Projekt Klassenanalyse mentioned earlier). Both draw on Marx's critique of political economy and the presentation within it of the economic determinants of capitalist social relations. Critics of Wright's class theory have concentrated on the relations of economic categories and social classes, but Carchedi (1986) argues that Wright has also misunderstood the relationship of individual and class consciousness.

Carchedi (1986) is a good example of the severe criticism that has been presented against Wright's rejection of the Marxian concept of exploitation: his critique is primarily concerned with the consequences of this decision. It means, first, that the basis of Wright's class theory lies not in "production" but in "distribution." The general theory of exploitation leads to the formulation of ahistorical categories which are not based on abstractions à la Marx but on analytical distinctions. At the same time, Carchedi is critical of the use of the game-theory method and of adopting ungrounded fantasies of a "debt market island" and "labour market island" as a starting-point for a theoretical analysis. Carchedi argues that actors should be understood as personifications of structures (Marx's concept of character mask). It is only on such a premise, he says, that people can be understood as agents of change, as actors who bear the internal contradictions of structures. The structural positions themselves should not be seen as static, but as societal processes: as an example, he mentions the rising and falling tendencies of qualifications.

Carchedi's criticism that Wright's class theory is essentially ahistorical is justified and well-grounded. Above we have in the same spirit criticized Wright's theoretical turnabout by reference to the loss of historical dynamics. In our view it is possible to elaborate upon the relationship between Marx's theory of capitalism and the theory of class structure. On the basis of the value categories included in the critique of political economy, it is not possible to proceed directly to constructing a class theory. These categories merely describe the preconditions for the economic existence of social classes, that is, the economic determinants under which members of a particular class on average have to live in capitalism. But in addition to economic conditions there are also a number of social conditions which affect the details of classes' existence and, above all, their opportunities for action. This further implies that the economic preconditions for class existence at the same time define the basic structure of classes' everyday life, i.e. the average structural coercion under which the members of social classes must live (Marquardt 1974; 1976; Ottomeier 1974; 1977; Rasmussen 1978).

Ottomeier's theory is based upon the dilemma of *Verhältnisse* (objective social relations) and *Verhalten* (interaction). He discusses the process of identity-formation in everyday life, which under capitalism is characterized by the independence of structures from actors and a strict differentiation of different life spheres. People are involved in two separate processes of reproduction, i.e. capital reproduction and individual reproduction. In the building of his identity, the wage labourer must accommodate himself to the requirements of different structural spheres: the sphere of production (work), circulation (markets), and individual reproduction (consumption, leisure time). Without going into the details, we may note that the main argument of Ottomeier's theory is that the everyday life of the wage labourer is basically structured by the conflicts between these different structural coercions and requirements. The basic reason for this is that the reproduction of everyday life *(Verhalten)* forms an integral part of the process of capital reproduction *(Verhältnisse)*. – The main concern of Ottomeier's theory (and other similar theories, such as Marquardt's) is thus with the structural conditions that regulate the everyday life of the wage labourer and with the restrictions these impose upon social action. In a more theoretical perspective, the focus is not so much on "role behaviour" or on the psychological aspects of identity, but on their structural basis.

If the basic structure of the daily life of social classes under capitalism is described by the concept of *life-form* (Rasmussen 1985), then the *starting-points* provided by the critique of political economy for sociological theory of class structure can be summarized in two points: (1) the economic preconditions for the existence of social classes and (2) the life-forms of these classes. From this point of view, the major difficulty of the class theory of analytical Marxism concerns its ability to grasp the dynamics of change in and of capitalism, a dynamics which may be seen as being based on the total process of capital reproduction and its historical nature, which finds expression in changing types of accumulation (Aglietta 1979; Gordon et al. 1982); this dynamics of change, in turn, is the basis, albeit not deterministically, of the change of class structure and the life-form of classes.

Class theory should not and cannot be conceived as one integrated, logical system reducible to one type of theoretical work and one theoretical construct. The basis of the theory of class structure lies in Marx's critique of political economy. However, from the existence of a given class under certain structural conditions, under certain life-forms we cannot reach a causal explanation of the determination of class consciousness and class action. We need theoretical constructs to explain the other preconditions for class action as well. This idea is presented in schematic form in Table 4.

Table 4. Problems, Levels, and Theoretical Constructs of Class Theory

Class Theory	Consciousness and Action	Hegemony
Critique of political economy	Class structure and situation of classes → consciousness and action	Theory of hegemony, theory of the state (theory of society), role of classes in the formation of social forces → social change
Value categories → economic preconditions of class existence ↓ Life-forms of classes ↓ Sociological theory of class structure	Theory of consciousness, theory of collective action, (theories of the political, ideological and culture) → "other" conditions of consciousness and action	

Class theory and class research advances through consecutive cycles (see Finnish Class Project 1985: 39–42; Blom 1983) and involves theoretical breaks both with regard to the questions and problematics dealt with and with regard to the theoretical constructs. Class theory does proceed straightforwardly only towards the final problem of class action; it is important and indeed necessary also to examine the class structure as well as the position and situation of classes, regardless of whether or not this predicts class action. Our diagram also aims to show that when social change is understood as the theoretical and practical focus of class research, problems relating to the state and politics are also central to class theory.

4.2 Class Action: An Excursus

Jon Elster points out that the main concern of Marxist class theory is with explaining collective action. He says that Marx was not particularly interested in the texture of everyday life. Elster (1985 b: 349) himself is concerned to study the preconditions for collective action at different levels, from cognitive and informational preconditions to motivational factors. In considering the rationality of collective action, he declares that his aim is "to anchor these correlations in a theory of individual behavior" (1985 b: 359). An important instrument in the combining of collective action and individual behaviour is game theory.

The perspective from which collective action is explained also defines the concept of class. In market economies classes are defined "by the activities in which they are compelled to engage by virtue of the endowment structure" (Elster 1986: 145). In this case coalition behaviour "is not what agents can do, or do do, but what they must do to optimize". "The endowments include tangible property, intangible skills and more subtle cultural traits" (Elster 1986: 147). Elster concludes that classes, when defined from this point of view, provide an explanation for collective action.

According to Elster one of the three central challenges to class is presented by cultural identity, which is based on language, religion, ethnicity or nationality. In other words, he is actually saying that in the formation of collective actors attention should be paid not only to class but also to the processes of civil society. Elster thus rejects two theories. One is the theory which simply states that classes tend to become collective actors and non-class collective actors tend to disappear; the other, somewhat more complex theory states that "whenever the set of classes differs from the set of collective actors, class itself provides an explanation for the deviation". (Elster 1986: 161)

In Elster's and Roemer's thinking, the updating of class action (collective action) and more generally of class theory is intimately bound up with methodological questions, with the carrying out of a programme of methodological individualism (see Elster 1985 b: 3–48; Elster 1982 a and Roemer 1982 b; cf. Cohen, G. A. 1982). Roemer says: "I argue that class analysis requires microfoundations at the level of individuals to explain why and when classes are a relevant unit of analysis" (Roemer 1982 b: 513). These micro-foundations are required to overcome the aggregation gap between society and individual behaviour (Roemer 1982 b: 516).

Elster's analyses of class action are not necessarily very interesting reading. For example, in discussing the determinants of motivation connected with the interaction structure of collective action, Elster (1985 b: 354) says he has singled out five variables: group size, the distance between group members, the turnover rate in group membership, the degree of group homogeneity and the technology of collective action. How he has arrived at these five variables which are often used in social psychological studies of group action, remains a complete mystery.

Analyses based on game theories may well make it easier to understand the consequences arising from certain action strategies adopted by given actors (or groups of actors). However, these analyses are still far removed from the structural and institutional preconditions for class organization and class action in the societal context. True, the explanation of class action as collective action is an important task for class research (cf. Carchedi 1986); but this task must be undertaken by analysing, through the perspective of classes" life-forms, their class situation and the structure of their everyday life and action. Additionally, the existing organizations must be dealt with as independent, institutional preconditions for class action. And third, the concept of class action itself needs to be further elaborated (cf. Therborn 1986).

The only fruitful perspective on the (structurally determined) action of class members as individuals is that of group behavior: it must be understood as a generalization of average individual acts. The model of rational gains-oriented action is applicable to economic class action, but the group behaviour of classes involves other qualititative aspects as well. Second, the action of classes as collectives consists in action based on common community values and social characteristics (cf. the discussion of Weber in the following section). The prototype of this kind of action is represented by traditional, socially isolated working-class communities.

These two different types of action are mediated by institutional social action, which is based on an orientation – as Weber showed – to social order *(Ordnung)*. In this type of action the "other actors" required by the reflexive orientation of social action towards "others" has been replaced by "social orders" (from law to religion and morals). When class action is considered as a form of activity which carries the potential of social change, then the analysis of none of the types of action outlined above is a priori primary; they must be examined relative to each other as preconditions of activity aiming at and capable of social change. It is important to bear in mind that this kind of precondition is in structural terms the most determined type of class action: the action of class members in production and in social reproduction.

4.3 Weber and Analytical Marxism: A Comparison

The rationale of comparing the class theories of analytical Marxism and Weber lies in two similarities: both theories are based on the concept of utilitarian market gains and on methodological individualism.

Weber discusses the problem of social class in his book *Economy and Society;* more specifically, under Chapter IV "Status Groups and Classes" in part one "Conceptual Exposition," and under Chapter IX "Political Communities" in part two, entitled "The Economy and the Arena of Normative and De Facto

Powers." The subtitle of the latter analysis is: "The Distribution of Power Within the Political Community: Class, Status, Party."

Weber's definition of class is based on the concept of class situation *(Klassenlage)*. Class situation means the typical probability of (1) procuring goods, (2) gaining a position in life, and (3) finding inner satisfactions *(des inneren Lebensschicksals)*. Class situations differ according to the degree and type of utilizing goods or services, and according to their income-producing uses within a given economic order. In this definition Weber is referring, first, to the *individual* conditions for prospective activity (procuring goods, finding inner satisfaction), and second, to the relative control *(Verfügungsgewalt)* that can be gained over goods or skills. Class situations are thus determined through a certain type of action, which in other contexts we would identify as forms of rational-instrumental action (Jones 1975: 734).

Class, then, means all persons in the same class situation (Weber 1978: 302). Weber's theory of class situation is in essence a general theory of *market capacities*. The decisive moment, Weber writes, is not property or the ownership of economic resources, but the chances of utilizing these resources in the *market*, which present a common condition for the individual's fate. In this sense, he continues, class situation is always ultimately "market situation." Further, Weber adds that "the fact that creates 'class' is unambiguously economic interests, and indeed, only those interests involved in the existence of the market" (Weber 1978: 928). Classes are stratified according to their relations to the production and acquisition of goods (Weber 1978: 937); thus the concepts of economic action and markets provide a central basis for the concept of class. Weber even speaks of an analysis "within the area in which pure market conditions prevail" (Weber 1978: 928).

Weber's class theory must be interpreted within the framework of his theory of action and, in particular, his analysis of economic action. Economic action acquires its planned and rational nature through its orientation to the market. The power of capital lies with economic enterprises, which are constitued by autonomous action capable of orientation to capital calculation, to calculating the probable risks of loss and the chances of profit. In the last instance economic action is oriented to expectations of prices and their changes as they are determined by the conflicts of interests in bargaining and competition and the resolution of these conflicts. At the same time, economic action concerns and moves the most important classes and class groups, the owners of capital and workers. (For interpretations and critiques of Weber's concepts related to economic action, see Bader et al. 1976: 193–320; Clarke 1982: 204–220, Gronow 1978.)

The fundamental counterargument against Weber's theory of class situation concerns his failure to make any distinction between different goods and commodities which provide actors with market capacities. Ownership of land, industrial means of production, education, and technical qualifications all carry equal weight as long as they produce control on the markets. In short Weber's class theory, as one of class situations, is a general theory of market capacities. Rather than offering criteria for defining social classes, it equates different kinds of "market resources" and collapses into an analysis of relative control on the market.

There have been some attempts to elaborate upon Weber's class theory and to add new dimensions to it by using his own concept of status. However in many cases these efforts have failed to realize that these two concepts apply to completely different spheres of action.

Weber (1978: 305) defines status as an effective claim to social esteem and social honour. The individual's status position is typically based on his (1) style of life *(Lebensführungsart),* (2) formal education, and (3) hereditary or occupational prestige. Weber says that whereas the "genuine place" of classes is within the economic order, the place of status groups is within the social order, that is, within the sphere of the distribution of honour (Weber 1978: 938).

Economic monopolization can take place both on the basis of class position and on the basis of status position. These, however, are two completely different processes. The formation of status groups, Weber writes, is the exact counterpart to rational economic action. Capitalist monopolies differ from monopolies of status groups by their purely economic and rational character: they are based upon an entirely rationally calculated mastery of market conditions, but nonetheless they can retain their formal freedom. The formation of status groups, then, represents a threat to free enterprise, fetters the free market, and creates economically irrational consumption patterns (Weber 1978: 307).

In short, then, we may summarize Weber's discussion of class and status by noting that these two categories are based upon different structural orders, i. e. the economic and the social order. From the point of view of free enterprise and rational economic action, status positions undermine the preconditions for rational economic action and therefore represent irrationality. Class action and status action are based upon different kinds of basic orientations.

Bryn Jones draws our attention to an interesting paradox in Weber's concept of class. The mode of action typical of classes, he writes, is in conflict with action to attain class advantages (Jones 1975: 738). Class action, as economic action, is a form of rational-instrumental action which aims at appropriation through the markets. But when classes are successful in their monopolizing action and exclude others from a certain economic interest activity, they are actually engaged in "status activity." This is because class and status pertain, as was already mentioned, to different spheres. The kind of action which is typical of classes is rational-instrumental activity on the markets; status groups are typically engaged in normative, value-oriented activity.

The implications of the problem are clear when we consider the chances of classes to take political action. If political action is always a priori concerned with normative interests, then, by definition, class action cannot, as a form of non-normative, rational action, extend to the sphere of politics. The concept of class cannot be extended into an instrument of political analysis. Weber writes: "As a separate structure, a political community can be said to exist only if, and in so far as, a community constitutes more than an 'economic group'; or, in other words, in so far as it possesses value systems ordering matters other than the directly economic disposition of goods and services" (Weber 1978: 902; Jones 1975: 74).

For Weber, communal relationships are based on a subjective feeling of the parties involved that they belong together. These relationships are the exact counterpart to economic relationships. Class actors cannot, in any sense, be "communal actors."

There are three points we need to consider in our comparison of Weber's class theory and that of analytical Marxism. First, the constitution of class theory; second, the conceptualization of super-individual structures; and third, the relationship between class action and communal (or political) action.

When Weber is interpreted from the point of view of stratification theory, the class theory of analytical Marxism comes very close to Weber's, at least in formal terms. It equates different types of resources on the basis of game theory's concept of exploitation and adopts these as its class criteria. As we just saw, it is wrong to interpret Weber as a stratification theorist. Class and status are concepts which derive from different spheres, and they cannot be arbitrarily combined to form a tool for selecting stratification criteria. What is more important, a class theory which is based on the general concept of exploitation cannot solve Weber's "unsolved problem": how essentially different types of market capacities are equated and converted into criteria for making class divisions.

Weber, adhering to the premises of methodological individualism, attempted to reconstruct super-individual social structures (such as the markets or the state) on the basis of the *"als – ob"* category: by conceiving structures as if they were based on an agreement between individuals. Elster and Roemer try to solve the same problem directly by a theory of micro-action. This solution correctly emphasizes the importance of the choices and strategies adopted by individual actors, but it still fails to incorporate the dimension of objectivity which in Marx is visible in the idea of individualized social relations and the fetish forms of social relations; or in Weber, in the pessimistic critique of culture directed against objective progress of the rationalization process (capitalism as an "iron cage").

According to Weber, there is a genuine break between class action taking place as market activity and (political) communal activity. These are two different types of activity which cannot be directly combined or reduced to each other. In this respect the investigations by analytical Marxists of class action and collective action and Weber's argumentation are complete opposites. No attempt has been made to conceptualize the break mentioned by Weber or the problems that the two types of action originate in different spheres. The same problem, incidentally, has remained largely unsolved in interpretations of Weber which are based on the theory of closure (see Parkin 1974, 1979; Murphy 1984, 1986).

4.4 Class-theoretical Critique of Analytical Marxism: Conclusions

(1) An adequate class theory must be anchored in a theory of the constitution of capitalist society and in certain categories which characterize capitalism. The same requirement applies to the basic concept used by analytical Marxism to define classes, i.e. that of exploitation. However, analytical Marxism does not meet this basic requirement: methodological individualism does not provide a sufficiently solid basis for constructing such a theory. For a sociological theory of classes, Marx's critique of political economy with its value categories only defines the economic preconditions for the existence of classes and the average structural coercions of the everyday life of classes (i.e. their "life-forms"). The theoretical starting-points of analytical Marxism can be criticized for their ahistoricity, their exclusive concern with distribution, and their hypothetical nature (or game-theoretical building of concepts).

(2) Analytical Marxism lacks the relevant mediations between class structure and class action. Its concept of class action, defined as the average economic action of individuals, is far too narrow; it is a utilitarian concept which omits to consider other important types of class action, i.e. value-based communal action and institutional action guided by social orders (as defined by Weber). This means that analytical Marxism fails to grasp the relationship between class action and social change. Also, analytical Marxism has no concepts for hegemony or hegemonic projects and is therefore unable to analyse the role of classes in the formation of social forces.

(3) From the point of view of class research, the starting-points of analytical Marxism are reductionistic: first, it lacks the basic understanding of class research as a cyclic process moving between different levels of analysis; second, it fails to recognize that different theoretical concepts and formations are applicable to different phases of class research and different levels of class theory; and third, it is limited to one type of social action, i.e. individual economic action.

(4) The more general problems of analytical Marxism, particularly its relation-ship to Marx's theory of capitalism, are clearly visible in Erik Olin Wright's class theory. On the other hand, the capital-logical class theory which is based upon Marx's critique of political economy also lies open to criticism. Its main short-coming is that it fails to analyse the processes of class relations. Therefore the first version of Wright's theory, which was essentially based on Braverman's analysis of the labour process, represents an important step forward in the elab-oration of Marxian class theory.

(5) The problems related to the first version of Wright's theory can be traced back to the shortcomings of Braverman's analysis. The attempts to develop a Marxist labour process theory "beyond Braverman" show that even at the level of the labour process it is impossible to analyse merely "classes in themselves"; it is always necessary to include in a class theory different power resources and

strategies. However, in the conceptualization of these resources it is not sufficient to examine the relationship between two antagonistic subjects. The power resources of the new middle classes must also be taken into account. This line of reasoning leads to the discovery of specific forms of mental labour and various related processes of class relations. At the same time, the historical anchorage of class criteria becomes evident.

* Acknowledgement

This article is based on the work of a comparative class structure and class consciousness project financed by the Academy of Finland. It is part of an international research project with 13 participant countries. The international leader of the project is Erik Olin Wright. The basic questionnaire has been the same for all countries. The Finnish Project is headed by Raimo Blom, and it has been carried out at the University of Tampere. Markku Kivinen has participated in the project since 1981. Other researches are Liisa Rantalaiho, Marja Järvelä, Harri Melin, Jouko Nikula and Elisa Mikkola. A preliminary version of the Finnish final report has been published in English (Finnish Class Project 1985).

References

Abercrombie, N. and J. Urry, *Capital, Labour and the Middle Classes.* London. 1983
Aglietta, M., *A Theory of Capitalist Regulation.* London. 1979
Aglietta, M. World Capitalism in the Eighties, *New Left Review* 136, 5–41. 1982
Bader, V. et al., *Einführung in die Gesellschaftstheorie: Gesellschaft, Wirtschaft und Staat bei Marx und Weber.* Frankfurt. 1976
Beckenbach, N. et al., *Klassenlage und Bewußtseinsformen technisch-wissenschaftlichen Lohnarbeiter.* Frankfurt. 1973
Bischoff, J. *Gesellschaftliche Arbeit als Systembegriff.* Westberlin. 1973
Blom, R., Classes and the State. Department of Sociology and Social Psychology, University of Tampere, Research Reports. 1983
Blom, R. and M. Kivinen, The Relevance and Dimensions of Class Theories. Comparative Project on Class Structure and Class Consciousness. Working paper series 35. Department of Sociology. University of Wisconsin, Madison. 1987
Bohman, J., Making Marx an Empiricist: On Recent "Analytic" Marx Interpretations, *Praxis International* 6, 341–352. 1986
Bourdieu, P., *La distinction.* Paris. 1980
Braverman, H., *Labor and Monopoly Capital.* New York. 1974
Brenner, R., The Social Basis of Economic Development, in: *Analytical Marxism,* John E. Roemer (ed.). Cambridge, pp. 23–53. 1986
Burawoy, M., Toward a Marxist Theory of the Labour Process: Braverman and Beyond, *Politics and Society* 3–4, 247–311. 1978

Burawoy, M., *Manufacturing Consent*. Chicago. 1979
Burawoy, M., Between the Labour Process and the State: The Changing Face of Factory Regimes under Advanced Capitalism, *American Sociological Review* 5, 587–605. 1983
Burawoy, M., *The Politics of Production: Factory Regimes under Capitalism and Socialism*. London. 1985
Carchedi, G., *The Economic Identification of Social Classes*. London. 1977
Carchedi, G., Two Models of Class Analysis, Capital & Class 29, 195–215, 1986.
Carling, A., Rational Choice Marxism, *New Left Review* 160, 24–62. 1986
Clarke, S., *Marx, Marginalism and Modern Sociology: From Adam Smith to Max Weber*. London. 1982
Cohen, G. A., *Karl Marx's Theory of History: A Defence*. Princeton. 1978
Cohen, G. A., The Labour Theory of Value and the Concept of Exploitation, *Philosophy and Public Affairs* 8, 338–360. 1979
Cohen, G. A., Reply to Elster on "Marxism, Functionalism, and Game Theory," *Theory and Society* 11, 483–495. 1982
Cohen, J., *Class and Civil Society: The Limits of Marxian Critical Theory*. Oxford. 1982
Crompton, R. and G. Jones, *White-Collar Proletariat. Deskilling and Gender in Clerical Work*. London. 1984
Cutler, T., The Romance of "Labour", *Economy and Society* 1, 74–95. 1978
Edwards, R., *Contested Terrain: The Transformation of the Workplace in the Twentieth Century*. London. 1979
Ehrenreich, B. & J. Ehrenreich, The Professional-Managerial Class, in: *Between Capital and Labor*. P. Walker (ed.). New York, pp. 5–45. 1979
Elger, T., Braverman, Capital Accumulation and Deskilling, in: *Skill and Deskilling: The Degradation of Work*. S. Wood (ed.) London, pp. 23–53. 1982
Elster, J., Marxism, Functionalism and Game Theory: The Case for Methodological Individualism, *Theory and Society* 11, 453–482. 1982 a
Elster, J., Reply to Comments, *Theory and Society* 12, 111–120. 1982 b
Elster, J., Drei Kritiken am Klassenbegriff, *Prokla* 58, 63–82. 1985 a
Elster, J., *Making Sense of Marx*. Cambridge. 1985 b
Elster, J., Three Challenges to Class, in: *Analytical Marxism*. J. Roemer (ed.). Cambridge, pp. 141–161. 1986
Finnish Class Project, The Reality of Social Classes in Finland. Comparative Project on Class Structure and Class Consciousness. Department of Sociology and Social Psychology. University of Tampere, Working Papers 13. 1985
Friedman, A., *Industry and Labour: Class Struggle at Work and Monopoly Capitalism*. London. 1977
Giddens, A., In Place of Emptiness, *New Society* 29, 383–384. 1985
Goldthorpe, J., On the Service Class, its Formation and Future, in: *Social Class and the Division of Labour*. A. Giddens and G. MacKenzie (eds.). Cambridge, pp. 162–185. 1982
Gordon, D. et al., *Segmented Work, Divided Workers. The Historical Transformation of Labor in the United States*. Cambridge. 1982
Gronow, J., Formaali rationaalisuus ja pääomasuhde. Max Weberin "Wirtschaft und Gesellschaftin" ideaalityypit ja ymmärtävän sosiologian metodi. Helsingin yliopiston sosiologian laitos, Working papers 9. 1978

Gronow, J., *On the Formation of Marxism: Karl Kautsky's Theory of Capitalism, the Marxism of the Second International and Karl Marx's Critique of Political Economy*. Commetationes Scientiarum Socialum 33. Helsinki. 1986

Hirsch, J., Auf dem Wege zum Postfordismus? *Das Argument* 151, 325–342. 1985

Hodgson, G., A Theory of Exploitation Without the Labour Theory of Value. *Science and Society* 44, 257–273. 1980

Hodgson, G., *Capitalism, Value and Exploitation*. Oxford. 1982

Hunt, I., A Critique of Roemer, Hodgson and Cohen on Marxian Exploitation, *Social Theory and Practice* 2, 121–171. 1986

Jones, B., Max Weber and the Concept of Social Class, *Sociological Review* 4. 729–757

Järvelä, M., The Generation of the Social Need for Education. Joensuun korkeakoulu. Karjalan tutkimuslaitos. 1978

Kivinen, M., The New Middle Classes and the Labour Process. Paper Presented at the International Meeting of the Comparative Project on Class Structure and Class Consciousness. Madison, Wisconsin, August 1987. 1987 a

Kivinen, M., *Parempien piirien ihmisiä – näkökulma uusiin keskiluokkiin*. (People who Move in Better Circles – A Perspective on the New Middle Classes). Jyväskylä. 1987 b

Kostede, N., Kritik neuerer Analysen zur Klassenstruktur der BRD. Rezension der Studien des IMSF und des PKA, in: *Gesellschaft. Beiträge zur Marxschen Theorie 7*. Frankfurt, pp. 119–132. 1976

Lappe, L., Technologie, Qualifikation und Kontrolle. Die Labour-Process Debatte aus der Sicht der Deutschen Industriesoziologie, *Soziale Welt* 2/3, 310–330. 1986

Larson, M. S., *The Rise of Professionalism*. Berkeley. 1977

Littler, C. R., *The Development of the Labour Process in Capitalist Societies,* London. 1982

Lockwood, D., *The Blackcoated Worker: A Study in Class Consciousness*. London. 1958

Marquardt, O., Konjunkturforløb og klassebevidsthed, *Jyske Historiker* 1. 1974

Marquardt, O., Tesen til klassebevidsthed som et teoretisk problem, *Bidrak* 3–4, 82–95. 1976

Marshall, G. and D. Rose, Constructing the (W)right Classes. *Sociology* 20/3, 440–455. 1986

Marx, K., *Grundrisse. Foundations of the Critique of Political Economy*. Harmondsworth. 1973

Mauke, M., *Die Klassentheorie von Marx und Engels*. Frankfurt. 1970

Murphy, R., The Structure of Closure: A Critique and Development of the Theories of Weber, Collins and Parkin, *British Journal of Sociology*, 547–567. 1984

Murphy, R., The Concept of Class in Closure Theory: Learning Rather than Falling into the Problems Encountered by Neomarxism, *Sociology* 2, 247–264. 1986

Offe, C., Bemerkungen zur spieltheoretischen Neufassung des Klassenbegriffs bei Wright und Elster, *Prokla* 1, 83–82. 1985

Ottomeier, K., *Soziales Verhalten und Ökonomie im Kapitalismus: Vorüberlegungen zur systematischen Vermittlung von Interaktionstheorie und Kritik der Politischen Ökonomie*. Gaiganz. 1974

Ottomeier, K., *Ökonomische Zwänge und menschliche Beziehungen: Soziales Verhalten im Kapitalismus*. Hamburg. 1977

Parkin, F., Strategies of Social Closure in Class Formation, in: *The Social Analysis of Class Structure*. F. Parkin (ed.). London, pp. 1–18. 1974

Parkin, F., *Marxism and Class Theory: A Bourgeois Critique*. London. 1979

Poulantzas, N., *Klassen im Kapitalismus – heute*. West-Berlin. 1975

Projekt Klassenanalyse. *Materialien zur Klassenstruktur der BRD. I–II*. West-Berlin. 1973

Projekt Klassenanalyse. *Oberfläche und Staat*. West-Berlin. 1974

Przeworski, H., *Capitalism and Social Democracy*. Cambridge. 1985

Rasmussen, F. D., *Arbejderens situation, de sociale problemen og revolution*. København. 1978

Rasmussen, F. D., Velfaerdstatens klasser, *Tidskriftet Kurasje* 37, 83–105. 1985

Ritsert, J., Braucht die Soziologie noch den Begriff der Klasse? Über Max Webers Klassentheorie und neuere Versuche, sie loszuwerden, *Leviathan* 1, 4–38. 1987

Roemer, J. E., *Foundations of Marxian Economic Theory*. Cambridge, Mass.. 1981

Roemer, J. E., *A General Theory of Exploitation and Class*. Cambridge, Mass.. 1982 a

Roemer, J. E., Methodological Individualism and Deductive Marxism, *Theory and Society* 11, 513–520. 1982 b

Roemer, J. E., New Directions in the Marxian Theory of Exploitation and Class, *Politics and Society* 3, 253–287. 1982 c

Roemer, J. E., A Reply, *Politics and Society* 3, 375–394. 1982 d

Roemer, J. E., *Introduction in Analytical Marxism*. Cambridge pp. 1–7. 1986

Schanz, H.-J., *Antikritik – reflektioner over kritikken af kapitallogikken*, Aarhus. 1977

Stark, D., Class Struggle and the Transformation of the Labor Process – A Relational Approach, *Theory and Society* 9, 89–130. 1980

Therborn, G., Class Analysis: History and Defense, in: *The Sociology of Structure and Action*. U. Himmelstrand (ed.). London, pp. 96–132. 1986

Urry, J., Scientific Management and the Making of the American Service Class. Paper presented at the World Congress of Sociology. New Delhi. August 1986

Weber, M., *Economy and Society*. Berkeley. 1978

Wood, A., *Karl Marx*, London. 1981

Wood, S., The Deskilling Debate: New Technology and Work Organization, *Acta Sociologica* 1, 3–24. 1987

Wright, E. O., *Class, Crisis and the State*. London. 1978

Wright, E. O., *Classes*. London. 1985 a

Wright, E. O., Wo liegt die Mitte der Mittelklasse, *Prokla* 58, 35–62. 1985 b

Between Rational Choice and Durkheimian Solidarity

Frans Kerstholt

1. Recent Stratification Research: The Continuing Relevance of Class

During the 1960s and the greater part of the 1970s stratification research was dominated by the functionalist status attainment model. Since the path-breaking work of Blau and Duncan, many research projects have focussed on the extent to which occupational opportunities are determined by ascription and/or by achievement. Apart from some later qualifications concerning the direct effects of family background variables, the hypotheses of "heightened universalism" and of "increasing openness" as fundamental features of modern society have been accepted by most researchers (Blau and Duncan 1967: 430).

However, satisfaction with the results obtained gradually declined. This happened for several reasons. The first reason was that more and more investigators came to judge the amount of variance explained by status attainment model as disappointingly low; e. g. with income as the dependent variable, approximately 20% of the variance could be explained. Another reason was that political and cultural properties of societies turned out to be of significant relevance for the explanation of the size and patterns of mobility (Heath 1981, chap. 7). Finally, the existence and growing popularity of rival theoretical approaches to social inequality was an important reason. Of course, the varieties of Marxism and non-Marxist conflict-theory are the obvious examples here.

Thus, the results of research together with the existence of rival theoretical orientations compelled sociologists to a reconsideration of the current theoretical models.

1.1 Reactions to the Status Attainment Model

Two reactions to the status attainment model proved to be important both for the development of more powerful explanatory models of social inequality as well as for the renewal of the insight that class must be considered an important factor in the operation of systems of inequality.

Robinson and Kelley (1979) proposed to supplement the status attainment model with class variables from "rival" theories. They added Marx' "control of the means of production" and Dahrendorf's "position in the authority relations".

Wright and Perrone's (1977) main aim was to show that the Marxist explanatory model was at least as suitable as the usual status model for the explanation of income inequality. Consequently, they conducted analyses in which they used Marxist class categories along with variables of the status model.

The most important results can be summarized as follows:

(1) The explanatory power of the models had increased considerably.

(2) Class had important effects independent of status.

Robinson and Kelley arrive at the conclusion of the co-existence of two distinguishable and loosely connected stratification-systems in modern society: "a status system centering on education and occupational status" and "a class system centering on the control of the means of production and authority" (Robinson and Kelley 1979: 51 and 54).

The studies were replicated in several countries (Colbjörnsen et al. 1982; Kerstholt and Luijkx 1984; Terwey 1984). The findings generally confirmed the above-mentioned conclusions. The most conspicuous results were found in the Dutch study:

(1) In the Netherlands, the status system was found to play a considerably more important role in explaining income inequality than in the other countries.

(2) In comparison to the class system, the Dutch status system also had stronger effects on income. This result also seems typical for the Dutch case.

The main conclusion to be drawn from these reactions to the status attainment model is that stratification theory and research should not be confined to either class or status models. Repeatedly, class has been empirically proven to be of much greater salience than many writers seem to assume.

1.2 Recent Mobility Research

In some recent papers John Goldthorpe has assessed the extent to which the rates and patterns of mobility in the industrialized countries have or have not undergone change during the last decades (Goldthorpe 1983, 1984a, 1984b). He did so on the basis of a survey of the available internationally comparable research on social mobility. His main conclusion was that the results of international mobility research do not support the hypothesis that the openness of the industrialized countries has increased to any substantial extent. Observed increases in social mobility can almost completely be explained by changes in the occupational structure and by changes in fertility rates. Goldthorpe observed a surprisingly strong measure of self-recruitment of classes, which in some cases seems to be still increasing.

Goldthorpe evaluated these results of mobility research in terms of his class-analytic perspective and concludes that the mobility conditions of class formation have not been weakened. One still has to reckon with the possibility if not the reality of the political economy of class. The class-analytic perspective of Goldthorpe will be discussed in the next section.

1.3 Conclusion

With regard to the question of the relevance of class in modern society the conclusion must be the following. Both the reaction to the status attainment model and the results of mobility research point to the continuing relevance of class.

2. Neo-Weberian Class Theory as Improved Marxist Theory

Ever since the publication of Max Weber's views on class theory the field of class theory has been divided in two generally hostile camps: Marxist versus Weberian class theory. Though scarce, the main explanatory differences between the approaches of the founders were frequently reproduced in the writings of their followers; most recently and with exemplary clarity in the Weberian book by Giddens (1973) on the one hand and the Marxist book by Crompton and Gubbay (1977) on the other hand.

In his essay *Class, Status, Party* Weber tied classes – just as Marx did, broadly conveived of as economic interest groupings – to market positions. In that way the decisive distinction between Weber and Marx seemed to lie in his emphasis on markets in contrast to Marx' emphasis on production. According to his Marxist opponents, Weber had made a double mistake. His emphasis on markets implied an unjustified restriction of class analysis to market economies. Furthermore, he is said to have missed the workings of exploitation in production.

In his later *Status Groups and Classes* and unnoticed by many commentators Weber removed the reason for the first Marxist objection to his view of class. Classes are now defined as groupings of people with similar life-chances as a consequence of similarities in the disposal of goods or skills, *within a given economic order*. Only the second objection remains. For his alleged neglect of exploitation in production consists exactly in his conscious orientation on distributive matters, the distribution of life-chances. Since the Marxist conception of exploitation in production is founded on the labour theory of value and its elaboration into a political economic theory of (objective) surplus value, anyone who rejects these theories has no choice but to focus on questions of distribution. This is what Weber did, which I think, was quite justified.

However, there is a second difference between Weber and Marx that bears some relevance to class theory. Weber dismisses Marxist economic determinism. This seems irrelevant today. But this determinism had a recent revival in structuralist Marxism, where under the guise of the rejection of economism it took the form of the theory of the relative autonomy of the political and ideological superstructures (Althusser 1970–1973). At the same time, this disguised determinism produced a theory of the operation of modes of production in which, as Frank Parkin correctly remarked, the notion of the productive system as causal agency was effectively put to flight: "Since all major institutions are directly implicated in the mode of production, and are indeed part of its very definition. There is no separate, external realm of social life upon which it could make its impress. It is indistinguishable from the social system as whole" (Parkin 1979: 7). Apparently, the elimination of explanatory power was the price for the continued, though concealed, adherence to economic determinism.

The preceding brings me to the conclusion, that the Weberian class theory must be seen as an improved Marxist theory. The overall definition of explanatory problems is roughly the same. Yet, it is exactly through his rejection of the labour theory of value and of economic determinism that Weber is able to retain the explanatory potential of class theory. As we will see below from the discussion of some recent developments in neo-Weberian and neo-Marxist class theory this situation has not changed since the days of Weber. I will discuss the neo-Weberian class theories of Goldthorpe, Parkin and Ingham/Ultee. Then some shifts in the views of the Marxist sociologist Wright will be given special attention. They seem to confirm Parkin's dictum: "Inside every neo-Marxist there seems to be a Weberian struggling to get out" (Parkin 1979: 25).

2.1 John Goldthorpe: A Frank Weberian

Recently Goldthorpe summarized his conception of class analysis as follows:

(i) Class analysis aims first to establish how far classes are formed as relatively stable collectivities.

(ii) To the extent that classes are in this way identifiable, the question arises of the degree of socio-cultural differentiation of these collectivities – together with that of how such differentiation is affected by mobility between classes – and further of the degree to which classes form the basis of socio-political mobilization and conflict.

(iii) From the standpoint of class analysis, how far variation in any particular aspect of social behaviour or relationships, within the population at large, can actually be accounted for in terms of class membership is entirely a matter for investigation

[. . .] it has never been supposed by class analysts that the variable of class membership itself – or even if supplemented by that of class mobility – can provide the basis
for any complete mapping of socio-cultural patterns. Indeed, one of their preoccupations has been with the way in which the effects of class in this respect are cut across
both by the effects of stratification within classes as, for example, by income, and by
those of other affiliations – religious, ethnic, regional etc. (Goldthorpe 1984 b:
491–492).

Stable collectivities exhibit a strong measure of "continuity with which, in consequence of patterns of class mobility and immobility, their members have been
associated with particular sets of positions over time."

In this conception of class-analysis, which goes back to Max Weber's view of
"social class," mobility processes are constitutive for the formation of classes.
According to Goldthorpe, mobility analyses should focus on "certain social relationships in which individuals and groups are daily involved and which are believed to exert a pervasive influence in their lives." Goldthorpe locates these
relationships in the social division of labour and derives the relevant socio-economic positions as follows:

the social division of labour [. . .] is usually being constituted in two main ways:
    in basic employment relationships which differentiate employers,
    self-employed workers and employees; and
    in varying employment functions and conditions of employment which differentiate
categories of employee – most importantly (a) those in subordinate positions who,
via a labour contract, exchange more or less discrete amounts of labour for wages on a
short-term basis and (b) those in positions involving some exercise of authority or
expertise, whose conditions of employment imply the exchange of "service" for
"compensation" in a more diffuse and long-term fashion.

In this manner Goldthorpe distinguishes between the "working class" and the
"service class." He regards class structures as an inevitable source of social
conflict (Goldthorpe 1984 b: 467).

Application of this class-analytic perspective to the results of mobility research
leads Goldthorpe to conclude that the mobility conditions of class formation have
not been weakened. One still has to reckon with the possibility if not the reality
of the political economy of class.

In another recent paper Goldthorpe makes a strong case for the reality of class
politics (Goldthorpe 1984 a). He argues that the decisive explanatory variable for
the so different performances (growth, unemployment) of the European
economies during the present-day crisis has to be found in the varieties of class
relations.

Goldthorpe explains the economic crisis as the result of economic inefficiencies
which in their turn came into being as a consequence of the postwar shift of
power to the advantage of organized labour. Further, Goldthorpe discusses the
corporatist and dualistic tendencies in modern Western societies which he sees as
responses to the economic crisis. He interprets these tendencies as different

forms of class politics. Corporatism stands for a compromise between the forces of organized labour and capital. Power blockades are avoided and labour accepts efficiency-restoring measures in exchange for active employment policies. Dualistic tendencies are initiated by capital. Their aim is the elimination of inefficiencies through the weakening of labour. On theoretical and empirical grounds Goldthorpe argues that the corporatist solution has the most favourable socio-economic consequences.

2.2 Frank Parkin: "Social Closure" as the Basic Process

Parkin is perhaps the most original of the contemporary class theorists. He takes his central concept from Max Weber. It is worth noting though that Weber himself did not use the concept of social closure in his explicit class theories (1922: 184). This is striking because the concept directly refers to the process that is perhaps central in Weber's economic sociology. At least, according to Collins, the process of monopolization should be regarded as such (Collins 1986: 125–133).

Parkin introduces the concept as follows:

By social closure Weber means the process by which social collectivities seek to maximize rewards by restricting acces to resources and opportunities to a limited circle of eligibles. [...] virtually any group attribute – race, language, social origin, religion – may be seized upon provided that it can be used for "the monopolization of specific usually economic opportunities." [...] its purpose is always the closure of social and economic opportunities to outsiders (Parkin 1979: 44).

Parkin sees social inequality, i. e. the unequal distribution of life-chances, as the outcome of strategic action of members of social groups. He employs a view of social action that combines two elements. He assumes rational actors and thinks in terms of what could be designated as a typically Weberian conflict perspective. Parkin contrasts his view with the liberal as well as with Marxist theory:

The neo-Weberian position advanced here is that the relation between classes is neither one of harmony and mutual benefit, nor of irresolvable and fatal contradiction. Rather, the relationship is understood as one of mutual antagonism and permanent tension: that is, a condition of unrelieved distributive struggle that it is not necessarily impossible to "contain" (Parkin 1979: 112).

In my view, Parkin in this way brings about an elegant supersedure of the unfruitful opposition of harmony and conflict. Distributive struggles are not exclusively considered non-cooperative games.

Many social groups are involved in processes of social closure. Parkin distinguishes three kinds of closure: exclusion, usurpation and dual closure. Exclusion is directed downward, usurpation is directed upward as it is normally mounted by an outsider group in response to its status and its collective experiences of exclusion. Dual closure typically refers to the strategies of the middle classes which usually simultaneously practice exclusionary and usurpationary closure.

Regarding closure in contemporary modern society, Parkin's position is as follows: "In modern capitalist society the two main exclusionary devices by which the bourgeoisie constructs and maintains itself as a class are, first, those surrounding the institutions of property; and, second academic or professional qualifications and credentials" (Parkin 1979: 47–48). He concludes: "[. . .] the dominant class under capitalism can be thought of as comprising those who possess or control productive capital and those who possess a legal monopoly of professional services" (Parkin 1979: 58).

Parkin's theory includes the following attractive elements:
– The theory suggests an explanation of mobility processes as the outcome of strategic action of social groups trying to improve or defend their life-chances.
– The combination of the explicitly elaborated Weberian conflict perspective with the assumption of rational action implies that Parkin's theory shares a number of important premises with the "rational choice-theory." The last-mentioned theory has emjoyed increasing attention from sociologists during the last decade. The subject of the significance of the rational choice theory will be taken up in the next sections.

2.3 The New Weber Interpretation: The Ingham/Ultee View

The "new interpretation of Weber" was introduced by Geoffrey Ingham (1970). In the Netherlands its main proponent is Wout Ultee (1983). It mainly consist of a reversal of the "classic interpretation of Weber" that used to be most influential among American functionalist sociologists.

The outstanding feature of the classic interpretation is that it takes the three Weber dimensions of stratification – class, status and party (power) – as three kind of scarce goods people strive after. Income, status and power are essentially seen as socially available rewards.

In the new interpretation class, status and power are considered to be the most important resources that individuals use in order to improve their life-chances or, what amounts to the same, their living conditions. The assumption is that individuals pursue the improvement of their life-chances. The basic proposition is: To the extent that a person has more resources at his disposal, he has better life-chances. Then the three kinds of resources are specified as economic, symbolic and political power.

The dimensions of Weber have been transformed into independent, explanatory variables. The point of the new interpretation is the following. It hypothesizes independent effects of any of the three kinds of resources on a person's living conditions. Economic and political power are included within the scope of sociological theory.

The new interpretation has at least four significant advantages for empirical-theoretic research.

(1) It provides an excellent framework for the successful derivation of hypotheses (see e. g. Ultee 1983).

(2) It seems possible to link the theory to rational choice theory.

(3) The results of a great deal of reported research allow fruitful interpretations in terms of the new reading of Weber. The reactions to the status attainment model which were discussed in the first section of this paper are excellent examples in this respect. The interpretation of the Wright/Perrone research would run as follows. They have conducted successful research that focussed first of all on the estimation of the independent effects of economic power (class) and of symbolic power (status) on a not unimportant aspect of a person's living conditions (income).

(4) Finally, the new interpretation yields an important expansion of the scope of Weberian stratification theory. Weber's concept of "estate" ("*Stand*") has considerable historic-specific connotations from which ensue some limitations to its applicability. These limitations are eliminatated by the replacement of "estate" by the more general concept of "symbolic power".

2.4 Erik Olin Wright: From Marx to Weber

Wright is one of the rather few Marxists who regard the formulation of testable hypotheses as an important goal of theoretical work. His constructive critique of the class theory of Poulantzas resulted in a Marxist class theory that has at least one very attractive property. Wright avoided unescapable problems of operationalization by not charging the basic concept of exploitation with the usual notions of surplus production and productive labour. He developed a domination-centred concept of exploitation. In that way the original Marxist concept of exploitation assumed mere metaphoric significance (Wright 1979).

Later Wright became increasingly dissatisfied with his domination-centred concept that "should now be replaced by a rigorous, exploitation-centred conceptualization" (Wright 1985: 105). His new theory of class can be characterized as a sociological application of the models of class and exploitation which were developed by the economist John Roemer (1982a, 1982b).

I will first discuss the changes in Wright's ideas. Then I will argue that Wright's first theory rightly deserves the label Marxist and that his later theory is before anything else a nice elaboration of the economic part of Weber's theory of social inequality.

2.5 Wright's First Bid

The first theory starts from a conception of exploitation relations in which exploitation is defined as a "relation of domination within which people in the dominant position are able to appropriate the surplus labor of people in the subordinate position" (Wright 1979: 15). Classes are common positions within the social relations of production that comprise intrinsically antagonistic positions.

As it is sufficient for my purposes, I will restrict my discussion to Wright's conception of the capitalist relations of production. He breaks these relations of production down into three interdependent dimensions or processes. He then defines the classes implied by the capitalist relations of production:

The fundamental class antagonism between workers and capitalists can be viewed as a polarization of each of these three underlying processes: capitalists control the authority structure as a whole, decide how the physical means of production are to be used, and control the accumulation process. Workers, in contrast, are excluded from control over authority relations, the physical means of production, and the investment process (Wright 1979: 25).

In between the objectively polarized positions of capitalists and workers Wright places a cluster of "contradictory positions" consisting of managers and supervisors. Contradictory positions are described as positions that simultaneously, be it to differing degrees, have certain characteristics of each of the two classes between which they are situated. In general, managers and supervisors occupy intermediate positions on the three dimensions of capitalist production relations. Consequently, in Wright's view they exhibit bourgeois and proletarian characteristics at the same time. The intermediate positions represent a wide range of combinations of bourgeois and proleterian characteristics. It is for that reason that according to Wright some contradictory positions are closer to the bourgeoisie while others are closer to the proletariat: "The contradictory quality of a particular position within class relations is a variable..." (Wright 1979: 41–42). This is a rather striking description of contradictory positions. Wright maintains his relational starting point (fundamental class antagonism) although going on to describe the contradictory quality of contradictory positions as a variable characteristic.

Note that in this conception of classes and class relations the notions of the production and appropriation of surplus do not have any operational meaning.

2.6 The Revised Class Theory

As mentioned above, Wright's new class theory leans heavily on Roemer's game theoretic models of class and exploitation. Wright summarizes Roemer's approach as follows:

The basic idea of this approach is to compare different systems of exploitation by treating the organization of production as a "game". The actors in this game have various kinds of production assets (i. e. resources such as skills and capital) which they bring into production and which they use to generate incomes on the basis of a specific set of rules. The essential strategy adopted for the analysis of exploitation is to ask if particular coalitions of players would be better off if they withdrew from this game under certain specified procedures in order to play a different one. The alternative games differ in the ways the assets are allocated. Different types of exploitation are defined by the particular withdrawal rules that would make certain agents better off and other agents worse off (Wright 1985: 68).

Roemer defines four kinds of exploitation; feudal exploitation, capitalist exploitation, socialist exploitation and "status" exploitation.

The distribution of productive assets under capitalism is defined in the usual way: "What Roemer demonstrates is that if the coalition of all wage-earners were to leave the game of capitalism with their per capita share of society's assets, then they would be better off than if they stayed in capitalism, and capitalists would be worse off" (Wright 1985: 70–1). So not surprisingly, a radical redistribution of the means of production would put an end to capitalist exploitation.

The withdrawal rule for feudal exploitation prescribes leaving the game with one's *personal assets* (rather than one's *per capita* share of total assets).

Socialist exploitation results from an unequal distribution of skills: "A coalition will be said to be socialistically exploited if it would improve its position by leaving with its per capita skills while its complement would be worse off under such circumstances" (Wright 1985: 70). From this analysis it follows that the incomes of the higher skilled are not a direct consequence of their skills. Rather, these incomes are explained as the result of the unequal distribution of skills. The implication is: "The highly skilled [. . .] thus have an interest in maintaining skill differentials, and this is what underpins the claim that their income reflects exploitation" (Wright 1985: 70). This conception further implies that sociological research on the relationships between education, occupation and income has to be regarded as investigation into "socialist exploitation."

Roemer's concept of "status" exploitation undergoes a slight transformation in the new theory of Wright. Referring to Smith and Marx, he proposes to treat the factor "organization" as a productive asset. Its unequal distribution is then seen as the basis of "organization asset exploitation":

The claim that the effective control over organization assets is a basis of exploitation is equivalent to saying (a) that non-managers would be better off and managers/ bureaucrats worse off if non-managers were to withdraw with their per capita share of organization assets (or equivalently, if organizational control were democratized); and (b) that by virtue of effectively controlling organization assets managers/ bureaucrats control part or all of the socially produced surplus (Wright 1985: 80).

Class locations and the interests they involve are considered to be unambigiously determined by the positions people occupy with respect to the different kinds of exploitation.

Ownership or non-ownership of means of production defines the position in relation to capitalist exploitation.

Differentials in *skills (education)* do the same for socialist exploitation.

Finally, the position in the organizational hierarchy *(management)* is decisive with respect to organizational exploitation.

Wright is of the opinion that as a consequence of the central role of the concept of exploitation the revised class theory has a solid Marxist foundation.

2.7 Some Evaluative Remarks

It is striking that Wright has included the factor "occupational level" (skills, education) in his model. Apart from the rhetoric, this fact alone contributes to a considerable reduction of the difference with non-Marxist theories.

The Weberian conception of class is perfectly compatible with Wright's list of class criteria. Giddens (1973: 107) used ownership of property in the means of production, possession of educational or technical qualifications and the possession of manual labour-power. Among the sources of what he calls "proximate structuration of class relations" Giddens even lists the authority relationships within the enterprise (Giddens 1973: 108). What else could be expected of a Weberian class theorist? After all, wasn't Weber one of the great pioneers of the theory on bureaucracy?

My conclusion must be that Wright's revised class theory implies an explanatory model displaying the main characteristics of a Weberian model. This may seem a bit of a surprise, since the new theory is explicitly said to be founded on a genuine theory of exploitation and Weber determinedly denied the possibility of a scientific theory of exploitation. Yet, things take a different look when we turn our attention to the operational meaning of the Roemer/Wright theory of exploitation. All the theory predicts is that given the distribution of the productive assets mentioned, a positive relationship between control over an asset and income is to be expected. Well then, neo-Weberian theories predict exactly the same. The new interpretation of Weber provides us with the clearest example.

Indeed, Wright has presented a nice elaboration of the economic part of Weber's model of inequality. Unwittingly, he has made the transition to the Weberian camp. The neo-Marxist concept of exploitation that he uses is operationally redundant. Thus, Wright has effectively covered the theoretical trajectory from a metaphoric to a superfluous concept of exploitation.

In contrast, Wright's earlier class theory may be considered genuinely Marxist, because it is certainly based on the most important dimensions of the relations of production that emerge from the Marxist tradition.

The observed change in the ideas of Erik Olin Wright clearly supports my view that the Weberian way of defining class theoretical problems must be seen as improved Marxism.

3. The Future of Stratification Research: Issues and Problems

In the first section of this paper some results of recent stratification were briefly discussed. They point to the desirability of theoretical models in which processes of the formation of classes and of status-groups are paramount. The relationships between both processes should also receive special attention.

Recent theoretical developments seem to indicate that the building materials for such theories are rather scarce. Only the new interpretation of Weber utilizes both the concepts of class and status. The explicit orientation on individuals and the resources at their disposal, however, seems to divert attention from the group processes involved. It can hardly be accidental that this theory is especially attractive to researchers with a strong preference for techniques of causal analysis.

The other theories advance at best some theoretical notions concerning the formation of classes. It seems necessary to look at other fields of sociological and anthropological activity in order to find starting points. Two fundamental theories on the formation of social groups promise to be useful. Rational choice theory as aplied to "the logic of collective action" (Olson 1965, but also in game theoretic Marxism) is the first one. The other theory has been repeatedly called to our attention by Randall Collins (1975, 1981a, 1981b, 1985). This theory is the Durkheimian theory of the formation of solidary groups through rituals. Both theories of group formation have the advantage of being built on explicit micro-foundations.

The Durkheimian theory is expected to be of use for the development of a theory of the formation of status-groups. The rational choice theory promises to be particularly helpful in the explanation of the formation of classes as social groups, and in the explanation of the action of classes or status-groups in the arena of social conflicts. The affinity between rational choice theory and the typically Weberian conflict perspective will receive special attention.

3.1 The Formation of Groups Through Rituals: The Durkheimian Micro-Tradition

Durkheim's theory of group formation through rituals is the starting point for what Randall Collins calls the Durkheimian micro-tradition: "Durkheim presented a powerful model of the ritual aspects of social behavior as the key to emotional solidarity and to our most fundamental conceptions of reality" (Collins 1975: 43).

The theory is based on Durkheim's "law of social gravity" (Durkheim 1964 [1893]: 339; Collins 1985: 124–131), that explains social phenomena as resulting from the structural relations between individuals. "Social density" – "the actual, physical pattern of who is in the presence of whom, for how long, and with how much space between them" (Collins 1985: 125) – is the fundamental factor behind the social, mental and moral phenomena that make up the subject matter of sociology. Durkheim describes processes of group formation in terms of social density: "What bring men together are mechanical causes and impulsive forces, such as affinity of blood, attachment to the same soil, ancestral worship, community of habits, and so on. It is only when the group has been formed on these bases that..." (Durkheim 1964 [1893]: 278).

The subject of the theory of rituals is the operation of the sociological law of gravity under conditions of high "social density." The basic idea is that interaction situations involving high social density lead to ritual behaviours which in their turn are of fundamental importance for the development and the functioning of solidary groups. Durkheim (1971 [1912]: 214–216) distinguishes between everyday situations of low density and unusual interaction situations that are characterized by a strongly increased social density. The latter situation is likely to give rise to forms of collective exaltation. Under these conditions the fundamental interplay of the ritualization of behaviour and the genesis of social solidarity is to be expected.

The analysis of behavioural variation under different conditions of social density further leads to the distinction between the profane and the sacred. Sacred things or persons ought to be approached in a ritually prescribed way and with required respect or disrespect. In the case of a taboo, the prescription is of course to abstain from approaching. Sacredness is not restricted to the religious sphere in the narrow sense of the word. Phenomena of this kind can be expected in all situations of increased density. In that connection Durkheim points to "That general effervescence [...] characteristic of revolutionary or creative periods [...]." He remarks:

Under the influence of the general exaltation, we see the most mediocre and inoffensive bourgeois become either a hero or a butcher. And so clearly are all these mental processes at the root of religion that the individuals themselves have often pictured the pressure before which they thus gave way in a distinctly religious form.

The leaders of large organizations with an ideological message are aware of these relationships:

This is why all parties, economic or confessional, are careful to have periodical reunions where their members may revivify their common faith by manifesting it in common. To strengthen those sentiments [...] it is sufficient to bring those who hold them together and to put them into closer and more active relations with one another (Durkheim 1971 [1912]: 210–211).

One effect of such reunions is that different persons are invested with different degrees of sacredness. As a consequence, they may expect different gradations of deference.

In this way Durkheim formulates the starting points of a theory about the ritual causation and continued existence of solidary social groups. The references to the activities of leaders of large ideologically oriented organizations and to the different degrees of ritually prescribed deference reveal the potential importance of this approach for stratification theory. Rituals may be used as weapons in struggles, including the struggle over the distribution of life-chances. Moreover, status inequality, the unequal distribution of prestige, may originate in rituals as well as be preserved by them.

Collins summarizes Durkheim's theory as follows:

the ritual [. . .] also heightens the contact: by going through common gestures, chants, and the like, people focus their attention on the same thing. [. . .] they become overwhelmingly conscious of the group around them. As a result, certain ideas come to represent the group itself by becoming its symbols. The tabooed object of the primitive tribe, the altar of a religion, the flag of a modern political ritual – for that matter, the football team of a college crowd – takes on a sacred significance, transcending the ordinary and enforcing respect.

Durkheim referred to this aspect of interaction as moral density (Collins 1985: 128).

3.2 Rational Choice Theory and Group Formation: The Logic of Collective Action

Rational choice theory is the general theory of action that is implied in the concept of the "homo economicus." Recent developments in micro-economics have made it possible to extend the framework of rational choice outside the realm of traditional economics. The development of concepts like transaction costs, information costs and the game theoretic exploration of market imperfections, to mention only some examples, have increased the relevance of rational choice models to organizational and stratification theory (Barney and Ouchi 1986; Fitzpatrick 1986).

Below I will argue that these developments have even practically led to a theoretical fusion of recent game theoretic or "analytic" Marxism (Elster 1985; Roemer 1986) and the typically Weberian conflict perspective.

A central theme running through the sociological applications of rational choice theory is that of the logic of collective action (Olson 1965). Olson's classical study raises the question of the conditions under which rationally acting individuals will combine in order to realize or defend common interests. In a sense this is the recruitment problem faced by any organization that tries to induce people to make a contribution to the realization of a generally available provision (collective good, public good). Skillfully preparing a game theoretic formulation of Olson's problem, Heath concludes: "Olsons's major achievement is to show that the public goods may not be provided even if everyone concerned might actually be better off making the required contributions and receiving the benefits in question" (Heath 1976: 31). The sociological significance of Olson's problem is that it clearly pertains to questions of the organization of cooperation and of the growth of solidarity. Thus, the problem has a direct bearing on the problem of the formation of cooperative and solidary groups.

3.3 The Organization of Solidarity

Elster has reformulated Olson's problem in game theoretic terms:

The basic problem confronting any group of people trying to organize themselves is that of the Prisoner's Dilemma. In its simplest form it is a strategic game between any given individual and "Everyone else". To each of these actors, two strategies are available: to engage in the collective action or to abstain. For any pair of strategies chosen by the actors, there is a well defined payoff [. . .] to each of them. In the matrix below the first number in each cell represents "my" payoff and the second the payoff to each of the individuals included in "everyone else".

		Everyone else	
		Engage	Abstain
I	Engage	b,b	e,f
	Abstain	c,d	a,a

Here b-a represents the gain from cooperation, [. . .]. Similarly c-b represents the free-rider gain and a-e the loss from unilateralism. Clearly, whatever everyone else does, it is in my interest to abstain. If all others engage in collective action, I can get the free-rider benefit by abstaining and if everyone else abstains, I can avoid the loss from unilateralism by abstaining too. Since the reasoning applies to each agent, in the place of "I", all will decide to abstain and no collective action will be forthcoming (Elster 1985: 359–360).

Then Elster raises the question of the possibility of cooperative solutions (e. g. the production of a public good or the realization of collective action) to the prisoners' dilemma. In other words, he ask for solutions to the free rider problem. In accordance with the assumptions of game theory he envisages three possibilities: ". . . if the interaction is repeated several times: if the payoffs that motivate the actors differ from the [. . .] reward structure and if the behaviour is less than fully rational" (Elster 1985: 360). He explicitly concedes the feasibility of any of the three distinguished possibilities.

With respect to repeated interactions he gives the example of capitalists and workers interacting over long periods of time. Their chosen actions reciprocally determine each other. This implies the possibility of threats or promises. He then states:

These can be formalized into such meta-strategies as "always choose the same strategy as your opponent did in the preceding game", that is retaliate with abstention against abstention and answer cooperation with cooperation. It can be shown that if all parties adopt this meta-strategy the ensuing situation will be stable against defectors. The free-rider gains will not tempt the individual to break out of the collective action (Elster 1985: 360).

This formulation of the well-known tit-for-tat meta-strategy includes a superfluous reference to "abstention against abstention". In that way the cooperative solution to the repeated prisoners' dilemma seems to be restricted to the rather trivial situation in which the first player starts with cooperative behaviour. However, Taylor (1976) has shown the existence of less trivial combinations of meta-strategies that lead to stable cooperation of rationally acting players, and in which "abstention against abstention" really plays a role.

Elster's final judgment on the possibility of cooperative solutions to the repeated prisoners's dilemma is cautious: "...for collective action to take place so many conditions must be fulfilled that it is a wonder it can occur at all. The window of acceptable parameter values may be very narrow indeed" (Elster 1985: 361).

The results with respect to repeated prisoners' dilemma games have received some interesting applications. Relevant examples are game theoretic Marxism and the work by Raub and Voss, who argue for the possibility of a rational choice foundation of solidarity (Raub and Voss 1985, 1986).

Game theoretic Marxism carries at least one fundamental theoretical implication. Contrary to traditional Marxism, more or less durable cooperation between classes is considered a serious possibility. Indeed, class compromise is seen as the normal case:

The basic sense in which there is a need for cooperation between workers and capitalists is that the means they use to increase their share of the total product, such as strikes or lockouts, also disrupt production and hence reduce the total to be shared. Also, the capitalists have an interest in the survival of the workers, and the latter an interest in high profits that will ensure economic growth and future gains (Elster 1985: 377).

3.4 The Growth of Solidarity

In avowed opposition to the Durkheimian theory of solidarity, Raub and Voss have outlined the contours of a rational choice theory of social solidarity. The relevance of such a theory to class formation and the action of any interest group may be immediately evident.

Raub and Voss (1985, 1986) build on Friedman's work (1977) concerning the problem of the iterative prisoners' dilemma. From Friedman they borrow four stringent conditions under which cooperative behaviour of rational individuals is provocative. They then suggest sociological interpretations of these conditions. For the purpose of presentation, I will combine Friedman's conditions and the sociological interpretations by Raub and Voss:

(1) An endogeneous sanctioning mechanism should stabilize all acors' willingness to cooperate. It is essential that this mechanism comes into being as an adaptation to the situational characteristic "iteration". This condition ensures that cooperation does not depend on supervision, coercion or unconditional commitments to normative obligation (Raub and Voss 1985: 20–21).

Raub and Voss argue that this mechanism requires a measure of ("perfect") information. Thus, they suggest as a sociological condition a high degree of visibility of behaviour as, for instance, made possible by frequent and intensive interactions (Raub and Voss 1985: 21).

(2) Expected stability of the social situation is the next condition. Raub and Voss translate this condition into sociological variables such as community closure and homogeneity of the population (Raub and Voss 1985: 22).

(3) The condition of a strong interdependency can be realized by the institutionalization of opportunities for reciprocity. (Raub and Voss 1985: 24). Raub and Voss seem to use here the well-known "norm of reciprocity".

(4) Problems of the coordination of possible strategies must have been overcome. With respect to this condition Raub and Voss refer to factors such as the availability of unambigous rules and a common history of the population involved (Raub and Voss 1985: 29).

3.5 Rational Choice and the Typically Weberian Conflict Perspective

Above several references were made to a typically Weberian conflict perspective. The keyword was permanent tension and it was praised for its elegant supersedure of the antithesis of harmony and conflict.

I will very briefly indicate how this perspective can be given a rational choice foundation. Weede (1986) has shown that in principle a society without conflicts cannot exist. He uses the modern micro-economic concept of externalities. These exist "when the economic activity of consumers and producers causes benefits or costs to third parties without any equivalent compensation" (Fitzpatrick 1986: 28). Of course, Weede uses the concept in a sociological manner.

According to Weede, conflicts between people generally arise when actors do not take into account the negative externalities of their selected courses of action for others (Weede 1986: 11). He mentions three possibilities; egoistic behaviour, lack of information perhaps originating from short-sightedness, and the objective opposition of interests possibly implicated in the (strategic) interdependence of actors.

In the opinion of Weede, it is especially the consumption of "positional goods" that leads to conflicting interests. The defining characteristic of a "positional good" is that its consumption by any person inhibits by that fact alone the opportunities of other persons to consume that kind of good. Social positions are the most important sociological positional goods. The example is a privileged occupational position (Weede 1986: 11 and 47).

The existence of a conflict of interests does not in itself lead to overt conflict. The occurrence of overt conflict depends on the subjective cost-/benefit calculations of the individuals involved, i. e. on Olson's logic of collective action. Weede's general judgment is that the objective conditions (especially the neglect of negative externalities) and the subjective conditions of conflict (Olson's logic) will normally be fulfilled. His conclusion is that in principle a conflict-free society is inconceivable (Weede 1986: 47).

Social conflicts require internally cooperative conflict parties. Latent conflict parties have different capacities for cooperation and for the mobilization of resources. One of the major factors is the intensity of common interests that in its turn is mainly determined by the degree of attachment to the positions involved. Here the idea of "mobility closure" that is so characteristic of the Weberian approach to social inequality is given an explicit rational choice foundation. The implication of the argument is: "Social mobility of the individual is an alternative to solidary class action" (Weede 1986: 48).

In an actual conflict, parties are dependent on each other in the sense of the strategic situations that are the subject of game theory. The strategic structure of the situations that emerge in the course of the conflict process determine whether conflicts will or will not be resolved in a way which is acceptable to all parties involved.

The first conclusion must be that Weede's rational choice foundation of conflicts rather accurately corresponds to the typically Weberian conflict perspective. In the discussion of that perspective the elements of "permanent tension" and the "supersedure of the contradiction of harmony and conflict" received special emphasis. Moreover, the Weberian idea of "social closure" appears to play an important role in Weede's argumentation.

Another equally important conclusion concerns the relation between Weberian class theory and game theoretic or analytic Marxism. Both approaches have the same rational choice foundation and transcend in the same way the unfruitful opposition of harmony and conflict. The inescapable conclusion seems to be that analytical Marxism and Weberian class analysis have fused into a single explanatory framework.

4. Class and Status: Between Rational Choice and Durkheimian Solidarity

At first sight it seems clear that the rational choice approach is pre-eminently suited for the analysis of processes of the formation of classes whereas the theory of group formation through rituals can be of special use in the analysis of the formation of status-groups. Analytical Marxism can among other things be seen as devoted to the study of questions of class formation on the basis of rational choice models. Collins, on the other hand, has made explicit use of the Durkheimian micro-perspective for the analysis of the development of status-groups (Collins 1975, 1979).

However, things appear in a slightly different perspective if the question of the relationships between classes and status-groups is raised. With the aim of exploring somewhat further the applicability of both theories of group formation, I will briefly examine the three most distinctive positions on the relationships between classes and status-groups; interplay of class and status, priority of class, priority of status-groups.

The first position can be found in Haller (1983). He describes class formation as processes in which individuals or groups pursue their economic interests through the use of consciously built and if possible further strengthened power positions (Haller: 146). Stratification or the formation of status groups is defined as the unequal distribution of "social honour" among the members of a society. (Haller: 100). The basis for stratification processes is seen in long-lasting and intimate relations between individual persons (Haller: 146).

The interplay of class and status is then approached in terms of a distinction between effects of class formation on stratification and effects of stratification on class formation.

It should be clear that Haller's theory comes close to the above-mentioned division of labour between rational choice theory and the Durkheimian micro-theory. Haller's conception of class formation clearly points to rational choice theory as the appropriate explanatory device. Long-lasting and intimate relations between individual persons imply frequent situations of intensive co-presence, i. e. heightened social density. This means that it should be possible to establish a link between Haller's conception of the stratification process and the Durkheimian theory of group formation through rituals.

The second position is typical of traditional Marxism. In as far as the existence of status-groups is recognized, they are essentially seen as manifestations of class. Although not quite clear, the connected theory of group formation certainly displays strong similarities to rational choice ideas.

The third position has recently been advanced by Randall Collins. With respect to economic structures in general he states: "At their core: a *social* tie must always be negotiated before the bargaining for social advantage can take place

[...] *Status groups are more fundamental than classes, as the latter can emerge only on the basis of the former"* (Collins 1985: 166–167). According to Collins, calculating, self-interested individuals "are never very effective unless they can relate to non-rational feelings of solidarity that hold people together" (Collins 1982: 25). He considers solidarity a crucial weapon in the struggle for advantages in which the groups with the most internal solidarity usually win: "Which interests win out [...] is not a matter of rational calculation. It depends on something deeper: on moral feelings that bind people together in a group. The procedures that produce these moral feelings [...] are *social rituals"* (Collins 1982: 28).

To recapitulate, Collins does not rule out the rational pursuit of self-interest altogether. But the nonrational foundations come first. What is of prime importance is membership of more or less solidary groups.

An interesting parallel to the view of Collins can be found in the writings of Wallerstein who is usually regarded as a Marxist author. He has expressed his view on the relationships between classes and status-groups several times. His view still is: "I believe 'class' and what I prefer to call 'ethno-nation' are two sets of clothing for the same basic reality" (Wallerstein 1979: 224). The idea behind this formulation is that groups come to present themselves either as classes or as status groups. Their "choice" depends on some judgment on what will best further their interests under the circumstances they find themselves in.

In a more recent article this basic view is given a somewhat more explicit elaboration. Processes of class formation and processes of status-group formation are seen "on occasion as fused and reinforcing sets of processes [...] groups are in fact constantly being recreated such that over time we have genuinely new wine in old bottles [...]" (Arrighi et al. 1985: 152–153). The authors conclude: "The actual history of the construction [...] of classes, nations, and ethnic groups [...] is a history of the constant fall and rise of the intensity of [...] claims in cultural clothing" (Arrighi et al. 1985: 156).

Like Collins, Wallerstein seems to base the rational pursuit of self-interest on the pre-existence of more or less solidary groups. In contrast to Collins, though, Wallerstein conceives of status-groups as normally striving after well-defined political or economic advantages.

4.1 A Paradox of Collective Action?

We seem in this way to have arrived at a paradox of collective action, or perhaps better of the theory of collective action. For Collins the fundamental issue is Durkheimian solidarity facilitating among other things the rational promotion of interests. Wallerstein, on the other hand, sees economic and political interests as the basic issues. Classes and status-groups, though perhaps expressions of Durkheimian solidarity, are somehow rationally devised means to fundamental ends.

The problem is whether this paradox can be resolved in a theoretically rational manner. In my view, it is possible to propose a rather simple solution to this problem. Following Elster, a collective actor can be defined "as an interest-group that has succeeded in overcoming the freerider obstacle to concerted action" (Roemer 1986: 142). Elster does not require that the free rider problem be resolved in a rational way. If we accept this stand-point, it becomes possible to regard the Durkheimian theory of the formation of solidary groups through rituals as a means to treat an important way in which the free rider problem can effectively be overcome.

This implies that rationally operating collective actors can arise in at least two ways:

(1) Through the mechanism of Durkheimian solidarity.
(2) As a rational solution to the repeated prisoners' dilemma.

An interesting implication is that the scenarios outlined by both Collins and Wallerstein can actually occur. If Wallerstein is correct in pointing to the possibility of the formation of status groups on the basis of common interests, the following conclusion seems justified. The two fundamental theories on the formation of social groups are useful for the explanation of the rise and functioning of classes and status-groups, but in a broader sense than is usually anticipated. On the one hand, the Durkheimian theory can be extended to classes. Likewise, rational choice theory can be useful in connection with status-groups. So, it seems sound enough to conclude that collective life is enacted between rational choice and Durkheimian solidarity, perhaps most visible in the field of stratification theory and the organization of collective action.

References

Althusser, L., *Lire le Capital*. III Volumes, Paris: Maspéro. 1970–1973

Arrighi, G. et al, Rethinking the Concepts of Class and Status-group in a World-System Perspective, in: R. Collins *Three Sociological Traditions: Selected Readings*. New York: Oxford University Press, 140–158. 1985

Barney, J. and W. G. Ouchi (eds.), *Organizational Economics*. San Francisco and London: Jossey-Bass. 1986

Blau, P. and O. Duncan, *The American Occupational Structure*. New York: The Free Press. 1967

Colbjörnsen, T. et al., *Klassestruktur och Klasseskiller*. Bergen: Universitetsforlaget. 1982

Collins, R., *Conflict Sociology*. New York: Academic Press. 1975

Collins, R., *The Credential Society*. New York: Academic Press. 1979

Collins, R., Micro-translation as a Theory-Building Strategy, in: K. Knorr-Cetina and A. Cicourel (eds.): *Advances in Social Theory and Methodology: Toward an Integration of Micro- and Macro-Sociologies*. Boston: Routledge and Kegan Paul, pp. 81–108. 1981 a

Collins, R., On the Micro-Foundations of Macro-Sociology, *American Journal of Sociology* 86, f: 984–1014. 1981 b

Collins, R., *Sociological Insight: An Introduction to Non-Obvious Sociology*. New York: Oxford University Press. 1982

Collins, R., *Three Sociological Traditions*. New York: Oxford University Press. 1985

Collins, R., *Weberian Sociology*. Cambridge: Cambridge University Press. 1986

Crompton, R. and J. Gubbay, *Economy and Class Structure*. London and Basingstoke: Macmillan. 1977

Dahrendorf, R., *Class and Class Conflict in an Industrial Society*. London: Routledge and Kegan Paul. 1959

Durkheim, E., *The Division of Labor in Society*. New York: The Free Press (1893). 1964

Durkheim, E., *The Elementary Forms of the Religious Life*. London: George Allen and Unwin (1912). 1971

Elster, J., *Making Sense of Marx*. Cambridge: Cambridge University Press. 1985

Elster, J. (ed.), *Rational Choice*. Oxford: Basil Blackwell. 1986

Fitzpatrick, G., *Microeconomics: New Theories and Old*. Oxford: Oxford University Press. 1986

Friedman, J., *Oligopoly and the Theory of Games*. Amsterdam: North-Holland Publishing Company. 1977

Giddens, A., *The Class Structure of the Advanced Societies*. London: Hutchinson. 1973

Goldthorpe, J., Social Mobility and Class Formation, Paper, Amsterdam. 1983

Goldthorpe, J. (ed.), *Order and Conflict in Contemporary Capitalism: Studies in the Political Economy of Western European Nations*. Oxford: Clarendon Press. 1984 a

Goldthorpe, J., Women and Class Analysis: A Reply To The Replies, *Sociology* 18, 4: 491–499. 1984 b

Haller, M., *Theorie der Klassenbildung und sozialen Schichtung*. Frankfurt and New York: Campus-Verlag. 1983

Heath, A., *Rational Choice and Social Exchange: A Critique of Exchange Theory*. Cambridge: Cambridge University Press. 1976

Heath, A., *Social Mobility*. London: Fontana Books. 1981

Ingham, G., Social Stratification: Individual Attributes and Social Relationships. *Sociology* 4: 105–113. 1970

Kerstholt, F. and R. Luijkx, Class, Status and Income Inequality, *The Netherlands' Journal of Sociology* 20,2: 134–149. 1984

Olson, M., *The Logic of Collective Action*. Cambridge, Mass.: Harvard University Press. 1965

Ordeshook, P., *Game Theory and Political Theory: An Introduction*. Cambridge: Cambridge University Press. 1986

Parkin, F., *Marxism and Class Theory: A Bourgois Critique*. London: Tavistock. 1979

Raub, W. and T. Voss, *Bedingungen der Kooperation im Licht der Theorie Rationalen Handelns*. Utrecht: State University: unpublished paper. 1985

Raub, W. and T. Voss, Die Sozialstruktur der Kooperation rationaler Egoisten: Zur "utilitaristischen" Erklärung sozialer Ordnung, *Zeitschrift für Soziologie* 15, 5: 309–323. 1986

Robinson, J. and J. Eatwell, *An Introduction to Modern Economics*. London: McGraw-Hill. 1973

Robinson, V. and J. Kelley, Class as Conceived by Marx and Dahrendorf: Effects on Income Inequality and Politics in the United States and Great Britain, *American Sociological Review* 44: 38–57. 1979

Roemer, J., *A General Theory of Exploitation and Class*. Cambridge Mass.: Harvard University Press. 1982 a

Roemer, J., New Directions in the Marxian Theory of Exploitation and Class, *Politics and Society* 11, 3: 253–287. 1982 b

Roemer, J. (ed.), *Analytical Marxism*. Cambridge: Cambridge University Press. 1986

Taylor, M., *Anarchy and Cooperation*. London: Wiley. 1976

Terwey, M., Klassenlagen als Determinanten von Einkommensungleichheit, *Zeitschrift für Soziologie* 13, 2: 134–144. 1984

Ultee, W., Machtsverhoudingen en inkomensongelijkheid, *Sociale Wetenschappen* 26, 2: 101–138. 1983

Wallerstein, I., *The Capitalist World-Economy*. Cambridge: Cambridge University Press. 1979

Weber, M., *Wirtschaft und Gesellschaft*. Tübingen: J. C. B. Mohr. 1922

Weede, E., *Konfliktforschung*. Opladen: Westdeutscher Verlag. 1986

Wright, E., *Class Structure and Income Determination*. New York: Academic Press. 1979

Wright, E., *Classes*. London: Verso. 1985

Wright, E. and L. Perrone, Marxist Class Categories and Income Inequality, *American Sociological Review* 42: 32–55. 1977

"New" Social Inequalities and the Renewal of the Theory of Social Inequalities

Reinhard Kreckel

1. Introduction

Classical Marxist class theory and non-Marxist stratification theory share three common background assumptions which are becoming increasingly untenable in the light of "new" social inequalities: (1) they start from a *vertical* image of society; (2) their concept of society is restricted to the *nation-state*; (3) they concentrate on the *occupational structure* as the backbone of social inequality. Against the limitations of this "classical" view an alternative approach is advocated. It starts from the metaphor of *centre and periphery* and analyses social inequality in the context of a complex set of interwoven *fields of power*. The centre-periphery-model aims at integrating both vertical and non-vertical aspects of social inequality; it is based upon a global world-society perspective; and it includes types of inequality not primarily rooted in the occupational structure, such as gender and ethnic discrimination.

2. Critique of the Classical Concept of Social Inequality

The opening assumption of the present paper is that classical theories of social inequality have lost a good deal of their explanatory power, as well as of their political relevancy and plausibility in everyday discourse. By "classical" theories of social inequality I mean the entire range of Marxist and non-Marxist models of class structure and social stratification which have dominated academic and political discussions for a long time. My contention is that, today, the historical conditions which have given rise to the classical perspective have undergone substantial changes. Therefore, a change of theoretical orientation is indicated.

The very starting point of my argument, the notion of a "classical" model of social inequality, includes Marxist as well as non- and anti-Marxist viewpoints and ignores their fundamental disagreements. This may be somewhat disconcerting. But, with the coming of age of the time-honoured controversies between

Marxists and Weberians, functionalists and conflict theorists, empiricists and structuralists, reformists and revolutionaries etc., a common and largely taken-for-granted set of background assumptions shared by all of them becomes visible. I shall single out three of these shared background assumptions which, due to historical changes, are becoming increasingly untenable: supporters of the "classical" view conceptualize social inequality in advanced societies as *vertical* inequality; they analyse social inequality within the frame of *solitary* societies; and the social relations of *work or production* are taken as the basis of social inequality.

(1) The first taken-for-granted assumption I would like to comment upon concerns the conception of advanced society as *work society*. That is, according to the "classical" view, an individual's position in the class structure or stratification system of a society is considered as being determined by his or her position in (or relationship to) the world of work. "The backbone of the class structure [. . .] is the occupational structure" (Parkin 1971: 18). Thus, traditional research on social inequality has been mainly concerned with employed and self-employed income earners and persons living from capital returns. Persons not (or not any more) having an income status of their own, i. e. economically "inactive" persons (children, adolescents), were either subsumed under the status of those on whom they were economically dependent, or they were graded according to their past (retired or unemployed persons) or future (students, trainees) positions in "active" life. Housewives without independent work income were considered as "inactive," too. Inasmuch as inequality research took any notice of them at all, they were given their husbands' (the "breadwinners'") social status. Thus, in fact, the analysis of structured social inequality was only based upon the activities of a numerical minority of the population. All "private" activities not mediated by the market were excluded. That is, the "work society" was narrowed down to a *paid work society*.

Jürgen Habermas had recognized this as early as 1968. In his widely read paper "Science and Technology as Ideology" he put forward the thesis that class antagonism has become latent in advanced capitalist society and that traditional Marxist class analysis was thereby rendered obsolete. One of the reasons he gave was that the most highly deprived groups in society were not to be found any more among the wage earning population which disposed of the "strike weapon" as a basis of counter-power. The members of society most hardly hit by disfranchisement and pauperization were, therefore, to be found in social groups not directly involved in the process of production. They lacked conflict capacity, "because the system does not live off their labour" (Habermas 1972: 371). According to Habermas, the crucial question for social theory therefore is how, within a given society, the problem of distributing "wealth *and* labour both unequally and yet legitimately" is solved (Habermas 1972: 357). The unequal distribution of (paid) work and (unpaid) non-work is thus recognized as being of high theoretical significance. In Habermas' most important work "Theorie des kommunikativen Handelns" these ideas are advanced even further. He writes, with reference to late capitalist societies:

A line of conflict is emerging between the *centre* comprising those directly participating in the process of production whose interest is to defend capitalist growth as the basis of the welfare state compromise, and a mixed and checkered *periphery* at the opposite end. It embraces groups standing at a distance from the "core of productivistic efficiency" (*J. Hirsch*) which are more sensitized to the self-destructive consequences of the growth in complexity, or more affected by them (Habermas 1981, vol. ii: 477; my translation).

Habermas thus joins André Gorz in taking his "adieux from the proletariat" as subject of history and from class conflict as the prime mover of societal transformation (cf. Gorz 1980). It is replaced by the conflict between work and non-work.

Even if one is not prepared to accept this conclusion completely, one will have to agree that "to be working" today is almost synonymous with being in dependent and salaried employment. As official statistics reveal, around 90% of the labour force of the most advanced capitalist societies are working in dependent jobs. Whereas in earlier stages of capitalism considerable proportions of the "active" population never entered the labour market at all, wage labour is the predominant form of work in our type of society. It is true, however, that the average life-time spent at work has become shorter during the last decades; but at the same time, dependent employment has grown to be a more important factor in the life of more people. Their economic as well as their social and personal identity is decisively shaped by wage labour. It suffices to mention the crises of identity affecting unemployed and retired persons and, increasingly, housewives without a "real" occupation (cf. Beck 1986; Negt 1984).

Thus, on the one hand, more than ever before, the analysis of traditional social inequality is obliged to focus on the asymmetrical relationship between capital and labour, mediated by the labour market (Kreckel 1980; Offe 1984). But on the other hand, "new" forms of social inequality gain in significance: *first*, there is the growing field of inequalities of access to various forms of welfare benefits and of public goods and services. These are distributive inequalities of a predominantly politial character which, as Rainer Lepsius (1977) has argued, may be considered as being the basis of a new form of classes, the "welfare classes." A *second* "new" area of social inequality arises from the differentiation between occupational work and housework which to a certain extent coincides with a sexual division of labour. With the growing impact of the women's liberation movement the sociology of social inequality, too, has begun to recognize the importance of this problem. *Finally*, I recall Habermas' mixed and checkered group of shadow workers, blacklegs, subsistence producers, "new self-employed" on the one hand, the unemployed on the other, some of whom have begun to search for an alternative economic, social and personal identity outside the official world of work.

(2) Attempts at including these fields into inequality research are hampered by a second problematic presupposition of the "classical" approach: traditionally social inequality was understood and described as *vertical* inequality. That is, the metaphorical notion of a "stratified" society is taken for granted as linguistic, and thus conceptual, frame of reference for the analysis of social inequality. Against this, I want to posit that the conceptual equation of "social" and "vertical" inequality was only justified as long as there were good reasons to assume that the main conflicts concerning distributive inequality and its legitimacy are derived from the vertical structure of society. As soon as additional, non-vertical disparities gain importance, which is now the case, the metaphor of verticality itself turns into a hindrance to the further advancement of knowledge. This is even more strongly so if the restrictive model of "stratified" society is maintained, which both Marxist and non-Marxist sociologists are inclined to do, as Ossowski (1963) showed. Besides the "new" inequalities already mentioned above, there are further important inequalities which hardly fit the vertical model: regional disparities, including the disparities between town and countryside, the discrimination of stigmatized (racial, religious, sexual etc.) minorities and marginal groups, the peripheral situation of so-called "guest-workers" etc.

(3) The example of the "guest-workers" leads on to a third limiting presupposition of traditional stratification and class analysis: the empirical frame for the investigation of structured social inequality was usually the *solitary society*, in practice: the nation-state (cf. Giddens 1985). Contrary to this presupposition I wish to emphasize the notion of international dependency and inter-dependency in world society. *Today*, social inequality can only be adequately analysed within a global context. International labour migration is just one example for this: obviously, the presence of large numbers of foreign workers and their families in advanced capitalist societies is highly pertinent to the analysis of national structures of inequality. Yet, a satisfactory analysis of the significance of this international group within the national context is hard to achieve as long as the (implicitly ethnocentric) perspective of traditional inequality research is maintained (Heckmann 1981). On the other hand, as soon as one starts thinking in global terms, it becomes clear that the world-structure of inequality provides the labour markets of the rich capitalist societies with poor "external hinterlands". This is where the "guest-workers" come from and where, inversely, certain labour intensive processes of production are frequently transferred to, according to the logic of the so-called "new international division of labour" (Fröbel et al. 1977; 1986). The example of the "external hinterlands" clearly demonstrates that it is insufficient to treat the international context of national structures of inequality as a mere environmental factor; both are interdependent. The same holds true with respect to the position of "national" economies within the world-economic system and national states within the global power system: the economic and political strength or weakness of a national society relative to the overall structure cannot but have a strong impact upon the size of the "pie" of wages and the

quality of the jobs available for distribution among its citizens (and "guests"). Thus, without taking into account the international context, sociology lacks the theoretical basis to distinguish to what extent a national working class has acquired the characteristics of a "labour aristocracy", and to what extent it remains close to the ideal type of the "proletariat" which has nothing to lose but its chains. One is reminded of Lenin's (1967) theory of imperialism according to which colonial exploitation provided the material means allowing parts of the working class in the imperialist countries to lead a petty bourgeois life. In the contemporary post-colonial and post-Keynesian world this is certainly somewhat more complicated. Still, it is hard to deny that in advanced capitalist societies the amount of national wealth available for (unequal) distribution is not only to be seen as resulting from high industrial productivity, but also from international relationships of *unequal exchange*:[1] labour intensive products are imported at low costs from underdeveloped countries; in return, capital intensive goods are exported at high prices, the terms of trade being schewed. Seen within a global perspective, the living standard in First World societies is a privileged one which hardly anyone among the working population is inclined to put in jeopardy.[2]

Thus, conceiving of advanced western societies as of relatively autonomous entities amounts to analysing only the tip of an iceberg. Unsurprisingly, those staying on top would prefer to keep it that way. By preserving a self-indulgent and ethnocentric "view from above", the situation below the waterline remains unclear and is unlikely to be realistically appreciated. On the other hand, if one adopts the perspective of the "wretched of the earth" (Fanon 1961), the vast majority invisible from the tip of the iceberg, it becomes clear that the "historical subject" able to break their economic, political, military, technological and cultural dependency is unlikely to be found in the richer countries of the world, whether capitalist or socialist. One may well agree with Jürgen Habermas (1981; 1985) that in advanced capitalist societies "vertical" class conflicts have lost their power of shaping the life-world of social groups and that new lines of conflict are emerging on the fringes of the "core of productive efficiency". But in arguing that these conflicts are not derived any more from problems of distributive inequality, but from the "colonization of the life-world", Habermas' view is limited by the perspective he deliberately adopts, the perspective of the "rationalized" western world. Looking at it from a more global standpoint it would seem to me

---

[1] The finer points of the on-going debate about "unequal exchange" need not to be discussed here. For an easily accessible summary of the crucial arguments, cf. Harrington (1977: chaps. 2, 4, 5).

[2] One might argue that the Marxist conception of the development of capitalism clearly forbids any isolated treatment of national societies; therefore, Marxist class analysis ought not to be included in my criticism. But the practice of Marxist research on social classes is somewhat different: its models of class structure in modern capitalism refer to "monadic societies," just as those of the non-Marxist sociology of social stratification d. Cf. e. g.: IMSF (1972–1974); Projekt Klassenanalyse (1973–1974); Herkommer (1983); Poulantzas (1975); Wright (1985).

that, for a long time to come, we will still be faced with the very tangible after-effects of the colonialization of the world, not just the life-world. I think it likely that structural conflicts will be increasingly, not decreasingly, centred around problems of distributive inequality, albeit on a global rather than national level.

3. Historical Roots of the Vertical Image of Society

I now return to the metaphor of "vertical society." At least since Stanislaw Oslowski's book *Class Structure in the Social Consciousness* has become a taken-for-granted part of the curriculum of virtually every sociologist of social inequality, it is generally recognized that the language of vertical classification, apart from shaping images of society in everyday life, also has a strong impact on sociological theorizing and, beyond this, on political practice. In his resent study on "Vertical Classification", Barry Schwartz argued, using methods adapted from Claude Lévi-Strauss, that the vertical imagery is "more than an arbitrary linguistic convention": it is "the 'natural language' of social inequality" (Schwartz 1981: 150). Up to a certain point, I would agree with this interpretation. When one tries to translate theoretical arguments about structured social inequality into everyday language, it seems very difficult indeed to avoid using a vertical terminology. The polarity of "higher" and "lower" facilitates the thinking of, the communication about, and the orientation in social structure. However, although it may appear natural to talk about superiors and subordinates, about high status positions and low qualifications, top management and bottom income, the "upper ten" and the "down and out", it does not follow that the common conceptual denominator of these inequalities must also be bound to the vertical metaphor. Rather, the more an everyday construction of reality has become compulsory, and compulsive, the more important it is that sociological analysis tries to free itself from this linguistic spell.

One of the reasons explaining the strong social compulsion connected with vertical terminology certainly is that vertical social differentiations are explicitly *institutionalized* in many societies. It suffices to remind the reader of the Indian caste society or the European *Ständegesellschaft*. They are "vertically structured" indeed; but the prime reason for this is surely not that vertical classification is a compelling feature of human cognition. Rather, it is firmly institutionalized by means of mobility barriers, rules of homogamy, inheritance laws etc. That is, we need not return to naturalistic explanations of the fact that vertical classifications tend to be taken for granted in everyday life, as long as the possibilities for socio-historical explanation are not exhausted. To those socially embedded in them, vertical social constructions appear natural and inevitable, yet they can be understood as being as historical and man-made as any social institution, however "sacred" they may appear to be. The sociologist should not fall prey to this.

Let us now turn to the world of advanced capitalism, the world of bureaucracy and hierarchy we experience ourselves. In factories and schools, in hospitals, armies and administrative bodies, even in sports and the arts, the hierarchical distinction of ranks, grades, titles etc. implying an unequal distribution of rights and duties is crucial. *The hierarchical co-ordination of human action is a central organizing principle of our type of society. It is purposely erected and consciously upheld and defended.* The main precursor of the modern principle of hierarchical organization in the Western World may be found in the Roman Catholic Church, especially in the medieval monasteries, both influenced by antique traditions. The most influential step towards the modern bureaucratic form of domination and subordination probably was the setting up of post-feudal mercenary armies, instruments of power purposely constructed according to the logic of hierarchical control. Thus, it was no accident that the Jesuit Order, consciously founded as a tool of catholic counter-reformation, was organized in a quasi-military fashion. The further progress of purposive-rational organization towards the modern form of industrial production and bureaucratic administration need not be depicted here. It suffices to recall Max Weber's thesis of the steady growth of bureaucratic rationality, supposedly the most efficient way of "getting things done". But obviously, bureaucracy is not just about "getting things done", but about getting things done by persons who obey orders. In this way, bureaucracy always implies hierarchy.

These historical references are meant to give some support to my thesis that whenever social relations are organized in an explicitly hierarchical way, they may well be described by means of a vertical terminology. In this case, very common in our type of society, the vertical concepts are hermeneutic concepts taken from, and adjusted to, an empirical reality of institutionalized verticality. However, it would be completely unjustified to conclude from this that forms of inequality *not* commonly recognized as "vertical" in a given cultural and linguistic context are thereby to be excluded from the conceptual field of the sociology of social inequality (Kreckel 1987).

It is my impression that precisely this has happened in classical stratification and class analysis. The historical experience of the vertical structure of traditional *Ständegesellschaft* and of the bureaucratic hierarchies of our time has lead to a *conceptual over-generalization*. The empirically plausible metaphors of verticality and stratification were stylized into theoretical concepts and equated with social inequality in general. This is now beginning to take its toll. Classical (Marxist as well as non-Marxist) inequality research is not able to come to terms with the emerging "new" inequalities. It will have to overcome the conceptual limitations of its vertical background assumptions in order not to sink into irrelevancy.

What I describe as *"new" inequalities* are by no means new phenomena (cf. Berger 1986; Hradil 1987). They are new only insofar as their ascent to social and political saliency, and the awareness thereof, is comparatively recent: sexual inequalities, regional disparities, the discrimination of minorities and marginal groups, the unequal distribution of access to public goods and welfare benefits, the imbalance of social burdens, the peripheral position of foreign workers etc. on the one hand, and the global relationships of inequality and dependency on the other are such "new" inequalities. None of them fit easily into the metaphor of vertical society. Thus, it seems consequent that an earlier critique emphasizing the inability of classical inequality research to come to terms with "non-vertical" inequalities suggested the notion of "horizontal disparities" (Offe 1970) as a way out of the deadlock. This was a first step in the right direction; but the notion of "horizontal disparities" is a residual category only, added on to the vertical metaphor. It indicates where the problem is, but does not yet solve it.

My contention is that *all social inequalities, no matter whether they are "old" or "new", national or international, vertical or non-vertical, require a common conceptual and theoretical frame*, because *today* they have all become part and parcel of the same set of problems. In the world of today the demand for equality between people of all races, sexes, religions, nationalities etc. is no longer bound to the vertical dimension alone, and it has increasingly found recognition as a major motive of political legitimation as well as of political contestation. None other than Talcott Parsons, one of the main promotors of the functionalist theory of stratification, has recognized this development and, as a consequence, partly revised his earlier views. In his 1970 paper, "Equality and Inequality in Modern Society," the institutionalization of social inequality is no longer presented as an inevitable functional requirement for the maintenance of social order. Rather, it is seen as being accompanied by the institutionalization of the principle of equality. Parsons now speaks of the "dialectical" aspects of the problem of order, and he concludes that "all societies institutionalize some balance between equality and inequality" (Parsons 1977).

Whatever the theoretical merits of this solution may be, there is strong evidence that in the present age of decolonization, racial egalitarianism, women's liberation, welfare policies etc., the claim that goods and life-chances ought to be distributed equally and that individuals and peoples of all kinds ought to be treated as equals has become a basic norm of almost universal recognition. But there is also strong evidence that this norm is in continuous conflict with the real world of persistent inequalities. The battle about inequality and its legitimacy is becoming increasingly more general and inclusive. As a consequence, a more inclusive conceptual framework is required in order to allow a synoptic view of the various forms of inequality as well as of the efforts to overcome them and the devices to defend or conceal them. Without it, the empirical splitting-up of the social and political forces of resistance against the various forms of inequality and exploitation in the present world risks to be merely mirrored by the conceptual splitting-up of sociological analysis.

4. Centre and Periphery

As a first step towards a common conceptual framework covering the various inequalities occurring in the world today, I suggest an alternative metaphor, the metaphor of *centre and periphery*. It is better suited for theoretical generalization *and* differentiation than the old vertical model. The image of centre and periphery gives immediate access to the crucial insight that social inequality is always rooted in an *asymmetrically structured field of power*. The sociology of social inequality may thereby return to its origins as a political sociology of social inequality, whereas orthodox stratification research seems to be drifting further and further away from openly facing its political implications (cf. Kreckel 1980; 1982).

Certainly, the metaphor of centre and periphery is not a new invention. It is quite well established in a number of specialist fields in the social sciences. My aim, however, is to generalize its applicability: in human geography and urban sociology, for example, the distinction between core and peripheral zones or regions is quite common. Sociologists and economists of development and under-development, especially writers influenced by "dependency theory," distinguish between central, semi-peripheral and peripheral economies, nation or societies, between "metropolitan" and "peripheral" capitalism. The theory of labour market segmentation is built upon the assumption of a dualism between core workers, core firms, core sectors and their marginal counterparts, etc. These few examples may suffice to demonstrate a first advantage of using the centre-periphery-model: it refers to a field of power typically characterized by a *concentration of forces* near the centre and an increasing *dispersion of forces* towards the periphery (Galtung 1971). That is to say, those occupying the central positions in national and world societies do not only benefit from the obvious advantages of material superiority and cultural hegemony, they also hold the strategic "inner line" in all distributive conflicts, whereas efficient horizontal communication, cooperation and coordination between marginally located actors is more difficult to realize.

As soon as the conceptual "switch" from the vertical metaphor to the centre-periphery-model is made, it becomes transparent that the vertical image of society is geared towards a *very specific historical constellation* and hardly makes sense when applied to a different situation: thinking about social inequality in terms of vertical concepts implies that one expects to find only *one* major "line" or "dimension" of distributive conflict in society, the conflict based upon the tension between "top" and "bottom", or "higher" and "lower" ranks. Given the wide variety of empirical possibilities revealed by comparative historical research, the likelihood of empirical social structures coming close to the ideal type of consistent vertical structuration is not very high. Vertical integration is not the only possible form of structured social inequality, not even in advanced industrial or capitalist society. To the extent that the interplay between "old" and "new", national and international inequalities gains importance, the vertical model becomes increasingly deficient.

Indeed, most of the classical empirical studies of class structure and social stratification may be taken as witness of this problem. After all, the empirical multitude of dimensions and levels of inequality which hardly fit the one-dimensional vertical model is by no means a new phenomenon. The theoretical and methodological difficulties arising from this state of affairs must be faced by all sociologists sharing the "classical" conception of social inequality. Typically, they are circumvented through the introduction of a *purified model of "normal society"*: macro-sociological surveys concerned with social inequality tend to concentrate their attention upon native, male persons of working age, living within an administratively defined (national or regional) territory. Excluded are the young and the old, the housewives and the foreigners; also omitted are handicapped, sick or institutionalized persons, often even agricultural and family workers and farmers. Regional and international disparities are only of marginal interest. That is, the desirable degree of homogeneity of the empirical field of investigation is largely achieved through the exclusion of "difficult cases". What is left over after such a process of elimination is some kind of "normal" or "core" population more or less synonymous with the economically active citizens of a nation-state or of a part thereof. It follows that the theoretical generalizations of classical inequality research are based upon the, more or less tacit, assumption that various "marginal" groups of the resident population may be safely omitted from systematic consideration – although they usually add up to a numerical majority. Looked at it from this point of view, classical inequality research appears to be concerned mainly with "normal," not "deviant" inequalities.

In order to avoid being forced by one's own conceptual presuppositions to have to accept paradoxical consequences of this kind, I would like to introduce the notion of *peripheral situation* as a less exclusive conceptual basis of inequality research. Its epistemological status is that of a "guiding hypothesis" or "theoretical orientation" (Kreckel 1975: 37 ff.) whose aim it is, among others, to facilitate the theoretical integration of the endeavors of classical stratification and class analysis with those of hitherto excluded fields of research, such as the sociology of delinquent behavior, of youth and old age, of gender differentiation, of international migration, of development and underdevelopment etc., as well as of the sociology of politics and international relations:

Peripheral situations, i. e. structurally determined situations generating disadvantages in the possibilities of access to generally desirable material and/or symbolical goods and limiting the possible range of autonomous action, are locations within social or world structures occupied by individuals, groups or nations lacking conflict capacity to the extend that they are excluded from the dominant resources of power and unable to establish a basis of counter-power.

This formula does, of course, not wish to forestall the answer to the question of what the "dominant resources of power" are in a particular case, and of why there may be a deficit in counter-power. It allows for a functionalist solution, seeking the sources of power in the inevitability of value consensus and legitimate order, as well as for a Marxist solution according to which the development of counter-power in a situation of class domination can only be successful, if a fundamental conflict between productive forces and relations of production arises. That is, the centre-periphery-model is meant to be a formal, yet historically rooted theoretical orientation, a "proto-theory", not a substantive piece of theory of society in itself. However, in attempting to turn the analyst's attention into a specific direction, it is not entirely "innocent". In particular, it rather strongly emphasizes one line of thought hitherto largely neglected: the very geometry inherent in the centre-periphery-model suggests that peripheral locations are more disunited than central ones. Hence the assumption that the development and sustenance of a coherent "periphery consciousness" and of an efficient "periphery organization" will generally meet with difficulties, given the variety and structural dispersion and the multitude of peripheral situations.

5. Towards a Renewal of the Theory of Social Inequality

As was said before, the metaphor of centre and periphery is in regular use in a number of specialist fields of the social sciences. The variant of the centre-periphery-model I find particularly useful as a starting point for my own argument is the model connected with the work of authors such as Galtung, Frank, Amin, Wallerstein and Senghaas. Whatever the controversial points between these authors may be, their common frame of reference is the "dependency theory," i. e. the attempt to explain the underdevelopment of the Third World as a consequence of its dependence on the First World. It seems quite clear, however, that the aim of the present paper, namely, to extend the applicability of the centre-periphery-model to the entire field of social inequality, would suffer if this model could not be detached from the immediate connotations of the dependency debate. I therefore suggest that the only premise to be borrowed from dependency theory is the assumption that, today, *world society* has to be the most general level of analysis for all social inequalities. Apart from this presupposition, I preserve the common assumption of classical stratification research and class analysis that politico-territorial units, in particular the nation-state or administratively defined parts thereof (regions, countries, cities etc.), are of fundamental importance for the analysis of structured social inequalities. One of the reasons is that all social inequalities are backed up by relations of power (cf. Kreckel 1982). To the extent that the exercise of power is domesticated by

constitutional and legal institutions, which is typically the case in modern politically defined territories, these territories may well be taken as the "natural"
frame of inequality analysis – provided the fact is taken into account that on the
level of modern world society, inequalities are not upheld and legitimized by an
integrated legal and constitutional order holding the monopoly over the means of
violence. In world society, power is still largely exercised through the "rule of
might," not "the rule of right" (cf. Giddens 1985).

However, very often the sociological significance of this anarchic state of international affairs is not recognized. As a consequence, social inequality, especially
social stratification, is analyzed within a limited territorial framework only. Implicitly, the world is conceived of as a patchwork of national or sub-national units
which can be treated more or less independently, each "having" its own class
structure or system of stratification. Analyses of this kind may become very
misleading if the relations of interdependence between the various (local, regional, national, international, global) levels of territorial organization, as well as
those between units located on identical levels, are not considered. As soon as
the centre-periphery-model is adopted, this danger is more easily avoided. It
obliges to distinguish between "dominant centres", "intermediate centres",
"subcentres" etc., each being accompanied by more or less overlapping
"peripheries" and "semi-peripheries". That is, the question of mutual inter-
dependences, of partial identities and partial differentiations between various
levels and units of analysis imposes itself almost automatically.

Once the problem is set up in this way, it becomes quite clear, too, that the
empirical occurrence of an ideal-typical concentric (or "planetary") constellation
is highly unlikely – of a constellation, that is, where a number of "intermediate
centres," each dominating an equal and equidistant number of "subcentres", are
arranged in a symmetrical way around one "dominant centre". What is to be
expected instead are intricate patterns of competing, mutually interfering forces.
Yet, surprisingly, it is hard to deny that the image of society tacitly adopted by
the various forms of classical inequality research corresponds more or less with
the simple model of a concentric constellation. It presupposes that, as a rule,
unequally structured societies are characterized by one unified hierarchy of classes or strata only, reaching from "top" to "bottom" and allowing an unambiguous classification of all "typical" members of society.[3] On the basis of the centre-
periphery-model, a different guiding hypothesis seems more appropriate,
namely, to expect a variety of relationships of interdependence between the
various levels and units of local, regional, national, and global inequalities. Just
as in the case of interstellar systems, the "fields of force" surrounding competing

---

[3] The very fact that "status inconsistencies" are a specific field of interest in stratification
research underlines this point. The notion of status inconsistency only makes sense, if it is
based upon the tacit assumption that the standard situation is one of "consistent," one-
dimensional stratification. Cf. R. Kreckel (1986).

centres and subcentres may overlap and interfere with one another. If the global asymmetry between First and Third World is to be taken as the most general constellation constructed according to the principle of centre and periphery (with the Second World, rather awkwardly, interfering), we find further subcentres and sub-peripheries within each of the global centres and peripheries, and so forth. Whatever level is singled out for detailed analysis, it can only be adequately grasped, if its degree of autonomy, dependence and/or domination vis-à-vis the other levels and units is taken into consideration.

The traditional industrial proletariat of the capitalist centres may be used as an example to illustrate this. Seen within the context of their own national societies, the position of the industrial proletarians clearly is a peripheral one. But from a global perspective, in comparison with the poor masses of the world periphery, their position reveals itself as being rather "central". That is, there is an asymmetrical, albeit more or less indirect relationship of interdependence between peripheral positions in the First and in the Third World. This is not just an abstract argument: it points to the structural conditions which prevent the workers of the First (and Second) World from becoming reliable allies of the "Wretched of the Earth" (Fanon). From the perspective of the Third World, they are nothing but a "labour aristocracy" (Lenin).

Thus, to sum it up, the use of the metaphor of centre and periphery directs the attention towards the *interdependence of various levels and aspects of social inequality*. Empirical research alone can ascertain to what extent they actually are connected and interdependent in a particular case, and whether the interdependence is a mutual and symmetrical or a lop-sided and asymmetrical one.

The notorious absence of clear-cut lines of class polarization and class conflict in advanced capitalist societies, one of the facts most irritating to sociologists holding orthodox Marxist persuasions, may also be seen in a new light once the centre-periphery-perspective is adopted. The classical situation of class struggle where a dominant minority is confronted by a disadvantaged, but solidary majority reveals itself as a historically exceptional and rather unlikely constellation, not as the rule. Theoretically much more likely, and empirically more frequent, are situations where clear dividing lines are missing and unambiguous interests are exceptional. Different levels and dimensions of social inequality tend to overlap. Being disadvantaged and socially peripheral in one's capacity as a woman, for example, or as an unskilled worker, an inhabitant of a deprived area etc., and at the same time enjoying the advantages of life in the First World is not a firm basis for a revolutionary "class consciousness" or an unambiguous "periphery loyalty". A second reason pointing into the same direction follows directly from the logic of the centre-periphery-model, too: once this model is adopted, one is obliged to operate with a multitude of more or less overlapping polarities, but one is not forced to assume that this must lead to clear empirical polarizations. Rather, the field of force between a centre and its periphery should be ideal-typically imagined as a series of concentric circles. This means that one would normally expect to find various *intermediate or mediating positions*, such as "middle classes" or "semi-peripheries".

One of the most influential writers emphasizing the high improbability of a unified class consciousness emerging from the multitude of particularized and often ambivalent interests separating the various disadvantaged groups in society was, of course, Max Weber (1964). His view that the development of a revolutionary class consciousness was very unlikely, especially in advanced capitalist societies, was supported by two basic arguments. One argument referring to the empirical differentiation of class situations and class interests more or less converges with the considerations derived above from the centre-periphery-model. Weber's second argument may also be related to this model. He emphasizes the integrative and pacifying powers of shared *beliefs in the legitimacy* of an existing social order. Once a social status quo, including its structures of social inequality, is generally recognized as being legitimate, the organization of an efficient counter-power challenging the status quo becomes very difficult. The logic of "all in one boat" prevails. Edward Shils (1975), certainly no radical, has developed this line of thought further, making use of the centre-periphery metaphor. According to his view, every society has a *central value-system* represented by certain central institutions. Among other things, these institutions fulfill the function of legitimizing and stabilizing the existing power relations and distributive inequalities. According to Shils, it is one of the distinguishing features of advanced societies that their entire population, including peripheral groups and classes, is integrated into the central value system. Peripheral value-systems are relics from earlier stages of historical development, bound to vanish and/or to be integrated into the central value-system. Antonio Gramsci (1971), certainly a radical, wrote from a very different theoretical perspective. However, his central concept of *hegemony* amounts to much the same thing: class domination in capitalist society implies an institutionalized domination over the minds and wills of the dominated. Whether we call it "hegemony" or "value integration", their common function clearly is the ideological obliteration of structural cleavages. It follows that, apart from the "objective" ambivalences of interest stemming from the diversity of levels, units and dimensions of inequality, "subjective" distortions of perception may erect additional obstacles against the development of a powerful and unified periphery consciousness.[4]

One of the initial assumptions of the present paper was that the notion of world society is gaining theoretical weight; the modern world is increasingly dominated by one "central" or "hegemonic" set of general values. There can be little doubt that these values have much in common with the euro-centric view of the world: high on the priority list are values such as nationalism, bureaucracy, meritocracy, and technological efficiency, but there are also values like equality and liberty

---

[4] For a more fully developed discussion of the interplay between ideology and inequality, cf. Kreckel (1985).

which give rise to some cautious optimism. In other words, whereas Shils and Gramsci had national societies in mind, my contention is that the world society as a whole is moving towards a morally (or, if one prefers, towards an a-morally) integrated structure. That is, the centre-periphery relations in the modern world are not only objective relationships of military superiority, unequal exchange, technological advantage or cultural tutelage, but also a subjective bond based upon the recognition of a common destiny. This, indeed, is a precondition of the full sociological applicability of the centre-periphery metaphor. The relationship of centre and periphery is not simply an "objective" asymmetrical constellation opposing friends and enemies, but an *internal* relationship between opponents sharing a common "subjective" frame of reference. This is the case in modern world society. It is engaged in a global discourse. One of its topics is the question of the legitimacy of persistent inequality and injustice in the world. In this sense, the existence of genuinely "foreign" affairs among men, between "us" and "them", has become morally untenable. The demand for equality has reached the remotest corners of the globe. The last barbarian has been transformed into a fellow human being. This, at least, is both the theoretical and the normative premise of my argument.

In the world of today, an ever-increasing number of individuals are able to decide between various simultaneous memberships and loyalties, be it in the politico-territorial domain (commune, region, nation, political alliance etc.) or in other respects (linguistic, sexual, religious, ethnic identities etc.). Each of these memberships may become the basis of a common perception and dramatization of social disadvantages and, consequently, of solidarity and political action.[5] Of course, the success or failure of such action does not only depend upon the "subjective" factor, i. e. the common perception of deprivation and the readiness to fight against it. "Objective" structural conditions play a decisive role, too. The overall location of a "subjective" conflict within a given field of interaction of central and peripheral forces determines whether such a conflict touches upon problems too fundamental to be resolved locally, or whether it amounts to a mere "storm in a tea-cup". The so-called North-South conflict certainly is the most fundamental confrontation of our time. The objective conditions for a successful solidarization of the dispersed and scattered forces of the world periphery are not very favourable, given structural advantages of the central powers.

The practical consequences of the application of the centre-periphery model must be quite depressing to anyone interested in overcoming deeply rooted structures of inequality. By insisting upon the necessity of theoretical differentiation, the model directs the attention to the empirical multitude and ambivalence of interests in social life which, according to the logic of centre and periphery, favour the actions of the centre, and thus the status quo. Traditional Marxism, of

---

[5] Cf. our comparative study on regionalist protest movements in Scotland, Occitania and Catalonia: R. Kreckel et al. (1986).

course, puts its hope upon the built-in self-destructive dynamics in the capitalist centres themselves. But the powers of destruction and self-destruction available in the modern world certainly are no reason for hope of whatever kind. Those experiencing oppression and exploitation may have clear ideas who their oppressors and exploiters are – from the point of view of the centre-periphery model the problem of social inequality presents itself in a more complex way. Although extreme inequality of economic, political and military power are in clear evidence in world society, the emergence of equally clear-cut lines of conflict opposing "centres" and "peripheries" is quite unlikely, except in specific situations, such as wars.

Given this state of affairs, one may almost look back with regret to the times when the parsimonious metaphor of the vertically structured and monadic work-society still seemed to cover the essential problems. In comparison, the centre-periphery model is much more complex. Once the degree of complexity of the conceptual model is increased, more facets of social inequality become visible and relevant to the sociologist's theoretical eye. The perceived world, including its problems and the possibilities of their solution, becomes more complex. Thus, it is certainly no accident that people in everyday life prefer simple metaphors, such as the polarity of "above" and "below". This simplifies matters. Simplification facilitates communication, and it is instrumental in identifying the "broad issues" upon which politically successful action is usually based. But its prize is the loss of cognitive substance which, eventually, influences the outcome of practical action. The dilemma now is that sociology, as a communicative science, is neither allowed to adopt the conceptual simplifications of everyday language completely, nor to disregard them entirely, as the natural sciences do. Indeed, language is the only way to transfer sociological findings and insights into everyday life, whereas the results of the natural sciences find their way into industrial products or technical devices which the user need not "understand".

If we accept Barry Schwartz' (1981) survey of empirical evidence, vertical classification is a simplification almost universally applied. Even if we do not agree with him that this is to be explained with reference to universal characteristics of the human mind, it is certainly safe to predict that vertical thinking is so deeply rooted in the institutions and power relations of the present world that it is unlikely to vanish all of a sudden.[6] The sociologist is obliged to take this into account, especially as the centre-periphery-metaphor seems to go somewhat against the grain of everyday language and thought. It therefore is a metaphor located on a middle level of abstraction. On the one hand, it should be concrete enough to be translatable into everyday life; on the other hand, it is meant to be

---

[6] The interplay between (vertical) classification and class structure is also central to the important work of another, more critical follower of Durkheim and Lévi-Strauss, Pierre Bourdieu (1979; 1984). I share his scepticism against universal theories in sociology as well as his conception of society as a field of power.

sufficiently abstract to free sociology from some narrowing thinking habits and to provide it with a more comprehensive theoretical perspective. After all, there is always hope that conceptual innovation may have some enlightening impact upon everyday constructions and reconstructions of the world.

References

Amin, Samir, *La déconnexion. Pour sortir du système mondial.* Paris: Découverte. 1986

Beck, Ulrich, *Risikogesellschaft. Auf dem Weg in eine andere Moderne.* Frankfurt: Suhrkamp. 1986

Berger, Peter A., *Entstrukturierte Klassengesellschaft?* Opladen: Westdeutscher Verlag. 1986

Bourdieu, Pierre, *La distinction. Critique social du jugement.* Paris: Minuit. 1979

Bourdieu, Pierre, Espace sociale et genèse des "classes," *Actes de la recherche en sciences sociales* 52/53: 3–15. 1984

Fanon, Frantz, *Les damnés de la terre.* Paris: Maspéro. 1961

Fröbel, Folker, Jürgen Heinrichs, and Otto Kreye, *Die neue internationale Arbeitsteilung.* Reinbek: Rowohlt. 1977

Fröbel, Folker, Jürgen Heinrichs, and Otto Kreye, *Umbruch in der Weltwirtschaft.* Reinbek: Rowohlt. 1986

Galtung, Johan, A Structural Theory of Imperialism, *Journal of Peace Research* 8: 81–118. 1971

Giddens, Anthony, *A Contemporary Critique of Historical Materialism.* London: Macmillan. 1981

Giddens, Anthony, *The Nation-State and Violence.* Oxford: Polity Press. 1985

Gorz, André, *Adieux au prolétariat. Au delà du socialisme.* Paris: Galilée. 1980

Gramsci, Antonio, *Selections from the Prison Notebooks.* London: Lawrence and Wishart. 1971

Habermas, Jürgen, Science and Technology as Ideology, in: *Sociology of Science.* B. Barnes (ed.), 353–375. Harmondsworth: Penguin. 1972

Habermas, Jürgen, *Theorie des kommunikativen Handelns.* (2 vols.). Frankfurt: Suhrkamp. 1981

Habermas, Jürgen, Die Krise des Wohlfahrtsstaates und die Erschöpfung utopischer Energien, in: *Die Neue Unübersichtlichkeit.* Frankfurt: Suhrkamp, pp. 141–162. 1985

Harrington, Michael, *The Vast Majority. A Journey to the World's Poor.* New York: Simon and Schuster. 1977

Heckmann, Friedrich, *Die Bundesrepublik: Ein Einwanderungsland?* Stuttgart: Klett – Cotta. 1981

Herkommer, Sebastian, Sozialstaat und Klassengesellschaft, in: R. Kreckel, 75–92. 1983

Hradil, Stefan, *Sozialstrukturanalyse in einer fortgeschrittenen Gesellschaft.* Opladen: Leske. 1987

Institut für Marxistische Studien und Forschung (IMSF), *Klassen-und Sozialstruktur der BRD.* (3 vols.). Frankfurt: E. V. A. 1972–4

Kreckel, Reinhard, *Soziologisches Denken.* Opladen: Leske. 1975

Kreckel, Reinhard, Unequal Opportunity Structure and Labour Market Segmentation, *Sociology* 14: 525–550. 1980

Kreckel, Reinhard, Class, Status and Power? Begriffliche Grundlagen für eine politische Soziologie der sozialen Ungleichheit, *Kölner Zeitschrift für Soziologie und Sozialpsychologie* 34: 617–648. 1982

Kreckel, Reinhard (ed.), *Soziale Ungleichheiten.* Göttingen: Schwartz. 1983

Kreckel, Reinhard, Ideology, Culture and Theoretical Sociology, in: *Power and Knowledge.* R. Fardon (ed.). Edinburgh: Scottish Academic Press, 151–169. 1985

Kreckel, Reinhard, Status Inconsistency and Status Deficiency in Meritocratic Society, in: *Status Inconsistency in Modern Society.* R. W. Hodge and H. Strasser (eds.). Duisburg: Sozialwissenschaftliche Kooperative, 188–203. 1986

Kreckel, Reinhard, Friedrich von Krosigk, Georg Ritzer, Gerhard Sonnert and Roland Schütz, *Regionalistische Bewegungen in Westeuropa.* Opladen: Leske. 1986

Kreckel, Reinhard, Neue Ungleichheiten und alte Deutungsmuster. Über die Kritikresistenz des vertikalen Gesellschaftsmodells in der Soziologie, in: *Soziologie der sozialen Ungleichheit.* B. Giesen and H. Haferkamp (eds.), Opladen: Westdeutscher Verlag, 93–114. 1987

Lenin, Vladimir I., Imperialism, the Highest Stage of Capitalism, in: *Selected Works.* Vol. I. Moscow: Progress. 1967

Lepsius, M. Rainer, Soziale Ungleichheit und Klassenstrukturen in der Bundesrepublik Deutschland, in: *Klassen in der europäischen Sozialgeschichte.* K. U. Wehler (ed.). Göttingen: Vandenhoek, 166–209. 1977

Menzel, Ulrich and Dieter Senghaas, *Europas Entwicklung und die Dritte Welt.* Frankfurt: Suhrkamp. 1986

Negt, Oskar, *Lebendige Arbeit, enteignete Zeit.* Frankfurt – New York: Campus. 1984

Offe, Claus, Politische Herrschaft und Klassenstrukturen, in: *Politikwissenschaft.* G. Kress and D. Senghaas (eds.). Frankfurt: Fischer, 137–162. 1970

Offe, Claus, *Arbeitsgesellschaft.* Frankfurt – New York: Campus. 1984

Ossowski, Stanislaw, *Class Structure in the Social Consciousness.* London: Routledge. 1963

Parkin, Frank, *Class Inequality and Political Order.* London: MacGibbon & Kee. 1971

Parsons, Talcott, Equality and Inequality in Modern Society, or Social Stratification Revisited, in: *Social Systems and the Evolution of Action Theory.* London: Collier Macmillan, 321–380. 1977

Poulantzas, Nicos, *Classes in Contemporary Capitalism.* London: N. L. B. 1975

Projekt Klassenanalyse, *Materialien zur Klassenstruktur der BRD.* (2 vols.). Berlin: Verlag für das Studium der Arbeiterbewegung. 1973–4

Schwartz, Barry, *Vertical Classification.* Chicago – London: University of Chicago Press. 1981

Senghaas, Dieter, *Weltwirtschaftsordnung und Entwicklungspolitik.* Frankfurt: Suhrkamp. 1977

Shils, Edward A., *Centre and Periphery. Essays in Macrosociology.* Chicago – London: University of Chicago Press. 1975

Wallerstein, Immanuel, *The Capitalist World-Economy*. Cambridge: University Press. 1979

Weber, Max, *Wirtschaft und Gesellschaft*. Cologne-Berlin: Kiepenheuer and Witsch 1964

Westergaard, John and Henrietta Resler, *Class in a Capitalist Society*. London: Heinemann. 1975

Wright, Erik Olin, *Classes*. London: N. L. B. 1985

Classes, Collectivities and Corporate Actors

Barry Hindess

1. Introduction

Nobody would deny the importance in the modern world of actors other than human individuals – capitalist enterprises, churches, political parties, state agencies, trades unions, etc. I call these social actors and I argue that all too often modern social thought has failed to take seriously their status as actors. I also argue that class theory is generally mistaken in treating classes as being in some sense collective actors.

One of the most striking features of the modern period has been the development of corporations. There were corporate actors in the world well before the emergence of modern capitalism, but their numbers and significance have grown considerably from around the middle of the nineteenth century (Coleman 1982, chapter one). Many, but by no means all, of these new corporate actors have been capitalist enterprises – or rather, their owners. The joint-stock company is a legal person separate from its stock-holders or employees – and it is perhaps the most common example of a capitalist employer who is not a human individual. The rise of the joint-stock company has sometimes been presented as a process of the separation of ownership (in the person of the stock-holders) from control (in the person of the managers), most famously in the work of Berle and Means (1968). That presentation is misleading (Hadden 1977; Thompson 1986; Tomlinson 1982). Stock-holders own stock, which may give them certain voting rights over the appointment of directors and other matters affecting company policy, but they do not own the company's assets. In some cases, of course, a small minority of the stock-holders do occupy a dominant position. They may then be regarded as effective owners of the company's assets. As for managers, they do indeed exercise control, but they do so in their capacities as agents of the corporation that employs them.

The growing importance of corporate actors throughout the modern period gives rise to two obvious sets of problems for class analysis. First, most forms of class analysis treat classes as collectivities consisting only of human individuals. How, if at all, do corporate capitalists fit into such classes? In the Weberian tradition the answer is clear. First, class situation is defined in terms of a concept of life chances, which effectively restricts class membership to human actors. Secondly, of course, corporate actors are not real actors, since their actions are reducible in principle to those of human individuals. For Marxism, the question is more problematic. The dominant tendency has been to treat classes as consisting of human individuals, with share-holders and senior management as the capitalists involved in the case of joint-stock companies. But if classes are identified in terms of the occupation of positions in relations of production, then there are strong grounds for arguing that the capitalist class contains corporate actors as well as human individuals (Cutler et al. 1977; Scott 1979). The effect of that argument is to undermine analysis of classes in terms of some subjective referent like consciousness or a shared perception of class interests (see the discussion of the corporate ruling class in Clegg et al. 1986).

The second set of problems for class analysis follows from the ways in which the very existence of social actors depends on their relationships with others. Corporations exist as actors by means of executives and other employees, some of whose decisions and actions are legally recognised as those of the corporation itself. Agents who perform such services are an important part of what has been called the new middle class, and debates over their class positions continue to generate a considerable literature. The significance of such questions has been much over-rated. What makes class membership seem important is the prior assumption that it is the structural foundation of interests, consciousness and some potential for collective action. I have argued elsewhere that that assumption is false (Hindess 1986). It remains significant only as a consequence of the part it plays in certain forms of political and social scientific discourse, but it has no extra-discursive foundation in an "objective" structure of society. What matters then, is the question not so much of what the class position of some section of the new petty bourgeoisie is (in some supposedly objective sense), but rather what role conceptions of its class position play in particular social or political analyses.

This paper raises questions about the concept of actor with serious implications for class theory. What is required for something to be an actor at all, and in what sense can actors other than human individuals be said to make decisions, have objectives and so on? An actor is a locus of decision and action, and in that sense human individuals are far from being the only important actors in the world. It is sometimes suggested that all action is reducible to the actions of human individuals. Coleman (1982), on the other hand, has argued against such reductionist claims. In his view there are two kinds of persons in the world, natural and corporate, and a clear conflict of interests between them. I argue first that the question of reductionism is a non-issue and secondly that Coleman's counterposition of the interests of natural and corporate persons is misleading.

There are important actors other than human individuals, but I argue that classes are not amongst them. This raises a further problem for class theory. The imagery of struggle is a central feature of the most important forms of class theory, and it suggests that classes are, in some sense, collective actors. What remains of that imagery if classes as such are not actors? Here again, I argue that the imagery is misleading, and that it remains important only as a consequence of the part it plays in a number of political and social scientific discourses.

In a loose sense the claim that there are important actors in the modern world other than human individuals would not be disputed. But that loose acceptance can obscure very different views as to how precisely the notion of actor is to be understood. I argue against three views in particular. The first is any treatment of social actors as if they were themselves reducible to human individuals. Weber's explicit methodological individualism is the most obvious example, but there are many others. The second is the view that there are essentially two kinds of actor, human and corporate, with a clear conflict of interests between them. Finally, there is the extension of the concept of actor to collectivities (like classes) that have no identifiable means of formulating decisions, still less of acting on them. Before proceeding to these arguments it is necessary to consider the concept of actor.

2. A Minimal Concept of the Actor

An actor is a locus of decision and action, where the action is in some sense a consequence of the actor's decisions. Actors do things as a result of their decisions. We call those things actions, and the actors' decisions play a part in their explanation. Actors may also do things that do not result from their decisions, and their explanation has a different form. This is a minimal concept of the actor. Most accounts of action build considerably more into their concept of actor than is provided here. Actors are said to be characterized by their possession of a more or less stable portfolio of beliefs and desires, they are frequently supposed to be rational and to posses a utilitarian structure of preferences, and more often than not they are assumed to be human beings. Giddens, for example, suggests that a serious problem with discussion of action in terms of intentions, reasons, and so on, is that it tends to abstract from features that are central to human activity:

"Action" is not a combination of "acts": "acts" are constructed only by a discursive moment of attention to the duree of lived-through experience. Nor can action be discussed in separation from the body, its mediations with the surrounding world and the coherence of the acting self (Giddens 1984: 3).

Here the minimal concept of actor is taken up and modified by the addition of several further assumptions. In particular, Giddens takes it for granted that actors are human individuals.

The minimal concept of actor incorporates none of the additional assumptions noted in the last paragraph. It says that a capacity to make decisions is an integral part of anything that might be called an actor, and it says that those decisions may have consequences. Other entities, like the moon or the river Thames, do things but they would not normally be described as making decisions and acting on them. This concept is formal and abstract. It tells us nothing about the conditions that make it possible for something to be an actor, except that it must be capable of reaching decisions and of acting on some of them. By the same token it says nothing about the other characteristics that actors may possess. To say that actors' decisions play a part in their actions is not to deny that other conditions might also be involved in the determination of action – for example, that unconscious processes might play a part in human activities.

Human individuals are certainly actors in the sense outlined here, but there are many others. Capitalist enterprises, state agencies, political parties and universities are all actors in the minimal sense that they have means of reaching decisions and of acting on some of them. I call these social actors, for reasons to be explained below. For the moment, a word of warning is in order. I have presented action as a function of the actor's decisions or intentions. Now, these intentions are themselves generally supposed to result from the actor's beliefs, desires and other states of mind[1]. The relevant states of mind here are propositional attitudes: that is, they

are identified most naturally by reference to propositions that, in some sense, constitute their objects. Thus the belief that Paris is in France is a state of mind, conscious or unconscious, identified by reference to the proposition appearing in the that-clause, which tells us what in fact is believed: Paris is in France. A parallel story goes for desire (Macdonald and Pettit 1981: 59).

What is at stake here is the idea that actors' decisions follow from beliefs and desires by virtue of their meanings, that is, by virtue of what Winch calls "logical" or "internal" relations. We therefore have a notion of reaching decisions or forming intentions as a process of following the "logical" order of meaningful relations between propositions – and it is in this sense that actors are normally supposed to be rational.

The problems with this general approach to human action need not concern us here (Hindess 1988). For present purposes we can suppose that discussion of action in terms of propositional attitudes is reasonable enough in the case of human actors. Many of their decisions involve propositions that are formulated and may (or may not) be spoken or written out. But the treatment of action as a function of such "states of mind" pre-empts consideration both of what is to count as an actor and of the processes by which decisions are made. In particular, it is to insist on a considerable refinement of the minimal concept of actor proposed here. It seems odd to attribute propositional attitudes and other conscious or unconscious states of mind to capitalist enterprises and other social actors. At best it is an allegorical convenience, and it is certainly no substitute for analysis of the processes by which capitalist enterprises do make decisions. The identifica-

---

[1] This assumption is taken for granted in most forms of rational choice analysis and in analytical philosophy's treatment of intentional analysis. For the latter, see Macdonald and Pettit 1981, and Doyal and Harris 1986.

tion of decisions with states of mind can be avoided if we say simply that some decisions involve propositions that are formulated, some involve states of mind such as beliefs and desires, and some involve both.

3. Reductionism

Now consider Weber's assertion that the actions of corporate actors

must be treated as solely the resultants and modes of organization of the particular acts of individual persons, since these alone can be treated as agents in a course of subjectively understandable action (Weber 1978: 13).

There are usually two aspects to the claim that social actors are reducible to human individuals, as if the latter were the only real actors. One concerns the attribution of a unitary subjectivity to humans, but not to other actors. The decisions of corporate actors are frequently dispersed within the organization (see Thompson 1986, esp. chapter 7). We are concerned, say, with the pattern of investment displayed by a large corporation, and we try to understand that behaviour as resulting from a mixture of standing policies and recent decisions. Intentional analysis in this case is hardly going to lead us to interpret those policies as resulting from the consistent application of some more or less stable collection of beliefs and desires. Decisions are made and policies laid down at a variety of points within the organization, and we are more likely to interpret them in terms of the application of particular accounting practices, institutionalized techniques of information gathering and assessment, decision-making procedures, and their relationships to decisions and policies emanating from elsewhere.

The decisions of corporate actors, in other words, cannot be seen as the products of a unitary consciousness. Yes – but we should be wary of the presumption that human individuals are in contrast characterized by a unitary consciousness: that their decisions are not also the dispersed products of diverse and sometimes conflicting objectives, forms of calculation and means of action. The advantage of the abstract concept of actor proposed above is that it forces us to consider the processes by which decisions are produced, by humans as much as by social actors, rather than simply refer them to a supposed unitary subjectivity.

The other aspect of the reductionist claim concerns the fact that human individuals are the only actors whose actions do not always depend on the actions of others. The actions of capitalist enterprises or trades unions always depend on those of other actors – executives, managerial and other employees, elected officials, legal representatives, and sometimes other organizations. They therefore depend not just on those other actors but also on the specific character of the social relationships in which they are implicated with them. I call such actors "social actors": each and every one of their actions involves social relations with other actors.

There is, of course, an important sense in which human individuals are constituted as actors in and through their relationships with others – and in that sense human actors are necessarily also social actors. But they are nevertheless not social actors in the sense that I am using the term here. Some of the actions of human individuals depend on the actions of others in the way I have just noted, but not all of their actions do so. This is a significant difference between human individuals and other actors.

Does it follow that social actors can be discounted as actors on the grounds that their actions are reducible to the actions of human individuals? In fact, such reductionist claims rarely amount to more than a gesture and they do nothing to reduce the importance of analysing social actors and their conditions of action. Even if we were to accept in principle that social actors were always reducible to human individuals, we should still be concerned with investigating the decisions and actions of social actors and with their consequences.

There are indeed actors other than human individuals, some of whom have important consequences in the modern world. Considered in terms of their social impact, many of the most significant decisions are taken by actors other than human individuals – by governments, large corporations, unions, churches. If human individuals were the only real actors, then these social actors would have to be regarded as the instruments of some other set of interests – as in Marxist accounts of the state, managerialist and many Marxist accounts of the corporation. A different example is Friedman's (1980) account of the corporation as a mere intermediary for its stock-holders, which enables him to treat legal restrictions on corporate behaviour as infringements of individual liberty, and of government agencies as the irresponsible instruments of politicians and public servants. To say that human individuals are not the only real actors is to argue, on the contrary, that social actors should be regarded as actors with concerns and objectives of their own. It may be possible to subject these actors to controls and restrictions of various kinds. Some could even be dispensed with without any great loss to the rest of us. But it is impossible to conceive of a complex modern society in which such actors did not play a major role. Any approach to the analysis of modern societies that admits only human individuals as effective actors must be regarded as seriously incomplete.

4. Two Kinds of Persons?

In *Power and the Structure of Society* and more recently in *The Asymmetric Society* Coleman provides a striking contrast to reductionist treatments of social actors. Coleman argues that there are two kinds of persons: natural and corporate. In his view the importance of corporate actors in the modern world indicates the emergence of a fundamentally new kind of society characterized precisely by what he calls asymmetric relationships. Relationships between natural and corporate persons are asymmetric partly because they are different in kind, but also because of differences in power, resources and interests. This new kind of society is asymmetric because relations between natural persons have been displaced first by relations between corporate and natural persons and secondly by relations between natural persons in their capacities as occupants of roles within corporate persons.

Coleman begins his story in the European middle ages. Social organization was then a matter of the organization of persons and "those forms of organization which were fruitfully conceptualized as corporate actors were structures themselves composed of persons" (1982: 14). The crucial feature of this characterization is the emphasis on persons, rather than roles. Where the modern corporate actor is made up of roles or positions, corporate actors of the past were made up of persons. In that respect Coleman regards the family as "the prototype of the corporate actor around which the old social structure was built" (1982: 123). Of course, the family can also be seen as a structure of roles. The important point here is that the occupants of those roles are, in general, not readily interchangeable: a family is identified by the persons who are its leading members.

In the old kind of society then, social structure was a structure of persons who occupied fixed positions. The key change was the emergence of a concept of corporate actor of a qualitatively new kind, a legal person distinct from its members. The formation of such corporate actors and their growing importance had the consequence that natural persons were freed from the fixity of the old social structure. In effect:

the structural stability of society was provided by new, fixed functional units, the corporations [. . .]. It was the positions, as components of the new elements of society which provided the continuity and stability of structure (Coleman 1982: 15).

Roles and positions in corporations are the functional equivalent of persons in fixed positions! Natural persons can be freed from their fixed positions only because a new kind of fixity has emerged to take their place.

However, what matters for present purposes is that Coleman presents the modern corporation as a double-edged invention. On the one hand, it makes possible the growth of individual freedom and social mobility, both of which depend on the possibility of seeing a person simply as the occupant of a role or position. Authority has ceased to be absolute: it is no longer authority over persons as such but is limited to positions or roles. These are all positive developments, but they have their price. On the other hand, then, Coleman finds several disturbing features of the new society. We have been freed

from a sometimes oppressive structure of the sort that existed in the Middle Ages. Yet the resulting situation is one in which most natural persons are employed by those impersonal corporate actors, and thus find themselves working for ends that are not their own (Coleman 1982: 37).

The freedom of natural persons has been bought at the price of their subordination to the ends of (unnatural) persons.

Furthermore, the growing importance of asymmetric relationships produces changes in patterns of responsibility and dependency. The decline in (natural) person to person relations leads to a decline in personal responsibility amongst humans and to their increasing dependence on the state and other corporate actors. New personality types appear as the reduced importance of person to person relations leads to a reduction in personal concern for others. Where norms were once maintained through networks of personal relations, these are now breaking down and we find new modes of imposition and development of norms through the advertising and other activities of corporations. Finally, the rise of schooling (in the hands of corporate actors) involves new patterns of interaction between adults and children and a general reduction in the extent and intensity of adult involvement in child socialization.

Coleman finds many of these developments disturbing, and he clearly regards the asymmetric society as raising matters of grave concern for natural persons. The problem we face is how to get "that balance of rights and that balance of responsibilities among the different kinds of actors which will prove in the end most satisfactory to natural persons" (Coleman 1982: 42). We have to evaluate our modern asymmetric societies, and we should do so in terms of the interests of natural persons. Of course, Coleman recognizes that there are differences between natural persons. Nevertheless, we should "exclude the benefits to corporate actors per se as criteria for evaluation" (Coleman 1982: 43). Corporate actors may be necessary but their interests should be subordinated to those of natural persons. A difficulty here is that the most obvious candidate for the role of protector of the weak, namely, the state, is itself a corporate actor. We have to find ways of protecting the interests of natural persons that do not increase the power of the state.

What are we to make of these arguments? Coleman insists on the importance of social actors in the modern world and he maintains, correctly in my view, that social theory has paid them insufficient attention. Nevertheless, there are problems with his account of the two kinds of persons. I have already noted a disturbing element of functionalism in Coleman's treatment of structures of persons and structures of roles as if they played equivalent parts in the maintenance of structural stability. There is a related problem with the explanatory ambitions of Coleman's discussion of the growing significance of corporate actors and the correlative decline of (natural) person to person relations. In effect, he presents us with an updated version of the old story of *Gemeinschaft* and *Gesellschaft*, in which an excessive weight of explanatory significance is loaded on to a single historical polarity.

More important for present purposes is his account of the interests of corporate and natural persons and of what should be done to protect the latter. Notice first that the idea of evaluating social systems in terms of the interests of natural persons assumes a unity of interest amongst natural persons as such, distinct from corporate actors. Why should we accept that assumption? Coleman recognizes that natural persons may have different interests. This means that what is at stake in his reference to the interests of natural persons is not necessarily a matter of what individual natural persons recognize as their interests at some particular point in time. It is a matter, in other words, of interests that are "objective" – in the sense that they pertain to persons simply by virtue of their status as natural persons.

Here Coleman provides us with yet another attempt to derive actors' interests from their social location. In that respect it suffers from many of the problems of Marxist and other accounts of objective interests. Marxists will talk of distinct and opposed class interests while recognizing that there are differences within the working class and within the bourgeoisie. In much the same way, Coleman recognizes differences between natural persons, and between corporate persons, but nevertheless talks of the interests of natural persons as providing a criterion for the evaluation of social systems.

Once we question the presumption that natural persons share a unity of interests simply by virtue of their status as natural persons, then Coleman's criterion of evaluation must collapse. Of course there are social conflicts around opposed conceptions of interests, but it is a mistake to suppose that these must reflect "objective" or "structural" differences in the social locations of the actors involved in those conflicts (Hindess 1986). By the same token their statuses as different kinds of persons are no reason to suppose an objective conflict of interests between them. In contemporary Britain many natural persons would see their interests as being with the defence of some corporate actors (trades unions, hospitals, schools and universities) against others. Other natural persons continue vote to in a government which sees things rather differently.

There is, finally, a curious air of unreality in the suggestion that we (natural persons) should consider changes in the balance of rights and responsibilities "among the different kinds of actors" (Coleman 1982: 42) without taking the interests of corporate actors into account. The problem here is not that Coleman denies the reality of corporate actors or that he effectively reduces them to human individuals. Quite the contrary, he insists that they have concerns and objectives that are not reducible to those of human individuals. It is precisely because of their importance and irreducibility that Coleman invites us to do something about them while we can. The problem rather lies in the implicit assumption of an effective political community consisting entirely of natural persons.

Coleman, of course, is by no means alone in making that assumption. It also appears in a rather different form in much of contemporary democratic theory and again, for example, in those discussions of corporatism which present it as undermining our democratic institutions. What is involved here is the view that the interests of citizens, individually or in groups, are the only interests legitimately involved in the determination of the policies and personnel of government. We then have the assumption of a political community consisting exclusively of natural persons (citizens) in which the political activity of corporate actors is presumptively illegitimate. (There are left-wing and right-wing versions of this fantasy.)

On the one hand, it is recognized that corporate actors are an important part of our society – who could possibly deny it. On the other, they are not recognized as part of our political community. The problem is, of course, that corporate actors are part of our political community, whether we (natural persons) like it or not. Capitalist enterprises, trades unions and other corporate actors all have an interest in, say, the economic policies of governments. If those interests are excluded from formal channels of political influence, they will make themselves felt in other ways. It is impossible to imagine a parliamentary democracy in which both government and the electorate are not subject to the machinations of social actors[2]. What those social actors are may change, but there is no prospect of a complex modern society without them. It follows that we (as citizens or as natural persons) cannot expect to make collective decisions without social actors also being involved. In particular then, there is no sense in which we could seriously consider changes in the balance of rights and responsibilities between different kinds of persons, without corporate persons also being involved. *The Asymmetric Society* is published by one of them.

5. Classes

My final argument in this paper concerns those extensions of the concept of actor to cover entities that are actors only in the most allegorical of senses – classes, societies, men as a collectivity subordinating women as another collectivity and so on. These are all spurious actors, and they are frequently invoked in political and social scientific discourses. In particular, the analysis of politics in terms of relations between competing classes usually involves one or both of two elements, both of which I dispute. One is a notion of classes as collective actors. The other is a conception of class interests as objectively given to individuals by virtue of their social location, and therefore as providing a basis for action in common.

Consider first the idea of classes as collective actors. The problem here is that even the minimal concept of actor outlined in the first part of this paper requires

---

[2] I have discussed this issue in another context in Hindess 1983, chapter 2.

that the actor possess means of taking decisions and of acting on them. Capitalist enterprises, state agencies, political parties and trades unions are all examples of actors in at least this minimal sense – that is, they all possess means of taking decisions and of acting on at least some of them. There are other collectivities, such as classes and societies, that have no identifiable means of taking decisions, let alone of acting on them. There are, of course, actors who claim to take decisions and to act on behalf of classes and other collectivities – but the very diversity of such claims is reason to be wary about accepting any one of them.

The point of restricting the concept of actor to things that take decisions and act on some of them is simply that actors' decisions are an important part of the explanation of their actions. To apply the concept of actor to classes or other collectivities that have no means of taking decisions and acting on them, and then to explain some state of affairs (say, the emergence of the welfare state or its current crisis)[3] as resulting from their actions is to indulge in a kind of fantasy. Such fantastic explanations may well be thought to serve a polemical function, but they can only obscure our understanding of the state of affairs in question, and political decisions as to what can or should be done about them.

The other element in the idea of classes as social forces is the view that there are structurally determined class interests. These interests are supposed to be given in the structure of social relations, with the result that the parties, unions and other agencies of political life can then be seen as their more or less adequate representations. There are many well-known problems with this conception of interests, and I have discussed them at length elsewhere (Hindess 1986, 1987). For the moment notice that such a concept of interests may be used to perform several theoretical roles, of which two are particularly worth noting here.

One is that it appears to provide an explanatory link between action and social structure. Interests provide us with reasons for action and they are derived from features of social structure. On this view, people have interests by virtue of the conditions in which they find themselves, as members of a class, gender or community, and different elements of those conditions may then be seen as giving rise to different, and sometimes conflicting, sets of interests. Functionalist sociology treats norms and values as if they provided an explanatory link of a similar kind.

Unfortunately for class analysis the situation is rather more complicated. Most of those to whom objective interests are attributed by class analysis rarely acknowledge those interests as their own[4]. The idea that structurally determined class interests provide an explanatory link between social structure and action is a principle honoured more in the breach than in the observance. Far from provid-

---

[3] This is the standard Marxist account, but there are more sophisticated versions. For example, Clegg et al. 1986, and many of the essays in Goldthorpe 1984.

[4] Przeworski (1986) is unusual among contemporary Marxists in arguing that class analysis has often been mistaken in the interests it has ascribed to the European working classes.

ing an effective explanatory link the idea of structurally determined class interests generates a host of explanatory problems. Why, for example, do the British working class not acknowledge their objective interest in socialism?

The idea of objective interests that are real but not recognized leads to the posing of an entirely imaginary problem: why do the working class, and others, not pursue their real interests?[5] An imaginary condition in which real interests are pursued is posed as a measure of the present in which they are not pursued, and the problem is to explain away its non-existence. Conceptions of objectively determined class interests may well have consequences in other ways, for example, in the actions of parties or sects who claim to represent those interests, but in general they do not provide the explanatory link between action and social structure that they appear to promise.

The other significant theoretical role of the idea that there are structurally determined interests is that it seems to allow us to bring a variety of relationships and struggles into a larger pattern. For example, the 1984–85 miners' strike, the dispute in 1986–87 between the NGA, SOGAT and the Murdoch newspapers, and diverse other particular conflicts between groups of employees on the one hand and their employers and other agencies (e. g. the police) may be regarded as instances of a wider struggle between one class and another. The cases cited here do indeed have features in common but that does not mean that there is such a wider struggle into which they can all be subsumed.

What is involved in this manoeuvre is the idea that a variety of different relationships can be lumped together as so many instances of the one more general relationship on the basis of characteristics ascribed to the participants – in this case, the class interests that are supposed to be represented on one side or the other. Something similar is involved above in Coleman's treatment of the interests of natural and corporate persons. This manoeuvre makes sense only on the assumption that each class (or each kind of person) can be treated as a unified group simply because they happen to share those ascribed characteristics.

Since the classes in question are not actors they cannot, as classes, enter into relations with each other. In effect, then, the use of class interests as a device for bringing together a variety of distinct relationships and struggles requires that we treat the participants in each one of those relationships (for example, those miners who supported the 1984–85 strike) as surrogates, that is, as standing in for the classes as such. This returns us to the fantasy of classes as collective actors.

Nevertheless, if classes are not collective actors, the idea that they are remains significant both in the academic social sciences and in the political discourses of sections of the left. There are groups in most contemporary societies who analyse politics and act at least in part in class terms, and in some cases these groups have

---

[5] The Gramscian notion of rule by consent is usually invoked at this point. Miliband (1969) is still the most thorough discussion of the British case. An interesting recent variant is *Marxism Today*'s discussions of Thatcherism – see the essays in Hall and Jacques 1982.

been extremely influential. Doesn't that show that there is more to the class analysis of politics than I have suggested? Perhaps, but it would be a mistake to confuse questions of the political significance of a mode of political analysis with its validity. (Consider the example of Shi-ite Islam.)

The point rather is that where conceptions of class interests are significant elements of political life then that fact may require explanation. Support for movements and organizations operating in terms of class interests, or some other way of conducting and analysing politics is one of the outcomes of competition between movements for support. It is never a mere reflection of social structure. It is impossible to account for the relative strength or weakness of class-based politics in, say, Britain and Sweden without reference to the outcomes of past struggles over the policies and internal structure of particular organizations and conflicts within and between competing movements and organizations.

Conceptions of class interests may well be significant elements of political life, even though class interests as such (as distinct from conceptions of them) have no explanatory role. This point is frequently acknowledged in the literature of class analysis. Everyone now writes of the need to avoid reductionism, and many authors insist that interests are not sociological givens. To take just one example, Clegg, Boreham and Dow argue that

without organization there can be no "class interests." The notion of a class having a collective interest can only ever gain credence inasmuch as organizations are formed whose mandate entails the representation of "class interests" (1986: 259–260).

The implication here is that parties, unions and other organizations cannot be seen as mere instruments of some set of class interests given in advance of their articulation. However, they also write of the capitalist and working classes as if they were engaged in struggle for "greater control over the capitalist system as a whole," and suggest that reference to classes and their real interests may perform "an important heuristic function" (Clegg et al. 1986: 260).

The heuristic function is, as I noted above, that talk of classes and their interests enables political analysis to bring together a wide range of discrete conditions and struggles into a unified pattern. In the final chapter of *Class, Politics and the Economy* Clegg, Boreham and Dow, for example, take up the argument that the development of social policy in the advanced capitalist economies can be understood in terms of a struggle between classes[6]. Classes have different interests in the institutional character of social policy and they can be expected to pursue distinct policy objectives. How social and economic policy develop in a particular society will therefore depend on the organizational and other resources at the disposal of the classes and on the success of the tactics they employ.

I have discussed this argument elsewhere (Hindess 1987). Let me conclude this

---

[6] There are many different versions of this argument. In addition to Clegg et al. 1986 and Goldthorpe 1984, see Esping-Anderson 1986; Korpi 1983; and Stephens 1979.

paper by noting what the heuristic function of the invocation of classes as if they were actors amounts to in this case. It enables us to discuss the development of social and economic policy in terms of class relations without getting caught up in the details of policy discussion and of the factions, parties and other organizations involved, and of the confused and conflicting objectives that they pursue. It would be difficult not to conclude that Britains's high level of unemployment and its deteriorating social services have come about largely because of the relative weakness of the working class and the strength of its opponents. The problem with that conclusion is not so much that it is wrong as that it is uninformative. If popular and organizational support for a politics conceived in terms of the interests of the working class is weak, we should not assume that there is a real working class collective actor just waiting to be revived. But without that assumption, reference to the weakness of the working class is merely allegorical. It suggests that something should be done, but offers precious little guidance as to what should be done to change the complex of parties, unions, employers associations at work in British society, the ideologies and forms of political calculation in terms of which they conduct their activities and the patterns of support they emjoy. The heuristic invocation of classes as if they were actors carries a heavy theoretical and political cost.

References

Berle, A. A. and G. C. Means, *The Modern Corporation and Private Property*. New York: Harcourt, Brace & World. 1968

Clegg S., P. Boreham and G. Dow, *Class, Politics and the Economy*. London: Routledge & Kegan Paul. 1986

Coleman, J. S., *Power and the Structure of Society*. Pittsburgh: University of Pennsylvania Press. 1973

Coleman, J. S., *The Asymmetric Society*. Syracuse: Syracuse University Press. 1982

Cutler, A. J., B. Hindess, P. Q. Hirst and A. Hussain, *Marx's "Capital" and Capitalism Today*. (vol. 1). London: Routledge & Kegan Paul. 1977

Doyal, L. and R. Harris, *Empiricism, Explanation and Rationality*. London: Routledge & Kegan Paul. 1986

Esping-Anderson, G., *Politics against Markets*. Princeton: Princeton University Press. 1985

Friedman, M. and R. Friedman, *Free to Choose*. Harmondsworth: Penguin. 1980

Giddens, A., *The Constitution of Society*. Oxford: Polity Press. 1984

Goldthorpe, J. (ed.), *Order and Conflict in Contemporary Capitalism*. Oxford: Clarendon Press. 1984

Hadden, T., *Company Law and Capitalism*. London: Weidenfeld and Nicolson. 1977

Hall, S. and M. Jacques (ed.), *The Politics of Thatcherism*. London: Lawrence and Wishart. 1982

Hindess, B., *Parliamentary Democracy and Socialist Politics*. London: Routledge & Kegan Paul. 1983

Hindess, B., Interests in Political Analysis, in: J. Law (ed.), *Power, Action and Belief.*
London: Routledge & Kegan Paul. 1986

Hindess, B., *Politics and Class Analysis.* Oxford: Blackwell. 1987

Hindess, B., *Choice, Rationality and Social Theory.* London: Allen & Unwin. 1988

Korpi, W., *The Democratic Class Struggle.* London: Routledge & Kegan Paul. 1983

Macdonald, G. and P. Pettit, *Semantics and Social Science.* London: Routledge &
Kegan Paul. 1981

Miliband, R., *The State in Capitalist Society.* London: Weidenfeld & Nicolson. 1969

Przeworski, A., *Capitalism and Social Democracy.* Cambridge: Cambridge University Press. 1985

Scott, J., *Corporations, Classes and Capitalism.* London: Hutchinson. 1979

Stephens, J., *The Transition from Capitalism to Socialism.* London: Macmillan. 1979

Thompson, G., *Economic Calculation and Policy Formation.* London: Routledge &
Kegan Paul. 1986

Tomlinson, J., *The Unequal Struggle.* London: Methuen. 1982

Weber, M., *Economy and Society.* Berkeley: University of California Press. 1978

II. Management in Class and Organization Structures

Ownership and Management Strategy

Glenn Morgan

1. Introduction

A number of articles have recently argued for the need to decompose the "black box" of the firm (the phrase used by Tomlinson 1986). In these perspectives, the firm is analysed as the site of the complex construction of "organizational interests"; although structured by capitalist relations, these interests cannot simply be read off from capital itself. They are produced and reproduced within the organization through the interplay between various managerial groups. (For various attempts to conceptualize these processes see Armstrong 1984; Tomlinson 1986.)

Whilst these approaches have provided a fruitful starting point for debate regarding the conditions under which "organizational interests" are constructed and corporate strategies formulated, they are in general weakened by a failure to adequately theorize the impact of the environment on these internal processes. In particular, they have not emphasized sufficiently the way in which ownership and share market conditions penetrate into the organization. This is not simply a question of the perception of the actors *within* the organization; it also relates to the way in which actors *outside* the organization, in particular owners (but also government, professional associations and financial intermediaries of various sorts) provide resource and support for certain managerial groups as opposed to others in the construction of a particular discourse concerning the "real interests" of the organization.

The paper considers these issues at both a theoretical and empirical level. In the first section of the paper, the categories of ownership and management are subjected to a critical analysis initially through an examination of Berle and Means' (1932) thesis on the separation of ownership and control. It is argued that Berle and Means create a false dualism incapable of accounting for the dynamic interpenetration of ownership and management. This argument provides the basis for a more extended discussion of the ways in which management is influenced and constrained by ownership relations in modern Britain. The second section provides empirical support for these arguments through examining in detail corporate strategy in the Imperial Group in the period from the mid-1970s to the company's takeover by Hanson Trust in 1986. The central importance for managers of retaining the support of shareholders in order to pursue major strategic change is demonstrated. Furthermore, the general point is developed that the interests of major shareholders may not coincide with the interests and expectations of the dominant managerial group within the company. This in turn can be related to the more general debate in Britain regarding the relationship between the "City and Industry". The concluding section reviews the previous arguments and argues that the study of management must be linked at the top level to the study of ownership relations and the way in which these work in particular social contexts.

2. The Debate on Ownership and Control

The idea that management is crucially affected by the ownership context in which it is located is in many ways a simple and obvious one. Nevertheless, until recently it has been significantly absent from much of the literature. The reason for this can be traced back to the continuing influence of Berle and Means' contribution on *The Modern Corporation and Private Property* (1932). This book was premised on the emergence of a clear distinction between ownership and control in the modern corporation. In Berle and Means' own work, this distinction becomes elevated to a dualism in which ownership and management are two radically separated phenomena that no longer interact. How does this come about?

Berle and Means' main empirical point was to examine the diffusion of share ownership in the USA in the early decades of the 20th century. They argued that fewer American firms were owned by one ruling group of shareholders than previously had been the case. They distinguished between two situations of shareholder control; majority control where over 50% of shares were owned by one individual or group and minority control where between 20–49% of shares were owned by an individual or group. In a situation of majority control, the major shareholder would in any conflict be able to override all other shareholders simply by virtue of owning the most shares. In a situation of minority control, Berle and Means argued, the large shareholder would still be likely to get its own way for two reasons. Firstly, many small shareholders would be unlikely to vote. Secondly, the many that did would be influenced to follow the large shareholder. If there were no shareholdings above 20%, Berle and Means argued that there would be a situation of management control. The existing management of the company would be able to use their influence over situations of dispersed shareholding to ensure that they effectively ran the organization without any challenge from the legal owners. Berle and Means argued that it was this latter situation which was to become significant in the USA. As a result, they argued, a dispersed and relatively powerless group of shareholders faced unified and powerful management. Berle and Means' characterization of management assumed that, with shareholders less significant, managers would act in a more socially responsive way. They would not be driven simply by the need for profit maximization but would rather consider the interests of society as a whole. Thus they created a dualism where previously ownership and control had been unified in the person of the owner-manager. Now according to Berle and Means, capitalist organizations were no longer controlled by their legal owners; indeed legal ownership was irrelevant to understanding the organization. Since managers controlled organizations with no interference from owners, the key to understanding was the characteristics of the managers. Thus the issue of ownership began to drop out of sight in the analysis of management and organizations.

There have been extensive criticisms of Berle and Means' arguments which I shall not repeat here (see e. g. De Vroey 1975; Nichols 1969; Zeitlin 1974 and for an overall analysis Scott 1985). Instead, I will confine myself to two aspects of their thesis – their concepts of ownership and management, which because of the radical separation made between the two have in my view contributed to the neglect of the interrelationship between the two. With regard to ownership, first of all, Berle and Means operated with a highly restricted definition. Their understanding of ownership was that by virtue of holding a large number of shares, a shareholder would be able to control or influence key decisions in a company on an almost day-to-day basis. Thus the way in which the shareholder "controlled" was through directing the management. Management would have no choice but to listen to somebody who owned 50% or more of shares; where a shareholder owned between 20–50%, management would also be likely to follow the instructions of the shareholder according to Berle and Means. Why however, pick on 20%? There is no theoretical justification for this number; it remains an intuitive guess on the authors' part. Other authors have argued that holdings as small as 10% or even 5% can still be sufficient for shareholder control. The reason why it is possible to reduce the number is that the notion of control begins to change. Berle and Means' notion of shareholders directing management is a very limited case. In large scale organizations, it is more likely that shareholders will influence managers than they will control them directly.

The author who has done most to develop these ideas in the British context is Scott (see especially Scott 1985, 1986). Scott argues that rather than looking at individual shareholdings in isolation, it is necessary to consider the extent to which groups of large shareholders constitute what he terms "constellations of interests". Whilst even the largest of shareholders in major companies may not own more than 1% of the entire share stock, if sufficient of them act in concert at certain key moments, they can exert a critical influence over managers. Scott also opens up the notion that critical moments are not just at the point at which shareholders interests are formally consulted, e. g. an Annual General Meeting. Rather, critical points are part of the ongoing nature of capitalist share owning. This necessitates a consideration of the institutional framework of share ownership and a rejection of Berle and Means' static conception of ownership, in favour of a more dynamic approach.

In contemporary Britain and the USA, ownership is mediated through the turbulent and tumultuous environment of the stock exchanges. A number of key features are relevant here:

(1) In the UK and the USA, shareholding is highly concentrated in the hands of pension funds, insurance companies, investment trusts, merchant banks and the clearing banks. The savings of individuals are brought together by a small group of key institutions who through these savings manage funds in a wide variety of different investments. Share ownership is one form of such investment, and because these organizations deal in such large sums of money and stock, their policies of buying or selling shares in particular companies is reflected in the rise and fall of the share price on the market.

(2) The market for investments is highly complex and diversified offering the potential for different absolute and relative income and capital growth rates over short-, medium-and long-term planning horizons. Thus investing institutions are continually evaluating their "exposure" in the different fields of investment and adjusting them in the light of their own needs (as defined both by current expenditure requirements, e. g. on pensions or insurance claims, and by their own competitive position relative to others in the same sector of the market). Investing organizations may sell and re-buy shares in a particular company over a short period of time in order to provide liquidity for another investment which is higher yielding by some company defined target.

(3) The fund managers' horizons tend in the main to be dictated by short-time cycles ranging between three months and a year. If investments are not yielding expected rates of return within this period, they may be sold. Selling, however, brings its own pressures. Too much selling at one go may, as has been pointed out, cause a share's price to drop so far that it becomes counter-productive to try and sell it off.

These institutional factors mean that ownership is not a stable phenomenon with a clearly defined purpose. At the minimum, ownership in the legal sense will be continually changing. Furthermore, the reason why it changes is not simply a matter of fund managers' perceptions of the adequacy of one particular investment, but rather their assessment of market trends as a whole. Thus there is a potential for wide fluctuations in the share price of any particular company. Berle and Means fail to consider this at all, yet it is possible to argue that it is through the continuous change in share prices that shareholders have their greatest influence over managers, not through any direct pressure either on the board of directors or in the AGM of a company.

The reason why this is so relates to two further key features of the environment. The first relates to debt provision, the second to takeovers. In relation to the former, the lower the share price, the more difficult it will be for the organization to raise loans at the best interest rates which are available. Since few major companies are nowadays able to raise sufficient capital internally to finance expansion either based on organic growth or on an acquisitions policy, they need to generate capital through access to the money markets. There are various ways in which money can be raised: two are most important – loans and rights issues. In relation to the former there is now a worldwide market in the provision of various forms of loans; this means that firms are not simply faced with one type of loan at one fixed interest rate. They can find loans offered at different interest rates, in different currencies, to be repaid over different periods. As well as the skill of their own internal finance departments, a company's ability to get the best deal is dependent upon the lender's assessment of its creditworthiness and future earnings capacity. Here the share price and associated figures such as a high share price then affects the company's ability to borrow and may lead to unwanted conditions being placed on loans. (See Stearns 1986; Mintz and Schwartz 1985; 1986 for more detailed discussions of this in the American case.)

In relation to takeovers, it is generally the case that the lower the share price, the more vulnerable a company is to hostile takeover. This is particularly the case where a low share price reflects either general share price falls or poor management, but where the underlying values of assets, particularly in physical terms but also to an extent in goodwill terms, remains high. Companies where significant gaps arise between the value of real assets and the overall company value as expressed in share price have over the last decade in the UK and the USA become sitting ducks for takeover. Once again, then, management's future is intimately tied up with rise and falls in the share price. Consequently, Berle and Means' concept of ownership is totally inadequate to understanding the current situation in the UK. By identifying the influence of shareholding solely with long-term ownership, they failed to predict the extent to which management would be dependent on short-term fluctuations in share prices brought about by the buying and selling practices of a small number of institutional shareholders.

Taking the other side of Berle and Means' equation – that of management –, Berle and Means assumed that, separated from the pernicious influence of owners, managers would become the benevolent servants of the social interest. They elevated the category of management to an unproblematic unified entity. Whilst numerous criticisms can be made of this, I wish to concentrate on the issue of the possible schism within management between the circuit of financial capital and the circuit of industrial capital. I will not seek here to elaborate on the theoretical basis of this distinction which has been developed elsewhere (Morgan and Hooper 1987; Thompson 1977). Instead, I will seek to describe its meaning and relevance to the argument in hand. The circuit of financial capital refers to those processes whereby profit is produced through the manipulation of capital *per se*; thus interest payments on loans, profits generated from speculation in currencies, commodities, shares and any other form of security, both come under the heading of the circuit of financial capital. Industrial capital refers to those processes whereby profit is produced through the valorization process, i. e. where capital is used to purchase labour power which in turn generates surplus value.

It has in the past been common to identify these two circuits with two distinct institutional spheres, i. e. banking with financial capital and manufacturing with industrial capital. This, in my view, is an oversimplification, paralleling the dualism of Berle and Means' argument. On the contrary, there is a significant amount of evidence which supports the view that both circuits exist within particular organizational settings (see e. g. Armstrong 1984; Morgan and Hooper 1987; Scott and Griff 1985; Thompson 1985). If both these circuits exist within organizations, i. e. companies are simultaneously seeking to generate profits from the circuit of financial capital and the circuit of manufacturing capital, what does this mean for the unitary view of management? At this point, it is necessary to employ a comparative perspective. Within large-scale organizations in the UK and the USA, there is reason to believe that there is a basic tension within management between those concerned with the creation of profit through financial manipulation and those concerned with the creation of profit through industrial production. In countries like Japan and West Germany, on the other hand, this does not seem to be the case (Armstrong 1984). The reason seems to lie in the much greater significance of stock market and money market dealings in the UK and the USA than in West Germany and Japan, where investors take a more long-term approach to their money. Thus in the UK, in order to satisfy the short-term requirements of fund managers and in this way to keep share prices up with all the advantages this gives to management, managers are constrained to play the game of financial manipulation. This in turn reduces the opportunities for the company to make long-term investments in manufacturing and other processes, where gains are uncertain. The result is the emergence of conflict within management that reflects these external pressures. In conclusion, then, it can be seen that Berle and Means' characterization of owners and managers – the former dispersed and powerless, the latter unified and powerful –, locked in a zero-sum battle which management inevitably wins, is a gross oversimplification. Instead, both groups consists of a variety of interests and intersect with each other in complex ways. What holds this together is its location within a system of capitalist market relations, structured in a historically specific manner in the UK and the USA. If we are to properly understand the actions of top management, their formulation of corporate strategy and the constraints under which they work, we need to comprehend their position within this framework. Similarly, if our focus is on ownership, we cannot disentangle it from issues of markets and management. There is a continuous interpenetration of these elements which defies the simplistic dualism of Berle and Means. In the case study which follows I will attempt to illustrate these issues.

3. Imperial Group: Strategy, Ownership and Corporate Survival

Imperial Group was the name of the holding company which had grown out of the old Imperial Tobacco Company. First founded through an amalgamation of smaller U. K. tobacco companies in response to US competition in the early 1900s, Imperial still maintains a dominant position in the U. K. cigarette market with its Players, Silk Cut and Embassy trade marks. However, with the growth of awareness of the link between smoking and ill health, it became clear to Imperial management that it needed to diversify into new areas. Thus in the 1960s and early 1970s Imperial made a number of important purchases, including Golden Wonder Crisps, Ross Foods and Courage breweries.

It is important to note that Imperial's cigarette business always generated high profits, even after the link between smoking and cancer was established. Although it faced increasing competition during the 1960s and 1970s from companies such as Rothmans and Grand Metropolitan as well as the entry of some of the American cigarette giants (particularly American Brands via its production of Benson and Hedges), Imperial's sustained period of dominance in the UK from the early 1900s to the 1950s gave it a hold on the market which, although reduced, still remained predominant. Imperial ensured it retained this position through aggressive advertizing and continued rationalization of production processes. As a result, although the market for cigarettes in the UK failed to grow as quickly, Imperial's tobacco division continued to generate high levels of profit. This made the company one of the blue chip stocks of the London Stock Exchange. Through to the 1970s it was on everybody's list of good investments.

Imperial's cash pile in the mid-1970s was further expanded by the gradual sale of its stake in BAT (formerly British American Tobacco). The sale of this stake and associated joint holdings with BAT which dated back to the early part of the century, brought in almost £ 450 m to Imperial in the period 1975–79. (See Morgan and Hooper 1987 for further details.) This huge cash mountain which was continually being augmented by profits from Imperial's tobacco division (the other divisions – brewing, leisure and foods – never made much profit in comparison) was invested by Imperial in government gilts. At a time when there was high inflation, the real yield on gilts remained good in comparison to most other investments. So large was the cash mountain which Imperial had accrued that the Times (23. 9. 79) estimated that of Imperial's 91p. share value, 35p. per share derived from its gilt portfolio.

At this stage it is possible to discern emerging tensions between and within the categories of owners and managers. Most clear of all was the desire of leading managers in Imperial to put their cash to productive use. Imperial's Chairman, Sir John Pile argued in his 1979 statement to shareholders that the company needed to make another major investment in a productive outlet:

Whether in the form of dividends from BAT or interest from government securities, the investment income from these sources has been useful to us. The drawback of this situation however is that sizable assets generating this investment income were not and are not under our direct control and left where they are, they would not be available to us to secure the future prosperity of what is essentially a trading company. From 1975 onwards we have therefore indicated our intention of acquiring with these funds new trading assets which would add further to our growth prospects [. . .]. It is this same compelling need to move our funds from indirect to direct management to invest them in growth assets of our own choosing preferably overseas and to derive the benefits of full earnings and not just the dividend income from them which led us to dispose of our 50% holding in Mardon (Imperial Group: Reports and Accounts 1979).

The extent to which this view differed both from that of other managers in Imperial and from the shareholders of the company is a key question. Pile expresses what has been termed an approach stemming from the industrial circuit of capital. He wished to invest in new productive enterprise. When the name of that enterprise was announced as the Howard Johnson motel group (known in the press as HoJo and referred to by that term in the following pages), what had until then been an academic debate came out into the open.

Although there was not in the end either a shareholder or management revolt, the financial press was full of the internal differences that the takeover of HoJo was creating in Imperial. In the boardroom it seems that the argument against HoJo was led by Geoffrey Kent; for his pains Kent became Chairman of Imperial in the early 1980s when it became clear that HoJo was in a mess and Pile's immediate successor had been unable to staunch the outflow of funds. His appointment was referred to as a "boardroom coup" and represented a belated and eventually inconsequential victory for those who had opposed HoJo's purchase. Outside the boardroom amongst large shareholders there was also concern about the acquisition. A number of institutions expressed doubts, and Imperial management was forced to make strenuous efforts to keep them on its side.

The fact that in the end only a small number of individual shareholders voted against the deal going through may have related less to the immediate pros and cons of the purchase and rather more to a feeling amongst institutional investors that self-interest necessitated they support Imperial for the time being. A major withdrawal of support would have undoubtedly sent Imperial's share price falling with consequent effects on the portfolios of the institutions, since it would have been seen as a vote of no confidence in Imperial's management as a whole and not simply a tactical withdrawal of support in a particular area. Thus at this stage, no matter what their misgivings, the institutions had little choice but to stay behind the Imperial Board. It is important to note that this was the high point of influence of a certain management group within Imperial both over other managers and over shareholders in general. In distinction to a growth strategy based on financial success (such as the Group had been achieving in the period 1975–79 with its purchase of gilts and other investments), it was now committed against a background of considerable dissent to a strategy based on the acquisition and management of another company. In other words, it was committed to expanding the circuit of industrial capital and the associated valorization process. Any failure with the HoJo purchase would be likely to reduce the power and influence of this group.

The HoJo deal soon proved to be as risky as most commentators had expected. Within a couple of years, these difficulties which were necessitating Imperial spending huge amounts of capital on HoJo in order to improve its performance, had led to the boardroom coup which installed Kent as Chairman. Kent in turn put his own nominee, Michael Hostage, into the hot seat at HoJo in a further bid to stem the losses. There were many adverse factors which were affecting the HoJo deal, amongst them unfavourable currency movements, the US recession of the early 1980s, changes in US motel tastes and styles, and a more highly competitive environment in the hotel/motel industry. All of these were compounded by the failure of Imperial management to implement a successful turnaround strategy. Instead, losses continued to mount and Kent, originally an opponent of the deal, found himself saddled with its failure. Although Imperial continued to make optimistic noises, by 1985 it was clear that HoJo was "still making a pitiful return on capital and a disposal even for $ 300 m would greatly enhance earnings per share in the current year" (Financial Times 15. 2. 85). HoJo was a black hole into which Imperial poured funds for a period of about 5 years. The effect on its stock market standing was clear. Its failure to make its huge cash mountain work was a big negative mark against it: Its reputation as a blue-chip investment faded and instead the financial press began to talk about it as a possible takeover target. So long as Imperial kept HoJo, however, possible buyers would stay away, such was the reputation of HoJo as a "poison pill". Eventually, however, Imperial did find a buyer in the US for HoJo; the Marriott corporation bought HoJo from Imperial for $ 162 m (£ 113 m). The Guardian commented: "The sale involves a substantial write-down of all the HoJo assets bought in 1980 for £ 280 m, leaving Imperial shareholder funds £ 127 million the poorer". (25. 9. 85)

By this time Imperial was in a considerably different position to the one it had occupied in the late 1970s. It now had a demoralized management at the top. More importantly, it now had a changed relationship with its shareholders which placed constraints on the actions management might want to now take. Firstly, the HoJo failure had kept the company's share price down, although the company's real asset value remained high. As a result, the gap between stock exchange value and real asset value that opened up was an open invitation to a takeover bidder. Secondly, the failure of Imperial management severely dented the confidence of the institutional shareholders in Imperial's future plans. It was unlikely that they would again fall in so easily behind the Board's plans as they had done in 1979 in spite of their own misgivings. Together these things added up to Imperial being highly vulnerable to a bid once they had got rid of HoJo.

In order to protect itself against possible predators and to try to reassure its shareholders, Imperial moved quickly following its sale of HoJo. It made an agreed bid for United Biscuits (known as UB hereafter), led by Sir Hector Laing. It very quickly became common in the financial press to refer to the bid as a "reverse takeover." A number of reasons for this description emerged. Firstly, it was made clear that UB managers would be soon taking on the most significant positions in the merged company. Secondly, the industrial logic of the merger seemed to clearly favour UB. The aim, the companies proclaimed, was to create an international foods group – an aim which left little room for many of Imperial's other interests. Thirdly, the central idea of the merger seemed to be that Imperial's tobacco division would generate cash which UB desperately needed in order to invest in the production capacity necessary for it to be successful in the so-called "cookie wars' that it was involved in in the USA, in order to gain a significant foothold in the massive North American biscuit market. Finally, UB shareholders would be receiving a premium on their own shares because of the Imperial bid whilst Imperial shareholders would be facing earnings dilution.

Imperial shareholders, although pressed by their board to accept the logic of the merger, were not going to be as easily won over as in 1979. The financial press interpreted the merger as basically a defensive ploy on the part of Imperial management. As such it could be expected that the institutional shareholders would hold their hand and wait to see if any other possibilities emerged. From the start, the press published rumours that Hanson Trust might be interested in Imperial, and when it came to light that stakes in Imperial were being bought by speculators such as the Barclay Brothers (Times 25. 11. 85) and more ominously an unnamed "American arbitrageur" (Daily Mail 29. 11. 85), it seemed likely that a serious takeover bid might be in the offing.

In December, Hanson Trust did indeed launch a bid for Imperial, which the Board immediately rejected, preferring to persevere with its agreed merger. The nature of Hanson Trust is important to the discussion which follows. From small beginnings in the early 1960s, Hanson Trust had grown through a series of major acquisitions in the 1970s, its most well-known and successful being those of Ever Ready Batteries and the London Brick Company. The strategy was usually the same. Companies with failing managements but with a continuing basic market potential were targeted. Operating costs were severely trimmed back; extraneous businesses reorganized and sold off at advantageous prices; decision making devolved to the operating unit level where clear and specific targets were set; capital expenditure tightly controlled and limited. Hanson's growth had been continuous throughout the 1970s and early 1980s. Institutional shareholders had become heavily involved in it through rights and loans issues. The Sunday Times commented on the announcement of Hanson's bid for Imperial: "Imperial is a classic Hanson target; asset rich with mature markets and a management that has failed to convince the City it knows where it is going" (15. 12. 85).

In the summer of 1985, however, Hanson itself had started to run into some difficulties of its own. It had not yet recovered from its first major rebuff in the UK takeover field when it failed to acquire Powell Duffryn following a spirited campaign by the Board, which persuaded the City institutions to back Powell Duffryn's existing management. Further, in 1985, Hanson had made yet another rights issue, this time of £ 500 m. The City institutions, already "awash with Hanson paper", as certain financial commentators reported, were not keen and the issue was only saved from embarrassing the underwriters through the Kuwaiti Investment Office purchasing a larger than expected proportion of the issue. Finally Hanson was in trouble in the USA where its bid for SCM had resulted in court proceedings. In spite of these difficulties, Imperial, which by this time so closely fitted Hanson criteria for acquisition, was still targeted by Hanson and in early December a bid was put in.

By this stage then there were three managements involved in Imperial's future – Imperial's own management, demoralized and discredited by the HoJo affair; UB's management, a traditional manufacturing company seeking to expand its productive base through merger with a cash rich company; Hanson's management where financial and industrial circuits existed within the same organization though not in conflict because of the hegemonic position of financial concerns. At the same time, there were three sets of shareholders involved, though here the matter of differentiation is more complex. Although there were small investors who had a stake in each company but were unlikely to hold shares in all three, for the institutional investors the situation was different. It was more than likely that they would hold shares in all three companies and it would be their decisions that would make or break particular managements and their strategies.

In the aftermath of Hanson's bid both sides began fierce publicity battles attacking the others' plans. From the start, the financial press seemed to feel Hanson would succeed though not with its initial offer. The Observer commented;

Lord Hanson's bid for Imperial looks unlikely to succeed at the current price of 236 ½ pence which represents a 27 ½ p discount against Imperial's market price of 259 p. But that is not to say that the City has not made Hanson the favourite to win through. Why? The reasoning is as follows; certain institutions may have lightened their weighting in Hanson Trust but for the best part they are heavily committed. Should Hanson lose out on SCM and Imperial, the image may crack and with it the share price (22. 1. 85).

The Investors Chronicle similarly noted this tie:

Any institution which holds both Imperial and Hanson – and the overlap in share register is considerable – will be inclined to back Hanson for fear that if the bid fails the value of shares in Britain's most acquisitive company will drop sharply (10. 1. 86).

Thus there was a considerable feeling that many city institutions were locked into Hanson to a greater extent than the other companies involved.

In early February the situation was clarified further by the government's decision to refer the Imperial plan for merger with UB to the Monopoly and Mergers Commission on the grounds that putting together the snack and crisp empires of the two companies might be against the public's interest. The Hanson bid was not affected and they now had a free run. Imperial decided to withdraw its bid for UB and in return the government immediately dropped the reference to the MMC. This allowed the true situation to reveal itself in that UB now bid for Imperial. The reverse takeover was now itself reversed. In order to avoid another MMC reference, UB and Imperial agreed to sell Golden Wonder to another company.

This left Hanson and UB in head-to-head confrontation. Although the exact details of the two bids need not be set out here, a crucial feature was the extent of paper involved in the bids. In any bid situation, the bidder may either offer straight cash for the shares of the other company or some form of paper. (A third alternative is cash plus paper, but for ease of presentation I will discuss the two clear alternatives.) Usually paper bids involve the shareholders of the acquired company receiving a paper interest in the acquiring company. This in turn can take a number of forms; for example, the shareholder of the acquired company may receive ordinary shares in the acquiring company, or loan notes or convertible stocks. In a paper bid, the value of the bid becomes moveable since it depends on the way in which the acquiring company's shares move. If over the period of a bid the acquiring company's shares fall in price, the bid becomes less valuable and vice versa. On the other side, the shares of the company to be acquired will almost certainly change, though this is not so crucial to the success or failure of the bid. The bids of Hanson and UB both included a substantial paper element as well as some cash. Only Hanson, however, had an alternative straight cash offer, something which gave it an advantage. In mid-February, Hanson's revised paper bid was worth 301 p per Imperial share (its straight cash offer was 293 p per share) whilst the UB paper bid was worth 332 p per share. With Imperial's shares trading on the market at 320 p per share there was also effectively another cash possibility for investors.

At first sight the difference in bid values might lead one to make UB slight favourites but over the next month the values changed. One key factor was that Hanson won its court case over SCM and it looked like the takeover could now go ahead without delay. This certainly helped to push up Hanson's share price. Other factors may also have been involved. If city institutions judged they would lose more from a Hanson defeat than it would cost them to buy into Hanson now and push its price up, thus ensuring a Hanson victory, they might have increased their weighting in the company. It is worth remembering that the Imperial battle was going on at the same time as the Guiness-Distillers affair where concerted insider efforts to hold up the Guiness share price were allegedly being made in order to beat off the Argyll challenge. Although no such allegations have ever been made regarding Hanson, the fact that its share price steadily rose through the month thus increasing the value of its paper bid was important to its eventual success.

By mid-March the financial press were noting that Hanson's offer was now valuing Imperial higher than UB. Although there was a certain amount of further fluctuation for the rest of the period, the value of the bids remained in the same general area. Thus shareholders were not given a clear financial incentive to accept one or the other. The issue was increasingly narrowing down to which style of management shareholders and fund managers in particular preferred. The Financial Times described the struggle as follows;

The battle for Imperial can lay more claim than most to the description "epic". It is partly the sheer scale of the fight, partly the cast of characters headed on the one side by Lord Hanson. [...] aggressive capitalism incarnate and on the other by Sir Hector Laing representing a more paternalistic form of industrialism (8.4.86).

Lord Hanson embodies what accountants term the "proprietary approach" to a company, Sir Hector the "entity" approach. The essence of the proprietary approach is that companies are in business to make money not things. The shareholder is sovereign and the managers' principal duty is to make the largest possible return on capital; no strong distinction is made between "organic" growth and expansion through acquisition, no particular effort is made to stay in or dominate particular markets. The entity approach by contrast takes the short-term demands of shareholders less seriously. Managers are encouraged to look to the needs of employees and the wider community. The function of business is seen as providing real goods and services. This requires specialisation. There is an emphasis on the need for long-term planning; financial ratios may have to take a back seat as management insists on measures that will not boost earnings per share (10.4.86).

These quotes make clear the perceptions of the city analysts. To use my terms, UB is unequivocally located in the circuit of industrial capital, looking for expansion of profit primarily from productive investment. In Hanson on the other hand, the circuit of financial capital is clearly dominant. Making the money work in whatever way is necessary is the fundamental concern. Within this framework, the circuit of industrial capital clearly has a role but equally clearly it is subordinate to that of the circuit of financial capital.

By this time then, the issue was clearly set up in strategic terms – which sort of company would the institutional shareholders most trust with their money. The immediate financial issue of whose bid was more valuable was downplayed. Lex of the Financial Times wrote;

It would be nonsensical for any institution to take a decision based on the market value of the 2 offers. The few half pence which may separate them on Friday afternoon will seem an irrelevance even by Monday morning. The institutions must for once take a decision which is as much commercial as it is financial. Either they endorse Sir Hector Laing's vision of an international consumer product group fit to take on Nestle and Nabisco or they opt for the proven conglomerate of Lord Hanson (9.4.86).

Within days, the outcome was clear. Hanson Trust had won; UB's offer lapsed with it only having 34% of acceptances. Hanson with a week of its bid left to run already held between 42–45 according to the Financial Times (12.4.86). Three

days after, the Imperial board accepted defeat and recommended Hanson's bid
to its shareholders. The financial press generally felt that the decision was not an
easy one for fund managers though "many said the factor that had finally
clinched a difficult decision was the belief that Hanson would do more with
Imperial's assets in the short to medium term" (FT 12. 4. 86).

However, a more detailed analysis which appeared in the Scotsman a week
later casts doubt on this. According to this account, the major institutions were in
the main (though not unanimously) against the UB offer and for Hanson. This
accords well with the dominant impression throughout that Hanson was going to
win:

Of the major Imperial holders – the Pru, Norwich Union and Legal and General
Insurance Groups – accounting for about 12% of Imperial in total, all rejected the UB
offer. UB and Imperial supporters included the B & B Investment Group and two of
the largest pension funds, PosTel and the National Coal Board. Other institutions
with smaller stakes did back UB but they were vastly outnumbered by Hanson supporters and abstainers. Why did the institutions come down so heavily against UB in
what many of them acknowledged to be a close decision? Their desire not to adminis-
ter another rebuff to Hanson, a group in which many of them have a sizable investment must have counted for something but does not explain their central choice.
Fundamentally the institutions went for the recognizable, the predictable, benefits
Hanson would wring out of Imperial – against the uncertainty implicit in the UB/
Imperial extra, global dimension [. . .]. The current pressures on fund managers to
prove their success every 2–3 months are hardly conducive to producing such a radical
change of directions (21. 4. 86).

What appealed to the Institutional investors was the relative certainty of the
financial strategy pursued by Hanson. In contrast, a strategy based solely on
industrial expansion appeared uncertain and risky.

In the end it was the crucial intervention of the institutional shareholders that
won the day for Hanson. Unlike other takeover situations where the loyalty of
small shareholders to a long-term and well-linked company had been mobilized
to effect a defence against a company like Hanson, in the case of Imperial there
was no such group which came forward. Probably this is indicative of the extent
of disillusion the small shareholders felt with Imperial management as well as
their ability to get a good cash price on the market for their shares. According to
the Financial Times (12. 4. 86), small investors, who had originally held about
25–30% of Imperial shares at the beginning of the period, had sold almost half of
them on the open market by the end of the period.

Hanson's victory was soon followed up in typical Hanson manner by financial
and managerial restructuring of the acquired company.

Classic Hanson. That is the strategy that has emerged at Imperial with the sale of
hotels etc. and expected sale of Golden Wonder and possibly Courage. Other elements include an immediate attack on the target company's bureaucracy and central
overheads coupled with the devolution of responsibility to line managers. At Imperial

[...] some 260 out of 300 of the Group's central office staff have been made redundant and surplus divisional London properties are being sold. Hanson itself is expected to move into Imperial's main London office at Hyde Park Corner with some of the floors let to other tenants. Second there is usually much tightened control over capital expenditure with outlays strictly monitored and approved by Hanson's central management team. Third there is often a rapid disposal of assets – usually at very good prices – which Hanson does not deem part of its core activities (FT 23.7.86).

In terms of sales, Hanson sold Imperial's hotels (to THF for £ 190 m) in mid-July; in mid-September, it made its major sale of Courages breweries to Elders IXL for £ 1.4 bn and also negotiated the sale of Golden Wonder Crisps for £ 87 m. Within 5 months, Hanson had recouped £ 1.7 bn of its £ 2.8 bn outlay on Imperial whilst still retaining the most profitable element of the Imperial operation, its tobacco division. These sales allowed Hanson to renegotiate at more favourable rates the loan facility it had taken out with a consortium of international banks headed by the Chemical Bank of the US in order to fund its acquisition. Eighteen months later Hanson sold the Ross Foods part of Imperial to UB for £ 335 m, further rubbing salt into the wounds for Sir Hector Laing.

4. Conclusions

This chapter has sought to address the issues of ownership, control and management strategy. I have argued that ownership is of major importance in the formulation of management strategy. Managers cannot go beyond the bounds set for them by ownership. However, it is important not to conceive of this in a static manner. Rather the impact of ownership is a continuing and dynamic phenomenon which makes itself felt on managers through share price movements. It is these movements that managers have to take account of. These movements in their turn are predominantly determined by the decisions of the large institutional shareholders, whose actions in turn are oriented towards short-term gain. All of this means that the circuit of financial capital predominates over industrial capital.

Thus in contemporary Britain, managements are pushed towards emphasizing financial issues over manufacturing ones by their need to secure their survival and growth; failure in this regard will lead to a low share price and therefore likely takeover. This trend is not without its contradictions. Some firms remain firmly wedded to the circuit of industrial capital; within others such as Imperial in the period under analysis it is possible to discern emerging conflict between the two circuits. Still others such as Hanson and other conglomerates such as BTR have become structured in such a way as to cope with these issues. Financial manipulation and financial growth is the main target, but industrial companies are acquired and made more profitable, though, it is important to note, not by expansion and growth into new markets but by tighter systems of cost control and better margins in existing markets. Finally, of course, there are those which in direct terms are completely separate from the circuit of industrial capital i. e. the financial services sector – banking, insurance etc. Overall, however, the linkage between ownership and management encourages firms to move away from grappling with difficult issues such as capturing market share in manufactured products from international competitors and instead turn towards ways of financially manipulating profits. In this way the process of deindustrialization is reproduced within the firm.

It would be wrong to see this process in terms of one set of institutions, e. g. banks, controlling and dominating the activities of another set of institutions, e. g. manufacturing firms. Rather what exists at the moment in Britain is a particular structure of ownership which reproduces itself through management strategies which are seeking to accommodate to that ownership. Because this is the case it would be futile to imagine that Britain's manufacturing decline could be halted by the creation of a new set of institutions providing capital at lower rates and with fewer strings. This would not break the links in the chain that binds management strategy and ownership together. Only a much wider re-organization of social relations which fundamentally changes the institutions of the City and their counterparts in companies could achieve that. Such a re-organization is not on the political agenda at the moment, so until then it is necessary to reiterate that any failures of British management are simultaneously failures of the current system of ownership and the way it is operationalized through the Stock Market. Thus the proper study of management must involve the examination of that ownership context. To do otherwise is to repeat Berle and Means' artificial and inaccurate dualism between ownership and control.

References

Armstrong, P., Competition between the Organizational Profession and the Evolution of Management Control Strategies, in: *Work, Employment and Unemployment*. K. Thompson. London: Open University Press, 97–121. 1984

Berle, A. A. and G. C. Means, *The Modern Corporation and Private Property*. New York: Macmillan. 1932

De Vroey, M., The Separation of Ownership and Control in Large Corporations. *Review of Radical Political Economics* 7, 2: 68–90. 1975

Mintz, B. and M. Schwartz, *The Power Structure of American Business*. London: University of Chicago Press. 1985

Mintz, B. and M. Schwartz, Capital Flows and the Process of Financial Hegemony. *Theory and Society* 15, 1: 77–101. 1986

Morgan, G. and D. Hooper, Corporate Strategy, Ownership and Control. *Sociology* 21, 4: 609–627. 1987

Nichols, T., *Ownership, Control and Ideology*. London: George Allen and Unwin. 1969

Scott, J., *Corporations, Classes and Capitalism*. 2nd ed. London: Hutchinson. 1985

Scott, J., *Capitalist Property and Financial Power*. Brighton: Wheatsheaf. 1986

Scott, J. and C. Griff, *Directors of Industry*. Cambridge: Polity Press. 1985

Stearns, L. B., Capital Market Effects on External Control of Corporations. *Theory and Society* 15, 1: 47–75. 1986

Thompson, G., The Relationship between the Financial and Industrial Sector in the United Kingdom Economy. *Economy and Society* 6, 4: 253–283. 1977

Thompson, G., *Economic Calculation and Policy Formation*. Mimeo. 1985

Tomlinson, J., Democracy Inside the Black Box? Neo-Classical Theories of the Firm and Industrial Democracy. *Economy and Society* 15, 2: 220–250. 1986

Zeitlin, M., Corporate Ownership and Control: the Large Corporation and the Capitalist Class. *American Journal of Sociology* 79: 1073–1119. 1974

International Management and the Class Structure

Jane Marceau

1. Introduction

Organising the management of the productive and service organisations on which their collective and individual fortunes depend has long been and remains a major preoccupation of the privileged classes of Europe. Over the post-war decades in particular, as technology has been transformed in line with intellectual and socio-economic developments, so new organisational forms have been devised and entrusted with the dual task of ensuring both the smooth transfer of resources from one set of products to another and increasing the profitability of productive investments made. Corporations have been restructured to take account of new productive and competitive conditions and to respond adequately to new challenges. In many cases, companies have begun to demand new skills of their managers, sometimes skills formally credentialled by a degree in business administration, such as the MBA. When new markets have been opened up, and especially when expansion has taken place on an international scale, a prime concern of those investing has been to devise the organisational forms which would best ensure the best return, protecting both the short and the longer-term interests of investors. New organisational forms have often led hirers to develop new managerial technologies and to demand new skills of international managers.

For the managers themselves, the new organisational forms created have come to provide the framework in which they must make their careers and achieve other ends. For the ambitious among the managers, and hence perhaps those most likely to be successful, these goals centre on reaching control positions and doing so as quickly as possible. In practice, therefore, the new forms developed in multinational companies have become the framework for playing out older games on the way to the top. The enterprise structures in which the players act both shape and are shaped by their incumbents, and frequently outcomes can only be understood in terms of the characteristics of the main players. The argument of this paper is that, despite all the changes made, in organisational positions, in rhetoric, in objective skills recognised and rewarded, the new structures created in many multinational companies in Europe have continued to provide career paths to the top which particularly favour the characteristics and values held by the sons of the business fractions of Europe's national bourgeoisies.

In terms of careers, the internationalisation of business in Europe has had two major effects. First, the growth of transnational European enterprises has served to broaden the arena of competition for top places and to provide more top positions through the addition of Europe-wide activities. Secondly, however, the managerial technologies and organisational structures developed have effectively determined the relative chances of success of socially different competitors across European nations. In particular, the new structures very frequently offer a "challenge-success" career path to the top. This path is intended to link rapid promotion to objective performance criteria. Moving up the path depends at each step on each contender visibly making profits. This profit dependence often means in practice that the actors who play best in the competition for the top are those best endowed with the resources which have underlain success in organisations more usually associated with entrepreneurial capitalists. These resources include the characteristics, attitudes, skills, and values which have long been developed within traditional bourgeois families. The players thus depend on access to an array of social and economic capital derived from families of origin as much as they depend on their formal educational achievements, including the high-level cultural capital inculcated in international business schools, despite the fact that the game is now played on a much larger stage and in an international arena. The new organisational forms associated notably with the development of international business and international management have in effect thus provided a particularly suitable forum for the sons of each national bourgeoisie in Europe to reach out from their bastions of origin and move into an expanding game. Doing so, the "new managers" bring the attitudes, values and many practices of each national group into the international arena. It is argued here that those who best bring together the different resources will do better in the new and more complex arena than those who are less well endowed with any one resource. The winners in this game will form the core of an international business class now emerging in Europe and which will consolidate its position after the abolition of all trade barriers in the Common Market in 1992.

The emerging international business class as a whole will thereby contain many of the essential attributes of each national group of origin. Despite this continuity, however, individual managers' experiences in the international arena do modify their national perspectives, and as they collectively begin to form an international business class, some elements of both practice and ethos will be different and in some cases conflict quite markedly with the more particularistic views of each group of origin.

It is not just values, attitudes and practices which link national bourgeoisies into the beginnings of an international business class. The contention of this paper, as stated above, is that the new organisational structures facilitate access to the top positions in major European companies for the sons of the business fraction of each national bourgeoisie. This means more than a simple social "reproduction" of the personnel in top business positions. First, it means, that individually bourgeois sons personally link the productive organisations of their families of origin to the usually much larger groups controlling international businesses. This is partly because, since success along the new routes seems to demand the use of a range of resources derived from families of origin, while the sons leave family enterprises to work in multinational corporations they never wholly leave their families behind. Indeed, in very many cases, they reinforce their personal links to the business fractions of the upper classes of their countries of origin by the marriages which they make (see Marceau 1989). The links between national and international business men are also made through the portfolios of investments made over a lifetime. For example, Scott (1982) has shown how in Britain over the last few decades family businesses have frequently sold out and diversified their investments and the same processes seem to have occurred elsewhere (Morin 1974). The growth of the international arena suggests that the portfolios which are managed by European business "sons" will contain *mélanges* of both national and international capital, linking the fortunes of national business families into those of multinational enterprises.

There is yet another link too. Recent evidence (Herman 1981; Lewellen 1971; Useem 1984) suggests that in the most senior positions in large companies, at top management and Board level, ownership and control *re-merge*. In other words, evidence on share-holding suggests that at the very top of a company the controllers of industry are also the owners, at least in part. If it is the case that sons from the business fraction of each national bourgeoisie in Europe are more likely to reach these top positions than are others because of their greater likelihood of success in the new organisational forms, then the separation of "ownership" and "control" occurs essentially only over a period along individual career trajectories.

For these reasons, if Scott (1982) and other observers are correct in saying that most family enterprise owners have diversified their capital holdings so that their collective fortunes depend on the success of a variety of enterprises, then collectively too the sons all their lives represent the interests of capital, even though holding formally managerial positions, since they too depend on the success of a variety of enterprises. From their families of origin they receive one portfolio of investments, or at least the income from family investments. As they rise to the top in particular businesses, the sons' own portfolios come to include large capital stocks, both in the enterprises they come to control and in others. The extent of their ownership is manifest in the "wealth creation" (remuneration) packages now offered to senior and top executives in every major industrialised country (personal communication, remuneration consultant, 1987) and which have been well documented, notably in North America by Lewellen (1971) and Herman (1981). As these authors show, as they reach the top, the most successful managers receive a direct remuneration handsome enough to mean that much is invested and a portfolio of stock options and assets in the enterprise in which they serve. These investments both complement those of their families of origin and contribute to the economic strength, and hence the social position, of their family group as a whole, both at "home" and across national frontiers.

In these ways, therefore, the new organisational forms of international businesses, legitimated by reference to new managerial technologies and techniques, constitute the new framework for an old game – namely the making of profits through a series of business investments – played by traditional players on a broader stage, and in the process links national and international capital together. This paper uses an empirical study carried out in the late 1970s and in 1980 to illustrate this process (see Appendix A on the population concerned and the sources of the data used).

2. Changes to the Opportunity Structure

The key changes in the structure of business organisations which provide the framework for our respondents' careers have been well summarised by Dyas and Thanheiser (1976), by Franko (1976), by Horovitz (1980) and others. The general need for "reconversion strategies" by bourgeois sons in response to the changes has been outlined by Bourdieu and his colleagues (1973). Their descriptions of the changes are set against the background of the reorganisation of productive property-holding in Europe which saw the share of enterprises wholly owned by individual families decline throughout the twentieth century, though at different rates in each country (see, e. g. Morin 1974; Bauer and Cohen 1981). As Dyas and Thanheiser and Franko see it, the late 1960s and the 1970s were the heyday of the expansion of European firms which transformed themselves into multinational enterprises by extending operations, first in manufacturing and later in banking (Steuber 1976), across Europe to take advantage of both the increasing wealth and the increasing economic unity of European nations. These enterprises grew vastly in size, however measured, they undertook direct investments outside national frontiers, largely in contiguous nations, and they created links between companies in different countries. The growth of the EEC and, to a lesser extent, of EFTA, saw massive alteration in international investment and production patterns. These took place notably in aluminium, glass, metals, processed foods, chemicals and electrical and electronic goods, but also in business services, such as insurance, banking and consulting (Jacquemin and de Jong 1977; Cahiers Français 1979; Steuber 1976).

In concert with the development of these new areas of activity, enterprise internal structures were reorganised. They began to converge in each country, moving towards divisionalised structures since the traditional mother-daughter subsidiary model with one chain of command to the president at home often proved unable to cope with the control demands made by hugely expanded operations (Horovitz 1980). Thus, for the first time in the late 1960s, British, French and German enterprise structures began to look much alike (Horovitz 1980).

Management opportunities also changed, following the creation of divisions as profit centres and shifts in the relative importance of different functions. Notably, finance and marketing came to the fore, a move perhaps not unexpected in an era where major firms were often selling almost identical consumer products, fabricated with mature industrial technologies, thus creating a need to penetrate ever new markets (Bourdieu et al. 1973). At a time of new spatial and internal investment patterns, companies also needed to keep sharper eyes on which investments paid and which did not; hence the rise to prominence of the financial analyst and controller, a function whose importance increased in the crisis conditions of the 1970s (see, for instance, diverse articles in business journals such as *L'Expansion* from 1974 onwards).

These changes offered new opportunities for the ambitious sons of Europe's national bourgeoisies who had been displaced by the same processes of capitalist development from pursuing careers in the enterprises controlled by their families of origin. At the same time, the universalisation of company structures and procedures across Europe encouraged international demand for managers with skills transferable from enterprise to enterprise, sector to sector, country to country. Demand especially increased for professional managers who also possessed multicultural and multilingual skills, as well as an acceptable business ethic (see INSEAD publicity and the annual reviews of executive salaries published by *L'Expansion*). The curriculum of the business schools, and notably that of the Institut Européén d'Administration des Affaires (INSEAD) at Fontainebleau, which grew up in Europe at the same time encapsulated the appropriate intellectual management technology and incorporated it into the training offered to candidates for the Master of Business Administration. As an international business school, the Institute also offered necessary multicultural skills. It is therefore graduates of INSEAD that form the population whose careers are reported in this paper.

It is this population whose experiences in the business world after graduation suggest that the business organisational structures which developed over the postwar decades, far from changing chances of access to top positions, essentially provided a framework for altered class action.

Possession of considerable social, economic and cultural capital resources continues to be important for success because, as was indicated earlier, reaching the top in these new organisations, at an age which the ambitious consider appropriate, seems to involve the development of high-risk, challenge-success, career strategies. Rapid progression seems to be achieved less often by "loyalty" than by rapidly becoming visible by visibly making profits for the company. The necessary visibility can only be ensured through risk-taking. While success implies a majority of good judgements, the visible manager must also take responsibility for the bad ones. Making *visible* profits usually involves placing oneself in exposed positions. From this exposure comes the need to cushion the risk as well as enhance the chances of good judgements by drawing to the full on the armoury of resources derived from membership of the privileged classes.

3. The Players

The questionnaire survey of the social origins of a section of the players in the international business arena showed that very large proportions were from business owner backgrounds. In virtually every country except the Scandinavian nations, the largest single proportions were born into families where the father owned, partly or wholly, one or more businesses and usually had an important share in the management of them. These groups, those of *Fabrikant* and *Unternehmer, industriels* and *impresari,* formed 19 per cent – 39 per cent of every national cohort. Adding to this possessory *patronat,* the *controllers* of business (many of whom are substantial shareholders), the *Présidents-Directeurs-Généraux,* the *administrateurs de société,* the Directors General and their equivalents across Europe, raises the proportion of respondents drawn from owning or controlling business families to at least half everywhere and in most countries around two-thirds. Moreover, this pattern remained essentially the same across two decades, 1959 to 1978. The sons of bourgeois Europe, it seems, were taking advantage of a training in the skills newly greatly in demand in international business.
The position of solid entrenchment within the business world of many of the managers studied was equally clear after analysis of the occupations of grandfathers, uncles, brothers and male cousins and the spouses of female members of the extended family. Varying somewhat across categories, between a quarter and two thirds of these held positions in the business world, mostly quite senior ones. In contrast, their relatively low penetration into the public, cultural or political sectors of their society is equally outstanding. The rising managers of the new international business arena are overwhelmingly drawn from the existing national business world although their families have some representatives in the other fields of power. Recruitment to top positions in businesses expanding into the new international forum for the sons of bourgeois Europe is thus essentially following a well-established path. Similarly, without giving details in the limited space available here, the overwhelming majority had been educated in Europe's most socially and intellectually exclusive secondary schools and universities. Of the hundreds potentially available, only forty university institutions across twelve

Table 1. Father's Occupation, Percentage

Father's Occupation	British	German	Belgian	Scandin.	Swiss	Dutch	Austrian	Spanish	Italian	French
Bus. owner/independ. serv. PDG, Chairman of Board, Director General	26	39	28.5	22	29.5	31	34	19	32	22
	2	2.5	2.0	4	8	10	2	9.5	7	9
MDs, GMs, *Directeurs*	6	4	1	21	8	23	7	9.5	5	6
Senior management	6	5	3	4	1.5	1	5	–	2	8
Other management	6	3	3	5	3	4	5	5	3	6
Profs. in business	5	9	9	6	11.5	–	8	–	2	8
Total business	51	62.5	64.5	62	60.5	68	63	43	51	50
Senior civil service	8	6	5.5	2	1	1	3	9.5	7	6.5
Army/Navy	8	2	5	2	1	1	3	–	2	4
Teaching/cultural/research	8	7	5	8	6	3	2	–	7	4
Doctors & other 'medical'	5	5	5	8	4	8	3	9.5	7	1
Lawyers	3	3.5	2	3.5	2	5.5	3	9.5	7	1
Total non-business 'upper middle class'	32	23.5	22.5	23,5	14	18.5	16	28.5	30	16.5
White-collar & technician	8	3	1	3	5	–	8	–	5	4
Shopkeepers/artisans	2	1	8	4	9	2	3	19	8	5
Manual	2	1	1	–	4	2	2	5	–	2
Farmers/landowners	3	2.5	2	3	3	1	3	–	5	4
Miscellaneous	4	2	3	4	3	5.5	10	5	3	2
N =	301	302	109	169	130	90	59	21	59	579
% sample	85%	81%	85%	91%	88%	96%	85.5%	91%	81%	87.5%

MD = Managing Director. GM = General Manager.
Profs. in business = Professionals in business.
Directeurs = top management.

Table 2. Occupations of male Respondents' Fathers and Grandfathers*, Percentage

Occupation	Fathers	PGF	MGF	French** PGF	MGF
Own business (patron)	33	28.5	26	25	17
Top management	13)	6)	4)		
	)24	)14	)8	7.5	13
Senior management	11)	8)	4)		
Total senior business	57	42.5	34	36.5	30
Senior civil service	8	5	4	7.5	12.5
Military and naval	3	4	10	1	1
Law	3)	4)	4)		
	)13	)10	)9.5	7.5	14
Medicine and similar	10)	6)	5.5)		
Other professional	3	4	3	–	–
Writers and other cultural	0.5	1	1.5	5	1
University teachers/ research	3	1	3	0.5	1
Other teacher	2	3	3	1	2
Routine non-manual/ lower mgt/tech./white-collar	1	5	6	6	8
Shopkeepers/artisans	4	7	7	14	12.5
Manual workers	1	6	4	7	5
Farmers and land-owners	1	10	11	13	6
Misc. (clergy, organist, etc.)	1	2	2	5	6
N =	292	276	273	173	152

PGF = paternal grandfathers
MGF = maternal grandfathers
** Data from first French study only.

countries of Europe had trained the 2110 managers studied. Respondents had largely trained in the traditionally prestigious disciplines of engineering, law and economics, supplemented by some commercial studies, as had many of their fathers before them. Moreover, following a well-trodden path, few had ever seriously considered a career in anything but business and in their chosen domain they were ambitious. Almost all considered that the only interesting posts in business were those at the top and these they almost universally intended to reach. At INSEAD, they had received the supplement to the earlier education received and this combination of credentials, they felt confident, would improve their chances not just of access but of *rapid* access to senior posts in major businesses operating in the European international arena. Armed with this new credential, they moved out from home to conquer new territories.

4. Moves in the Game

The challenge-success career route, the track to the top posts and high salaries coveted by young high-flyers and favoured especially by the sons of the *patronat,* is not a simple path. Pursuing that course involves many moves and many risks. In their race to the top, the ambitious young men – whether engineers, econo- mists or lawyers – in the study find that they must move sideways by function, sector, size and nationality of firm and leapfrog over each other as they moved up, and sometimes down, and across. They find they must cut corners by taking risks and juggle their relative advantages and handicaps, their educational cre- dentials and their track records, in highly complex ways. Their ambitions interact with hirers' requirements to encourage them to make moves which weave a web of tracks upwards, sideways and sometimes downwards, tracks which cross na- tional boundaries, mix cultures and overcome barriers of distance and language. The choices made are often high risk, involving taking cuts in salary or learning new jobs while exposed to continual scrutiny. Each post on the way up is usually considered only as the period between the last and the next. For the ambitious, careers in this arena are thus not straightforward; they involve searching and being sought in a game in which, at the highest levels in particular, the rules are not explicit, the opportunities are unpredictable and the rewards are various.

The secret of success in these high risk but high speed career routes is the translation of "responsibility" into "profit." The trek to the top necessitates searching around for the right position in which to use one's entrepreneurial talents to achieve results which are noticed by top management while, at the same time, as we said above, getting noticed involves taking considerable risks. Many respondents described how it had been necessary to drop salary, begin again in a new sector, firm or country or accept a job at a lower initial level in order then to jump much further upwards once their worth had been seen in concrete financial results. They sometimes have to do this not once but several times within a few years.

So, in organisational terms, which are the fast tracks? They are fashioned from experiences which at the same time as they involve taking risks to make the necessary profits, also give the occupant of a position a global view of enterprise activities. One respondent, a highly successful one, summed up the best route to the top, as follows:

The fast tracks? Where functions are concerned:
• marketing *used* to be;
• export today and certainly tomorrow still;

- finance, and the social in the future perhaps;
Where sectors are concerned:
- electronics;
- information technology;
- new energies.
In general, the *international above all!*

While marketing may have been the go-getter during the consumer boom of the 1960s, in less propitious times, finance and external relations came to the fore. Finance was cited by many respondents who said for instance that the "fast tracks are the financial and trade department", "business development in banks and financial management in general" and, most significantly here, "all the positions where you are most exposed". Success in finance may offer the opportunity to be the visible hand running another area of activity. Not only are sound financial results important in establishing credibility, but the positions which are used to gain them, such as assistant to the Director General for Europe, give their holders the particular advantage of the global view of a large and complex firm that top managerial tasks require and a chance to increase visibility by influencing the organisation of the company. The high-flying risk-taking career typically involves taking over a profit centre (such as a division or subsidiary) which is in trouble, making a financial success of it and then either moving on and up to run a larger and more important subsidiary or moving out of the group to run a business elsewhere if the right offer in terms both of power and remuneration is made.

The following example shows how important in doing this successfully are the specific management skills which a business school teaches.

I was taken on by E. (a large British multinational) in July 1975 through INSEAD. I was then assistant to the Director General for Europe. My task was to perfect a system of budgetary control for the headquarters of all the subsidiaries in Europe (60 companies in 14 countries, 5000 employees). It was a financial task but at the same time it was more than that, it was really the whole reorganisation of the company headquarters and its operations [. . .] In July 1976, I became Director of Marketing, based on Switzerland.

After making a success there the respondent was sent back to France to get the situation of a French subsidiary back into profitable order and in the course of doing this he became Director General of the subsidiary. That seemed promising but things could have gone wrong since the Director General for Europe retired and the British closed the Swiss offices. He was offered the chance to go to London but decided to stay in France.

In this case, several risks were taken in fairly quick succession, involving company reorganisation, change of function and moves between countries, all within four to five years. Taking these risks paid off handsomely for a while but then problems elsewhere in the group arose and promotion possibilities in the short term looked bleak. So yet another new departure had to be chosen. The respondent when interviewed was about to leave for a new job in Switzerland, in a large company operating in a totally different and socially very prestigious field, wine.

I got a job through a headhunter who organised the meetings. I will be Secretary General to the firm and then will become Chief Executive Officer (*administrateur délégué*). It's a promotion because it's a firm whose turnover is twenty times greater than the company where I am now.

The following is a second example of a manager successfully pursuing a similar career, taking risks, changing direction and ultimately making profits for a firm. The respondent is a Dutchman, who, after INSEAD, worked first for a French multinational, ultimately taking over the running of a German subsidiary before returning to the headquarters in Paris, and then taking on another subsidiary in difficulty. On leaving INSEAD he had several offers and had finally chosen a French company, which offered what many INSEADs seek, "adventure".

I met the new Director General who had just arrived from the USA and who wanted to create a team that he thought would be young, full of initiative, keen to take risks. In short, it sounded a fascinating adventure for three years.

During that period he rose through the sales side to be *Chef de Groupe* in control of a group of existing products, and at the same time to be New Business Manager, in charge of creating and developing new products and deciding on product orientation for the future. After a while, however, internal problems arose in the enterprise and the team broke up. The respondent decided to move on and chose another French firm,

which offered me a huge increase in salary and a new function [. . .]. I stayed there for four years. During those few years I created the post of Marketing Manager. My team was responsible from A to Z for the profitability of our product lines. Sales increased enormously. In spite of this, because we were only a subsidiary we suffered a lot from the silly decisions taken by the mother-company. We had four years of constant struggle.

Already working outside his home country, the respondent decided to go on playing on the international stage but to change the products with which he worked and move out of mass market goods. With this aim he joined another French company in the International Affairs Division. Then disaster struck, but a disaster soon turned to good effect. A motoring accident forced him to take a new direction. He was asked by his firm to make a study of a German subsidiary of the company which was in bad financial shape. The study took a year and following it, once he had recovered from the accident, the company asked him to run the subsidiary in Germany. "It was suggested that I took the subsidiary over. Profits were quickly made". Soon after this, another part of the Group was found to face financial troubles and on the basis of his track record, the respondent was asked to move once again, back to Paris, to take over the firm in difficulty.

So then another sector began to fail. This was the export section of the "brown products" of the Group [. . .]. I took it over. I'm still there. Next year for the first time we shall make profits. You have to persevere.

Success in a task or series of tasks of clear financial benefit to the company is thus the secret of many fast promotions. Even though in some cases studied here the functions held by the promotee were in fields such as marketing, it was the financial result from the whole operation of the enterprise, the creation of profits for the firm, which was crucial. Success in this is seen by supervisors as indicating clearly general management ability, leads upwards fast and gives rapid access to positions with a fully recognised general management content and power. A final example can be seen in the experience of a Belgian high-flyer who, having internationalised himself by working for a Swiss company in North Africa, returned home to Belgium with a mission to take over and "mend" an ailing company.

Then I joined this company [a manufacturing firm] [. . .] which was bankrupt when I arrived. I came to get it back on its feet. I was taken on as a consultant to organise a new structure and then I was appointed Chief Executive Officer (*Président Directeur Général*). By 1976, the firm had been reorganised and had become financially sound [. . .]. I am now a member of the Board of Directors (*Conseil d'Administration*). There are two groups, ten companies in all [. . .] I am in charge of everything [. . .]. I prefer to work in a small firm (here there are 600 people) and be totally in charge [. . .]. Our turnover doubled in two years and tripled in five years [. . .]. My plans for the future? To create new businesses. In another two years I'll leave – there's nothing more interesting than taking over a business.

Thus, a decade only after receiving his MBA from INSEAD, this respondent was Chief Executive Officer and a member of the Board of Directors of a medium-sized manufacturing company, itself a member of a larger group, with profit control of ten companies. Leaving a successful international career to take a financial risk at home he had acquired a top job at a very young age. The doubling and tripling of turnover was the basis of a financial success visible to all and appropriately rewarded.

5. Reaching the Top

Success on the "challenge-success" road to top positions in particular seems to depend greatly on the judicious use of personal and familial capital resources of all kinds. While, in looking at the moves made, it is hard to study directly the use of social capital in making a success of different positions, and the research described here was also designed for other purposes, it is clear from the study that upper class families provide important back-up resources which both encourage entrepreneurial initiative and cushion the risks taken by their members. First, they provide the attitudes, values and expectations which make risk-taking a "normal" approach in business life. An upbringing in the entrepreneurial classes ensures that offspring absorb the values and role models provided by senior family members, notably fathers but also uncles and elder brothers, as the IN-SEAD study showed. By their teenage years sons of the business fraction of the bourgeoisie already both understand the entrepreneurial ethos and are well-versed in the basic essential techniques of private enterprise.

Second, upper class families maintain extensive and intense relationships with a wide network of relatives. Many of these relatives both occupy now and have occupied in the past, thus multiplying their influence, important positions in many areas of the business world across Europe. They are people who are important sources of the information on which the proper working of the *pifomètre*, business "nose" or flair depends. They can often provide privileged information which leads to actions whose results are registered as objective career performance as, for example, when they suggest new approaches, discuss inventions or changed product needs, indicate new or cheaper suppliers, point to market opportunities at home or overseas, propose deals that might be done, provide banking business, or advise on possible changes to or interpretations of government policies and regulations. Access to such information on the privileged basis which kinship encourages increases the obvious organisational value of a position holder and makes him appear a likely candidate for senior positions at an early age.

Similarly, families of this kind are important channels for the transmission of information "out" by an individual. Very many, perhaps most, senior management positions are never formally advertised. At senior levels companies prefer to recruit discreetly and the transmission of potentially useful information by a roundabout route on a candidate can be crucial – and can be done on an international scale, as one Swedish respondent to this study, working in an American bank in London discovered when summoned to an interview in Paris for a job for which he had not applied. Moreover, many senior jobs are created with particular people in mind, as Granovetter (1974) has shown, while top jobs are modified to suit the people available, as Glickman and his colleagues have indicated (1968: 27). Getting one's qualities known abroad is thus particularly welcome and who better knows a person than his relatives?

Finally, in both recruitment to existing posts and the creation of new ones, emphasis on "personal" suitability is often a disguised demand for "social" acceptability. Being *"quelqu'un de bien"* means in France, for instance, "having a house in Cannes, a chalet in the Alps or a hunting stretch in the Sologne" as one respondent said. The economic capital available through an extended family in the upper class ensures access to these and other elements of the good life so that direct ownership of the facilities is unnecessary. This enables the ambitious to acquire at a young age the social impedimenta which are still essential to success in many business arenas. Possession of access to them enables the young not only to live in the right way but also to interact with the right people, again multiplying chances of visibility. Moreover, the same possession may be taken as an indication of adherence to a system of values supportive of those of established business and society at the same time as it indicates the material possibility of maintaining villas and chalets in places which permit strategic initiatives, both given and received, once more multiplying an employee's value to his enterprise.

So far we have been referring to families based on ties of consanguinity and marriage. But parallel "families" are created in other ways: through relationships established not by blood but by common experience and membership of an exclusive body. The *annuaires* of Europe's prestigious educational establishments, including that of INSEAD, are the manifestation of a parallel family which is almost as powerful as those of blood and marriage. Alumni of INSEAD not only look each other up in the Address Book when visiting another city or country but when possible attend the monthly meetings and fund-raising dinners at which they meet not only each other but also some of the most powerful business and political leaders, such as senior members of the Conservative Party in Britain. A report of one such dinner in London, for example, showed that the guest list included Edward Heath, Roy Jenkins, Lord Hankey, Lord Farnham, Sir Donald Barron, Sir Robert Clark, Sir Jaspar Hallam, Sir Kenneth Keith and Sir Arthur Knight (Daily Telegraph, 5. 11. 76). In these ways an elite institution forms the basis for making other elite contacts on a regular basis.

Such contacts are vitally important because, as Glickman and his colleagues showed in 1968 and Useem emphasised in 1984, as did Bauer and Cohen in 1981, the development and succession of the very few top officers in a corporation is more than an extension of the same processes lower down, At the top, the group of individuals who work together is quite small and its members have highly personal relationships. With regard to selection and placement they operate much as they would in a small firm, and there is a high proportion of group input into choices of new members. Informal procedures supplant formal ones. Common consensus on candidates ranks high. In the top positions, clear-cut measures of performance are less frequently available: top managers must therefore have confidence that those they promote are extensions of themselves and have a proven profit record. At the same time, increasingly, as Useem (1984) underlines, the spread of the corporate network in modern capitalism means that what other large companies are doing is of major concern to all. Companies are urged to increase their managerial outreach, to spread their contacts through encouraging top executives to accept outside directorships, to improve their scan of economic and political trends by belonging to business organisations. Possession of inter-corporate networks is vital and in succession to controlling posts in large companies, criteria of choice include possession of extensive external connections. These connections, according to Useem, run along the lines of old-boy contacts and kinship links built and developed long before high office is achieved. This is because at the very top of major enterprises "who" you "are" and what you believe are crucial, for it is at this point that ownership and control re-emerge. Organisational structures which encourage a "challenge-success" career give the best chances of access to that point since they both give the necessary visibility internally through the making of profitable decisions and allow scope for entrepreneurial drive and initiatives. Membership of the business fractions of the bourgeoisie developed in an earlier business world ensures possession of the essential external network of kin and other contacts which take much of the risk out of entrepreneurship.

It is, in short, the accumulation of credentials, track record and contacts which provide the key to reaching top positions early. Since at the heart of the concept of "track record" lies the visibility which comes from making profits, while the most successful respondents to my study were publicly defined as managers, in practice they were essentially risk-taking entrepreneurs. In developing their careers they concentrated through their choice of sector, function, type of company and place of work, on acquiring the skills and experience which allow them to bid effectively for the risky tasks that challenge the manager to prove his worth at what still lies at the heart of any enterprise's activity – the making of profits. At an earlier stage of capitalism such managers may have essentially turned their attention to the creation of new enterprises in the manufacturing or banking section or to expanding existing ones into "new areas". Doing this, their entrepreneurial activities would have been clearly seen as such. In an age where the bigger enterprises grow by expansion into new markets for existing products or by the accretion of other business activities, the entrepreneurial nature of the activities of these men is disguised to the general view.

It is this essential quality of entrepreneurship, of independence, of the wish to be effective in the making of profits which can then be translated into handsome remuneration and the transformation into controller-cum-owner which takes place at the top of such enterprises and which, if thwarted in a large firm, leads an MBA to leave and found new firms or take over existing smaller ones. In this move, too, the person seen at one stage of a career as a manager, returns to the entrepreneurial capitalist mode most consonant with his origins. As he moves he carries with him both the ideas, values and attitudes which he learned in his milieu of origin and those learned through business education and apprenticeship in larger enterprises. This new mélange is taken back to the enterprises he controls and becomes part of that business practice and, to the extent that he participates in the creation of a business class-wide rhetoric at national or international level, also becomes part of a more general renewal of business politics in the society. Similarly, to the extent, too, that managers with this entrepreneurial thrust and experience reach the top positions in major enterprises, so they will promote similar experiences for and attitudes in those they in turn employ and promote.

Thus, while major enterprises have modified their structures to cope with new productive demands, I suggest that these new organisational forms, typical of modern international management, far from requiring a change in the nature of the activities and values which led to success in an older form of capitalist organisation, demand and reward exactly the same qualities as the old. Success in the new structures continues to depend on a similar *ensemble* of qualities, skills and contacts and families retain their significance. For bourgeois sons the only moments of their career when they are not a professionally active part of a possessory bourgeoisie are the early stages. Even then, since they maintain an interest in the enterprises on which the economic fortunes of their families of origin depend, as do many of the aces in their own game, they hardly move far away. They may, indeed, be the active managers of the family investment portfolios concerned.

From this perspective, while one may clearly identify the growth of a new international business elite, trained in "modern" techniques and working in the *entreprises de pointe* of Europe, in firms at the forefront of both managerial and physical technologies, one can also see that this elite is essentially an offshoot of an older capitalist class formation in each country, developed, with the aid of capital of all kinds drawn from "home", through new business organisational forms. The new organisational forms are the new settings for traditional practices; they are the new frameworks which allow specific individuals to achieve traditional goals and to re-merge with the culture and interests of their national classes of origin. To be successful in the new structures, and especially to be successful at a youthful age, seems to involve pursuing a "challenge-success" career in which every move made depends on the making of visible profits. The managers competing most spend all their lives with profit-making at the forefront of their activities, and at the top of the tree they "re-join" their families of origin as members of a European entrepreneurial class. The only difference in their generation is the scale of operations: the enterprises they come to manage in the 1980s and beyond operate across national frontiers and the men who manage them see the whole of western Europe as the normal arena for their activities. To the extent, therefore, that from their positions they contribute to the development of a European class-wide business rhetoric, it is likely that the rhetoric will contain both the terminology of technocratic management and most of the essential elements of the "older" family capitalist ethic and values. The latter elements may, however, also be allied to a vision that is broader in scale and less nationalistic in tone since the speakers share an international management experience and most believe, as my study showed, in the future of a united "Europe" (see Marceau 1989). These new "managers" may thus provide a competing rhetoric to the purely national class-wide visions engendered "at home" and modify business positions taken in negotiations with governmental bodies, whether national or international, such as those associated with the European Economic Community. Finally, to the degree that their collective experience as international managers contributes to the transformation of their culture of origin, the adoption by the privileged sons of Europe of a new managerial technology and its use inside a new organisational framework especially suited to playing on an international stage may provide the opportunity for some change as the international business class develops, as well as much continuity.

References

Bauer, M. and E. Cohen *Qui gouverne les groupes industriels?* Paris: Le Seuil. 1981

Bourdieu, P., L. Boltanski and M. de St. Martin Les stratégies de reconversion. *Social Science Information* 12: 61–113. 1973

Cahiers Français Les Multinationales. *Cahiers Français* 190 (March–April): 5 and 23. 1979

Dyas, G. and H. Thanheiser *The Emerging European Enterprise.* London: Macmillan. 1976

Franko, L. *The European Multinationals.* New York: Harper and Row. 1976

Glickman, A., C. Hahn, E. Heishman and B. Baxter *Top Management Development and Succession.* New York: Committee for Economic Development. 1968

Granovetter, M. *Getting the Job: A Study of Contacts and Careers.* Cambridge, Mass.: Harvard University Press. 1974

Herman, E. *Corporate Control, Corporate Power.* New York: Cambridge University Press. 1981

Horovitz, J. *Top Management Control in Europe.* London: Macmillan. 1980

Jacquemin, A. and H. de Jong (1977) *European Industrial Organisation.* London: Macmillan. 1977

Lewellen, W. *The Ownership Income of Management.* New York: National Bureau of Economic Research and Columbia University Press. 1971

Marceau, J. *A Family Business? The Creation of an International Business Elite.* Cambridge: Cambridge University Press. 1989

Morin, F. *La structure financière du capitalisme français.* Paris: Calmann Lévy. 1974

Scott, J. *The Upper Classes.* London: Macmillan. 1982

Steuber, U. *International Banking.* Leyden: A. W. Sijthoff. 1976

Useem, M. *The Inner Circle.* New York: Oxford University Press. 1984

Appendix A. Methodology of the Study

The population described in this chapter is composed of alumni of the *Institut Européen d'Administration des Affaires* (INSEAD) located in Fontainebleau. The study covered alumni of 12 European nationalities who had entered INSEAD between 1959 and 1978. The data were gathered through the analysis of 2110 admissions forms, including those of all the West German, British, Dutch, Belgian, Austrian, Swiss, Italian, Spanish, Swedish, Norwegian and Danish students and a 75% sample of the French drawn by groups of years. The archival data were supplemented by 200 questionnaires returned by the French only in 1974 and by 304 returned by the other nationalities in 1979, all respondents being from the alumni population working in

Europe at the time. These were completed by the return of 134 questionnaires by the wives of the French and 169 by the wives of respondents of the other nationalities. In addition, 120 interviews were carried out with a sample of respondents to the questionnaire who had left INSEAD at least five years previously. They were working in companies in "new" manufacturing (pharmaceuticals, electronics etc.) and in the service sector, notably banking, and were located in Paris, Bruxelles, London, Basel, Zürich, Geneva, Frankfurt and München. These cities were chosen because of the concentration there of INSEAD alumni of different nationalities in the sectors selected and with the longer post-MBA careers appropriate to the study. The discussion in this chapter is based on the information drawn from all these sources.

Managers and Social Classes

Harri Melin

It is the purpose of this chapter to discuss certain lines of demarcation in the internal differentiation of wage earners; special attention is given to the category of managers. The empirical results that are presented below are based on analyses carried out within Erik Olin Wright's comparative project on class structure and class consciousness, and concern six advanced capitalist countries: the United States, Canada, the United Kingdom, Norway, Sweden, and Finland (Wright et al. 1987).

Who are managers and what do managers do? Who are today's companies and organizations run by? Over the past 20 years considerable debate has occurred over management and managerial strategies. Most of the studies have been primarily concerned with organizational control and with the development and differentiation of forms of control.

1. A Short History of Management

In early capitalism the functions of management and ownership were not separated in the same way they are today, but were personified in one and the same owner-manager. According to Hill (1981), the capitalist who owned the factory was also responsible for its management. In the biggest factories he would have a few hired foremen to take care of supervision on the shopfloor, or alternatively an independent contractor who would be responsible for certain parts of the production process and at the same time for supervision of these workers. These contractor arrangements represented a kind of "system of co-exploitation." There were very few hired managers (cf. Clawson 1980).

Inside the factories, workers were kept under strict control by means of both economic and non-economic sanctions. There were considerable differences in how different worker groups were treated: craftsmen were given a much better treatment than unskilled labourers, who were usually women and children. The concept that is best suited to describe the type of management strategy applied in the early days of industrialism is that of direct control. In other words, the workers were controlled personally, either by the owner of the company or by the contractor who had hired the workers. The emergence of modern manufacturing industry and management is discussed in a number of studies (e. g. Chandler 1977; Chandler and Daems 1980; Clawson 1980; Marglin 1974; Marx 1977).

With the expansion of production and technological development, the capitalist had to make certain organizational and administrative changes. In addition, the bourgeois state became a major influence in labour relations as legislation on employment relations began to increase in the early 19th century. There were a number of revolutionary technological innovations such as the conveyer belt, which was first introduced in the textile industry in the mid-19th century, and these had a significant effect on the size of factory units. One single factory could have a payroll of several thousand workers. These changes meant that the owner-manager was no longer capable of running his factory on his own: he needed to hire managers who would share his responsibilities. Consequently, company organizations became far more complicated. The original capitalist enterprise, in which the owner-manager had sole control and power over the company, was beginning to hinder development and the expansion of production. In order to ensure continued growth of capitalist production, it was necessary to separate ownership from management (cf. Clegg et al. 1986: 104).

Scientific management was the first influential theory of management in capitalism. Harry Braverman has described Taylorism as an explicit verbalization of capitalism (Braverman 1974: 86). From the point of view of social development, Taylorism was closely bound up with the rapid growth of markets for mass-produced consumer goods in the United States, and especially with the growth of the automobile industry.

Big factories, increasingly complex production machineries, and expanding management were the key factors that shaped the factory organization as it entered the present century. At the top there was still the owner-manager, but below him he had engineer-managers who were responsible for the company's technological development and for supervising the foremen. There was no strict division of labour in company management: the same managers would take care of supervising production and the workers and also of marketing. In the class structure, these changes had many important consequences. Most importantly, the wage-labouring middle class was born.

The growth of the wage-labouring middle class – a process which is still continuing today – first became a burning social issue in Germany. Val Burris has analysed the emergence of the new middle class and the theoretical debate which has been going on around the new middle class in a recent article (Burris 1986). It was also in Germany, more specifically in the Republic of Weimar, where the question of the new middle class was first taken up as an important question of class theory, where, Marxist scholars and politicians entered a heated debate about the class position of the new category of salaried employees and about their social identification (Burris 1986: 324–331).

In the early 20th century the expansion of industrial production, the considerable growth of company size, and economic monopolization finally put an end to the system of combined ownership and management. In all large companies the organization of production and the supervision of labour was now the responsibility of hired managers. The manager-owner withdrew from the actual production process into the role of owner.

The highly fragmented production system which was developed at the Ford factories may be regarded as representing the beginning of a completely new stage in the organization of production and management. The aim was to reach maximum productivity through the standardization of production and technical and bureaucratic supervision of labour. Technical control had many advantages compared with the previous systems. The supervision of workers engaged in line production was far simpler: the conveyer belt itself became an immediate supervisor, which also meant that manning in supervision could be reduced. At the same time, it was possible centrally to adjust and control the pace of work in the whole factory (Edwards 1979: 113–123).

Raija Julkunen (1987) has dealt extensively with Taylorism and Fordism in her study of new forms of work organization. According to Julkunen, there is a specific Taylorist-Fordist strategy of supervision in which the control and supervision exercised by company management becomes more efficient throughout the production process at least on the following dimensions:

(1) the time-space dimension of the work process – this makes it possible to intensify work and to control the flow of the work process more efficiently;

(2) the wage-performance relationship – the output produced by workers can be increased without a corresponding increase in payroll expenses;

(3) the qualifications required by the work process – company-specific skills and qualifications mean an increasingly homogeneous labour force, which further strengthens the power and control of management;

(4) worker resistance becomes less significant because rising wages and increased consumption are conducive to social harmony (Julkunen 1987: 95–98).

These characteristics of Taylorism-Fordism made it in certain fields of production far superior to earlier forms and methods of work organization.

In the 1930s it was widely believed, especially in the United States, that the new method of technological control could solve the whole problem of labour supervision. However, this was not what happened. The methods so well-suited to controlling labour in the manufacturing industry were in fact not at all applicable to part of industrial production, the growing public sector, or to various service industries.

In bureaucratic control, the emphasis is on the social and organizational structure of work. Its methods include the forming of closely defined work categories, rules, career procedures, discipline, wage systems, definitions of responsibilities, etc. (Edwards 1979: 130). Bureaucratic control was therefore a way of institutionalizing hierarchic use of power in organizations. It did not replace technical supervision, but appeared as a complementary form of control. It is widely used, especially in the public sector.

2. Control of the Labour Process

According to Andrew Friedman (1977), there are two widely used forms of organizational control in contemporary capitalism:

(1) direct control (technical control), where the aim is to control the workers by Taylorist methods; and

(2) responsible autonomy, where the aim is to integrate the workers to the company's goals by giving them independence and by encouraging them to adapt to possible changes at work and in work organization; the main methods in this strategy are giving rewards, status, responsibility, etc. (Friedman 1977: 6–7).

Company management will adopt one of these two strategies depending on the strength of the resistance presented by the workers. If there is an organized and powerful resistance, the latter method will be used, but when the workers are weak, the method of direct control will be applied.

In contrast, Edwards has argued that the most commonly used method of control in modern companies is bureaucratic control (Edwards 1979: 141–142). The primary purpose of this strategy is to prevent the trade union from influencing the workers and to integrate them to the company's/organization's objectives. Bureaucratic control has meant a very clear stratification of workforces within individual companies and also a significant increase in the number of foremen and supervisors relative to the number of workers. In this model the company's line organization remains unaffected but its content changes. The performance of subordinates is subjected to constant and systematic evaluation. Foremen receive their instructions for evaluation in writing. Positive sanctions are also applied to influence the workers' behaviour.

Friedman and Edwards draw our attention to important aspects of labour control in contemporary capitalism. However, both give too much emphasis to the predominance of one single form of control, because in practice companies apply several different strategies at the same time. Also, both writers fail to take into account one important economic sanction inherent in capitalism: the need to sell one's labour power in order to reproduce it, which in itself is a highly efficient method of labour control. In the assessment of the resistance represented by the working class, one should pay more attention than Friedman does to the variations between different countries in political organization and in political conjunctures. Compared with Britain or Holland, for example, where unionization levels are around 50% and 30% respectively, the role of the trade union movement is surely quite different in countries like Finland, where over 80% of the workers are members of the union.

Andrew Friedman has pursued further the debate on managerial strategies, responding to the criticism presented against his theory and elaborating it (Friedman 1986). He writes: "perhaps the most important criticism has been the charge that too much rests on a simple dichotomy. Management groups rarely pursue 'pure' strategies." He presents a concrete example to specify his description of the tasks of management and defends his own position regarding the control of labour.

Julkunen criticizes Friedman and Edwards for their too heavy emphasis on the function of control in management: work process theorists, she argues, tend to identify organization of work with control strategy. However, the control of labour is not central to the company's operations. A far more important role is played by the management's decisions concerning production strategies and production technology; their decisions regarding the use of labour power are secondary. According to Julkunen, the use of labour power lacks all the distinctive marks of strategy. In the theory of work process, company management is assigned a rationality it does not possess (Julkunen 1987: 194–200).

The case has been made by various writers that in capitalism we can find a distinct, uniform doctrine or theory of control. This is not true. At the different stages of capitalism owners and managers have adopted different strategies in controlling production and labour; the conditions of control have been different at the different stages of development. Companies have also adjusted the work process according to the markets and their market strategies, and made changes in the work organization depending on the type of production technology. In international comparisons we can see several differences in how labour power is utilized, yet in the research these have been almost completely ignored. Most of the studies have been carried out in the United States, but the results are often considered applicable to the entire capitalist system. Furthermore, the work process debate has paid far from sufficient attention to the economic and political conjunctures prevalent at different stages of social development.

The case of Japan has received a great deal of attention in the recent debate on work organization. "Japanization" has been proposed as a new alternative to organizing work and to controlling the work process. This strategy is understood as consisting of at least the following elements:

(1) the dualization of the company's internal labour markets;

(2) the creation of company-specific interest representation systems (or the abolishment of national collective bargaining); and

(3) establishing direct contacts between company management and workers (leaving the trade union movement out of negotiations) (Julkunen 1987: 360, 367).

3. Managers and the Class Structure

Managers form a wage-earner category who hold a large part of the decision-making authority in each company or organization. The managerial question is central to the debate on the new middle classes, the new petty bourgeoisie, or contradictory class locations. Different theories have applied different criteria to slot managers in different class groups.

Nicos Poulantzas holds that managers belong either to the bourgeoisie or to the new petty bourgeoisie, depending on the extent to which they have economic or ideological dominance (Poulantzas 1975). He categorizes actual business managers and leading officials in public administration in the bourgeoisie, because they make important economic decisions and are responsible for the reproduction of the bourgeoisie's ideological dominance. Nevertheless, the majority of managers are new petty bourgeoisie.

In his study of the economic identification of the new middle class, Carchedi makes an important distinction according to whether labour power bears the functions of the collective worker or the functions of global capital. Of the basic classes, the proletariat bears the functions of the collective worker, and the bourgeoisie the functions of global capital. The wage earners who bear both functions simultaneously are classified as belonging to the new middle class (Carchedi 1975). The majority of managers meet these criteria. Carchedi believes that the new middle classes are becoming increasingly proletarianized. By this, he does not mean to say that their living conditions are becoming worse, but that in their work the functions of the collective worker are increasingly taking over from the functions of global capital.

Projekt Klassenanalyse (PKA 1973) places managers into two categories depending on who they are employed by: either in the category of wage workers of capital, or in the middle class who are paid by derived income. In addition, PKA holds that the middle class includes all state employees regardless of their position or tasks in the respective organization. Managers belong for the most part to the class of unproductive wage workers of capital, but some of them are also classified as productive workers, or as aggregated personnel: these are involved in management, planning, and control. PKA's theory is a comprehensive attempt to describe the connections of class structure and class consciousness. Its main contribution to class theory is its detailed analysis of the internal differentiation of wage workers. The basic criterion for class dividions in PKA is derived from the economic structure of the social formation: the form of income. Nevertheless, there are significant further divisions both within the wage workers of capital and within the middle class. As far as its analysis of managers is concerned, there are a number of problems in PKA's theory. Although all members of the middle class share the same form of income, this class does not represent a uniform category: on the basis of autonomy and dominance, one can identify several subcategories. Similarly, the group of unproductive workers is internally differentiated according to these same criteria. Secondly, the theory fails to pay any attention to the implications of the different tasks in which aggregated personnel are engaged.

The Soviet scholar Valentin Peschanski has argued in his article on middle managers (Peschanski 1985) that this group of company workers represents part of the wage-working middle strata. According to Peschanski, these strata are very heterogeneous. They have no common social and economic basis, and they also differ in terms of their relationship to the means of production. In addition, they differ in terms of their position in social reproduction (Peschanski 1985: 245). Therefore the middle strata should not be regarded as constituting a uniform middle class. Middle managers in companies form one such middle stratum in the class structure of modern capitalism because of their dual position in capitalist reproduction.

Abercrombie and Urry (1983) have made a significant contribution to the debate on the new middle classes. They argue that wage earners can be divided into three main categories: the working class, the deskilled white-collar workers, and the service class. In structural terms, deskilled white-collar workers belong to the working class. In functional terms, the members of this class are unproductive workers who take part in the execution, control, and reproduction of the work process.

The service class differs from the rest of the middle class in that it is responsible for the conceptual execution of the work process and for its control and reproduction. In contradistinction to the deskilled white-collar workers, it is characterized by the unity of its tasks and class position. The service class is not undergoing a process of proletarianization. It has specific causal powers, which distinguish it from the proletarianizing groups. Also, the interests of the service class differ from those of other wage workers: among these are the emphasis of the role of training and education, ensuring that their share of GDP in the reproduction sector is as high as possible, and fostering professionalism.

Abercrombie and Urry's study has many merits but it may also be criticized for placing too much emphasis on the British case. Many of the generalizations they propose do not apply to the Nordic countries, for example. A more serious shortcoming is that their analysis of the state remains somewhat superficial.

Above I have briefly introduced some studies and theories on the new middle class. These, however, represent only a fraction of the debate which is now gathering momentum all over the world (see e. g. Carter 1985; Clegg et al. 1986; Johnson et al. 1982).

4. Wright and the New Middle Classes

Erik Olin Wright's theory of the class structure of capitalist society is perhaps the most influential contribution to class analysis during the last decade (Wright 1978). Wright has taken certain criticisms against his class theory so seriously that he has revised his concept in some very essential respects, and in fact created a whole new theory (Wright 1985). He does not discard the notion that different class criteria may apply to the same class locations, but his theory of the actual criteria is now different. The concept he employs to characterize the essence of contradictory class locations is that of exploitation. He states that the old theory was based solely on an analysis of domination relations, whereas the concept of exploitation was not involved in it except in rhetorical references. The reason why Wright considers it important to take exploitation under careful theoretical analysis is that it provides an objective basis for studying the connections or compatibility of class position and interests. This new perspective to classes is to a great extent based on John E. Roemer's game theoretical analysis of forms of exploitation (Roemer 1982).

Wright's new class theory is a bold attempt to overcome certain central problems of class analysis. He does not hesitate to reject his earlier systematics, nor to include his views on the foundations of the theory of history in his elaborations of class theory. Wright's new theoretical position has inspired a lively debate and many criticisms from a number of different angles (cf. Carchedi 1986; Giddens 1985; Kivinen 1986; Rasmussen 1985; Rose and Marshall 1986). Below are the main counterarguments that the theory has evoked within the Finnish Class Project.

(1) Wright argues that his new theory of contradictory class locations is not confined to capitalism, but moves within a broader framework of the theory of history. When constructing his theory through a conceptualization of the mode of production and the forms of exploitation that go with it, he fails to consider the problems connected with the relationship between the theory of history and the theory of capitalism.

(2) Wright makes no distinction between exploitation and repression. He does not consider the question of how the repression implied by class relations manifests itself in the structuration of class situations. The entire problematics of the structuration of class situation collapses into a comparison of incomes.

Table 1. Class Structure of the USA, Great Britain, Sweden and Finland

	USA	GB	Swe	Fin
self-employed	15	13	11	21
expert managers	4	6	4	4
semi-credentialled managers	6	7	4	6
uncredentialled managers	2	3	3	3
expert supervisors	4	2	4	1
semi-credentialled supervisors	7	4	3	1
uncredentialled supervisors	7	3	3	3
expert non-managers	3	4	7	4
semi-credentialled workers	12	14	18	17
proletarians	40	43	44	41

Sources: for USA and Sweden, Wright 1985; for Great Britain, Marshall 1987; and for Finland, Kivinen 1986.

(3) The replacement of the problematic class criterion of autonomy by professional akills leads to new problems of vagueness (see Blom and Kivinen 1987; Finnish Class Project 1985).

Table 1 describes the class structures of the United States, Great Britain, Sweden and Finland according to Wright's new theory. The most significant differences occur in the proportions of the categories of self-employed and supervisors. By contrast, in the category of managers there are no major differences between the four countries. Compared with the old theory, the working class is now substantially smaller.

5. Job Autonomy and Class Theory

Markuu Kivinen attempts in his recent study *Parempien piirien ihmisiä* (People who move in better circles) to develop a theory on the new middle classes (Kivinen 1986). He starts from a critique of Erik Wright's ideas on contradictory class locations. Kivinen's conclusion is that a relevant analysis and accurate class criteria can only be produced by concentrating on combinations of different forms of mental labour (types of autonomy) and domination relations.

The theoretical background of Kivinen's attempt lies, first, as mentioned, in a critique of Wright (Finnish Class Project 1985); second, in studies on the theory of the labour process; and third, in studies on the theory of civil society. Kivinen applies in his own analysis the research strategy of "successive cycles" proposed by the project (Finnish Class Project 1985: 41). Therefore, he is concerned not only with the question of class structure, but also with the structuration of the class situation of the new middle class and with the consciousness of this class. In his analysis Kivinen focuses particularly on different types of autonomy. He is also concerned with the relationship between autonomy and managerial position as a criterion of class structure. Kivinen does not accept semi-autonomous employees as an independent class group. Similarly, he argues that wage earners in managerial positions do not form a coherent class group. The answer, he says, lies in the relationship between autonomy and managerial position, as examined within the totality of class relations.

Kivinen crystallizes the main result of his study in the following theses:

The core of the new middle classes is composed of those who represent professional, capital-adequate and scientific-technical types of autonomy, irrespective of their managerial functions, and those who have managerial functions in office work. Those in performance-level office work with some degree of autonomy, as well as craftsmen, careworkers and workers in small enterprises who do have autonomy, form a group of contradictory class locations which fall in the middle ground between the core of the new middle classes and the working class. In the class situation of these groups, we can detect features which are characteristic of both the core of the new middle classes and the working class. Finally, within these types of autonomy, those in managerial positions come closer to the core of the new middle class (Kivinen 1986: 248).

The breakdown presented in Table 2 illustrates in detail this class structure typology.

Table 2. Class Position of Wage Earners (%)

	USA	Swe	Nor	Can	Fin
core of new middle classes	24	18	27	27	20
marginal groups of new middle classes	19	22	20	18	31
working class	57	60	53	56	49

The core of the new middle classes includes one fourth of all wage earners, and more or less the same amount belong to the marginal groups of the middle class. Half of the wage earners are thus classified as working-class.

Wright needed the criterion of job autonomy only to slot non-managerial workers into place. In contrast, Kivinen holds that a theory of the new middle classes cannot be based on the view that mental (autonomous) labour forms a residual criterion which is relevant only in the case of non-managerial wage earners. Rather, one must investigate the way in which managerial position and different forms of mental work are combined as class criteria.

Kivinen's analysis of the consciousness of the new middle classes leads to a surprising result. He argues that the label of contradictory consciousness can only be applied to the working class and to the marginal groups of the new middle class, whereas among core groups there are no signs of experiences of exploitation or subordination. According to Kivinen, the core of the new middle classes differs from other wage worker groups in that its consciousness is not marked by contradictions based on the wage worker's character mask.

The theory presented by Kivinen on the core and marginal groups of the new middle classes is an important step forward in research on the internal differentiation of wage earners. However, there are also a number of problems:

(1) Kivinen bases his conception on the connections that exist between different features of mental labour and domination relations. This, as such, is a perfectly plausible argument. The problem is that in practice, Kivinen identifies mental labour with autonomy and more specifically with the aspects of job autonomy that the Finnish Class Project has seized upon in its analysis. However, all the different moments of mental labour cannot be identified only through job autonomy.

(2) The theoretical concepts that Kivinen employs are at the same time the key concepts of his survey analysis.

(3) Kivinen holds that the core of the new middle class is not in a contradictory location. As far as the consciousness of the new middle classes is concerned, this

argument is tenable, but it is not so from the point of view of the class's formal position. As a whole Kivinen's results do not in my opinion provide sufficient evidence to refute Wright's central theses concerning contradictory class locations.

(4) It is necessary to analyse in greater detail the position of the new middle classes in the class structure and in the totality of class relations. Kivinen's definition of the marginal groups of the new middle classes rests heavily on distinctions in autonomy. However, in this context the use of autonomy as a criterion is not adequate because at the level of class situation the marginal groups of the new middle classes differ only very little from the working class.

6. Managers and Social Classes

The remaining part of this chapter is concerned to describe some empirical results of the comparative class project, particularly those relating to the organization of management tasks and to the organizational decision-making authority of managers. The following describes the use of organizational power at two levels. We shall first look at the supervisory authority of managers (i. e. over the labour of subordinates), and then present a comparative analysis of managers' decision-making authority in matters concerning the entire organization.

There are marked differences between the six focal countries in the relative proportions of managers and non-managerial workers in the total labour force. In this regard there is no consistent pattern of work organization across advanced capitalist countries.

Table 3. Managers and Workers in Six Countries (%)

	Managers	Workers
USA	55	45
Canada	47	53
Great Britain	41	59
Norway	43	57
Sweden	41	59
Finland	34	66

The proportion of managers is highest in the United States, where more than half of the active labour force is engaged in other than shopfloor or performance-level jobs. The figure is lowest in Finland, where only one third of all wage earners are classified as managerial. Canada ranks second in this comparison, whereas Great Britain, Norway, and Sweden form an in-between group with an average 40% of the labour force engaged in managerial tasks.

In all countries there is a clear bias in favour of men in the gender composition of managers.

Table 4. Managers by Gender (%)

	Men	Women
USA	58	42
Canada	63	37
Great Britain	67	33
Norway	70	30
Sweden	62	38
Finland	59	41

The proportion of male managers is highest in Norway, with 70% of all managers representing the male sex. The proportion of women is highest in Finland, but only by one per cent over the United States. In Canada, Sweden, and Great Britain, men represent about two thirds of all managers.

However, the comparison presented in Table 4 does not tell the whole truth about the gendered division of labour in these countries. Firstly, the proportion of women in the total active labour force is at a far higher level in the Nordic countries, which should obviously also be reflected in their relative share of managers. Secondly, American and Canadian employers tend to pursue a strategy whereby at least nominal authority is given to a large number of occupational groups, and this means that the proportion of what may be described as "nominal managers" is higher in these countries. We may assume then that a large part of women occupying managerial positions in the US and Canada would not qualify as managers in the Nordic countries. These questions are discussed in greater detail by Erik Olin Wright and Göran Ahrne in their comparative study of the American and Swedish class structures (Ahrne and Wright 1983).

Our data on supervisory authority describes organizational decision making on two dimensions: first, to what extent do managers participate in decision making on work tasks, working methods, and pace of work, and second, to what extent do they have decision-making authority with regard to disciplining, rewarding, warning, and dismissing their subordinates.

The sample of managers included in the comparative material is rather heterogeneous and ranges from top executives of large corporations to foremen responsible for shopfloor supervision. In the case of task supervision (work tasks, working methods, and pace of work), all managers have considerable decision making authority, although there are some minor differences between the countries concerned: Swedish managers tend to have more task authority than others, whereas in Finland managers have least decision-making authority on this dimension.

By contrast, individual wage earners occupying managerial positions do not have very much authority to sanction: only a relatively small number can decide

Table 5. Supervisory Authority of Managers

	USA	Can	GB	Nor	Swe	Fin
Decides on						
– work tasks	78	83	82	78	87	78
– work methods	69	69	65	69	77	72
– pace of work	60	64	64	49	62	53
Has influence on discipline/rewards	48	37	38	27	39	40
– final decision lies with higher management	76	54	78	78	88	52
Can prevent rise in wages or promotion	63	49	–	43	44	39
– final decision lies with higher management	71	53	–	70	79	47
Has influence on dismissing workers	50	44	54	28	31	36
– final decision lies with higher management	67	52	80	64	94	34
Has influence on giving warnings	63	61	63	59	57	48
– final decision lies with higher management	62	49	74	45	81	31

on their subordinates' wages, promotions, or discipline. In addition, the final decision in these cases is usually made by the respondent's own superior. American managers tend to have more authority here than their Nordic colleagues.

In all countries male managers have more supervisory authority than female managers. In particular, the authority of Swedish and Norwegian male managers to sanction is considerably greater than that of their female colleagues.

The wage earners investigated in the comparative study were asked whether they took part in decision making concerning the workplace in general, the products and services produced, the amount of work, working methods, budgeting, etc. There are clear differences between the six countries in what we call organizational decision making.

In Finland, more than four fifths of the managers reported that they could influence decision making in matters concerning the workplace in general. In the United States the figure was 60%, in Canada 62%, and in Great Britain and Sweden 70%. In Norway, two thirds of the managers are involved in company decision making. Again there are clear differences between the sexes: a far larger number of male managers participate in decision making. The difference between men and women is greatest in Norway, where some 70% of the male managers have decision making authority in these questions, whereas with women the figure is 60%. Sweden comes closest to full gender equality, with 70% of the male managers and 66% of the female managers involved in company decision making.

Table 6 cescribes the participation of managers in the six countries concerned in organizational decision making. The main finding here is that Nordic managers have greater authority than managers in the United States, Canada, and Great Britain.

In Finland, 80% of the managers decide on staff numbers employed by the company, in the United States only 41%; the other four countries fall in between. Around 60% of the managers in Canada and 80% of the managers in Great

Table 6. Organizational Power of Managers

	USA	Swe	Nor	Can	Fin	GB
Takes part in decision-making at workplace	60	69	66	62	83	70
Has influence on						
– staff number	41	71	66	45	80	70
– products/services	62	74	70	59	78	79
– work routines/amount of work	63	74	69	62	85	54
– working techniques	62	74	75	62	85	54
– company budget	52	77	52	66	57	48
– resource allocation	56	91	58	72	67	60

Britain take part in decision making concerning products or services produced. On this dimension of organizational decision making the Nordic countries come close to Great Britain, while the situation in the United States is rather similar to that in Canada. On the whole, however, there seem to be clear differences between the six countries as far as organizational decision making is concerned. The greatest differences occur in authority over allocation of budget resources. In Sweden more than 90% of the managers decide on resource allocation in comparison with only 56% in the United States.

Another concern of the comparative project was to find out in what ways or through what channels managers take part in decision making. That is, do they make their decisions independently or as part of some decision-making organ; are they required to submit their decision to their own superiors; or do they merely give advice to those responsible for the final decision? Once again we find clear gender differences, with male managers usually deciding on matters on their own and women acting as advisors.

Summing up the foregoing analysis, we may conclude that in the Nordic countries managers tend to have greater organizational authority than their colleagues in the United States, Canada, and Great Britain; this also applies to the channels of decision making. On the other hand, managers working in North America usually have more supervisory authority than Nordic managers.

A major concern in our comparisons of work organization was with the social division of labour and the development of labour markets in advanced capitalism in general. That is, we wanted to find out whether the recent structural changes in advanced capitalist societies are creating a work organization that is common to all these countries, or whether work organizations develop independently of these universal processes.

Our results suggest that capitalist economies continue to differ from each other in significant respects. At the same time, there would also seem to be a certain tendency towards uniformity, but this appears to be restricted to geographical regions: on the one hand, there are many similarities between the United States and Canada, on the other hand, the Nordic countries have rather similar work organizations. This same pattern has earlier been discovered in the cases of class structure and industrial structure as well (Black and Myles 1987; Julkunen 1986).

In the United States and Canada, the proportion of wage earners occupying managerial positions is far greater than in the Nordic countries. On the other hand, North American managers tend to have less decision-making authority in matters concerning the workplace. American and Canadian managers have subordinates more often than their Nordic colleagues, but these have a larger number of subordinates to supervise. In the Nordic countries wage earners who occupy managerial positions have considerable decision-making authority within their work community.

In an earlier context (Luokkaprojekti 1984: 85–86) I have presented a more detailed analysis of the internal differentiation of managerial wage earners with regard to participation in organizational decision making. Here, a distinction is proposed between three types of managers according to how much influence they have in important decisions concerning the organization or the company:

(1) Decision making or top managers decide alone or as a member of a group on investments, the use of the means of production, and the use of labour power.

(2) Task managers or middle managers decide on the use of the means of production and labour power, or only on the use of money capital.

(3) Nominal or lower managers decide either on the use of the means of production of on the use of labour power.

These distinctions provide a helpful basis for analysing the internal differentiation of managers. We no longer need to rely only on the wage earner's formal position in the organization or his formal participation in the decision-making process; the main criterion is now provided by real decision-making authority in questions which are of consequence to the organization or the company.

In the following comparisons I shall first consider involvement in decision making concerning the workplace. The focus is on wage earners who have organizational decision making authority, i. e. managers who decide on numbers of workforce, products or services produced, and resource allocation within the company budget.

Table 7. Decision-Makers by Country (% of Wage Earners)

USA	33
Canada	26
Norway	28
Sweden	30
Finland	28
Average	29

The proportion of decision makers is highest in the United States, but on the whole the differences between the six countries are not very significant. However, the figures in Table 7 clearly contradict our earlier argument that there is a distinctly North American and a Nordic pattern of work organization, in that the proportion of decision makers is lowest in Canada.

Examined at the societal level, decision making in the work organization may be of two basic types: centralized or decentralized. The growth of the number of managerial wage earners over the past twenty years has not necessarily resulted in a more decentralized decision-making process in capitalist companies and organizations.

Table 8. Wage Earners by Types of Managers (% of Wage Earners)

	USA	Can	Nor	Swe	Fin
top managers	4	3	6	4	7
middle managers	6	6	9	6	9
lower managers	19	14	11	14	11
non-managerial	71	77	74	76	73

If we divide managers or decision makers into the three types outlined above – top, middle, and lower managers – and then examine their relative proportions in different countries, we can get a clearer picture of the social division of labour.

The proportion of top managers is highest in the Nordic countries, especially in Norway and Finland. Similarly, there are more task or middle managers in the Nordic countries than in North America. On the other hand, the proportion of nominal or lower managers is highest in North America, particularly in the United States. Organizational decision-making authority is thus most centralized in Finland and Norway, and most decentralized in the United States.

Table 9. Internal Differentiation of Decision-Makers (%)

	USA	Can	Nor	Swe	Fin
top managers	13	12	24	17	24
middle managers	17	26	34	25	34
lower managers	70	62	42	58	42

One quarter of the managers in Finland and Norway classify as top managers; roughly one third are task managers. In the United States and Canada about 10% are top managers. Less than one fifth of all managers in the US are middle managers, in Canada middle managers represent two thirds of all managerial wage earners. Nominal managers represent over two thirds of all managers in the US and slightly less than two thirds in Canada. Here we find that the internal differentiation of managers differs very clearly between the Nordic countries and North America. In the former, decision making authority is to a great extent centralized, and the number of nominal managers is significantly lower than in the United States and Canada.

Certain countries involved in the comparative class project have also produced data on the employment of managers in different sectors of the economy. Here,

Table 10. Managers by Economic Sectors (%)

	USA	Canada	Norway	Sweden	Finland
private	64.6	–	52.1	48.6	51.4
public	23.8	–	44.0	45.3	46.6
other	11.8	–	3.9	6.2	1.9
Top managers in public sector					
	25	–	35	39	29

too, there are some very marked differences between the Nordic countries and the United States. In the Nordic countries, roughly half of all managers are employed in the private sector, in the United States more than two thirds; the respective proportions for the public sector are slightly less than half and less than one quarter. In the group of top managers, 40% of Sweden's managers, 35% of Norway's, and about 30% of Finland's are employed in the public sector; in the US about one quarter of all top managers earn their living in the public sector.

There are also other significant differences between Nordic and North American managers. Nordic managers have a wage-earner background more often than their American counterparts. Also, a smaller number of Nordic managers have been self-employed at some time during their work career than managers in the United States and Canada. In the US more than one quarter of all managers have worked as independent entrepreneurs; in Canada about one quarter; in Sweden less than one fifth; in Norway one in ten; and in Finland only 6%. There is also a greater willingness among North American managers to become self-employed: both in the United States and in Canada, more than half of the top, middle, and lower managers would want to have their own company.

Additionally, large numbers of non-managerial wage earners in North America would want to be self-employed. In the Nordic countries and especially in Norway, wage earners are less keen on the idea. In the group of top managers,

Table 11. Self-Employment in Managerial Groups (%)
Ever been self-employed (%)

	USA	Canada	Norway	Sweden	Finland
top managers	26	24	12	17	6
middle managers	17	17	8	12	7
lower managers	19	14	8	5	8
non-managerial	13	12	7	7	6

Willingness to be self-employed (%)

	USA	Canada	Norway	Sweden	Finland
top managers	59	55	21	44	37
middle managers	73	51	19	43	31
lower managers	58	54	24	37	36
non-managerial	53	49	18	36	24

only one fifth would want to be self-employed. In Finland about one third and in Sweden about 40% of the managers would want to work for themselves.

The position of managerial wage earners on the job market is more secure in the Nordic countries. For example, there are marked differences between the Nordic countries and North America in terms of how often managers have been unemployed: experiences of unemployment are much more common in North America.

Table 12. Trade Union Membership in Managerial Groups (%)

	USA	Canada	Norway	Sweden	Finland
top managers	9	16	57	66	51
middle managers	7	28	64	67	79
lower managers	14	32	67	80	80
non-managerial	19	36	62	81	81

The strong wage-earner identity of Nordic managers is also reflected in their high level of unionization (see Melin 1988). In Sweden, nine in ten wage earners are union members, and among managers unionization levels are also extremely high: two thirds of all top managers are members, and among middle and lower managers the proportion is even higher. In Finland and Norway managerial unionization is at a slightly lower level, particularly among top managers, but nevertheless even they are far ahead of the United States and Canada. In the US, less than 10% of top managers are union members, in middle managers the figure is 7%, and in lower managers 14%; in Canada the figures are slightly higher.

7. Summary of Comparisons

Our foregoing analyses of managers and the organization of managerial tasks in six advanced capitalist countries are summarized in Table 13. The most important finding is that the organization of management differs not only between individual countries, but also and above all between two main groups of countries: North America (the United States and Canada) and the Nordic countries (Norway, Finland, and Sweden). Great Britain would seem to fall somewhere in between these two groups.

The organization of managerial tasks in the six countries concerned may be summarized as follows:

United States: In the United States there are more wage earners occupying managerial positions than in any other country. There is also a high number of wage earners who are directly involved in company decision making. Decision making is decentralized in that there is a lower number of top managers than in

Table 13. Summary of Comparisons

	Decision-makers	Top managers	Middle managers	Sanction authority	Organizational authority	Wage worker career	Trade union membership
USA	+	−	+	+	−	−	−
Canada	−	−	+	+	−	−	−
Norway	−	+	−	−	+	+	+
Sweden	+	−	+	−	+	+	+
Finland	−	+	−	−	+	+	+
GB	−		+	+	+	+	+ −

the Nordic countries. There are many nominal managers. Managers tend to have considerable authority to sanction their subordinates, but they have less decision-making authority in matters relating to the organization than their Nordic counterparts. Managers have a wage-earner background less often than in the Nordic countries. A far higher proportion of American managers have been self-employed. Finally, unionization levels are very low.

Canada: In Canada there are fewer decision makers than in the United States. Management in general is decentralized in much the same way as in the United States. Canadian managers also have considerable authority to sanction their subordinates, but little organizational decision-making authority. The work career of Canadian managers is very similar to that of their American colleagues: there are many who have been self-employed, and unionization levels are low. On the whole, Canada and the United States resemble each other in several respects. These results support the earlier findings that have been presented within the comparative project (cf. Black and Myles 1987; Julkunen 1986).

Norway: In Norway there are fewer decision makers than in North America. Managerial tasks are to a great extent centralized; there is a comparatively large number of top managers and relatively few nominal managers. Managers do not have very much sanctioning authority, but on the other hand they have more organizational decision-making authority than North American managers. Managers typically have a wage-earner background. Relatively few have been self-employed, nor is there very much willingness among managers to become self-employed. Unionization levels are high.

Sweden: In Sweden there are more decision makers than in the other Nordic countries, but less than in North America. Management is organized in a more decentralized way than in the other Nordic countries: there are fewer top managers and more nominal managers than in Norway and Finland. In terms of sanctioning authority, Swedish managers have less control than their American colleagues, but on the other hand they have more organizational decision-making authority. Swedish managers have a strong wage-earners identity: large numbers have a wage-earner background, and unionization levels are extremely high.

Finland: The relative proportion of wage earners occupying managerial positions is lowest in Finland. Management in general is highly centralized. Together with Norway, Finland has the highest proportion of top managers and the lowest proportion of nominal managers. Managers tend to have less supervisory authority than in the other countries, but more organizational decision making authority. Finnish managers have a wage-earner background, and large numbers are union members.

Great Britain: Great Britain has less managers than the average for the countries included in this comparison. As yet we do not have access to data on the internal differentiation of managerial types in Britain. In the same way as their American colleagues, British managers have a high degree of sanctioning authority; on the other hand, they also have considerable organizational decision making authority. In this respect Great Britain differs both from the Nordic countries and from North America: managers have a high degree of authority on both these dimensions. Managers typically have a wage-earner career, and their unionization level is lower than in the Nordic countries but higher than in North America.

8. Conclusions

The first preliminary results of the international comparative project clearly indicate that there are significant differences between advanced capitalist countries in terms of the social division of labour, in the social position of managers, and in the consciousness of managers. The common argument that there is emerging a uniform work organization typical of all capitalist economies is therefore obviously exaggerated.

In this particular case we found marked differences between the North American and the Nordic work organization. The relationship of managers to society and to social forces has a completely different background: in the Nordic countries managers are more often employed in the public sector of the economy and more often have a wage-earner background than their American or Canadian colleagues.

References

Abercrombie, N. and J. Urry, *Capital, Labour and the Middle Classes.* London: 1983
Ahrne, G. and E. O. Wright, *Classes in the United States and Sweden.* Wisconsin: 1983

Black, D. and J. Miles, Dependent Industrialization and the Canadian Class Structure. *The Comparative Project on Class Structure and Class Consciousness* in Tampere on 1.–3. April 1987. Tampere: 77–114. 1987

Blom, R. and M. Kivinen, The Relevance and Dimensions of Class Theory. Comparative Project on Class Structure and Class Consciousness. Working paper series 35, Madison: 1987

Braverman, H., *Labour and Monopoly Capital.* New York: 1974

Burris, V., The Discovery of the New Middle Class. *Theory and Society* 3: 317–349. 1986

Carchedi, G., On the Economic Identification of the New Middle Class, *Economy & Society* 4: 1–87. 1975

Carchedi, G., Two Models of Class Analysis. *Capital & Class* 29: 195–215. 1986

Carter, R., *Capitalism, Class Conflict and the New Middle Class.* London: 1985

Chandler, A. D., *The Visible Hand: The Managerial Revolution in American Business.* Cambridge, Mass. 1977

Chandler, A. D. and H. Daems, *Managerial Hierarchies.* Cambridge: 1980

Clawson, D., *Bureaucracy and the Labour Process.* New York: 1980

Clegg, S., P. Boreham, and G. Dow, *Class, Politics and the Economy.* London: 1986

Edwards, R., *Contested Terrain.* New York: 1979

Finnish Class Project, *The Reality of Social Classes in Finland.* Tampere: 1985

Friedman, A., *Industry and Labour.* London: 1977

Friedman, A., Developing the Managerial Strategies Approach to the Labour Process. *Capital & Class* 4: 97–124. 1986

Giddens, A., In Place of Emptiness. *New Society* 29: 383–384. 1985

Hill, S., *Competition and Control at Work.* London: 1981

Johnson, D., et al., *Class and Social Development.* Beverly Hills: 1982

Julkunen, R., *Kansankoti ja oravanpesä.* Tampere: 1986

Julkunen, R., *Työprosessi ja pitkät aallot.* Jyväskylä: 1987

Kivinen, M., *Parempien piirien ihmisiä* (People who move in better circles). Helsinki: 1986

Luokkaprojekti, *Suomalaiset luokkakuvassa.* Jyväskylä: 1984

Marglin, S., What Do Bosses Do? *Review of Radical Political Economics* 6: 60–112. 1974

Marshall, G., Classes in Britain: Marxist and Official (manuscript). 1987

Marx, K., *Capital.* Vol. 1. New York: 1977

Melin, H., The Differentiation of Managerial Functions in Contemporary Capitalism. Paper presented at the 12th Nordic conference of sociology. Stavanger: 1983

Melin, H., Classes and Trade Unions, in: G. Ahrne (ed.), *Classes and Organization in Nordic Countries.* Uppsala: 1988

Peschanski, V., Middle Managers in Contemporary Capitalism. *Acta Sociologica* 3: 243–255. 1985

Poulantzas, N., *Classes in Contemporary Capitalism.* London: 1975

Projekt Klassenanalyse, *Materialien zur Klassenstruktur der BRD I.* Westberlin. 1973

Rasmussen, F. D., Velfaerdstatens klasser. *Kurasje* 37: 88–105. 1985

Roemer, J. E., *A General Theory of Exploitation and Class.* Cambridge, Mass: 1982

Rose, D. and G. Marshall, Constructing the (W)right Classes. *Sociology* 3: 440–455. 1986

Wright, E. O., *Class, Crisis and the State*. London: 1978
Wright, E. O., *Classes*. London: 1985
Wright, E. O. et al., *Comparative Project on Class Structure and Class Consciousness.
  User's Guide for the Machine-Readable Data File*. Madison: 1987

Technical Workers: A Class and Organisational Analysis*

Chris Smith

1. Introduction

This paper examines the relationship between theories of the class situation of technical labour and national and organisational structuring of technical occupations. It suggests that a deficiency in class theories of technical workers of the last two decades has been a failure to appreciate the diverse meaning attached to "technical labour" within advanced capitalist countries. National diversity is compounded by variations in the way technical workers operate at the firm level, both of which affect the relationship between technical workers, capital and the manual working class. The paper argues that a grounded approach to the class situation of technical workers, which is sensitive to cultural and organisational variations, is a necessary corrective to the global approaches of the 1970s.

2. Explanations for the Growth of White-Collar Workers

Theories explaining the growth of white-collar workers divide broadly into Weberian and Marxist positions. Weberian analysis emphasizes the growth of bureaucratic modes of organisation and employment sustained by diversification of market relations, and changes in the structure of power from traditional authority to rational-legal calculations under capitalism. As bureaucratic methods of organisation inevitably penetrate all areas of life, employment of white-collar "experts" and routine support staff accelerates. The expansion of the state into civil society generates the need for more administrators, technocrats, co-ordinators and managers (Mills 1953). Within enterprises the separation of ownership from control – the emergence of "managerial capitalism" – promotes the need for managers and their specialized administrative and technical staff. Increases in size, complexity and technological scale of enterprises requires the employment of commercial, marketing and distribution functions which are characteristically white-collar in nature. Finally there is the growth of financial

* I am grateful for the comments of Peter Meiksins on an earlier draft of this paper.

and insurance services to support large-scale enterprises. While many of these "factors" are also mentioned by Marxist writers, the core of Weberian explanations lies in changes in power and market relations, which, for Marxists, are more the outcome or effects of changes in the structure and relations of the capitalist production process (Crompton and Gubbay 1977; Hyman 1983). The logic of bureaucratisation as a continuous process is evident either explicitly or implicitly within the Weberian perspective.

The central focus of Weber's class analysis concerns the view that market capacities or properties, be they capital, specialised knowledge or skills, provide the criteria for drawing the boundary between different classes. While this may appear more refined than Marx's attention to ownership and production relations, Weberians tend to fashion a very "fragmentary class structure" from this approach and one that does not correspond with the institutions of political and economic action within capitalism. Hyman (1983: 20) has shown how Marx saw the "fundamental weakness of any model of class based on purely market criteria, 'because of the infinite fragmentation of interest and rank into which the division of social labour splits labourers as well as capitalists and landlords.'" Marx went on to say that "'any attempt to relate class to the identity of revenues and sources of revenues would imply the existence of an *infinity of classes*'" [emphasis added]. This was indeed, the problem that confronted Weber who was forced into adopting conventional descriptive rankings of skilled, semi-skilled, and white-collar into his class analysis, to impose some order on the class structure.

More recent Weberian approaches to class have been more sophisticated, but equally prone to this loss of dynamic. Wright (1985), developing a theory of class based on market capacities, such as skill and credential knowledge as well as property, produces a highly fragmented "class map." He severs any sense of social action within the class structure and produces a distributive classification of 9 groups of wage labourers defined by the degree of possession of organisational and skill/assets, together with 3 classifications of owners. This approach is concerned with labour market segmentation rather than class relations and action.

For Marxist writers the expansion of white-collar workers has to be tied into the internal dynamics of the capitalist economy and the state. The accumulation process, the increasing pressures of competition, the growth in the scale of reproduction of labour power and the drive to increase labour productivity have all swelled the numbers of white-collar workers. Against the standard assumption that this growth challenges Marx's alleged views on the simplification and polarisation of the class structure between workers and capitalists, it is now more widely accepted that in both his early and mature writings, Marx identified the expansion of non-manual workers as a definite tendency within the system. Rattansi (1985: 653) suggests that Marx located the expansion of "middle class" groups in the "growth in the *total* mass of surplus value and profits" which supports an increasing number of unproductive groups in the system. According to this view their is an increase in office workers "involved in calculation, administration and sales" in realising, rather than producing surplus value and managers, created through the "endemic pressure towards concentration and centralisation of capital" who are the main non-manual groups responsible for co-ordination and control in the modern enterprise (Rattansi 1985: 643).

Interest in technical labour through a Marxist perspective has been through two traditions. The first, developed in the 1960s through the work of Mallet, Gorz and others associated with the *new working class* thesis. This suggested that modern industry created integrated production and an increasingly collectivised workforce divided occupationally, but not in terms of class, between technical and manual components. The second approach developed in the 1970s by structural writers, such as Braverman, Poulantzas and Carchedi, who argued that technical workers formed a fraction, not of the working class, but a new and expanding middle class. I shall briefly review the perspectives of these writers and then examine their consequences for conceptualising British technical workers.

3. The New Working Class Thesis

Orthodox Marxist writers suggested that as white-collar workers lack economic ownership and are formally dependent on wages like manual workers, then they should be regarded as members of the working class. Their minor status advantages and more secure employment conditions would, it was argued, be eroded as their numbers expanded. The universal consequences of employment concentration, rationalisation and deskilling would, in effect, *proletarianise* white-collar positions. An associated strand of this argument appeared in the 1960s and suggested that technical white-collar workers were not only increasingly joining the ranks of the working class, but becoming a vanguard section within it. French proponents of this model, especially Mallet (1975) and Gorz (1967), argued against the established Marxist view that cadres and other technical groupings should be treated as part of the new petty bourgeoisie because of their supervisory functions. Instead, they were part of the working class, albeit a working class which is increasingly internally differentiated.

At the centre of the *new working class* thesis was the belief that advances in technology, automation and process production, were reconstituting the skills and character of the collective labourer, breaking down barriers between white- and blue-collar work, and widening the contradiction between the forces and relations of production. The emergent unionisation and collectivisation of technical workers in France and Italy produced industrial struggles that seemed to challenge the narrow economic claims of traditional trade unionism. It was argued by Gorz that technical workers would increasingly demand control over production for themselves and manual workers, because their knowledge and abilities were unfulfilled by the narrow commercialism of profitable production. This was under-consumptionist economic theory applied to the class structure. It was argued by Mallet, that the *technological basis* of new industry demanded group working, firm specific skills, and these eroded the barriers between the collective worker. It was the clash between the increasingly socialised and collectivised nature of production and the authoritarian managerial hierarchy of the firm that fuelled pressures towards workers' control spearheaded by those autonomous technical groups most challenged by this pattern of control within the industrial enterprise.

In both Gorz and Mallet there is some confusion over who constitutes the *new working class* and, more particularly, technical labour. However, the major problem of this school is its tendency towards seeing technology or new production techniques as automatically impacting on the class structure. Mallet is very much within the strong French tradition of labour process writing, and specifically the Proudhonian orientation towards the autonomy of skilled labour which tends to consider the abstract possibilities of machinery outside of definite social relations of production. Mallet's attention to the discontinuous impact of technology on the social division of labour led him to assume a wider constituency for the receipt of technical knowledge and training than actually took place. As Mandel (1978: 269–270) has observed, "the increased level of skill of the collective labourer takes the form under capitalism of only a slight increase in the average skill of each worker, combined with a substantial increase in skill of a small minority of highly qualified producers (polyvalent technicians and repair workers)". Poulantzas (1975: 243) has made the same criticism of technological models of the capitalist labour process. Empirical evidence from English and French oil refineries (Gallie 1978); English chemical plants (Nichols and Beynon 1977); and American plants (Halle 1984) stresses both the continuing tendency towards task and training specialisation, the powerful educational barriers between workers and the persistence of narrow manual operations within apparently sophisticated technical surroundings. Mallet, at both the theoretical and empirical levels, romanticised the extent of comprehensive knowledge of production residing in an enlarged, polyvalent workforce, and underestimated the specialisation and fragmentation of technical knowledge.

4. Braverman

The application of science to production and the emergence of scientific management are portrayed by Braverman as removing the conceptual dimensions from manual work and transferring these to the office, which under conditions of monopoly capitalism is dominated by management and its agents. Technical workers – engineers, designers and planners – are the creation of monopoly capitalism and the agents responsible for deskilling of the manual craftsman. Automation, far from signalling the reversal of this trend, accelerated the subordination of labour to capital by creating a technically impoverished working class. The technicians created through the application of science to capitalist production are not representatives of a working class vanguard, as argued in the new working class literature, but management agents charged with excluding manual labour from the conceptualisation of work.

Braverman considers technical labour through the labour market and the division of labour. Through the creation of distinct occupations responsible for designing and planning work, the wage labour form of these positions carries certain consequences regardless of the specific relationship between technical and manual labour. As wage labourers, technicians, like other "intermediate employees", are formally part of the working class.

That is, like the working class, [they] possesses no economic or occupational independence, [are] employed by capital and its offshoots, possesses no access to the labour process or the means of production outside that employment, and must renew [their] labours for capital incessantly in order to subsist (Braverman 1974: 403).

However, through their place in the division of labour, Braverman, following Lockwood (1958), suggests that white-collar workers' authority relations distinguish them from manual workers.

Since the authority and expertise of the middle ranks in the capitalist corporation represent an unavoidable delegation of responsibility, the position of such functionaries may best be judged by their relation to the power and wealth that commands them from above, and to the mass of labour beneath them which they in turn help to control, command and organise (Braverman 1974: 405).

Possessing oppositional labour market and labour process conditions, white-collar workers exhibit "the characteristics of the worker on the one side (and) manager on the other in varying degrees". Within what he sees as a continuum between these two positions, draughtsmen and technicians are located towards the working class, and engineering heads are part of management and the industrial bourgeoisie. Foremen, junior managers and certain technical specialists occupy the "middle ground" of this continuum. There is movement along or up and down this dynamic continuum, which also serves as a status ladder, a hierarchy of command, authority and privilege instituted and perpetuated by corporate management as a mechanism of "divide and rule" amongst employees.

Braverman's analysis of technical workers as intermediate labour in Chapter 17 of *Labor and Monopoly Capital* maintains that the massification of market conditions determines their work position. However, his central thesis is that the decline in craft regulation erects a structural barrier between technical and manual workers. Towards the end of the book he places technical staff within a managerial situation, monopolising "technical knowledge of production" and excluding the working class from this knowledge. "[T]he extreme concentration of this knowledge (scientific, technical and engineering) in the hands of management and its closely associated staff organisations have closed this avenue to the working population" (Braverman 1974: 443). For "working population" read manual workers and the working class. Within this context technical workers appear unambiguously to be part of capital, acting as gatekeepers to the single store of technical knowledge necessary for production.

My study of technical workers in a large aerospace company challenges Braverman's rather static notion of a single store of knowledge, which, like zero-sum conceptions of control, assumes management is omnipotent and labour passive and dependent (Smith 1987). Technical knowledge was organised through a technical division of labour that placed engineers above skilled manual workers. However this division of labour was nevertheless part of a broader craft tradition which reinforced social bonds across the shop-floor-office divide. Technical workers were part of a collective productive apparatus with more in their work situation that united with, rather than divided them from, manual workers. Other writers looking at the relationship between manual and technical modes of conceptualisation have noted more interaction and movement than Braverman recognises (Cooley 1980; Jones 1982). Braverman's world allows for no such interaction as the flow of knowledge is always *downwards* to manual workers, and their participation in conceptualisation or the coexistence of different types of conceptualisation is not acknowledged.

5. Structural Marxism and Technical Workers

The identification of white-collar workers as a "new middle class" is most closely associated with the structural Marxism of writers like Poulantzas (1975) and Carchedi (1977). Although there are differences between the two, which I briefly explore below, what unites this perspective is a view of the working class becoming a progressively smaller section of society, increasingly out-numbered by the expanding new middle class. Theoretically, this school was marked by a shift away from the attention given to the *conditions* of work evident in the new working class writers' focus on technology, work organisation and industrial sector. Neither is any central importance attached to the skill structure or positive ideological qualities of craft labour as in Braverman's work. For Poulantzas, Carchedi and others, the *place* or functional location occupied by the agents of capital and labour is of a higher theoretical value than either the consciousness or conditions of those within these positions.

6. Poulantzas

For Poulantzas, social classes are defined through economic, political and ideological relations, which in effect are given a similar power of determination. To be within the proletariat, workers must perform productive labour, what Poulantzas re-defines as production of *material* commodities, and be excluded from supervision and mental labour. Those "agents" which lack ownership or control over capital, but are nevertheless implicated by political or ideological relations in serving capital, are part of a *new petty bourgeoisie*. With this narrow definition, the working class – which does not receive any treatment under a separate section in his influential *Classes in Contemporary Capitalism* – is becoming a minority force increasingly replaced by the new petty bourgeoisie. Sections within the new petty bourgeoisie may exhibit a polarisation towards a proletarian position through economic or political or ideological determination, but without discharging supervisory or mental labour, they remain outside the working class.

Technicians for Poulantzas are part of productive labour, but excluded from membership of the working class because of their role as agents of capital in politically supervising the labour process and operating within the ideological apparatus of mental labour. Technicians are responsible for the work of management and supervision, thereby controlling the "efficiency of workers and the achievement of output norms" (Poulantzas 1975: 239–40). They are also indirectly part of the process of separating workers from the conditions of work and subordinating them to an ideological class knowledge. This aspect of their class placement relates to their ideological position, and means that whether technical workers are aware or critical of their role in production, does not negate their complicity as agents of capital. Their consciousness or the content of their work is irrelevant to the form in which it takes place, namely within mental labour. This distinguished Poulantzas from Gorz, Mallet and British writers on technical labour, such as Cooley (1980), as these latter writers would argue that consciousness does have implications for class position.

For Poulantzas the separation between mental and manual labour presents an irresistible class barrier, it is the form of the "capitalist subordination of the working class to the hierarchy of bourgeois factory despotism." Like Braverman, Poulantzas sees social closure, monopoly and exclusivity between possessors and non-possessors of technical knowledge. Technicians' and engineers' "mental labour separated from manual, represents the exercise of political relations in the despoticism of the factory, legitimised and articulated through the monopolisation and secrecy of knowledge, i. e. the reproduction of ideological relations of domination and subordination" (Poulantzas 1975: 240).

Poulantzas, like Braverman, makes some significant advances in our understanding of the political role of supervision and control, and the elevation of mental over physical labour under capitalist relations of production. However, both also share too rigid a delineation of the relations between productive "mental" labourers and manual workers, which exhibit marked variations across national and sectoral boundaries. British technical workers do not supervise manual workers, and have historically been closely allied to skilled workers through craft socialisation, unlike the situation in France, which is Poulantzas's implicit model. At a different theoretical level Poulantzas operates with a non-Marxian definition of productive labour and uses a revision of Marx's approach to class differentiation, which, as Clarke (1977) has pointed out, is closer to Weber. The abstract placement of technical labour overrides all considerations of the organisational design or corporate management strategies towards employing such labour or the specific conditions under which it operates. Such trans-national and trans-historical structuration has a necessarily limited validity, given the lack of room it offers for *interaction* between condition and function in the division of labour.

7. Carchedi

Carchedi (1977) builds on Marx's analysis of modern industry where the "collective labourer" progressively increases and so enriches the cooperation and complexity of the capitalist labour process, and the delegation of capitalist functions to a variety of agents reduces the personal or individual character of factory relations (Marx 1976: 643 and 1040). The production of surplus value requires certain functions which the socialisation of capital and labour has transformed into global rather than individual forms. These Carchedi calls the *global functions of capital,* surveillance and control of the labour process for the purpose of exploitation; and *collective labour functions,* the production of surplus value. The proletariat for Carchedi are those who perform collective labour functions, are exploited or economically oppressed, lack ownership of the means of production and are dependent on a wage to subsist. The bourgeoisie are the exploitiers, owners and oppressors, the non-labourers engaged in the global functions of capital. The *new middle class* is composed of agents who perform *both* the global functions of capital and the collective functions of labour, who lack economic ownership of the means of production and are hence dependent upon the wage to subsist. Where technical labour is engaged in the surveillance and control of the labour process, performing capital as well as productive labour functions, it is part of this new middle class.

The strengths of Carchedi's analysis are in terms of locating the functional supports and contradictions in occupational bands where class identity is not clear-cut. The problem with the method is that is assumes that class relations can be imposed simply through reference to the technical division of labour via job descriptions, when similar occupations may contain divergent forms of association with other workers and managers, different patterns of socialisation and culture, which cannot be read through *functional* classification. This is not to suggest that these cultural factors override functional or structural placement, but rather that structure rather than structural*ism* requires a careful integration with concrete history and empirical reality. Carchedi's functionalism applied to a concrete context, relegates class to a mere reflex of structure and therefore overdetermines social "behaviour" in the classical functionalist manner.

8. Technical Workers and Class

How do we characterise the place of technical workers in the class structure? Their location in "mental labour," and their political role in supervision over manual workers created for Poulantzas a class divide between the two groups. For Carchedi, advancing a more complex model, there is a constant recomposition of those intermediate workers whose work is characterised by a combination of capital and labour functions. Some elements were driven into the proletariat through loss of capital functions, while others are drawn into the new middle class by absorbing displaced capital functions. In both models the subjective and historical relations between technical and manual workers are ignored, which makes for a "purer" model, but one constantly qualified by national variations in class structures. Mallet and the school of new working class writers are at once more empirical and idealistic, projecting onto the formal inter-dependencies between sections of the collective labourer a *necessary*, not *contingent* co-operation and unity.

In my view, a humanist Marxist perspective which approaches class through social relations in production and encompasses ideological and political relations has greater analytical depth than a one-dimensional focus on structure, or a narrow attention to particular conditions, like types of technology of production systems. Such an approach requires historical and comparative dimensions which seek to integrate, rather than suppress, those distinctive legacies attached to occupational structures and reproduced into the experience of class relations. The growing imprecision of terms like "manual" and "mental" labour and greater internal diversity within waged labour in advanced capitalism, requires a more *grounded* approach to the question of class. Most British technical workers are productive, non-supervisory wage labourers, working within social and institutional practices that foster a working class identity. They are, but may not remain, overwhelmingly concentrated within collective work situations alongside manual workers and have historically borrowed trade union practices from skilled manual workers.

For Braverman (1974) and Poulantzas (1975), a class divide existed between mental and manual workers, where the conceptualisation of work was separated into technical and manual labour camps. My analysis of the British craft tradition has indicated the continuity between manual and technical modes of conceptualisation (Smith 1987). This continuity existed because technical occupational roles were defined alongside and not against manual skills, and the conditions of recruitment supported rather than blocked manual workers transferring into the technical office. The occupational socialisation of technical workers maintained the connection with the workplace rather than the college, and confirmed the value of practical experience, which prevented technical education assuming an autonomous, alternative source of authority over manual labour. This meant technical workers' occupational identity continued to be informed by manual workers' perceptions of their competence, rather than through an independent knowledge base which excluded this evaluation. The dominance of craftism as the main avenue of training across the collar divide made it inevitable that most British technical staff should share with skilled manual workers a sense of being the aristocracy of *labour* rather than the poor relations of *capital*. This cultural legacy continues to inform the broad engineering labour process, despite the decline in the apprenticeship route and the growth of a graduate barrier within the hierarchy of technical work.

However, the work situation of technical workers is complicated by two sets of experiences: office life and technical workers' relations with manual workers. Technical workers work in departments and contexts containing a mixture of class positions not so clearly differentiated as on the shop floor. Technical managers and supervisors, because of their surveillance and control functions, "command during the labour process in the name of capital" (Marx 1976: 450). Where "the work of supervison becomes their established and exclusive function", they are a "special kind of wage labourer" distinguished by a class division from those in non-supervisory positions. The office also contains many who have been downwardly mobile, ex-owners or managers, as well as aspirant managers with ideological attachments to capital functions. Consequently, there exists a material support for a mixture of ideological practices, reflecting different class interests of the groups in the office. Moreover, working class technicians share certain common *conditions* – autonomy, responsibility, absence of rigid job controls – with managerial or new middle class labour, which structures their everyday experience and generally reduces their awareness of a rigid class division between themselves and managers.

Technical workers experience their relations with manual workers through three primary contradictions: their position as part of "office" or "mental" labour; their indirectly productive position; and the relative autonomy fostered by their working conditions. Although not evidence of a *class division* between technical and manual workers, these conditions structure everyday relations and experiences and support common-sense distinctions which can *in practice* assume the position of a class barrier. Moreover, capitalism continues to elevate "mental" over "physical" labour, therefore technical workers' position within formal conceptualisation means they share with all "mental" labour a common status over manual labour. Where technical workers are unlike other non-manual groups is their engagement with production and the stress placed on practical as well as abstract knowledge. The precise nature of the relationship between the two groups will depend on national and contingent factors which need to be integrated into any class analysis.

9. Technical Workers: Comparative Position

There is considerable confusion over the term "technical worker" in the literature. Within different institutional and national contexts divergent functions are embraced by the term "technical" – specialist skills, expertise, conceptual knowledge, supervision and authority. It is clear that French writers assume technicians or cadres will have supervisory authority over manual workers and possess qualifications which guarantee a certain social status within the hierarchy of the firm. Similarly, American writers stress the professional and managerial aspects of technical work. In the British context neither model applies. It is therefore important to uncover the *particular* meaning of the term in different contexts. There is also the related question of the social valuation of technical and engineering activities across countries. On the continent engineering technique is elevated as an abstract process, whereas in Britain engineering has a practical and implicitly manual meaning (Ahlstrom 1982; Albu 1980; Lawrence 1980; Whalley 1986 a). Finally, there is the question of technical workers' location by type of production and place in the production cycle. The relative size of the technical component within a particular sector or company is relevant to any assessment of the relationship technical workers are likely to enter into with either other workers or management. In consumer goods sectors technical workers tend to form an elite, close to managers, since by function, skill and usually gender division, they will be strongly differentiated from the largely unskilled manual workforce. Within capital goods sectors, skill ratios may be more equal and the barriers between a technician and craftmen less tightly constructed.

The generic term "technical" carries little generalisability without these qualifications, although there is an equal danger, evident in Whalley (1986 a) and those adopting a culturalist perspective on class, of eliminating universal factors and generalisation and replacing these with comparative institutional, training and occupational analysis. The neglect or suppression of cultural factors in structural Marxism has provoked this retreat into cultural relativism.

There is a need to theoretically locate technical workers both within *capitalism* and specific *capitalist societies*. We also need to examine how technical workers are *managed* within the firm, how structural forces are mediated through *managerial strategies* towards technical workers. Proletarian or bourgois polarisations for groups within technical labour are not simply provided by a given set of structural forces external to social action as implied by Poulantzas and Braverman. Both managers and workers operate upon these determinations, and hence we need to catalogue the choices or responses available to both sides. These, I would argue, are influenced by sectoral practices and wider developments within business policy. Many of the assumptions present in theories of the 1960s and 1970s took for granted the continued bureaucratic integration of technical labour within the firm. However, I will suggest that these beliefs have recently been challenged in business policy, and these have certain consequences for understanding class relations in the workplace.

10. Technical Workers and the Organisation

The structuralist Marxist attention to the division of labour and abstract relations of production within capitalism as a whole inhibited both comparative and empirical studies of technical workers in the workplace. Weberian writing has been preoccupied with the occupational formation of engineers who are implicitly seen as "professional" or part of management. This ignores the productive nature of technical jobs, which increases their labour content and association with skilled manual workers, while simultaneously weakening their connection with non-technical white-collar workers and non-productive managerial and administrative functions. There is also a tendency in the literature on occupational formation to assume a necessary not contingent relationship between qualifications, occupational training and the actual work experience and place in the division of labour occupied by technical workers (McLoughlin 1983). This is particularly problematic in Britain, where occupational credentialling has been resisted by employers who are concerned to maintain their own power over the allocation and utilisation of qualified technical labour.

More recent neo-Weberian writing has attempted to enter the workplace and examine the role of managerial strategies in shaping the social organisation of technical labour. Whalley (1986a) in particular has been concerned to explore the labour market position of British technical workers *within* the firm. In his two case studies of companies located in hi-tech and traditional engineering product markets, Whalley distinguishes two organisational design strategies open to corporate management to control their technical staff: *insulation,* which is oriented towards R & D, engineers, giving them autonomy within technical constraints which are already imbued with market principles. And *exposure,* which is applied to the less innovative groups of technical staff, designed to weaken their attachment to technical expertise as a narrow specialism, by exposing them to market, commercial and financial pressures in a direct way. Whalley notes:

The tension between the technical expertise and profit maximisation is continually generated within the structure of capitalist firms since it is one expression of the contradiction between the development of the forces of production and the attempts to maximise capital accumulation. Both the "insulation" and "exposure" strategies in place at Computergraph [a hi-tech company] and Metalco [a traditional mechanical engineering company] were designed, in their different ways to deal with this problem (Whalley 1986 b: 231).

In seeing this tension between "expertise" and "profitability" Whalley is returning to the under-consumptionist thesis best articulated by Gorz. Whalley makes many favourable references to his work and pays particular attention to the under-utilisation of technical knowledge held by engineers. But whereas Gorz saw in this gap the unfulfilled desires of technical labour and potential for a radical challenge to the capitalist hierarchy that frustrated their technical knowledge, Whalley claims that engineers have to learn the "rules of the game", namely that "non-technical" managerial skills are needed to get on. He believes the social position of engineers is not determined soley by the division of labour, but also shaped by their performance of functions that demand discretion and responsibility as "trusted employees". "Engineers [. . .] are not trusted by management because they are engineers, they are engineers because they are trusted" (Whalley 1986 a: 70). By which Walley suggests that discretion is not dependent on their technical knowledge, but willingness to work within an environment controlled by managements' concerns.

Whalley rightly brings out the shared and cooperative character of the technical division of labour in British engineering, where the craft tradition ensures a weakly structured divide between manual and mental skilled engineering workers. Unfortunately, he all too easily abandons the division of labour and structural forces altogether, for a micro-organisational theory of technical worker's class position. In reacting against structural Marxism, Whalley's conceptualisation of technical workers' class position is reduced to "the phenomenological reality of class in the workplace" (Whalley 1986 a: 185). He says:

If there is a common denominator underlying the range of activities performed by [. . .] engineers [. . .] it is not a coherent body of intellectual knowledge, but the degree of discretion that is built into their jobs [. . .]. Instead of understanding the hierarchical division of the technical workforce – craftsman, technician, engineers – as a hierarchy of skill categories, we need to see it instead as a hierarchy of discretion, a segmentation of employees by varying degrees of "trust" (Whalley 1986 a: 59).

From this concern with discretion in their work situation, Whalley defines the class identity of *all* technical labour through the concepts of trust, responsibility, and service – all aspects of organisational autonomy within internal labour markets – and abandons structural models based on relations of production. But the question is whether autonomy is *designed* and therefore contingent on such things as management planning, or is rather an *inherent* or *universal* feature of engineers' work, as Whalley says "built into their jobs"? Whalley does not really resolve this question, although implying that autonomy is "built into" technical jobs does also beg the question of whether this is conscious design, or a structural *given*. The thrust of Whalley's approach is towards the "social construction" of occupations, and a world of voluntary action where human agency overrides wider structural forces. Hence his concern with "the phenomenological reality of class in the workplace."

A phenomenological approach to class is one in which work situations can be manipulated and designed, where determination is abandoned and voluntarism embraced. This ignores the influence of important elements in technical workers' function within the capitalist division of labour, chiefly their productive labour position. Technical workers enter into conflict with capital, regardless of cultural or organisational design, because of pressures by management to increase their productivity or exploitation. Such attempts can be with conventional direct controls such as lengthening the working day, intensifying their work through new technologies like Computer Aided Design, introducing work measurement or weakening occupational controls with task fragmentation and deskilling. There is growing evidence of these measures appearing in technical departments (Smith 1987). However, job autonomy still remains an important characteristic of technical jobs, and increasing direct supervision is often an inefficient method of control, so the organisational designs observed by Whalley may be more appropriate. But it is important to see the autonomy that exists as contested, the use of capital equipment in the technical departments raising identical questions of control, over-specialisation, increasing operating time, boredom, task standardisation etc. as its introduction on the shop floor. This is because management in introducing such equipment are concerned with labour productivity, and thus treating technical workers not as a *permanently autonomous* and trusted group, but the same as other workers, except with jobs in which direct controls may be inefficient. This economic condition explains the stress on production evident in technical trade unionism and is evidence of their waged labour condition or function (Smith 1987: 269–270). Whalley understands this rationale for trade unionism when he notes that "engineers may be trusted workers, but they are still workers none the less, and may therefore need a union" (Whalley 1986 a: 197). But he does not explain why, if engineers are workers, they are not simply a section of the working class rather than part of a "service class."

The existence of both direct and indirect organisational controls, and competition between different management groups in pursuing these, as Baldry and Connolly (1984) observe, indicates that it is not technical workers' "trusted" or "responsible" position that is the common denominator stimulating these designs. Rather, as Whalley suggests but does not sustain, it is the concern for profitable production, and hence devising ways of maximising the productivity of technical workers. By focusing solely upon indirect designs, and neglecting the competition from more direct and traditional techniques, Whalley overplays the stability of autonomy and trust, and underestimates its contested and contingent nature within capitalist relations of production. Technical workers at British Aerospace I interviewed were acutely aware of the potential for direct control of some new technologies, and sought to maintain their job autonomy through collective representation. Early attempts to introduce CAD into the drawing office on terms that threatened these conditions were met with resistance in organised sectors. The expanded use of CAD came at a time of labour market and trade union weakness, when new conditions, especially shift working, could be imposed (IDS 1982). By ignoring the common pressures and controls that other workers experience, and only concentrating on the unique elements of organisational design for technical workers, Whalley is separating these workers from their condition as productive wage labourers. This allows him to suggest that all technical workers are in a different class, not a section of the working class.

When Whalley locates engineers within the class structure, it is their autonomous place in the organisational structure and not their engagement with production that defines their class position. Engineers are "trusted employees, part of a wider service class in industrial capitalism" (Whalley 1986 a: 13). In elaborating what is meant by "service class", Whalley says: "The key feature of this world are the twin characteristics of discretionary work and an employment matrix of careers, contracts, salaries and fringe benefits" (Whalley 1986 a: 186). Salaries versus wages, autonomy versus control, career versus job; these are the oppositional couplets that capture the experience of office and works "employees". But these appearances of difference, significant as they are, are also contradictory and variable, and do not provide a satisfactory basis for class identification. His central concept of "trust" captures these difficulties.

Trust is essentially a two-dimensional category which tells us little about social relationships between oppositional groups, conflicts over resource distribution or the struggles in the labour process over the generation of surplus value. Trust as a social category is undynamic, loaded with inter-personal not collective connotations, that chiefly concern aspects of labour market closure, recruitment and selection. Whalley suggests that trust relations are at the basis of the differentiation between "office" and "works" employees in British industry. Office labour is a "trustworthy" pool from which to recruit management. But is this true of all office labour? Moreover, does the technical office provide such a key site for managerial careers? Armstrong (1987) has arrived at the opposite conclusion by noting that British management "culture" is anti-productivist, built on a nexus of finance and marketing decision making, and hostile to the productive position of engineers. Hence engineers' low representation, at least in manufacturing industry, within the higher echelons of management. Trust would seem more a contested feature of job autonomy than a universal basis for management selection.

Micro or organisational design can effect the potential for technical workers identifying themselves with management of manual workers, but it does not offer an adequate basis for building a theory of class. Whalley's work remains an advance because of its focus on organisational design strategies. But these need to be integrated into class theory. Leaving aside the direct control strategies used against technical workers, indirect controls express the specific *terrain* upon which the new middle class confront capital. Corporate management strategies to reduce the size of supervisory hierarchies, length of career ladders, autonomy of specialist functions, centralisation of control over these functions, the size of internal-functions against those bought-in from the market, are all questions of organisational design over which the new middle class struggles against corporate management. Drawing from different sources, I shall examine strategies related to *internal* controls and those concerned with the *externalisation* of the transactions between technical workers and management to the market.

11. Management Strategies and Technical Workers

Internalising intermediate workers within the firm has been the dominant organisational response to the increasing complexity in management, the impact of technology and the other determinants on the growth of white-collar workers discussed at the beginning of this paper. The problem of controlling the expansion of white-collar workers within the firm produced bureaucratisation, task standardisation and deskilling through technological means. These elements are most stressed by new working class and deskilling writers who see proletarianisation as the major outcome of these developments. However, in order to maintain control over technical specialists and simultaneously weaken their attachments to labour organisations, the creation of specialist career structures, staff status and other rewards have been granted to technical and other white-collar groups by corporate management. These elements are most stressed by Weberian writing in the area. In addition, it has been suggested that in order to ensure greater identification between technical workers and profitable production, it has been necessary for management to weaken technical workers' attachment to narrow specialist career hierarchies and expose them to the pressures of production and market forces (Whalley 1986a). With the development of new technologies, changes in the labour market and business policy, these internal strategies – which retain technical workers in collectivities, however fragmented and controlled – have been supplemented by attempts to remove specialist skills from inside the firm to the external market, a shift from direct controls to contracting relations. This atomises workers, lowers union density and solidarity by increasing self-employment and petty bourgeois places.

12. Internalisation

12.1 Exposure to Production

In a study of the re-organisation of technical workers at the confectionery division of Cadbury-Schweppes, a major capital investment programme provided the reason for changing the autonomous place of technical and craft workers in the factory (Smith et al. 1989). Specialist hierarchies and career structures which reinforced the autonomy of these groups, and their credential or qualified power base, were broken up and exposed to a task not status hierarchy. From being a centralised grouping within a technical hierarchy, simply *servicing* the production environment, they were relocated into integrated project groups under the direct control of production management. Although these changes did not take place on a systematic basis until the late 1970s, the ideological rationale for the change was pin-pointed by corporate management a lot earlier. Sir Adrian Cadbury, writing in the late 1960s, rejected the then dominant organisational design for white-collar specialists based on status provision, specialist autonomy and independence from production and other workers, in favour of project management:

[T]he basic form of organisation will increasingly become the group and it will be more concerned with the task in hand, which is the bond between members of the group, than with job descriptions or status in the hierarchy. The working group will be drawn from various disciplines and functions that can contribute to a particular objective [...]. The project team is a natural example of this pattern of organisation (Cadbury 1969: 12).

Under the old system technical workers at Cadbury's operated in a socially cohesive and centrally located environment, which in the late 1960s contained 75 draughtsmen, engineers and technicians. Between 1969 and 1972 TASS membership grew from 20 per cent to 100 per cent of technical workers below management status, which represented the majority in the office. Unionisation was a response to redundancies within the supervisory levels of the firm, a major shock to Cadbury tradition. The changes in the late 1970s, dramatically reduced concentration and membership of TASS, which was down to only 15 members in the early 1980s, and increased the managerial element in their work and lowered the line separating managerial from staff status. Most importantly, it exposed technical workers to the direct pressures of production by destroying the insulating and mediating organisational structures which had reinforced a strictly technical specialist identity and their independence from production management.

The capital investment programme was largely completed by contractors, supervised by Cadbury engineers. This represented a major change, from internal to external management of investment, and was only introduced after opposition from technical workers. It is the intention of the company to move engineers into production management functions, largely because of the contracting-in of technical functions and the decline in supervisory and bureaucratic controls, and the necessity in the new large capital-intensive production plants for more technical skills. The previously autonomous engineers were a pool of labour identified by corporate management as being available to fill these new managerial posts.

12.2 Exposure to Markets

Whalley (1986 a) describes the way management at Metalco, a traditional engineering firm in the West Midlands, faced with a deteriorating product market shifted its engineers away from long-term research towards more routine production functions:

A major part of its [Metalco] strategy involved organisational changes [which internalised market forces]. Instead of channeling commercial pressure through managerial hierarchies, Metalco had begun to provide its technical staff with financial information, and impose cost constraints on them by "internalizing the market" (Whalley 1986 b: 236).

By establishing internal profit centres and increasing competition for resources between sections and divisions of the same company, engineers became engaged in commercial as well as technical decision making. Whalley describes how previously centralised and integrated departments were separated into individual profit centres and forced to compete with each other:

Each of these operated under a separate management, was responsible for its own financial well-being, and expected to trade with all the other units only on open-market terms, competing with non-Metalco companies even for intra-corporate business. Their links with Metalco corporate structure were therefore not dissimilar to those that many small companies have with their banks (Whalley 1986 b: 236).

The consequences for engineers was that the majority were aspiring to managements posts, a higher percentage than at the other company studied by Whalley. They were aware of commercial and financial pressures, and over 50 per cent wanted to participate in running the company within its existing structure. There did not exist the aspirations for radical control over production identified by new working class writers. Like Whalley's example, part of the re-organisation of engineering workers at Cadbury's was designed to integrate and expose some to the pressures of production, while others were moved to servicing the Cadbury Schweppes Group independently of the demands of production within the factories. It was envisaged that eventually such group resources would be commercially independent, increasing, as with the Metalco example, market relations between engineers and the firm. Autonomous group technical resources have been established at other food companies, United Biscuits for example, turning bureaucratically integrated facilities into consultancy and commercial resources, and engineers into commercially conscious managers.

These developments suggest that corporate management have been *active* in the struggle to transform technical workers from positions of autonomy into managerial agents. These formal changes in job titles and tasks may serve to make more complex the nature of "management". Granting managerial status to engineers at Cadbury's was motivated by a desire by corporate management to control more directly the allocation of engineers in the factory. What is significant is that these processes did not occur automatically, but through the mediation of management within the firms. Exposure is not something that has happened universally in the confectionary sector in Britain; Mars and Rowntrees, for example, maintain centralised technical resources, therefore indicating divergent strategies for handling technical workers, and hence the role of managerial choice in this process.

13. Externalisation

Creating autonomous working environments, granting special status provisions, exposing technical staff to production or commercial pressures remain strategies for *internal* organisational design. They do not fundamentally affect the class position of technical workers who remain in collective, waged labour situations, albeit with considerably more exposure to managerially defined views of work. However, recent trends in business strategy have favoured the break-up of centrally integrated bureaucratic organisations into smaller, federated production units, and alongside this an increase in the buying-in of technical specialists rather than retaining them in direct employment. The consequences of these moves shift intermediate workers from wage labour to self-employment or a petty bourgeois class position. Similar trends in managerial hierarchies, such as management buy-outs, have shifted managers from new middle class to capitalist positions. These changes are not uniform, surveys revealing a mixed picture[1], and it is difficult to know whether we are simply witnessing conjunctural responses to the weakened market position of labour, or a real structural shift in capitalist organisation. However, it does appear that subcontracting is increasing amongst specialist labour groups, including sections of technical workers.

---

[1] The ideology and advocacy of contracting out and manipulating labour contracts to give management greater control over labour utilisation and exchange has gone together with employer or management influenced research into the actual incidence of such practices. For a critical assessment of this see Pollert (1987). Examples of this type of survey are CBI (1985) and NEDO (1986). More independent surveys are at once more cautious about trends, Marginson et al. (1986).

Sectors like aerospace have traditionally relied upon a large number of contract draughtsmen who, due to union pressure from within the contracting firms, have been unionised. The pool of contract draughtsmen expands with orders and reduces with downturns, hence the employer avoids redundancy and other costs of directly employing more technical staff. The expansion of subcontracting, which was regarded as an antiquated mode of control by most writers on the labour process outside of sectors like construction, reflects changes in the balance of forces between capital and labour in the recession. It has also been hastened by technological changes, the wider availability of cheaper distributed information technology, and the increasing scale of international competition. In Britain legal changes have meant unions can no longer lawfully struggle to insist on employers only using unionised contract workers. Such changes have strengthened the hand of the employer and weakened trade union opposition to subcontracting. Sir Adrian Cadbury expresses the view of corporate employers in wishing to extend contracting, which he sees as tied to creating the fragmented and federal structures for business units expressed above:

Each business unit in its turn will be looking for ways of cutting costs and will only retain under its direct control those activities which are essential for the continued survival of the enterprise. One of the characteristics of the small firm is that it does not seek to provide its own services, like computing, design, security, machinery installation and so on, it buys them from outside. I would expect tomorrows' companies to follow this example and to concentrate on the core activities of their businesses, relying for everything else on specialised suppliers who would compete for their custom. Computer programmers and system analysts for example could work from home under contract, rather than directly employed in large offices and so decide for themselves when and for how long they will work (Smith et al. 1989).

The decline in collectivised working environments for specialist technical staff identified here by Cadbury, and the support for the expansion of self-employment and small firms by corporate capital, has elsewhere been associated by him with a challenge to the continued viability to trade union organisation:

It raises enormous problems for the trade union movement everywhere because the individual will want to make his private bargain with the company [. . .]. I would suggest that we are moving away from collectivism, which is what the trade union movement is all about, to a much greater degree of individualism. Indeed you could argue, certainly in Europe, that one of the reasons why a number of people have moved out of large scale industry and commerce and moved into small scale, particularly service enterprises is precisely to get away from the rules and regulations of collectivism and to have greater freedom to run their lives as they would like (Smith et al. 1989).

Within his own firm those "leaving" have not gone voluntarily to expand their individual life chances, but through the pressure of corporate redundancy, mechanisation and rationalisation programmes. This quote expresses the *ideology* of contracting, and a new way of controlling new middle class labour for corporate capital. The push factors affecting the creation of the small firm – high unemployment and business policies of the corporate sector – have had a more significant impact than voluntary action by individuals. Shutt and Whittington (1987) have suggested that large firm fragmentation strategies in the recession have expanded the number of "dependent" small firms, in order to reassert control over the labour process, spread innovation risks and face up to intensified competition.

Again, while not wishing to give overdue significance to these trends without more sustained empirical evidence, reducing the bureaucratic stability and security of new middle class groups through externalisation does appear as a growing option if not strategy of corporate capital. Specific case study evidence from the new hi-tech firms by Winstanley (1986) found evidence of subcontracting but also a "division between those for whom it is a symbol of their labour market strength through scarce skills, such as software consultants, and those less powerful and on the casualised periphery, such as draughtspeople." My own work on the aerospace industry revealed a degree of mobility between direct employment, self-employment and contract status in periods of boom. However, in the recession management appear more conscious in their manipulation of labour contracts – consultancy in this area has been booming – and, consequently, drifting between types of employment may not exist to the same degree.

Technological change, particularly the cheapening of information technology, may be allowing the externalisation of technical functions out of the firm. Lee (1986) in a study of information technology in some West Midlands manufacturing companies, found some evidence of the buying-in of expertise from small, specialist software houses, as an alternative to in-house systems departments. However, for design work the stress remained on retaining staff in-house not only because of the absence of ready-made design packages but also, more importantly, the need to create stability between design and production. Baldry and Connolly (1984) and Campbell and Currie (1987) in case studies of the social impact of Computer Aided Design in drawing offices in Britain, did not encounter any marked expansion of subcontracting, although specialisation was a definite trend, and Rader (1982: 173) has suggested that the option of externalisation increases if knowledge and training in CAD becomes exclusive to a limited number of technical staff in the design offices.

British engineers have traditionally come under the control of the employer, lacking an autonomous professional base. Watson (1975: 50) noted that in 1960 only 2 per cent of engineers were in private practice, compared with 33 per cent of principal accountants, 25 per cent of architects and 62 per cent of solicitors. The absence of a client-practitioner relationship for engineers has fostered a bureaucratic identification with a single employer. However, with the changes mentioned above this may no longer hold to the same extent. Lee (1986) found that while self-employed and consultant engineers constituted only 2.8 per cent of the membership of the Institute of Electrical Engineers in 1977, this figure had increased to 7.5 per cent by 1985. Unionising engineers is impossible in this situation, moreover evidence from Winstanly (1986) suggests that in hi-tech sectors where the *ideology,* if not the total experience of technical staff, is orientated towards self-employment, then trade union density is considerably lower amongst technical workers. Self-employment encourages individualism and weakens collectivist pressures in the workplace. A TASS organiser, reflecting on the difficulty of unionising a hi-tech company, INMOS, in the Bristol area, told me that "a lot of these new technology firms are very difficult to crack, all the engineers have a vision of themselves as entrepreneurs and think they're going to make a packet out of it" (Smith 1987: 189).

14. Conclusion

This paper has examined the theoretical relationship between global, national and organisational contexts for approaching the class situation of technical workers. Technical workers in different national contexts have been shaped by particular education and training systems, and within divergent modes of conceptualising their place in the division of labour and their relationship with both management and labour[2]. But after we have made this very necessary step of signalling these comparative differences, which global theorising of structural Marxism sought to gloss over, we are left with two possible conclusions. Either, all theories and ideas are *reducible* to national practices and experiences, or alternatively the local structuring and formation of technical skills, identities and boundary relationships must themselves be located in a more global context. Adopting the first position of cultural relativism suggests we cannot make any generalisations about technical or any other group of workers. This I have rejected because it does not explain the way political and economic trends produce very similar agendas

---

[2] A comparative historical account of the development of engineers in Britain and selected European countries is found in Ahlstrom (1980). The only contemporary empirical comparative research has been undertaken by Peter Whalley, Stephen Crawford and Robert Zussman, coordinated by Allan Silver from Columbia University. This involved examining two new and old engineering sectors in each of the following countries, France, the USA and Britain. Whalley (1986 a) has produced the British research; Zussman (1985) the American and Crawford (1985) in (PhD form only) the French findings. As yet, apart from references to comparative data in summary form in individual pieces, and a conference paper by Silver et al. (1985), the promised comparative book has not appeared. My own work has examined in summary form the historical development of British technical occupations (1987); Armstrong (1987), using secondary sources, has summarised the historical development of British and German engineers within managerial hierarchies; and Boltanski (1987) has examined the origins of cadres in France. But in general, the literature has been singularly uncomparative and impressionistic on national cultural differences.

across countries, as in the 1960s when the imminent proletarianisation of white-collar workers appeared part of an implicit assumption of class homogenisation. Similarly, the agenda in the 1970s was around the break-up of the collective labourer into competing segments which could not coalesce into a single form but required combining in particular alliance and coalitions.

I have argued for the second interpretation, that institutional and national characteristics must be re-positioned within a more responsive structural theory based on global dynamics which are always mediated through national contexts. Relatedly, I have suggested that sector and managerial strategies towards technical labour must recieve a similar integration. Against those that assume a self-sufficient technological, organisational or economic logic driving technical labour towards set polarisations, I have argued in favour of a more contingent relationship between environmental dynamics and managerial policies towards controlling technical labour. This is not suggesting voluntarism, as the pressures on intermediate workers remain those of capital or labour. While some writers, in embracing micro-organisational analysis and fieldwork, find it a welcome and exciting relief from the greyness of structural Marxism of class of the 1970s, I would caution against the limitations of embracing what Whalley celebrated as the "phenomenology of class in the workplace". This cannot substitute for general class analysis. Trends in business policy suggest a greater variety in the methods of securing technical labour than previously recognised by class theorists, but an understanding of these new strategies can only be adequately conceptualised within general theory, and not, as suggested by Whalley, through concepts such as trust which remain simply the outward social expression of the organisational or labour market position of new middle class labour.

There remains a need for more comparative historical and empirical research into the formation and current class position of technical labour across capitalist societies. My fieldwork at British Aerospace in the late 1970s and early 1980s suggested a growing educational segmentation within technical labour, alongside continued interaction and cooperation in the work relations between manual and technical groups. I found that the craft tradition which had continued to ensure a contradictory cooperation was being challenged by technological change in both manual and technical areas. It was evident from that research that diverse pressures would continue to operate in the concentrated and collective work environments most British technical workers continue to inhabit. More research of this type and that of Whalley is needed in the newer industrial sectors, and the non-engineering areas, to increase our knowledge of the workplace relations between technical, managerial and manual groups. Such research should seek to integrate the developments in class theory of intermediate workers produced over the last three decades, recognising the implicit cultural assumptions of certain theorists, Mallet, Gorz and Poulantzas in particular, while avoiding the problem of celebrating cultural or organisational relativism to answer the evident structural reductionism of much of the 1970s writings.

References

Ahlstrom, G., *Engineers and Industrial Growth,* London: Croom Helm. 1980

Albu, A., British Attitudes to Engineering Education: A Historical Perspective, in: K. Pavitt (ed.), *Technical Innovation and British Economic Performance,* London: Macmillan. 1980

Armstrong, P., Engineers, Management and Trust, *Work, Employment and Society* 1/4: 421–440. 1987

Armstrong, P., B. Carter, C. Smith, and T. Nichols, *White-Collar Workers, Trade Unions and Class.* London: Croom Helm. 1986

Baldry, C. and A. Connolly, Drawing the Line: Computer Aided Design and the Organisation of the Drawing Office, paper to 2nd Annual Aston/UMIST Conference Organisation and Control of the Labour Process, March. 1984

Boltanski, L., *The Making of a Class: Cadres in French Society.* Cambridge: Cambridge University Press. 1987

Braverman, H., *Labor and Monopoly Capital.* New York: Monthly Review. 1974

Cadbury, G. A. H., Our Technological Future, paper to Institute of Production Engineers, 29th October, University of Leicester. 1969

Campbell, A. and W. Currie, Skills and Strategies in Design Engineering, paper to 5th Annual UMIST/Aston Conference Organisation and Control of the Labour Process, 22–24 April. 1987

Carchedi, G., *On the Economic Identification of Social Classes.* London: Routledge and Kegan Paul. 1977

Clarke, S., Marxism, Sociology and Poulantzas's Theory of the State, *Capital and Class* 2: 1–31. 1977

CBI (Confederation of British Industry), *Managing Change: The Organisation of Work.* London: CBI. 1985

Cooley, M., *Architect or Bee: The Human/Technology Relationship.* Slough: Hand and Brain. 1980

Crawford, S., The Work and Values of French Engineers in Traditional and Advanced Industries, unpublished Ph. D. thesis, Columbia University. 1985

Crompton, R., Approaches to the Study of White-Collar Unionism, *Sociology* 10/3: 407–426. 1976

Crompton, R. and J. Gubbay, *Economy and Class Structure.* London: Macmillan. 1977

Gallie, D. *In Search of the New Working Class.* Cambridge: Cambridge University Press. 1978

Gorz, A., *Strategy for Labour: A Radical Proposal.* Boston: Beacon Press. 1967

Halle, D., *America's Working Man.* Chicago: University of Chicago. 1984

Hyman R., White-Collar Workers and Theories of Class, in: R. Hyman and R. Price (eds.), *The New Working Class? White-Collar Workers and Their Organisations,* London: Macmillan. 1983

IDS (Incomes Data Services), *CAD Agreements and Pay.* IDS Study 276, London: Incomes Data Services. 1982

Jones, B., Destruction or Redistribution of Engineering Skills? The Case of Numerical Control, in: S. Wood, *The Degradation of Work.* London: Hutchinson. 1982

Lawrence, P., *Managers and Management in West Germany*. London: Croom Helm. 1980

Lee, G., The Adoption of Computer Based Systems in Engineering: Management Strategies and the Role of the Professional Engineer, Work Organisation Research Centre Working Paper Series, no. 16. University of Aston. England 1986

Lockwood, D., *The Blackcoated Worker*. London: Allen & Unwin. 1958

Mallet, S., *The New Working Class*. Nottingham: Spokesman. 1975

Mandel, E., *Late Capitalism*. London: Verso. 1978

Marginson, P., P. Edwards, J. Purcell, and K. Sisson, *The Workplace Industrial Relations Company Level Survey*. University of Warwick: Industrial Relations Research Unit. 1986

Marx, K., *Capital (Volume One)*. Harmondsworth: Penguin. 1976

McLoughlin, I., Industrial Engineers and Theories of the New Middle Class, unpublished Ph. D. thesis, University of Bath. 1983

Mills, C. W., *White Collar*. New York: Oxford University Press. 1953

NEDO (National Economic Development Office), *Changing Working Patterns: How Companies Achieve Flexibility to Meet New Needs*. London: NEDO. 1986

Nichols, T. and H. Beynon, *Living with Capitalism: Class Relations and the Modern Factory*. London: Routledge & Kegan Paul. 1977

Noble, D., *America by Design*. New York: Knopf. 1977

Pollert, A., The Flexible Firm: A Model in Search of Reality (or a Policy in Search of a Practice)? Industrial Relations Research Unit, Working Paper Series, University of Warwick. 1987

Poulantzas, N., *Classes in Contemporary Capitalism*. London: Verso. 1975

Rader, M., The Social Effects of Computer Aided Design: Current Trends and Forecasts for the Future, in: L. Bannan, U. Barry and O. Holst (eds.), *Information Technology: Impact on the Way of Life*. Dublin: Tycooly International Publishing. 1982

Rattansi, A., End of an Orthodoxy? The Critique of Sociology's View of Marx on Class, *Sociological Review* 36/1: 641–661. 1985

Shutt, J. and R. Whittington, Fragmentation Strategies and the Rise of Small Units: Cases from the North West, *Regional Studies* 19/1: 13–23. 1987

Silver, A., S. Crawford, P. Whalley, and R. Zussman, Knowledge, Organization and Politics: Engineers in Three Nations, Paper to Conference of Council of European Studies, October 18–20, Washington. 1985

Smith, C., Engineers, Trade Unionism and TASS, in: P. Armstrong et al., op. cit., pp. 160–197. 1986

Smith, C., *Technical Workers: Class, Labour and Trade Unionism*. London: Macmillan. 1987

Smith, C., J. Child and M. Rowlinson, *Innovations in Work Organisation: The Cadbury Experience*. Cambridge: Cambridge University Press, 1989

Watson, H. B., Organisational Bases of Professional Status: A Comparative Study of Engineering Professions, unpublished Ph. D. thesis, University of London. 1975

Whalley, P., *The Social Production of Technical Work*. London: Macmillan. 1986a

Whalley, P., Markets, Managers and Technical Autonomy, *Theory and Society* 15/1–2: 223–247. 1986b

Winstanley, D., Recruitment Strategies and Managerial Control of Technological

Staff, paper to Aston/UMIST 4th Annual Conference on the Organisation and Control of the Labour Process, April. 1986

Wright, E. O., *Classes*. London: Verso. 1985

Zussman, R., *Mechanics of the Middle Class: Work and Politics among American Engineers*. California: University of California Press. 1985

III. Class Restructuring and Organizations

Disorganised Capitalism and Social Class

John Urry

1. Introduction

Marx and Engels wrote of capitalism that the:

Constant revolutionising of production, uninterrupted disturbance of all social conditions, everlasting uncertainty and agitation distinguish the bourgeois epoch from all earlier ones. All fixed, fast-frozen relations [...] are swept away, all new-formed ones become antiquated before they can ossify. All that is solid melts into air, all that is holy is profaned [...] (1888: 53–4; see Lash and Urry 1987, for further discussion).

Bourgeois or capitalist society, then, is one of intense change, particularly of where people live and how their lives are organised over time. According to Marx and Engels, as production is revolutionised in order to bring about massive savings of labour-time, people's relationships to each other across space are transformed. First, capitalism has 'pitilessly torn asunder the motley feudal ties that bound man to his "natural superiors" (all quotes from Marx and Engels 1888: 65). Second, the need for a constantly expanding market "chases the bourgeoisie over the whole surface of the globe and destroys local and regional markets." Third, the "immensely facilitated means of communication draws all [...] nations into civilisation" (by "civilisation" we can read "modernity"). Fourth, enormous cities are created, and this has "rescued a considerable part of the population from the idiocy of rural life." Fifth, political centralisation is generated as independent, loosely connected provinces "become lumped together into one nation." Sixth, masses of labourers "organised like soldiers" are "crowded into the factory" and the proletariat "becomes concentrated in greater masses." And finally, the development of trade unions is "helped on by the improved means of communication that are created by modern industry and that places the workers of different localities in contact with one another."

Marx and Engels in the *Manifesto* are very much the analysts of "modernity" and indeed see the bourgeoisie as a profoundly revolutionary class, setting in motion an exceptional train of events, creating more massive and sophisticated forces of production than all the previous centuries had managed (see Berman 1983). People's lives are thus controlled by a revolutionary bourgeois class, by a class with vested interest in change, crisis and chaos. The citizen in this modern era must learn not to long nostalgically for the "fixed, fast-frozen relationships" of the real or fantasized past, but to delight in mobility, to thrive on renewal, to look forward to future developments in their conditions of life. As a world of change, it is a world which swings wildly out of control, menacing and destructive. The bourgeoisie thus moves within a profoundly tragic orbit. It has unleashed tremendous powers, but these are powers which are destructive as well as constructive, conflict producing as well as releasing. Within this uncontrollable maelstrom the temporal and spatial structuring of people's lives are continuously transformed.

What Marx and Engels thus set out in the *Manifesto* is an analysis of an exceptionally influential set of social developments which have characterised western societies roughly from the end of the 19th century onwards. However, what I want to suggest is that the era of "organised capitalism" that they outline has, in certain societies, come to an end, and that there are a set of tremendously significant transformations which have recently been literally "disorganising" contemporary capitalist societies, transformations of time and space, of economy and culture, which disrupt and dislocate the patterns that Marx and Engels so brilliantly foresaw.

In this claim that organised capitalism is – if sporadically and unevenly – coming to an end, in my claim that we are moving into an era of *disorganised* capitalism, I am arguing against the conventions, not just of "orthodoxy," but of a good deal of conventional social science. Both Marxists and Weberians will generally contend that we are living in increasingly *organised* societies. Marxists speak of "monopoly capitalism," characterised by the increasing concentration of constant and variable capital complemented by the unidirectional tendency towards centralisation of money capital. Weberians will similarly claim that contemporary society is imbued with increased levels of organisation. They will point to the seemingly teleological growth of state bureaucracy in both capitalist and apparently socialist countries. They will point to an ineluctable rationalisation in our whole gamut of institutions – of the school, the police, the civil service, the factory, trade unions and so on. They will view this process of further organisation as the obverse side of secularisation, in which the dissolution of internal constraints are progressively replaced by normalising, individuating and ordering external constraints. I thus aim to argue against some of the best Marxist and Weberian opinion in the contention that contemporary capitalism is undergoing a process of disorganisation.

2. Organised Capitalism

This concept has a considerable pedigree dating back to Hilferding and was particularly developed by Jürgen Kocka and several other contemporary social historians (see Winckler 1974). For these writers, organised capitalism begins in most countries in the final decades of the nineteenth century. Organised capitalism consists of the following interrelated features:

(1) the concentration and centralisation of industrial, banking and commercial capital – as markets became progressively regulated; in comparison with the preceding epoch of "liberal capitalism," special growth in producers' goods industries; the increased inter-connection of banks and industry; and the proliferation of cartels;
(2) the growth of the (famous) separation of ownership from control, with the bureaucratisation of control and the elaboration of complex managerial hierarchies;
(3) the growth of new sectors of managerial/scientific/technological intelligentsia and of a bureaucratically employed middle class;
(4) the growth of collective organizations in the labour market, particularly of regionally and then nationally organised trade unions and of employers' associations, nationally organised professions etc.;
(5) the increasing inter-articulation between the state and the large monopolies; and between collective organisations and the state as the latter increasingly intervenes in social conflicts; and the development of class-specific welfare-state legislation;
(6) the expansion of empires and the control of markets and production overseas;
(7) changes in politics and the state, including the increasing number and size of state bureaucracies, the incorporation of various social categories into the national political arena, the increased representation of diverse interests in and through the state, and the transformation of administration from merely "keeping order" to the attainment of various goals and national objectives; and
(8) various ideological changes concerning the role of technical rationality and the glorification of science.
I would also add to Kocka's enumeration the following further features:
(9) the concentration of industrial capitalist relations within relatively few industrial sectors and within a small number of centrally significant nation-states;
(10) the development of extractive/manufacturing industry as the dominant sectors with large and growing numbers of workers employed;
(11) the concentration of different industries within different regions, so that there are clearly identifiable regional economies based on a handful of centrally significant extractive/manufacturing industries;
(12) the growth of numbers employed in most plants, as the economies of scale dictate growth and expansion within each unit of production; and
(13) the growth and increased importance of very large industrial cities which dominate particular regions through the provision of centralised services (especially commercial and financial).
Clearly not all of these developments occurred either simultaneously or in the same way in all western countries. It is useful to distinguish between organisation

"at the top" and organisation "at the bottom". Organisation at the top here includes the concentration of industry, increasing interarticulation of banks, industry and the state, and cartel formation; organisation "at the bottom" includes, for example, the development of national trade union bodies, working class political parties, and the welfare state.

The following are three of the factors which determine the timing of, and the extent to which, the capitalism in each of these countries becomes organised. First, is the point in history at which it begins to industrialise; the earlier a country enters its "take-off", the less organised *mutatis mutandis* its capitalism will be. This is because countries which are later industrialisers need to begin at higher levels of concentration and centralisation of capital to compete with those which have already been industrialising for some time. Secondly, there is the extent to which pre-capitalist organisations survive into the capitalist period. On this count, Britain and Germany became more highly organised capitalist societies than France and the USA. This is because the former two nations did not experience a "bourgeois revolution" and as a result, guilds, corporate local government, and merchant, professional, aristocratic, university and church bodies remained relatively more intact. Sweden interestingly occupies a mid-way position, inasmuch as the high level of state centralisation during Swedish feudalism did not allow for the same flourishing development of corporate groups. And the third factor is size of country. For the industry of small countries to compete internationally, resources were channelled into relatively few firms and sectors. Co-ordination between the state and industry was then greatly facilitated, if not necessitated. At the same time, there would tend to be higher union densities, more "organisation" of labour, where there were relatively few firms and sectors.

Overall, Germany is closest to approximating the ideal type outlined above of organised capitalism, achieving high levels of organisation very early on both at the top and the bottom.

By contrast, central to the British economy have been the absolute size and international scope of the financial sector, the early export of capital goods, the early shift into production of services, and especially a sectoral profile in which concentration was focussed not in the characteristically organised-capitalist sectors, but in consumer industries such as food and drink. It was the absence of horizontal and vertical integration, of diversification and modern managerial structures in the key organised-capitalist sectors which was the decisive feature of Britain's middleman (or *Makler*) economy. At the same time, it was organised at the bottom earlier than it organised at the top and earlier than many other societies.

In the USA, to take a third example, the early and thorough organisation of American capitalism at the top was unmatched by such organisation at the bottom, and the American polity in organised capitalism at the end of the nineteenth century was characterised by the state acting as very much the instrument of the economically dominant class. Subsequently the "progressivism" of the New Deal

helped American capitalism to organise much later at the bottom and lent relative autonomy to the state for a period in the 1930s and 1940s. The notion of
"progressivism," an ideology and a movement associated with the rising service
class and related middle classes from the beginning of the twentieth century, is
key to the understanding of American capitalist organisation and disorganisation.
In the twentieth century some variety of "progressivism" has always been the
main source of opposition to unregulated capitalist accumulation in the US.
"American exceptionalism" is due, not as much to an ethnically divided and
weak working class, as to the very early presence, size and access to organisation
of the American new middle classes, especially the "service class" which articulated a progressive ideology.

I shall now consider some of the tendencies to disorganisation.

3. Towards Disorganisation

(1) The growth of a world market combined with the increasing scale and internationalisation of industrial, banking and commercial enterprises means that
national markets have become less regulated by nationally based corporations,
particularly as corporations have become much less market-specific. From the
point of view of national markets, there has been an effective *de*-concentration of
capital. This tendency has been complemented by the nearly universal decline of
cartels. Such deconcentration has been aided by the general decline of tariffs and
the encouragement by states, particularly the USA, to increase the scale of
external activity of large corporations. In many countries there is a growing
separation of banks from industry.

(2) The continued expansion of the number of white-collar workers, and particularly of a distinctive service class (of managers, professionals, educators,
scientists etc.) which is an effect of organised capitalism, becomes an increasingly
significant element which then disorganises modern capitalism. This results both
from the development of an educationally-based stratification system which fosters individual achievement and mobility and the growth of new "social movements" (students, ecological, women's movements etc.) which draw energy and
personnel away from class politics.

(3) Decline in the absolute and relative size of the core working class, that is,
of manual workers in manufacturing industry, as economies are de-industrialised.

(4) Decline in the importance and effectiveness of national-level collective
bargaining procedures in industrial relations and the growth of company and
plant-level bargaining.

(5) Increasing independence of large monopolies from direct control and regulation by individual nation-states; the breakdown of most neocorporatist forms of

state regulation of wage bargaining, planning etc., and increasing contradiction between the state and capital (cf. fiscal crisis etc.); a development of non-class specific, universalistic, welfare state legislation and subsequent challenge from left and right to the centralised welfare state.

(6) The spread of capitalism into most Third World countries which has involved increased competition in many of the basic extractive/manufacturing industries (steel, coal, oil, heavy industry, automobiles etc.) and the export of part of the first world proletariat. This in turn has shifted the industrial/occupational structure of first world economies towards "service" industry and occupations.

(7) The decline in the salience and class character of political parties. There is a decline in the class vote and the more general increase in "catch-all" parties which reflect the decline in the degree to which national parties simply represent class interests.

(8) An increase in cultural fragmentation and pluralism, resulting both from the commodification of leisure and the development of new political/cultural forms since the 1960s. There has been some decodification of existing cultural forms. The related reductions in time-space distanciation (cf. the "global village") likewise undermine the construction of unproblematically national subjects.

(9) The massive expansion in the number of nation-states implicated in capitalist production and the large expansion in the number of sectors organised on the basis of capitalist relations of production.

(10) Decline in the absolute and relative numbers employed in extractive/manufacturing industry and in the significance of those sectors for the organisation of modern capitalist societies. Increased importance of service industry for the structuring of social relations (smaller plants, less changeable labour process, increased feminisation, higher "mental" component etc.).

(11) The overlapping effect of new forms of the spatial division of labour has weakened the degree to which industries are concentrated within different regions. To a significant extent there are no longer "regional economies" in which social and political relations are formed or shaped by a handful of centrally significant extractive/manufacturing industries.

(12) Decline in average plant size because of shifts in industrial structure, substantial labour-saving capital investment, the hiving off of various sub-contracted activities, the export of labour-intensive activities to "world-market factories" in the Third World, and to "rural" sites in the First World etc.

(13) Industrial cities begin to decline in size and in their domination of regions. This is reflected in the industrial population collapse of so-called "inner cities," the increase in population of smaller towns and more generally of semi-rural areas, the movement away from older industrial areas etc. Cities also become less centrally implicated in the circuits of capital and become progressively reduced to the status of alternative pools of labour-power.

Generally speaking, the greater the extent to which a nation's capitalism was organised, the more slowly and hesitantly its capitalism, *ceteris paribus,* will disorganise. Thus such disorganisation is to be found in Britain and the USA from the 1960s, France from the late 1960s/early 1970s, Germany from the 1970s, and Sweden from the late 1970s/early 1980s. I cannot demonstrate that in detail, but I will refer briefly to changes in the three main classes of western capitalism, the capitalist, the service and the working classes.

3.1 Capitalist Class

It is important to note that the concept of disorganised capitalism is not the same as that of a post-industrial society thesis. The former rather involves the claim that centrally significant to the structure of contemporary societies is the economic and financial power of large, oligopolistic companies, i.e. monopoly capitals. Furthermore , the so-called shift to service employment in contemporary capitalism does not mean that people are disproportionately buying services – on the contrary, they increasingly buy sophisticated domestic goods which enable people to "self-service" themselves (see Gershuny and Miles 1983). The production of such commodities, however, involves substantial increases in "service" employment, either directly or increasingly hived off from the large corporations. It is, however, the development of such global corporations which has been central to the development of disorganised capitalism. What happened, very briefly, was that multinational corporations gradually took over the firms which themselves operated multinationally, often producing different products and based on different industrial processes. The attachment to any single economy was more tentative, as capital was free to expand (and to contract) on a global basis. A much more complex spatial division of labour developed in which different parts of different production processes were separated off and developed within different national economies depending, in part at least, on relative wage rates and worker organisation. The spatial division of labour, which in the earlier phases resulted from the unplanned patterns established by a considerable number of legally separated enterprises, becomes, under disorganised capitalism, a planned development *internal* to the vast global corporation.

The changes here have been truly momentous. In 1950, 75% of the leading 180 American multinationals and 86% of the leading 135 European multinationals had subsidiary networks in only six countries or less. By 1970 these figures had fallen to 5% and 23% respectively, as corporations expanded into dozens of countries as they pursued a worldwide strategy. Much of this expansion has been into other western economies as there has been a substantial interpenetration of capital across those economies. These global corporations have been very important in restructuring international trade – trade is now substantially organised within corporations and not nations. The flows of trade, their direction, volume and pricing, are more and more at the discretion of global corporations, which make these administrative decisions internally for the purpose of maximising global profit. This greatly increases the vulnerability of single *national* states which are unable to regulate and direct such flows of international trade, which take place under the visible hand of the global corporation; and yet at the same time all the major economies are increasingly dependent on the earning of "exports."

A number of processes that have contributed to these developments include: the break-up during the 1950s and 1960s of the old empires and spheres of influence (which were very much part of "organised capitalism"); the development of computerised systems of information storage and retrieval, and of satellite-based communications which transcend the nation-state; the long-term fall in the rates of profit in manufacturing industry in the western economies and the rising proportion of profits generated from "finance", and the consequential necessity for restructuring; the growth of new international money markets (particularly in Eurodollar and Eurobond markets), which permitted large companies to engage in financial speculation and indeed to become, in a sense, bankers as they took advantage of differential exchange and interest rates – a growth of astonishing proportions, so that there is now accumulated an international debt five times greater than the entire stock of money in the USA; and the general acceleration in the movements of capital which has become less government-regulated as a new loci of economic and financial power developed towards the end of the post-war boom – particularly as banks became de-regulated, and de-controlled. The most important form of "privatisation" has, in fact, been the growth of the private international money markets which now dwarf the financial power of the IMF or the World Bank (see Brett 1983; Hogan and Pearce 1984; van der Pijl 1984).

3.2 Service Class

Crucial to my argument here is that apparently similar societies develop different trajectories of economic and social development. Elsewhere I have tried to show that one factor that makes a major difference to such trajectories is the relative importance of a "service class" (see Urry 1986; Lash and Urry 1987, chap. 6; Goldthorpe 1982). There are five central points to note about this "service class":
(1) It consists of those dominant positions or places within the social division of labour which do not principally involve the ownership of capital, land or buildings.
(2) Those places are located within a set of interlocking social institutions that "service" capital through meeting three functions: to conceptualize the labour process; to control the entry and exercise of labour-power within the

workplace; and to orchestrate the non-household forms under which labour-power is produced and regulated.

(3) Those places enjoy superior work and market situations: incumbents thus exercise authority within each institution; typically enjoy well-defined "careers" in which work and market situations improve side by side; and enjoy medium to high levels of trust and discretion often stemming from forms of professional control and closure.

(4) Entry into such places is generally regulated by the differential possession of credentials, which are either organization-specific or are general. Such credentials serve as the main demarcation between the service class and "de-skilled white-collar workers", although changes occur in exactly where the demarcation is to be found.

(5) The relative size, the power, and the composition (male/female, public/private) of the service class vary substantially, depending upon class conflicts between capital and labour; gender conflicts, particularly over attempts to professionalize/masculinize occupations; struggles to extend educational credentialism; attempts to "professionalize" particular sets of work tasks; conflicts over the size, functions and organization of the state; sectoral changes in the national economy, and so on.

The society in which such a service class has had the most significant impact is the USA. Central to its trajectory has been the growth of a powerful service class in the early years of the century. This class possesses considerable "causal powers" which were initially realised in the USA. These powers are to restructure capitalist societies so as to maximise the divorce between conception and execution and to ensure the elaboration of highly differentiated and specific structures within which knowledge and science can be developed and sustained. The powers thus involve the deskilling of productive labourers, the maximising of the educational requirements of places within the social division of labour and the minimising of non-educational/non-achievement criteria for recruitment to such places, and the enhancement of the resources and income devoted to education and science (whether this is privately or publicly funded).

In the USA the service class substantially realised these powers, beginning with the move to scientise management at the turn of the century. The rise of modern management involved a substantial break in the logic of capitalist development, and was by no means inevitable. Until it emerged employers had employed a variety of other means of control over their workforces. It was in the USA that there was a major shift in these techniques with the growth of modern management. Indeed there was in effect something of a "class struggle" in American society around the turn of the century, and that was a struggle *between* existing capital and "modern management." In that struggle existing capital lost. Complex managerial hierarchies developed in many American companies and this led to the extensive growth of white-collar employment. Such processes helped in turn to produce an interlocking complex of new institutional developments, of colleges and universities, of private foundations, of professionalizing occupations in both the private and public sector, and large corporate and state bureaucracies. They developed and extended themselves between labour and capital, constituting a kind of wedge or third force in American society. There was then a process of "the making of the American service class", a process beginning with the initial development of modern management in the years before the First World War. Paradoxically then what is understood as the archetypal capitalist society, the USA, is that in which its structure has been most transformed by the development of an influential third force apart from those of capital and labour. It is the growth of this American service class which in part accounts for the particular character of American capitalism.

More recently, in the post-war period, similar developments have occurred in all the major western societies and have opened up new lines of social division, particularly involving the so-called "new" social movements, changing the patterns of "class versus class" social conflict, and affecting the powers of the working class in particular.

3.3 Working Class

While the process of organisation meant the spatial concentration of the means of production, distribution and social reproduction, disorganisation has meant a spatial scattering or de-concentration of this gamut of social relations. This spatial scattering has been translated in terms of a decline of not just the city, but of the "region" and of the nation-state. Crucial transformations occurred in the spatial distributions of social classes, away from the "inner cities," out of the conurbations and large cities and away from the previously dominant extractive/manufacturing industry (see Lash and Urry 1987, chaps. 4 and 5, for details).

These points can be clearly seen in connection with the spatial distribution of British trade unionism (see Massey and Miles 1984, on many of the following points). In the immediate post-war period, at the height of organised capitalism, union membership was concentrated in the cities, the coalfields and the regions of industrial concentration. Many unions were predominantly based in a few parts of the country. This was not only true of the unions which organised particular industrial sectors (the Association of Textile Workers, for example), but was also the case for the large general unions. Union strength was concentrated in the "heartlands" of industrial Britain.

Recently, however, the decline in union membership (2 million since the late 1970s) has particularly affected the old bases in these very industrial heartlands. There has been a flattening out of membership between different areas. Massey and Miles note that in 1951 the AUEW had 3500 more members in its base areas (London, Lancashire, Birmingham/Coventry, South Wales, Glasgow/Paisley) than in the rest of the country; by 1979 these "central" areas had 120,000 *fewer* members than the remaining areas. Total membership fell by 17% over the same period. This pattern of spatial dispersal has also affected unions which were initially more widely distributed. Between 1951 and 1983, NALGO, for example, mainly contracted in those areas in which 10% or more of its membership had been concentrated at the beginning of the period. Likewise in NUPE the share of membership of the periphery (North, South West and Wales) increased from 7% to over 20% between 1971 and 1983. Moreover, the increasing numerical importance of public sector and white-collar unions, which are spatially more even in their distribution, has itself served to effect an increased spatial levelling of British trade unionism overall.

This is connected with the decline in the manufacturing employment significance of the "city". Lane summarises how cities had been singularly important for British trade unionism:

What the city has provided has been quick and easy communication via an elaborate network of informal meeting places and formal organisations. The city, too, has a large and diverse population and this bestows on the individual a certain social invisibility, an immunity from the sort of scrutiny and social censorship that is more evident in the small town. The city [. . .] has provided both a range of organisation and a high degree of personal "protection" (1982: 8).

With the locational changes noted above, the plants remaining in the larger cities will be those which are less likely to be centres of militant trade unionism; while the plants established in the smaller towns and cities, although unionised, will be unlikely to develop as centres of militancy. This is partly because of the employment of a "green" labour force, but also because of the distance from the previous centres of militancy in that union, the difficulties of worker organisation in a large number of spatially dispersed plants, and the general lack of a radical culture in many smaller towns and cities in Britain.

Moreover, the development of multinational and global corporations has made the workforce particularly hard to organise. This is for a number of reasons: (1) it is very difficult for local shop stewards to discover how their company is, in fact, organised and the real financial standing of different plants; (2) there is a fairly high degree of financial autonomy (between divisions or even plants) which sets one group of workers against another, especially with the general growth of *plant* bargaining; (3) companies now produce an enormous range of different products and workers are again divided in terms of the different labour process involved in different product lines; and (4) the spatial redistribution of plants, even within a single country, has made the process of organising a section of the labour force very hard to achieve, requiring large travel and financial resources.

Partly as a result there are important spatial differences in strike activity. In the later 1970s, for example, the incidence rates of industrial disputes were two or three times as high in the North, Yorkshire and Humberside, the West Midlands and Scotland, compared with East Anglia, the South East and the South West. However, for all that these spatial changes are of importance, it is not the case that strike activity will itself disappear with the development of "disorganised capitalism". This is partly because of the decline of the national structures within especially the private sector in which labour had been organised. Since the later 1950s there has been a marked increase in shop-floor organisation, especially within some sectors of manufacturing, but also within parts of service employment as well. Cronin talks of the "extensive character of organisations on the shop floor", and this has been linked with the increased tendency to sectionalism within British trade unionism (Cronin 1983: 153). So long as collective bargaining was industry-wide or national, the pursuit of sectional interest could be partly held in check. With the growth in plant-level bargaining, itself a very clear response to the growth of massive *multi*-plant corporations, sectional competitiveness has become far more marked, and hence the prospects for corporatist-type national bargaining compromises has become jeopardised.

This can be interestingly seen by considering the historical patterning of British strike rates: there are five waves of strikes – 1910–13, 1919–20, 1957–62, 1968–72 and 1984–85. It is important to note that these waves have, roughly speaking, characterised the periods of transition, the first two from the liberal to the retarded organised phase, and the latter three from the organised to the disorganised phase. There was no major wave of strikes during the main period of British organised capitalism, between the 1920s and the later 1950s. The onset of disorganised capitalism has led to some considerable development of plant-based industrial conflict, particularly between the late 1960s and the mid-1970s, although this was substantially infused with non-class specific radical-democratic discourse.

4. Conclusion

To conclude, then, it was the characteristic of organised capitalism that the basic parameters of politics were set by social class, particularly by the struggle of labour and capital. Although some of the features of such struggle remain, they are now overlain by a variety of alternative bases of organisation, of new social movements, of a widespread group-based instrumental collectivism, of an internationalised classless culture, of a market-based neo-conservatism, and of the growth of the institutional and cultural resources of a powerful service class intermediate between capital and labour. The structures of the "modern" world are being transformed well away from Marx's prognostications in the *Manifesto,* and although the social relations between labour and capital structure those developments internationally, the patterns of social life and social struggle within different advanced *nation*-states are becoming decidedly disorganised. Indeed, it is part of the disorganising of western capitalism that relatively "classless" cultural forms have become of greater importance in the structuring of contemporary social life. If social action always involves an intermingling of presence and absence, modern culture permits an extraordinarily heightened "presence-availability", of social situations, events, myths and images which cohere around and "construct" diverse "subjects". With the sea change in modern society, with the fact that large organisations, workplaces and cities, are no longer getting more and more powerful for each individual, the processes of forming, fixing and reproducing "subjects" is increasingly "cultural," formed in diverse ways out of a myriad of myths and images, of consumer products, of available "life-styles" not at all based on where one lives or who one knows, that is, on those who are immediately present in one's class milieu. Thus, to paraphrase the *Manifesto of the Communist Party,* the fast-frozen relations of organised capitalism – which were structured around class, city, region, nation and even the world – are melting into air.

References

Berman, M., *All that is Solid Melts into Air. The Experience of Modernity.* London: Verso. 1983

Brett, E., *International Money and Capitalist Crisis.* London: Heinemann. 1983

Cronin, J. A., Politics, Class Structure and the Enduring Weakness of British Social Democracy, *Journal of Social History* 16: 123–42. 1983

Gershuny, J. and I. Miles, *The New Service Economy.* London: Pinter. 1983

Goldthorpe, J. H., On the Service Class, its Formation and Future, in: *Social Class and the Divisions of Labour.* A. Giddens and G. Mackenzie (eds.), Cambridge: University Press, pp. 162–85. 1982

Hogan, W. P. and I. F. Pearce, *The Incredible Eurodollar.* London: Unwin. 1984

Lane, T., The Unions: Caught on an Ebb Tide, *Marxism Today.* September: 6–13. 1982

Lash, S. and J. Urry, *The End of Organized Capitalism.* Cambridge: Polity. 1987

Massey, D. and I. Miles, Mapping out the Unions, *Marxism Today* May: 6–13. 1984

Marx, K. and F. Engels, *Manifesto of the Communist Party.* London: Foreign Languages. 1888

Urry, J., Capitalist Production, Scientific Management and the Service Class, in: *Production, work, territory.* A. Scott and M. Storper, London: Allen & Unwin, pp. 43–66. 1986

van der Pijl, K., *The Making of an Atlantic Ruling Class.* London: Verso. 1984

Winckler, H. (ed.), *Organisierter Kapitalismus.* Göttingen: Vandenhoeck and Ruprecht. 1974

Managing the Multinationals: The Emerging Theory of the Multinational Enterprise and Its Implications for Labour Resistance

Harvie Ramsay and Nigel Haworth

1. Introduction

In recent years, contrasting views have emerged of the prospects and obstacles facing labour in its efforts to respond to the internationalisation of capital. At one extreme lie numerous naively optimistic accounts associated with certain official presentations by labour organisations themselves, or with academics jumping on the fleeting bandwagon of conferences on cross-frontier collective bargaining in the mid-1970s. Cumulative lists of formal and informal transnational contact, promotion of intergovernmental agencies and codes of corporate behaviour, and general invocations of the functional requirements of pluralism fund an evolutionary image of progress. Capital is depicted as powerful and dangerous, but its ability to adapt, respond and counteract goes almost ignored.

At the other pole are found far more pessimistic, almost fatalistic perceptions of the ability of labour to combat international capital. A structural analysis of constraints and determinants is fuelled by a harshly realistic empiricism, recounting the defeats, inadequacies, retreats, reactiveness and general impotence of a divided and parochial labour movement. The pioneers of the analysis in a sophisticated form were Olle & Schoeller (1977). On the flip side of this perspective, multinationals themselves are depicted as highly rational, co-ordinated and inventive entities, acting with a unity of purpose and coherence of logic that labour is hardly able to conceive, let alone resist, and developing ever more effective strategies for control and for disabling its opponents.

If we had to choose between these two approaches, we would opt for the second. It starts from realities (though not necessarily from the whole of reality, as we shall be arguing below), and at least initiates a dispassionate, objective assessment of possibilities. Of course, this is a disingenuous choice, since work with which we have been associated adopts very much this angle of attack (Baldry et al. 1983, 1984; Haworth & Ramsay 1984, 1988). Yet the greatest fault this pessimistic approach has is that it squeezes out any possibility whatsoever for effective labour organisation against international capital, so appearing fatalist and defeatist. If there were no hope, this would be reasonable (though reason has often been a great enemy of the indispensable will to win). But such a view can itself be attacked on two empirical fronts. Firstly, the experience of effective labour action – local, international or both – may be argued to be less depressing than it has been given credit for. For instance, the empirical claims for two American disparagers of international labour efforts (Northrup & Rowan 1979) have been gloomily accepted by many radical commentators. In one recent reappraisal, however, a selection of their assertions is examined and found to be factually suspect on several counts, consistently understating labour achievements (Press 1984). Moreover, genuine gains have been made in at least some instances both through the extension of orthodox collective bargaining, and by means of more innovative strategies for international solidarity (as with the successful challenge to Coca Cola in Guatemala).

Secondly, and complementarily, the side of capital may be argued to have been misrepresented, concealing critical weaknesses behind a curtain of gloom. It is this second possibility on which we focus in this paper. Observations pertaining to the first will intrude, nonetheless, above all because the two are in an intimate "dialectically conditioned" relationship (see Haworth & Ramsay 1988), notwithstanding the failure in most texts, management or radical, to treat labour as an active variable rather than in mere human resource terms. Our self-critical reexamination begins with a recapitulation – and worse still extension – of the catalogue of the formidable powers and strategies of international capital. From there it will proceed to a reevaluation of those powers and strategies. We seek to lever open this area with the help of what might be thought an unexpected and reluctant resource, namely the developing management literature on the dilemmas of multinational enterprise in making its strategic and organisational choices.

2. The Power of International Capital

A multinational corporation as "traditionally" conceived is an enterprise engaged in production through directly owned (whether by acquisition or new investment) branches in more than one country. It has been suggested that a further qualitative leap takes place when the multinational ceases to be just a large company in a single country, and becomes so widely dispersed and international in its operations that it becomes a "global corporation" (Taylor & Thrift 1986). Although this unilinear and evolutionary model is called into question by several of the analyses on which we will touch later, it does describe certain outward features of the trends in corporate size and spatial spread, and in economic concentration. Thus the average foreign content of the largest industrial corporations internationally in 1980 amounted to 40% of sales (30% in 1971), 33% of net assets (31%), 53% of net earnings (49%), and 46% of employment (39%). Becoming a global corporation reputedly enables the enterprise to make

full use of a number of areas of advantage relative to nationally-based capital (Haworth & Ramsay 1986; Ramsay 1986), including:
- removal of decision-making to an HQ not accessible to nationally organised labour or to governments;
- ability to switch production temporarily (e.g. during a dispute). This lessens the impact of labour sanctions, and is supported by simpler economies of capital resistance, enabling companies to bear severe but localised losses within a larger and perhaps a diverse operation;
- ability to relocate or threaten to relocate production in the longer run enabling companies to play off one labour movement, or government, against others;
- access to a wide range of sophisticated techniques, and an ability to invest in management strategy formulation to outmanoeuvre opposition;
- access and leverage through numerous channels at a political level in host countries or prospective hosts;
- a logic of operations not reducible to the performance of individual plants and so beyond the ability of organised labour to confront and debate in bargaining terms at all effectively (Baldry et al. 1983, 1984);
- the use of transfer pricing and other methods which reflect an "internalisation" of trade and prevent ready monitoring and understanding of operations by labour, often also rendering information disclosure almost meaningless (Murray 1981; Rugman 1981).

The power of multinationals was implicitly assumed to grow at a rate fairly well proportional to their measured size (whether measured in sales, employment or capital value) in the eyes of the standard critiques of the 1950s onwards. The literature was full of doomsday forecasts of the proportion of total world production that would take place within the establishments of the largest global corporations by the end of the century or earlier, and the small number of top executives in what were taken to be hierarchical and tight-run economic ships who would run the world market economy between them. In many ways this led directly to the waning concern with the issue from the late 1970s, which seems to have either buried fears under the wider concern about the recession, or to have seen a markedly slower relative rate of growth of MNCs than erstwhile predicted as equivalent to a vanishing of problems altogether.

The following reasons for dissenting from this supposition that the issue has gone away should be noted:
- MNC growth may have been slower than some expected, but it has not ceased by any means. By 1980, the United Nations monitoring organisation on multinational capital found 104,000 affiliates in total, and reported that the largest 382 corporations had 25,000 affiliates between them, accounting for 28% of the GDP of non-socialist countries. These companies employed 25 million, including one-quarter of the manufacturing sector of the developed market economies (UN 1983). Other calculations suggest that the share of the top 200 corporations in the GDP rose by 50% between 1970 and 1980 (Clairmonte &

Cavanagh 1984a). Although the recession from the mid-1970s coincides with a moderation in what seemed a headlong advance of MNCs, it remains the case that direct investments in foreign markets outperformed domestic investments throughout the market economies (Michalet 1983). Indeed, when other factors noted below are taken into consideration, the recession will almost certainly be found to have increased the real pace of multinationalisation.

– The process of internationalisation mentioned earlier puts a far more striking perspective on the scale of MNC influence. Not only is at least four-fifths of the trade of countries such as the USA and UK actually trade by MNCs, but almost half of this is estimated to be within individual companies (UN 1983; Clairmonte & Cavanagh 1984a).

– MNCs should not just be understood in terms of the activities of manufacturing concerns. The burgeoning role of service MNCs is still more striking, as international companies move to control a sector which has grown markedly faster than either primary or secondary production. The total international trade in services was estimated at between $550bn and $800bn for 1980 (not far short of manufactured exports at just over $1000bn) (Clairmonte & Cavanagh 1984b). Especially significant for the control of overall economic activity are developments in the finance sector, wherein the role of transnational banks and other financial institutions through ownership and particularly control of debts in non-finance corporations has expanded apace (Clairmonte & Cavanagh 1984a; Grou 1985). Finance organisations are found at the centre of networks tying large corporations together at the international as well as national level (Fennema & Schiff 1985). This kind of structure seems certain to make real decision making progressively more remote from any influence by labour organisations, and increasingly difficult even to ascertain and decipher.

The international service sector is for the most part particularly amenable to the restructuring of communication and control flows through the medium of information technology, in this respect at least enhancing the capacity for centralised control of corporate activity.

– The role of finance and other operations more "remote" from production takes us onto another set of MNC developments which seem to stem from adaptations to the pressures of the recession amongst other things, and may be seen as marking a further qualitative leap in the problems of labour or governments gaining any purchase on the effective seat of control of establishments employing their members/citizens. These developments, which involve the use of strategies far less tied to direct investment and so to control through ownership, also incidentally entail that the standard measures of the scale of MNC activity and influence become of progressively less value.

The methods in question include subcontracting, joint ventures, management contracts, and a variety of related arrangements (UN 1983). Subcontracting may be allied with outwork in some industries, and offloads many of the problems of fluctuation and the need to change production onto suppliers.

Latterly it has gained increasing attention as a form of "Japanization," spreading the economic dualism characteristic of Japan across the market economies, and entailing such attendant strategies as "Just-in-Time" component deliveries. Such arrangements can operate internationally as well as nationally, and (as in the electronics sector at present) may entail the subcontracting of operations to other MNCs, even competitors in other contexts, as well as to local firms. Joint ventures with local firms (or governments) may be varied through licensing or technical aid agreements and the like. Management contracts may include the provision of consultancy services (up to and including the actual running of a venture) for the local nominal owners. Brooke (1985) finds that such methods are rapidly increasing, though from a small base that means they remain as yet a small proportion of activity at least if measured by directly attributable remittances.

All of these methods aim to increase the flexibility of MNC production without many of the attendant risks. Some recent radical analyses see them as such a competitive advantage that the labour movement cannot hope to fight them, and must instead adapt them in their own policies (Murray 1985).

3. Dilemmas, Contradictions and Weaknesses in Management Strategy and Control

A characteristic feature of Marxist and like-minded analyses of the driving logic of capital is that its defined subject matter is first and foremost just that: the "logic" of "capital." This refusal to begin from a reductionist analysis of individual firms or units has well-rehearsed strengths that have enabled those writing in this genre to identify issues concerning the international social division of labour and the dynamics of class relations which the orthodox economic/management literature has been both unwilling and unable to address. In seeking a full understanding of the power of particular managements to evaluate, act upon and control their environment, and in particular their dealings with labour, such an approach has important defects, however. These may be identified (see Haworth & Ramsay 1988) as abstraction from empirical realities to represent management as "agents" of "capital," entailing simplification and editing of reality, which most importantly elides any sense of MNCs as sites of uncertainty and contradictory decision making.

The effect of this editing becomes of critical importance when one seeks to confront not the comfortable armchair questions ("how exactly can we comprehend what is happening out there?"), but the concrete ones which face the would-be adviser to labour organisations ("what is to be done?"). The abstracted conception of "capital" leads to the conclusion that very little can be done. "Capital," including the particular "fragment" under scrutiny by the adviser, is either driven ineluctably by material forces beyond its own control, or it is sentient, cohesive and rational to an extent which enables it to choose and pursue strategies to outguess, and overpower any labour response in the long run. Meanwhile "Labour", in contrast, is viewed "realistically", with all its internal divisions, limits of perception, problems of cross-frontier communication, conflicts of interest, lack of resources and organisational failings exposed. The result is a sense of hopeless impotence.

To rectify the balance of this analysis, the obvious corrective must be a "realistic" assessment of the capacity of real-world managers in actual MNCs to formulate and implement strategies to control the world around them. Since radical-Marxist approaches have with a few honourable exceptions (see e.g. Elson 1986; Jenkins 1984) tended to disregard the problematic aspects of the internal working of capital, we must turn first to those who have not done so. Inevitably, this trail leads to those seeking answers to the problems identified by and for top management (i.e. they tend to a greater or lesser extent to be "servants of power"). This engenders, *inter alia,* a tendency to overemphasise difficulties, or to focus on dilemmas which afford little potential advantage to labour. Nonetheless, the more searching and extensive contributions to this literature yield a number of invaluable insights. The contributions in this area interestingly tend to take the form of a critical appraisal of orthodox organisational and/or economic literature, both of which share with the structural radical perspective a tendency to assume perfect knowledge, rationality and co-ordination by the international firm.

A fairly eclectic and catholic approach allows us to sample the work of various writers in order to pinpoint the key areas for re-evaluation. In an earlier contribution (Haworth & Ramsay 1988) a reconsideration of the work of Dunning led us to suggest that there are a number of moments in the organisational priorities of MNCs, and that these will often be in contradiction. The reconciliation of location-specific factors (such as material supplies, labour traditions, market access and product tailoring to local demands), ownership-specific factors (including corporate technological or financial advantages from international organisation, for instance), and internal management perceptions and interests (e.g. as between different functions and/or locations of units of the company) will not only often be second-best, but may be impossibly complex to assess in "optimising" terms at all.

A further examination of work in this area suggests that economic theory may be unable to gain any purchase on the realities of MNC decision making and implementation, given the "pollution" introduced by intra-organisational factors and political questions among others (Teece 1984). Our intention in what follows is to begin to look a little more closely inside some of these problems for management as they manifest themselves in practice. Although our discussion focuses on the multinational, many of the issues raised apply equally to management activity in any large company; since almost all of the large enterprises in developed economies are now multinational in some degree at least, the distinction seems fairly unimportant at this stage of analysis.

4. The Logistics of Intelligence and Control

A technical view of the world might incline the outside observer to imagine that communication advances have for some time sufficed to allow satisfactory co-ordination and control within international organisations. This would hold true only within an organisation conforming to functionalist, unitarist images, of course. When the obstacles to flows of accurate and timely information are not primarily ones of distance (though they may still be partially spatial in the sense that organisations embody spatially shaped conflicts and obstructions), this view rapidly crumbles. The obstacles to setting up computer-based information systems even in one location in organisations, on which there is a large literature of documentation and discussion, should warn us of the inadequacies of assuming communication to be relatively unproblematical.

The logistics of transnational data flows, even before considering organisational obstacles, are anything but simple. While most large MNCs now probably boast international computing networks, the problems of selection, interpretation, presentation and utilisation of information are all far greater than those of collection or transmission. The sheer volume of potentially relevant data, and of alternative nuances of interpretation, added to the complexity of the matrix of factors (local and global) to be considered in a fully informed and rational decision, mean that hunch, feel, and the prejudices which underlie these are always likely to come to the fore in top management judgements. Even outwardly extremely internationalised organisations are likely to be controlled by individuals who are more comfortable with some kinds of decision than others – e.g. with investing in territory considered "safe" rather than locations for which ignorance/ uncertainty/stereotype creates a sense of insecurity (see Boddewyn 1983, on the differences between foreign and domestic investment or divestment for US companies). Fayerweather (1982) identifies a number of types of "communication gaps" for such organisations, including those created by distance, culture, national frontiers and environmental differences.

Alternatively, a decision to encourage local autonomy will obviate the need for all but the most skeletal briefing to the centre, with assessment left to a consideration of "hard" business results. Such a decision is likely to be shaped by other factors than the burden of judgement alone, however – considerations such as market profile, economies of production scale and co-ordination, and, far from least, by organisational tradition. National and international government efforts to legislate on or otherwise regulate cross-border data flows may also be factors, since formally at least these have proliferated since the 1970s, and these will affect centralised companies most severely (Samiee 1984). So too, will the problems of a career circuit which rotates trainee executives around subsidiaries and so reduces tenure and thereby familiarity with the local scene (Porter 1986). In any case, the choice of whether to appoint technical experts or politically skilled managers to run things locally will be a difficult one, the latter being deemed more appropriate where the strategies are "consumer-driven" or in publicly visible contexts as opposed to being based on technological advantage (ibid).

While these narrowly logistical problems are important, the potential for intra-organisational conflicts seems of greater interest and potential for the purposes of this analysis. As Brooke observes (1984: 90), the amount of co-operative behaviour necessary to make a large-scale organisation at all viable is massive. The literature on internal political conflict in organisation is well-established, and it is reasonable to expect its impact to be particularly great in a vast and international enterprise, especially one reliant on "globalised" strategies to press its advantage over competitors. Brooke suggests a number of dimensions of division, including functional departments (marketing, finance, production etc.), product groups, and geographical location. The last is complicated by the fact that a national subsidiary, once established, becomes an entity in its own right with its own axes to grind on future investment priorities and so forth.

Given these divisions, it is not surprising that organisational information-gathering is suspect. After all, its sources are chiefly the local or functional managers who have their own perceptual filters at least, if not more deliberately their own corners to defend. Most MNCs also boast intelligence units, a fact that fuels the sense of conspiratorial omniscience presented by allies of labour movements. However, Ghoshal & Kim (1986) report that these are rarely influential for a number of reasons: they form an interest group themselves and so attract the hostility of other managers supposed to supply and draw on them; they are usually staffed by inexperienced (if well-qualified) individuals; and their report enters the decision-making process near its end, as a dossier for top-level arbiters, and in circumstances where proposals have already gained a good deal of organisational momentum, thus frequently becoming rationalisations for decisions already effectively made rather than initiating anything.

Finally, organisations on the scale of MNCs find themselves constrained by their own traditions and contemporary structures, often unable to change even when they (i.e. certain key figures) can see the need for it. Bartlett & Ghoshal (1987) cite several examples: the inability of ITT to co-ordinate long-established autonomous subsidiaries to pool resources for catching up in the use of the new digital technologies, for example; or the failure of the Japanese company, Kao, to shift from its uniform and face-to-face system of management to allow local autonomy to meet differentiated demands. The latter indicates that the much-admired (or feared) Japanese style may be less appropriate and work less well outside of globally homogenised product market industries (see Jaeger 1983; Kujawa 1983), although this generalisation remains as yet overly simplistic and underdeveloped. In general, it is worth remembering that the logistics of control in the face of any divergence of interests are immense, and should be familiar to all those friends of free enterprise who are so ready with their scorn of the "distortions" of planned economies. We have heard accounts of corporate planning in large consumer-product conglomerates which bore remarkable similarity to the interactions and target-setting (and to the attendant management career assessment) of the Soviet planning system; similarly, it has been observed that General Motors is a larger planned economy than most East European states.

5. The Icon of Structure and Other False Gods

Almost all the practically-orientated textbooks on MNC organisation these days insist that structure has no role of its own, but must follow from and serve strategy. Their authors are also aware that structure retains a potent flavour of magic unto itself, however, sustaining the notion that organisational form holds the key to most problems. As a result, mechanically constructed architectures have always tended to emerge around apparently functional solutions to environmental demands. Formalism commonly prevents realisation of a need to apply different organisational principles to parts of the company with different needs (Hout et al. 1982), or of the need to change structure to accommodate and make workable a change of strategy. An example of the latter impediment is provided by Chrysler's failure for a long time to establish a means to monitor its distributors, or to decentralise and extend its design team in line with its decision to match General Motors' range (Miles & Snow 1984).

Typically problems of process in structural proposals are lacquered over with free-flowing pronouncements of teamwork, pooled resources and shared information. The exposure of this shortcoming has been prevented by another feature of prescriptive and functional approaches – for the writer to report and celebrate (bask in the reflected glory of) putative success, and rarely to acknowledge, let alone analyse, failure. An outstanding example of misdirection in recent times has been seen in the rise and fall of the "Matrix" system of management adopted by many MNCs in the 1970s. The Matrix model emerged as an angularly logical response to a dilemma which has sharpened in many ways since – whether to organise to meet the demands of geographical location (local market configuration, host government demands and so forth) or product (which leans to a global and centralised approach). This dilemma will be addressed more directly below. The structural solution that concerns us for now was to propose that local managers should be integrated into both organisational chains of command, regional and functional/product-based. The language was of organic mutality, maximising co-operation, understanding the information flows in all directions.

More recently a number of writers have recognised the failure of the Matrix; companies such as General Electric, Ciba-Geigy, Texas Instruments and Citibank are reported to have retreated from it. The recantation by a senior executive of the consultancy company most closely associated with its promulgation (Hunsicker 1982) is particularly revealing. He reports that rather than benefitting from integration, lines of authority became confused, waiting for meetings froze decision making, paperwork proliferated, and imagination and initiative were stifled. The symptoms are all familiar to those who have read the account of pathological adjustments by mechanistic organisations in Burns & Stalker's classic study, *The Management of Innovation* (1961). Other examples of the failure of global, matrix and like complex models of corporate administration are provided in an effective critique of "the reorganization merry-go-round" (Bartlett 1983), though even here the internal conflicts of interest are neglected, and unitarist solutions for renewed effective management teamwork predominate. Hunsicker's own new "rosy glow" is sought in the same direction as that of many other writers (especially those celebrating the widespread effort to copy what are seen as Japanese methods): "the human dimension of management". We shall have a little more to say on this as well. Meanwhile companies continue to wriggle around in the hook of competitive crisis by searching for solutions in organizational structure – as with IBM's decision in 1988 to undergo a massive restructure by subdivision and decentralisation in an effort to overcome problems rooted in a technological and market shift from large, profitable mainframe-based computer systems.

In general, it must be said that management appear to have retained a stout ability to rely on fads, warmly nurtured pet theories, and in short on ideologies and prejudices in their pursuit of organisational nirvana. This is fed rather than cooled off by the vested interests of a huge "strategy industry" working in consultancy companies, business schools and in the career system of companies themselves. The latest development here has been the agglomeration of Saatchi and Saatchi in an explicit effort to build a "consultancy supermarket" with all lines of service on its shelves.

The sophistication of the MNC has thus far from immunised it against this propensity, although it has led to some striking embroidery work on the policy needling front. The material force of dubious, chimerical or plain erroneous views of the world have led *inter alia* to the vagaries of accounting described by Thompson (1978) and criticised by Higgins & Clegg (1988). Unfortunately, this example also illustrates the fact that management misdirection is not necessarily a welcome weakness ripe for exploitation by labour, another observation to which we will return.

6. To Direct or not to Direct

One particularly salient dilemma faced by MNCs concerns the degree of central-isation/decentralisation appropriate to their operations. Brooke (1984) quotes his own remark that "A decentralizing ideology masks a centralizing reality." How-ever, he reports that his later investigations had led him to modify this view somewhat, and proceeds to chart the contrary pressures and possibilities which push different organisations in very different directions across distinct dimensions of operations. Nonetheless, most observers seem agreed that the more firms are dominated by a move to a global production strategy, the more they are likely to adopt a centrally co-ordinated and directive structure of decision making.

Two extremes may be identified in this context: "multidomestic" industries, where each country is a separate competitive and so organisational sphere (until recently the approach of Unilever, for instance); and "global" industries where competitive position in one country reflects and affects intimately competitive position elsewhere (Porter 1986). In general, writers in this field seem to agree that the imperatives of production and marketing in almost all industries are in the direction of globalisation (a move most radical writers seem to take further and view as universal, inevitable, unproblematical and well-advanced), to gener-ate economies of scale in R&D, manufacture (where appropriate), and market-ing. For Stopford & Turner (1985), the microelectronics revolution and its ac-celerating repercussions for almost all products is a particularly potent force, and although they question the additionally canvassed force of homogenised con-sumer tastes, others believe that the flexible manufacturing systems emerging from computerisation and advanced automation provide a basis for meeting local demands within a globally co-ordinated system (Meredith & Hill 1987). At this stage we are inclined to wonder whether this claimed flexibility and variability, together with a lessening of economies of scale allowing closer location to mar-kets of smaller factors, is at least in some degree another example of idealised presentation by managerial futurologists.

Although many top managers, imbued with similar outlooks to academic econ-omists, are inclined to see the commercial case for centralisation as paramount (Brooke 1984: 236), and to regard administrative or national barriers as irritants (irrational imperfections which distort operations), others have recognised that these constraints are no less material or obdurate in their impact on appropriate decision making. The logistical problems of control aired earlier also have a role to play here, sometimes making it impossible to bring a subsidiary into line with headquarters perceptions and plans (see e.g. Prahalad & Doz 1981a, and other discussion in Otterbeck 1981). Reorganisations such as the move towards di-visionalisation by ICI reflect the opposing pulls of international coordination and the need to simplify the product focus of management objectives. Without this, one alternative is the "retreat to basics" accepted by Levi Strauss in an effort (apparently successful for now) to cut the losses from diversification, or by Massey Ferguson at the start of the 1980s in their abandoment of an abortive entry into the construction equipment field. Again the capacity for organisation is far more restricted than radical analyses of capital allow, and the contribution of sophisticated "decision support systems" seems at times further to tangle the managerial jungle.

In addition, the demands of host countries exert a major centrifugal force, as discussed in the next session, as do the requirements of responding to local market conditions effectively. Certainly the global car, loudly (and on the left gloomily) proclaimed in the 1970s, has not exactly proved its unqualified viability. Indeed in the Australian market the decision of Ford, one of the pioneers of the global car idea, to continue to develop models to local demand (initially largely fortuitous due to a delay in replacing the dated but persistently successful Falcon), had played a major part in their displacement of GM as local market leaders (due to the initial fleet-market failure of the Commodore, a global model at the base of GM's revival in the UK under the name of the Cavalier). Both companies retreated somewhat internationally from their bold globalisation plans in the early 1980s, though Ford has subsequently announced fresh plans to centralize world medium-sized car production in Europe from the early 1990s.

The use of licensing, subcontracting and other such methods, which it was noted earlier have been seen as fresh weapons in the MNC search for flexibility and control, may be regarded as a clever adaptation to the dilemmas of centralisation versus local presence and responsiveness. As such, they appear as an inevitable evolution of MNCs. In contrast, however, they may be seen instead as a cop-out with its own problems (e.g. of lost control over flexibility of global production when cutbacks or revised sourcing is called for). Davidson & Haspelagh (1982) suggest that such global tactics actually had had the effect of leading companies to downgrade foreign investment and to use licensing and other such distancing arrangements, rather than undertake integrated and planned rationalisation. Brooke (1985) finds that most exercises of this sort to date are rather ad hoc, and play a defensive rather than aggressive role in management strategy.

Joint ventures carry the longer-run risk of fostering new competition – as with Italian scooter manufacture, confronted by independent local Indian production made possible by a shared project (Porter 1986), while in the short run the problem of controlling production quality and quantity may become greater. This difficulty was faced by Massey-Ferguson when it sought to cut back international output of its models after 1980, for instance. Examples such as Benetton may not be typical, then, dealing as they do with multiple discoordinated and extremely weak secondary suppliers (and their ill-organised workforces). The implications of these stretched links and controls for organised labour are obviously considerable and very much two-edged, likely to vary markedly with the specific circumstances of each separate instance.

7. Sovereignty Unleashed?

The previous section highlighted the difficulties of meeting the local demands of particular markets with a centralised system geared to the economics of design and production. A related strand of research by management writers emphasises the problems raised for MNC management by host country demands. Contrary to radical theory, this perspective insists that these are growing in importance as governments seek to constrain MNC flexibility in employment and location of component and materials sourcing, administration facilities and the like (i.e. to limit the "branch plant" effect). Moreover, as recalcitrance becomes more widespread, and as competition intensifies in an industry, the bargaining power for nation states to batter concessions from an MNC is enhanced. This geographical factor above all others is seen as promoting the cause of subsidiary autonomy, compounded by its mediation through the attitudes and divided loyalites of local management.

The most sustained work on this dilemma of contradictory demands on MNCs has emphasised the indeterminacy of any fixed solution, given the changing latticework of national politics, competition, technological possibilities and pressures and so forth (see Doz 1978, 1979, 1986; Doz & Prahalad 1980, 1984; Doz, Bartlett & Prahalad 1981; Prahalad 1976; Prahalad & Doz 1980). From the viewpoint of the "capital logic" approach, the most striking aspects of these and other contributions are the solidity of the threat they depict from capitalist nation states (which it usually sees as helpless victims of MNC power and manoeuverability, or purely and simply as collaborators in the expropriation of their citizens), and the materiality and depth of the administrative dilemmas in resolving them (which is usually defined away by the presumed organic nature of management).

As with other writers reviewed earlier, Doz & Prahalad recognise the economic attractions of developing global strategies by many firms. The countervailing pressures to respond to host country demands involves an attempt to encompass not only visible market response and legal requirements (the official "company-as-good-citizen" approach), but also an awareness of unspoken or *sotto voce* threats and openings. These can only be picked up by politically sensitive and well-connected local managers, who will find themselves almost powerless to act within a globally-driven, production-orientated organisation. While a move to geographical organisation opens the possibilities of greater sensitivity to such opportunities, it cannot readily weigh these against global considerations. Where MNCs attempt to reconcile this dilemma, they have to allow strategic decision making to turn into a complex advocacy process between the two perspectives. Most efforts to institute this not only face the problem of judging the correctness of decisions in the hard terms needed for modern decision making theory, but also encourage the internal micropolitical manoeuvers required to muster support for different arguments. A great deal of weight and pressure may end up resting on the arbitration powers of the top executive. Moreover, the successful solution is seen to depend either on a fortuitous rarity of major decisions (which Doz & Prahalad see as the key to the much-celebrated success of the Swedish telecommunications company, L. M. Ericsson) or on the legitimation of argument and of the bargained solution through a powerful system of inculcation of managers into a shared value system (often attributed to Japanese companies or American counterparts such as Digital or Wang). This "solution" seems to us another example of the necessity for consultant-academics to offer piously hopeful answers, which in this case are likely to depend in turn on corporate success and the lack of more deep-rooted and divisive crises. Only those who treat Japanese companies as "models" will be blind to the already sometimes fragile and changing nature of those supposed paragons. (see e.g. Sethi et al. 1984).

The response of a labour movement strategist must be to seek points of leverage within these areas of MNC uncertainty, vulnerability and reluctant responsiveness (none of the management writers reviewed here regards local concessions as more than an expedient of the moment). The potential for government intervention which in some degree supports the interests of labour is supported by observations of the recent Caterpillar decision to withdraw from their Scottish plant (Caterpillar being feted in some quarters as an exceptionally successful "global competitor" – cf. Hout et al. 1982). It has been noted that controls over redundancies operated in other countries would have made it far more difficult and expensive for the company to act thus almost anywhere in Europe outside the UK (Haworth 1987). This in turn suggests that state policy may create a potential for labour struggles well within the framework of national capitalism, where otherwise even a well-organised, determined and highly popular factory occupation proved of limited value. Despite our scepticism on the scope for action within a capitalist state expressed elsewhere, these arguments lend force to proposals for efforts to build alternative economic and social strategies within countries and at least regionally wherever possible (e.g. between countries in the EEC or more widely, or in the South Pacific Basin, for example).

8. Human Resources as Labour

In the management writings reviewed here so far, it is noteworthy that attention to labour has been treated at best as a residual issue. The active agents discussed in this literature are companies, host and home governments, and to a lesser extent consumers. The "management of human resources" (MHR) is listed, if at all, as a secondary or support function. This is a rather startling stance given the attempts made to deal with issues problematical to management, although it may do no more than reflect managerial perceptions in an era of recession.

Nevertheless, the area of personnel strategy which so many radical theorists regard as parcelled up by MNCs also proves to be far more problematic for management practice. Personnel trends towards increased flexibility through the use of temporary/part-time/female/"unskilled" cheap labour in the peripheries of capitalism provide powerful and plausible generalisations that bear up poorly under scrutiny, for example. An equally plausible case can be made for a trend to more capital-intensive, automated production runs by expensive, skilled labour attracted and held with promises of strong employment security. Both policies face problems encapuslated in the attractions of the other (nor, or course, is the choice so one-dimensional or black and white) and both can be found, as can moves in either direction. These uncertainties of MHR strategy emerge clearly from Findlay's study (forthcoming) of "Silicon Glen" (electronics in the central belt of Scotland), providing an example in an industry often regarded as exceptional in the formulation of its employment policies. Flexibility may prove to be more an ideology than an identifiable set of practices, attractive to the New Right tone of politics in many countries, and partially taken on board by executives from those countries at least in their official statements of policy (Pollert 1987). "Flexible" practices may merely reshuffle contradictions and rigidities in MHR policy (Bruno, 1987; Hyman 1988).

Another example of severe difficulties lurking below the veneer of reported MHR success may be found in the often indifferent-to-disastrous results of international QWL programmes in the late 1970s (and in similar vein the "Learn-from-Japan" wave of the '80s, including quality circles and related involvement techniques). The variability of this strategy illustrates both the problems of misconceived management outlooks (the negative effects of unitarism, for example), and the proactive role of labour in such problems of management. The clamour to report success in most sources likely to be read by managers paradoxically also illustrates once again the power of and failings attendant on faulty management theories, produced by a combination of the ideology of unitarism and the pressures on consultant-academics to provide a good public relations account of their products. If MHR is a problem for MNCs, it is because labour is itself an active and often resistant force, ironically perhaps to a much greater extent than pessimistic advocates of employee interests have tended to realise.

In toto the implications of the above observations, and the more detailed investigations for which they suggest the need, lift some of the fatalistic gloom referred to at the start of this article. If capital is not supremely knowledgeable and coordinated in its actions, there is after all some hope for labour to find points of leverage. We will address this further in our conclusions.

Several caveats are necessary, however (and we will state them now to break our habit of ending papers on downbeat notes). Firstly, as we have observed elsewhere (Haworth & Ramsay 1984, 1986), unions are singularly ill-equipped to analyse or to act on effective analysis of MNC weaknesses at the present time; whilst the above reassessment of management removes the inclination to talk as if they operated in a different universe of competence to labour, the recession has forced many unions even further back into reflex, fire-fighting or even surrender mentalities, from which there is a long way to go to informed and effective resistance. The second reservation is that labour may not benefit from the observation that many companies make decisions on ill-founded, even myth- und prejudice-laden grounds. These companies, or rather their decision-makers, may well be prone to arbitrary choices profoundly affecting the lives of employees who find themselves even less able to comprehend or influence that decision than if it were made "rationally" and with a willingness to reconsider in the light of reasoned argument or determined resistance. Thirdly, and further to this last point, large-scale capital can for the most part afford to be irrational or in serious strategic error; its power to weather mistakes, or to redefine its environment to alter the outcome, will usually enable it to survive with only mildly ruffled feathers. Contrary to the ideologies of the New Right, it is more likely to be particular groups of workers who bear the brunt of the internal readjustments occasioned by such policies, in circumstances almost entirely beyond their scope to control or even, in many cases, to ascertain. It should be added that some of the more recent and realistic analyses advanced within the labour movement internationally have recognised and sought to grapple with these and other limitations facing the mounting of counter strategies to those of capital.

9. Conclusions: Some Implications for Labour Movements

At this stage of our analysis we have scarcely begun to work through the full strategic implications of the material we have reviewed, let alone to subject the ideas to their litmus test by providing concrete recommendations to labour involved in particular struggles. In this we acknowledge our continuing vulnerability to our own earlier strictures concerning the presentation of largely academic observations, even if these may have become less fatalistic than some alternatives.

To conclude this paper, therefore, we will conjecture briefly on some of the implications of the management literature for labour as an active force. At this stage we will not pour fresh cold water by questioning the ability of labour organisation at present to ascertain and take advantage of the possibilities raised, though many of these limitations remain intact from our earlier assessments.

The prime implication is that MNCs are not, after all, impassable monoliths, driven by an impenetrable, unwavering and unambiguous pursuit of an optimal global strategy. Their revealed vulnerabilities, and the extent to which these are specific to time, place and internal condition, warn against simplistic depictions of multinational capital as all of an unresponsive piece to labour demands and pressures. There is no substitute for as detailed as possible a knowledge of the firm's management culture and philosophy, organisational structure, and competitive position and strategy, and of the location of the subsidiary with which a union must deal within this structure and strategy. "Know thine enemy" is not an idle injunction. Sometimes, of course, the most effective approach is to charge the opponent head down instead of wavering to consider the circumstances and consequences. But where the more likely choice is defeatism, the informed search for leverage through cracks in the monolith becomes crucial.

A number of possible areas for exploitation by labour may be evaluated. At present the use of persuasion through a sympathetic or for other reasons responsive government (e.g. over public sector custom or aid for company projects) is the most common method considered by unions. It may be, however, that an appreciation of internal management lines of authority and conflicting interests, together with an idea of the position of accessible management figures therein, could give unions a handle on developments through exploration of mutual advantage or threats to act in ways undermining the manager or management group in the corporate system. At the moment any such "deals" tend to be left to local management initiative, and so to be on terms defined and dictated by management priorities.

The strategic importance or marginality of a subsidiary to wider MNC plans is also of importance in assessing how far labour can play its hand through conflict. Again a lack of knowledge these days is usually reflected in a sense of labour's impotence or hyper-caution, which management will naturally seek to reinforce through warnings, misinformation, pressure on governments to restrain labour and so forth. One message which seems of general and countervailing importance in this context is our observation of the costliness and inertia of most MNC administration and decision making. This helps to explain the reported oppressiveness of host government restrictions, since the mobility of capital proves far less than economic theory or radical expectations would predict. In other words, unions can chance their arm more than is often realised. On the other hand, if an MNC does react in draconian fashion, the chances are this was already inscribed in policy. Indeed, the conflict may well have emerged as a consequence of planned marginalisation and rundown, following a management decision to be prepared to risk confrontation to squeeze all remaining value from the plant (or even to give them a public excuse for withdrawal, a common strategy in many countries in the 1980s). Overall these remarks also hint at the generalisation that while corporations are vulnerable to competitors in the late stages of a plant's life or that of a product cycle, within the MNC labour is greatly weakened vis-à-vis management by the need for rationalisation and restructuring.

While the existence of a decentralised MNC structure, and the usual attendant need for the MNC to attend to the demands of local markets and/or politics, at least puts MNCs more or less in the same power position relative to labour as domestic enterprises, the constrained and contingent nature of autonomy should be remembered and its limits ascertained. Sophisticated managements may decentralise particular functions even within global structures, and one good candidate for this is personnel/MHR. Such devolution may be more a matter of image than reality, of course: one recent study suggests suprisingly tight monitoring and constraints on local policy in this area (Purcell et al. 1987).

The public reason for decentralisation will probably be responsiveness to a particularly variable aspect of local circumstances and needs, as reported repeatedly in interviews with management in overseas companies in Australia, for example (Ramsay 1986). Another reason may be the insulation of local bargaining and MHR issues from international developments in wages and conditions, and the prevention of international labour links (see Beynon 1984 on Ford's country-by-country bargaining and implementation of their employee involvement programmes, for instance). As Harvey (1982) astutely notes, contrary to market theory the power of capital is enhanced in each locality by low mobility of labour and the maintenance of spatial divisions in the working class. This in turn revives the need for labour to look not merely at local possibilities for action, but at the possibilities of international cooperation at regional and global levels. Our reconsideration incidentally leads us to upgrade both the symbolic significance (and the volume of the message to management) from international combine gatherings, even though the substance of policy formulation at these is usually thin, and also the important potential even of merely informational exchanges.

If this restores some hope for the value of a programme of action, it only lays down the skeleton of a manifesto for a far more extensive and acute system of information gathering and analysis on MNCs. The task of producing a practicable and strategically worthwhile decision support system for labour remains in its infancy, and although the development of information processing and communications technology makes it more feasible than ever before, the resources and vision for its creation are still seemingly some way off. It will probably be necessary to demonstrate the concrete advantages to labour action to be gained from such a system before it will get the necessary support. That we have not yet demonstrated here, only that it is a possibility.

References

Atkinson, J. & D. Gregory, A Flexible Future: Britain's Dual Labour Force, *Marxism Today*, April: 12–17. 1986

Atkinson, J. & N. Meager, Is Flexibility Just a Flash in the Pan? *Personnel Management*, Sept.: 26–29. 1986

Baldry, C. J., N. Haworth, S. Henderson & H. Ramsay, Fighting Multinational Power: Lessons from the Closure of the Massey-Ferguson Factory, Kilmarnock, *Capital & Class* 20: 157–166. 1983

Baldry, C., N. Haworth, S. Henderson & H. Ramsay, Multinational Closure and the Boundaries of Resistance, *Industrial Relations Journal* 14 (4), Winter: 17–27. 1984

Baliga, B. R. & A. M. Jaeger, Multinational Corporations: Control Systems and Delegation Issues, *Journal of International Bussiness Studies* Fall: 25–39. 1984

Barnet, R. J. & R. E. Muller, *Global Reach: The Power of the Multinational Corporations.* New York: Simon & Shuster. 1974

Bartlett, C. A., Multinational Structural Change: Evolution Versus Reorganization, in: Otterbeck, L. (ed.), pp. 121–145. 1981

Bartlett, C. A., MNCs: Get off the Reorganization Merry-Go-Round, *Harvard Business Review* 6 (2) March–April: 88–146. 1983

Bartlett, C. & C. Ghoshal, Managing Across Borders: New Strategic Requirements, *Sloan Management Review* 28 (4) Summer: 7–17. 1987

Beynon, H., *Working For Ford,* Harmondsworth: Penguin. 1984

Boddewyn, J. J., Foreign and Domestic Divestment and Investment Decisions: Like or Unlike? *Journal of International Business Studies* 14 (3), Winter: 23–35. 1983

Brewer, T. L., The Instability of Governments and the Instability of Controls on Funds Transfers by Multinational Enterprises: Implications for Political Risk Analysis, *Journal of International Business Studies* 14 (3), Winter: 147–158. 1983

Brooke, M. Z., *Autonomy and Centralization: A Study in Organizational Behavior.* New York: Holt, Rinehart & Winston. 1984

Brooke, M. Z., International Management Contracts: Servicing Foreign Markets and Selling Expertise Abroad, *Journal of General Management* 11 (1), Autumn: 4–15. 1985

Bruno, S., Micro-flexibility and macro-reality: some notes on expectations and the dynamics of aggregate supply, *Labour* 1(2): 127–151. 1987

Burns, T. & G. M. Stalker, *The Management of Innovation.* London: Tavistock. 1961

Casson, M. (ed.), *The Growth of International Business.* London: George Allen & Unwin. 1983

Clairmonte, F. F. & J. H. Cavanagh, *Transnational Corporations and Global: Markets: Changing Power Relations.* Sydney: Transnational Corporations Res. Project, Univ. of Sydney, Res. Monograph No. 20. 1984a

Clairmonte, F. F. & J. H. Cavanagh, *Transnational Corporations and Services: The Final Frontier.* Research Monograph No. 19, Sydney: TNCRP, Univ. of Sydney. 1984b

Cray, D., Control and Co-Ordination in Multinational Corporations, *Journal of International Business Studies* 15 (2), Fall: 85–98. 1984

Curson, C. (ed.), *Flexible Patterns of Work.* London: IPM. 1986

Davidson, W. H., Administrative Orientation, and International Performance, *Journal of International Business Studies* 15 (2), Fall: 11–23. 1984

Davidson, W. H. & P. Haspelagh, Shaping a Global Product Organization, *Harvard Business Review* 60 (4), July–August: 125–132. 1982

Doz, Y., Managing Manufacturing Rationalization within Multinational Companies, *Columbia Journal of World Business* 13 (2), Fall: 82–93. 1978

Doz, Y., *Government Control and Multinational Strategic Management: Power Systems and Telecommunication Equipment.* New York: Praeger. 1979

Doz, Y., *Strategic Management in Multinational Companies.* Oxford: Pergamon. 1986

Doz, Y. & C. K. Prahalad, How MNCs Cope with Host Government Intervention, *Harvard Business Review* 58 (2), March–April: 149–160. 1980

Doz, Y. & C. K. Prahalad, Patterns of Strategic Control within Multinational Corporations, *Journal of International Business Studies* 15 (2), Fall: 55–72. 1984

Doz, Y., C. A. Bartlett & C. K. Prahalad, Global Competition Pressures and Host Company Demands: Managing Tension in Multinational Companies, *California Management Review* 23 (3): 63–74. 1981

Dunning, J. H. & R. D. Pearce, *The World's Largest Industrial Enterprises 1962–83.* London: Gower. 1985

Egelhoff, W. G., Patterns of Control in U.S., U.K. and European Multinational Corporations, *Journal of International Business Studies* 15 (2), Fall: 73–83. 1984

Elson, D., A New International Division of Labour in the Textile and Garment Industry: How far Does the "Babbage Principle" Explain It? *International Journal of Sociology and Social Policy* 6 (2): 45–84. 1986

Elson, D. & R. Pearson, The Subordination of Women and the Internationalisation of Factory Production, in: K. Young et al. (eds.) *Of Marriage and the Market.* London: CSE Books, 1981: pp. 146–166. 1981

Elson, D. & R. Pearson (eds.) (forthcoming), *Women and Multinationals.* London: Tavistock.

Enderwick, P., *Multinational Business and Labour.* London: Croom Helm. 1985

Fayerweather, J., *International Business Strategy and Administration.* Cambridge, Mass.: Ballinger. 1982

Fennema, M. & H. Schiff, The Transnational Network, in: F. N. Stockman et al. (eds.) *Networks of Corporate Power: A Comparative Analysis of Ten Countries.* Oxford: Polity Press: pp. 250–266. 1985

Findlay, P. (forthcoming), *What Management Strategy? Labour Utilization and Regulation at Scotland's "Leading Edge,"* DPhil thesis, Nuffield College, Oxford.

Franko, L. G., *The European Multinationals.* London: Harper and Row. 1976

Franko, L. G., *The Threat of Japanese Multinationals: How the West Can Respond.* Chichester: Wiley. 1983

Frobel, F., J. Heinrichs & O. Kreye, *The New International Division of Labour.* Cambridge: Cambridge University Press. 1980

Ghoshal, S. & S. K. Kim, Building Effective Intelligence Systems for Competitive Advantage, *Sloan Management Review* 28 (1), Fall: 49–58. 1986

Grou, P., *The Financial Structure of Multinational Capitalism.* Leamington Spa: Berg. 1985

Hahlo, H. R., J. G. Smith & R. W. Wright (eds.), *Nationalism and the Multinational Enterprise: Legal, Economic and Managerial Aspects.* Leiden: Sijthoff. 1977

Hamilton, F. E. I. & G. J. R. Linge (eds.), *Spatial Analysis and the Industrial Environment Vol. II International Industrial Systems.* Chichester: John Wiley & Sons. 1981

Harvey, D., *The Limits to Capital.* Oxford: Balckwell. 1982

Haworth, N., Making Tracks: Caterpillar's Crawl from Scotland, *Fraser of Allander Institute, Quarterly Economic Commentary* 12 (4), May: 67–71. 1987

Haworth, N. & H. Ramsay, Grasping the Nettle: Problems with the Theory of International Trade Union Solidarity, in: Waterman, P., 1984: 60–87. 1984

Haworth, N. & H. Ramsay, Matching the Multinationals: Obstacles to International

Trade Unionism, *International Journal of Sociology and Social Policy* 6 (2): 55–82. 1986

Haworth, N. & H. Ramsay, Labour and Management Strategies in the World Market: The Plot Thickens, in: T. Dickson & D. Judge (eds.), *The Politics of Industrial Closure*. London: Macmillan: pp. 141–164. 1988

Hertner, P. & G. Jones (eds.), *Multinationals: Theory and History*. London: Gower. 1986

Higgins, W. & S. Clegg, Manufacturing Decline and the Sociological Critique of Enterprise Calculation, *Organization Studies* 9 (1): 69–89. 1988

Hood, N., D. Stewart & S. Young, Monitoring Multinationals in Scotland: Some Preliminary Evidence in Appraising Corporate Behaviour, *Managerial & Decision Economics* 3 (3): 164–171. 1982

Horn, N. (ed.), *Legal Problems of Codes of Conduct for Multinational Enterprises*. Deventer: Kluwer. 1981

Hout, T., M. E. Porter & E. Rudden, How Global Companies Win Out, *Harvard Business Review* 60 (5), Nov.-Dec.: 98–108. 1982

Hunsicker, J. Q., The Matrix in Retreat, *Financial Times* 25 Oct. 1982

Hyman, R., The Fetishism of Flexibility, paper to conference on Strategies of Flexibilisation in Western Europe, Roskilde Universitetsonter, 6–10 April (mimeo). 1988

Hymer, S., *The Multinational Corporation: A Radical Approach*. (papers edited by R. Cohen et al.) Cambridge: Cambridge University Press. 1979

Jaeger, A. M., The Transfer of Organizational Culture Overseas: An Approach to Control in the Multinational Corporation, *Journal of International Business Studies* 14 (2), Fall: 91–113. 1983

Jenkins, R., Divisions over the International Division of Labour, *Capital & Class* No. 22: 28–58. 1984

Kim, W. C., Competition and the Management of Host Government Intervention, *Sloan Management Review* 28 (3), Spring: 33–39. 1987

Kujawa, D., Technology, Strategy and Industrial Relations: Case Studies of Japanese Multinationals in the United States, *Journal of International Business Studies* 14 (3), Winter: 9–22. 1983

Levinson, C., *International Trade Unionism*. London: George Allen & Unwin. 1972

Litvak, I. A. & C. J. Maule, Foreign Subsidiaries as an Instrument of Host Government Policy, in: Hahlo et al. (eds.): pp. 195–206. 1977

Mathur, S. S., Strategy: Framing Business Intentions, *Journal of General Management* 12 (1) Autumn: 77–97. 1986

Meredith, J., The Strategic Advantages of the Factory of the Future, *California Management Review* 29 (3), Spring: 27–41. 1987

Meredith, J. R. & M. M. Hill, Justifying New Manufacturing Systems: A New Managerial Approach, *Sloan Management Review* 28 (4), Summer: 49–61. 1987

Michalet, C. A., Multinationals: Change of Strategy in the Face of Crisis, *Multinational Business* 1983 (1): 1–10. 1983

Miles, R. E. & C. C. Snow, Fit, Failure and the Hall of Fame, *California Management Review* 26 (3), Spring: 10–28. 1984

Murray, R. (ed.), *Multinationals Beyond the Market*. Brighton: Harvester. 1981

Murray, R., Benetton Britain: The New Economic Order, *Marxism Today* November: 28–32. 1985

Newby, H., J. Bujra, P. Littlewood, G. Rees & T. L. Rees (eds.), *Restructuring Capital: Recession and Reorganization in Industrial Society*. London: Macmillan. 1985

Northrup, H. R. & R. L. Rowan, *Multinational Collective Bargaining Attempts: The Record, the Cases and the Prospects*. Philadelphia: University of Pennsylvania Press. 1979

Olle, W. & W. Schoeller, World Market Competition and Restrictions upon International Trade Union Policies, *Capital & Class* 2: 56–75, (reprinted in P. Waterman (ed.) 1984: pp. 39–59). 1977

Organisation for Economic Cooperation & Development, *Disclosure of Information by Multinational Enterprises*. Paris: OECD. 1983

Otterbeck, L., *The Management of Headquarters – Subsidiary Relationships in Multinational Corporations*. Aldershot: Gower. 1981

Pascale, R. T., Perspectives on Strategy: The Real Story behind Honda's Success, *California Management Review* 26 (3), Spring: 47–72. 1984

Peccei, R. & M. Warner, Industrial Relations Decision Making in Multinational Firms, *Journal of General Management* 4 (1): 66–71. 1976

Pollert, A., "Flexible" Patterns of Work and Ideology: The New Right, Post-Industrialism and Dualist Analysis, paper to British Sociological Assoc. Annual Conference, 6–9 April. 1987

Porter, M. E., Changing Patterns of International Competition, *California Management Review* 28 (2), Winter: 9–40. 1986

Poulantzas, N., Internationalisation of Capitalist Relations and the Nation State, *Economy & Society* 3 (2): 145–179. 1974

Poynter, T. A., Managing Government Intervention: A Strategy for Defending the Subsidiary, *Columbia Journal of World Business* 21 (4) Winter: 55–65. 1986

Prahalad, C. K., Strategic Choices in Diversified MNCs, *Harvard Business Review* 54 (4), July–Aug.: 67–78. 1976

Prahalad, C. K. & Y. Doz, Strategic Management of Diversified Multinational Corporations, in: A. Neghandi (ed.), *Functioning of the Multinational Corporation*. New York: Pergamon. 1980

Prahalad, C. K. & Y. Doz, Strategic Control – The Dilemma in Headquarters – Subsidiary Relationships, in: L. Otterbeck (ed.): pp. 187–203. 1981a

Prahalad, C. K. & Y. Doz, An Approach to Strategic Control in MNCs, *Sloan Management Review* 22 (4), Summer: 5–16. 1981b

Press, M., The Lost Vision: Trade Unions and Internationalism, in: P. Waterman (ed.): pp. 88–107. 1984

Purcell, J. & A. Gray, The Management of Industrial Relations in Multinational Companies in Britain: An Interim Report on Policy and Practice, paper to British Sociological Assoc. Annual Conference, Bradford. 1984

Purcell, J., P. Marginson, P. Edwards & K. Sisson, The Industrial Relations Practices of Multi-Plan Foreign-Owned Firms, *Industrial Relations Journal* 18 (2), Summer: 130–137. 1987

Radice, H. (ed.), *International Firms and Modern Imperialism*. Harmondsworth: Penguin. 1975

Ramsay, H. E., *Transnational Corporations in Australia: Issues for Industrial Democracy*. Policy Discussion Paper, Working Environment Branch, Department of Employment and Industrial Relations, Canberra: AGPS. 1986

Remmers, L. & J. Delatorre, *The Impact of the OECD Guidelines*. Paris: INSEAD. 1981

Rowan, R. A. L. & D. C. Campbell, The Attempts to Regulate Industrial Relations Through Codes of Conduct, *Columbia Journal of World Business* 18 (2), Summer: 111–121. 1983

Rugman, A. M., *Inside the Multinationals: the Economics of Internal Markets,* London: Croom Helm. 1981

Samiee, S., Transnational Data Flow Constraints: A New Challenge for Multinational Corporations, *Journal of International Business Studies* 15 (1), Spring/Summer: 141–150. 1984

Sethi, S. P., N. Namiki & C. L. Swanson, The Decline of the Japanese System of Management, *California Management Review* 26 (4), Summer: 35–45. 1984

Sethi, S. P. & K. A. N. Luther, Political Risk Analysis and Direct Foreign Investment: Some Problems of Definition and Measurement, *California Management Review* 28 (2), Winter: 57–68. 1986

Stopford, J. M. & L. Turner, *Britain and the Multinationals*. Chichester: Wiley. 1985

Taylor, M. & N. Thrift (eds.), *Multinationals and the Restructuring of the World Economy*. London: Croom Helm. 1986

Teece, D. J., Economic Analysis and Strategic Management, *California Management Review* 26 (3), Spring: 87–110. 1984

Thompson, G., The Relationship between the Financial and Industrial Sector of the United Kingdom Economy. *Economy and Society* 6 (3), 235–283. 1977

Thompson, G., Capitalist profit calculation and inflation accounting. *Economy and Society* 7 (4), 395–429. 1978

Thompson, G., The Firm as a "Dispersed" Social Agency, *Economy & Society* 11 (3), Aug.: 233–256. 1982

Tudyka, K. (ed.), *Multinational Corporations and Labour Unions*. Nijmegen: Univ. of Nijmegen. 1973

Van Tulder, R., Technology and the Changing Structure of European Multinationals, paper to 8th EGOS Colloquium, Antwerp, 21–29 May 1987. 1987

UN (United Nations Centre on Transnational Corporations), *Transnational Corporations – A Code of Conduct: A Composite Text*. New York: United Nations. 1979

UN (United Nations Centre on Transnational Corporations), *Transnational Corporations in World Development: Third Survey,* New York: United Nations. 1983

Warner, M. & R. Peccei, Management Decentralization and Worker Participation in a Multinational Company Context, in: B. Wilpert et al. (eds.): pp. 65–83. 1978

Waterman, P. (ed.), *For a New Labour Internationalism*. The Hague: ileri. 1984

Wilpert, W., A. Kudat & Y. Ozkan (eds.), *Workers' Participation in an Internationalized Economy*. Kent, Ohio: The Comparative Administration Research Institute, Kent State University. 1978

Work Organization Under Technological Change: Sources of Differentiation and the Reproduction of Social Inequality in Processes of Change

Wolfgang Littek and Ulrich Heisig

1. Stratification on the Basis of Group Specific Differences in Working Conditions and Within Relations in Production as Decisive Preconditions of Change

Our argument is drawn from empirical research on the transformation of working and employment conditions through technological and organizational change and its behavioural consequences on professional male white-collar workers in three industrial firms of West Germany in the early 1980s strongly affected by economic recession. (More detailed descriptions of this research and its findings are to be found in Littek (1986) and Littek and Heisig (1986)). This research confronted us with the fact that, although for the first time since the 1950s white-collar workers had to deal with radical alterations in working conditions and redundancies due to strong technological restructuring and economic decline, *high trust relations, social exchange and responsible autonomy* in white-collar sectors nevertheless remained operative. Thus, there was *no* adjustment of social relations in qualified white-collar work to a level comparable to those in skilled blue-collar work. The latter, in contrast, is organized more on the basis of *low trust, economic exchange and direct control.* Intraorganizational differences in social relations and the organization of work between white-collar and blue-collar workers did not diminish. Proletarianization of white-collar workers, in the sense of adjustment to the same working conditions as prevailed in blue-collar work, could not be observed.

Starting with this observation the chapter seeks to provide an explanation of the fact that even radical technological and organizational restructuring of work, on the basis of new information technologies and redundancies, accentuated by economic recession, occurred with relatively little overt resistance. On the contrary, technical and organizational measures were often welcomed and supported actively by large groups of qualified white-collar employees (as sometimes by better skilled blue-collar workers, too). These groups took the opportunity of change to appropriate for themselves additional elements of work and new relevant functions in the labour process in order to strengthen their occupational position inside the firm, mainly at the cost of their colleagues with less initiative and less relevant qualifications. Far-reaching technological change obviously was made possible by maintaining and securing social stability (i.e. no dramatic conflicts or resistance) through deepening differences in working conditions, status and social relations and by unequally distributing losses and gains in favour of central white-collar groups. This expansion of inequality had the relevant social effect of stabilizing the already established relations in production inside each sector of employment. It led to high trust sectors growing larger within companies during times of economic recession while in many companies the labour force *in toto* was shrinking.

In constructing our argument, we sometimes refer to topics and positions broadly discussed in the "labour process debate" but employ deviating centres of gravity by stressing *educational differences* among workers, which have far-reaching consequences for the development of relations *in* production as well as the organization and quality of work. Thus, our interpretation of the "facts" showed that analysis which deals with the dynamics of production has to take into account the differences in social relations inside a work organization because they shape and influence the technical and organizational transformation of work processes (i.e. the rationalization of work). Furthermore, the differences in social conditions for different groups of workers influence the styling of work contents, the discretionary margins of a job, and beyond that affect the specific economic and social results of change far more than is anticipated by most "objectivist" Marxist theory which is influenced by the theory of the "real subordination of labour" to capital. (An informative criticism of real subordination theroy is to be found for example in Cressey and MacInnes' (1980) contribution to the labour process debate). Such traditional positions of Marxist class analysis – dominant in West German industrial sociology of the 1960s and 1970s – follow the premise that, under capitalist conditions, the transformation of the means of production will adjust the work situations of blue-collar workers and white-collar workers and level all differences in social relations in production. (On the basis of a comparative study on reactions to technological and organizational change by blue-collar workers and white-collar workers, Kudera et al. (1983) present a rather feuilletonistic but brilliant critique of the assumption that the work situations of both groups of workers, as well as their modes of behaviour, will adjust.) In these arguments a general tendency for the deskilling of labour is assumed to be inherent in the capitalist mode of production in the development of the means of production, which, in the long run, will "automatically" lead to a homogeneous proletarianized working class.

This class structural perspective is widespread even today. In this respect, the German debate has been different from Great Britain and the United States where Braverman (1974), who is one of the most prominent representative of the class structural position in these countries, already by the mid-1970s had unleashed a controversial and inspiring labour process debate. Braverman's book – which was published in German in 1977 – almost completely fitted into the German tradition of theorizing capital-labour relations (for an example of German theorizing see: Mendner 1975). The book was positively received in Germany as one further mosaic piece in an ongoing debate. Similar positions dominated there until the mid-1980s, when the Kern and Schumann study of 1984 questioned this paradigm of industrial sociology. (An excellent example of such unbroken "structural" theorizing is given by Schmiede 1983.) As a result of Kern and Schumann's thesis of "the end of the division of labour", a controversy on the future of wage work and a reception of the British labour process debate has begun among West German industrial sociologists (see: Malsch and Seltz 1987; Hildebrandt and Seltz 1987). Class structuralist perspectives fail to recognize that an industrial enterprise is, in fact, a terrain of struggles between different hierarchical, functional and positional groups, which, in order to secure their own specific interests in the course of action, mobilize their resources, temporarily form coalitions and compete against one another. This contest nearly always overlaps class boundaries and causes the outcomes of rationalization, such as the adaptation of technology and the formation of working conditions, to be socially structured by coalitions crossing hierarchical and class dimensions. This prevents the formation of cohesiveness between the different groups of workers and extenuates class conflict to a level that enables the functioning of the labour process on the basis of consent. Technical and organizational changes are not resisted collectively by the whole of the workforce, but rather are accepted or welcomed by parts of the workforce, namely the qualified and functionally relevant groups of employees, who in processes of change are quite often able to strengthen their position in order to improve their working and employment conditions.

In the course of change, the qualified members of established white-collar groups behaved in a way in order to ensure that their knowledge and their know-how would be secured, because both are the bases of their influence and privileges. As a matter of fact, these groups make use of the social positions as well as of the "areas of uncertainty" (Crozier and Friedberg 1979), which they control inside the labour process, as resources to influence management decisions and measures. Sometimes, this is achieved by defensive blockades but mostly by active participation in order to maintain their privileged positions. In this way, stratification is reproduced and stabilized not by management itself but by the self-interested strategic actions of qualified central white-collar groups whose members behave as if they were in an "antagonistic" class relation to all other working groups. Within the institutional context of the firm, economically determined antagonistic class relations between capital and labour on the level of society are modified by ideological and political relations, so that the working class within the labour process is segmented. This segmentation leads to the prevention of solidarity among the different factions, because, instead of acting as a homogeneous class when confronted by the management, the factions behave as competitive groups. (For further arguments on this see also: Clegg, Boreham and Dow 1986: 187ff.)

2. The Bilateral Reproduction of Segmentation Through Work Games Within the Labour Process

The splitting of the working class into various groups contributes to the overall social stability of an enterprise because social inequality, once established, counteracts the cohesiveness of the workforce and spirits away hierarchical conflicts by reversing them to competition between different groups which laterally struggle for the distribution of losses and gains. This competitive structure is the result of differences in modes of relations *in* production and of differences in working and employment conditions established by management, which aim at segmentation in order to maintain its domination over the labour process. Friedman (1977: 168), for example, emphasizes the stabilizing effects of stratification in the workplace that can be achieved by "splitting workers into various groups and applying different types of managerial strategies towards those groups which represents a major method whereby flexibility is gained and the capitalist mode of production itself is maintained". However, differences in working conditions and social inequality are to the same extent also the effects of labour power strategies oriented to intraorganizational conditions. In order to secure their own interests, workers themselves reproduce their segmentation by performing competitive work games. Members of the strongly established groups aim at the reproduction of functional and influential differences from which they derive advantages by voluntarily participating in these work games. In contrast, the members of the comparatively weaker marginal groups feel themselves forced to participate in these competitive work games by holders of stronger positions, if they do not intend to lose ground in the organization.

In order to explain the existing complementary interaction of management strategies and employee behaviour, one broadly discussed aspect within labour process theory serves only as a starting point: namely management's domination over the labour process being limited by the *use-value aspect of labour* together with the need for cooperation in the production of useful products or services. This aspect may in all kinds of economic situations force management to establish cooperative relationships with all groups represented within the white-collar and blue-collar sectors. Thus, it is commonly anticipated that in fact all labour processes will contain elements of consent. However, this basic general statement proves to be deficient in that it fails to explain the fundamental difference in the intraorganizational modes of relations in production and working conditions between the white-collar and the blue-collar sectors. In addition, this perspective fails to explain inter-organizational and inter-cultural differences in the organization of labour processes which, besides differences in industrial relation system and other general cultural particularities, are to a large extent due to the differences in systems of education and vocational training. Clear-cut segmentation between the two sectors is the basic social precondition which the management's strategies of work organization and change apply to. It is the difference in conditions which is essential for the specific strategies that different groups of workers develop. Differences in conditions determine the courses of action as well as their outcome. To explain these phenomena further, we hold it necessary to stress the importance of each individual's attained educational and training resources and to differentiate between skill and knowledge as subjective attributes of workers. While *skill* may be seen as the ability to carry out more or less complex prescribed work, knowledge is the prerequisite to perform more or less complex work in which personal decisions and flexibility are required.

Our research showed that differences in work games and their outcomes are attributable to the nature of the qualifications of work groups, i.e. whether they are grounded in knowledge or in (tacit) skills. In order to reach its productive aims by constantly transforming the technical and organizational foundations of the labour process (the means of production), management is highly dependent on the personal commitment and cooperation of experts, specialists and large groups of professional white-collar workers, who are required to master abstract unforeseen problems and to use their knowledge and qualifications actively. This is in contrast to the mere performing of duties or exercising of skills which is typical for skilled production workers who do prescribed work: management's dependence on their personal commitment is relatively minimal.

Inside each subgroup of workers vertical stratification is modelled by the degree of the knowledge or skill of each worker. As a result, work organizations are first of all stratified on the basis of educational differences into a white-collar and a blue-collar sector, between which there is little or no mobility. On the basis of differentiated knowledge, in white-collar sectors, and on the basis of skill in blue-collar sectors, a variety of power centres exist with different grades of influence. Apart from a host of superficial similarities, one decisive distinction exists between the two sectors. In the white-collar sector single groups or individuals control relevant "areas of uncertainty" on the basis of occupational knowledge and professional know-how and are therefore able to have a bearing on management decisions and rationalization measures. By contrast, in blue-collar sectors, where work is largely done on the basis of skill, workers control "uncertainty" and gain influence only as a collectivity.

In this way the educational differences lead to relevant behavioural differences, which are institutionally reflected in distinct relations between work contexts and bargaining contexts. This important distinction between two practical action frames of reference which workers have inside the labour process was introduced by Daniel (1973). He shows that in *bargaining contexts* workers primarily lay stress on extrinsic, mainly economic rewards, while in *work contexts* the selfsame workers refer to intrinsic rewards by measuring job content, work satisfaction and so on. White-collar workers mainly compete against one another for their individual advancement and the strengthening of their relative positions by getting more interesting, more important and more influential, as well as better paid, jobs in the social system on the basis of self-interest via work games. The actions they perform in the work context are based on a bargaining context structured by social exchange which is characterized by individual trading. Blue-collar workers, on the contrary, usually show more solidarity. They find themselves far more in opposition to management: if they want to influence management, they need to act collectively. The work games they carry out in work contexts are therefore defensive in that they primarily aim at securing mostly small margins of action inside the labour process, the "informal" improvement of their working conditions and the direct economic improvement of income. Behaviour shown in work contexts is coupled with a bargaining context defined by economic exchange, characterized by collective bargaining which seeks to directly link higher income to higher achievement.

Established groups are mostly offered advantages by management voluntarily, or they have the opportunity of pursuing advantages and personal interests by trading ("informal" bargaining). In contrast, groups whose work implies only (tacit) skills are usually in a far more defensive position. Their general experience is that management never offers them advantages voluntarily. They have to fight for their interests and only have a chance of not being deceived if they act collectively. Collective action is therefore the main instrument that blue-collar workers have for representing and securing their interests on the shop floor. A major means of doing so is by using the works councils *(Betriebsrat)* established in West German industry. It is the differences in the modes of social relations in production and the different experiences white- and blue-collar workers have inside the labour process, which form different expectations on both parts of the labour force and form different behavioural styles, which are decisive (beyond intraorganizational dimensions) for the cultural cleavage of the working class in society.

3. Distribution Patterns of Workers to Modes of Relations in Production

On the basis of the distinction between knowledge and skill, we have developed some basic characteristics of two fundamental modes of social relations in production coinciding with fundamental patterns of organizational behaviour which we can discern according to the attributes represented in Table 1.

Table 1. Two Types of Labour-Management Relations (Relations in Production)

Mode of Social Relations in Production	High Trust	Low Trust
Mode of conduct	Social exchange	Economic exchange
Basis of qualification	Occupational knowledge and professional know-how	Tacit or explicit skills, abilities to do a prescribed task
Behaviour within the labour process	Personal involvement and engagement, active participation in the rationalization of work	Defensive resistance against all kinds of management measures
Representation of interests	Trading in regard to working conditions in an individual and informal way, mostly on shop floor level	Collective bargaining of working conditions between unions, works councils and members of management in institutional contexts on enterprise level (on the basis of collective agreements between unions and employers associations of an industry).

Different vocational groups are incorporated in the social system of the firm according to the differences in the educational basis of their work. Their categorization as belonging to the high or the low trust sector is defined thus: first, by whether the performance of their work is grounded in knowledge or skill; second, by the amount of knowledge or skill required, and third, by the overall relevance of the performed task for the labour process. Beyond that, distribution to one of the sectors or positions occupied creates behavioural priorities which can be differentiated according to the degree of individualistic or collective strategies. High trust groups overwhelmingly utilize individualistic behaviour and competitive strategies to advance their position and establish their interests, whereas low trust groups prefer cohesive behaviour and collective strategies to defend their position and to secure their interests. The different relevant dimensions are summarized and brought into relation to each other in Figure 1.

As Friedman (1977: 97) argues, established white-collar groups are viewed "by top managers as more crucial to the working order of the firm, either because they contribute specialized knowledge which cannot be easily bought on the labour power market, or because they partake in the maintenance of managerial authority". This "has encouraged a hierarchy of workers in terms of their importance as individuals to top managers" (Friedman 1977: 109). White- and blue-collar workers in enterprises are treated differentially by management according to their position in the dimensions of Table 1 and Figure 1, with an unequal

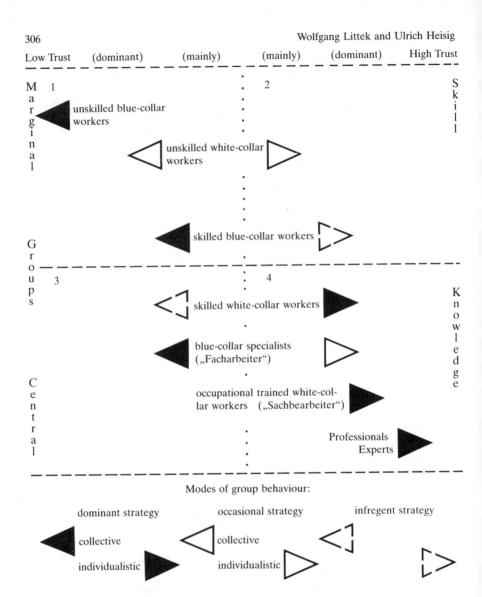

Figure 1. Workers' positioning in the Organized Labour Process in Relation to the Skill or Knowledge Basis of Their Work Roles and Modes of Behaviour

Low Trust Relations
– economic exchange
– "Taylorism" and direct control
– collective bargaining

High Trust Relations
– social exchange
– responsible autonomy
– trading of working conditions

distribution of chances and risks, gains and losses between both groups and subgroupings. This visible inequality causes a fundamental segmentation of the labour force into competing segments on the enterprise level. This intraorganizational segmentation and its permanent reproduction through inter-group competition in processes of change is the key element of the overall social stability of work organizations under technical and organizational change. One major reason for this is the transformation of conflict along hierarchical lines into lateral competition, and the continuation or rather deepening of stratification and class conflicts within the working class. (See also Burawoy (1979) on the transformation of conflicts.)

4. Dynamics of High Trust Relations

The development of social relations in production and their reproduction in strategic games is a mutual process, as Silverman (1970) and Knights and Collinson (1985) have demonstrated. High trust relations produce consent. Low trust relations likewise are accepted as modes of relations in production by both sides and are used as conditions for mutual behaviour in work contexts, and function as accepted forms to settle conflicts and guarantee the clearing of interests in bargaining contexts. Social conflicts erupt if changes in production relations and exchange relations are initiated by one side alone and not commonly attuned to.

In high trust contexts, trust, like money, is a management means of coordinating and controlling behaviour, and it is understood as such by workers. As trust is not one-sided but a mutual relation, it can only function if workers are also interested in high trust relations. In social exchange situations, where trust is offered as a reward, the ratio between work performance and economic return is not contracted formally and is not sued for legally. Hence workers who accept trust as an offer always bear a certain risk of being deceived. Because of this, high trust relations are usually only entered into by groups of employees who control relevant areas of uncertainty inside the labour process, and who, because of their specialized knowledge and know-how, cannot easily be substituted. Since their intraorganizational position in relation to management is quite strong, they can afford to deliver additional work not normally required and not necessarily remunerated. We found this to be a typical form of behaviour in that sector. Workers in high trust sectors can be sure that management will not risk disappointing their expectations, because management very much depends on their personal commitment and cooperation. To exercise control over working conditions and social exchange relations, qualified workers use their occupational knowledge and professional know-how as well as their active cooperation towards management as bargaining chips to strategically influence working conditions and exchange relations.

From the position of the workers who enter high trust and social exchange relations, strategic influence serves the reduction of uncertainties on the basis of occupational knowledge and superior information and aims at prestige and status. The gaining of influence seems to be a strategic game performed by qualified workers, in which their stake is loyalty. Loyalty is used as a means of exchange inside the labour process, which in the course of its transformation is bound to compensations. These may be won through concessions in the form of increased margins of action; through concessions in competence and discretion, through favourable treatment and consideration of their interests by management. In this context of action the gaining of influence is a work game based on "informal" power which is strategically directed towards success: the game is entered by qualified white-collar workers to give proof of their expertise, as the pre-condition for winning prestige, status and, in effect, income. (For further arguments on the relations between power, influence, trust and communication in the context of the coordination of actions within work organizations, see Zündorf (1986).)

5. Competitive Behaviour and Constraint Inside High Trust Relations

As stated above, high trust positions are secured or even advanced by their occupants on the basis of their occupational knowledge and professional know-how through personal control over important areas of uncertainty in the labour process. This control enables workers to individually exercise influence on management and to trade working conditions and benefits. Inside high trust sectors established groups gain influence on management decisions, the design of jobs and working conditions by active cooperation in work tasks and by participation in processes of change. As much as active behaviour is cooperative in the vertical dimension, it is competitive in the lateral direction. By cooperating with management, established groups gain influence and enjoy success mostly at the cost of weaker groups, who are also forced to behave in a competitive way as long as cooperative and participative modes of conduct dominate in white-collar sectors. In effect, in white-collar sectors cooperation and participation remain the central means of all established and marginal workers to secure or advance their interests. Defensive behaviour, resistance and insubordination, for example, by blockades of information, are the exception. Such "strategies" are mostly practiced stealthily by lower qualified marginal white-collar groups in a disadvantaged position in white-collar sectors in relation to similar groups in the blue-collar sector. Their weakness is due to the fact that while in low trust sectors no particular group is able to achieve important gains at the cost of colleagues, and the "balance of interests" in bargaining contexts is achieved by collective bargaining on a class level, in areas structured by high trust the trading of interests on the basis of qualificational and positional differences dominates.

For marginal groups of white-collar workers who are in a position between high and low trust relations, it is problematic to be non-cooperative in labour processes, to be defensive in processes of change and to participate in collective bargaining, for two reasons. First, it would be a "dangerous" self-admittance of weakness and a crossing of the borderline from the privileged high trust fraternity to the unprivileged low trust sector. This causes marginal groups to often stick to individual competitive behaviour, even if there seems to be no longer an "objective" reason to do so. Second, as long as individualism and competitiveness are still the dominant and successful patterns of behaviour used by established white-collar groups, the switching over of weaker marginal groups to collective forms of resistance and bargaining could be undercut by stronger groups and colleagues, because they refuse to act as partners in solidarity.

As a result, marginal white-collar workers are the helpless victims of a twofold competitive structure mostly in the sense that they are ground between the mill-stones of a stable high trust sector they never really belonged to, and a similarly stable low trust sector which they themselves never accepted they were to be part of. Inside high trust sectors competition and displacement of comparatively low qualified members is keener than in low trust sectors, because in low trust sectors intra-group struggles are mitigated by the acceptance of a common proletarian class position and an overall opposition to management.

In high trust systems a self-strenghtening double pattern exists. High trust relations do have their "objective" *raison d' être* in the existence of occupational knowledge and professional know-how which qualified groups of workers control. This fact is accepted equally by management and by workers. Knowing this, management on the one hand aims to appropriate this knowledge and know-how, because it is the basis of employees' resistance and counter-power, and sometimes it is successful in doing so. On the other hand, management cannot destroy this knowledge because it is these personal capacities which are the main preconditions of capital's (additional) productivity, creativity and adaptability. As employees well know, specific knowledge and know-how are the material basis of their influence, their status and their privileges. The conduct of skilled employees is normally aimed at securing this basis. In effect, the established groups make use of their knowledge, their controlled areas of uncertainty and their social position as resources to influence management measures by active participation aimed at maintaining favourable conditions. As a main result, the mutual dependence and intimate fellowship of management and established white-collar groups creates a tacit collusion which, in effect, causes established high trust relations to act continually at the cost of weaker white-collar employees and blue-collar groups.

6. Uncertainty, Stability and the Strengthening of Professional White-Collar Work Under Recession

Under economic recession the growing complexity and competitiveness of markets demands greater control of market conditions and production targets, necessitating high flexibility in production processes and a quickening in the transformation of the means of production as well. Under these conditions, management is even more dependent upon workers' creative, positive, and adaptive abilities, their knowledge, know-how and active cooperation, than it is in times of economic prosperity when the overall expansion mitigates competition, and even badly and ineffectively organized enterprises are able to survive. In order to gain flexibility in times of stiffening economic conditions, management therefore increases creativity and engagement, by means of heightening its efforts to motivate the diverse types of workers by carefully and selectively withdrawing authoritarian control of working conditions and granting workers trust and responsible autonomy.

Management strategies which aim at mobilizing personnel capacities work in favour of qualified white-collar workers for essentially two reasons: first, it is the middle stratum of occupational knowledge represented by qualified white-collar employees *(Sachbearbeiter)* that contains important capacities for problem solving. Success and profitability of an organization, especially in highly competitive situations, depends to a large extent upon its ability to make use of these capacities in order to gain higher productivity, flexibility and adaptability. The cut-back of these middle level capacities by discharging employees in times of recession, by fragmenting work and by centralizing problem-solving and decision-making capacities, would be short-sighted, as management well knows. It may increase profit in the short run, but in the long run it will create an economic situation that is even worse, because it creates inflexibilities in adaptation to external uncertainties and leads to overloads in the higher echelons of management. The delegation of competencies and responsibilities to qualified white-collar workers becomes even more important in situations characterized by intensive external and internal changes.

The second reason is a social one: offering trust seems to be problematic in blue-collar sectors. Here low trust social relations and modalities of economic exchange are institutionalized and are completed by stable forms of non-cooperation, defensive behaviour and collective bargaining. In this sector motivational measures aiming at cooperation and participation tend to give rise to even further distrust rather than to a strengthening of trust (for an example refer to the excellent study by Knights and Collinson 1985). Such "positive" management intentions would be misunderstood in low trust sectors and could cause a degree of social instability which would hinder the modernization of the means of production and of the organizational structure. It therefore seems to be easiest for management to strengthen and keep intact already existing high trust relations in white-collar sectors, where personal involvement, individually based cooperation in the execution of power, and participation in the gains arising from the rationalization of work are traditionally on the agenda.

These two reasons indicate a situational context largely structured by the management's risk demeanour which is evidently decisive for the strengthening of the white-collar workers during times of recession. Management, especially in situations of great external and internal uncertainty, fast-changing market conditions and far-reaching technical and organizational change, is very much interested in social stability, because during situations of great external uncertainty it has little interest in adding internal uncertainty by initiating social experiments. In the words of Burawoy, management is not very much interested in intensifying an externally generated profit crisis through shaping an internal legitimation or motivational crisis (see Burawoy 1979: 80ff.). Because of this, management avoids political intervention in established inequalities, as such intervention bears the risk of unrest and upheaval. In highly competitive situations, social stability is of central importance: that means, that the social system of an organized labour process has to maintain stability, while personal configurations inside it (i.e. which group or person holds which position) may change. While in processes of technological and organizational change the relative positions that persons and groups occupy on the basis of modernization of knowledge and skills may alter, and exchange of groups and persons may take place, a change of the modes of social relations in production is to be avoided.

To ensure stability, high trust should not be arbitrarily denounced or withdrawn by management. Such conditions of stability only exist where the groups bound into high trust relations personally dispose of power potential and influence which they can mobilize in cases where their interests are threatened. Beyond that they are not interested in high trust relationships. Dynamics of modernization within high trust therefore cause a self-regulation on the basis of positions and influence tied to educational and qualificational differences. While in the context of technical and organizational innovation high trust relations in production remain intact, the heavy competition processes caused by change result in the recomposition of the "high trust fraternity": the membership sometimes changes dramatically. The professionally trained, highly qualified and more vigorous groups take the opportunity of further strengthening their positions at the cost of the less qualified colleagues by actively participating in management measures. As a result depending on how far the technological organizational change alters the qualification requirements, there is a constantly ongoing exchange of established and marginal components: this exchange takes place on the basis of the modernization of knowledge and know-how.

7. Changes in the Composition of the Labour Force in Economic Recession and Its Effects on Relations in Production

According to the two reasons developed above, the situation of qualified white-collar workers in recession quite often develops contrarily to the average working class situation. Certain groups of white-collar workers very often have the gains of the rationalization of work within the enterprise of which the working class as a whole is the victim. The cohesiveness and solidarity of the working class thus is weakened even further during times of economic recession. Two reasons especially are of importance.

First, while the winners of technical and organizational change (the rationalization of work) are mainly recruited from the functionally important sectors, where highly influential groups of skilled white-collar workers or skilled blue-collar workers dominate, the losers are mostly to be found in marginal sectors. In addition, inside each sector the members of the comparatively lower skilled groups are faced by negative effects. Hence, in the restructuring process, workers in white-collar sectors, where high trust relations, active participation and trading of working conditions prevail, are better off than those in blue-collar sectors, where low trust relations, defensive resistance and collective bargaining prevail. In each sector, existing high or low trust relations and the predominant orientations and behaviour are confirmed and strengthened.

Second, in phases of prosperity when low trust sectors grow large as a consequence of an overall expansion of the workforce, and both weak and strong groups participate in the economic success (for example, by higher income), in times of economic recession, by contrast, the organizational margins of distribution become narrow. As a consequence, the competition between different groups of employees either to gain advantages or to prevent risks becomes stronger. Under recessionary conditions, restructuring of work initiated by management as a reaction to external constraints causes a Darwinian "survival of the fittest" struggle between the different groups of employees. As a result, hierarchical conflicts are overshadowed by lateral competition, and sometimes seem to vanish completely. Far from strengthening the cohesiveness of the working class, economic crises corroborate existing cleavages inside the working class and destroy solidarity even further. Beyond that, crises verify the individualistic orientations and competitive modes of conduct significant for qualified white-collar workers, because they demonstrate that such behaviour may be successful in economic recession.

The fact that under severe competition blue-collar workers and unqualified white-collar employees are dislodged to a great extent and substituted by better educated or higher qualified workers leads to an increase in the proportion of skilled and qualified members of staff. The paradox arises that in times of recession these groups grow larger in weight: because of this increased strength, massive restructuring of work and extensive redundancies obviously do not destroy industrial consent and harmony but conversely improve high trust relations between management and employees inside the firm. This phenomenon is relevant in order to explain recent observations that the "Taylorian" paradigm of fragmentation and direct control of work in central parts of industry in the 1980s seems to be superseded by "new" production concepts *(Produktionskonzepte)* which are founded on more complex work tasks and high trust and which aim at responsible autonomy. This observation has been introduced in Kern and Schumann's (1984) study with the rhetorical title "the end of the division of labour?," initiating a vehement debate in West German industrial sociology. The phenomenon is also relevant for an evaluation of Piore and Sabel's (1985) argument that from the 1980s onwards the old "Fordist" paradigm of mass production will in the long run be replaced by a renewal of the "old" handicraft paradigm throughout industry as a whole. These positions miss the point because they overlook the fact that the parallel existence of high and low trust sectors, "old" and "new" paradigms of production, are constitutive for the social stability of the capitalist mode of production, because it enables management to react flexibly according to the changing constraints of markets and needs of production. Both positions underestimate the importance of the economic conjuncture for the development of the labour process and relations in production: whereas the Fordist paradigm overemphasized phenomena like market expansion, increasing fragmentation of work and deskilling which connected boom with a unique capitalist logic of development, the "renewed" handicraft paradigm overgeneralizes phenomena like gaining higher productive flexibility, de-fragmentation, re-skilling and the growth of high trust relations reinforced by recession.

References

Berger, Ulrike and Claus Offe, Das Rationalisierungsdilemma der Angestelltenarbeit, in: *Angestellte im europäischen Vergleich, Geschichte und Gesellschaft. Sonderheft.* Jürgen Kocka (ed.), 7: 39–58. Göttingen. 1981
Brandt, Gerhard, Bernard Kündig, Zissis Papadimitriou and Jutta Thomae, *Computer und Arbeitsprozeß.* Frankfurt am Main/New York. 1978
Braverman, Harry, *Labour and Monopoly Capital.* New York and London. 1974
Burawoy, Michael, *Manufacturing Consent. Changes in the Labour Process and Monopoly Capitalism.* Chicago and London. 1979
Clegg, Stewart, Paul Boreham and Geoff Dow, *Class, Politics and the Economy.* London, Boston and Henley. 1986
Cressey, Peter and John MacInnes, Voting for Ford: Industrial Democracy and the Control of Labour, *Capital and Class* 11: 5–33. 1980

Crozier, Michel and Erhard Friedberg, *Macht und Organisation. Die Zwänge kollektiven Handelns,* Königstein/Ts. 1979

Daniel, William W., Understanding Employee Behaviour in its Context. Illustrations form Productivity Bargaining, in: *Man and Organization.* John Child (ed.), London. 1973

Friedman, Andrew, *Industry and Labour. Class Struggle at Work and Monopoly Capitalism.* London and Basingstoke. 1977

Hildebrandt, Eckart and Rüdiger Seltz (Eds.), *Managementstrategien und Kontrolle. Eine Einführung in die Labour Process Debate,* Berlin. 1987

Kern, Horst and Michael Schumann, *Industriearbeit und Arbeiterbewußtsein.* Frankfurt am Main. 1970

Kern, Horst and Michael Schumann, *Das Ende der Arbeitsteilung? Rationalisierung in der industriellen Produktion.* München. 1984

Knights, David and David Collinson, Redesigning Work on the Shopfloor. A Question of Control or Consent? in: *Job Redesign. Critical Perspectives on the Labour Process.* David Knights, Hugh Willmott and David Collinson (Eds.), pp. 197–226. Aldershot. 1985

Kudera, Werner, Konrad Ruff and Rudi Schmidt, Blue collar – white collar: grey collar? Zum sozialen Habitus von Arbeitern und Angestellten in der Industrie, *Soziale Welt* 2: 201–227. 1983

Littek, Wolfgang, Rationalisation, Technical Change and Employee Reactions, in: *The Changing Experience of Employment.* Kate Purcell *et al.* (Eds.), Houndmills, Basingstoke, Hampshire and London, pp. 156–172. 1986.

Littek, Wolfgang and Ulrich Heisig, Rationalisierung der Arbeit als Aushandlungsprozeß. Beteiligung bei Rationalisierungsverläufen im Angestelltenbereich, *Soziale Welt* 2/3: 237–262. 1986

Malsch, Thomas and Rüdiger Seltz, (Eds.), *Die neuen Produktionskonzepte auf dem Prüfstand. Beiträge zur Entwicklung der Industriearbeit.* Berlin 1987

Mendner, Jürgen H., *Technologische Entwicklung und Arbeitsprozeß.* Zur reellen Subsumtion der Arbeit unter das Kapital. Frankfurt am Main. 1975

Piore, Michael and Charles Sabel, *Das Ende der Massenproduktion. Studie über die Requalifizierung der Arbeit und die Rückkehr der Ökonomie in die Gesellschaft.* Berlin. 1985

Schmiede, Rudi, Abstrakte Arbeit und Automation: Zum Verhältnis von Industriesoziologie und Gesellschaftstheorie, *Leviathan* 2: 28–57. 1983

Silverman, David, The Theory of Organizations. London. 1970

Zündorf, Lutz, Macht, Einfluß, Vertrauen und Verständigung. Zum Problem der Handlungskoordinierung in Arbeitsorganisationen, in: *Organisation als soziales System.* Rüdiger Seltz, Ulrich Mill and Eckart Hildebrandt (Eds.), Kontrolle und Kommunikationstechnologie in Arbeitsorganisationen, Berlin. 1986

The New Rise of Self-Employment and Industrial Structure*

Timo Toivonen

1. Introduction

Until roughly 1980, discussion about social classes and strata in this century seems to have been dominated by one question: what is the position of the growing wage-earning middle class in the class structure? Does it belong totally or partially to the new middle class, to the new working class or to the traditional working class? (See e.g. Przeworksi 1985.) Contrasting to this debate there traditionally has been a consensus on the decline of small employers and own-account workers (petty bourgeoisie, old middle class, etc.) and the corresponding increase in employees. The beginnings of this consensus date to the classics of economics and sociology. J. S. Mill, Gustav Schmoller, Alfred Marshall, Max Weber, and of course Karl Marx have all observed the decline of small entrepreneurs.

In the early 1980s, some books and articles noted that this longstanding trend, at least in some cases, was no longer so clearly downward. For example, Szymanski notes that the United Kingdom as early as the 1960s and the United States as early as the 1970s were exceptions to the trend. He proposes that, in both cases, merely a temporary plateau has been reached. "It might well be the case that, at the prevailing level of technology and risk, capital finds it more profitable to indirectly exploit small business until such a time as there are major technological breakthroughs" (1983: 165–166; also Poulantzas 1975: 145). During the 1980s, more and more articles and books have questioned the decline of the petty bourgeoisie and have submitted the problem to closer analysis. The OECD has issued one of the latest and most extensive of these reports (1986). Some authors seem delighted with this trend, because social reality no longer conforms with the old theories. Still, the construction of new theories has been quite modest to date. Few new explanations are offered in statements such as "An adequate theoretical treatment of the class position of the owners of small capital requires the development of schemata that do not squeeze empirical observation into theoretical contradictions in order to remain true to some sacred texts" (Curran and Burrows 1986: 268) and "Petty bourgeoisie persists because of its

---

* I thank Arto Kankaanpää for helpful comments on an earlier draft.

important ideological and material functions within contemporary capitalism"
(Scase 1982: 160).

Perhaps one explanation for overestimation of the rate of decline of self-
employment in studies concerning class structure is that scholars have not differentiated between the agricultural type and other types of the petty bourgeoisie.
In the beginning of the 1970s, close to 15% of the total economically active
population was involved in agriculture and forestry even in many industrialized
countries – although this percentage was sharply declining. In agriculture, the
percentage of self-employment (independent farmers and their helping family
members) has been very high, and thus overall self-employment has diminished.
In the United Kingdom, where the changing trend in the petty bourgeoisie was
first evident, the percentage of agriculture had already been low for a long time.
Therefore this article is restricted to the development of self-employment outside
agriculture. The objects of this study are nine developed OECD countries. Limits
in the availability of data were the only reason for restricting the number of
countries considered to nine.

2. The Problem

First, trends in the percentage of self-employment outside agriculture are examined separately in each country. In this way it is possible to estimate to what
extent the development in the industrialized OECD countries has been similar.
Second, the impact of changing industrial structure on the percentage of self-
employment is explored. Study of the importance of structural changes for social
and occupational mobility has a long tradition (see, e.g. Blau and Duncan 1967;
Pöntinen 1983; Singelmann and Browning 1980), but the impact of change in
industrial structure on change of class or stratification structure has been investigated in only a few cases (e.g. Ahrne and Wright 1983; Toivonen 1985; Wright
and Singelmann 1981). If the possible increase has been due only to structural
changes, then the "old theories" follow the social reality within industries. Third,
correlations between the change in self-employment which is *not* due to the
structural factor, in unemployment, and the political composition of governments
and parliaments are examined. Other possible factors behind the change are also
discussed briefly.

3. Data

OECD National Accounts 1970–1982, 1971–1983, and 1972–1984, (vol. II Detailed Tables) were used as the main empirical data source, because its classifica-

tions are almost completely[1] standardized. Public sector employment is also documented, but unfortunately not according to industry. A more significant gap in the OECD data is that the gender division of labor is not documented. This is a pity, not only because of the growing participation of women in the labour market in general, but especially because their role in small business revival is documented to be important. For example, it has been indicated that women are standing small businesses at a rate of five times that of men in the USA (White 1984: 133). A minor deficiency is that the OECD times series do not begin before 1970. In addition, complete time series are available only from nine countries; unfortunately, the United Kingdom is not among these. (The UK's share of self-employed with industries is not detailed enough.)

It must be stressed that the percentages of self-employment in official statistics are considerably lower than those reported, for example, in the "Comparative Project on Class Structure" (Luokkaprojekti 1984: 74; Wright et al. 1982: 712). This may be due both to differences in definitions of entrepreneurs and to the "underground economy." The range of the "underground economy" is 4–12% of the registered GDP in the Nordic countries and 6–22% of GDP in the USA. The most important part of this economy concerns self-employment, which is about one third of the total (Tanzi 1983: 13). The larger problem is differing definitions of self-employment among different countries and between different surveys *within* countries. The glossary of OECD National Accounts does not give any definition of the entrepreneur, the self-employed, etc. But the definition is evident on the basis of the OECD definition of employee:

All persons engaged in the activities of business units, government bodies and private non-profit institutions, *except the proprietors and their unpaid family members in the case of unincorporated business.* Members of armed forces are included irrespective of duration of their service (National Accounts 1972–1984, 536, italics mine).

Thus, the proprietors of an incorporated business are classified as wage earners and salaried employees (but not always), because in a legal sense they are regarded as employees of their companies. The proportion of self-employment in incorporated businesses compared to total civilian employment was 2.8% in the USA in 1982 (Becker 1984). But this definition of self-employed is likewise vague because it is based on the method of payment of social security contributions and income tax or on self-definition such as in Britain or Finland (Dale 1986: 430; Central Statistical Office of Finland 1986). For example, data from the 1981 British Labour Force Survey show that of those women classified as "self-em-

---

[1] The deviations in industrial structure are as follows:
- restaurants and hotels are included in community, social and personal services in Japan and the Netherlands
- producers of government services include other producers in the data for France
- real estate and business services are included under community, social and personal services in Germany

ployed without employees," 47% either worked in their own home or used their home as a base, and of this 47% one quarter stated that they worked for an outside firm or organization (Dale 1986: 431). In the Finnish Labour Force Survey of 1980 there are 13% more entrepreneurs than in the Population Census from the same year. This is first of all because the reference period in the former study is one week and in the later one entire year. Second, the former is based on a sample and the latter on the total population. And third, in the Labour Force Survey only self-definition is used.

This vagueness is, however, not terribly important, if the main purpose is not to compare the actual percentages in self-employment between countries but so compare the *change* in percentages in self-employment. This is because the definitions can be assumed to be consistent in different years for a country. This can be observed, for instance, if in some country the definition or the method of data collection has changed; the figures of earlier years are then adjusted and made comparable to the later ones. The self-employed in this article consist of all employers, own-account workers, and helping family members, because the data material does not permit any differentiations. However, the majority of the self-employed consists of small employers and own-account workers. This is evident because, first, the percentage of helping family members varied in 1970 between 10% and 20% of all the self-employed outside agriculture, and in 1982 between just 2% and 10%. A clear exception is Japan, where the proportion has remained one third (OECD Labor Force Statistics 1963–1984). Second, the proportion of employers to total self-employment in nine OECD countries was mainly between one quarter and one third. And third, of all employers (including farmers), 80% employed fewer than 11 workers in Finland in 1981 (Luokkaprojekti 1984: 75). But because the exact composition of the group in different countries is not known, the neutral expression "self-employed" is used throughout.

Some researchers have stressed that unpaid (helping) family members should be excluded from the petty bourgeoisie because they consist of wives and adolescents who contribute their labor to the petty bourgeois family business without exercising ownership rights over the means of production (Cuneo 1984: 294). In some countries this may be true, but at least in the case of husband and wife this is not generally true in most advanced societes. In the small family business, husband and wife exercise almost equal power, but in the Census, the husband is counted as an own-account worker and the wife as a helping family member.

However, it is self-evident that the possible growth in self-employment is not due to growth in the numbers of helping family members, because in all OECD countries the general trend since 1969 has been a gradual decline or stability in the proportion of unpaid family workers (OECD 1986: 48).

The concept "self-employed" is used also because entrepreneur and small business owner must be distinguished. An entrepreneur is characterized principally by innovative behaviour. A small business owner is an individual who simply establishes and manages a business. Therefore, the latter concept is recommended (Carland et al. 1984: 358). But this proposal does not take into account the large portion of "small business owners" who own nothing. The term "employer" is also questionable, because an employer has employees – a relatively unusual case among the self-employed. And the concept "self-employed" perhaps points too much to the own-account worker. But because there is no better alternative, the concept "self-employed" is used in this paper.

4. General Trends in the Share of Self-Employment

Figures 1–12 show the development in the proportion of self-employed to total employment outside agriculture in twelve OECD countries since 1970. The percentage declined, in general until the mid-1970s, but they have stagnated or even risen slightly since then. So the percentages largely follow a U-curve (2nd-order polynomial function). Nevertheless, it can be stated that it is a matter of taste if we take this change as an historical turning point, because the percentages in 1984 are still clearly lower than in 1970. Thus the whole "new rise" could be merely a random peak, typical of all long-term trends of this kind. But we see that in most cases the development follows a U-curve very closely; this suggests that the phenomenon must be taken seriously.

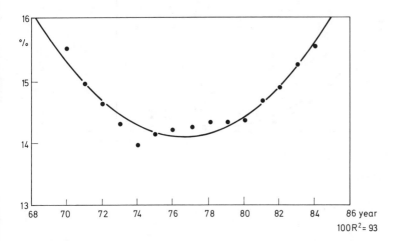

Figure 1. Percentages of self-employment to total employment outside agriculture and forestry in OECD countries, Belgium

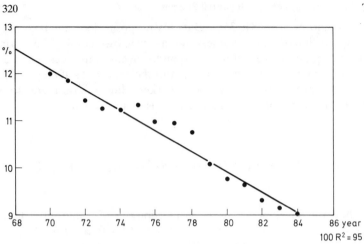

Figure 2. Denmark

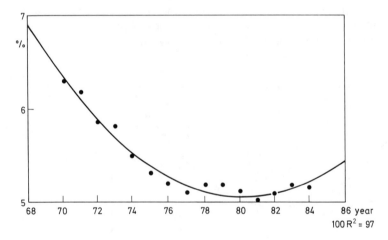

Figure 3. Finland

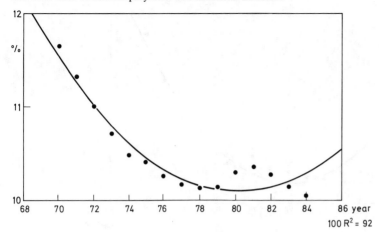

Figure 4. France

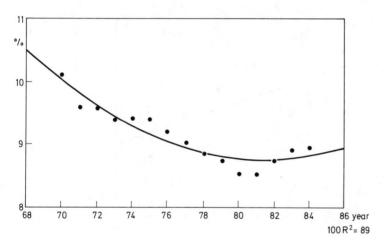

Figure 5. Germany

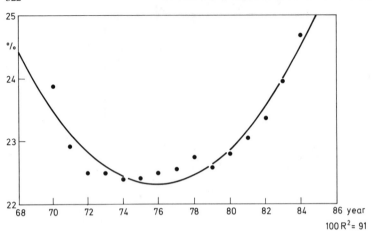

Figure 6. Italy

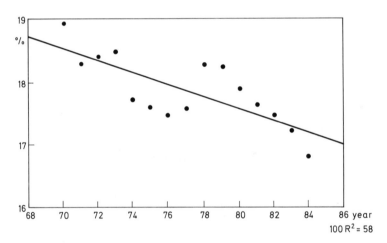

Figure 7. Japan

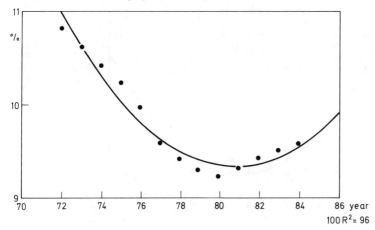

Figure 8. Netherlands

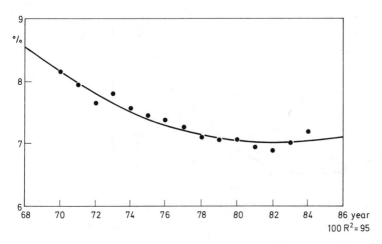

Figure 9. Norway

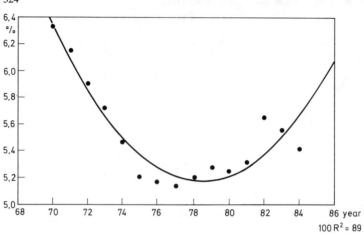

Figure 10. Sweden

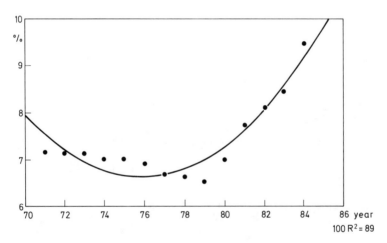

Figure 11. United Kingdom

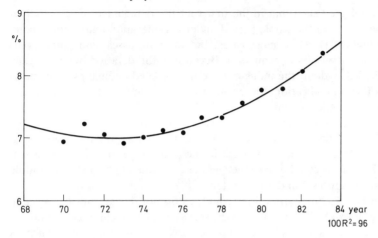

Figure 12. USA

Between different countries, however, there are differences in this development. The U-curve fits very well in the cases of Belgium, Finland, France, Germany, Italy, the Netherlands, Norway, Sweden, the United Kingdom and the USA (explanation percentages are at least 89). But Denmark and Japan are exceptions. In both countries no curve can be found, but the linear trend is downwards. In addition, in the case of Japan the trend is very inconsistent and the fit is therefore poor: the explanation percentage is only 58. However, for most countries this implies that there has been a tendency for the proportion of self-employment to increase as a function of time. Figure 1 also reveals that there are large differences in the percentages of self-employment (although these kinds of comparisons are quite questionable, see above). In Italy and Japan the percentages have remained over 20%, but in three Nordic countries, Finland, Norway and Sweden, they are only 5–7%. It is worth mentioning that the figures are not only due to large amounts of public sector employment. Without the public sector, the proportions are 7–9%.

5. Industrial Structures and Percentages of the Self-Employed

In identifying the components of the change in the percentages of self-employment, changes in the industrial structures were examined. Because the object of the analysis was in particular "the new rise", the years for comparison from each

country were selected such that in the first year the percentage of self-employment was the lowest in the whole period under consideration and in the second
year it was highest (1984 in most cases, but in some cases some other year
because data for 1984 was unavailable). Because in the data for Belgium, Italy
and the United Kingdom, the industries are not detailed enough even at the 1-
digit level of ISIC-classification, these countries are not included in further analysis. The earlier year for Finland was 1981, for France 1978, for Germany 1981, for
Netherlands 1980, for Norway 1982, for Sweden 1977 and for the USA 1973. The
selection of the earlier year for Denmark and Japan was difficult, because in
these countries there was no "new rise" in the percentage of self-employment.
The year 1975 was selected because the "new rise" seemed to begin in the middle
of the 1970s, as Figures 2 and 7 illustrate.

The industrial structures of various countries do not deviate much from one
another (Appendix 2). The exception is the service sector – including community,
social, and personal services (in continuing services). In some cases, such as
Japan, the percentage is much higher than in some others such as the Nordic
Countries. At the same time there are differences in the percentages of producers
of government services[2], but in the opposite direction. This leads to the conclusion that differences result mainly because in some countries services are mainly
public while in some others they are mainly private (see also Scharpf 1986: 8–11).
There are also other smaller differences between countries. One of these is the
high share of manufacturing in Germany.

The changes in industrial structures in most cases are very small because of
very short time-periods; but, in general, the direction of change is similar. The
shares of finance, insurance, real estate and business services (in continuing
finance etc.) and services of total employment have increased. At the same time
the share of manufacturing has decreased.

The differences in the percentages of self-employment are large between different industries and different countries (Appendix 3). In most cases the percentages are highest in trade, construction and services, and smallest in mining and
energy production. To some extent, the differences between countries can be
accounted for by problems with definitions as mentioned above, but there are
also other reasons. In Japan the percentage of self-employment was remarkably
higher than in all other countries except Italy. Especially in manufacturing, Japan's percentage of self-employment is high in comparison with other countries.
It was almost 13% in both years in Japan; whereas in the USA, in Finland and in
Sweden it amounted to only 2–3%. The structure of Japanese manufacturing is a

---

[2] The definition of producers of government services is: "All departments, establishments and
other bodies of central, state and local governments which engage in such activities as administration, defence, health, educational and social services and promotion of economic growth."
Other producers are "domestic services, producers of non-profit services to households (sport,
social and similar clubs, eating and drinking facilities etc., not too small)."

factor of some importance. For example, in 1984 the share of the sector "paper and paper products" of total employment in manufacturing was 16.2% in Finland, but in Japan it was only 2.2%. In this branch the percentage of entrepreneurs is exceptionally low; however, in Japan it was 4.1% and in Finland only 1.1%. There is another special feature of Japanese manufacturing, subcontracting, which perhaps explains some of the differences and the broken trend line (Fig. 8). In 1966, 54% of all small- and medium-size manufacturing firms (employment less than 300) were subcontracting. In 1981 the figure was already 66%. This is much more than for example in Sweden (le Grand 1986: 35–38).

In general, Appendix 3 reveals that the percentages of self-employment have increased in every industry. But one can also see that there are exceptions. For example, in the case of Japan the percentage of self-employment in total employment decreased, yet of eight industries taken separately it had increased in four, stayed unchanged in one, and decreased only in three industries. But in general, the data indicates that the increase in percentages of self-employment is not only structural.

Yet it is impossible to know without some more exact method to what extent the changes in percentages of self-employment are due to changes in distribution of employment across economic sectors, and to what extent the composition within industries is responsible.

6. The Shift-Share Analysis in the Change in Self-Employment

The shift-share-analysis method was used to explore this problem. It has generally been used as a method in comparative studies of regional developments (Moore and Rhodes 1973), and of occupational change (Singelmann and Browning 1980) and lately in comparisons of class structures as well (Ahrne and Wright 1983; Wright and Singelmann 1981).

The strategy of analysis is presented in the following phases. (For computing formulas, see Appendix 1.)

(1) *The hypothetical or expected number* of self-employed is counted. This is the number that would have occurred from an employment increase (or decrease) if the share of self-employment had remained unchanged.

(2) The difference between the actual and hypothetical amount is counted. This is *the net change.*

(3) *The structural component (shift)* is counted, imagining that the share of self-employment within economic sectors had remained unchanged, but assuming that the distribution of total employment across industries had changed

as it actually did. From this the expected number of entrepreneurs is subtracted.

(4) *The internal shift* is counted imagining that the share of industries of total
employment had remained unchanged, but assuming that the share of self-
employed within industries had changed as it actually did. From this the
expected number of self-employed is subtracted.

(5) *The interaction shift* is a residual term, obtained by subtracting the structural
and internal component from the net change.

Interpreting the interaction term is somewhat complicated. It can be expected
to be remarkable if the shares of industries of total employment and *simultaneously* the shares of self-employment within industries both change considerably.

The calculation of structural and internal shifts is based on the ten-sector
disaggregation (1-digit level of ISIC): mining and quarrying, manufacturing, electricity, gas and water, construction, trade with hotels and restaurants, transport
and communication, finance etc., services, producers of government services and
other producers.

Table 1. Net changes in the number of self-employed and its components (%)

	structural shift	internal shift	interaction shift	total	net change (000)
Denmark 1975–84	+53	+ 54	− 7	100	− 53.4
Finland 1981–83	−10	+112	− 2	100	1.6
France 1978–81	+58	+ 51	− 9	100	46.6
Germany 1981–83	− 2	+102	− 1	99	89.6
Japan 1975–84	−83	+167	+16	100	− 420.3
Netherlands 1980–84	−37	+150	−13	100	14.7
Norway 1982–84	+ 3	+ 95	+ 3	101	3.1
Sweden 1977–82	−44	+150	− 6	100	18.3
United States 1973–83	+39	+ 62	− 1	100	1493.6

Source: OECD National Accounts

The plus-signs mean that the component exerted an influence in the same
direction as the actual net change did. And correspondingly, the minus-sign
means an influence in the direction opposite to the actual net change. For example, in the case of Denmark this means that both structural and internal shifts
have had a positive influence on the decrease of self-employed, but that the
interaction shift has had a negative influence i.e. a simultaneous change in industrial structure and occupational status.

The general result of this analysis is simple: in every case except France the
impact of internal shift has been stronger than the impact of structural shift and
the impact of interaction shift in every case is negligible. In Finland, Germany,
the Netherlands and Sweden the net change should have been negative if the
change had been due only to the change in industrial structure. This means, for

example, that when the percentage of self-employment in the Netherlands rose by 0.4 percentage units from 9.2 to 9.6 between 1980 and 1984, it should have been only 37% of the actual rise and in the opposite direction, if the change had been due only to the change of industrial structure, i.e. the percentage should have *decreased* from 9.2 to 9.1. In Sweden the actual rise in percentage was from 5.2 to 5.6. The percentage should have been only 5.0 if the change had been simply structural. In both the Netherlands and in Sweden, the percentage should have risen by 150% if the percentages within industries had grown as they did but the industrial structure had remained unchanged i.e. they should have been 9.8 and 5.9. In Japan the percentage of self-employment actually fell from 17.6 to 16.8 between 1975 and 1984: a change of 0.8 percentage units. The change should have been 83% of that, or 0.7 percentage units, and in the opposite direction if it had been due only to the industrial change, i.e. the percentage should have *risen* from 17.6 to 18.3.

In two Scandinavian countries, Denmark and Sweden, changes in industrial structure had quite a strong influence decreasing the percentage of self-employment. The source of this change is easy to locate: it is the strong increase in public employment, i.e. the sector without self-employment (see Appendix 2). In the Netherlands the negative structural change in self-employment is only partly due to the public sector: the decrease in the proportion of construction to total employment is another important reason. In contrast, in France and the USA, where the change in industrial structure has had a positive influence on the increase in self-employment, the public sector has only grown slightly (France) or diminished (USA). In France, trade was an important source of a positive structural effect. Although the expansion of industry was relatively small, it was important, because 42% of French self-employment was concentrated in trade.

The impact of the internal shift was more important than the structural one. It amounted to approximately 100% or more in Finland, Germany, the Netherlands, Norway, Sweden (and in Japan, too, but for a decreasing percentage). In absolute figures, most often the main source for this was the increase of self-employment in construction. In relative terms, the strong growth of self-employment was actualized in finance also (more precisely, in real estate and business services) and in communication; but its absolute meaning is not so large. This is because the shares of these sectors in total industry are smaller than that of construction. In absolute and relative terms, most often the *decline* in self-employment compared to total employment was realized within the wholesale and retail trade, restaurants and hotels sector (unfortunately wholesale and retail trade is not treated separately in the statistics). This result is in accord with the OECD report, though the time periods were different (1986: 52–53, 64) (in the OECD study, the first year in the comparison was not the year when the percentage of self-employment was lowest, except in the case of the USA).

The shift-share analysis has been criticized for being responsive to the frequency of structural classification. The more frequent the industrial classification, the less the share of the internal component of the net change (e.g. Richardson 1978: 205). This possible defect was controlled by using the more dense classification (21–23 classes) for the calculation of shifts in cases where this was possible. This method yielded approximately the same results as in the earlier calculations. Only in the case of the USA was there a slight difference but not in the direction expected. The percentage of structural shift actually fell from 39 to 31.

It is reasonable to argue that the internal shifts are in general considerably more significant than structural shifts in the change of percentage of self-employment. This result is in agreement with the conclusions of Wright and Singelmann (1981: 30–33), although in the USA during the period these authors examined, from 1960 to 1970, the trend in small employers and petty bourgeoisie was downwards.

7. Internal Shift, Unemployment and the Composition of Parliaments and Cabinets

The changes in proportions of self-employment are thus only partly due to changes in industrial structures. Therefore the impact of two additional (in principle) easily quantifiable influences on internal shifts was examined (where internal shifts consisted here of *both internal and interaction shifts* as is usual in regional studies). The working hypothesis is that factors can have an influence most of all on that part of the net change which is not structurally conditioned. But one big problem is that the structural conditions change over time; for example, new technology may require a new mode of production, which may reflect different distribution between the self-employed and employees. Therefore, to study the period from 1970 to 1984, it would not be correct to calculate the structural and internal shifts for each succeeding year by keeping the distributions of the beginning year 1970 as the basis. Here the problem was solved by using the preceding year as the basis for the year under consideration. For example, for the year 1971 the year 1970 was the basis of calculations, for the year 1972 the year 1971 was the basis, etc. This strategy can be criticized as overestimating the rate in change of the structural shift (component) because in each case the structure of the previous year is seen as the "normal one." But this solution was selected because it was quite simple, and there was no theoretical basis for selecting some other year or some kind of moving average of years as the basis.

The first factor considered was the rate of unemployment[3], which is often

---

[3] In the context of an unemployment rate, the figures may be quite incoherent, based sometimes on labour force studies, sometimes on registered unemployment. However, there has been an attempt to adjust the time series within countries on the same basis.

mentioned in these contexts though relevant literature is in some disagreement on the direction of its impact. On one side unemployment has been seen to decrease small business because unemployment is linked with general economic stagnation. With decreased levels of per capita income, the demand for goods decreases and a smaller amount of savings is available for investments (Wilken 1979: 7). On the other side of the debate, unemployment is seen to increase self-employment, mainly for two reasons. First, it has been stressed that the high level of unemployment in the 1970s has forced people to create their own means of survival (Szymanski 1983: 166). This is probable in sectors such as construction, in which the cyclical changes are considerable and where professional skills are more important than capital requirements (Linder 1983: 262). Second, small firms are seen to be responsive to change, and since change is required during periods of economic stagnation, small firms tend to grow at such times. According to Bannock, an upsurge in small-scale economic activies occurred in the 1930s because of the Great Depression (Bannock 1981: 51). But data on labour force flows shows that the probability of an unemployed person becoming self-employed is low. It is low not only because the pool of self-employed is small compared with that of employees, but that probability is also *disproportionately* far lower than the probability of becoming a wage or salaried worker (OECD 1986: 60, 65). Also, in the studies where direct questions were asked of the self-employed about their motives in establishing a business of their own, the security of their own employment has not been the most important factor (e.g. Kankaanpää and Leimu 1982). According to another Finnish study, 70% of new entrepreneurs had never experienced unemployment (Aho and Ilola 1985: 47). And even in the cases where the lack of opportunity in labour market has been greatest, as among ethnic minority groups, this lack does not push them into self-employment (Rainnie 1985: 161).

Therefore it is not reasonable to think, if there is correlation between unemployment and self-employment, that the former variable is the direct cause for the later one. Probably this is because the unemployed people are often depressed (both financially and mentally) and unable to plan their own business. For this reason it is better to suppose the impact of unemployment to be more indirect. People who are getting into self-employment are still employed, but fear for their present employment and have enough personal and economic facilities to start their own businesses.

The second factor in the revival of small business is government measures. Government incentives have obviously been incorporated in all developed capitalist (and socialist) economies as regional policies, tax concessions, employment subsidies, counselling courses, "business clinics," campagins to shape attitudes towards self-employment etc. And these measures have been directed not only to the creation of new firms in old entrepreneurial sectors but even to open up previously regulated sectors and state monopolies, as the OECD Council recommended in 1979 (OECD-Observer 1986: 14–17). However, the last

measures mentioned, deregulation and privatization, do not necessarily lead to
an increase in the number of enterprises and entrepreneurs. Deregulation may
also lead to intensified concentration, as happened in the American railroad
industry.

As the scope and extent of actual government measures cannot easily be con-
strued as comparable quantitative indicators, one has to rely on indicators of the
potential for incentives. While governments of most political colors have supported small business, it can generally be assumed that conservative parties are
more inclined to do so than others are. But there are many alternatives to
measure this potential. In some cases a single and simple indicator is used, such
as "left wing cabinet seats as a percentage of total cabinet seats" (Paloheimo
1986: 14). In some other cases many indicators are used, as "the left share of total
classified votes in general elections, the left share of seats in legislature, the left
share of cabinet seats and the weighted cabinet share of left parties (where the
left share of cabinet seats is multiplied by the left share of seats in the legislature)" (Korpi 1985: 106). In this study the following index of right influence was
selected after some experiments:

$$R = 100 \times \frac{2 \times \text{cons. seats in legisl.} + a \times \text{total seats in legisl.}}{3 \times \text{total seats of legislature}}$$

where a = 1 if conservatives alone in cabinet,
        1/2 if conservatives with some other party in cabinet,
        0 if conservatives outside cabinet.

This index equals 100 if all the seats in legislature are occupied by conservatives
and they are alone in cabinet. Because this index takes into account both parliament and cabinet composition, it can reflect possible changes in the political
content of a cabinet with the similar composition after elections. This is possible
in a situation when the opposition party wins the elections but does not reach a
majority, or when there are many parties with equal power.

All correlations between the internal shifts in self-employment and the change
of unemployment are positive (Table 2, col. 1), although in the case of Japan the
correlation is close to zero. Columns 4 and 5 in the table show correlations
between the change in unemployment and the change in the percentage of self-
employment (total net change in percentage units) (4) and the change in the
numbers of self-employed (5). Comparing these columns, one can see that the
change in unemployment in general shows higher correlations with the internal
shift than with the change in percentage or with the number of self-employed (in
exceptional cases differences are quite small and correlations low).

These results thus support the hypothesis that unemployment and growth of
self-employment are positively connected with each other, although the mediating mechanism cannot be shown by this kind of data.

Table 2. Correlations between the internal shift of the change of self-employment (I), change in unemployment (U), right influence (R), the change in percentage of self-employed (Ep), and the change in the number of self-employed (E)

	IU	IR	UR	EpU	EU
	1	2	3	4	5
Denmark	.49	− .18	− .39	.41	.00
Finland	.26	− .11	− .09	.13	− .37
Germany	.82	.34	.09	.70	.05
Japan	.03	− .28	.35	.13	− .13
Netherlands	.74	.45	.01	.64	.02
Norway	.54	.76	.43	.01	− .30
Sweden	.43	.37	.18	.44	.26
USA	.33	− .18	.24	.42	− .38

(The French data was available only from 1975 and therefore left out)
Sources: OECD Labor Force and National Accounts Statistics; Mackie and Rose 1982, 1983, 1984 and 1985; Day and Degenhardt 1980; Paloheimo 1984.

The correlations between the right influence and the internal shift are in general low, and in four cases even negative. Consequently, the hypothesis that the new rise of entrepreneurs is the result of the growing influence of conservative politics is questionable. Correlations seem to be high in some countries where the correlations between unemployment and internal shift were high. In some cases the correlation between unemployment and right influence were also high (col. 3 in Table 2), which suggests multicollinearity. To control this, multiple regression analyses were calculated to study how much the change of unemployment and right influence simultaneously explain the internal shift in the change in self-employment (Table 3).

The differences between countries in explanation percentages are large. In the cases of Germany, the Netherlands and Norway the percentages are over 50%, but in the cases of Finland (1), Japan (1) and the USA (1) they were very low, under 20%. The signs of the coefficients of the change of unemployment are all positive; however, t-values are so low that the coefficients are not significant – only Germany, the Netherlands and Norway being exceptions. In general, the right influence has a weaker effect on the internal shift of self-employment than does the change in unemployment. Only two of the coefficients are statistically significant and in three cases the negative sign holds (Japan and the USA). However, it must be remembered that the low t-values may be due to the small number of cases (at most 14 in this analysis).

The examination of residuals in Finland, Japan and the USA reveals that the observations from the beginning of the 1970s seem to lie mainly below the regression line between the change in unemployment and the internal shift; i.e. it seems to be the change in the level in regression of U on I. Therefore, some experiments were made with a dummy-variable. In the case of Finland, a dummy-variable (1 for the years 1977/78 to 1983/84 and 0 otherwise) was added to the equation.

Table 3. Regression analyses for internal shift (I), change of unemployment (U), right influence (R) and dummy (D, see text) as independent variables (t-values of coefficients in brackets)

	constant	U	R	D	
Denmark	I = −2.20	+1.20	+.01		100 R^2 = 24
	(1.10)	(1.73)	(.06)		D-W = 2.97[1]
Finland (1)	I = −.44	+.62	−.04		100 R^2 = 7
	(.19)	(.86)	(.28)		D-W = 1.73
(2)	I = +1.05	+1.01	−.06	+2.74**	100 R^2 = 39
	(.52)	(1.60)	(.46)	(2.30)	D-W = 2.72
Germany	I = 101.51**	+32.03***	+2.03		100 R^2 = 74
	(2.45)	(4.88)	(1.61)		D-W = 2.00
Japan (1)	I = +143.80	+.14.04	−2.25		100 R^2 = 10
	(1.00)	(.47)	(1.07)		D-W = 1.82
(2)	I = +174.73	+19.46	−2.84	−13.83	100 R^2 = 27
	(1.28)	(.69)	(1.41)	(1.57)	D-W = 2.26
Netherlands	I = −29.44***	+4.97***	+.35**		100 R^2 = 74
	(3.65)	(4.27)	(2.58)		D-W = 2.03
Norway	I = 2.02***	+1.68*	+.05*		100 R^2 = 56
	(3.06)	(1.79)	(2.07)		D-W = 2.38
Sweden	I = −4.10	+4.97	+.20		100 R^2 = 27
	(1.32)	(1.42)	(1.18)		D-W = 2.32
USA (1)	I = +111.50	+47.40	−1.37		100 R^2 = 18
	(1.02)	(1.36)	(.94)		D-W = 2.34
(2)	I = +75.75	+44.37	−.20	+102.03	100 R^2 = 28
	(.67)	(1.28)	(.11)	(1.10)	D-W = 2.67

Significance levels: *** = 1%
               ** = 5%·
                * = 10%

[1] If the Durbin-Watson value is over .94 or less than 3.06 with two independents, there is no evidence (at 5% Level) of positive or negative autocorrelation of residuals. If it is over 1.53 or less than 2.47, there is evidence of randon distribution of residuals. With three independents, the corresponding figures are 0.81, 3.19, 1.74 and 2.26.
Sources: see Table 2.

Correspondingly, for the USA the dummy had values 1 for 1976/77 to 1982/83 and 0 otherwise, and for Japan 1 for 1979/80 to 1983/84 0 otherwise. In all cases explanation percentages rose, most of all in Finland and Japan. However, the wrong signs and low significances of the coefficients of right influence remain. The coefficients of the dummy are more significant. The problem lies, however, in the interpretation of these dummies. It is probable that they consist of many factors which are not identified in the present equations. It may be that they exist in all of these countries, but their influence varies, and therefore the explanation percentages of quantifiable variables also vary between countries. In the following section some speculation concerning these factors is presented.

8. Discussion of Other Influencing Variables

Japanese subcontracting systems were mentioned above. In other countries as well, the subcontracting has increased in recent times in manufacturing and also in building (Irsch 1983: 146–156). In most countries the growing percentages of self-employed, especially in construction, can be seen as a reflection of this trend. Closer examination of this possibility is impossible, because constructing is not presented separately in the data source. But subcontracting can only partially explain the increase in the percentage of self-employment, because even though the total growth of self-employment in construction is supposed to be the growth of subcontracting, only in one case is the share of construction in total net increase of self-employment due mostly to the construction sector.

Franchising has expanded rapidly in North America and around the world during the 1970s and 1980s. Total franchise sales for the United States and Canada in 1981 were estimated to be about one third of all retail sales (Knight 1984: 53). But there are no exact numbers about franchisee entrepreneurs in different countries. This is a pity, because some of the latest ones report that the position of franchisee is not as marginal in relation to the independent entrepreneur as it is usually thought: franchisees clearly perceive themselves as independent owners (e.g. Curran and Stanworth 1983; Knight 1984). Nevertheless, the net effect of the increase of franchise holders to the increase in the percentage of entrepreneurs can not be decisive. In the USA the percentage of self-employment in wholesale and retail trade, restaurants and hotels (where franchisees mainly operate) was 12.1 in 1970, in 1973 (when the percentage of self-employment to total employment was lowest) it was 11.0, and in 1983 it was just than 10.5. This means that the expansion of franchising has not been able to replace the disappearing traditional shop-keeper group. Of the eight countries studied in the shift-share analysis, only in Sweden and the Netherlands had the percentage of self-employed in trade etc. grown during "the new rise."

New technology is often mentioned as a creator of new possibilities for small firms. The developments in electronics, for example, have favoured small printing firms, just as automation has benefited the small machine tools industry and biotechnology the small cheese-making industry etc. (Bollard 1983: 42–49). This discussion has become very fashionable in recent years. Politicians, local authorities and also big corporations around the world have tried to establish new technology parks and the like by providing low-interest government money or venture capital for new technology-based firms. The direct effect on employment and entrepreneurship up to now, however, has been marginal. Only 4% of all new jobs and 3–5% of all business start-ups in the USA are supposed to have been provided by new technology-based firms (Hunsdiek 1985: 11). This is also confirmed by our data. The net increase in self-employment in manufacturing was only 11% of the total net increase in self-employment in the USA between 1973 and 1983. However, of these 11% the majority (80%) took place in the activities in which the role of new technology is probably important (printing and publishing, fabricated metal products, machinery and equipment and other manufacturing).

But perhaps the impact of new technology is more indirect. For example, the number of self-employed has grown very strongly in real estate and business services (i.e. accounting, book-keeping, etc.), which may well be connected with the introduction of microprocessors. Between 1973 and 1983, the increased involvement of entrepreneus in these activities was 24% of all net increase of self-employment in USA. In Sweden the corresponding increase was 22% between 1977 and 82, and in Finland even 38% between 1981 and 83.

9. Concluding Remarks

This article has attempted to present the development in the proportion of non-agricultural self-employment in OECD-countries in the 1970s and 1980s. The development has followed a U-curve in most countries, so that we can speak of the "new rise" of self-employment, but not without reservations, because in most cases the proportions of self-employed are still lower than in the beginning of the 1970s. The impact of industrial structure on this new rise was important only in few cases. In most cases it was negative or negligible, which means that the growth in the percentages has occurred within industries (i.e. internal change). This internal change was studied using regression analyses, the change in unemployment, and right-wing political influence as independent variables. The range of variation in explanation percentages was large between countries, and only in some cases were the coefficients clearly significant, even though the coefficient of the change in unemployment always showed a positive sign (indicating that the rise in unemployment and the growth of the internal shift in self-employment are positively connected). In addition, there was some discussion on possible influential factors which were not quantifiable in this study.

The new rise of entrepreneurs is a complicated matter. Even among societies with approximately the same social system and the same advanced economic level, the development routes of self-employment deviate from one other, as do the explanations of these routes. Further study is needed, beginning with the borderline between the self-employed person and the employee in different countries. Also the category of the self-employed is extraordinarily heterogeneous as a socioeconomic stratum. More structural data is needed: about gender, age, education and unemployment, as well as about concrete measures taken by governments to foster new entrepreneurship.

One of the most interesting questions is the future structure of modern advanced societies. If unemployment, public sector employment and self-employment all continue to grow, will we then in the next century be in a situation where a remarkable proportion of people of working-age is either outside employment, employed in the public sector or self-employed? Have traditional theories about classes and organizations gone totally astray?

References

Aho, S. and H. Ilola, *Lapin pienyritystoiminnan tukemiskokeilu. Työvoimapoliittisia tutkimuksia* 57. Helsinki: Työvoimaministeriö. 1985
Ahrne, G. and E. O. Wright, Classes in the United States and Sweden: a Comparison, *Acta Sociologica* 26: 211–235. 1983
Bannock, G., *The Economics of Small Firms: Return from the Wilderness*. Oxford: Basil Balckwell. 1981
Becker, E. H., Self-Employed Workers: An Update to 1983, *Monthly Labor Review* July: 14–18. 1984
Blau, P. and O. Duncan, *The American Occupational Structure*. New York: Wiley. 1967
Bollard, A., Economic Change and Small Firms, *Lloyds Bank Review* 147: 42–56. 1983
Carland, J., F. Hoy, W. Boulton and A. Carland, Differentiating Entrepreneurs from Small Business Owners: A Conceptualization, *Academy of Management Review* 9: 354–359. 1984
Central Statistical Office of Finland, *Yrittäjäkäsite tilastoissa*. 1986
Cuneo, C. J., Has the Traditional Petite Bourgeoisie Persisted? *The Canadian Journal of Sociology* 9: 269–301. 1984
Curran, J. and R. Burrows, The Sociology of Petit Capitalism: A Trend Report, *Sociology* 20: 265–279. 1986
Curran, J. and J. Stanworth, Franchising in the Modern Economy – Towards a Theoretical Understanding, *International Small Business Journal* 2: 8–26. 1983
Dale, A., Social Class and Self-Employed, *Sociology* 20: 430–434. 1986
Day, A. and H. Degenhardt, *Political Parties of the World*. Trowbridge & Esher: Longman. 1980
Hunsdiek, D., Financing of Start-Up and Growth of New Technology-Based Firms in West Germany, *International Small Business Journal* 4: 10–24. 1985
Irsch, N., Die kleinen und mittleren Unternehmungen in der strukturellen Krise seit

1974 am Beispiel der Bundesrepublik Deutschland, *Internationales Gewerbearchiv* 31: 146–156. 1983

Kankaanpää, A. and H. Leimu, *Yrittäjien käsitykset yritystensä perustamissyistä ja merkityksestä pienteollisuudessa.* Publications of the Turku School of Economics A-8. 1982

Knight, R. M., The Independence of the Franchisee Entrepreneur, *Journal of Small Business Management* 22: 56–61. 1984

Korpi, W., Economic Growth and Welfare State: Leaky Bucket or Irrigation System? *European Sociological Review* 1: 97–118. 1985

Labour Force Survey 1980. Official statistics of Finland XL: 5.

le Grand, C., Företagsstorlek som stratifieringdimension – en analys utifrån japansk industri, *Sociologisk Forskning* 23: 28–48. 1986

Linder, M., Self-Employment as a Cyclical Escape from Unemployment: A Case Study of the Construction Industry in the United States During Postwar Period, *Research in Sociology of Work: Peripheral Workers* 2: 261–274. 1983

Luokkaprojekti, *Suomalaiset luokkakuvassa.* Tampere: Vastapaino. 1984

Mackie, T. and R. Rose, *The International Almanac of Electoral History.* London: Macmillan. 1982

Mackie, T. and R. Rose, General Elections in Western Nations During 1982, *European Journal of Political Research* 11/3: 345–349. 1983

Mackie, T. and R. Rose, General Elections in Western Nations During 1983, *European Journal of Political Research* 12/3: 335–342. 1984

Mackie, T. and R. Rose, General Elections in Western Nations During 1984, *European Journal of Political Research* 13/3: 335–339. 1985

Moore, B. and J. Rhodes, Evaluating the Effects of British Regional Economic Policy, *The Economic Journal* 83: 87–110. 1973

OECD Employment Outlook. September 1986. Paris: OECD.

OECD Labor Force Statistics 1963–1984. Paris: OECD.

OECD National Accounts 1970–1983. vol. II Detailed Tables. Paris: OECD.

OECD Observer, May 1986: 14–17.

Paloheimo, H., Governments in Democratic Capitalist States 1950–1983. Studies on Political Science no 8. Department of Sociology and Political Science. University of Turku. 1984

Paloheimo, H., The Effect of Trade Unions and Governments on Economic Growth. Paper prepared for the Workshop an "National Models in Economic Policy." ECPR Joint Session of Workshops. Gothenburg, 1–6 April, 1986. 1986

Pöntinen, S., *Social Mobility and Social Structure.* Commentationes Scientarum Socialium 20. Societas Scientiarum Fennica. Helsinki. 1983

Poulantzas, N., *Classes in Contemporary Capitalism.* London: New Left Books. 1975

Przeworksi, A., *Capitalism and Social Democracy.* Cambridge. Cambridge University Press. 1985

Rainnie, A., Small Firms, Big Problems: The Political Economy of Small Business, *Capital & Class* 25: 140–168. 1985

Richardson, H. W., *Regional & Urban Economics.* Suffolk: Penguin. 1978

Scase, R., The Petty Bourgeoisie and Modern Capitalism: A Consideration of Recent Theories, in: Giddens, A. and G. MacKenzie (eds.), *Social Class and Division of Labor.* Cambridge: Cambridge University Press, pp. 148–161. 1982

Scharpf, F. W., Strukturen der post-industriellen Gesellschaft, *Soziale Welt* 37: 3–24. 1986

Singelmann, J. and H. L. Browning, Industrial Transformation and Occupational Change in the U.S., 1960–1970, *Social Forces* 59: 247–264. 1980

Szymanski, A., *Class Structure: A Critical Perspective*. New York: Praeger. 1983

Tanzi, V., The Underground Economy, *Finance & Development* 20/4: 10–13. 1983

Toivonen, T., The Entrepreneurs in Denmark, Finland and Sweden 1930–1970, *Acta Sociologica* 28/3: 193–205. 1985

White, J., The Rise of Female Capitalism – Women as Entrepreneurs, *Business Quarterly* 49/2: 133–135. 1984

Wilken, P. H., *Entrepreneurship: A Comparative and Historical Study*. Norwood: Ablex. 1979

Wright, E. O. and J. Singelmann, Proletarianization in the American Class Structure. Comparative Project on Class Structure and Class Consciousness. Working paper number 7. University of Wisconsin. 1981

Wright, E. O., C. Costello, D. Hachen and J. Sprague, The American Class Structure, *American Sociological Review* 47: 709–726. 1982

Appendix 1. Computing formulas for shift-share-analysis

(1) $\dfrac{\Sigma \; e_i^0}{\Sigma \; t_i^0} \; * \; \Sigma \; t_i^1 = $ hypothetical number of self-employed (H)

(2) $\Sigma \; e_i^1 - H = $ net change (N)

(3) $\Sigma \; \dfrac{e_i^0}{t_i^0} \; * \; t_i^1 - H = $ structural shift (S)

(4) $\Sigma \; \dfrac{e_i^1}{t_i^1} \; * \; t_i^0 \; * \; \dfrac{\Sigma \; t_i^1}{\Sigma \; t_i^0} \; - H = $ internal shift (1)

(5) $N - S - I = $ interaction shift (1a)

where e_i = self-employed in industry i
        t_i = employment in industry i
        $0,1$ = the years under consideration

Timo Toivonen

Appendix 2. Industrial structures[1] of OECD-countries in the years when the percentage of self-employed was lowest and highest respectively

	year	1	2	3	4	5	6	7	8	9	10	total
Denmark	75	.1	23.8	.7	9.0	17.5	7.5	7.5	6.1	26.1	1.6	100
Denmark	84	.1	21.3	.7	6.6	14.6	7.6	9.2	6.0	32.8	1.2	100
Finland	81	.5	28.1	1.4	8.8	16.3	7.9	6.4	4.8	21.1	4.9	100
Finland	83	.4	26.6	1.4	8.9	16.5	7.8	6.6	4.8	22.2	4.7	100
France	78	.8	27.6	.9	9.3	17.1	6.7	7.2	10.7	19.7	–	100
France	81	.7	25.9	1.0	9.0	17.4	6.7	8.0	11.3	20.0	–	100
Germany	81	1.0	35.6	1.1	8.3	17.2	6.0	3.0	8.6	16.1	3.3	100
Germany	83	1.0	34.1	1.1	7.9	17.2	6.0	3.2	9.1	16.9	3.6	100
Japan	75	.4	30.0	.8	11.2	20.4	6.9	4.2	16.7	7.7	2.0	100
Japan	84	.3	27.4	.7	10.5	20.0	6.0	4.9	20.4	7.4	2.4	100
Netherl.	80	.2	21.9	1.0	9.9	19.2	7.1	8.0	15.9	15.7	1.0	100
Netherl.	84	.2	20.4	1.1	7.7	19.1	7.3	8.6	17.4	17.2	1.0	100
Norway	82	1.0	22.5	1.1	9.0	16.7	10.8	5.9	8.2	24.7	–	100
Norway	84	1.1	20.7	1.2	8.6	17.0	10.6	6.5	8.7	25.5	–	100
Sweden	77	.5	25.6	.8	7.7	15.5	7.5	5.2	6.2	29.5	1.5	100
Sweden	82	.4	22.6	.9	7.3	14.5	8.7	5.6	6.1	33.7	1.3	100
USA	73	.7	22.8	.8	5.6	22.2	4.6	9.0	14.4	18.0	–[2]	98
USA	83	.9	18.1	.8	5.0	23.7	4.3	12.2	16.1	17.2	–[2]	99

[1] Deviations between countries, see note 1
[2] US figures do not include data from "other producers", but "statistical discrepancy" is approximately 2 percentage units
  1 mining and quarrying
  2 manufacturing
  3 electricity, gas and water
  4 construction
  5 wholesale and retail trade, restaurants and hotels
  6 transport, storage and communication
  7 finance, insurance, real estate and business services
  8 community, social and personal services
  9 producers of government services
 10 other producers

Appendix 3. Self-employed as percentages in industries in the year when the percentage was lowest and highest respectively

	Year	1	2	3	4	5	6	7	8	total
Denmark	75	0	6.9	0	20.9	23.5	11.9	10.8	31.8	11.3
Denmark	84	0	5.1	0	19.9	20.5	10.9	10.8	29.9	9.0
Finland	81	0	2.5	0	6.8	8.6	12.7	3.1	25.3	5.0
Finland	83	0	2.8	0	7.2	8.4	12.1	3.7	25.7	5.2
France	78	2.7	4.9	0.5	16.7	25.6	4.5	9.4	17.4	10.1
France	81	3.6	5.0	0	19.6	24.9	4.8	9.3	16.5	10.4
Germany	81	0	4.7	0	9.6	22.3	6.3	0.1	21.8	8.5
Germany	83	0	5.0	0	9.9	23.2	6.4	0.1	22.7	8.9
Japan	75	4.2	12.9	1.9	18.8	26.8	6.2	10.7	31.7	17.6
Japan	84	4.2	12.7	2.0	20.0	22.2	7.6	11.5	28.2	16.8
Netherlands	80	0	4.4	0	10.9	23.6	7.5	7.4	9.6	9.2
Netherlands	84	0	5.0	0	12.8	24.3	7.7	7.7	9.8	9.6
Norway	82	0	3.1	0	17.5	12.8	9.9	10.6	10.8	6.9
Norway	84	5.6	3.0	0	18.2	12.8	10.5	10.6	10.8	7.2
Sweden	77	5.6	2.4	0	14.1	9.0	8.7	5.4	17.9	5.2
Sweden	82	0	2.8	0	15.4	11.1	8.5	7.1	20.1	5.6
USA	73	2.6	1.5	1.1	18.3	11.0	5.1	11.9	12.1	6.9
USA	83	3.4	2.3	0.8	25.4	10.5	8.1	14.5	12.4	8.3

Notes, see Appendix 2

IV. The Labour Process, Class Structure and Gender

Exploring the Class and Organisational Implications of the UK Financial Services

David Knights and Hugh Willmott

1. Introduction

The empirical focus of this chapter is upon the organisation of financial services in the context of changing relations of political and economic power. Taking the form of a series of reflections upon "organisation" and "class," the chapter was prompted by a concern to appreciate the wider context and significance of an intensive field study of management control in a medium-sized UK life insurance and pensions company (Knights and Willmott 1987a, 1987b). Theoretically, our focus is upon the constitution of subjectivity, a dimension of social relations which has been comparatively neglected in radical organisation theory (Knights 1989; Willmott 1989). In this project, we share the aspirations of a number of contemporary thinkers who, while disagreeing fundamentally with each other, draw upon the inspiration and develop the insights of a Marxian critique in ways which seek to overcome its perceived limitations (for example, Baudrillard 1988; Foucault 1980, 1982; Habermas 1984; Lyotard 1984). Before we explore the relevance and impact of financial services in understanding the dynamic development of capital-labour relations, we sketch some background to the industry and outline our perspective on "class" and "organisation".

Historically, the ownership of capital (that is, the means of production) has provided the most reliable form of material protection against the instabilities of capitalism[1]. In the early stages, opportunities for enhancing financial security through direct capital investment were limited to a minority of quite wealthy property owners. Gradually, risk was spread through the provision of limited liability and the construction of share portfolios. More recently, many have found it useful, as a second line of risk management, to participate in institutional investments (that is, insurance policies, pensions, bonds, unit trusts). This indirect participation in the capital markets has been promoted and extended more widely as a consequence of the tax advantages accruing to these products, the growth of personal financial planning and, not least, the aggressive marketing of financial services.

---

[1] As a result of excess demand and tax incentives, domestic property has also provided protection against the devaluation of money over recent years, particularly in the UK.

Since the Second World War, increasing affluence, tax incentives, and fiscal privileges have all contributed to a rapid expansion of financial services in the UK[2]. Assisted directly by the state in the form of the partial privatisation of pensions (Social Security Act 1986), this expansion has accelerated recently. Growth has also been stimulated by media attention to the financial services resulting from the state intervening as a deregulatory (for example, the Building Societies Act 1986; "Big Bang" 1987) and regulatory (the Financial Services Act 1986) catalyst. Indeed, in the effort to promote their money commodities, the financial insitutions have created a climate in which a refusal or failure to participate in the markets for financial services is being defined as personally incompetent and socially irresponsible as well as materially damaging. In short, in the UK context (and elsewhere in the advanced capitalist world), financial service institutions are now strongly exerting their power upon an ever-broadening spectrum of the population, thereby contributing to the further commodification of relations (Offe and Ronge 1984) and the individualisation of subjects (Foucault 1982).

Let us take the example of life insurance. In its early days, when not simply a form of gambling (Knights 1988; O'Donnell 1936), life insurance was largely concerned with protecting life against death. Today its attraction resides in a capacity to defend or extend the standard and quality of life of, and for, the living by encouraging the growth of savings through the investment of excess earnings. Other financial services have a similar effect by facilitating consumption through the provision of credit, thereby stimulating the enforced saving of future incomes. Either way, subjective involvement or obligation generate industrious and financially self-disciplined subjects. In this respect, we argue, financial services are positive, productive and disciplining in their power effects. They not only maintain but also *improve* the material well-being of subjects (Knights and Vurdubakis 1988). Furthermore, they are integrative of populations and obscuring of class divisions and conflicts, for everyone is seen to share in the same strategy of protecting self and the domestic household from the risks of unpredictable and unstable environments through "a design predicated on the accumulation of capital and the calculation of goods" (Racevskis 1983: 100).

Turning now to consider our perspective on "class" and "organisation", it is necessary to emphasise that we are not using the term "organisation" to describe an entity. Nor are we using "class" to describe a common position or stratum within the social structure. Rather, for the purposes of this chapter, we are considering organisation as a process, and class as a principle which shapes and reproduces this process. In the context of contemporary UK society, we regard the *dynamic* nature of the capital-labour *relation* as the most significant expres-

---

[2] For example, life insurance and pensions have typically grown by as much as 20% per annum over recent years (ABI 1984).

sion of class[3]. However, an adequate analysis of the dynamics of this relation, we argue, must incorporate a theory of the constitution of subjectivity. That is to say, it must be attentive to how human experience is organised through relations of power in ways which both stimulate and impede their ability to overcome socially unnecessary constraints upon human development. In our view, the penetration of Marxian insights into the contradictions within processes of social reproduction is deflected when guided by a productivist philosophical anthropology or a deterministic political economy. For, in each case, the significance of critical dynamics and interdependencies within the capital-labour relation is marginalised. Thus, Marxism has been inattentive to the importance of other struggles (for example, career, gender, race); it has also embraced an economistic conception of (objective) class boundaries which is separated from the process of (subjective) class formation. More generally, the invidious choice between an essentialist philosophical anthropology, in the early writings, and the treatment of individuals as "personifications of economic categories" in the later work (Marx 1976: 92) inhibits an appreciation of the importance of the constitution of subjectivity in understanding the dynamics of continuity and change in capitalist society, a process which we examine in this chapter though an exploration of the development and impact of the financial services industry.

The chapter is organised into four sections. First, we situate our study intellectually. This we do by presenting a brief synopsis of relevant developments in organisational theory. Having noted that the hegemony of functionalist theorising, currently represented by varieties of contingency theory and population ecology theory, has been exposed and disturbed by varieties of phenomenology and radical structuralism, we focus upon the contribution of left-radical organisation theorists who have argued that an adequate analysis of organisations requires an appreciation of the role of class and power in their reproduction. Briefly, we review the key differences between Weberian and Marxian analyses of capitalist organisation, concluding in favour of the greater penetration achieved by the latter.

Then, in the second section, we review the relevance and limitations of a Marxian framework for understanding the role of financial services in the reproduction of capitalist (that is, class) institutions and organisations. First, when considering Marx's analysis of the dynamics of capitalist development, we focus on the polarisation thesis which, we argue, is a distraction in terms of understanding how capitalist relations of production are sustained. This we illustrate through a brief discussion of the ownership-control debate concluding that the significance of insurance and pensions companies for contemporary capitalism resides

---

[3] This relation is articulated in a variety of sites where it selectively exploits and reforms (and is reformed by) other kinds of power and status relations and their associated struggles, such as those of gender, career, lineage and race. In this chapter we concentrate only on the general aspects of power and class and therefore give no direct attention to these other important relations.

no less in their role as mobilisers of diffuse savings than in their impact upon the structure of ownership and its implications for the autonomy of corporate management. An important but neglected aspect of the transformation of savings, or excess income, into capital through the medium of popular institutional investment is that it promotes a mode of subjectivity which is highly conducive to the reproduction of capitalist (that is, class) relations.

In the third section, our focus is upon insurance as a commodity. We begin by analysing the original Marxian conception of the commodity form in relation to money as contrasted with material goods. This provides a basis for considering whether the products of insurance and pensions companies can be analysed as commodities, a question which prompts a discussion of the distinction between "productive" and "unproductive" labour. Underlying this distinction, we argue, is an overly materialist conception of products as consisting only of direct transformations of nature. While rejecting the Marxian notion that production for exchange denies workers their essential humanity, we subscribe to a view of commodification as obscuring the social character of production and consumption. This commodification, we contend, contributes to the general individualisation of subjects which we associate with the pursuit of social security through financial commodities promoted by modern power regimes.

Finally, in the fourth section, we examine the significance of financial services as insurantial technologies. Their promise, we suggest, is to resolve the problems of social insecurity; but their effect is to intensify the anxieties surrounding the separation of individuals from one another. The central argument is that no amount of financial independence can ameliorate let alone eradicate the insecurity which social relations dominated by instrumental power promote. Indeed, it can be argued that the very preoccupation with financial independence reflects and yet, through its reinforcement of the individualisation of relations, reproduces social insecurity.

2. From Orthodoxy to Marxian Analysis in Organisation Studies

Organisation theory offers a variety of responses to the question of how to account for the social reality of organisations. Within orthodox organisational analysis, now dominated by varieties of the contingency approach and population ecology theory (Aldrich 1979), it is assumed that their reality can be grasped without recourse either to a *theory of action* through which this reality is produced or to a *theory of society* in which it is located. Indeed, the most stoical defenders of the orthodoxy, have defined the status of theory *in distinct opposition* to that generated by approaches which are attentive to "action" and "society" in organisation[4]. Insofar as "action" and "society" are acknowledged as conditions of organisational reality, orthodox analysis formulates their significance as subjective or objective variables, that have to be taken into account in developing any specific study. Child (1972), for example, perceives actions as "strategic choice" variables that are contingent upon the values of managers and the situations with which they are confronted. Similarly, theorists have defined the environment as comprised of variables such as location, market, ownership etc. (Pugh and Hickson 1968) to which the organisation is obliged to adjust if it is to survive and succeed. Accordingly, where the significance of choice is recognised in orthodox analysis, it is associated with "ideological values" without any attempt to theorise their social conditions or consequences. In parallel fashion, where attention is given to organisational adjustments to the environment, there is little appreciation of how the resulting practices actually *condition* "external" circumstances, as well as being a consequence of them.

In recent years, orthodox theory has been criticised most vigorously for abstracting its analysis both from the mundane, practical accomplishment of action within organisations (Elger 1985; Silverman 1970) and from an appreciation of the wider historical and political-economic context of society (Clegg and Dunkerley 1980; Eldridge and Crombie 1974). Whereas those concerned with "action" have drawn upon the tradition of phenomenology, radical organisation analysts have been guided by the writings of Marx and Weber in their exploration of the political and class character of organisations. Although theoretically quite diverse, as Salaman (1981: 35) has observed, the latter analysts broadly share the understanding that:

the purposes of organisation (or of those who dominate them) and the structures of work and control to which they give rise, reflect more general purposes, cultures, interests and priorities in the society at large. They firmly reject the widely prevalent view that organizational structure follows from the application of neutral, apolitical priorities – such as efficiency, technology, etc., – and insist that such concepts be exposed for their political purposes and assumptions, and focus attention on the nature and function of organisational ideologies.

---

[4] In the most systematic of such defences, Donaldson (1985: 118) argues that "The study of society reveals larger structures and processes of stratification, socialisation, conflict and international relations, all decidedly worthy of enquiry, but already central to the programme of general sociology [. . .]. To require that all sociological studies "begin with a research problem relating to the structure of society rather than to the organisation itself" (Silverman 1980: 224) is to prevent the build-up of the sort of knowledge which comes from study of "the organisation itself". Questions about the consequences of variations in size on structure, technology on satisfaction, diversification on divisionalisation, or complexity on innovation might never have been posed let alone answered if organisation-level enquiries had not been pursued". It is worth noting that Donaldson contrives to omit all reference to the Bravermanian tradition of labour process analysis when castigating (Marxian) sociology for its failure to theorise organisational phenomena. For a critique of middle-range theorising, see Johnson, Dandeker and Ashworth 1984: 66–71. See also Willmott 1988.

Although Marxian and Weberian forms of analysis each seek to illuminate continuity and change in class relations, they differ fundamentally in their understanding of the motor of capitalist development and, relatedly, of the forces which condition the reality of organisations. At the core of these differences lie their contrasting assessments of capitalism as a mode of production. For whereas Marx identifies the capital-labour relation as the key to understanding society's dynamics, Weber highlights the demystifying impact of science and technology and the associated privileging of rational calculation as both a condition and consequence of capitalism's emergence and development.

We now continue by examining Weber's perspective more closely in relation to an evaluation of its strengths and weaknesses compared to the Marxian thesis. Weber assumes that technical rationality will continuously transform productive relations such that "the performance of each worker is mathematically measured, each man becomes a little cog in the machine and, aware of this, his one preoccupation is whether he can become a bigger cog" (Mayer 1956: 127). Stressing that processes of rationalisation (for example, modernisation, bureaucratisation) transcend the demands of particular economic systems, and indeed are intensified in a command economy, Weber argues that it is the *grinding, irreversible logic* of instrumental rationality, and not that of class struggle, which provides the most convincing explanation of the historical emergence and development of capitalist societies. Given this understanding, it is not surprising that Weber's appreciation of class is restricted to an examination of how the market distributes life-chances amongst individuals into a multitude of "class situations" – situations which are further differentiated by power deriving from their distinctive "status" attributes and party affiliations. Nor is it surprising that Weber's counsel is one of resignation and despair in the face of the crushing power of technical rationality which is expressed and secured in bureaucracy.

In contrast, Marx's analysis is attentive to the *contradictions* in the very structure and dynamics of the capitalist system. According to Marx, it is these contradictions which, in the trajectory of capitalist development, represent the seeds of its own destruction. Of course, Marx is not blind to the oppressive forces of capitalism. Commenting upon the transformation of feudal society accomplished by the bourgeoisie, Marx (Marx and Engels, 1970: 38, emphasis added) observes how this class has

pitilessly torn asunder the motley feudal ties that bound man to his "natural superiors", and has left remaining no other nexus between man and man than *naked self-interest, than callous "cash payment"* [. . .]. It has resolved personal worth into exchange value, and in place of the numberless indefeasible chartered freedoms, has set up that single, unconscionable freedom – Free Trade. In a word, for exploitation, veiled by religious and political illusions, it has substitued naked, shameless, direct, brutal exploitation.

However, whereas Weber stresses the relentlessness of rationalisation under the iron grip of instrumental reason, Marx identifies instabilities and irrationalities within the capitalist system which, over time, will be compounded to promote the only rational solution: a revolutionary transformation into socialism. Associated with the unrestricted and irrational play of market forces and the crippling degradation of factory work, the power and monopoly of capital is expected to create a polarisation of interests between capitalists and wage labourers[5]. Culminating in a revolutionary cataclysm, Marx anticipates that bourgeois bureaucratic practices which can repress fundamental conflicts of interest between capital and labour will be replaced by socialist strategies of production and distribution based upon economic need.

There can be little doubt that history has broadly vindicated Weber's counsel of despair. Industrialised capitalist societies more closely resemble his pessimistic prognosis than they do the optimistic projections of Marx. Despite this, it is arguable that Marx provides the more solid foundation for analysing the dynamics of advanced capitalist societies. For, in comparison to Weber, he penetrates beyond the dominant institutions and processes – such as the market, rationalisation and meaning-oriented action – to develop an historical understanding of their political conditions and consequences. More specifically, Marx reveals how the institution of the market and the application of rational calculation in the subordination of labour each promote and secure the priorities of the owners of capital to the comparative disadvantage of the sellers of labour. Of course, Weber also acknowledges the substantive "irrationalities" associated with the production and distribution of resources by the market when, for example, it fails to satisfy the basic needs of *individuals* who are denied full participation. But he does not recognise the market as a *class institution* in the sense that it systematically secures (and obscures) the exploitation of labour by capital. As Johnson (1980: 345) observes:

The market is, as Weber argues, a relationship of power, but power relationships do not originate in the market [. . .]. In Weberian theory exchange is a relationship of

---

[5] When analysing the labour process, Marx interprets organisational processes and transformations as media of class struggles in which capitalists, or their agents, strive to develop and sponsor forms of work organisation which are perceived to secure and advance the accumulation of private wealth. The history of organisational change is thereby understood as a steady process through which the accumulation of private capital involves its ever-increasing concentration and centralisation to the point of monopoly or oligopoly. Practices under monopoly regimes then have the self-defeating effects of undermining the competitive efficiency and innovatory strategies that were the motive-force of capitalism's abounding success. But more importantly for Marx, the centralisation and concentration of capital is seen to have a double, and potentially contradictory, impact on labour. At one and the same time, it increases "the mass of misery, slavery, degradation and exploitation" for the working class yet also, with the development of large scale production, it ensures that labour is "trained, united and organised by the very mechanism of the capitalist process of production" (Marx 1976: 929). In short, Marx would argue, capitalism "sows the seeds of its own destruction" for the preoccupation with capital accumulation necessarily impoverishes the working class while facilitating the development of social and organisational conditions through which workers potentially can effect a revolutionary uprising.

equality which functions to create inequalities only because individuals bring differential capacities to the relationship, while Marxian theory attempts to explain why exchange is unequal.

For Weber, class is just the distributional outcome of a set of competing market relations rather than the fundamental condition of their existence. By contrast, the concept of class is used by Marx to highlight the existence of a distinctive and fundamental *politico-economic relation* within capitalist societies: the capital-labour relation. The structure of this relation enables the owners of capital to monopolise the means of production such that labour is obliged to sell its productive capacity in return for a wage. In turn, the ownership of the means of production provides the opportunity to organise and control the labour process in ways which ensure that a surplus is appropriated, a surplus which is realised in the market when the exchange-value exceeds the costs of production and distribution, including the wages of labour.

For Marx, the institution of the market is an expression of the structure of the capital-labour relation through which the polarisation between two major classes – the bourgeoisie and the proletariat – is simultaneously reproduced and concealed. In one class are the owners of the means of production, landowners and capitalists, who live off the surpluses produced by labour. In the other class, there are the workers who depend for their subsistence upon the sale of their labour.

Although Marx allocates members of capitalist society to different class positions, class as a social position is significant only insofar as it grounds the process of emancipatory struggle towards a society in which divisions based upon the private ownership of the means of production are transcended. More concerned with the analysis of the *dynamics* of class relations and struggles than with the *occupancy* of class positions (Thompson 1968), he gives comparatively little attention to the definition of boundaries between classes and the significance of those occupying "intermediate" positions[6]. Thus, there are comparatively few passages where Marx discusses the structure of class, as contrasted with the dynamic reproduction of class relations. In the final pages of the third volume of *Capital*, one of the few places where Marx (1976) directly confronts the issue of class boundaries, his belief in the inevitability of polarisation is reaffirmed:

The owners of mere labour-power, the owners of capital and the landowners [. . .] or in other words, wage-labourers, capitalists and landowners, form the three great classes of modern society based on the capitalist mode of production [. . .]. Intermediate and transitional strata obscure the class boundaries [. . .] though very much less in the country than in the towns. However, this is immaterial for our analysis. We have seen that the constant tendency, the law of development, the law of the capitalist

---

[6] It is necessary to stress here that Marx's understanding of the polarisation of the classes is not as crude as it is frequently portrayed (Rattansi 1985). He anticipated the growth of "a special kind of wage labourer" (that is, the constituents of a middle class) where the capitalist would no longer be directly or personally responsible for the functions of "directing, superintending and adjusting" the labour process (ibid: 450, 449).

mode of production, is to separate the means of production increasingly from labour, and to concentrate the scattered means of production more and more into large aggregates, thereby transforming labour into wage-labour and the means of production into capital (Marx, final page of *Capital*, III).

In our view, a major problem of Marxian anaylsis is a tendency to conflate the continuous expansion of capitalist wage labour with the process of class *polarisation* and the growing pauperisation of the proletariat. There is a failure to anticipate and/or acknowledge the significance of productive power to mediate and institutionalise tensions within the capital-labour relation. Relatedly, Marx was unable or unwilling to admit, except by way of false consciousness, the space within subjectivity for a diverse range of interpretations of capital-labour relations. It is this space, we argue, that helps to account for the paucity of Marx's prediction that class struggle would inevitably transform capitalist social relations. For, in advanced capitalist society, subjects occupy multiple positions and are invested in a variety of identities (Henriques et al. 1984)[7]. While the fragmented and contradictory experiences associated with this development may stimulate a search for coherence and continuity, the simultaneous impact of individualisation, whereby subjects are separated off from one another, generates a vulnerability that tends to be managed through partial, sectarian indentifications – associations which offer a sense of subjective security. These differentiated identities severely limit the development of more broad-ranging class identifications and associated unifying forms of collective action.

In this regard, it is relevant to recall Weber's concern to compliment the analysis of class with considerations of "status" and "party." Clearly, this move reflected a recognition of how power exercised by members of populations is conditioned by symbolic, non-economic affiliations. However, as we argued earlier, his analysis fails to penetrate how these "phenomena of the distribution of power in a community" (Weber 1978: 137) are a medium and outcome of the capital-labour relation. As a consequence, class as an expression of the capital-labour relation is translated into a multitude of positions determined by the market. Despite his attentiveness to issues of "status" and "party" which are not determined by the market, Weber's theory of action *does not* permit an appreciation of how subjectivity becomes fragmented, with contradictory consequences

---

[7] The polarisation thesis is problematic from both sides of the class divide. In the literature, attention was first given to the capital side in the form of a heated and controversial debate about the significance of the separation of ownership and control within the modern joint-stock corporation. Since this debate impinges directly upon our subject matter of the financial services, it is examined in the next section. More recently, a greater concern has been directed towards analysing and accounting for the growth and proliferation of middle groupings within the class structure. Both of these developments create major difficulties for the assumption within Marxism that the class system would polarise around ownership and non-ownership of the mass of production with the latter increasingly becoming more pauperised and impoverished.

for the reproduction of advanced capitalist societies. Instead, his vision is one-dimensional: capitalism and systems of rationality are so uniformly oppressive in Weber's analysis that individuals are constrained by their cog-like status and demand nothing more than the opportunity to become a bigger cog in the machine of life. Although this preoccupation is undoubtedly widespread in advanced capitalist society, Weber is pessimistic about the potential of contradictory tensions and undercurrents to stimulate people to challenge the authority and value of this vision even whilst participating within it. Yet, it is possible – albeit perhaps unlikely in the current ideological climate – that subjects caught up in the "rat race" of status and economic competition will become dissatisfied with the ephemeral and transitory benefits of material and symbolic success. Whether such doubts can be mobilised into collective action designed to transform a society which offers such shallow fulfilments is questionable. It seems more likely that minor, unco-ordinated resistances will dissipate political energies in reformist directions that only serve to strengthen and stabilise capitalist social relations.

Another source of this stability, it is often argued, has been the transition from owner- to management-controlled corporations in contemporary capitalism. In the following section, we reflect upon debate which questions whether the robustness of capitalism is attributable, in large part, to the control of corporations passing from the class of owners to a new class of professional managers who strive to mediate the interest of a plurality of stakeholders who include employees and consumers as well as shareholders[8]. Here we argue that the strategic importance to the reproduction of a capitalist class society of institutional share-ownership, through life insurance and pensions, has been overlooked because of the preoccupation with ownership and control. Although not wishing to underemphasise their role in facilitating the expansion of circuits of capital, of equal if not more significance for the reproduction of capitalism is the role of the financial services in constituting a subjectivity of petty capitalism and in reinforcing the commodification of relations.

3. Financial Services and the Ownership-Control Debate

Parallelling the post-industrial society thesis (Bell 1974; Kerr et al. 1960), liberal theorists have drawn upon the seminal work of Berle and Means (1932) concern-

---

[8] In origin, the debate was less a concern with institutional participation in equities than absentee ownership as a result of the joint stock company, limited liability and the spreading of investments through share portfolios. However, the challenge to the polarisation thesis of Marxists was considerably strengthened when liberals pointed to the growing share of equities owned by insurance companies and pension funds on behalf of individuals who would not ordinarily be thought of as owners of the means of production.

ing the separation of ownership from control in the joint-stock corporation to conclude that the Marxist conception of class polarisation is no longer applicable to a contemporary social analysis of Western economies. Their thesis is that dispersed share-ownership has left power in the hands of managers whose task is to balance or reconcile a variety of interests in a socially responsible fashion (Galbraith 1952; 1967; Walton 1967). However, in presenting this thesis, evidence of the comparative historical stability of the skewed distribution of income and wealth as and between capital (profits) and labour (wages) throughout the twentieth century is disregarded. Alternatively, structured social inequality is assumed to be a necessary condition of universally beneficial wealth generation (Blackburn 1972: 183–4; 1973: 17–39; Hyman 1975)[9].

Responding to evidence of the continuity and stability of class inequality, Marxists have suggested a number of reasons why the dispersal of ownership has not prevented large shareholders from controlling business policy through a variety of means. First, those with substantial minority holdings can dominate shareholder meetings because of the difficulties of organising a mass of widely dispersed holdings. Moreover, managers are shareholders to a greater extent than any other single occupational group (Nichols 1969) and therefore will tend to pursue policies that are at least not inconsistent with the interests of ownership. More generally, owners and managers share similar social, ideological and political values as a result of class background and aspirations. Second, interlocking, directorship, kinship and educational links between large shareholders (Lupton and Wilson 1973; Urry and Wakeford 1973) result in a complementarity of values and practices not only between owners and managers but also often between independent companies. Third and most important of all, however, is the operation of the market which encourages managers to treat profit as a primary objective and acts as a limit on sacrificing dividend distribution to other objectives because of its effect on the share price and the danger of attracting predators. In the UK context, this has been a more important factor over recent years when there has been something of a merger mania. But even when dividends were comparatively "poor", corporate self-financing was conducive to capital growth and, at that time, was preferable to shareholders because of the less favourable tax treatment of income as against capital gains.

Having stimulated a lot of heat, numerous interesting arguments and a good deal of empirical research, the controversy on ownership and control eventually fizzled out in advance of any conclusive outcome. Not surprisingly, Marxists and liberals remain sceptical of one another's arguments. Our own sympathies lie with the Marxists insofar as they stress that class inequality is hardly affected by the development of absentee ownership in capitalist corporations. However, we

---

[9] This pluralist perspective, as one of its earlier exponents (Fox 1966) soon began to realise (Fox 1973), was a convenient ideology for a democratic state within a capitalist economy since it provided the illusion that the former had eliminated the exploitative conditions of the latter.

are critical of their failure to examine the broader impact of financial developments that have accompanied the formal separation of ownership and control. It
is to a remedying of this omission that our analysis now turns.

For us, the historical significance of the joint-stock corporation is not restricted
to its effect of enabling a delegation of managerial control from the owners of
capital to a new "middle" class of corporate executives and technocrats. In
addition, it is necessary to appreciate how the legalisation of limited liability
strengthened and rendered more adaptable the institutional complexes which
legitimate and sustain the principle and practice of capital accumulation (Gilmore
and Willmott 1988). For example, the spread of joint stock companies and the
associated equity modes of investment has provided one of the conditions of
possibility for dramatic growth in the financial services sector. There is not just
the positive effect on the financial strength of this sector from investing in capital-
appreciating equities. Of equal, if not greater, importance is the attractiveness to
consumers of sharing in the financial benefits on offer through institutional investment. This has had the effect of constituting the modern subject (that is the
citizen) as one who voluntarily, indeed often enthusiastically, engages in his/her
financial self-discipline (Knights 1988; Knights and Vurdubakis 1988) in ways
that quite clearly reinforce and reproduce the values and institutional arrangements of capitalism. In turn, the financial services industry has played a central
role in the development of capital markets which facilitate the realisation of
surplus and the spread of capitalism throughout the economy. These aspects of
the changes in the structure and organisation of capitalist corporations, we argue,
are of considerable importance for the reproduction of class relations in advanced
capitalist societies.

More specifically, a focus on the strategic role of the financial services can turn
to advantage the criticism that private ownership is of dwindling significance now
that the financial institutions hold more than 40% of UK equities. Institutional
investment on this scale, argue the liberals, makes nonsense of the class polarisation thesis since the beneficiaries of the income and capital growth of capitalist
enterprises are increasingly the general population of wage and salary earners. In
responding to this criticism, we can begin by conceding that the financial rewards
of indirect participation of citizens in capital markets does indeed create some
difficulty for traditional Marxist notions of a rigid demarcation between owners
and non-owners of the means of production. However, as we have argued, class
is a principle that structures organisational processes in ways that reflect and
reproduce the capitalist mode of production. Consequently, the mass consumption of financial commodities secures participation without power and yields
financial reward without effort – precisely the mechanisms that will assist in
maintaining contemporary capital-labour relations, with only minor modifica-
tions, in perpetuity. The limited share and distribution of capital resources
among the population does nothing to puncture the principle of class, whereby
capital induces labour to produce surplus value that is readily appropriated. It

does a great deal, on the other hand, for extending the docility and compliance, if not consent, of labour to the conditions of its own exploitation.

For by sharing, albeit unequally, in some of the affluence created by capitalist production, the employed working class enjoy considerable material comforts and feelings of security at least in comparison to previous generations of labour. This participation renders them more amenable towards, if not necessarily committed to, the demands of the system which provides such comforts. Relatedly, it reduces the attractiveness of an alternative, socialist system wherein a continuing rise of living standards as well as opportunities for individual advancement are by no means assured. In sum, when seeking to understand the role of financial services in the reproduction of capitalist (that is, class) society, their effect in constituting subjects and commodifying relations is of most crucial importance. Unfortunately, this phenomenon has been neglected in the debate over the separation of ownership and control. Yet, as we have argued, the opportunity to derive unearned income through the investment of savings in joint-stock companies is highly significant in providing comparatively cheap forms of capital as well as in constituting subjects as petty-capitalists. In the following section, we draw upon Marx's analysis of the commodity to elaborate our argument that financial service products contribute to the reproduction of class society through their impact on the commodification of social relations.

4. Insurance as a Commodity

One of Marx's major concerns was to penetrate the "appearances" of equal exchange within the marketplace to reveal the hidden "reality" of exploitation endemic to capitalist relations of production. In market exchange, the products of human labour take on the appearance of being independent of the social relations of their production. Describing this phenomenom as a fetish of commodities, Marx (1971: 43) observes how "a definite social relation between men assumes [. . .] the fantastic form of a relation between things." Only by revealing the nature of value as the socially necessary labour time involved in the production of usefull goods, Marx argues, is it possible to dispel the "fantasy" that "exchange value is the only form in which the value of commodities can manifest itself or be expressed" (ibid: 5)[10]. In this section, we address the adequacy of

---

[10] While this can be achieved through critical reflection, Marx stressed that it is only the practical working out of the contradictory structure of capitalist relations of production – where the means of subsistence for a majority of the population (that is, labour and its dependents) are merely a vehicle for the accumulation of surplus by a minority (the owners of capital) – that can actually set society upon a rational, socialist basis by exploding the myths and mystifications associated with commodity production.

Marx's analysis of the commodity form and the ontology of labour in relation to the "manufacture" of life insurance and pensions products.

4.1 The Commodity Form

In the first chapters of *Capital* Marx (1976) outlines his thesis on commodities and money as preparation for the critique of capitalist production. According to Marx, "objects of utility" become commodities as a consequence of "the social character of the labour which produces them" (ibid: 165). More specifically, objects become commodities when they are produced by "private individuals who work independently of each other" (ibid)[11]. In these circumstances, objects are produced principally for their exchange value rather then their immediate use-value. Once established, the commodification of objects of utility within markets generates one of the conditions crucial to the development of capitalist economic organisation in which, through the development of markets in which commodities are exchanged, the extraction of surplus value is *systematically* privileged over the use-value of the product.

4.2 Money as a Commodity

Money is a commodity because, in common with other commodities, it is "an object of utility" which must have "use-values for others, social use-values" (ibid: 9). Indeed, money is perhaps the ultimate commodity since it provides a continuous measure to facilitate comparable valuations of discrete goods. Not only is it an important condition for the development of the capitalist mode of production (Haug 1986) but, for our purposes, its significance resides in the fact that financial institutions sell products which are surrendered for money.

In the context of capitalist societies, money assumes a central importance for at least two reasons. In its apparent neutrality money helps to defuse the potential for antagonism associated with blatant inequalities. For example, the life insurance cover or pensions provision available to the executive is much more advantageous than that affordable by the clerk who processes the policies. However, the experience of this inequality and the antagonism it may generate is moder-

---

[11] In the process of uncovering the substance behind the appearance of commodity production, Marx broke down the exchange relation to its simplest constituent elements. Goods must first of all be qualitatively different from one another and "non-owning need on the one side must coincide with not-needing ownership on the other" (Haug 1986: 13) otherwise there is no basis for exchange. Secondly, it is necessary that the goods are equal in value – a measure only made possible by the presence of a third element through which to express their equivalence.

ated by the depersonalised nature of the financial transaction. Second, money has the virtue of lacking the constraints on accumulation present in respect of ordinary commodities whose "worth is limited by their usefulness" (ibid: 18). Transcending the limits of material satiability, money becomes a commodity that at once facilitates, and constitutes an imperative to the demand for, the accumulation of "abstract wealth" (ibid) as an end in itself.

The uniqueness of money as a commodity resides in its ability to represent exchange value which is independent of any specific commodity, even precious metals. This characteristic means that it can serve as security against future consumption in an uncertain and unpredictable capitalist market place. As Marx (1973: 165) puts it:

By possessing the *property* of buying everything, by possessing the property of appropriating all objects, *money* is thus the *object* of eminent possession. The universality of its *property* is the omnipotence of its being.

For these reasons, money provides an exceptionally valuable form of material security. More than any other commodity, even precious metals, it has a universal exchange value. Whereas other commodities require their purchaser to search out specialist buyers, the purchaser of money knows that it is very widely acceptable. Having said this, the security value of money can of course be undermined by a decline in its purchasing power over time, a condition which stimulates a demand for financial products designed to maintain or increase the underlying exchange value of money. Insurance and pensions are examples of financial products which fall into this category.

4.3 Insurance and Pensions as Commodities

So far we have presented an outline of Marx's analysis of the commodity form. A concern here is to defend our argument that life insurance and pensions policies are legitimately analysed as commodities. In doing so, we question the adequacy of Marx's distinction between productive and unproductive labour which leads him to view labour within financial institutions as wholly unproductive. Following Marx, critical analysts are disinclined to examine the finance sector in terms of its contribution to the commodification of relations largely because they are preoccupied with distinguishing productive from unproductive labour and demonstrating what they see as the fundamental contradiction: the domination of productive capital by finance capital (Anderson 1964; Longstreth 1979; Nairn 1977; 1979). Financial service companies are organised in a parallel fashion to other capitalist corporations in that they employ labour for purposes of producing commodities for exchange in the market and, in the process, extract a surplus which is passed on to shareholders[12]. Despite certain employment privileges, there is little doubt that, whether by default or design, financial service organisations are beginning to intensify the labour process (Knights and Sturdy 1989). There is in our view, therefore, little reason to exclude financial service products from being classed as commodities. Indeed, not to do so is to cling onto an historically superceded and essentialist conception of need which links it to an exclusively material or expressivist understanding of use value rather than seeing it as "induced by the exchange value system and" [functioning] "according to the same logic" (Baudrillard 1988: 86). Indeed, if we are to grasp the way in which human subjects are gripped by the desire for financial security we have to understand how the commodification of relations separates individuals off from natural and social objects only to offer a continous supply of commodities that claim to provide a reunification. But in reuniting individuals with the objects from which commodity production separates them, it has to be remembered that both commodities and the needs which they are deemed to fulfill are constituted through the commodification of relations.

Yet, for orthodox Marxists, at least, financial institutions are not real producers of commodities. Rather, they are simply intermediaries between two capitals: finance capital which provides the investment and the industrial capitalist who secures the surplus. As Ingham (1984: 81–2) points out, this orthodox perspective views the commodities (for example, money, loans, mortgages, investments, stock) in which the finance sector deals as merely a "sign or representation of the movements of the "real" components of the capitalist mode of production – productive capital, commodities and their underlying social relations". In so far as they are parasitic upon real commodities from which surplus value is extracted, the financial service institutions are seen to be populated by unproductive labour. Deriving from Marx's labour theory of value, this view precludes any conception of value arising from goods (for example, services) that do not involve some transformation of nature by labour. Our response to this is that it mistakenly equates productive labour exclusively with the production of material commodities. In de-valuing the production of nonmaterial goods, attention is deflected from the contribution that, for example, financial services make to the reproduction of capitalism through their solidification of commodity relations wherein life is conflated with the discounted value of a subject's anticipated future – or calculated past – earnings. Having argued the case for treating financial service products as commodities, we turn in the final section to an examina-

---

[12] Within the financial services industry (for example, life insurance, building societies) there are a large number of mutual companies which do not conform directly to the capitalist model. However, in competing with the proprietary companies, the mutuals behave exactly like them. The only difference is that the policyholders share in the distribution of profits thus reinforcing the extent to which consumers of financial services might be seen as mini-capitalists.

tion of their social significance and, more especially, the contribution they make to the reproduction of capitalist (class) relations.

5. The Social Significance of Financial and Insurantial Commodities

As commodities, life insurance and pensions policies are marketed as means of averting the risks of poverty and destitution or diminishing the effects of unwelcome fluctuations in material standards of living. In the context of contemporary capitalist society, such risks are associated with the traditional family dependency upon a single breadwinner, employment instability, the atomisation of social relations and the accompanying ethic of individual responsibility. Life insurance and pensions products are attractive to those who can afford them because they possess a potential to provide more adequate protection against future adversities than other forms of saving, such as deposit accounts in banks and buildings societies. More specifically, they are bought because they hold out the prospect of relieving anxieties aroused by the unpredictability and personal/familial exposure associated with the operation of capitalist labour markets. Although endemic to human beings by virtue of a self-conscious awareness of our own finitude, these anxieties are intensified by processes of individualisation and privatisation in advanced capitalist societies.

In response to these anxieties, the financial institutions have developed products which are seemingly more effective than mere money in proffering the possibility of eradicating social and economic insecurity. By itself, money can provide only limited security or guarantees on future consumption when, as a result of continuous demands for capitalist surplus and the limited resistance of labour to forces that would ordinarily lead to the relative decline of wages, the prices of commodities, and therefore money values, are unstable. In contrast, *money commodities* offer the buyer a means of participating directly in the inflation-hedged "fruits" of capital investment. In contrast to the physical and psychological limits on material consumption, the pursuit of security through abstract wealth knows no limits. It is unceasing in an economy that, on the one hand, is dependent on the insecurity of market relations and, on the other, undermines, displaces or precludes communal means of managing that self-same uncertainty and unpredictability. Indeed it could be argued that the spread of commodity relations, through the mass consumption of financial services, heralds the ultimate bourgeoisification of populations wherein, as financially self-disciplined, individualised subjects, they live through and for their asset wealth.

Participation in the market for such commodities itself serves to transform a public necessity for protection against the risks of a market mode of resource allocation into the pursuit of accumulation as private virtue. Ideally and materially, the presence of insurantial techniques and the commodities they engender both serve to sustain the capitalist mode of production. Insurance and pensions companies channel private savings, which are otherwise widely dispersed within the population, into the capital markets as they act as a vehicle for personal accumulation. In this way, they provide comparably cheap "fuel" to maintain the growth of capitalism (and thereby reduce the risk of economic crisis). Moreover, their existence has an important *disciplinary effect* in reinforcing and rewarding the bourgeois values of self-help and participation in the extension of commodity relations through institutional investment.

The more intensive and extensive the involvement of the population in the exchange of commodities, the more we become constituted as subjects whose sense of our own identity and self-worth becomes wrapped up in the pursuit of material and symbolic possessions. Materially, the greater our participation in the private provision of insurance and pensions, the less is the pressure on public welfare and state finances as individuals are encouraged, materially and ideologically, to take responsibility for their personal and family welfare. Seemingly everyone is a beneficiary. The state is relieved of the burden and risk of welfare provision. The policy holder has an opportunity to make substantial capital gains. And the financial markets are provided with a cheap and otherwise inaccessible supply of capital[13]. Nothing, however, changes at the level of capitalist production other than it being strengthened by the increasingly universal, individualised preoccupation with social security through the accumulation of financial assets.

These observations lead us to the conclusion that the significance of insurance and pensions companies is not confined to their impact upon the structure of ownership and the autonomy of control enjoyed by corporate management. The very existence of these companies both reflects and sustains a particular kind of materialist practice. In the name of social security (that is, personal and family welfare), insurantial practices promote the "commodification of self" as an extension of the possessive individualistic accumulation of money as an end in itself (i. e. as a profitable investment). In the language of Foucault (1980), the spread

---

[13] To make the point, we have emphasised the benefits of reliance on the private sector for the provision of financial services. It should be noted that the shift towards the private provision of social security could exacerbate the (political) unrest which usually accompanies economic recession since the value of financial service products (for example, pensions) is more directly linked to the performance of commercial corporations. The opportunity to make capital gains in a bull market must be measured against the potential for losses in a bear market. There is also the issue of the quality of advice received about the past and projected performance of different insurance and pensions companies and their products. In the UK the promotion of the private sector provision of these products has been accompanied by attempts to provide greater protection for the investor through the mechanism of the Financial Services Act and the establishment of the Securities and Investments Board. Finally, the supply of capital from individual policy holders is subject to greater variation, especially as companies develop more flexible products where there is no requirement for the payment of a regular premium.

of insurance and other investment commodities as a form of mass consumption represents a political investment in the social body. In contemporary capitalism, money management has become a technology of power wherein the population seeks security through its own financial self-discipline (Knights 1988).

6. Conclusion

We have used this chapter as vehicle for exploring the potential application of Marxist analyses of organisation and class in relation to contemporary developments in the financial service sector of the economy of capitalist societies. We began by examining the contribution of the Marxist literature to studies of class and organisation comparing and contrasting it with Weberian analyses where appropriate. In relation to our focus upon the financial services, it was concluded that Marx offered the more penetrating insights. Turning to his thesis on class polarisation and the associated ownership-control debate, we argued that the full significance of the financial sector had been occluded by too heavy a concentration on materialist rejections of its unproductive role. We also argued that the tendency of Marxists to focus upon the changing identity of the owners of capital (from personal possession by wealthy individuals and families to impersonal possession by corporations and financial institutions) has distracted attention from the critical role of financial institutions as mobilisers of cheap capital. At the same time, such perspectives neglect the importance of financial services in constituting subjects (that is, consumers) whose sense of what it is to be human involves (however limited) capital accumulation and financial self-discipline. Moreover, this emphasis overlooks the impact that a subjectivity of financial independence and individual self-responsibility has for the continuity of values and practices compatible with capitalist (that is, class) relations.

While resisting the functionalist trap to which Offe (1984: 121) seems to subscribe when he argues that the stability of "political and economic [. . .] substructures depends upon the universalization" of the commodity form, we do view the commodification of family and personal relations through financial products as contributing to the smooth running of capitalism. The mass consumption of financial services as a principal means of generating social security not only involves populations more directly in the circuits of capital. It also stimulates capitalist virtues of accumulation for their own sake.

Our critique has stressed the importance of appreciating social relations as the medium and outcome of the constitution of subjects and, by implication, their interest. It has to be recognised that subjects are constituted through their positioning in a diverse range of practices only some of which are directly a reflection and reproduction of class relations. Nonetheless, we argued that the development of mass consumer financial services is conditioned by the individualisation of subjects and their commodified relations. In offering commodified solutions to the anxieties and insecurities that these conditions arouse, the financial services reflect and reinforce the practices which reproduce them. When, as subjects, we are turned in on ourselves and unable to rely on the secure sense of identification with a group or collective set of meanings, we are rendered extremely vulnerable to an existential anxiety that blinds us to the technologies of power and class strategies which arouse or aggravate it. The effect of this is to reinforce preoccupations with private consumption and to deflect subjects from reflecting upon, or struggling against, the organisation of class relations.

References

Aaronovitch, S. *The Ruling Class*. London: Lawrence Wishart. 1961

ABI *Life Insurance in the United Kingdom 1980–84*. London: Association of British Insurers. 1984

Aldrich, H., *Organisation and Environments*. Englewood Cliffs, New Jersey: Prentice Hall. 1979

Anderson, P., Origins of the Present Crisis, *New Left Review* Jan.-Feb.: 25–42. 1964

Baudrillard, J., *Selected Writings*. Edited and introduced by M. Poster. Oxford: Polity Press. 1988

Bell, D., *The Coming of Post-Industrial Society*. London: Heinemann. 1974

Berle, A. A. and C. G. Means, *The Modern Corporation and Private Property*. New York: Macmillan. 1932

Blackburn, R., The New Capitalism, in: R. Blackburn (ed.), *Ideology in Social Science*. Bungay, Suffolk: Fontana. 1972

Blackburn, R., The Unequal Society, in: J. Urry and J. Wakeford (eds.), *Power in Britain*. London: Heinemann. 1973

Building Societies Act London: HMSO. 1986

Child, J., Organisational Structure, Environment and Performance: The Role of Strategic Choice, *Sociology* 6: 1–22. 1972

Clegg, S. and D. Dunkerley *Organisation, Class and Control*. London: Routledge and Kegan Paul. 1980

Donaldson, L., *In Defence of Organisation Theory*. Cambridge: Cambridge University Press. 1985

Eldridge, J. and A. D. Crombie *A Sociology of Organisations*. London: Allen and Unwin. 1974

Elger, T., Industrial Organizations: A Processual Perspective, in: J. B. McKinley (ed.), *Processing People: Cases in Organizational Behaviour*. New York: Holt, Rinehart and Winston. 1985

Financial Services Act, London: HMSO. 1986

Foucault, M., *Power/Knowledge*. Ed. C. Gordon. Brighton: Harvester. 1980

Foucault, M., The Subject and Power, in: H. L. Dreyfus and P. Rabinow (eds.), *Michel Foucault: Beyond Structuralism and Hermeneutics*. Brighton: Harvester Press. 1982

Fox, A., Industrial Sociology and Industrail Relations, *Royal Commission on Trade Unions and Employers' Associations*, Research Paper No. 3, London: HMSO. 1966

Fox, A., Industrial relations: a social critique of pluralist ideology, in: J. Child (ed.) *Man and Organisation*. London: Allen and Unwin. 1973

Galbraith, J. K., *American Capitalism: The Concept of Countervailing Power*. New York: Houghton Mifflin. 1952

Galbraith, J. K., *The New Industrial State*. London: Hamish Hamilton. 1967

Gilmore, C. and H. C. Willmott, Company Law and Financial Reporting: A Sociological Analysis of the U. K. Experience, Working Paper, Aston Business School. 1988

Habermas, J., *Legitimation Crisis*. New York: Beacon Press. 1975

Habermas, J., *Theory and Practice*. London: Heinemann. 1984

Haug, F. *Critique of Commodity Aesthetics*. Oxford: Polity Press. 1986

Henriques, J., W. Hollway, C. Urwin, C. Venn and V. Walkerdine, *Changing the Subject; Psychology, Social Regulation and Subjectivity*. London: Methuen. 1984

Hilferding, R., *Finance Capital*. London: RKP, 1981 edition. 1910

Hyman, R., *Industrial Relations: A Marxist Introduction*. London: Macmillan. 1975

Ingham, G., *Capitalism Divided? The City and Industry in British Social Development*. London: Macmillan. 1984

Johnson, T. Work and Power, in: G. Esland and G. Salaman (eds.), *The Politics of Work and Occupations*. Milton Keynes: Open University Press. 1980

Johnson, T., C. Dandeker and C. Ashworth *The Structure of Social Theory*. London: Macmillan. 1984

Kerr, C., J. T. Dunlop, F. H. Harbison and C. A. Myers, *Industrialism and Industrial Man*. Cambridge, Mass.: Harvard University Press. 1960

Knights, D., Risk, Financial Self-Discipline and Commodity Relations: An Analysis of the Growth and Development of Life Insurance in Contemporary Capitalism, *Advances in Public Interest Accounting* 19, 1: 47–70. 1988

Knights, D., Subjectivity, Power and the Labour Process, in: D. Knights and H. C. Willmott (eds.), *Labour Process Theory*. London: Macmillan. 1989

Knights, D. and A. Sturdy, Shifting Work: New Technology in the Insurance Office, in: I. Varcoe, M. McNeil and S. Yearsley (eds.), *Deciphering Science and Technology*. London: Macmillan. 1989

Knights, D. and T. Vurdubakis, Insurantial Technologies and the Social Constitution of Risk and Subjectivity, paper delivered at the Interdisciplinary Perspective on Accounting Conference, July, Manchester University. 1988

Knights, D. and H. C. Willmott, The Executive Fix, in: J. McGoldrick (ed.), *Business Case File in Behavioural Science*. Workingham: Van Nostrand Reinhold. 1987a

Knights, D. and H. C. Willmott, Organisational Culture as Management Strategy: A Critique and Illustration from the Financial Services Industry, *International Studies of Management and Organisation* XVII, 3: 40–64. 1987b

Longstreth, F., The City, Industry and the State, in: C. Crouch (ed.), *State and Economy in Contemporary Capitalism*. London: Croom Helm. 1979

Lupton, T. and S. G. Wilson, The Social Background and Connections of "Top Decision-Makers", in: Urry J. and J. Wakeford (eds.) *Power in Britain*. London: Heinemann. 1973

Lyotard, J. F., *The Post-Modern Condition: a Report on Knowledge*. trans. G. Bennington and B. Massumi. Minneapolis: University of Minnesota Press. 1984

Marx, K., and F. Engels, The Communist Manifesto, in: *Marx and Engels*, Selected Works. London: Lawrence and Wishart. 1970

Marx, K., *Capital: A Critical Analysis of Capitalist Production*. London: Allen and Unwin. 1971

Marx, K., *Capital, Vol. 1*. Trans. by Moore and Aveling. London: Allen and Unwin. 1973

Marx, K., *Capital, Volume 3*. Harmondsworth: Penguin. 1976

Mayer, J. P., *Max Weber and German Politics*. London: Faber and Faber. 1956

Nairn, T., The Decline of the British State, *New Left Review*. Mar.-Apl.: 101–102. 1977

Nairn, T., Britain's Perenniel Crisis, *New Left Review*. Jan.-Feb.: 113–114. 1979

Nichols, T., *Ownership, Control and Ideology*. London: Allen & Unwin. 1969

O'Donnell, T., *History of Life Insurance in its Formative Years*. Chicago: American Conservation Co. 1936

Offe, C., *Contradictions of the Welfare State*. London: Hutchinson. 1984

Offe, C., and V. Ronge, Theses on the Theory of the State, in: C. Offe, *ibid*. 1984

Pugh, D. and D. Hickson, The Comparative Study of Organisations, in: D. Pym (ed.), *Industrial Society*. London: Harmondsworth. 1968

Racevskis, K. *Michel Foucault and the Subversion of the Intellect*. Ithaca: Cornell University Press. 1983

Rattansi, A., End of an Orthodoxy? The Critique of Sociology's View of Marx on Class, *Sociological Review* 33: 641–669. 1985

Salaman, G., Towards a Sociology of Organisational Structure, in: M. Zey-Ferrell and M. Aiken (eds.), *Complex Organizations: Critical Perspectives*. Glenview, IU.: Scott, Foresman and Company. 1981

Silverman, D., *The Theory of Organisations*. London: Heinemann. 1970

Thompson, E. P., *The Making of the English Working Class*. Harmondsworth: Penguin. 1968

Urry, J. and J. Wakeford, (eds.) *Power in Britain*. London: Heinemann. 1973

Walton, C. C., *Corporate Responsibilities*. Belmont, California: Wadsworth. 1967

Weber, M., *Economy and Society: An Outline on Interpretive Sociology* (3 vols). New York: Bedminster Press. 1978

Willmott, H. C., Beyond Paradigmatic Closure in Organisational Analysis, in: J. Hassard and D. Pym (eds.) *The Theory and Philosophy of Organizations*. London: Croom Helm. 1988

Willmott, H. C., The Dialectics of Praxis: Opening Up the Core of Labour Process Analysis, in: D. Knights and H. C. Willmott (eds.), *Labour Process Theory*. London: Macmillan. 1989

Willmott, H. C. and D. Knights, The Problem of Freedom: Fromm's Contribution to a Critical Theory of Work Organisation, *Praxis International* 2,2: 204–225. 1982

Organization and Class: Burawoy in Birmingham

Dennis Smith

1. Introduction

In his latest book, *The Politics of Production: Factory Regimes under Capitalism and Socialism* (1985), Burawoy speculates about the ways in which "factory regimes" – in other words, political practices and ideological assumptions embedded in the labour process and related aspects of production – are shaped and how they, in turn, shape the experience of labour on the shopfloor and the development of working-class struggles within capitalist societies.

In the light of this central concern, the present paper will pay particular attention to Burawoy's discussion of tendencies within Western capitalist societies, especially Britain. In the next section the pertinent aspects of Burawoy's argument will be indicated. In subsequent sections two comparisons will be carried out. First, a comparison will be made between aspects of nineteenth and early twentieth century Birmingham and Sheffield as a way of exploring the relative importance of factory regimes in shaping the development of working-class participation in social and political conflict. Second, the development of two large factories in South West Birmingham – the Austin car factory and the Cadbury chocolate factory – during the twentieth century will be compared in order to assess the plausibility of Burawoy's analysis of the impact of "external" change (especially in the sphere of social reproduction) upon factory regimes.[1] Finally, some tentative conclusions will be drawn.

2. Burawoy on Factory Regimes

Burawoy argues that the character of factory regimes reflects the institutional relationship between the apparatuses of factory and state (do they tend towards separation or fusion?) and the way the state intervenes in the factory regime (is it

[1] The author is principal investigator of the South West Birmingham project which has been examining the consequences of economic restructuring in that locality, with particular reference to local factories of the firms of Austin Rover and Cadbury Schweppes. The research is financed by the Economic and Social Research Council (D04260006).

direct or indirect?). Alongside the part played by the state is another factor, the degree to which the workforce is separated from the means of subsistence. Are workers able (for example) to produce food directly on family smallholdings or are they almost completely dependent upon wages received in return for the sale of labour power? This variable directs attention to the relationship between the workers' bargaining power within the factory and the means whereby the domestic economy, local welfare arrangements and local schooling are supported and regulated.

The two factors just mentioned – the form of state intervention and the degree of wage dependence – are high in the "causal hierarchy" (90). Within the limits defined by these two factors, two other independent variables operate. They are the play of market forces (e.g. the degree of inter-firm competition and the state of the local labour market) and the nature of the labour process (e.g. whether the subordination of labour is merely "formal" as in the putting-out system or whether it is "real" as in the case of factory labour subject to direct managerial discipline)[2].

In his discussion of modern cases Burawoy deliberately chooses examples – e.g. Allied in Chicago and Jays in Manchester – which have similar labour processes and, indeed, similar renumeration systems and market contexts (128). This allows him to concentrate his argument upon the factors which are highest in his "causal hierarchy". The comparative and historical arguments which emerge from an initial discussion of Allied and Jays largely depend upon the dynamic interplay among three relationships: the intervention of the state within the factory regime; the impact of the factory regime upon the reproduction of labour power; and the intervention of the state in the reproduction of labour power.

Within this context, three conjunctures are of particular relevance to the British case. The first is characterised by *despotic* regimes. In this case the factory regime and state apparatus are institutionally quite separate and state intervention in the factory regime is indirect (e.g. entailing legislation protecting market relations and the external labour market). Historically, such regimes vary in the degree to which operatives are excluded from control over the labour process, the degree to which factory owners regulate the sphere of reproduction (e.g. housing, schooling and moral behaviour of workers), and the degree to which employees are treated as having rights and obligations beyond the contractual exchange of labour power for wages. The main point, however, is that the state

---

[2] There is a slight ambiguity over the relationship between labour process and factory regime as concepts in Burawoy's scheme. His initial definition of factory regime encompasses "the organisation of work – that is, the *labour process* – (and) [...] distinctive political and ideological *apparatuses of production* which regulate production relations. The notion of *production regime* or, more specifically, factory regime embraces both these dimensions of production politics" (Burawoy 1985: 8; italics in original). However, later in the book Burawoy identifies "labour process" as one of "four variables (with) [...] independent effects on the form of factory regimes" (90).

does not intervene directly within the factory regime or the sphere of reproduction. By implication, the state has relatively little effect upon the capacity of capital and labour to exercise influence upon each other.

The second conjuncture is characterised by *hegemonic* regimes. This case differs from the despotic case in three ways. First, although the apparatuses of state and factory remain separate, the degree of state intervention within the factory increases, especially regarding the regulation of conflicts between capital and labour (e.g. by insisting on recognition of trade unions, imposing pay norms, enforcing health and safety standards). Second, state intervention in the reproduction of labour power increases, mainly through the provision of welfare rights, unemployment benefits, public housing, state pensions and so on. Third (and consequentially), large-scale capital concedes to its "industrial citizens" (10) increased rights within collective bargaining and greater opportunities to advance within an internal labour market. Higher wages feed back into buoyant product markets to the advantage of capital.

The third conjuncture, recently appearing and discussed only briefly, is *hegemonic despotism*. This case has the following characteristics. First, "withdrawal of the state as an arena in which struggles between capital and labour can be fought out" (264). This movement seems to encompass not only a lessening of state support and regulation in the sphere of reproduction (schools, welfare, housing) but also a loosening of state controls over the internal affairs of factory regimes. Second, the readiness of capital to be geographically mobile as demonstrated by transfers of manufacturing capacity to peripheral societies and regions. Third (and consequentially), a radical shift of the balance of power between capital and labour within the inherited "hegemonic" institutions of factory regimes, enabling concessions from labour to be won through persuasion rather than conflict. In such circumstances, resistance from labour to sub-contracting, temporary contracts and home-working is reduced.

Some general comments are in order before making a detailed critical response. First, a great deal of explanatory weight is attached by Burawoy to the factory regime as a determinant of the development of working class struggles. One very strong expression of this assumption is his statement that "variations in factory regime are *sufficient* to explain both working-class reformism in England and a revolutionary movement in Russia. Other factors enter into the analysis only as determinants of factory regimes" (88; italics in original). Bold assertions of this kind provide a clear target for critics, sympathetic or not. It is a target pinned on the shirt front close to the heart since Burawoy is clearly keen to show that "the industrial working class has made significant and self-conscious interventions in history" (5).

By focusing his attention so closely upon the factory regime Burawoy is reduced to treating his various "independent variables" as givens which may be taken at face value. This can produce misleading results. For example, Burawoy treats increases in state support for the reproduction of labour as an externally imposed "penalty" whose most significant consequence was a raising of the cost to employers of eliciting the compliance of workers since the latter became less wholly dependent upon wages. However, this ignores the possibility that state action in this sphere might to a considerable degree be a response to pressure from employers themselves.

To give one instance, when the provision of labour exchanges and national insurance schemes was widely discussed in Britain between 1905 and 1914 "one of the most consistent and active proponents of social legislation were the members of the Birmingham Chamber of Commerce" (Hay 1977: 442). The employers represented in such a body were, typically, local residents. They had domestic property to protect and spouses and children who travelled the highways. If the standard of living of the working men and women had to be raised as one means of "civilising" them, why not transfer part of the burden onto taxes rather than bearing it on payroll costs? Of course, this is only part of the story but it is a part which gets screened out by the relatively narrow range of motives and consequences to which Burawoy pays attention.

It is perfectly reasonable to present an argument about social and political change which directs particular attention to a single explanatory factor. However, the most successful enterprises of this kind are backed up with rich empirical data drenched in comparative and historical argument. An obvious example is Barrington Moore's *Social Origins of Dictatorship and Democracy* (1969). Moore places great emphasis upon the extent and type of commerical exploitation of agriculture by the landed aristocracy as the major determining variable of the processes of economic and political modernisation leading towards, respectively, bourgeois democracy, revolutionary communism and fascism. The commercialisation of agriculture is decisive mainly through its impact upon relationships among the state, the landed aristocracy and the urban bourgeoisie. Moore pays considerable attention to what might be labelled the "agricultural regime" – in other words, the political practices and ideological assumptions embedded in the forces and relations of production binding peasant to landlord. The parallels with Burawoy's "factory regime" are obvious. However, even though the peasantry in agrarian societies consituted a far higher proportion of the population than the factory proletariat has ever done in industrial societies, Moore does not simply "read off" the propensity for, say, peasant revolution or bourgeois reformism from the state of landlord/peasant relations within the "agricultural regime". Instead, he examines the interplay *between* the development of these relations and the working out of accomodations and struggles among dominant or would-be dominant classes (or class fragments). This element is missing from Burawoy's argument and leaves him open to the suspicion of having "tunnel vision," able to perceive factors external to the factory only as "independent variables" whose dynamics do not require close examination.

These comments may be considered over-censorious on the grounds that they make too many demands on Burawoy's historical and comparative analysis which is, at best, a tentative and speculative development of a few case studies. If so, then perhaps the following sections may be considered as a series of further tentative speculations which explore some of Burawoy's general formulations in the context of further case studies.

3. Two Cities

The term "factory regime" should really be expanded to "workplace regime" in the case of early and mid nineteenth-century Birmingham. The broader term would encompass domestic industry and workshop production which were intimately tied in with the relatively few factories which existed. "Garret masters" served as head craftsmen in small work teams made up of kin and apprentices. In good times they were able to expand their labour force. Some leading craftsmen acted as sub-contracters on a piece-work basis either within the walls of specialised steam-driven factories or in their own smaller premises. Within this highly differentiated system, factors served as intermediaries, arranging orders and distribution, supplying raw materials and capital.

It is relevant to notice that the above description applies equally to Sheffield and to Birmingham.[3] The skilled artisan was the key figure in the occupational structures of both cities before 1850. E. P. Thompson notes that in the early nineteenth century "important groups of privileged artisans or skilled workers will be found in the provinces [...]. This was true, in particular, of the Sheffield cutlery and Birmingham small-ware industries" (1968: 265). Contemporary recollections of artisan life in that early period, rather highly coloured, indicate a similar pattern of work and leisure in the two places. Birmingham's craftsmen worked early in the morning and late at night: "At noon they rested; many enjoyed their siesta; others spent their time in the workshops eating and drinking, these places often turned into taprooms and the apprentices into pot boys" (quoted in Reid 1976: 77). In Sheffield the "ale pot not infrequently stood on the anvil, and the men gossipped and drank instead of working" (Leader 1905: 47).

In the light of these comments, the question arises: do these two cities represent, perhaps, a version of what Michael Burawoy calls the "patriarchal" regime based upon widespread sub-contracting arrangements involving to some degree the employment of kin by sub-contractors? Burawoy argues that "operatives sought to defend rather than transform the existing patriarchal factory regime" and that this "defense was carried into the wider political arena" (1985: 95).

In his *History of Labour in Sheffield* (1959), Sidney Pollard drew attention to

---

[3] The discussion of Birmingham and Sheffield in this part of the paper is based upon research carried out for Smith (1982). Supporting references may be found there.

certain similarities between political movements in the two cities, especially with respect to cooperation between working men and the local middle class. He wrote that in Sheffield "There was [...] close cooperation between organisations of the two classes during the agitation preceding the Reform Act of 1832 in striking parallel with the developments in Birmingham" (41–2). Peter Mathias has also stressed the similarity of the two cities, contrasting their social tendencies with the "class consciousness [...] and class bitterness" of radically divided towns such as Merthyr Tydfil, with its huge iron works, and the Lancashire mill towns:

The secondary metal trades, centred on the Birmingham district, Sheffield and many Lancashire villages, were very different in their structure of production and collateral social relationships. The average size of workshop (in the midnineteenth century) still had less than ten employees [...] (and) a man could set up as a small master fairly easily, if he saved £ 60–£ 100, renting "rooms and power" for his workshop. [...] A feeling of solidarity existed in the (Birmingham) region and hostility was expressed more against the distant monopoly-seeking copper and iron magnates forcing up raw materials prices by collusion, as the Birmingham men believed, rather than against the owners of property within Birmingham. The great crises came from fluctuations in export markets for which no local people could be held responsible. The same was true of the Sheffield edge-tool and cutlery industries [...]. The trend in both places was toward a gradual increase in the size of plant, which had been the case long before 1851 (1983: 247–8).

In both cities traditional craft skills were succeeded by mass production – from the 1860s in the case of Sheffield steel, from the 1880s in Birmingham with the development of automatic cutting and stamping machines. However, Mathias adds, "At the end of the century, and even in the mid-twentieth century, the small firm prospered among the giants more easily in the Sheffield and Birmingham trades than almost anywhere else" (248).

Do we have in this comparison between Birmingham and Sheffield confirmation of Michael Burawoy's suggestion that the character of the factory/workshop regime is the major determinant of the way in which the working class participates in society and politics? Unfortunately, this conclusion is difficult to sustain.

Working-class politics developed in very different ways in the two cities. In Sheffield the Chartist movement had a strong strain of anarchism, expressed in the attempt by local radicals to inaugurate a system of "ward-motes" or popular neighbourhood councils during the 1850s. During the next decade, the Sheffield trade unions were subjected to a governmental inquiry and widespread attacks in the press for their violent methods of enforcing their rules on members. A prolonged strike against mechanisation by the prestigious and powerful local unions in the file trade was bitterly fought and utterly lost. From the 1860s onward, massive steel works, employing huge amounts of incoming capital and immigrant labour swamped the residual influence of the craft unions within Sheffield society. Nevertheless, the local anarchist tradition persisted. It resurfaced in the syndicalist pamphlets of the Sheffield Workers" Committee of 1917 which were intended to appeal to the aspirations of skilled engineers coming to terms with the influx of unskilled dilutees. By that date, the planting of the steel works in the city and the retreat of middle-class Sheffield to the suburbs had produced very marked residential segregation by class. As a consequence, Sheffield became over much of its area a solidly working-class city prepared to support Labour candidates in local and national elections.

By contrast, Birmingham had become the major stronghold of Unionism during the late nineteenth century and many of its local labour leaders were well described as "cloth-capped Chamberlainites." As a political movement, Unionism in Birmingham was, crudely expressed, the outcome of a conscious appeal by professional and business interests in the Liberal party to "respectable" skilled working people followed by a gradual fusion of the Liberal leadership with local Conservative interests. Not until 1924 did Birmingham acquire its first Labour MP, fifteen years after Sheffield. In 1926 Sheffield became the first large provincial city to have a Labour Council, an achievement denied to Birmingham till after World War II. The gap of fifteen to twenty years between the swing to Labour in the two cities might, on one reading, be explained as a consequence of variations in the timing of the shift from a "patriarchal" regime to a succeeding ("despotic"?) factory regime. After all, as the quotation from Peter Mathias indicates, in both cities large firms employing sophisticated machinery and a mix of craftsmen and semi-skilled labour were well established by the latter part of the nineteenth century but Birmingham lagged perhaps twenty years behind Sheffield in this development. Unfortunately, such an explanation would not account for the fact that (for example) the anarchistic tendency, the sharp social polarisation and the entrenched resistance to mechanisation so characteristic of Labour politics in Sheffield were quite foreign to Birmingham. There are other important differences also, as will be seen shortly.

Another explanation will be proposed. The great significance of the factory regime is acknowledged but this factor should be considered in a broader framework relevant to a commercialised agrarian society undergoing the transformations associated with the development of industrial capitalism. The parts played by labouring men and women in the factory or workshop must be considered alongside their simultaneous involvements in religious, political and educational movements. Also relevant are fissions and accomodations within and between the working class, the petty bourgeoisie, and, not least, the big bourgeoisie of major capitalists and their leading professional associates. Furthermore, the dynamics of these relationships must be considered with reference to their interplay with the still-very-powerful social, commercial and political forces deriving from an older order, only very gradually being superceded.

The case of Sheffield may be considered first, necessarily briefly. In the early nineteenth century the city was, in effect, a dense cluster of toolmakers' and cutlers' villages, relatively isolated and surrounded by large aristocratic estates.

Adult males, organised in dozens of unions within a narrow range of trades, dominated the labour market. There was a thin layer of professional and commercial families but its members were effectively excluded from the heart of either the highly-localised, craft-based working-class institutions of Sheffield or genteel circles in the surrounding countryside. There was virtually no civic tradition of "public service".

As the city grew in population during the 1840s and 1850s working-class activism was directed at preserving or enhancing the autonomy of local people and resisting attempts at domination from "outside". Apart from the anarchism of the local Chartists, expressions of localism included: resistance by local trade unions to regulation by the Cutlers' Company (controlled by the larger masters); enthusiasm for the democratic tendency within Methodism (against the more centralist Wesleyans); and a strong preference for the freer atmosphere of "their" Sunday schools as opposed to the larger and more bureaucratic Anglican day schools. However, the political, religious and industrial movements were not tied together. Instead, their supporters ignored or opposed each other. Meanwhile, a split developed between working-class adherents of two alternative strategies of industrial regulation, especially in larger enterprises: one strategy envisaged cooperation between "just" masters and "respectable" working men; the other wished to conserve and strengthen the capacity of the artisan community to regulate its own affairs.

Splits within the working class were a major source of weakness as from the 1860s onward the growth of the steel industry in Attercliffe and Brightside radically altered the face of Sheffield capital. Mighty new masters such as John Brown and Charles Cammell established strong links with the richest and most powerful sections of landed and metropolitan society. By the 1890s the "heavy" trades had become the main local employers. They were vigorously anti-union. Efforts by labour leaders to establish local arbitration machinery were unsuccessful. The Labour party's capture of the city council in the mid-1920s institutionalised a fundamental dichotomy in Sheffield society: between an industrial sector dominated by capitalist interests with major allegiances outside the region and labour-controlled local governmental bodies serving a predominantly working-class city.

Turning to Birmingham, a factory/workplace regime broadly similar to the Sheffield model in the early nineteenth century was set in a very different context. For example, the range of occupations within the general area of hardware manufacture and "toy" – (or, in modern parlance, gadget –) making in Birmingham was much wider than in the Sheffield trades. Also, there was a much higher incidence of female and child labour, especially in the less-skilled button and steel-pen industries. The families of working people in Birmingham were unlikely to be dependent upon a single income or the fortunes of a single trade. There was less pressure to defend craft demarcations. An upsurge of union organisation in the 1820s, 1830s and 1840s failed to prevent erosion of traditional craft privileges accompanying the steady increase in larger, more mechanised establishments with lower wages and fewer apprentices. Unable to resist change unaided or by industrial means, artisan leaders turned to the strategy of cooperating with "their betters" in political, religious and educational enterprises as a means of establishing a relatively influential "voice" in the emerging civic order.

Unlike isolated Sheffield, Birmingham was a busy regional and national crossroads, for people, goods and ideas. Its urban big bourgeoisie – manufacturers, bankers, wholesalers, leisured gentlefolk, doctors, lawyers, ministers and so on – were much thicker on the ground, more "clubbable" and exercised greater influence than their counterparts in the northern city. Working men found their way into the ranks of radical middle-class enterprises such as the Birmingham Political Union (whose members dominated the newly-elected town council in the 1830s) and, later, the Complete Suffrage Union. Many joined in protests against church rates, picked up basic literacy at the Quakers' First Day Adult School, attended People's Chapel (founded by, among others, the self-made manufacturer John Skirrow Wright), and became involved in Liberal politics through the Birmingham Reform Association (founded 1858) and Birmingham Liberal Association (1865).

This strategy was rational in view of the weakness of autonomous working-class industrial organisation and also because Birmingham's big bourgeoisie had much more influence in relation to the surrounding county aristocracy and within national networks than had its counterpart in Sheffield. Between 1830 and 1870 the balance of power swung steadily away from rural hierarchies – genteel, landed, Anglican – and towards the city. The higher circles of money, power and prestige in Birmingham were fundamentally divided during this period between those who wished to retard this development and those who wished to encourage it. In other words, just as the Sheffield bourgeoisie faced an increasingly disunited working class, so the skilled artisans of Birmingham benefited from a split within the local establishment.

Liberal politicians such as George Dixon and Joseph Chamberlain drew legitimacy from their commitment to a "civic gospel". They said they wanted to build up and exercise the powers of the municipality on behalf of all the local people. Although the gap between promise and performance was very great, especially in the sphere of housing, labour leaders gave their support to the Liberals, especially during the 1870s and 1880s. Their adherence was strategically important during this period in building up the legitimacy of the new political regime. In return, union organisers such as W. J. Davis of the Brassworkers managed to encourage the widespread introduction of conciliation and arbitration machinery in Birmingham trades. In this way, "rights" were conceded to labour which they could never have won through the exercise of their weak industrial muscle.

Labour politics in early twentieth-century Birmingham was shaped by three factors: progressive disillusionment with the Chamberlainite regime, especially regarding the provision of housing and the protection of tenants' rights; an increase in the proportion of semi- and unskilled labour in local industry, especially large concerns such as GEC, Dunlop, Cadbury and Austin on the northern and southern boundaries; and a gradual healing of the split within the big bourgeoisie as property of all kinds closed its ranks against labour. These factors will enter the analysis once more in the next section of this paper. However, this section has, hopefully, sustained the argument that similar factory or workplace regimes may lead to very different modes of working-class participation in social and political struggle.

4. Two Factories

At this point the focus will shift from the impact of factory regimes on broader social change to the impact of "external" factors on factory regimes. Particular attention will be paid to two enterprises located in the south-western suburbs of Birmingham: the chocolate factory established by Richard and George Cadbury at Bournville in 1879 with 230 employees and the car factory opened by Herbert Austin at Longbridge in 1905 with a payroll of 270.[4] By 1962 the Bournville shopfloor workforce had increased to nearly 9 000. By the late 1970s the figure stood at about 7 000 but subsequent drastic cut backs reduced it to a little over 3 000 (1987). The Austin factory shopfloor provided work for about 20 000 people in the late 1970s but this fell to 11 000 by 1982, a further thousand jobs being lost in the subsequent five years.

The history of the two factories has been closely related to the development of South West Birmingham as a distinctive locality. From the turn of the century of the recent past, South West Birmingham has been an attractive destination for capital and labour. Metal and engineering industries, especially car-making and component suppliers, have been prominent. Skilled artisans from the crowded city centre invested their savings in nice terraced houses out in Kings Norton, Northfield, Stirchley and Selly Oak, convenient for the suburban railway. Some found their way into Bournville Village, a Cadbury model development which embodied an implicit criticism of the inadequate implementation of the civic gospel by followers of a rival dynasty, the Chamberlains. Semi-skilled machine minders and unskilled labourers also came to the expanding-south-western sub-

---

[4] Initial reading on Cadbury would include (for example) Williams (1931), Gardiner (1923), Cadbury Bros. (1947), Cadbury Bros. (1964), Rogers (1931), C. Smith (1987), Bournville Village Trust (1955) and Dellheim (1987). Soon to appear are Smith, Child and Rowlinson (forthcoming), a doctoral thesis on Cadburys by Michael Rowlinson and publications from the South West Birmingham project. On Austin see (for example), Church (1979), Wyatt (1981), Willman and Winch (1985), Williams, Williams and Haslam (1987) and Marsden et al. (1985) and forthcoming publications from South West Birmingham project.

urbs. Tensions between skilled and semi- and un-skilled workers were liable to become exacerbated by ethnic and religious conflicts in the inner areas, as manifested by the violent anti-Irish feelings which broke surface in the "no-popery" riots of the late 1860s. Suburban dispersal gave more room to breathe, allowing minorities (if they were white) to merge within the mass.

People came not just from inner Birmingham but from much farther afield, especially during the 1930s. Tyneside, Welsh and other regional accents mixed with native Brummie and near-by Black Country twangs. Large council house estates were laid out between the wars and after 1945. Some of them, especially on the periphery, received exiles from demolished sub-standard housing in the inner city. As in the case of Bournville Village, these last housing enterprises represented attempts at planned community improvement. These efforts were a counterpoint to the individualistic striving for self-improvement (more money, more pride, more choice) by the restless people who made the treck to South West Birmingham in the hope of being "taken on" at "the Austin" or Cadbury and, perhaps ("if you keep your nose clean") even being "made up" to foreman.

In view of some obvious differences between the factory regimes at the Longbridge and Bournville works, to be discussed shortly, it is worth stressing some less obvious similarities. Both managements were committed at the highest levels to exploiting new technology in spite of the fears of labour that this would lead to job losses and changed working practices. This was evident in the course of a brief correspondence in *The Times* at the end of 1932. Sir Herbert Austin, founder and principal director of the Austin Motor Company, wrote to the newspaper in order to expose "two fallacies," one being that industry was overproducing, the other that machines were responsible for the world's unemployment problem: "The machine, rather than decreasing employment, has been the means of enormously increasing it [. . .]. Personally, I consider it a dangerous policy, absolutely against national interests, to keep raging that there is overproduction, and that a shorter number of hours should be worked. Of course, we can work fewer hours, but by the same line of argument, why work at all?" In Austin's view,

All this cry of "over-production" unfortunately tends to create in the minds of those workers in employment an impression that the less work they do the better matters will become for their less fortunate fellows. No more destructive doctrine could be devised. If only it were possible to make our trade unions realise that upon the speed and efficiency at which the men in employment work depends the survival of the whole of our industrial structure, I am sure a good deal of unemployment in this country would disappear (The Times, 26 Nov. 1932)

Within a week Laurence J. Cadbury, one of the firm's leading directors, had responded, adding his support. His argument was more academic and theoretical than Austin's, referring as it did to Ministry of Labour statistics and the views of Professor Sargent Florence. Briefly, he argued that where there was high elasticity of demand sales would increase in response to the lower prices resulting from reduced labour costs. Demand-led expansion would lead to increased employment. In other words, "it is incorrect to assume that machines are everywhere displacing men". Instead, there was hope "that this century will succeed, as did its predecessor, in solving the problem of labour displacement". (The Times, 1 Dec. 1932).

In fact, both factories underwent fairly radical restructuring between the wars. Following the revival of the car trade in 1922 and Sir Herbert's visit to the United States that year both the opportunity and the method of strengthening the Austin Motor Company became apparent. A comprehensive reorganisation of production methods was carried out ensuring that "work should proceed from machine to machine and from process to process without any backward movement [. . .] and that it should flow directly on to the assembly line" (Engelbach 1927–28: 68). Technological innovation was accompanied by the inauguration of a system of close monitoring of operations by an efficiency department and a cost office. At roughly the same time Cadbury, which also had a planning department and cost office, was adopting advanced "mass-production methods" in which "America has led the way" (Cadbury Bros. 1947: 17). A primary consideration was "the flow of production through the works" (20). The inter-war restructuring and the successes of products such as Cadbury Milk Chocolate and the Austin Seven provided a momentum which carried both firms through to the post-war period.

When Harry Hopkins visited South West Birmingham in the mid-1950s he spent time in both the Bournville and the Longbridge works. He concluded that "in both the conveyor belt was king. In Bournville's Milk Tray building it stopped five minutes in every hour; in the Longbridge Car Assembly Building it halted not at all in working-time" (1957: 67). There were other similarities, readily recalled by shopfloor employees whose careers began before World War II. At both firms, for example, family connections with existing workers were perceived as being very useful if you wanted to "get in" and "get on".

At both firms, before and after the last war, there were several clubs – especially for hobbies and sports – attended by shopfloor enthusiasts during lunch breaks and before or after work. At this point differences in factory regime begin to emerge clearly. In both cases, many meetings were held on the factory premises but only at Austin would the company actually charge workers for the use of premises. At Cadbury, by contrast, luxurious facilities were provided free (or for a very modest and very highly-subsidised club subscription), especially in the sphere of sport. Just as the rolling acres of Rowheath, the Cadbury sports complex, are among the first memories to surface for retired Bournville employees, so the rough tactics of the "works police" with men caught smoking in the toilet is typically mentioned by elderly ex-Austin workers. The difference between the orientations of the two company managements could be expressed as the contrast between two sets of questions: "what can you do for us? and why should we pay for more than we get?" (Austin) as compared with "what can we do for you? and why should we not spend a little extra if it makes for all-round contentment?" (Cadbury). As one Cadbury ex-employee remembered: "If you suggested (in the Works Councill) that there should be a little more sugar in the tea they would happily oblige [. . .]. They were very obliging in that way".[5]

It is time to dig a little deeper. Apart from wartime, when government directives shaped production, Austin and Cadbury were both manufacturing goods for markets which were greatly affected by fashion, taste and seasonality. The managerial styles just mentioned represented contrasting responses to the need to minimise risk and uncertainty. The factories at Bournville and Longbridge were both established on greenfield sites, away from entrenched working-class communities. George Cadbury's local property development which became the Bournville Village Trust – very much under the influence and eye of the Cadbury family even though it was legally separate from the company – provided a powerful means of shaping the culture of the local area. This was the case even though, for most of its existence, only some forty per cent of householders in trust property have been Cadbury employees.

The implicit message of the trust was the need for respectability, dependability, sobriety, moderation and orderliness. Within the factory, employees were given practical encouragement to "make the best of themselves" educationally (through day continuation and evening classes), in their health (through the medical department), as citizens (through paid time off for service on the city council, for example), and so on. Trade union membership was openly tolerated and, from 1918, a structure of shop committees feeding into Men's and Women's Works Councils was in operation.

In return for such consideration, loyalty and hard work were expected. Moral and social improvement of the workforce was one objective of these arrangements. If you were young, female and semi-skilled, you could certainly expect better treatment at Cadburys than in the pen nib or button trades of central Birmingham. However, another objective was to guarantee continuity and flexibility of production in the light of the changing commercial judgements of the directors.

At first sight, the early years of the Austin works in Longbridge seem to have had uncanny resemblances to the Bournville experience. The Bournville Village Trust had been established in 1900 (over two decades after the factory was opened) on part of the three hundred or so acres of land that George Cadbury had purchased in the area. Herbert Austin's company purchased over one hundred acres in Longbridge in 1917 and built upon it an estate of 252 dwellings complete with a village hall, clubrooms, a laundry and a Church of England mission room. In the same year the Austin Technical Society was established with

---

[5] References to individuals working in South West Birmingham, past and present, are based upon interviews carried out as part of the author's ongoing research, including the South West Birmingham project.

its own library and cinema in order to encourage improved scientific and commercial skills among employees. Works apprentices received pay for attending classes run by the company. From 1919 they attended a newly-established company engineering college. The brightest could compete for a company scholarship at Birmingham University.

Furthermore, although Herbert Austin is usually remembered as a dedicated engineer with a somewhat dour and Social-Darwinist view of the human condition, it is worth noting that he had suffecent sense of involvement in public life to stand (successfully) as parliamentary candidate for King's Norton (which he served as MP from 1918 to 1924) and act as chairman of the Greater Birmingham Employment Committee during the depression years of the 1930s.

Despite these potentially predisposing conditions, the Austin Motor Company did not adopt the Bournville strategy of minimising risk and uncertainty by cultivating loyal compliance with strictly-imposed standards within a culture carefully managed and monitored by the company. Instead of attempting to minimise uncertainty by "reaching out" to incorporate and control, within the limits of Christianity and honest Liberalism, the outer and "inner" environment of its workforce, the Austin approach was to try to limit risk by eliminating all avoidable commitments to employees while maximising demands upon them within the terms of the wage contract.

It is likely that this strategy appeared more feasible than the Cadbury approach in view of the sheer size to which the Longbridge force grew (from under three hundred to over twenty thousand in the first decade and a half) and the very shaky finances of the company in the early years (leading to the intervention of the Receiver in 1921). The task of coordinating and dominating communications within such a large collectivity was much more daunting than in the case of Cadbury. In any case, the resources to do it were not readily available. The high level of dependence by Austin on casual workers was consistent with the strategy of minimum commitment to labour. Their employment reinforced the argument against the adoption of the Bournville approach since such workers typically experienced many fruitless journeys to the factory gates, hours of frustration before being turned away, and months of unemployment over the winter.

Before World War II, trade unions were not readily tolerated at the Longbridge works though they had an intermittent covert existence. Significantly, strike activity was almost unknown in Cadburys before the 1970s, the major exception being the General Strike. By contrast, major stoppages occurred at Longbridge in, for example, 1918 (10 000 out), 1928 (5 000 affected) and 1936 (5 000 affected). The causes of these strikes were matters such as the regrading of jobs, proposed wage cuts and changes in piece-rates, all regularly recurring items of low-level dispute within the factory.

The atmosphere in the works by the mid-1940s is nicely conveyed by the experience of a maintenance tradesman who joined one of the Longbridge machine shops in 1946. Without ceremony, he was taken directly to a collection of machines in need of servicing and told to "get on with it". With the aid of a another worker he purloined a workbench from another department, banged a nail in the wall to hang up the coat in which he had just arrived, and "got on with it." There was little communication with fellow workers or foreman for several days and it was months before he was allowed into the "pen" along with the established maintenance team and given his own bench alongside them. He was told by the informal team leader not to communicate with the men on the other side of the shop and later discovered that he was the first man for a long time to be taken into that area who was not already connected in some way, mainly through kinship, with someone or other already working there. Through a mixture of natural engineering ability and political skill he later made his way up to become a senior foreman.

A straightforward reading of Burawoy's argument would, perhaps, suggest that up until at least the 1950s the Austin works was an example of "market despotism" and Bournville of "paternalism". This seems inadequate to capture the different dynamics of the two factories. Although the use of historical analogies is risky it is tempting to suggest that, in some respects, these dynamics resembled those of an early medieval feudal army (Austin) and, to take another institution common in the same period, a religious order attached to a cathedral, abbey or friary (Cadbury). The processes of pacification and secularisation of society which have swept aside these institutions in the intervening millenium have not dispensed with the social dispositions and psychological orientations which they encouraged as a means of coping with uncertainty.

On the one hand: an admiration of guts and craftiness; a habit of sticking to the security of the small face-to-face group and cruelly testing out potential comrades; and a readiness to bargain hard about the terms upon which the group engages in the next season's campaign (a new vehicle, a new piece rate). On the other hand: a sense of membership within a corporate body; an expectation that clear internal and external boundaries will be maintained so that each knows his or her proper place in the overall scheme of things; and willing subjection to a discipline which enjoins obligations in return for privileges and rights. These descriptions over-simplify matters. They ignore the common subjection to the dull grind of labour and the widespread alertness to the element of "bamboozling" at all levels in both factories. However, they pinpoint some central aspects of each factory regime which were profoundly affected by the expansion of the welfare state, especially after World War II, and the recession of the mid/late 1970s and early 1980s.

As has been seen, Burawoy argues that increased state support for the reproduction of labour power and greater state intervention in capital/labour relations within the factory encouraged a transition from (to oversimplify) a "despotic" regime based upon very directive managerial styles to a "hegemonic" regime based on persuasion and concession by capital. Subsequently, a reduction in the scope of state support and intervention combined with the readiness of capital to be geographically mobile leads to a shift in the balance of power back towards capital. In the ensuing phase of "hegemonic despotism", inherited techniques of managerial persuasion facilitate a reverse flow of concessions back from labour, recouping many losses of the previous phase.

The two phases just described belong mainly to the post-war period. During those four decades workers at the Bournville and Longbridge factories have benefited from the expansion of council housing and welfare services and the economic boom of the 1950s and 1960s. In that period, many local workers acquired their own cars, went on foreign holidays, moved into the private housing market and began to climb up the status hierarchy of residential estates in the locality. The bottom rungs of this hierarchy were occupied by residents of deprived households on some of the outer council estates. From the 1970s job losses and industrial depression increased the pressure on state subsidies at the bottom of the ladder and made it more difficult to advance up it.

The two factory regimes were transformed in different ways during the post-war years. As the welfare state developed, the insulating strategy of the Cadburys was gradually undermined. The distinctiveness of the facilities available in Bournville – factory and village trust – was reduced. To some extent, efforts were made to reach out beyond Bournville and shape the welfare state, especially in the early post-war years. Laurence Cadbury spoke out on (for example) family allowances, marriage, large families and industrial pension schemes (*The Times*, 14 Aug. 1946, 6 Nov. 1946, 4 Jan. 1947, 4 Jan. 1954). Paul S. Cadbury made his views known on (for example) housing, town and country planning, local government and problem families (*The Times*, 13 Oct. 1945, 1 April 1946, 20 Jan. 1947, 11 Jan. 1950, 24 Mar. 1950, 1 Oct. 1952, 2 Oct. 1954). However, by the late 1960s the directors of the chocolate firm were steadily reducing the proportion of their time and resources being devoted to "welfare," a process well under way by the time the merger with the mighty Schweppes company occurred in 1969. During the same period, the increased power and significance of shop steward organisation at Bournville was acknowledged, leading to the unionisation of the works council (or factory council) system in 1968.

These changes had an ironic effect. The employees had become thoroughly entrenched in a participation-cum-bargaining structure drawing upon the authority of Cadbury tradition reaching back to World War I at the same time as management were beginning to regard many aspects of that tradition as unnecessary costs diverting them from efficient profit-seeking. The company culture was becoming the "property" of the employees. The phase which Burawoy wants to label as "hegemonic" witnessed a gradual *erosion* of the legitimacy of management from the point of view of the workers, "guardians" of the company tradition. By the latter part of the 1970s union representatives had a great deal of day-to-day influence on the running of the factory. One line supervisor who took early retirement in 1978 recalls that at the end of his time at Bournville he was being informed by the shop steward when Saturday working was to be carried out and which men would be having the overtime. His own sphere of managerial initiative was very restricted in these circumstances.

Subsequently, the inherited participation structure and the conservatism of the labour force were largely overriden by a mixture of direct confrontation (leading to strikes in 1977 and 1979) and very generous financial compensation for workers made redundant or put onto new shift patterns. The right of management to demand loyalty above and beyond the labour purchased through the wage packet has been further eroded by acts such as the sale of much of the land previously used for sporting facilities. Reliance on temporary workers has increased, somewhat reducing dependence on disgruntled long-serving employees. During the 1980s a beginning has been made on the task of creating a new framework of expectations which stresses that the company can offer employees only very limited security and that the future well-being of all depends upon committed efforts by every worker. Some may have to be made redundant in the future but it is impossible to say who will be lost and who saved. There is a touch of Calvinism here. To recall the previous analogy, the Cadbury "priesthood" is now preaching the need for a puritan reformation.

The other case has a closer resemblance to the Burawoy model. At the Austin factory, the improved bargaining position achieved by labour during World War II crystallised in innovations such as the guaranteed working week and a piece work system based upon a negotiated price for each job. As in Bournville, the inter-war strategy of insulating the company was undermined: in the case of the Austin factory it was no longer so easy to trasmit the costs of uncertain or cyclical market demand onto the workforce. The influence of shop stewards increased markedly. They were able to insist on "mutuality" arrangements giving them bagaining rights over piece-work rates. Even after measured day work was introduced in the early 1970s the "effort bargain" had to be negotiated at shopfloor level. Management was, indeed, forced to shift from despotic discipline to persuasion and concession as a means of ensuring the continuing flow of production.

The culmination of this "hegemonic" strategy was the installation in 1975 of a "participation scheme", a complex committee structure with widespread union involvement alongside management. In effect, an attempt was made to reshape the "feudal army" into a kind of constitutional monarchy. The rewards for management included a positive commitment by senior shop stewards at Longbridge to the forthcoming Metro project with its implications of reduced manning levels and changed work practices. Michael Edwardes subsequently swept the participation scheme aside and arranged the sacking of the leading union convenor at Longbridge. However, his new despotism benefited from the commitments given by the shopfloor leadership to management in the preceding "hegemonic" period.

Recent managerial strategies at both Bournville and Longbridge have entailed an increasing emphasis upon engendering a sublte mixture of initiative and compliance within self-monitoring work teams able to exercise responsible autonomy within limited operational spheres. In other words, they have been trying to persuade individuals and groups to want to get things right and look good in the eyes of management. This has involved a mixture of technical training, education in the new rules of conduct associated with flexible working, and regular "psyching up" by enthusiastic line supervisors. There has also occurred, as a complementary exercise, a steady war of attrition against established union structures, gradually forcing influential stewards to compromise with the way the company wants things to be.

Both firms are building up their training programmes for new recruits and strengthening their contacts with local schools. In other words, an increasing investment is being made in the reproduction of labour power. The results of this investment will be embodied in the local labour force who will transmit the new expectations to their relatives and friends. Such an investment is heavily localised, being vested in the labour market in and around South West Birmingham. These factors must be weighed in the balance against the supposedly high mobility of capital within larger corporations. If Cadbury Schweppes or Austin Rover move away from the area much of the money now being spent will have been wasted.

5. Conclusions

Finally, four sets of conclusions. First, as the comparison between Birmingham and Sheffield was intended to show, Burawoy does not convincingly establish the point that factory regimes play the decisive part of shaping working-class participation in social and political struggle. It is necessary to locate the workplace within various sociopolitical contexts to which it is related in complex ways.

Second, certain aspects of Burawoy's argument about the implications of changes relating to state involvement in the reproduction of labour power are more plausible, especially when considering factory regimes characterised by "market despotism" such as the Austin factory in Longbridge. The case is far less convincing when considered with respect to the "paternalistic" regime at the Cadbury factory at Bournville. This may cast doubts on the adequacy of the theory in view of Burawoy's assumption that "market despotic" regimes have been "rare" (1985: 88). One potentially relevant line of inquiry, which has been neglected here (as by Burawoy), is the significance of gender within the internal labour market.

Third, examination of the South West Birmingham case suggests that it is useful to consider the interplay of factory regimes of different kinds within specific local labour markets with distinctive social and cultural characteristics. What happens in specific factories is likely to feed into and be affected by this larger context.[6] In the case of South West Birmingham, the locality has over the past century served as an expanding arena within which blue-collar workers and their families could pursue improvement. Within the area various collectivist (or community-based) and individualist strategies have both been available with respect to job and home: council house or private residence? union solidarity or individualist careerism? an employer who (in some matters, at least) said "what can I do for you?" or one who only said "what can you do for me?"; an employer who knew your first name or one who did not know you at all?; a close linkage between work and leisure (as was possible at Bournville) or the option of escaping into anonymity as soon as the factory gates were left behind? The element of choice within workers' lives may have been relatively small but it was valued. Immigrants to the locality had made an active decision to go there. Casual workers could decide which car factory to try their luck at each day (Austin? Singer? Wolsely?). Without romanticism, it is possible to acknowledge the opportunities that have existed in the area to cultivate a sense of the active self.

One example. Tradesmen who served their apprenticeship at Cadburys might elect to try and stay on at that firm or they might take their skills elsewhere in the area. The Austin maintenance tradesman mentioned earlier had served his time at Cadburys. He decided he "wanted to make it on his own" and got taken on at "the Austin." When he became a senior foreman, half a dozen of the men under his direction had previously worked at Cadburys.

Finally, throughout the period being discussed the factory regime was complemented in the experience of workers in South West Birmingham by the domestic regime, the household arena, and the networks of kin and friends to which it gave entry. For the casual worker and the skilled craft worker, used to moving between factories, the nodal point of his or her social networks was as likely to be the family as the work place. To speculate further, perhaps the factory regime had particular impact upon the semi-skilled machine operatives in the chocolate factory since they – more than most local workers – became highly adapted to a specific technology which was not duplicated in other firms in the area.

For most South West Birmingham workers, however, the job not only located you within a cultural and political system in the factory with its on-going battles (or "games") in which you readily participated but it also provided a ticket of entry to another sphere. This was the realm of the emancipated householder. As such, you expected to enjoy the material fruits of capitalism and the sense of controlling your own life as promised to all English citizens in the political charter proclaimed by Chamberlainite Liberalism and subsequently enacted by the high-spending Labour councils of Birmingham in the 1950s and 1960s. The early

[6] Since 1974 Austin Rover (previously BL and British Leyland) has been largely state-owned. In the last few years the Conservative government has made it clear that as much of the company should be privatised as soon as possible. This government has suffered no obvious electoral penalties in Northfield constituency (which contains the Longbridge plant) for its policies towards the firm.

middle-aged Brummie car worker who bought his council house in the 1970s or early 1980s was, in this sense, "coming into his inheritance". In the end, changes within the factory regime were less significant than the fact that he continued (or, in some cases, did not continue) to have a job. The worker who loses his or her job is in great danger of losing the ticket for entry to the world of the independent householder. Such people go right to the bottom of the ladder where risk and uncertainty are maximised.

References

Bournville Village Trust, *Bournville Village Trust 1900–1955*. Bournville. 1955

Burawoy, M., *The Politics of Production: Factory Regimes under Capitalism and Socialism*. London: Verso. 1985

Cadbury Bros., *Industrial Record*. Bournville. 1947

Cadbury Bros., *Industrial Challenge*. Bournville. 1964

Church, R., *Herbert Austin. The British Motor Car Industry of 1941*. London: Europa. 1979

Dellheim, C., The Creation of a Company Culture: Cadburys, 1861–1931, *American Historical Review* 92, 1: 13–44. 1976

Engelbach, C. R. F., Some Notes on Reorganising a Works to Increase Production, *Proceedings of the Institute of Automobile Engineers* 23: 64–74. 1927–8

Gardiner, A. G., *The Life of George Cadbury*. London: Cassell. 1923

Hay, R., Employers and Social Policy in Britain: The Evolution of Welfare Legislation, 1905–1914, *Social History* 2, 4: 435–55. 1977

Hopkins, H., *England is Rich*. London: Harrap. 1957

Leader, R. E., *Sheffield in the Eighteenth Century*. Sheffield: Chapman. 1905

Marsden, D. et al. *The Car Industry. Labour Relations and Industrial Adjustment*. London: Tavistock. 1985

Mathias, P., *The First Industrial Nation* (Second Edition). London: Methuen. 1983

Moore, B., *Social Origins of Dictatorship and Democracy*. Harmondsworth: Penguin. 1969

Pollard, S., *A History of Labour in Sheffield*. Liverpool: Liverpool University Press. 1959

Reid, D. A., The decline of Saint Monday 1766–1876, *Social History* 71: 76–101. 1976

Rogers, T. B., *A Century of Progress 1831–1931*. Bournville. 1931

Smith, C., Cadburys and the Management of Consent, WORC Working Paper No 27, Aston University. 1987

Smith, C., J. Child and M. Rowlinson (forthcoming), *Innovations in Work Organisation: The Cadbury Experience*. Cambridge: Cambridge University Press.

Smith, D., *Conflict and Compromise. Class Formation in English Society 1830–1914*. London: Routledge and Kegan Paul. 1982

Smith, D., *Barrington Moore. Violence, Morality and Political Change*. London: Macmillan. 1983

Thompson, E. P., *The Making of the English Working Class*. Harmondsworth: Penguin. 1968

Williams, I., *The Firm of Cadbury*. London: Constable. 1931

Williams K., J. Williams and C. Haslam, *The Breakdown of Austin Rover*. Leamington Spa: Berg. 1987

Willman, P. and G. Winch, *Innovation and Management Control. Labour Relations at BL Cars*. Cambridge: Cambridge University Press. 1985

Wyatt, R. J., *The Austin 1905–1952*. Newton Abbot: David and Charles. 1981

The Class/Gender/Organization Nexus*

Rosemary Crompton

1. Introduction

The study of organizations is an interdisciplinary field; the insights of sociology, social psychology, decision theory, operations research, and economics (this list does not claim to be comprehensive), have all been claimed to make a significant contribution to our understanding of "organizations." It is hardly surprising, therefore, that no single "Organization Theory" as yet exists. The picture is made even more complex by the fact that the various disciplines involved in the study of organizations have themselves been the subject of continuing internal discussion and debate.

This is particularly true of the Sociology of Organizations. Probably a majority of sociologists would reject the suggestion that a "revolution in Sociology" occurred in the 1970s (Goldthorpe 1973); but nevertheless, developments in the philosophy of science, together with a revival of interest in Marxist theory, had a significant impact within the discipline which was and is reflected in its contribution to organization theory (Reed 1985). One consequence of this wider debate within sociology, therefore, is that the study of organizations from a sociological perspective is multi-paradigmatic in both theory and practice – although the "single theory" approach does still have its defenders (Donaldson 1985).

Although a profusion of theories might initially appear as somewhat confusing, there have been a number of recent suggestions as to how the diversity of available perspectives might be classified. (For a useful summary, see Scott 1986.) Such exercises in classification are to be welcomed, not least because they suggest ways in which diversity can be ordered without the loss of insights generated by individual theoretical approaches. Indeed, it may be argued that the sociology of organizations is somewhat in advance of sociology more generally in its recognition that: "[...] sociology, in order to be scientific in its comprehension of a complex subject matter, necessarily must be multi-paradigmatic" (Himmelstrand 1986). The complexity of the subject matter of the sociology of organizations – indeed, of any social phenomena – is also emphasized in what Giddens has described as "structuration theory." This explicitly recognizes the fact that social structures – including organizations – have a *dual* reality. That is, they are simultaneously being created (by people), and at the same time have the capacity to shape and constrain the actions of those who create them.

The question of social class was first systematically addressed within organization sociology in the nineteen-seventies.[1] This "radical critique" of organization theory was much influenced by both structural Marxism and the debate on the labour process initiated by Braverman in 1974 (Clegg and Dunkerley 1977, 1980; Salaman 1981). It argued that the distribution of power and control within work organizations, the structuring of organizational places, and the behaviour of employers, management and the workforce, are all a consequence of the location of the organization in a class society – of which the organization is a microcosm. Thus concepts and definitions developed within Marxist class theory, such as exploitation, alienation, bourgeoisie, proletariat, and so on may, it is argued, be (relatively) straightforwardly brought to bear upon the analysis of organizations. It may be suggested that, although this approach has generated many useful insights into the workings of work organizations in capitalist societies, it does not sufficiently take into account the dual reality of organizations, and thus their structure, which was stressed above. It is true that the debate since Braverman has been replete with arguments to the effect that worker resistance has had a significant impact in shaping the structure of work organizations; that management have a number of strategies available via which control may be exercised, and so on (Friedman 1976, Thompson 1983). However, it would have to be conceded that the radical neo-Marxist approach to the study of organizations nevertheless takes as given the major factors structuring work organizations – that is, the demands of capitalist accumulation in a capitalist society.

There have been a number of criticisms levelled against the basic assumptions of this "critical organization theory" (see Donaldson 1985). However, the major argument of this paper is that work organizations are significantly structured by gender, as well as class variables. The fact that the significance of gender has been relatively neglected is a criticism, of course, that could equally be levelled at a whole range of theories which have purported to describe organizational structuring. However, as in the social sciences more generally, the intellecutal impact of "neo-" or second-wave feminism has begun to be felt and has been reflected in a number of commentaries and monographs. Recent work in the area of gender and organization theory, it may be suggested, has been developed within what Burrell and Morgan (1979) have labelled the "radical humanist" paradigm; that is, tending towards the interpretative, qualitative tradition in sociology. Much of the emphasis of this work has been on the regulation of sexuality within organizations (e.g. Hearn and Parkin 1987) – which is hardly surprising given its importance in mixed-sex establishments – although research such as Collinson and Knights (1986) has also demonstrated how gender power may be used to control access to organizational places. (In the example they investigated, a woman was "persuaded" of her unsuitability for a high level job within an insurance office.)

---

[1] As with most generalizations, this sentence over-simplifies. Long before Braverman, there existed a tradition which was critical of many of the assumptions of "industrial sociology." Such commentaries clearly recognized an opposition of interest between management and the workforce.

In this paper, the effect of gender upon the restructuring of organizational places will be explored within a single industry – the Building Society movement. Although there are considerable variations within the industry as to the type of depositor (i.e. customer) sought and business transacted, there are, nevertheless, significant continuities in the ways in which the industry has used female labour (see Ashburner 1987). It will be argued that this restructuring can only be adequately comprehended by taking into account the dual reality of Building Societies as organizations – that is as constraints on (men's) actions at the same time as they are deliberately being transformed and restructured. Before the examination of the empirical material, however, the theoretical issues raised by the question of gender will be examined in more depth.

2. Theorizing Gender

A major impact of contemporary feminist thinking on social science has been to establish that gender relations are not somehow "natural" (and therefore not requiring explanation) but are *socially constructed*. Once this has been recognized, however, the question is immediately raised as to how this construction takes place. An initially persuasive account is given by sex-role theory (Mead 1962, Oakley 1972), where "male" and "female" roles are, as it were, cultural "scripts" learned by individual men and women in particular societies. The problem with this approach, as with role theory more generally, is that it is not so much incorrect as circular. As Connell (1985) has argued, role theory does not ignore change; "the problem is rather that role theory cannot grasp social change as history, that is, as transformation generated in the interplay of social practice and social structure. Change is always something that *happens* to sex roles, that impinges on them" (p. 263).

The argument shifts, therefore, towards theories which seek to explain the determination of the social, and thus, gender relations and roles. Marxist-derived theories, in particular, have argued that, to a greater or lesser extent, gender relations are shaped by the prevailing structure of economic (or class) relationships, reflecting the dominant "mode of production". (Indeed, the overall strategy of such attempts to theorize gender may be paralleled with some instances of critical organization theory.) However, feminists have been swift to argue that the oppression of women pre-dates capitalism, and indeed, throughout recorded history, men have apparently dominated women. Thus Hartmann (1981) in an oft-quoted passage, has argued that "The marriage between Marxism and feminism resembles that between husband and wife in English common law: the two are one, and that one is Marxism."

Theories of patriarchy, in contrast, argue that women are oppressed by men.

Walby (1986) has defined "patriarchy" as "a system of inter-related social structures through which men exploit women" (p. 51). It is difficult to construct a theory of patriarchy, however, without slipping into what Connell (1985) has described as "categoricalism" – that is, the assertion that "men" (as a category) oppress "women" (as a category). Besides being a profoundly negative perspective, categoricalism, it may be suggested, is also the antithesis of social science thinking – unless the boundaries of the subject matter are shifted to include biological engineering.

A way out of this apparent impasse is offered by "dual systems" theories, where "capitalism" and "patriarchy" are seen as two systems simultaneously structuring social reality. "Capitalist development creates the places for a hierarchy of workers, but traditional Marxist categories cannot tell us who will fill which places. Gender and racial hierarchies determine who fills the empty places" (Hartmann 1981). This approach would be complementary with that of critical organization theory. Organizations, on this reading, would be the product not only of capitalistic, but also patriarchal, structures. Whilst there is much to commend this as a general approach, a weakness of "two systems" theory is that it implicitly assumes that "patriarchy" *is* a "system" which can be described in the same way as capitalism – i.e. it assumes, rather than demonstrates, the prior existence of a theory of patriarchy.

However, it has been argued that no satisfactory theory of patriarchy has yet been developed (Beechey 1979). In the strict sense, "patriarchy" implies the rule of the father, but is more often used to describe the domination of women by men. We may observe empirically that gender relations are commonly, but not universally, patriarchal. To describe this empirical reality, however, is not to have developed a theory of patriarchy (or gender relations), just as to observe that organizations are found within a wide variety of types of society and historical periods is not to have developed a theory of organizations.

Nevertheless, the very fact that patriarchal structures *are* virtually ubiquitous has convinced many that a theory of patriarchy is awaiting discovery even if it has not yet been found. Such an enterprise, it may be suggested, underpins recent attempts to develop a "realist" theory of patriarchy. Again, parallels may be drawn with developments in organization theory. As Reed (1985) has argued, much critical organization theory is informed by a realist philosophy of science. The realist approach has been described as follows:

For the realist, adequate causal explanations require the discovery both of regular relations between phenomena, and of some kind of mechanism that links them. So, in explaining any particular phenomenon, we must not only make reference to those events which initiate the process of change: we must also give a description of that process itself. To do this, we need knowledge of the underlying mechanisms and structures that are present, and of the manner in which they generate or produce the phenomenon we are trying to explain (Keat and Urry 1975, quoted in Reed 1985: 75).

Following these prescriptions, critical organization theory claims to have discovered in the neo-Marxist analysis of the capitalist labour process and the contradictions within capitalist society, the "underlying mechanisms" which structure organizations in capitalist society.

Realist accounts of a theory of patriarchy, however, have not, as yet, been particularly successful. A too-literal interpretation of the injunction to acquire knowledge of the "underlying mechanisms" may all too easily slip into an (elaborated) biological determinism (e.g. Foord and Gregson 1986). Walby (1986) has recently claimed to have theoretically demonstrated the presence of a "system" of patriarchy in a major *tour de force* which charts patriarchal processes (i.e. male exclusionary practices) in three industries in Britain (engineering, textiles and clerical work) from 1800 to after the Second World War. She has certainly massively documented "regular relations between phenomena" – whether or not the "underlying mechanisms" which would reveal a "system" of patriarchy have also been demonstrated is a moot point.

One of the problems besetting attempts to uncover a theory of gender relations is that, in addition to their expression in formal institutions and practices – e.g. in laws relating to marriage and divorce, workplace practices, the structuring of state benefits and so on – gender relations are simultaneously the continuous product of *lived experience*. The categories "bourgeois" and "proletariat" do not depend for their existence upon the *personal* interaction of individuals (see Abercrombie and Urry 1983). For men and women, however, interpersonal experience is inescapable. This renders gender relations dynamic and potentially fluid, and thus attempts to develop a single theory of gender or patriarchy become even more problematic. Gender relations can and do change. During this century, women in Britain have achieved the vote and, more recently, legislation outlawing overt discrimination in the "public" sphere of employment. It is not being suggested that equality has therefore been unproblematically achieved. It has not, and it *is* important to continue to document instances of male exclusion. However, it is equally important to theoretically examine that changes that *have* occurred.

The parallels which have been drawn between theorizing organizations and attempts to theorize gender may be extended to the strategies which have guided empirical research. In practice, it may be suggested, organization theory and research has involved the creation of an archive of theoretically informed *case studies*. (Even survey research such as the work of the Aston group may be viewed as an agglomeration of individual "cases.") It can be argued that it is also through the case study that gender *can* be simultaneously grasped as "lived experience" which is nevertheless occurring within a social *context*. It is through the case study that we can come closest to the interweaving of personal lives and social structure, the links between history and biography (Mills 1959). Case study research, it may be argued, is essential in order to grasp the notion of the dual nature of the structure, of structure as process, that is, "structuration" (Giddens 1981). It is via the case study method that one may go beyond the documentation of instances of male exclusion, and make moves towards the explanation of these instances. Such studies may not immediately reveal the inner practices of gender relations (and thus a "theory" of gender), but at the very least, our understanding of the structuring of gender will be enhanced.

3. Building Societies

In England and Wales, Building Societies are major financial institutions; £102 billion of assets were distributed between 190 societies at the end of 1984. However, their contribution to employment within the financial sector is relatively modest despite very rapid expansion during the 1970s. In 1981, the number of people employed by Building Societies was approximately 56,000 as compared to 293,000 in Insurance and 367,000 in Banking. The Building Society movement is also a female dominated industry; women are approximately 70% of all employees.

Building Societies borrow from investors (savers) and advance money for house purchase. (Investors and borrowers are often the same individuals). Historically, there has been no shortage of borrowers. Investors are recruited in part through a network of agents – estate agents, solicitors, etc. – who are paid a retainer and/or a small commission on investment brought to the Societies; smaller investors are also recruited through advertising compaigns, as passing trade, etc. Agents liaise with Building Society managers (who may be described as Area Managers, Regional Managers or Branch Managers) who are expected to possess a suitable level of financial expertise and professional standing. Managers are not paid commission. Investors – particularly small investors – are also serviced by a network of branches. The branch network expanded massively during the 1960s and 1970s. In 1962, there were 1070 building society branches, 2522 by 1972 and 5147 by 1979 (Davies 1981: 58). On a day-to-day basis much branch activity resembles that of savings banks. New technology, particularly the introduction of counter terminals, has been extremely important in facilitating the extension of "banking" services. The branches are staffed largely by women, who will often have a woman supervisor (who may be known as "Assistant Branch Manager," "Chief Clerk" or even, in the case of "satellite" branches, "Branch Manager"). Branches vary considerably both in size and the existent of functions carried out at the branch. The smallest and simplest are "satellite" or "feeder" branches, where a two or three woman team runs the computer terminal, linked to the decision-making centre. The decision-making centre could itself be a "branch office" or "processing centre" and would be under the direction of a "Branch Manager" or "Area Manager" or "District Manager" whose job it is to liaise with agents, authorize mortgage loans, etc.

A number of different factors combine to make the Building Society industry a particularly interesting case study.[2] The particular timing and nature of building society expansion supplies insights into both the emergence of newly sex-typed occupations (cashier-clerks in the branch offices) as well as the partial breakdown of established, gender-based exclusion practices (management trainees). Relevant factors include, first, the very rapid expansion of the financial sector, and the building society industry in particular from the 1960s; second, the expansion of women's labour market participation during the same period; third, the growth and patterning of educational and professional qualifications amongst women and, fourth, the impact of neo-feminism and equal opportunities legislation.

Table 1 indicates the pattern of growth in Building Society employment (the number of branches doubled during the 1960s, then doubled again during the 1970s). It can be seen that (a) growth in employment has been extremely rapid (during a similar period, employment in Insurance increased by 9% and in Banking by 35%), and (b) employment growth has been concentrated in the branches. The largest single category of employment increase, therefore, has been amongst cashier-clerks in the branch offices.

Table 1. Building Society Employment (Numbers)

	Chief Office			Branches			Total
	FT	PT	Total	FT	PT	Total	
1970	10.711	708	11.419	13.405	342	13.747	25.166
1980	14.237	1.129	15.366	32.181	5.180	37.361	52.727
% increase	33	59	35	140	1.515	272	110

Source: adapted from Davies (1981).

4. Cashier-Clerks

Building Society cashiering is a female occupation. In the Cloister Building Society, for example, 96% of field staff on clerical grades were women. As such, it might be cited as an example of a gender shift, as the job was once predominantly carried out by men (Craig et al. 1985). Further investigation, however, reveals that the process (i.e. male clerk-cashiers → female clerk-cashiers) has not been straightforward and, rather than women taking over what was once a man's job, the nature of the *job* has been transformed – and "feminized".

---

[2] In addition to secondary sources and data provided by the Building Societies Association, the empirical research for this paper also included interviews and firm-specific material gathered from two large and one medium-sized Building Society. We have used the pseudonyms "Cloister"; "Holyoake Permanent" and "Regional Plus" to refer to these societies.

As Table 1 illustrates, expansion in Building Society employment was largely a consequence of Branching which itself resulted from competition for investors. At the same time as Building Societies were expanding their branch network, the major clearing banks were undergoing a period of rationalization and branch closure. It has been suggested that the Building Societies are, in a sense, simply repeating a "natural history" in the growth and development of financial institutions which was largely accomplished by banks in the 19th century (Davies 1981: 71). However, this comparison is inappropriate. The expansion of branch banking occurred before computerization. Thus each bank branch represented a "microcosm" of banking, with a full range of staff including bank managers empowered to negotiate loans and investments (Crompton & Jones 1984). The structure of branch banking, therefore, was expensive to create and maintain in respect of both staff and facilities.

In contrast, the expansion of the Building Society branch network occurred at a time when computing technology was available. During the 1970s, efficient terminals linked to a mainframe at regional and/or head office were developed, and the further development of mini- and microcomputers means that advice on financial matters such as underwriting and mortgage quotes can be given by an efficient machine operator. These technical innovations have made possible the development of what are variously called "satellite," "feeder" or "retail" branches and much branching activity has been of this kind. As noted earlier, satellite branches are effectively shop-fronts, often run by an all-female staff, and controlled from the processing centre or regional office. It is difficult to gather accurate data on the extent to which the creation of the Building Society branch network has depended upon satellite branches. Figures on the number of staff per branch, however, suggest that well over half the branch network is composed of satellite branches, and amongst the smaller societies branching may have been entirely achieved via the creation of satellites (Boleat 1982: 10).

If the expansion of the Building Society branch network could not have been achieved without the introduction of successive generations of computer technology, neither would it have been possible without the thousands of women who were recruited to run the branches. In respect of feminization, Craig et al. (1985) have argued;

Probably the major explanation of the feminisation of this occupation (cashiering) lies in the expansion of education which provided a supply of sufficiently well-educated women at the same time as opportunities for upward mobility made male labour scarce at the established level of wage rates (1985: 80).

Whilst this explanation is not incorrect (girls' school-leaving qualifications were improving rapidly during this period, [Crompton and Sanderson 1987]), it is incomplete and therefore rather misleading. In particular, it obscures the point that the women recruited to the building society branch network were not recruited to the *same* jobs as earlier generations of male cashier-clerks. Both the rate of branch expansion, and the technical change which facilitated it, meant that the job of a building society cashier-clerk from the 1960s through the 1970s and 1980s would have been very different from in the 1940s and 1950s. In short, it is being argued that it would be more accurate to regard cashiering in the branches as being *created* as "women's work," rather than a situation where females were directly replacing male clerks. As a recent commentary has noted: "Counter work is traditionally seen as a woman's job, which is why so few men apply for clerical work" (Industrial Relations Review and Report 1985: 11).

In the three societies from which we gathered information, over 90% of cashiers were women, and the wages paid to female cashiers would not be sufficient to support a household – they are "component wage" jobs (Siltanen 1986). It may be suggested, however, that building society cashiering has been culturally, as well as economically, gendered. Reference has already been made to the expansion of personal savings which was both cause and effect of the expansion of the branch network. This expansion was largely in respect of working class accounts – the underbanked who were the targets of Branch expansion. Market research evidence suggests that working class customers do not like entering the major clearing banks (Gough 1982). On the other hand, working class customers might find themselves attracted by a small, cosy branch office staffed by a group of competent, cheerful, welcoming women. This is certainly the image of the branch office presented in the media such as television advertising, and our observations of branch activities would confirm that for many customers the transaction has important social, as well as financial, implications.

The period during which the branch network was expanded (the 1960s and 1970s) was one of growth and prosperity within the industry. As mutual institutions, Building Societies were not vulnerable to threats of takeover or shareholder pressures, and throughout this period mortgage interest rates were fixed by a cartel operated by the largest societies.[3] The expansion of the branch network has been explained as a "natural" expression of the competition for customers' accounts (Davies 1981); but it has also been described as an expression of managerial *"folie de grandeur"* (Barnes 1984). Whatever the "true" explanation might be, it would be generally agreed that the 1960s and 1970s was a period during which there was little in the way of economic pressure on building society management. In respect of organizational expansion and restructuring, therefore, the (male) building society management probably had a remarkably free hand. (The fact that one major society has grown at a rate similar to that of comparable

---

[3] The cartel was finally abolished in the early 1980s. The Building Societies Act, which came into operation in 1987, has been introduced with the aim of increasing competition between financial institutions – it allows, for example, for the creation of public companies. However, during the period under discussion, competition between the Societies took the form of competition for investors, and Building Societies were protected from competition with other financial institutions.

institutions without possessing a single branch may be cited as evidence in support of this argument.) Mass cashiering in the branch network, it is being suggested, was actually created as a "female" job in actuality, if not with absolute deliberation. Women so recruited would not normally expect to be promoted to managerial levels.

Indeed, in all three of the Societies we investigated, the most usual career route was via direct entry as a Management Trainee. There are exceptions – men and women can in theory progress from the clerical ranks to management but it would be relatively unusual for the move from clerk to full manager of a non-satellite branch to be achieved. There are, in any case, only a tiny minority of male clerks. The small societies will not usually have a management training programme, and will recruit non-satellite branch management and above from the larger societies who "home-grow" their trainees. In all of the three societies we investigated, management trainees were required to register for the Building Societies' professional qualification (or similar), but no strong sanctions appeared to accompany a failure to complete the course.

Building society cashiering, therefore, is a "woman's job" with little in the way of promotion prospects. As female resentment of enhanced male promotion prospects is less likely to be expressed in the absence of direct competition with men (Crompton and Jones 1984), this restructuring of employment along gender lines was achieved with little or no resistance. However, considerable evidence of gender conflict did occur at the point where women *were* in direct competition with men – the recruitment of management trainees.

5. Management Trainees

Building Society management, especially above the level of Office Manager, is generally an all-male occupation. Particularly amongst branches (and societies) which specialize in the larger accounts (i.e. customers), it is doubtless felt that the most appropriate person to deal with the bank managers, solicitors, accounts etc. should be male. However, masculinity is not in itself a sufficient qualification: the individual has also to be socially acceptable and of similar status to the professionals with whom he has to interact in the course of his work. Thus a competitive, standardised, and rational selection procedure has been established. The industry also sponsors professional examinations (the Chartered Building Societies Institute). The very rationality of these selection procedures, however, has proved to be problematic as far as male exclusion practices are concerned.

In April 1977 (a year after Equal Opportunities legislation in Britain), a woman who had been interviewed for a post as a Management Trainee with the Leeds Permanent Building Society complained that she had been discriminated against on the grounds of her sex during the course of the interview. The case was taken up by the Equal Opportunities Commission, who undertook a thorough going investigation of the process of recruitment in the Leeds in 1978. They found that, of the 412 women and 1382 men who applied for management traineeships, 58% of the men, but only 39% of the women were called for interview. Thirty percent of the men interviewed were offered a second interview, as compared to 4% of the women. No women were offered jobs as management trainees as compared to 145 of the men.

The evidence gathered by the EOC provides a rich and fascinating account of the processes of male exclusion. Let this be thought of as an isolated example, Table 2 gives details of the recruitment of management trainees by the Cloister Building Society – who seem to have been more aware of the potentialities of Equal Opportunities legislation than the Leeds Permanent.

Table 2. Cloister Buildung Society: Recruitment of Management Trainees by Gender

| | Men | | Women | | Total | |
	Nos	%	Nos	%	Nos	%
1960–69[1]	158	93	12	7	170	100
1970–74[2]	199	98	5	2	204	100
1975–79	169	67	84	33	253	100
1980–85[3]	30	35	57	65	87	100

[1] Data for 1961, 1962, 1963 not available
[2] Data for 1972 not available
[3] Between 1980–82 the Cloister virtually ceased recruitment of management trainees.

In 1974, 42 management trainees were recruited by the Cloister Building Society, of whom none were women. In 1975 (the year of Equal Opportunities Legislation) 39 management trainees were recruited, of whom ten were female.

Occupational segregation – that is, concentration of men and women into "men's" and "women's" jobs – is an important mechanism maintaining stability and continuity in gender relations. The most stable arrangements occur when segregation is maintained by recruitment – as in the Building Society industry, where counter work is "traditionally seen as a woman's job" and "so few men apply for it" (IRRR 1985). However, as the EOC report reveals, the gender/grade structure described in Table 3 was not simply a consequence of a process of self-selection and direction, but was also actively created via a process of male managerial exclusion.

In 1978, as we have been, nearly 1,800 people applied for 145 jobs. Direct discrimination on the basis of sex was illegal, universalistic criteria had to be employed in order to sift applicants. In the case of the Leeds, three criteria were laid down in the job advertisements: (1) age (precise specifications varied between the 20–30 age range); (2) educational requirements (a minimum of 4 "0" levels including Maths and English), and (3) a sound financial or commercial

Table 3. Number of staff employed by the Leeds Permanent Building Society in 1977

	Male Nos	%	Female Nos	%	Total Nos	%
Management & managers	281	27	1	–	282	14
Assistant managers & supervisors	50	5	17	2	67	3
Area representatives	39	4	0	0	39	2
Management trainees	80	8	0	0	80	4
Chief clerks	282	27	1	–	283	14
Clerical, typing general duties	314	30	897	98	1211	62
Total	1046	100	916	100	1962	100

Source: Adapted from Table 0.1 EOC Report 1985:3.

background. In respect of these characteristics there were no differences between the men and women who applied. However, women who possessed all three of the characteristics specified stood less chance of being offered an interview than men who had none of them. In the words of the Commission:

[...] since the singular lack of success of female candidates in gaining interviews and jobs could not be explained by any lack of the relevant criteria sought by the Society its Managers directly discriminated against women applicants because of their sex (EOC 1985: 26).

It is clear, therefore, that the process of male exclusion has historically shaped the gender/occupation structure within the Leeds Permanent and, it is probably reasonable to assume, within the Building Society movement as a whole. (It should be noted that following the EOC investigation, the Leeds has made a number of changes to its prescriptions for employment and instructions to Managers regarding interviewing practice.) However, of as much interest as the exclusion processes themselves is the way in which they had to be achieved using overtly rational criteria. It has been argued elsewhere that both particular occupations, and the qualifications they require, may be more or less firmly sextyped. A "male" or "gender neutral" occupation or qualification will usually receive enhanced status (and material rewards) as compared to a "female" occupation (Crompton 1987). The official criteria for selection were all gender neutral but the arguments employed by the Leeds Managers show ample evidence of difficulty in maintaining even a facade of rationality.

For example; "Shirley I" (EOC 1985: 89–90) was one of the seven female applicants who was recommended for a second interview. Nearly 23 and single, she had 8 "O" levels, 3 "A" levels, five years work experience with a major clearing bank and was an Associate of the Institute of Bankers. At her first interview, she was described as "very presentable" in appearance, "well spoken," "relaxed," and "confident." At her second interview, she was described as only "fair" in appearance, "nervous" and "lacking in confidence" – in short, it was necessary to re-define her personal qualities to provide a rational basis for exclusion. Some managers found this particular kind of rationality more difficult to achieve than others, as with the Branch Manager who reported that:

Miss N. is perfectly prepared to meet our mobility requirement and has no reservations in meeting professional people. As I *cannot* fault her academically, I feel I *should* put her forward to the Regional Manager for interview (EOC 1985: 326, my emphasis).

In short, when truly universalistic criteria are applied to men and women, "traditional" differences between the sexes are undermined. Thus the more the organization relies upon rational criteria to allocate individuals to positions within it, the more susceptible is the structure to the liberal feminist strategy of the "qualifications lever."

6. Concluding Remarks

In respect of debates concerning the location of women within the structure of organizations, this brief account of the Building Society industry has, hopefully, generated a number of insights. The "structuration" of gender within a single industry over the last twenty years or so has lent partial confirmation to some hypotheses, and thrown some doubt an others. It has been earlier suggested that it is rather misleading to view the "feminization" of the occupation of cashier-clerk as a *process,* in which women were directly substituted for men. Rather, the occupation was *restructured* as a consequence of a particular mode of competition (branching) combined with extremely rapid technological innovation. Women were recruited into what was effectively a new occupation. Murgatroyd (1985) has suggested that occupations become defined as female if they "were expanding at a time when the skills needed to do them were commonly held or easily learned, and when there was either a particularly high demand for labour or an especially large pool of women seeking work." As we have seen, all of these factors were relevant during the 1960s and 1970s, and a period of rapid business expansion accompanied by technological change has resulted in the creation of numerous routine, female clerical jobs – cashier-clerks in the branch offices[4]. These jobs have also been culturally stereotyped as feminine, and are represented as such in the media and in "common-sense" discussions of employment within the industry. It might be expected, therefore, that the general im-

---

[4] An interesting coda to the development of this "female" job can be found in recent developments in the arena of building society qualifications. A new "practitioner" qualification – the Certificate in Building Society Practice – has been introduced by the Chartered Building Society Institute. Those gaining the qualification are over 90% female, and it is widely regarded within the industry as a useful qualification for a woman who wishes to achieve "chief clerk" status (although she would probably be called an "assistant manager").

pact of this development will be to reinforce existing structures of gender relations.

However, although the emergence of a "woman's" occupation might be a source of stability in gender relations, considerable strain was evident at other points in the structure. Institutionally rational procedures have been developed to screen out unsuitable candidates in the recruitment of management trainees. (As in all selection processes, these rational procedures will be supplemented by the selectors' intuitive and/or informal awareness of "what the organization is looking for"). Up until the relatively recent past, being a woman would seem to have conferred instant unsuitability for management traineeships within the Building Society industry. (This phenomenon is not unique to the industry, the exclusion of women from internal hierarchies has been well documented (Walby 1986).) However, as we have seen, "rational" exclusion practices can be turned against themselves. Formal age, qualification and experience requirements are not sex-specific, and when women possess these qualities, the denial of access becomes problematic. In this particular case, the (created) structure itself constrained the actions of the men within it. (It is not being suggested that the question of equality of access has been unproblematically resolved. Legislation cannot fully take into account the influence of informal assumptions, and recent evidence suggests that although women are achieving promotion to "management" which involves the supervision of other women (for example, assistant branch manager), they are not yet established in "financial" management – i.e. area or non-satellite branch management (see IRRR 1985)).

The dual nature of the structure is thus well-illustrated, at the organizational level, by this example of managerial exclusion. However, in my final comments I will move (briefly) from the level of organization and industry towards the wider debate concerning the occupational structure of white-collar organizations, the location of women within them, and developments in the wider society.

In previous empirical work (Crompton and Jones 1984), it has been argued that the impact of deskilling and work fragmentation in white-collar bureaucracies has been "buffered" by both the recruitment of women and the persistence of internal labour market opportunities for men. That is, that although the clerical labour process may have been deskilled in a technical sense – tasks have become more routine, been mechanized etc. – the extent of the direct impact on the male labour force has been reduced. Indeed, the history of the development of clerical work in this century could be read as one in which the careers of male clerks have been "saved" by female labour. This generalization might at first appear paradoxical, as male clerks – like male workers more generally – have always been alive to the dangers of their substitution by cheap female labour (Walby 1986). However, in Britain the historical record reveals that a large number of female clerks were initially recruited into women-only grades, and the widespread requirement that women should resign on marriage effectively removed them from competition with men (Cohn 1986; Grint 1988). Although the poverty of the genteel (unmarried) female clerk was commented upon and generally deplored in the nineteenth and first part of the twentieth century, few active steps were taken to remedy the situation – which would have involved paying them at "male" rates and/or allowing access to "male" jobs.

The development, over the last twenty years, of the *de facto* feminized occupation of cashier-clerk in the Building Society industry might appear, at first sight, to be a case of history repeating itself. In the late twentieth century, women are still being recruited to sex-typed clerical jobs, thus posing no threat to the male white-collar career. However, as we have seen, the persistence and regeneration of sex-typing has been accompanied, in this historical period, by the active resistance of women to their exclusion from senior white-collar grades within the industry. The explanation of this resistance in contrast to the relative acquiescence of previous decades, lies in the historical changes in economic and social assumptions concerning women which have taken place since the Second World War. The explanation of these changes is properly the subject of another paper. However, the evidence of their impact is an expression of the continuing structuration of gender relations not only within individual industries and organizations, but also at the interface between the organization and the wider society.

* Acknowledgements

The research referred to in this paper was carried out with the aid of grants from the EOC, ESRC and the University of East Anglia.

References

Abercrombie, N. & J. Urry, *Capital, Labour and the Middle Class*. London: Allen & Unwin. 1983

Ashburner, L., The Effects of New Technology on Employment Structures in the Service Sector. PhD presented to the University of Aston. 1987

Barnes, P., *The Myth of Mutuality*. London: Pluto. 1984

Beechey, V., On Patriarchy, *Feminist Review* 3: 66–82. 1979

Boleat, M., *The Building Society Industry*. London: George Allen & Unwin. 1982

Braverman, H., *Labor and Monopoly Capital*. New York: Monthly Review Press. 1974

Burrell, G. & G. Morgan, *Sociological Paradigms and Organizational Analysis,* London: Heinemann. 1979

Clegg, S. & D. Dunkerley (eds.), *Critical Issues in Organisations*. London: Routledge & Kegan Paul. 1977

Clegg, S. & D. Dunkerley, *Organization, Class and Control*. London: Routledge and Kegan Paul. 1980

Cohn, S., *The Process of Occupational Sex-Typing*. Philadelphia: Temple. 1986

Collinson, D. & D. Knights, "Men Only": Theories and Practices of job Segregation in Insurance, in: D. Knights and D. Collinson (eds.), *Gender and the Labour Process*. London: Macmillan. 1986

Connell, R. W., Theorising Gender, *Sociology* 19, 2: 260–272. 1985

Craig, C., E. Garnsey & J. Rubery, *Payment Structures and Smaller Firms: Women's Employment in Segmented Labour Markets*. Research paper No. 48, DoE. 1985

Crompton, R. & G. Jones, *White-Collar Proletariat: De-skilling and Gender in the Clerical Labour Process*. London: Macmillan. 1984

Crompton, R. & K. Sanderson, Where Did all the Bright Girls Go?, *Quarterly Journal of Social Affairs* 3, 2: 135–147. 1987

Crompton, R., Gender, Status and Professionalism, *Sociology* 21, 3: 413–428. 1987

Davies, G., *Building Societies and their Branches: A Regional Economic Survey*, London: Franey. 1981

Donaldson, L., *In Defence of Organization Theory*. Cambridge. Cambridge University Press. 1985

EOC, *Formal Investigation Report: Leeds Permanent Building Society*, Manchester: EOC. 1985

Friedman, A., Responsible Autonomy versus Direct Control over the Labour Process, *Capital and Class* 1, 1: 43–57. 1976

Foord, J. & N. Gregson, Patriarchy: Towards a Reconceptualisation, *Antipode* 18, 2: 186–211. 1986

Giddens, A, *A Contemporary Critique of Historical Materialism*, London & Basingstoke: Macmillan. 1981

Goldthorpe, J. H., A Revolution in Sociology? *Sociology* 7, 3: 449–462. 1973

Gough, T. J., *The Economics of Building Societies*. London & Basingstoke. Macmillan. 1982

Grint, K., Women and Equality: The Acquisition of Equal Pay in the Post Office 1870/1961, *Sociology* 22, 1: 87–108. 1988

Hartmann, H. I., The Unhappy Marriage of Marxism and Feminism: Towards a More Progressive Union, in: L. Sargent (ed.), *Women and Revolution*. Boston: South End Press. 1981

Hearn, J. & W. Parkin, *"Sex" at "Work": The Power and Paradox of Organisation Sexuality*. Brighton: Wheatsheaf. 1987

Himmelstrand, U. (ed.), *The Social Reproduction of Organization and Culture*. London: Sage. 1986

Industrial Relations Review and Report (IRRR). November 1985

Mead, M., *Male and Female*. Harmondsworth: Penguin. 1962

Milkman, R., Female Factory Labour and Industrial Structure: Control and Conflict over "Women's Place" in Auto and Electrical Manufacturing, *Politics and Society* 12, 2: 159–230. 1983

Mills, C. W., *The Sociological Imagination*. New York: Oxford University Press. 1959

Murgatroyd, L., Occupational Stratification and Gender, in: *Localities, Class and Gender*, Lancaster Regionalism Group, London: Pion. 1985

Oakley, A., *Sex, Gender and Society*. London: Temple Smith. 1972

Pugh, D. S., D. J. Hickson & C. R. Hinings, *Writers on Organisations*. (3rd edition). Harmondsworth: Penguin. 1983

Reed, M., *New Directions in Organisation Theory*. London: Tavistock. 1985

Salaman, G., *Class and the Corporation*. London: Fontana. 1981

Scott, W. R., The Sociology of Organizations, in: U. Himmelstrand (ed.), *The Social Reproduction of Organization and Culture*. London: Sage. 1986

Siltanen, J., Domestic Responsibilities and the Structuring of Employment, in: Crompton, R. & Mann, M. (eds.), *Gender and Stratification*. Cambridge: Polity. 1986

Thompson, P., *The Nature of Work*. London: Macmillan. 1983

Walby, S., *Patriarchy at Work*. Cambridge: Polity. 1986

Masculine/Feminine Organization: Class versus Gender in Swedish Unions

Alison E. Woodward and Håkon Leiulfsrud

1. Introduction

Examination of the family and the union as organizations may be one way to unravel the complicated inter-relation of gender, social class and class action. The family is usually seen as part of "the female nexus," the activities and relationships concerned with social reproduction such as household tasks and child rearing (Prokop 1976; Strandell 1983). Unions as organizations have been seen as part of the "male nexus" connected to production and politics. They are structured, like many organizations, in "male" or patriarchal hierarchies that hinder the participation of women, and thereby perhaps women's class action. However, it is not only irresponsive union frameworks which structure and constrain female participation in labour action. Female union activity is shaped by a highly integrated complex of factors including the structure of the labour market, the nature of female jobs and working conditions, and the factor of the female nexus itself, the life connection in the family. With increasing female labour force participation, an understanding of women in the organizations of class action requires an approach linking rather than dichotomizing the spheres of production and reproduction (Beechey 1987: 11) and analyzing female strategies in each.

This chapter reviews recent research on the relation between gender and union activity as background to a consideration of results from Sweden where union organizational frequency is very high. In Sweden, factors influencing female participation and action are undergoing rapid change. We find growing individuation both in terms of union membership and union engagement. This may indicate that women increasingly see labour market activity as separate from their roles as family members. On the other hand, we also see some indications that party political preferences and class awareness among married women is mediated by everyday reality outside of production, i.e. within the family. However, factors such as full-time or part-time labour and union activity may mute family orientation. To examine individuation or autonomy among women in class organization, we look at men and women in class homogeneous households and compare them to those in class heterogeneous households. Results from a qualitative study of such families provide a supplement to this picture of families as an organized entity for actors in the class structure.

2. Women and Politics

The traditional approach to women in politics and union activity has been to see
women as passive (Siltanen and Stanworth 1984b). Even after the women's
movement had shaken up other areas of academic study, it took a long time for
studies of women in unions to really get underway (Creighton 1976; Milkman
1976; Wertheimer and Nelson 1975). Both the historical record of women's protest (Boston 1987, Milkman 1985) and the study of the situation today needed to
be written. The task of this recent research has been to challenge the pre-concep-
tion of the passive working woman.

The results support two main contentions. First, women's activity should be
seen as situationally dependent. Women work in different sectors and have different work histories than men. When women are in the same situation as men,
they react similarly. This has been called the Taylor thesis (Watts 1980, after
Taylor 1978; see also Simpson and Mutran 1981[1]). It holds that when women are
exposed to industrial culture, similar attitudes appear where work settings are
comparable. However, some scholars add an important sub-codicil: because of
the gendered structure in society or patriarchy, women will never be in precisely
the same position as men (Hartman 1979).

The second main contention is that women are active, but in different ways
than men. Politics and class action have usually been defined from the male point
of view (Goot and Reid 1984; Siltanen and Stanworth 1984b: 186–189). Women
are politically active as well, but in different forums and in different ways. In the
case of unions, this has been illustrated by the outpour of research about women's union activities in the past (Boston 1987; Bradley 1986; Grieco and Whipp
1986; Pollert 1982) and about women in today's changing labour process (Crompton and Jones 1984; Crompton and Mann 1986; Feldberg and Glenn 1979, 1983;
Gottfried and Fasenfest 1984; Knights and Willmott 1986). Detailed ethno-
graphic studies have provided new insights into women's conceptions of their
unions and frustrations when attempting to carry out labour action (Cavendish
1982; Cockburn 1983; Granath and Larsson 1985; Gunnarson and Ressner 1983;
Lindgren 1985; Rosendal 1985). Much of this research has been confined to a
single industry or sector. Drawn together there are some very important conclusions to be found:

(1) The traditional conception of women as passive is probably wrong. In the
past, women's activities in unions have frequently been concealed by the way history is written and union records kept (Beale 1982; Boston 1987; Bradley 1986).

---

[1] In American political science, Kristi Andersen has posed a similar thesis (1975). While American evidence presented by McDonagh (1982) draws into question the importance of women's
employment as opposed to derived status of the husband for women's political choice, Danish
evidence shows clearly the importance of female employment in explaining political positions
(J. G. Andersen 1984, 1986).

(2) Some comparative inactivity of women may be attributed to direct repression by males. Feminist writers see an interaction between patriarchy and capitalism. In this perspective, the power hierarchy within the unions is only a mirror of this interaction. Unions are not only class organizations, structured as a defensive response to the exploitation of labour by capital; but also a gender organization, reflecting the gendered segmentation of the labour market (Clegg and Dunkerley 1980; Gordon et al. 1982; Hearn and Parkin 1983).

(3) Even though the historical record may be incorrect about women as political actors, there is no reason to make that mistake today. The situation of women as workers is changing dramatically. Internationally, women account for the majority of new union memberships and in most countries the organizational frequency among female workers (in comparable industries) is fast approaching that of male workers (Cook et al. 1984; Karlsson 1983).

(4) When women are active they use a different approach. Often female class action is extremely local and may take forms outside the traditional organizational structure of the union (Purcell 1984). Their demands are also different. Women demand equal pay, but go beyond economism to make strong demands for better working conditions and better welfare provisions. Their demands frequently put labour in a broader perspective of community and the family (Cavendish 1982; Holmila 1986; Liljeström and Özgalda 1980).

What the evidence shows is definite. The working woman is not necessarily a "passive woman." However, the married woman's activity is often restricted to working hours, and located near home, due to her double burden of family and work. The weight of work at home for women has not lessened with the parallel increase of work in the labour market (Åkerman 1983; Berk 1985). This is in part due to another myth that accompanies the myth of the "passive woman", that of pin-money involvement in the labour market. According to the myth, women's involvement in the world of work is peripheral, hence her "passivity" in terms of union activity is rational.

Thus it is important to examine the experience in societies where the idea that women are working for "pin-money" has disappeared. In Scandinavia, the transition to seeing the two-partner family as composed of two wage-earners has been made. Increasingly, both partner's contributions become vital for the living standard of the household. In a country such as Sweden, the family can hardly be seen as a safe haven or separate sphere protected from the world of work.

3. The Case of Sweden

Historically Swedish women were less organized than men (Boman 1981; Kjellberg 1983: 142–147). In the post-war period, though, Sweden has seen women receive many structural guarantees for equality (Ruggie 1984). These have been accompanied and perhaps spurred by an increase in women's organizational frequency.

Notably, the Swedish working class, and with it, working class unions are becoming feminized. Women accounted for almost the entire membership increase in the *Landsorganisationen* (LO, Federation of Swedish Workers) in the 1970s and 1980s. An example of the changing complexion of the working class labour scene is that the Metal Workers, long seen as a key group in industry and the labour movement were passed in numerical size 1981 by the number of female workers alone organized in the Municipal Workers' Union. This "female"

Table 1. Membership and Labor Union Activity According to 1984's Swedish Living Condition Study*

Men and Women According to Individual Class Location (Percentages)

	Member in trade union	Never attended any meeting	Have attended a meeting during year	Have attended at least 4 meetings in this year	Have spoken at a meeting	Have a commission of trust
Men						
Workers						
Unskilled and semi-skilled workers	84.7	30.2	48.6	10.4	42.1	11.8
Skilled workers	90.3	26.4	44.8	15.0	43.5	15.6
(All m. workers)	87.2	28.4	46.2	12.5	42.7	13.5
Salaried employees						
Junior employees	80.7	19.0	46.9	13.4	66.0	19.7
Intermediate	85.9	14.1	52.4	18.7	70.4	19.4
Senior employees	80.3	10.5	60.2	23.2	80.1	23.9
(All m. employees)	82.9	14.3	53.1	18.6	72.1	20.7
Women						
Workers						
Unskilled and semi-skilled	83.6	34.2	37.9	7.0	26.6	6.6
Skilled workers	88.7	32.7	32.6	7.7	35.8	6.0
(All f. workers)	84.6	33.9	36.8	7.2	28.5	6.5
Salaried employees						
Junior employees	83.4	25.8	46.0	10.9	40.3	14.5
Intermediate	89.2	14.5	45.2	12.5	52.5	16.4
Senior employees	90.4	14.5	60.6	19.6	74.1	20.7
(All f. employees)	86.5	20.0	47.7	12.7	49.7	16.1

* Not previously published data. Age group 16–74. (N = 3130)

union is now the biggest in the LO group. In all at the end of 1984, 43 per cent of the members of LO unions, 61 per cent of TCO members (Swedish Central Organization of Salaried Workers) and 40 per cent of SACO-SR (Swedish Academic Central Organization) were female (see Appendix A). Today the organizational frequency and activity rate of men and women is virtually identical (see Table 1).

However, as noted above, women use their unions in different ways than men. Female-dominated unions in the health and clerical sectors are most active concerning specific local work issues. For example, women respond to new technology by questioning what consequences it will have for their health, personal relations at work and sexual equality (Boman 1981; Morgall and Vedel 1985) rather than only worrying about redundancy. Tonboe (1986) suggests that with increasing female dominance in public sector unions Scandinavia is seeing a change in union political action, from national level issues to local welfare state issues.[2]

The largest Swedish union (Municipal Workers' Union), which is dominated by female members, has been seen by some (Ressner and Svensson 1986) as expressing more militant and all-encompassing demands than the traditionally aggressive male-dominated metal trade unions.[3] The Municipal Workers demand radical wage redistribution between different categories of employees and sexual equality as well as campaigning for shorter hours, maintained levels of public health-care and social services and work place democracy. Male-dominated unions recurrently press what can be seen as narrower demands focused on the real wage package (Ressner & Svensson 1986).

The increasing presence of women and their more encompassing demands are positive news, but the negative news is that some things change very slowly. Women are still less likely to be in leadership positions, even though female-dominated unions are increasingly recruiting female leaders. At the local level, women are beginning to achieve representation in leadership roles (Gonegai and Thorsell 1985; LO 1984), but parity tails off, the higher one goes in the hierarchy. If we examine the situation more closely, we see that the question of union activity as presented in Table 1 is as much a question of social class as one of gender. Middle class females do nearly as well or sometimes better than working class males on all measures of activity. Further, the intra-sex differences are smaller, the further up the class hierarchy one travels. The differences between male and female junior and intermediate level salaried employees are very small indeed.

The tendencies in Table 1 indicate that the differences are strongly related to

---

[2] In Sweden in 1980, 61 per cent of female wage earners were to be found in the public sector as opposed to 34 per cent of male workers (Ahrne 1982: 20).

[3] A powerful description of the Metal Workers as a traditional male union is too be found in Korpi (1978). Lash and Urry (1987) describe similar processes of tactical and demand change in capitalism at large.

class and the structure of the labour market. If the extra work burden of the women is taken into account, as many authors argue (Cook et al. 1984; Siltanen 1986), one would expect the sex-related differences to lessen. It may be that women seem "passive" not because of their sex but because they live in a world where things are passed out according to gender, including tasks in the home.

4. Family Situation and Class Action

The Taylor thesis suggests that if women occupy the same positions as men, they will react similarly in terms of politics and union activities. We would like to amend the thesis, suggesting that the similar situation includes not only location in the class structure and similar work situations but also location in the family. A satisfactory explanation of organized class action and the issue of gender requires seeing production and reproduction not as a dichotomy, but as a whole.

Table 2. Swedish National Class Study: Membership in Unions, Union Activism and Political Engagement by Individuals in Couples with Differing Class Composition, Men and Women in Percentages

Couple Composition	Member of union (a)	Active in union[1] (b)	Politically active[2] (c)	n = a)	n = b)	n = c)
Men						
Worker	91	23.5	10.5	157	145	155
Middle	82	41	24	105	86	105
Non-traditional cross-class	100	23	18	27	26	27
Traditional cross-class	91.5	42.5	20.5	94	87	96
Total	89	32.5	17	383	344	383
Women						
Worker	86	14.5	13	118	103	119
Middle	79	21	27	80	66	81
Non traditional cross-class	94.5	23	21	18	22	22
Traditional cross-class	81	14.4	8	74	62	76
Total	83	17	16	290	253	298

[1] Union activity = union member either elected or appointed office holder at present or earlier.

[2] Politically active = has been part of some group or organization which attempted to influence decision makers, express viewpoints or participate in election.

Much in union structure and culture is prejudicial not only against women, but against the working class. Unions are the organ of class struggle, but they are also organizations, *formal* organizations, and those who do best in formal organizations tend to be non-working class and male. Table 2, based on information from the Swedish national class study,[4] further illuminates the findings in Table 1.

Individual social class is more powerful than sex in predicting union activity. At first glance, it may look as if the family in Sweden is of little relevance for examining the situation of the individual wage worker and his or her union. The results demonstrate an individuated response to wage labour for both men and women. The class situation in the family seems to play little or no role in an individual's propensity to join a union. We would like nonetheless to explore the interwoven network of family situation, class localization and gender as a pathway to understanding those differences between female and male political and labour activity that remain. One way to capture the interaction between family situation, class position and gender is to compare men and women with different class situations at the level of the family. We compare here class homogeneous family constellations[5] (with partners on the same side of the border between the working class and other classes) to class heterogeneous or cross-class families. These cross-class families include one partner who is either a semi-autonomous employee, a supervisor or a manager, and another one firmly in a working class position. As we are here concerned with unions and families, we include only employees in the analysis.

The traditional and most frequently found cross-class constellation is the non-working class male married to a woman working in a working class position. A non-traditional constellation is the non-working class wife married to a working class husband. People in cross-class families of either traditional or non-traditional types experience the everyday reality of class differently than their sisters and brothers in homogeneous relationships (Abbot and Sapsford 1987; Leiulfs-rud and Woodward 1987, 1989; McRae 1986). Conventionally, it has been assumed that women take the position and opinions of their spouse into account when deciding about politics or labour action. In contradiction to this conven-

---

[4] Data dealing with the Swedish class structure were collected within the "Comparative Project on Class Structure and Class Consciousness" led by Erik Olin Wright, University of Wisconsin, Madison. The Swedish Class Project provides a representative study of the Swedish class structure in 1980. The sample of 2025 was drawn from national census registers. The final number of respondents was 1145 with a response rate of 76 per cent (Ahrne 1982). We would like to thank Lars Häll, Statistics Sweden, for providing us with the data in table 1 and Appendix A.

[5] Here we employ the classification system first elaborated by Wright (1979) and used consistently throughout the Swedish national class study. Some 45 per cent of all Swedish two partner families exhibit a cross-clas pattern using a loose definition, that is to say a semi-autonomous employee married to a manager would be a cross-class couple. Almost a third are of the more extreme combination of one working class and one non-working class partner (Leiulfsrud 1985) to be treated here.

tional view of the malleable woman, we see that in Sweden at least, the individual class position itself must be used to account for degree of activity. This is an important result that challenges a number of assumptions that have been made in connection with the "unit of analysis" debate (Erikson 1984; Goldthorpe 1983, 1984) in Great Britain. According to these scholars, there is little today which would indicate that female social and political action is not mediated through their spouses. In Sweden, though, it seems that the spouse's class has little effect on the position his wife takes in relation to her union and union activity. Thus, we feel, in accordance with Stanworth (1984) and Marshall et al. (1988), that "family reductionism" is misrepresenting. The individuation of wage labour and the privatization of family life give rise to a long series of competing influences on the class subject at both the political and ideological level.

For example, increasing time per week at work can strengthen an autonomous relation to the union.

Table 3. Swedish National Class Study: Membership in Unions, Union Activism and Political Engagement for Women in Full- or Part-Time Employment in Families with Differing Class Composition, Percentages

Couple Composition	Member of union (a)	Active in union (b)	Politically active (c)	n = a)	n = b)	n = c)
Full-time Women						
Worker	92	16	6.5	61	56	61
Middle	87	32.5	29	45	40	45
Non-traditional cross-class	(100)	(21.5)	(21.5)	12	14	14
Traditional cross-class	89	18	10.5	37	34	38
Total	90	21.5	15	155	144	158
Part-time Women						
Worker	76	7.5	14	50	40	51
Middle	69	4.5	17	29	22	30
Non-traditional cross-class	(80)	(14)	(14)	5	7	7
Traditional cross-class	74	11	5.5	35	27	36
Total	74	8	12	119	96	124

Union activity = union member either elected or appointed office holder at present or earlier.
Politically active = has been part of some group or organisation which attempted to influence decision makers, express viewpoints or participate in election.

A comparison of full-time employed women and men shows no statistical differences in terms of organizational frequency, and only very small differences between male and female working class workers as far as union activity goes, regardless of family class composition. In the middle class as well, the differences between male and female employees are small, although family class may play a slightly greater role, as can be seen in Table 3.

Thus far, we seem to have to some extent verified a Taylor thesis. If women occupy the same positions as men, they will react similarly in terms of union activity. With fewer hours of work and thus a weaker connection to the labour market, we also find a lower degree of union activity. This seems to be an important distinction, for, as we see in our figures in Table 3, 43.5 percent of the married or co-habiting employed women worked less than 30 hours a week in 1980. Here women differ dramatically from men, who seldom work part-time (Sundström 1987). More than three fourths of the women in Table 3 holding union leadership posts worked full time.

Organizational contexts such as family and union can contribute to either reinforcement or weakening of the ties between social class and political and ideological values. Table 4 includes only results on the Swedish working class, due to limitations in the data set. We note that union organization in the Swedish case strengthens class-congruent attitudes for women. While the number of non-organized women is small, we hypothesize that the union works to heighten class awareness and socialist political identification for working class women. Those in mixed class situations show less class-congruent identification (socialist sympathy and working class identification) than their unionized sisters in homogeneous marriages, but are still more congruent than non-unionized women in either family situation.

One index of sympathy with Social Democratic policy is support for greater state spending on welfare issues. If we compare results from working class men and women in cross-class and class homogeneous family situations in Tables 4 and 5, we find that family situation or a "partner-effect" and even unionization matter little to women when it comes to support for the welfare state. However, men in varying family class constellations do differ in sympathy for welfare state issues. Middle class men married to working class women are slightly more sympathetic to increased public spending than their brothers in homogeneous situations. Here we suspect that the results for women may reflect an individuated response to political issues related to their sector localization. Females in different class positions are very similar in their support for the welfare state. This may be related to the fact that 61 per cent of female wage workers were employed in the public sector in 1980, as opposed to 34 per cent of all male workers. Figures from middle class partnerships demonstrate that the discrepency between male and female support for the welfare state is even more pronounced in the middle class.

It is not surprising that union organization, socialist party preference and support for the welfare state seem to be linked. Swedish Social Democracy has long had a close relationship with the LO (Federation of Swedish Workers) to the

Table 4. Swedish National Class Study: Unionized and non-Unionized Working Class
Women in Different Family Class Situations
Percentage who consider themselves to belong to a class, who express Strong sympathy with a Socialist party, who express a working class identity and who support
increased public spending on welfare

	Belong to Class	Socialist Sympathy	Working Class ID	Support Welfare
Unionized				
a) Working Class	49.5	56.5	76.5	87
b) Traditional cross-class	32	44	46	77
c) Total	43	52	67	83
Non-unionized				
d) Working Class	18	(18)	44	76.5
e) Traditional cross-class	(43)	(25)	(38.5)	(86)
f) Total	29	22	41.5	81

Number of respondents per category:
Belong to Class: N = a) 101 b) 60 e) 161 d) 17 e) 14 f) 31
Strongly sympathize with socialist party: N = a) 85 b) 48 c) 133 d) 11 e) 12 f) 23
Working Class id: N = a) 98 b) 46 c) 144 d) 16 e) 13 f) 29
Support for increased public spending on health services and education:
N = a) 101 b) 60 c) 161 d) 17 e) 14 f) 31

Table 5. Swedish National Class Study: Wage-Earning Men in Different Family Class
Situations
Percentage who consider themselves to belong to a class, who express Strong sympathy with a Socialist party, who express a working class identity and who support
increased public spending on welfare

	Belong to Class	Socialist Sympathy	Working Class ID	Support Welfare
Couple composition				
a) Working Class	44	52.5	77	81
b) Middle Class	28	29	34	58
c) Non-traditional cross-class	48	65	72	67
d) Traditional cross-class	39	44	38	66
e) Total	39	45	55.5	70

Number of respondents per category:
Belong to Class: N = a) 158 b) 105 c) 27 d) 96 e) 386
Strongly sympathize with socialist party: N = a) 137 b) 96 c) 23 d) 82 e) 338
Working Class id: N = a) 148 b) 94 c) 25 d) 90 e) 357
Support for increased public spending on health services and education:
N = a) 158 b) 105 c) 27 d) 96 e) 386

extent that for a number of years LO members were automatically also collectively attached to the party. What does surprise, given the conventional picture of the woman as her husband's political blotter, is that organized working class women married to middle class men tend to be closer in their political preferences to the working class than to the middle class male position. Non-organized working class women (with a reservation for the very small number of respondents) are as anti-socialist as middle class males in homogeneous situations! In Sweden, union organization in the working class is an important factor for the reproduction of working class political values for women.

These results are important as they indicate the problems in looking at women either as autonomous individuals outside of a family context, or with a solely family reductionist approach which treats women as mirror-images of their spouses. Organizations such as unions can play a powerful role. Union membership, whether active or passive may be an important mediating factor, just as the everyday reality of family life also mediates in the reproduction of class related values.

5. The Juncture of Class and Gender: The Cross-Class Family

That the cross-class family can be a fruitful place to examine the intersection of the world of the market and the family at the level of values and ideology has also been demonstrated by McRae (1986), who closely examined non-traditional cross-class families with a working class husband and non-working class wife. She found that virtually all the wives and more than half of the husbands were trade union members. Although her sample was small, and not all of the husbands would be classified as working class according to most recent models, her discussion provides some insights similar to ours. The wives are highly organized, and the husbands participate more often and in more social organizations than other manual workers (1986: 226). However, within the couple, channels of influence about attitudes towards unions can flow both ways. Some women have been galvanized by their husband's experiences at the factory. Others have been turned against unions after conversation with their spouse (notably husbands in nationalized industries). With a small sample it is difficult to discover unambiguous influences, but the family situation seems important in deciding whether to adapt a compartmentalized, individuated attitude to class action. Only one fifth of the middle class wives in McRae's sample had socialist or working class preferences and could find "intelligible links exist between their private, cross-class family lives and their public left-wing ideologies. Private and public life "make sense" as one realm creates and sustains the others" (1986: 211) for these women. Generally, however, cross-class data seems to indicate that women experience many disjunctions between their private and public lives.

The cross-class family stands the issue of class and gender on its head, and produces situations charged with ambivalence as well as revealing the range of strategies used by women and men to deal with contrasting class experiences. We pursued the issue of class within the family by intensively studying 30 cross-class families. Half the couples had a working class husband, and the other half had a working class wife[6]. Some women practiced what Watts (1980) describes as a "discrete" or individuated approach, carefully separating home and work. This was especially true of women in working class jobs. Equally and oppositely, non-working class women were influenced by their working class partner in discussions about union tactics and politics. Another pathway was the influence that cross-class experience provided in terms of class-related resources. The middle class spouse often had the organizational savvy and discipline (as can be noted in Table 1) which the working class spouse lacked and could provide tips or inspiration in union-related battles. The working class spouse had at times access to a long labour movement tradition, either through his or her own experience or through the family which could fire the non-working class spouse's resolve in a labour battle.

For example, within the smaller qualitative study, we had a virtually Pygmalion relationship. In this case the woman, Ann Marie, reveals an individuated strategy. For her, the situation at work and at home were quite separate. The key-punching wife claimed of her architect husband,

He basically formed me, really well. People who knew me ten years ago, don't recognize me when they meet me, in all ways as far as my way of life and my thoughts [...].

Yet, the woman revealed independent labour activity. While her husband, an adamant conservative, said, "in principle I am opposed to unions," she became one of the early union members at her American affiliate firm which had been resisting unionization. Only 15 of the 60 employees joined. In describing her job, her awareness of exploitation was high. She complained about everything from wages to work injuries. At work, Ann Marie picks up entirely different messages than those emitted by her conservative husband. She is stimulated and challenged by more ideologically coherent working class co-workers:

I think my mates are members to help push up our wages and then they are probably

---

[6] Families were selected from Stockholm and Södertälje census registers and contacted in 1984–85. They were legally married, two-income families with children no older than 12 years. After an initial mail questionnaire to 263 families so identified, we chose a group of 30 couples, selected to include half non-traditional and half traditional partnerships, including non-middle class partners from all the so-called "contradictory positions" and the capitalist position in the Wright (1979) class model. In all, each family was interviewed on at least two separate occasions resulting in total interview times from at least 6 to 10 hours per family.

afraid of getting unemployed. And then it is also true that Doris is really engaged and active [. . .], she's tried to talk to us, but she probably feels she doesn't get too much response. She's a red socialist so it stinks, but still [. . .].

Ann Marie, despite her admiration for her conservative husband's acumen in politics, accepts the analysis of her socialist co-worker as related to her exploitation on the job, and compartmentalizes the way she thinks and acts at work away from what goes on in her home.

The influence within the family may go both ways. A working class member may raise the middle class partner's consciousness, just as the middle class member may provide the verbal backbone to help a working class partner stand up for his or her rights. The working class partner, especially when male, is often a member of a powerful union. For these men, union membership comes naturally, as for this printer:

I'm in the union because there has never been any alternative. For me it is so self-evident that I have never even thought about why it is so. You never got anything for free in this country. You have to hang together and then you can be strong. You have to fight and it is easiest in an organized form.

His consciousness clearly influenced his teacher wife who wished her union were more aggressive:

It's so that when you work in a sector that is women's work, then the unions are worse. You can see that if you look at the union I am in, in comparison with the high school teachers' union which is male-dominated. They're much tougher, they issue strike warnings and such [. . .].

For the working class woman, on the other hand, the verbal resources of the husbands may rub off. Thus, an automated data process worker in a big automobile firm was the one who brought up most of the work complaints from her co-workers to management. She aired grievances at home to a manager husband who saw the consequences of her poor working conditions for their family. Each week she came back to work primed with anger. However, like many women she felt stymied by the male-dominated local. For example, compensation for child care had been lagging despite female demands. She commented with disillusion on the male hierarchy at her work place, saying, "the big union boss there is typical – if he coughs, everyone coughs" and continued,

We have been trying to get heard for years here, but it was first when the men had to start staying home with these sick kids that the demand began to get heard a little higher up – before, it was seen as a little local girls' demand and nothing happened.

A change in union sensibility, if this case is any indication, will come not only from women making their demands more effectively, but also from men experiencing at home the relevance of these demands. Union activity provides a forum which can be individuated. Working class women members demonstrate that their identity is not wiped out in the interchange with the middle class in the family sphere. On the contrary, in many cases it seems that the cross-class bond provides resources for strength as members in the labour movement, although partners act in their own class congruent union. Working class women in class-mixed marriages, facing the non-working class reality of their husbands every day, may compartmentalize their class awareness, yet still reveal it in specific work related and political situations.

6. Conclusions

Swedish unions themselves are aware of the influence families have on union activity. A study by the *Landsorganisationen* (Federation of Swedish Workers) in 1981 showed that activity of one partner in the household could affect the other positively, that "it doesn't seem to be the case that one partner is forced into passivity because the other is active" (LO 1981: 118–119). Their conclusion was that an integration of families and family interests into trade union policies was a precondition for the mobilization of women in general.

This realization signals a change from the historical position of unions which in this century have often been essentially mirrors of a masculine struggle. In any practical analysis of the reasons for the seemingly passive union woman and the prospects for change, we need a multi-dimensioned approach which illuminates various pathways and strategies both at work and at home. Changes in the division of labour at home may be a key to underwriting female activism above and beyond mere membership. Can one imagine a world where a man wielding a vacuum cleaner would see this activity as an act of class struggle?

Nonetheless, the organization of work and unions is a necessary adjunct. The recent studies of structural obstacles within the structure of the union itself and within jobs in sectors dominated by females, where low skill and isolated working conditions lead to low levels of organizational activity, suggest that the very ways of doing things within unions must change. Studies such as Cockburn's (1983), Gonegai and Thorsell (1985), Lindgren (1985), Ressner (1987) and Siltanen (1986) all reveal in detail problems with not only structure but attitudes among the primarily male leadership of unions.

However, as our findings indicate, awareness is built first and foremost in the work experience itself. As the material in this paper suggests, more intense wage labour activity in more varied positions on the labour market have been accompanied by women adopting a more individuated view of themselves as workers, and not simply and primarily as family members. As women become institutionalized as wage labourers, they take the first steps towards seeing the interests of all workers as their own. This is indicated by the high willingness to join unions. But to become active requires a following step, a step that must be reinforced not only on the job but in the home and in the community. When work issues spill into the home arena, partners can support each other in their struggles against poor work conditions and pay.

By seeing that the work place is not the only forum for struggle, and that change must occur at home as well, it becomes easier to understand why female organization has not directly led to female leadership in unions. Change in gender roles occurs slowly, but as female wage labour becomes a necessary component in nearly all families, one possible road will be an adjustment of the burdens at home, leading to possibilities for change in union leadership.

Unions in many countries are experimenting with new ways of organizing, holding meetings and making decisions. Some use affirmative action to recruit new female leaders, others provide separate channels for female advancement (Beattie 1986; Boston 1987; Cockburn 1984). This organizational experimentation may benefit not only women but all workers with family responsibilities. The key to leaving the mythology of the passive woman worker far behind is seeing that the organization of the family and the organization of work and class action hang together and must change together.

References

Abbot, Pamela and Roger Sapsford, *Women and Social Class*. London: Tavistock. 1987

Ahrne, Göran, *Report on the Swedish Class Structure*. Comparative Project on Class Structure and Class Consciousness. Working Paper Nr. 4. Madison: University of Wisconsin. 1982

Åkerman, Britta, *Den okända vardagen: Om arbetet i hemmen*. Stockholm: Förlaget Akademilitteratur. 1983

Andersen, Jørgen Goul, *Kvinder og politik*. Aarhus: Forlaget Politica. 1984

Andersen, Jørgen Goul, Political Behaviour in Denmark: The Invisibility of Class and Gender, Manuscript, Aarhus: August. 1986

Andersen, Kristi, Working Women and Political Participation 1956–1972, *American Journal of Political Science* 19 (August): 443–454. 1975

Beale, Jenny, *Getting It Together. Women as Trade Unionists*. London: Pluto Press. 1982

Beattie, Margaret, The Representation of Women in Unions, *Signs* 12/1: 118–129. 1986

Beechey, Veronica, *Unequal Work*. London: Verso. 1987

Berk, Sarah Fenstermaker, *The Gender Factory*. New York: Plenum Press. 1985

Boman, Ann, Omsorg och solidaritet. Ohållbara argument, *Kvinnovetenskaplig Tidskrift* 1–2: 51–54. 1981

Boston, Sarah, *Women Workers and Trade Unions*. London: Lawrence and Wishart. 1987

Bradley, Harriet, Technological Change, Management Strategies and the Development of Gender-Based Job Segregation in the Labor Process, in: David Knights and Hugh Willmott (eds.), *Gender and the Labor Process*. Aldershot, Hampshire: Gower, pp. 54–73. 1986

Cavendish, Ruth, *Women on the Line*. London: Routledge and Kegan Paul. 1982

Clegg, Stewart and David Dunkerley, *Organization, Class and Control*. London: Routledge and Kegan Paul. 1980

Cockburn, Cynthia, *Brothers: Male Dominance and Technological Change*. London: Pluto Press. 1983

Cockburn, Cynthia (ed.), Trade Unions and the Radicalizing of Socialist Feminism, *Feminist Review* 16 (April): 43–73. 1984

Cook, Alice H., Val R. Lorwin and Arlene Caplan Daniels, *Women and the Trade Unions in Eleven Industrialized Countries*. Philadelphia: Temple University Press. 1984

Creighton, Hanna, Tied by Double Apron Strings: Female Work Culture and Organization in a Restaurant, *The Insurgent Sociologist* 11/3: 59–64. 1976

Crompton, Rosemary and Gareth Jones, *White-Collar Proletariat: Deskilling and Gender in the Clerical Labor Process*. London: Macmillan. 1984

Crompton, Rosemary and Michael Mann (eds.), *Gender and Stratification*. Cambridge: Polity Press. 1986

Erikson, Robert, The Social Class of Men, Women and Families, *Sociology* 18: 500–514. 1984

Feldberg, Roslyn and Evelyn N. Glenn, Male and Female Job Versus Gender Models in the Sociology of Work, *Social Problems* 26/5: 524–538. 1979

Feldberg, Roslyn L. and Evelyn N. Glenn, Technology and Work Degradation: Effects of Office Automation on Women Clerical Workers, in: Joan Rothschild (ed.), *Machina Ex Dea*. New York: Pergamon Press, pp. 59–77. 1983

Goldthorpe, John H., Women and Class Analysis: In Defence of the Conventional View, *Sociology* 17: 465–488.

Goldthorpe, John H., Women and Class Analysis: A Reply to the Replies, *Sociology* 18: 491–499. 1984

Gonegai, Berit and Birgitta Thorsell, *Kvinnorna och facket: En studie om facklig aktivitet bland kvinnor i svenska kommunalarbetareförbundet*. Gothenburg: Department of Sociology, University of Gothenburg. 1985

Goot, Murray and Elizabeth Reid, Women – If not Apolitical then Conservative, in: Janet Siltanen and Michelle Stanworth (eds.), *Women and the Public Sphere: A Critique of Sociology and Politics*. London: Hutchinson, pp. 122–136. 1984

Gordon, David, Richard Edwards and Michael Reich, *Segmented Work, Divided Workers. The Historical Transformation of Labor in the United States*. Cambridge: Cambridge University Press. 1982

Gottfried, Heidi and David Fasenfest, Gender and Class Formation: Female Clerical Workers, *Review of Radical Political Economics* 16/1: 89–103. 1984

Granath, Erna and Lena Larsson, *Kvinnoplats: En arbetsstudie om kvinnors vardag på kontor*. Stockholm: Liber Förlag. 1985

Grieco, Margaret and Richard Whipp, Women and the Workplace: Gender and Control in the Labor Process, in: David Knights and Hugh Willmott (eds.), *Gender and the labor process*. Aldershot, Hampshire: Gower, pp. 117–139. 1986

Gunnarson, Ewa and Ulla Ressner, *Från hierarchi till kvinnokollektiv*. Stockholm: Swedish Centre for Working Life, Research Report 40. 1983

Hartman, Heidi, Capitalism, Patriarchy and Job Segregation by Sex, *Signs* 1/3 (2): 137–169. 1979

Hearn, Jeff and P. Wendy Parkin, Gender and Organization: A Selective Review and a Critique of a Neglected Area, *Organization Studies* 4/3: 219–242. 1983

Holmila, Marja, Life Style Issues-Debate Between Men and Women in the Finnish Trade Union Movement, *Acta Sociologica* 29/1: 3–12. 1986

Karlsson, Gösta, *Vrouwen in de vakbeweging*. Brussel: Europees Vakbondsinstituut. 1983

Kjellberg, Anders, *Facklig organisering i tolv länder*. Lund: Arkiv. 1983

Knights, David and Hugh Willmott (eds.), *Gender and the Labor Process*. Aldershot, Hampshire: Gower. 1986

Korpi, Walter, *The Working Class in Welfare Capitalism*. London: Routledge and Keagan Paul. 1978

Lash, Scott and John Urry, *The End of Organized Capitalism*. Cambridge: Polity Press. 1987

Leiulfsrud, Håkon, Familie og klassestruktur, in: Jens Hoff (ed.), *Stat, kultur og subjektivitet – Elementer til en moderne klasseanalyse*. Copenhagen: Forlaget Politiske Studier, pp. 207–235. 1985

Leiulfsrud, Håkon and Alison Woodward, Women at Class Crossroads: Repudiating Conventional Theories of Family Class, *Sociology* 21/3: 393–412. 1987a

Leiulfsrud, Håkon and Alison Woodward, Cross-Class Encounters of a Close Kind. *Acta Sociologica* 32/1: 75–94. 1989

Liljeström, Rita and Elisabeth Özgalda, *Kommunals kvinnor på livets trappa*. Stockholm: Svenska kommunalarbetareförbundet. 1980

Lindgren, Gerd, *Kamrater, Kollegor och Kvinnor: en studie av könssegregeringsprocessen i två mansdominerade organisationer*. Research Reports from the Department of Sociology, University of Umeå RR no 86. Umeå: Umeå University. 1985

(LO) Landsorganisation i Sverige, *Vem är aktiv i facket? En undersökning från LO 80 utredningen*. Jönköping: LO. 1981

(LO) Landsorganisation i Sverige, *Kvinnor i facket – En undersökning om kvinnorepresentationen inom fackföreningsrörelsen 1983*. Stockholm: LO. 1984

Marshall, Gordon, David Rose, Carolyn Vogler and Howard Newby, *Social Class in Modern Britain*. London: Hutchinson. 1988

McDonagh, Eileen, To Work or not to Work: The Differential Impact of Achieved and Derived Status upon the Political Participation of Women, 1956–1976, *American Journal of Political Science* 26/2: 280–297. 1982

McRae, Susan, *Cross-Class Families*. Oxford: Clarendon Press. 1986

Milkman, Ruth, Women's Work and the Economic Crisis, *Review of Radical Political Economics* 8/1: 73–97. 1976

Milkman, Ruth, *Women, Work and Protest*. London: Routledge and Kegan Paul. 1985

Morgall, Janine and Gitte Vedel, Office Automation: The Case of Gender and Power, *Economic and Industrial Democracy* 6: 93–112. 1985

Pollert, Anna, *Girls, Wives, Factory Lives*. London: Macmillan. 1982

Prokop, Ulrike, *Weiblicher Lebenszusammenhang*. Frankfurt am Main: Suhrkamp. 1976

Alison E. Woodward and Håkon Leiulfsrud

Purcell, Kate, Militancy and Acquiescence among Women Workers, in: Janet Siltanen and Michelle Stanworth (eds.), *Women and the Public Sphere*. London: Hutchinson, pp. 54–67. 1984
Ressner, Ulla and Lennart Svensson, Kvinnors osynliga revolt, *Dagens Nyheter*. 20 February, 3. 1986
Ressner, Ulla, *The Hidden Hierarchy*. Aldershot: Gower. 1987
Rosendal, Mona, *Conflict and Compliance: Class Consciousness among Swedish Workers*. Stockholm: Studies in Social Anthropology, Stockholms University. 1985
Ruggie, Mary, *The State and Working Women: A Comparative Study of Britain and Sweden*. Princeton: Princeton University Press. 1984
Siltanen, Janet, Domestic Responsibilities and the Structuring of Employment, in: R. Crompton and M. Mann (eds.), *Gender and Stratification*. Cambridge: Polity Press, pp. 97–118. 1986
Siltanen, Janet and Michelle Stanworth (eds.), *Women and the Public Sphere: A Critique of Sociology and Politics*. London: Hutchinson. 1984a
Siltanen, Janet and Michelle Stanworth, The Politics of Private Woman and Public Man, in: J. Siltanen and M. Stanworth (eds.), *Women and the Public Sphere: A Critique of Sociology and Politics*. London: Hutchinson, pp. 185–208. 1984b
Simpson, Ida Harper and Elizabeth Mutran, Women's Social Consciousness: Sex or Worker Identity, *Research in the Sociology of Work* 1: 335–350. 1981
Stanworth, Michelle, Women and Social Class Analysis: A Reply to Goldthorpe, *Sociology* 18: 159–170. 1984
Strandell, Harriet, *Kvinnosocialisation och lönearbetets betydelse: kvinnor i fabriks-, kontors- och omsorgsyrken*. Helsinki: University of Helsinki, Department of Sociology (Licentiat-thesis). 1983
Sundström, Marianne, *A Study in the Growth of Part-Time Work in Sweden*. Stockholm: Swedish Centre for Working Life/Almqvist and Wiksell International. 1987
Swedish Official Statistics (SCB), *Politiska resurser- Preliminära resultat från 1984 års undersökning av levnadsförhållandena.* Statistiska meddelanden Be 40 SM 8601. Örebro: Statistics Sweden. 1986
Taylor, Stan, Parkin's Theory of Working Class Conservatism: Two Hypotheses Investigated, *Sociological Review* 26/4: 827–842. 1978
Tonboe, Jens Chr., On the Political Importance of Space. The Socio-Spatial Relations of Trade Unions, Gender and the Decentralized Danish Welfare State, *Acta Sociologica* 29/1: 13–30. 1986
Watts, Ian, Linkages Between Industrial Radicalism and the Domestic Role Among Working Women, *Sociological Review* 28/1: 55–74. 1980
Wertheimer, Barbara M. and Anne H. Nelson, *Trade Union Women: A Study of Their Participation in New York City Locals*. New York: Praeger. 1975
Wright, Erik, O., *Class, Crises and the State*. London: New Left Books/Verso. 1979
Wright, Erik O., *Gender, Classes and Families*. Comparative Project on Class Structure and Class Consciousness. Working Paper No. 34. Madison: Department of Sociology, University of Wisconsin. 1986

Appendix A Swedish Living Condition Study 1984: The Gender Composition in Selected Labor Unions in Sweden 1984, Percentage of women members

	Predominantly* Male Unions	Less Gender Segregated	Predominantly* Female Unions	Total % Female Members
LO				
	Construction workers (6.5)	Food manufacture (40)	Commercial workers (65.5)	
	Manufacturing workers (22)	Government workers (32)	Municipal workers (80.5)	
	Wood manufact. workers (10)			
	Transport workers (13)			
	Metal workers (14)			
	Subtotal LO			43
TCO				
		Commercial white-collar (55)	Bank employees (69)	
		Industrial white-collar (42)	Spec. Teachers (74)	
			Teacher Union (75.5)	
			Health service (95)	
			Municipal employ-ees (73.5)	
			Government em-ployees (65)	
	Subtotal TCO			61
SACO-SR				40
Percent female members: all unions				49

N = 3130. These selected unions cover 84% of the members of LO and 91% of the members of TCO.
LO (Federation of Swedish Workers), TCO (The Swedish Central Organization of Salaried Workers) and SACO-SR (Swedish Academic Central Organization)
* Predominantly male unions here defined as those with less than 31% female members. Less gender segregated ones have at least 32% but maximally 64% female members, while predominantly female unions are defined as 65% female or more.
Source: 1984 Swedish Living Condition Study (ULF). Not previously published.

V. Classless Organizations?

Between Class Analysis and Organization Theory: Mental Labour

Guglielmo Carchedi

1. Introduction

The labour process debate has three shortcomings. It (a) ignores the distinction between labour and non-labour, (b) does not theorize the difference between material and mental labour and (c) ignores the class nature of mental labour. The same shortcomings can be found in the Second International's notion of socialist organization as well as in present "non-class reductionist" approaches. Thus, from this angle, present debates do not go any further than the theoretical limits of the Second International. This paper submits some basic principles of a socialist organization and argues that central to such an organization there is a fusion of material and mental labour. It then proceeds to sketch a theory of material and mental labour and of the class nature of mental labour.

2. Class Analysis and Socialist Organization

The potential for social critique offered by Marx's analysis of the labour process has been rediscovered towards the end of the 1960s in the wake of anti-authoritarian social movements critical not only of capitalism but also of "realized socialism." This has been an important reason for the renewed interest in this field of research since the publication of H. Braverman's *Labor and Monopoly Capital* (1974). This work rediscovers the centrality of the labour process in Marxist theory[1].

In spite of its fundamental importance for reviving the interest of Marxists in the labour process, Braverman's work and the discussion around it retain some lacunae. The first is the lack of development and application of a dialectical method to understand both labour and the labour process. Almost without exception, there is practically no concern in this debate in developing dialectics as a method of social research. The second is the failure to distinguish between labour and non-labour and the economic significance of non-labour. The third is the lack of inquiry into what mental labour is, both in general and in specific types of

---

[1] The literature is enormous. For a good introduction to the labour process debate see Thompson 1983. See also Carchedi 1987; Clegg, Boreham and Dow 1986.

production relations (Carchedi 1987). Concerning this latter point, there is a void when it comes to the theorization of (a) the difference between material and mental labour and (b) the class nature of mental labour. It is this third point which is of particular relevance for our present purposes.

The same shortcomings can be found in the Second International's notion of socialist organization. Bernstein, in his famous attack on orthodox Marxism, theorized the inevitability of oligarchy in large-scale organizations (1899: 111–119), a theme which would be elaborated upon by Michels twelve years later (1911). Kautsky (1899), in his critique of Bernstein, did not even consider this argument. This is because he did not properly theorize the relation between theory and practice. For Kautsky, "class struggle, when fought on all sides, scarcely stimulates the theoretical mind" (p. 13). Thus, the more time devoted to theory, the less time left to practice and vice versa. Kautsky did not see (and this would have been the proper answer to Bernstein and to all those after him, like Michels, who hold to the inevitability of oligarchy and bureaucracy) that theory and practice are two aspects of the development of the collective labourer, both of them being necessary and complementary. But, for this dialectical complementarity to emerge, a proper, different, organization is needed – one which struggles *continuously* to give *all* its members the opportunity to engage in practical activity and to reflect on it, i.e. to theorize it.

It is interesting to note that this theoretical inability was the reflection of a real situation. Basically. Kautsky had become the spokesman and theoretician of a party, the SPD, in which there was no dialectical relation between theory and practice for all its members, i.e. no internal democracy. This accusation (that of authoritarianism) had been brought against the SPD by H. Müller as early as in 1892 in his little known but very important *Der Klassenkampf in der deutschen Sozialdemokratie*. It becomes thus understandable why Kautsky could write in 1901–2 that "socialist consciousness is something imported in the class struggle of the proletariat from outside, and not something which forms itself spontaneously" (p. 80). It is clear that an organization in which there is no dialectical relationship between theory and practice cannot theorize the generation of its consciousness from within itself and must theorize the importation of consciousness from outside. If the moment of action is separated from that of reflection, this latter moment is brought back to the masses as directives (authoritarianism) and from outside (i.e. first from outside the moment of action, as a separate moment, and then from outside the masses, as a separate layer of specialized intellectuals).

The notion of the importation of a proletarian consciousness "from without" heavily influenced Lenin's theorization, as it is clear in *What is to be Done?* (1902). For Lenin, revolutionary consciousness cannot be the proletariat's spontaneous product. Left to itself, the proletariat can only develop "trade union" consciousness. The theory of socialism, however, can only be elaborated by "educated representatives of the propertied classes, by intellectuals" (p. 375).

Thus, for Lenin, the task of the socialist organization is to transform a trade-union consciousness into a revolutionary one, i.e. "to combat spontaneity" (p. 384). If, as submitted above, the Kautskian position is the theorization of the SPD's lack of internal democracy, then the application of this principle as theorized by Lenin cannot but tend to reproduce that lack of internal democracy by justifying, stimulating and reproducing an internal division of tasks between intellectuals and non-intellectuals, between mental and material labour.

The Leninist interpretation is the one which, for obvious historical reasons, has become the orthodox, and dominant, one. There are, in the history of Marxism, important examples of "heretics" who understood the reactionary implications of the Leninist position and fought for a different type of organization. The two theoreticians and leaders of the socialist movement during the Second International who stand out in this respect are R. Luxemburg and A. Pannekoek.

Contrary to Lenin, Luxemburg conceives of the relation between spontaneity and organization, between mental and material labour in a positive way: the one becomes a condition of reproduction and of enlargement of the other (1904). For Luxemburg, contrary, to Lenin, it is the artificial separation of socialist struggle and trade union struggle which is the cause of reformism and revisionism (1906: 215). A socialist organization must express radically different social relations and thus must be radically different from the organization of the bourgeoisie: this new, different, form of organization is the workers' committee (p. 176). This theme will be picked up and developed by the Council Communists, of which A. Pannekoek is the best-known representative.

The view that a socialist organization can work according to the same principles as those of a capitalist organization is shared (either implicitly or explicitly) by authors who stand at the opposite end of the Leninist position. A useful example is E. Laclau and C. Mouffe's *Hegemony and Socialist Strategy* (1985). To say, as Mouffe does, that we need a "redefinition of socialism as the extension of democracy to all fields of social exisence" (quoted in Slater 1987: 162) is unqestionably true but in a way begs the question: What kind of democracy is meant here? If by democracy we mean bourgeois democracy, then how does Mouffe's redefinition of socialism differ from Bernstein's conclusion that "the liberal organizations of modern society [...] do not need to be destroyed, but only to be further developed" (Bernstein 1899: 163), i. e. extended to all fields of social existence? If that redefinition rests upon or at least also encompasses principles of socialist democracy, then: what are they, how are they related to bourgeois democracy, should these latter be used only in a transition period, etc.? These, it would seem, are fundamental questions for the "non-class reductionist" project. Yet, they are missing.

This, in a way, is not surprising since Laclau and Mouffe reduce the development of Marxism to the official Marxism of the Second and Third International, thus downplaying the theoretical developments (and the social movements of which they were the expression) which were opposed to Kautsky in the Second

International and to Lenin in the Third International. There is no mention of, say, Council Communism in *Hegemony and Socialist Strategy*. Yet, a great deal can be learned from it concerning the principles of socialist democracy.

In short, if what must be extended to all fields of social existence is bourgeois democracy, then we shall never reach socialism (aside from the question concerning the extension of bourgeois democracy as a tactical move; but this does not seem to be the preoccupation of Laclau and Mouffe). If it is socialist democracy which must be extended, then we have there a tautology. In my opinion, the task is to "redefine" socialism by defining the principles upon which a socialist organization should be built. These principles are radically different from the ones characterizing the capitalist-authoritarian organization. They are not figments of imagination but are extracted from an analysis of real social movements and of their protagonists' theorizations. Let me briefly mention them.

First, socialist development requires that the development of one member, or group or labouring class, must be the condition for the development of the other members, or groups or labouring classes, rather than being built on the lack of development of the other members, groups or labouring classes. It follows that a socialist organization must be the organization of all labouring classes, not only of the collective labourer (i.e. all those employed by capital in order to transform use values) or even less of the industrial, urban proletariat. It also follows that a socialist organization must be one in which co-operation, and not authoritarian discipline, is the link uniting the individual members.

Second, socialist development requires that an individual be exposed to the widest range of experience. This in turn requires that people must perform not only one task but must rotate among many different tasks. Rotation must be the condition of an all-round development of the individuals, instead of being a condition for their increased exploitation and alienation (e.g. labour's mobility as dictated by capital). But this maximum exposure also requires that the tasks themselves are not fixed but changeable in order to meet the individual's needs. Or, tasks must be changed in order to allow the labourers' maximum development rather than to increase domination and exploitation of labour. This maximum exposure also requires that all tasks encompass both the transformation of reality (natural and social) and the mental conception (production of new knowledge) which goes with it. This organization must thus be based on a radically different technical division of labour, a division of labour functional for the all-round, and not to the one-sided, development of the individual. As already mentioned, it is this aspect which is particularly important for our present purposes.

Third, socialist development requires that everybody participate in the process of collective decision making. This means that representative organs must be the condition for the continued reproduction and enlargement, rather than for the stifling, of direct democracy; i.e. that the organization must be the condition for the continued reproduction of social movement rather than being its brake.

In short, a socialist organization must ensure that all labourers participate in the process of collective decision making concerning the performance of tasks designed and continuously changed in order to develop all aspects of the individual's personality (thus encompassing both material and mental labour) and carried out in a spirit of co-operation, without control and surveillance. This is not a "utopian" notion, it has been extracted from the demands which are recurrently thrown up by socialist movements in all countries.

Socialist democracy must be based upon a socialist, and not upon a bourgeois or liberal, type of organization. This implies that the extension of bourgeois democracy must be subordinated to the development of socialist democracy and is desirable only if compatible with it. Thus, the question is whether the social content of the principles of bourgeois "democracy" can be changed and given a socialist content when immersed in the context of a concrete socialist organization. This question cannot be decided upon in the abstract. The answer hinges upon an analysis of the concrete situation. However, this concrete analysis presupposes that we are aware of the characteristic features of a socialist organization and of its radical differences with the bourgeois type of organization. Particularly important for our present purposes is the notion that in a socialist organization each member must engage both in changing reality and in the theorization of this change.

Thus, it is essential that we engage in the theorization of material and mental labour and of the class content of mental labour. However, as far as these topics are concerned, present debates do not go any further than the theoretical limits of the Second International. Braverman is far more sensitive to them than orthodox Marxism, the "non-class reductionist" position, and his commentators (the labour process debate). But he too fails to theorize a concept, mental labour, which plays such an important part in his work. The remainder of this paper will attempt to partly fill this lacuna.

3. Elements of a Theory of Material and Mental Labour

For reasons of exposition, this section has been subdivided into four sub-sections.

3.1 Material and Mental Transformations as Conceptual Building Blocks of Labour

No matter how one chooses to define it, human labour is always conscious activity. More precisely, the transformation of material objects, or *material transformation,* both requires some previous knowledge of the transformation (no matter how vague, tentative, hypothetical or incomplete that pre-figurative knowledge might be) and cause new knowledge[2] of that material transformation to emerge. Alternatively, the transformation of existing knowledge, or *mental transformation,* both requires some material objects (even though they might only be pencil and paper) and causes their transformation (consumption). In short, material transformations necessarily require mental transformations, production of knowledge, and mental transformations necessarily require material transformations. Or, labour is always a combination of material and mental transformations.

Thus, in reality, material and mental transformations do not exist separately from each other. However, we can *examine* them in isolation. In fact, the *objects* of transformation differ: they are material objects in the case of material transformations and knowledge in the case of mental transformations. Or, to use Marx's terminology (1973), the object of the former process of transformation is the real concrete (material reality, as it exists independently from our perception of it[3]), while the object of the latter process of transformation is knowledge. We are therefore warranted in analyzing these two types of transformations in isolation from each other. We are also warranted in making material and mental transformations the *conceptual* building blocks of the notion of labour. Let us then examine these two types of transformations.

Material transformations are the transformation of material objects into different material objects. Since the use of the new material objects is different from the use of the old objects (and this is the purpose of the transformation), we can say that a material transformation is the transformation of a material use value into a different material use value. In symbols

$$MAT = MAU \rightarrow MAU^*$$

where MAT stands for material transformation, MAU means material use value, MAU* indicates a new material use value and $\rightarrow$ symbolizes the transformative process which changes MAU into MAU*. The transformed material use value is the outcome of the incorporation of the labourer's concrete, i.e. specific, labour (and, through this, of the use value of the means of transformation) into the use value of the objects of labour.

Let us now consider mental transformations, or the production of knowledge. Conseptually (and thus neither chronologically not psychologically), the production of knowledge can be separated into two steps. The first is *observation,* which – to begin with – is sensory perception, perception of the real concrete through our senses. But observation is not independent of social conditioning, it

---

[2] The notion of new knowledge will be dealt with further down. For the time being an intuitive understanding is sufficient. It should be anticipated that new knowledge also includes reconfirmation of already existing knowledge.

[3] In fact, the real concrete is given by both material and social reality. However, the focus in what follows will be on material reality in order to contrast it to our perception of it and to limit the scope of this article.

is socially filtered. The "filter" is given by the mental producers's previous knowledge[4] and social practice. Thus, observation is the socially filtered sensory perception of the real concrete. The result of observation is the *imagined concrete*. In symbols

$$O = (RC, SS) \rightarrow IC$$

where O stands for observation, RC for real concrete, SS for socially filtered sensory perception, the symbol $\rightarrow$ for the process of transformation, and IC for the result of that process, or imagined concrete.

The second step is *conception*. Once observation has given the real concrete a mental shape, this imagined concrete is transformed by the conscious application of the previous knowledge[5] of reality into new knowledge. This is the *concrete-in-thought*, i.e. the result of conception. In symbols,

$$C = (IC, CIT_o, MA) \rightarrow CIT_n$$

where C stand for conception, IC for imagined concrete, CIT_o for the old, i.e. previously existing, concrete-in-thought, MA for the material aids to mental transformations (e.g. word processors), $\rightarrow$ for transformation, and CIT_n for the new concrete-in-thought, the result of conception. Notice that previous knowledge has now been given the precise meaning of previous concrete-in-thought, or CIT_o.

Even though analytically we can separate observation from conception, in practice this is not possible. A mental transformation is always both observation and conception, i.e.

$$MET = (O, C)$$

where MET stands for mental transformation, O for observation and C for conception. This can also be written as

$$MET = (RC, SS, CIT_o, MA) \rightarrow CIT_n$$

which indicates that the production of new knowledge is the transformation of the socially filtered sensory perception of the real concrete and of the already existing knowledge of the real concrete, with the aid of material instruments, into the new knowledge of the real concrete.

Since for the present purposes it is the transformation of existing knowledge into new knowledge which interests us, from now on we shall use an abridged form of the process of mental transformation, i.e.

$$MET = K \rightarrow K^*$$

where MET means mental transformation, K existing knowledge (in the limited meaning of concrete-in thought) and K^* new knowledge (also only as concrete-in-thought)[6].

---

[4] As we shall see shortly, this previous knowledge is the previously produced concrete-in-thought.

[5] Again, this is previous concrete-in-thought.

[6] There are at least two important differences between material and mental transformations which should be mentioned. The first is that existing knowledge (K) is both an object of mental transformation and a means of transformation. In material transformations, on the

However, we are not interested in the transformation of knowledge, i.e. in the production of new knowledge, for its own sake. We are interested in it inasmuch as we can conceptualize what a mental use value is. The problem, therefore, is twofold: (a) when do we have new knowledge? (b) what is the use value of knowledge, or what is a mental use value?

As far as the first question is concerned, the knowledge emerging at the end of the mental transformation can be different from the initial one (for example, it can be a refutation of the initial one or it can be more or less complete, adequate, correct, etc. than the initial one). In this case, there obviously is production of new knowledge. But the knowledge emerging at the end of the process of mental transformation can be "the same" as the initial knowledge in the sense that it re-confirms its adequacy, completeness, correctness, etc. In this latter case too there has been production of new knowledge, since there has been a re-confirmation of the previously existing knowledge. In this case, K* is different from K because it contains the reconfirmation of K, because, as it were, it is K plus the knowledge of its validity. Thus, *new knowledge* is not only different knowledge but also re-confirmation of existing knowledge. By (new) knowledge it is here meant any mental product which affects our perception of the real concrete. Thus, (new) knowledge encompasses science, superstition, art, etc.

As far as the second question is concerned, just as the use value of material objects is their ability to satisfy (real or imaginary) needs, the *use value of knowledge* is its ability to allow us to relate to the material world[7], thus allowing us to satisfy our needs by transforming material use values. We have seen above the two senses in which knowledge can be new. In case of different knowledge, its use value will be new too because that knowledge will allow us to relate differently to material reality by engaging into new transformations of material use values. In case of re-confirmation of existing knowledge, its use value will also be new since that knowledge will allow us to transform material use values into new material use values, albeit in the same way. Thus, a *new mental* use value is any knowledge which, directly or indirectly, allows us to relate to material reality by

---

other hand, there is always a strict separation between objects and means of transformation (something which does not preclude the transformed objects of a certain transformation to become means of the *following* material transformation). The second is that in material transformations there is always a logical as well as a chronological separation between production and consumption. In mental transformations, on the other hand, the separation is only analytical. A person engaged in conception both transforms knowledge (production) and incorporates it in his or her labour power (consumption). The non-materiality of the product imposes a chronological contemporaneity of production and consumption.

[7] In fact, we should say: its ability to relate to the material and social world, i.e. to the real concrete (see Note 3). Here, however, I focus only on the relation between material and mental transformations. It should also be clear that knowledge's ability to relate to the real concrete should be understood both in the sense of an immediate relation and in the sense of a mediated relation (i.e. in the sense that the ability to relate to the real concrete and thus to satisfy needs might emerge at the end of a series of intermediate mental transformations).

changing old material use values into *new material* use values, either in the same or in a different way.

3.2 What Are Material and Mental Labour Processes?

In the previous sub-section, I have submitted a theory of material and mental transformations and thus of material and mental use values. As repeatedly stressed, however, material and mental transformations do not exist disjointly. They can only exist conjointly, as elements of a labour process. Or, material and mental transformations *must* combine in a labour process. This will be the focus of this subsection.

The labour process in its general form, i.e. in the form common to all types of society, is the transformation of use values (both material and mental) into new use values (also both material and mental) through the application of concrete labour. Or, the labour process can be represented as follows

$$LPr = U \rightarrow U^*$$

where LPr is the labour process, U indicates the material and mental use values to be transformed and U^* indicates the transformed material and mental use values.

If material and mental transformations always exist conjointly, the question becomes that of specifying the nature of the relation binding them. There are two pre-requisites. Since we know that material and mental transformations do not exist disjointedly, this relation should be conceptualized in such a way that it reveals these transformations' mutual existential interdependence. Secondly, since we are interested in theorizing material and mental labour, this relation should also be able to account for material and mental labour as specific forms of combination of material und mental transformations. It is my contention that this relation should be conceptualized in dialectical terms.

The notion of dialectical relation is a complex one and I elaborate it elsewhere (G. Carchedi 1987: chapter 2). For the present purposes, it is sufficient to highlight only a facet of it. Given two elements (the material and the mental transformations) of a process, the relation tying them is said to be a *dialectical relation* if each one of them cannot exist without the other (i.e. if it is a relation of existential interdependence) in the specific sense that one of them (the determinant element) *calls into existence* the other element (the determined one) *as a condition of* the former's *existence or supersession*.[8]

This notion stresses that two elements (material and the mental transforma-

---

[8] It should be stressed that this is an incomplete formulation. Any critique of the notion of dialectical relation in this truncated form would be unfair. The complete formulation can be found in G. Carchedi 1987: chapter 2, section 2 ("Some Principles of Dialectics"). It should

tions) of a process (in our case, the labour process) are tied by a dialectical relation if each one of them cannot exist without the other (i.e. if it is a relation of existential interdependence) in the specific sense that one of them (the determinant element) calls into existence the other element (the determined one) as a condition of the former's existence. The first pre-requisite is satisfied because the determinant element cannot exist without calling into existence (i.e. determining) the determined element; and the determined element cannot exist without the determinant one since it is called into existence by this later. The second pre-requisite is equally satisfied because the determinant role can be assigned to either type of transformations. By assigning the determinant role to either one or the other type of transformations, we can theorize material and mental labour processes as specific forms of combinations of material and mental transformations.

Thus, a *material labour process* is one in which material transformations are determinant (i.e. there are mental transformations, or production of mental use values, but they are determined by the transformation of material use values) and a *mental labour process* is one in which it is the mental transformations which are determinant (i.e. there is transformation of material use values but this is determined by the production of knowledge in the sense that it is (a) the consumption of the material aids to the production of knowledge and (b), for some labour processes, their transformation into the material depositories of knowledge, as for example the physical qualities of a book)[9].

3.3 How Can We Recognize Material and Mental Labour Processes?

If the labour process has always a double nature (it is always a dialectical relation between material und mental transformations), we need a criterion on the basis of which to judge when the labour process is material or mental, i.e. when it is the material or the mental transformations which are determinant. If either one or the other of these two types of transformations is determinant, then the product will also have a double nature in which either the material aspect or the mental

---

also be stressed that there is no relation of determination between nature and our knowledge of it since knowledge is not a condition of existence of nature. But there is a dialectical relation of determination between material and mental transformations, between our transformations of nature and the conception determined by those transformations.

[9] Notice that there is no inconsistency between this notion of material and mental labour processes and the principle that, within a materialist theory of knowledge, material transformations are always determinant. The ultimate generation of knowledge by material transformations does not imply at all that in the actual combination of material and mental transformations the former are always determinant. Due to the social division of labour, the societal labour process splits into a variety of individual labour processes, some of which are material and other mental. But knowledge is always ultimately determined by material transformations.

one will be determinant. Therefore, we can trace back the nature of the labour process by considering the product. Usually the determinant aspect of a product is empirically given. Thus, in the production of a car it is the material aspect which is empirically given (and on this basis we know that the production process is a material one) and in the production of a concert it is the mental aspect which is empirically apparent (something which allows us to know that in this production process it is the mental aspect which is determinant).

However, this rule is not always accurate. The rule which allows us to adjudicate the determinant role to either the material or the mental transformation within a labour process is given by whether *the determinant aim of the individual labour process, as socially validated at the moment of exchange* is a material use value or new knowledge. In short, the nature of the labour process is revealed by whether the product is exchanged primarily because of its material qualities or because of its knowledge content. For example, a book would appear to be the product of a material labour process. However, the book is produced and exchanged primarily because of its knowledge content and the material transformations (the book must be clearly printed, graphically attractive, with a few printing mistakes as possible, etc.) are important but subordinate to the knowledge content carried by the book. The same applies to the labour process producing a game or a toy or a shop's sign-board. These are all examples of mental labour processes, i.e. of mental products for which a material shell is needed.

The principle submitted above stresses both the individual aim and social validation. The former element stresses the subjective, and the latter element stresses the objective, aspects of production. The former, the individual aspect, implies that the same person making the same thing can engage either in a material or in a mental labour process. If I make shoes as a form of art, I engage in a mental labour process. I.e. the fact that those shoes can be used as shoes is secondary. What is of primary importance, the aim of my activity, is the transformation of knowledge. The social use of those shoes resides in their knowledge content and it is because of this knowledge content that they will be exchanged. If, on the other hand, I make the same shoes because I want to create a material object which can be worn by human feet, no matter how beautiful that object might be, then I engage in a material labour process. They are exchanged as material use values, as shoes. The conception needed to make them, no matter how beautiful they may be, is determined by the material transformations.

This should not be read to imply that the intention, the aim of the producer, is the only determinant of the nature of the labour process. If this were so, a serious element of indeterminacy would be introduced since it would be difficult to know what the aim of the producer has been simply by looking at the nature of the product. Moreover, the individual aim of the producer could clash with the use aimed at by the consumer of the product at the moment of exchange. However, the material or mental nature of a labour process is also determined by social validation.

In a system in which products are made in order to be exchanged, individual production must be validated as social production, as socially useful production: the product of the individual producer (be it a person or an enterprise) must pass the final examination by society. Or, in a system in which products are exchanged (bought and sold), the realization of a use value takes place *after* the moment of exchange; however, *the moment of exchange is the moment at which the use value is validated not only as such but also as either material or mental*. I.e. this is the moment at which the buyers show whether they are interested in that use value either primarily because of its material qualities or because of its knowledge content.

Thus, *individual production* creates the material and mental qualities as well as the *individual nature* of a use value, but exchange must validate the *social nature* of that use value. Or, individual production takes on a social character, becomes social production, only at the moment of its social validation, i.e. when the product is exchanged on the market. It is at that moment that the *potential social* production (i.e. individual production) becomes *realized social* production. From a practical point of view, therefore, *we need only know the social validation* of the product in order to know the social nature of the labour process.

One point should be stressed. Consider the case of somebody designing and making highly fashionable and expensive shoes which can be bought by the rich either to be used as "status symbols" (thus, not to be used as shoes) or perhaps not used at all. Here the determinant aim of production is a material use value while the primary aim of the consumer at the moment of exchange is its knowledge content. Is this then a material or a mental labour process? The answer is that this is a material labour process. In fact, *it is the general, social validation of the use value* as revealed at the moment of exchange which should be looked at. Thus, it does not matter whether somebody buys those shoes not as shoes but as a status symbol. The fact is that those shoes have been produced as shoes, i.e. because of their physical qualities, and that their normal, social use is perceived to be as shoes. An anomalous validation does not change the labour process from a material into a mental one. Similarly, I can buy a book as combustion material and not because of the knowledge it carries. However, this anomalous validation does not change the process which has produced that book into a material one. Anomalous validation as revealed at the moment of exchange does not change the nature of the labour process and thus of the product.

Thus, social production is the social form taken by individual production. This implies that the latter might realize itself at the social level, as socially validated production, in a modified form[10]. If the aim of the labour process, i.e. the

---

[10] The relation between individual and social production is similar to that between individual and social values as analyzed in G. Carchedi 1984a: 437ff. There is no relation of determination between individual and social production. Rather, the latter is the socially realized form of the former through, and at the moment of, exchange.

determinant transformation, has been a material (respectively mental) transformation and if exchange validates the nature of the labour process (and thus of the product) as material (respectively mental), the individual nature of production realizes itself as its social nature. The individual and social aspects coincide. Conversely, if the determinant transformation (aim of) the labour process has been a material (respectively mental) transformation but exchange validates that product for its knowledge content (respectively material qualities), individual production realizes itself at the social level in a modified form. In this case, the material (respectively mental) nature of individual production has been changed, at the moment of exchange, into its opposite. In this case, too, all we need to know for practical purposes is the social realization of that use value[11].

3.4 What Is Material and Mental Labour?

The answer to this question follows logically from the analysis submitted above. Labour is material or mental according to whether the determinant transformations are material or mental, i.e. according to whether the principal aim of that labour is a transformation of material use values or of knowledge. We should distinguish between the case in which the transforming agent performs the whole of the labour process and the case in which he or she performs only a part of it.

In the former case, the transforming agent carries out material or mental labour according to the nature of the labour process in which he or she is engaged. Shoes are made and sold primarily because of their material qualities, i.e. the aim of the process of transformation is a material use value. Therefore, a cobber carries out material labour. This, to repeat, does not mean that he or she does not engage in mental transformations. Rather, this means that those mental transformations are determined by the material ones and not vice versa, that the knowledge produced in that labour process (which, as pointed out above, can be either different from, or a reconfirmation of, the initial knowledge) is a consequence of the need to produce a material use value. On the other hand, a shoemaker who would make models of shoes used in the Middle Ages and sell them to a museum for an historical exhibition, would engage in a mental labour process and thus in mental labour. Here the material transformations are determined by the mental ones.

Under capitalism, however, the typical production process is not carried out by one individual but is fragmented in a number, sometimes a very large number, of

---

[11] It should be pointed out that the fact that some objects (e.g. beautiful shoes), originally born as the result of a material labour process, might later be appreciated as works of art does not change the material nature of the labour process which has produced them and which has been validated at the moment those shoes have been exchanged on the market.

positions. In this case, both the material transformations and the mental ones are carried out collectively, by what Marx call the *collective labourer*. In a shoe factory, for example, there are workers who physically transform leather, glue, etc. into shoes. Each one of these workers carries out only a fraction of the whole process. They perform material labour within a material labour process. On the other hand, that labour process also needs, say, shoe designers who engage in the conception of shoes. They carry out mental labour within a material labour process.

The former category of agents is engaged in material labour because they carry out collectively the material transformations needed by that labour process. The latter category of agents carries out mental labour for similar reasons. Again, each one of those agents is engaged in both material and mental transformations. But, material labourers are such because, in their positions (jobs), it is the material transformations which are determinant, since those positions are a part of the collective material transformation needed by that labour process; and, mental labourers are such because their positions are a part of the collective conception needed by that labour process. In short, a certain position can be seen as requiring either material or mental labour only after it has been placed within the context of that labour process's technical division of labour.

Thus, to work at the assembly line means to perform material labour not because those agents do not think (of course they do), nor because they wear a blue overall, nor because they "work with their hands," but because the principal aim of what they do is the transformation of material use values, because, therefore, they are part of the collective transformation of material use values within that labour process. The researchers employed by a research and development enterprise perform mental labour not because they do not use their hands (of course they do), nor because they wear a white overall, nor because their labour is expenditure of "nervous" (as opposed to "physical") energy, but because the aim of their task is to transform knowledge and, therefore, because they are part of the collective conception, transformation of knowledge, within that labour process.

Lastly, consider a newspaper. In this mental labour process there are mental labourers (e.g. the journalists) and material labourers (e.g. those manning the printing-machines). These are clear examples of mental and material labour. What about a typist whose task is simply to type the journalists' articles? This person performs material labour because the aim of this labour is to give the journalists' conception a material shell. Of course, the typist too engages in conception. But, within that labour process, the typist's conception is secondary (determined) since it is needed only inasmuch as he or she can give a material shell to somebody else's conception. In this job (and within this technical division of labour), what is important is not what the typist thinks but what he or she transforms physically (white paper into typed paper). The typist's conception is obviously needed but it is needed only because he or she must engage in a material transformation. From the point of view of the labour process, the typist is there basically to perform a material transformation.

But the same transformation (typing), when done by the journalist, becomes a part of his or her mental labour. The same transformation, the creation of the material shell for the journalist's conception, can be both determined by that conception (and thus become a subordinated part of mental labour) if the journalist both writes and types, and the determinant transformation if typing becomes a separate activity, job, due to a change in the labour process's technical division of labour. Or, it is the technical division of labour within a labour process which decides whether a certain transformation is a determined aspect of a certain position or the determinant aspect of a different position. Thus, within the societal labour process, it is the social division of labour which structures the individual labour processes into material and mental processes; and, within each of these individual labour processes, it is the technical division of labour which structures the individual transformations into material and mental labour.

Throughout I have used the term "material" and not "manual" labour. It is impossible, both analytically and empirically, to draw a distinction between expenditure of physical energy (manual labour) and expenditure of mental energy, or between blue-collar and white-collar work, or between other similarly dubious categories. But it is possible and advisable to operate a distinction between material and mental *transformations* by looking at the objects of transformation; between material and mental *labour processes* by looking at the determinant type of transformation within each labour process after the labour process has been placed within the social division of labour and after social validation has been taken into account; between material and mental *labour* when the agent performs *the whole labour process* by considering the determinant aspect of the labour process; and between material and mental labour when the agent performs only *a fraction of the labour process* by looking at the determinant transformation within that position after that position has been placed within that labour processes's technical division of labour.

4. On the Class Content of Mental Labour

The importance of clearly conceptualizing mental labour is obvious. It is obvious from the point of view of political theory since a socialist organization – contrary to a capitalist one – must fuse in each position both material and mental labour. It is also obvious from a sociological point of view, since categories such as "manual labour" or "blue-collar vs. white-collar workers," etc. stand on theoretical quicksands. It is obvious from an economic point of view, from the point of view of exploitation, since mental labour has become a very important branch of the economy, an important source of surplus value not crystallized in material objects. And it is obvious from an ideological point of view, since not only the outcome of mental labour – i. e. knowledge at whatever level of complexity – but mental labour itself carries, by its very nature, an ideological content. Since this latter is perhaps the most controversial point of all, I shall try to illustrate it by briefly considering the example of information technology.

With the increasing computerization of the production process grows also the importance of a new type of mental labour: data processing and information technology. In my view, the specificity of this new form of mental labour resides not in the nature of the knowledge transformed and produced (data, symbols, signs, "formal" concepts, etc.). These are features common also to other types of mental labour. Rather, this specificity resides in the fact that for the first time *a machine,* the computer, and *a mechanical language* are *indispensable for mental labour and thus stamp with their nature the content of conception.* Let us elaborate on this fundamental point.

First, since the computer is indispensable for data processing and information technology, and since the computer is a machine which, like all machines, works on the basis of mechanical processes (and this applies both to the hardware and to the software), the *mental labour* necessarily required by it as well as the knowledge produced by this mental labour *rest upon a mechanical and formalized way of reasoning,* as opposed to a substantive and dialectical one. This mechanical and formalized way of reasoning is *inherent* in the computer and reveals the capitalist nature of this machine[12]. Elsewhere, I have called this way of reasoning "software reasoning" and I have stressed some features characterizing it (G. Carchedi 1987: 239). In short, just as certain machines force people to use their body in a certain way and only in that way, the computer forces people to reason (to use their minds) in a certain way and only in that way.

An analogy can be found in the development of the modern musical notation from the system of neumes in use before the ninth century. These signs vaguely indicated the outline of the melodic movement so that the singer had the utmost freedom of interpretation, and music had to be orally transmitted. It can be argued that the invention of the staff "freed music from its hitherto exclusive dependence on oral transmission" and that "it was an event as crucial for the history of Western music as the invention of writing was for the history of language" (Grout 1980: 63). This is true. But, at the same time, it can be argued that – contrary to the invention of writing – this new notation also set rigid limits to the singers' freedom of interpretation, i.e. on their ability to freely develop patterns of "musical thinking". The codifications of Guido d'Arezzo and of

---

[12] This point implies the thesis of the class character not only of machines but also of technique and of science. This is a very controversial point. Limits of space prevent me from properly arguing for this thesis. Two excellent collections of articles supporting the thesis of the social character of science can be found in Himmelstein and Woolhandler 1986 and in Levins and Lewontin 1985.

Philippe de Vitry forced people to "musically think" according to fixed patterns and only according to those patterns.

Second, the computer delimits not only the boundaries of mental labour and thus of conception; it also stamps with its character the way the products of mental labour are exchanged between people. For the first time in history, *communication must take place through a machine and through the language of the machine,* something which implies a great mechanization, impoverishment and standardization of language, communication and social contacts (B. Carchedi 1973–4). Moreover, this form of exchange of knowledge (communication) excludes *a priori* the incorporation in knowledge of both the "rational" and the "emotional" aspects of human personality.

The first two points have focused on the features inherent in the computer, i.e. on its *nature,* on the type of knowledge both required and produced by the computer and on the way in which that knowledge must be exchanged among people. Now I shall add a third and a fourth point on the capitalist *use* of the computer. Again, I shall focus on its specific features, rather than on the features it shares (even though in specific ways) with other machines (e.g. it is a "job killer", it is damaging to the labourers' health[13], it is a powerful element of ideological domination[14], etc.) when used by capital.

Third, the computer, unlike other machines, can be used at the same time both to depersonalize the individual labourer (since, as we have seen, he or she can communicate only through a machine and only through the language of the machine) and to personalize the control upon the individual labourer. In fact, this control takes place through the computer itself, i.e. the machine records with relentless precision all the data on the labourers' performance. Or, the computer is, at the same time, *both an instrument of labour and an instrument of control over labour*[15]. Moreover, the control made possible by the computer has the new and specific characteristic of being contemporaneous with production (e.g. data processing) instead of having to wait for the end of a pre-fixed period of time.

---

[13] But the study of these features can be highly instructive. For example, as B. Carchedi (1983–4) has found out, the computer requires high levels of concentration also for dequalified mental labour. This high level of nervous tension cannot be relaxed in the intervals of time during which the operator has to wait for the answers (commands) to appear on the screen. This is "dead" time for the labourer, time during which he or she does not work, at least according to the capitalist. Abnormal behaviours follow, like talking to the machine, threatening it, caressing it, etc.

[14] The computer spreads an ideology of competence: only those who have technical knowledge are entitled to take decisions for the collectivity (i.e. for those who have been excluded from that knowledge). Clearly, this is a mere justification of subordination. See, on this point, Rosanvallon (1976). Moreover, as Levins submit, "the ideology of expertise makes a matter of pride to consider only precise, quantitative information as real science while the rest is 'philosophy' (a bad word among positivistic scientists) or 'not my department'" (1986: 18. See also Siegel 1986).

[15] Something which does not imply that the time spent working with the computer coincide with the time spent, by other agents, controlling that work.

Fourth, the mental labour associated with the capitalist use of the computer is subjected to dequalification through the computer itself. Up to now, the deskilling of a type of labour using a certain machine (e.g. the production of food before the introduction of the assembly line) has always been the result of mental labour, conception, which did not need that machine as a material means of mental labour. The computer, on the other hand, both requires a certain type of mental labour and is one of the necessary means of mental labour through which that labour is dequalified[16].

As I have said above, it is not only the capitalist use of the computer and of the mental labour necessarily associated with it (information technology and data processing) which is in contradiction with a socialist organization of labour. This contradiction has deeper roots, it strikes roots in the capitalist nature of that knowledge, i.e. in the mechanical and formalized way of reasoning inherent in that type of mental labour (something which delimits the boundaries of conception) and in the impossibility to exchange the outcome of that conception other than through the machine and through the language of the machine. This, however, does not imply that the computer and its knowledge are only an instrument of domination of labour by capital; i.e. the computer can also be used to resist and fight against that domination.

To make this clear, a few remarks are needed on the class determination of science and technology. This is a very controversial and politically important subject with cannot be properly argued for here[17]. In what follows I can only give an indication of the argument supporting the thesis of the non-neutrality of science, technology and of knowledge as a social phenomenon (a) in general and (b) under capitalism.

Social phenomena[18] are determined, in a very complex and mediated way, by production relations. Under capitalism, production relations are contradictory. This means that the nature of social phenomena is also contradictory. More specifically, this means that social phenomena have dominant and secondary features. In terms of our analysis, this implies that they are instruments of domination by one class, group, etc. over another because of their dominant features; however, they can be instruments to resist that domination because of their secondary features. Or, in this view, the possibility for science and technology to be used by more than one class, group, etc. is explained not by abandoning the thesis of the class determination of knowledge but by developing that thesis.

It is because of these primary features that the computer and the mental labour

---

[16] As always, the introduction of a new machine in the production process dequalifies existing jobs (as a tendency) but also creates (as a counter-tendency) new qualified jobs. There is no space here to elaborate on this point. As far back as in Carchedi 1975, I have argued for a dialectical approach to the question as to whether the computer causes qualification or dequalification.

[17] The interested reader is referred to Carchedi 1987, especially chapters 1, 2 3 and 6.

[18] Thus not individual nor natural phenomena.

inextricably associated with it are ultimately incompatible with a socialist society (G. Carchedi 1984b, 1987: ch. 6). But it is because of the secondary features that information technology can be used to develop certain aspects of people's creativity, that computer aided instruments can be used to assist in navigation, that the diagnosis of rare illnesses can be facilitated by the use of computer programs, that computer aided machines can be used to lighten heavy, dangerous, unpleasant work, etc. But it should not be forgotten that these features are secondary and that in its dominant features the computer and its knowledge are instruments of domination over labour. It should, therefore, be clear that the alternative use of these elements of science and technique is possible and useful only on condition that this use is secondary and subordinate, that we never cease to develop the collective labourer's radically different view of reality (both social and natural) while, at the same time, using elements of existing knowledge to resist capital's domination and to operate a transition to a socialist system.

References

Bernstein, E., *Evolutionary Socialism.* New York, 1961. 1899

Braverman, H., *Labor and Monopoly Capital,* New York. 1974

Carchedi, B., Informatica come Tecnologia di Controllo Sociale, *Primo Maggio,* 19–20: 28–40 and 22: 3–16. 1983–4

Carchedi, G., On the Economic Identification of the New Middle Class, *Economy and Society* February: 1–87. 1975

Carchedi, G., The Logic of Prices as Values, *Economy and Society* 13, 4: 431–455. 1984a

Carchedi, G., Socialist Labour and Information Technology, *Thesis Eleven* 9: 74–97. 1984b

Carchedi, G., *Class Analysis and Social Research.* Oxford. 1987

Clegg, S., P. Boreham and G. Dow, *Class, Politics and the Economy.* London. 1986

Grout, D. J., *A History of Western Music.* London and Melbourne. 1980

Himmelstein, D. and S. Woolhandler (eds.), Science, Technology and Capitalism, *Monthly Review* July–August: 1–128. 1986

Kautsky, K., *Bernstein en het Sociaaldemokratisch Programma.* Amsterdam. 1899

Kautsky, K., Die Revision des Programms der Sozialdemokratie in Österreich, *Die Neue Zeit* 20: 68–82. 1901–2

Laclau, E. and C. Mouffe, *Hegemony and Socialist Strategy.* London. 1985

Lenin, V. I., *What is to be Done?* Moscow. 1902

Levins, R., Science and Progress: Seven Developmentalist Myths in Agriculture, in: Himmelstein, D. and Woolhandler, S. (eds.), pp. 13–21. 1986

Levins, R. and R. Lewontin, *The Dialectical Biologist.* Cambridge, Mass. 1985

Luxemburg, R., Organizational Questions of the Russian Socialdemocracy, in: Waters, 1970, pp. 112–130. 1904

Luxemburg, R., *The Mass Strike, the Political Party and the Trade Unions,* in: Waters (ed.), pp. 153–218. 1906

Marx, K., *Grundrisse.* London. 1973

Michels, R., *Political Parties.* New York, 1962. 1911

Müller, H., *Der Klassenkampf in der deutschen Sozialdemokratie.* Zürich. 1892

Rosanvallon, P., *L'Age de l'Automation.* Paris 1976

Siegel, L., Microcomputers: From Movement to Industry, in: Himmelstein, D. and Woolhandler, S. (eds.), pp. 110–118. 1986

Slater, D., Socialism, Democracy and the Territorial Imperative: Elements for a Comparison of the Cuban and Nicaraguan Experiences, *Antipode* 18 (2): 155–185. 1987

Thompson, P., *The Nature of Work.* London. 1983

Waters, M. A. (ed.), *Rosa Luxemburg Speaks.* New York. 1970

Against the Current: Organizational Sociology and Socialism

Stewart R. Clegg and Winton Higgins

The critical current in organization analysis has not only called into question the conservative assumptions of more orthodox organization theory, but also the purely cosmetic nature of what often passes for worklife reform. However, if has chosen to mount these attacks from essentialist starting points – the "division of labour" and "bureaucracy" – which circumscribe its theoretical critique of organizations in capitalist society. Consequently, critical organization theory has difficulty in being coupled to a political project which generates a confrontation with capitalism based on criteria of socio-economic re-organization, in which mutually dependent criteria of democracy and efficiency are operative. By default, it ends up endorsing functionalist fatalism.

1. Introduction

The debate between orthodox organization theory and its radical critics has degenerated into a dialogue of the orthodoxly deaf with the radically blinkered. The course of this degeneration is a constantly recurring one in intellectual life, which Weber identified, in "Science as a Vocation," when he noted that the world of scholarship unearths many facts which are "inconvenient" for deeply held values (Weber 1948: 147). Like many of their colleagues on other disciplines, some sociologists try to avoid the inconvenience by embracing the empiricism of small, unthreatening facts, while others retreat behind the cannons of tradition. In this article we invite the radical critics in organization analysis to squarely face a measure of inconvenience in some organizational aspects of late capitalism. Against the defenders of orthodoxy (Donaldson 1985; Shenkar 1984), we argue that the inconveniences are not insuperable obstacles to "socialism," as Weber imagined. Moreover, in overcoming them, the radical theorists could serve their own political values far more effectively, as well as add to the discomforts of orthodox theory.

Weber never anticipated that "socialism" could ever offer an antidote to bureaucracy. Despite his opinion (but through his legacy), a number of scholars in recent years have produced what have come to be called "critical" perspectives on organizations in opposition to empiricist and conservative conceptions. Instead of simply reporting evident "facts," these critical scholars have increasingly turned to a study of the structures and processes taken to underlie the existence and non-existence of certain possible facts, an enquiry whose method is somewhat similar to Umberto Eco's (1983) puzzle-solving method of "abduction." Sometimes, however, puzzles may be solved too readily, evidence found too close at hand or "inconvenient" facts avoided.

2. Critical Sociology, Socialism and Organizations

Critical sociology of organizations has honed in on the central concerns of the orthodoxy, the design and rational structuring of organizations (Benson 1985; Donaldson 1985). Drawing on Marxist perspectives, it has taken "rational structuring" in organizations to task as an effect of capitalist domination. It champions the goal of autonomy as emancipation from domination. The critical school argues that the practical achievement of autonomy presupposes overthrowing "capitalism." Strategic conception oriented to this end must rupture notions of organization whose constitutive interest is in the "control" of objects (Habermas 1971). This argument has its problems. In rejecting the concern with "rational structuring" as itself a delusion of "capitalist theoretical hegemony," little space is left in which critics might rationally re-construct organizations in practice. The catchcry of autonomy subverts existing organizational design while tacitly denying the need for redesign in aid of substantive goals like democracy and efficiency.

Critical organization theory, then, in spite of its real achievements, has not yet contributed to a generalizable alternative practice of organizations. Some justification exists for this negativity. An essential objective of the critical exercise is to alert us to the unexamined and implicit assumptions of existing frameworks. It was in this way that a certain eminent Victorian left-Hegelian, for whom "critique" was rarely absent from the title page, developed his own analyses. However, Marx, in a famous thesis, warns us against merely negative dialectics; indeed, such a warning against analysis without transformative application is engraved upon his tombstone. This should alert us to a second meaning of "critical," as being decisive with respect to outcomes, in which some positive alternative does require proposal.

A major reason for the shortcomings of Marxist critical theory in organization analysis is that its critique is far too narrow. Its deficiency in this respect has two aspects, both relating to Marx's lineage from utopian socialist thought. On the one hand, classical Marxism and its derivatives have been subjected to a critique both *by* utopianism and *for* utopianism, as Anderson (1983: 97) has noted. With respect to contemporary Marxism, utopian critics most frequently focused on its narrow and utilitarian development in Eastern Europe after 1917 (although in a modified form the same charge surfaces in accusations against the reformism of social democracy), while Western Marxism since Lenin, through its characteristic focus on aesthetic and cultural questions rather than the social relations of material and more mundane production, may similarly be characterized by default as "utopian" in the negative sense.

This present-day cleavage in Marxism's evolution goes back to the debates over revisionism in the Second International, even if the practical utopianism of Luxemburg's, Pannekoek's and Gorter's "council communism" got lost in the process (Bricaner 1978; Carchedi 1987; Smart 1978). This vision survived only in Gramsci's participation in the Turin workers' council movement of 1921, and remained unquelled even during his long imprisonment (Gramsci 1971). On the one hand, social democracy seemed to cultivate a narrow, utilitarian form of political calculation premised on an accommodation to, and management of, capitalism. On the other hand, Bolshevism simply absolved the more inhuman aspects of capitalist organizational practice (through Lenin's enthusiasm for Taylorism and its presumed efficiency) taking it eventually to the further extreme of Stakhonovism (see Corrigan et al. (1981) on "the Bolshevik problematic").

Faced with these alternatives, some, not surprisingly, attempted to return to Marx to find a way out of the stalled de-Stalinization in the East and the disintegrating "long boom" in the West. However, Marx himself was not much help. In his few remarks on the organization of a socialist society, the residues of impractical utopianism were all too apparent. He reproduced notions characteristic of French utopian socialists such as St. Simon or Fourier, who imagined an overthrow of complexity and divisions of labour (Anderson 1983: 98). Subsequent, orthodox Marxists could ignore organizational questions as they waited for capitalism to collapse.

Such an alternative was clearly not open to critical, Marxian, organization theorists. Their problem has not so much been capitalism's inevitable demise, but its present, compelling, exhaustive ascendancy. Consequently, critical theory in organizations has displayed an unwarranted essentialism as part of a "principle of totality", characterized by sweeping statements about "capitalism" as a first cause (e.g. Braverman 1974; Clegg 1975, 1977, 1979; Salaman 1979). Having reduced phenomena to this single essence, many writers go on to reduce the essence itself – capitalism – to no more than an order of domination and subordination, centred on control of the division of labour.

Braverman (1974) exemplifies the analytical reduction of capitalism and the organization of the capitalist enterprise to a system of (unchallengeable) domination and (inescapable) subordination. His pessimism has left its stamp not only on many subsequent analyses of capitalist control but also on alternatives that these analyses have generated, as, for instance, in a number of articles by Ramsay (1977, 1983a, 1983b; Ramsay and Haworth 1984).

The corpus of work by Ramsay is of considerable critical importance in at least two respects. First, it debunks a great deal of liberal-humanist concern gesticulating at "radical reform". Second, it demonstrates how organizational reforms have often been attempts (albeit inefficient and ineffective ones) at securing consent and building it into otherwise unchanged forms of control. However, Ramsay's essentialism wields too blunt an instrument in his amorphous notion of domination, something that rules out crucial differentiations between policies pursued through deceptively similar reforms. He thus uses a Marxist argument to reject reforms as such – including ones which, we will argue, derive from a wider Marxist critique. He and Howarth write:

> [...] in the actual creation of socialist relations, a change in ownership relations (or to Marxist hands on the levers of a state "machine") in isolation from other transformations has little meaning. The division of labour (particularly of mental and manual work), the experience of control at the workplace, the production of goods for use rather than exchange, and the very relations embodied in the nature of the state must all be transformed. To seek incremental changes as if these dimensions were separate spheres or their development could be raised notch by notch is, we believe, an absurdity as a means to create socialism in the real world of class struggles. To change ownership and leave the division of labour intact and unchallenged for example, merely recreates capitalist relations at the workplace. [...] workers cannot hope to transform their position in isolation from the political economy of the system in which they live, produce, and trade their labour and the wages received in return for it (Ramsay and Haworth 1984: 314).

Certainly British socialists in particular have found little to celebrate in the public corporation that constitutes a monument to their traditional obsession with nationalization (although as Tomlinson (1982) and Williams et al. (1985) show, its failure owes more to poor socialist policy than to the capitalist demon). But fundamental problems arise out of this widespread assumption that the division of labour belongs to the essence of capitalism and must also go when the latter is abolished; or at very least it must be so completely "transformed" as to lose its presently ubiquitous features of complexity, scale and hierarchy.

A basic theme of this chapter is that this view of the division of labour over-totalizes the power of capitalism in ascribing to it a seamless functional unity, establishes unrealistic criteria for organizational change, and thus prejudges all organizational reform. At times the prejudice takes explicit aprioristic form. For example, Ramsay and Haworth (1984: 311) justify their rejection of the Swedish wage-earners' funds scheme for collective ownership of capital (to which we shall return) because "if it should come to constitute a real threat to capital, the latent forces of repressive domination could be marshalled to eradicate or neutralize it." It sounds like *Catch 22* (Heller 1962; Perry 1984): defeat is the ultimate test of the system transforming potential of any reform. Logically, reformism cannot impinge on the essence of capitalism.

Ramsay and Haworth fail to distinguish between the form and intent of a particular *proposal*, like industrial democracy or wage-earners' funds, and the fragments of legislation and actual changes in routine practice in which it has to be implemented *over time*. Stop the clock at any moment and the results may not seem too impressive when measured against an ideal. But, as Etzioni (1960) advised us long ago, organiziational goals are better judged in terms of the effectiveness of their achievements by reference to past or competitor perform- ance, than to some ideal model. Only over the long term and in hindsight can one ever know where a line of development was leading, and even that knowledge needs revising from time to time as the historian's craft requires. The point of the ideal is not to stand in judgement on poor realities but to provide what Wigforss called a "provisional utopia," an achievable vision of a better future (Tilton 1984). Ramsay and Haworth's critique of reformist organizational creativity never comes to grips with the internal organizational dynamic, and the evidence against reformist proposals is purely circumstantial – they are products of the state, they appear when the – essentially capitalist – economy is in "crisis" (pre- sumably to save it from the latter), when the all-powerful bourgeoisie does not crush them, and so on. This leaves them with an awkwardness they are at pains to underplay but which they muse over explicitly at one point in their article (Ram- say and Haworth 1984: 311): why do those articulated capitalist interests (who positively embrace organization theory) wax so histrionic against reformist pro- posals like wage earners' funds?

3. Socialism and Organizations: Beyond Catch 22

Ramsay and Howarth take up the Swedish wage-earners' funds proposal to illus- trate the vanity of reformism. In the Swedish reformist tradition, the concept of collective capital formation comes from its leading theoretician, Wigforss, who fundamentally reworked Bernsteinian revisionism (Higgins 1985a and b). The doctrinal shift which Wigforss introduced illuminates not only the thrust of the recent fund proposal, but also the trajectory of the political unionism that launched it as part of the attempt to transform capitalism through piecemeal organizational redesign.

It is worth recalling here why Bernstein in particular took upon himself the odium of challenging "orthodox Marxism" in the international Marxist move- ment, for we would argue that many present-day Marxist theorists are caught in the same intellectual bind and political limbo as the old orthodoxy (even if they have done more than their forbears to raise their predicament to the level of an art form!). Working from deterministic theses about inevitable class polarization and crisis under capitalism, the orthodoxy announced three "guarantees" of history – capitalism's self-destruction, the working classes coming demographic dominance, and, given continued agitation and propaganda, socialist political dominance on that demographic basis (Salvadori 1979). For the orthodox, be it noted, it was capitalism's *macro*-economic irrationality that would precipitate the terminal "crisis" of mature capitalism: at the point of production the bourgeoisie ran a tight ship whose presumed technical sophistication and organizational efficiency would fall like ripe fruit into socialist laps. (This belief, of course, underpinned Lenin's conversion to Taylorism.)

In hindsight, this last point was an astonishing and self-defeating concession. For western labour movements this concession has left the bitter and enduring legacy of complicity in economic-liberal policy, with which it shares the implicit assumption that capitalist organization necessarily spells effective enterprise (Higgins 1985a, 1985b). Secure in the belief that the final, cataclysmic crisis of capitalism was only just around the corner, "orthodox Marxism" also remained secure in its disinclination to concede the importance of organizational questions. Its fatalistic vision led inexorably to a politics of abstention.

Bernstein demolished the "guarantees of history" to make way for a new interventionist socialist politics. His classic *Evolutionary Socialism,* though concerned mainly with an argument about social democracy's wider political role, contains suggestive *obiter dicta* on organizational questions (Bernstein 1961: 139; see also 163). But Bernstein stopped halfway. His attack on determinism did not extend to upsetting the orthodox assumption that capitalism had still to mature – that is, still had a progressive future – before it would be meaningful to propose transformative (as opposed to ameliorative) policies. Pending this mystical maturation, reformist interventions such as social policy or industrial democracy rested on a merely ethical-liberal basis. In other words, Bernstein stopped short of a critique of capitalism's organizational effectiveness and thus could not forge the link between democratization and economic renewal.

This is precisely the link that Wigforss latched onto in the 1920s. Armed with Marx's conceptualization of capitalism's "irrationality", Wigforss imbided the lessons of the then ongoing "rationalization movement" which uncovered – albeit sympathetically – the organizational roots of industrial dislocation and inefficiency in the capitalist enterprise. Two of the themes which the movement articulated drew Wigforss' attention. First, forms of financial calculation in the enterprise conflicted with the technical and organizational preconditions of an efficient manufacturing process. Second, typical authority relations and reward systems tended to produce inefficient work practices. Wigforss concluded that these disorders were *systemically induced,* flowing inescapably from two aspects of private ownership of industry – the profit principle and the necessarily authoritarian forms by which, as Weber (1978) had already noted, the outside owners' interests and prerogatives were imposed on a working collectivity. Here, then, was a whole new dimension of "critique" in addition to the critique of capitalism's macro-economic irrationality.

Where Bernstein had talked about "organized capitalism", Wigforss (later joined by his colleague, Gunnar Myrdal) repeatedly took up the cudgels against capitalist "*dis*-organization" (especially Myrdal 1934; also see Eyerman 1985). For Wigforss, these considerations completely reversed social democracy's programmatic presuppositions. Capitalism no longer had a progressive future and socialists had no business tinkering with ameliorative reforms while awaiting the great day of maturation (or "crisis") and leaving capital in control of the enterprise and resource allocation. The former had now to be democratized and the latter brought under social control. Socialism, in his celebrated phrase, had to be brought forward as "the working hypothesis" of day-to-day policymaking rather than left to Sunday outings to Utopia. Transformational reforms had to go on the immediate agenda. Wigforss was to bring together the issues of *organizational effectiveness* and *control*. "It is a curious blindness," he wrote, "not to see that the organization of economic life is at the same time a question of forms of control" (Wigforss 1981: IX: 63).

In the 1920s, leading elements of the Swedish union movement agreed with Wigforss that capitalism constituted a deteriorating basis for the organization of the modern industry it itself had created. The labour movement presented itself not simply as a challenger to capital's *control* of the economy and enterprise, but more particularly as the bearer of sounder *organizational principles* and social priorities upon which to place a more advanced economy and enterprise (de Geer 1978; Hadenius 1976).

None of this, of course, could make any sense to Marxists of an older school who still assumed that efficiency belonged to the essence of capitalism. Not unlike managers and management theorists then and now, they equated greater managerial control of the labour process with higher productivity, and they inevitably mistook the pursuit of organizational efficiency as subservience to capitalism, as class collaboration. Two perverse contemporary contrasts to Wigforssian social democracy make this point plain enough. In the early 1920s, while Wigforss himself was trying to generate an offensive for industrial democracy, that bastion of orthodox Marxism, Lenin, was introducing Taylorism into the USSR – its bourgeois credentials sufficed to establish its claim to technical efficiency. In the first years of the depression, while Wigforss was leading the onslaught against economic liberalism in Sweden, in Britain the leftist Labour leader and Prime Minister, MacDonald, was defending *laissez-faire* as "old, sound socialist doctrine" and declaring that his party was "not concerned with patching up the rents in a bad system, but with transforming Capitalism into Socialism" (cited in Winch 1969: 123–124). The actual outcome of posing socialism's choices in this way are too notorious to be laboured here.

The labour movement that consolidated its ascendancy in Sweden from the 1930s on, did not attempt to build socialism overnight. Rather, like good Marxists, they followed the text of the "Preface" and set themselves only such tasks as they could solve (Marx 1968). The early tasks thus posed were nonetheless impressive – reorganization of public economic management and of the labour market and intervention into the distribution of access to education and health care. But in the 1950s and 1960s Wigforss kept prodding the movement towards its central task, reorganization of the economy itself along democratic collectivist lines in order to eradicate "that economic organization, those forms of property rights and control over the material foundations of social life as a whole, which we are accustomed to call bourgeois' (Wigforss 1981: IX. 430). He revamped this central task in terms of "economic democracy" as a counterweight to the widespread complacency that held up welfareism as the harbinger of "post-capitalist" society, a complacency which begged the whole question of economic organization.

Wigforss broke this central task down into two *interdependent* parts – democratization of work life (industrial democracy) and democratization of control over productive resource (economic democracy). His work during the 1920's on the former anticipated the labour movement's offensive into worklife organization from the beginning of the 1970s. Strategically this was an offensive informed by the inseparable objectives of worklife democratization: on the one hand, greater productive efficiency than capitalist authoritarianism could achieve, and on the other hand, the intention of making workers fully fledged "citizens" in economic as well as political life (Wigforss 1981: V: 387). In the mid-1950s, in aid of economic democracy, he advocated experimentation with collective capital formation in terms that prefigure the Swedish union confederation LO's wage-earner fund proposal of 1976.

It is highly significant that both these initiatives were triggered by the greater salience capitalist "disorganization" assumed with the end of the long boom, as well as with the coming of the conglomerate and others forms of centralization and internationalization of capital. Both represent a serious, in some cases a mortal, threat to an industrial economy as such (but not to capital), with industrial disinvestment and technological dependence at home, and relocation of vital aspects of now internationalized production processes to the labour-repressive "Newly Industrial Countries." In this present period, it is not without interest to go back to Wigforss' intellectual strategy to see how the more percipient, industrially oriented friends of capitalism grapple with these problems.

In dramatic contrast to the ageless catalogue of woes, including unions, wages, taxes, "big" government and its "interference," which economic liberals are trotting out yet again to explain capitalism's nonfeasance, management theorists like those around the *Harvard Business Review* pin the blame on management itself, its self-defeating forms of calculation, and the elitist forms of organization it generates (e.g. Hayes and Abernathy 1980; and Hayes and Wheelwright 1984). Unless one believes in the resurrection of the dead, as they do in proposing the exhumation of Schumpeter's long-defunct hero-entrepreneur as the answer to manufacturing decline, one has to see these problems as endemic in capitalist industrialization and a suitable case for democractic-socialist re-organization (Higgins 1986; also see Higgins and Clegg 1988).

We are concerned here with the strategic thrust of the Wigforssian element in Swedish social democracy, rather than historical outcomes that have been conditioned by many extraneous factors. We would have to go well beyond the limits of this article to assess either how far this element has informed applied policy or its success in achieving substantive reformist goals. It is, in alliance with the union movement, the important element in the struggle against economic liberalism among the social democrats.

4. Radical Organization Theory

These political debates have hardly percolated through to the sociological field of organization analysis. Debate here has been largely theoretical rather than oriented to practice, above all in the confrontation between a set of "conservative" positions about the "sociology of regulation" and the radical response, the "sociology of radical change" (Burrell and Morgan 1979). The few gestures to practical alternatives have either sought all-embracing social change or enclaves within capitalism.

The first of these alternatives, obviously the more ambitious and idealistic, sees the division of labour itself as an expression of the capitalist essence as we have seen in Ramsay and Haworth (1984). This is a notion that comes down to us in particular from the youthful Marx and Engels' (1965) *The German Ideology* of 1845–6. Had the mice been left to complete their gnawing criticism of this unpublished manuscript, later generations might have been spared such a marked obsession with the obolition of the division of labour as an essential talisman of socialist rectitude. For the young Marx, alienation of labour constituted the central feature of capitalism, and expressed itself in the latter's specific division of labour, which had to be suppressed if capitalism were to be overcome. This privileging of labour consigned politics – and any political theory of organization – to a secondary role at best (Feher 1984: 68).

Marx not only left no theory of organization as such; he left little room for one to develop. This has proved an unhappy circumstance for his followers and for those societies that have seen revolutions, in the name. In Russia, for instance, organic forms of revolutionary organization, confronted by a war-torn state and economy, were barely able to cope with the contingencies of some routines that no longer worked, overlain by ones which functioned all too well but in ways which were repugnant to the new values. Almost inevitably the "new societies" fell back on some "old techniques" (documented in Clegg and Dunkerley 1980: 113–118).

Various writers have papered over the theoretical absence in Marx, as Burrell and Morgan (1979) describe, with "anti-organization theory" and "radical organization theory" paradigms, but neither have contributed much to organizational design. Since these "radical structuralists" begin by declaring war on "the problematic of rational structuring" (Benson 1983), this disability is quite explicable: they have had nowhere else to go but back to a somewhat romantic radical idealism (exemplified by Braverman's (1974) own "romance of labour" (Cutler 1978)). Consequently, radical organization theorists have sought either the construction of socialist alternatives to advanced capitalism or the construction of alternative organizational forms within advanced capitalism itself.

5. Alternative Totalities: Alternative Organizations?

Apart from those few western intellectuals who remain attracted to the state-collectivist bureaucratism of the USSR (the nature of which has been analysed in organizational terms by Hirszowicz (1980)), few would hold up Russian social theory as a likely source for an alternative organizational practice. The more recent tendency has been to look to Mao, rather than Marx's Russian heirs, as a source of anti-bureaucratic socialist construction.

Post-revolutionary China has exercised a similar fascination for western intellectuals opposed to bureaucracy as did the China of the Emperors for some, like Weber, who held less sanguine views about the imminent transcendende of bureaucratic forms. Radical argument in organization analysis has seen bureaucracy as in some way an essential adjunct of capitalism. So China presents an interesting case both for those regard bureaucracy as functionally necessary and irreducible beyond a certain level, and those who regard bureaucracy as less a response "to functional imperatives rather than a political action" (Child 1972: 2). The latter argument, as it has gained currency in critical organization analysis, has tended to equate bureaucracy with the political action of capitalists against workers (e.g. Braverman 1974; Marglin 1974), rather than considering it as a more general set of organizational relations, capable of deployment as a resource in almost all of the many arenas of organizational life. In contrast, the former argument, asserting the inevitability of bureaucracy, has rested on a general, functionalist theory of contingency: bureaucracy arises to handle those problems it is the best available solution to: hence bureaucracy is functionally irreducible (e.g. Donaldson 1985; Shenkar 1984). We will look at show Shenkar in particular mounts his argument.

Two minimal characteristics of any definition of bureaucracy are "a specialized division of labour and the use of multiple rules" as Shenkar (1984: 289) has observed. The minimization of these through forms of "anti-bureaucracy" in China during the Cultural Revolution has been seen by Shenkar (1984: 290) as one "example of what the dismantling of bureaucracy may imply." The "ruinous consequences" are clear, he argues (Shenkar 1984: 297) suggesting that there was a lack of contingent fit between these principles of anti-bureaucracy and the tasks that the organizational structures created during the Cultural Revolution had to cope with (Shenkar 1984: 298). What emerges from this period in history, according to this analysis, is the conclusion that "Bureaucracy [. . .] is inevitable" (Shenkar 1984: 303).

We disagree with Shenkar (1984) on a number of points. The Cultural Revolution clearly had organizational effects, but it opposed not so much bureaucracy *per se* as the *Stalinist form* of legal rational bureaucracy developed in China during the early 1950s whose own inefficiencies, failures and "ruinous consequences" are well documented (Henley and Nyaw 1986). Far from being an attack on bureaucracy as such, it focused on something much more specific: bureaucratically devised and implemented party policies and highly centralized decision making. Mao charged that the industrialization process under the Soviet model was creating a "new class." These cadres had vested interests in furthering statist industrialization, interests which control of administrative office in a non-market setting gave free reign to. In his attempts at a Cultural Revolution, Mao intended to oppose these tendencies by marshalling local as against central interests, particularly through the "revolutionary committees." It is important to observe that while the Cultural Revolution weakened and humiliated state bureaucrats, it did so through further expansion of state power over economic markets, culture and society (Krauss and Vanneman 1985: 119). None of this is clear in Shenkar's (1984) account.

In making his argument, Shenkar falls prey to the common idealist fallacy of mistaking the rhetoric of the Cultural Revolution for its practice and seeing its effect as contingent upon the rhetoric. Certainly the Cultural Revolution was disastrous in a number of ways: much less certain, however, is the claim that these disasters were the result of organizations not functioning bureaucratically in a contingently correct mode. Indeed Shenkar (1984) falls into the same trap as many western radical intellectuals in their initial response to the Cultural Revolution (King 1977: 364). They took its central policy initiatives as alternative models of organization structure, and as thus giving the lie to the orthodox Weberian view of bureaucracy. But its aspirations were really more modest, to reform the organizations of the party, not those of the state or organizations generally (Hearn 1978: 46–47).

The post-1976 revelations about the "disasters" of the Cultural Revolution and the failure of its organizational anti-bureaucracy relate more closely to increasing political struggles after the deaths of Mao Zedung and Zhou Enlai, than to technically irreducible facets of organization, much as Child's (1972) argument would have suggested. As Lockett (1983) shows, organizational practice merely provided the arena in which political struggles were waged. Consequently, with the defeat of the Gang of Four's radical line, the forms through which their supporters had waged their struggle were to come under increasing attack.

Shenkar (1984) interprets the Cultural Revolution as a revolution against bureaucracy. It failed. In this failure he reads the functional inevitability of "bureaucracy." Events since 1976, he maintains, support this argument. In the post-1976 period there has been a widespread re-adoption of legal-rational bureaucratic models which stress the overall responsibility of the factory director under the leadership of the enterprise Party Committee. But we would suggest that this should not be taken to signal either bureaucracy's or functionalism's triumph.

The failure of the Cultural Revolution's interventions into the division of labour and its minimal rules proves nothing about the failure of a socialist, critical practice of organizations. To suggest otherwise would only indicate a mistaken idealist emphasis on the feasibility and necessity of eliminating divisions of labour and rules altogether. In practice, in China as elsewhere, socialist reconstruction has not done away with these aspects of organization, but has rather promulgated *different* divisions of labour, *different* rules, *different* forms of organization, including a movement from central hierarchy to local control, and a mixture of collective leadership and democratic management by workers under direct leadership by the factory director.

In this part of our discussion, this distinction is our main theoretical point. Shenkar (1984) is wrong to suggest that the Cultural Revolution was a revolution against bureaucracy *per se*. Accordingly, we also reject his claim that the Cultural Revolution is a "critical" test. Defining bureaucracy in terms of structural organizational characteristics and then imagining an antithesis to these in terms of the absence of such structural characteristics produces a remarkably skewed contest in which presence invariably will be easier to establish than absence. And what such negativity could look like is never spelled out.

The Chinese experience proves nothing about the inevitability of some postulated, immutable aspects of bureaucracy. It suggests rather the malleability of organizational forms. And it is on the basis of malleability that a critical theory of organizations must bite, rather than the pure opposition of an anti-organization theory. However, such negativity is not only found in revolutionary, socialist construction. It also turns up in advanced capitalism.

6. Anti-Organization Theory and Alternative Organizations

Where alternative organizational forms have been constructed within advanced capitalism, research demonstrates that they conform closely to some aspects of what Burrell and Morgan (1979: 322–323) call "anti-organization theory." Empirically, such organizations have been researched by Rothschild-Whitt (1979). It is important to bear in mind some sampling limitations with respect to organisation size in the "collectivist-clemantic organizations" researched: "most are small in size, containing under 10 or 20 members [...] [and] [...] often choose to remain small so that they can retain their democratic structure" (Rothschild-Whitt 1983: 398). Moreover, niche space is also important as well as size: "cooperatives have done best where they provided goods or services that were qualitatively different from those provided by mainstream organizations, and for which they therefore had no direct competition" (Rothschild-Whitt 1983: 401). If smallness of size and uniqueness of niche space have to be defining characteristics of an alternative organizational practice, then it will obviously not be generalizable in a modern industrial society. To the extent that a "minimalist" view of both the division of labour and of rules is maintained, then one actually serves to strengthen the functionalist arguments for bureaucracy (see Clegg and Dunkerley 1980: Ch. 6, for a discussion of these). Democracy and bureaucracy become antithetical concepts, with the former applicable only to small-scale operations in unconstrained niche space, while the latter is accepted as unavoidable in large-scale organizations in competitively constrained niches.

To conclude from studies of small-scale collectivist organizations that bureaucracy is functionally necessary everywhere else, is an effect of the "ultimate values' vested in such organizations, as a sample of post-1960s collectives would suggest. Characteristically, they operated with ideals of not only self-management but also self-finance: such ideals can only by expected to work well in small-scale labour-intensive sectors of the economy (Abell 1983: 95). Self-financing restricts size; given restricted size, quite idealistic conceptions of democracy can operate, albeit with costs of extensive time spent making it work, in emotionally intense settings involving members who not only embrace the ultimate values but ensure that other members embrace them as well.

Idealistic conceptions of democracy have a legitimate critical pedigree, of course, particularly in Marx's (1971) assessment of the Paris Commune. The "organicist" conception of democracy implicit in both "alternative" organization practice and Marx's theory finds its unity in the latter's conception of democracy, which circumscribes democratic possibilities as surely as todays anti-organization theory. As Feher puts it:

In order for all political functions to be perforemd by all citizens (which is the only theoretically conceivable state in which the isolated political sphere is abolished or transcended), the following conditions would have to be met. Small, indeed, minimal, political units are vital. But everyone's perfect political freedom and political equality are equally necessary. So also absolute emancipation – not of labour, but everyone's absolute emancipation from labour, in other words, a non-working population. A total transparence of all political functions is equally a precondition, together with the indispensable training of everyone's political view. Finally, everyone should be a co-proprietor of each and every unit of property within a given framework. Not all of these requirements contain elements that would run counter to our contemporary vision and understanding of democratic socialism. However, several of them are unrealizable or hardly realizable in separation, and all of them in conjunction cannot represent a viable goal (Feher 1984: 72).

The least insuperable element of these requirements, although still problematic, is the property relation.

7. Property Relations/Economic Democracy

There are a number of ways, with associated problems, in which economic democracy, through collective ownership and control, can function. The simplest, most prevalent and most problematic are self-financed, self-managed organizations (such as those studied by Rothschild-Whitt (1979) and Sandkull (1984)). The problems with these, as has been argued, are that they tend to be an adequate organizational form only in small-scale, labour intensive, low capitalized and relatively uncompetitive sectors of the economy. These limitations can be overcome to some extent, by backwards and forward linkages with other collectivist producers/distributors, as well as through the support of a middle clas professional base, allied to a broader social movement orientation, such as feminism (Sandkull 1984), or an unusually large-scale cooperative movement like Mondragon (Bradley and Gelb 1983). But the amounts of capital raised will be small where self-financing is the norm; moreover, this practice concentrates risks of capital loss; loss of income, and loss of livelihood in the same labour managed process. Where capital inputs are allowed on some principle other than a fixed amount of capital per person, there will also be the potential for inegalitarianism to form within the organization.

One way of maintaining an egalitarian organization with a greater propensity for capital formation is, as Abell (1983) suggests, to move to some version of external financing through some form of collective or state capital. Equality needs to be not only intra-organizational, but also societal. The pursuit of equality and the pursuit of efficiency are, as Wigforss demonstrated, inter-dependent values. Where forms of calculation guide investment on these two principles, social capital can enforce technical-rational efficiency through input/output ratios in order to promote system-wide equity. Inefficient organization should not be subsidized. On this basis the formal properties of a collectivist organization and a macro-economic planning of efficient allocation of resources can be achieved. Morever, this does not restrict the possibility of economic democracy being extended to large, capital intensive as well as to small, labour intensive organisations. In the former case, however, the owner collectivity does not correspond to the worker collectivity, even if it overlaps it. Just as each of these collectivities is indispensable to the other, so democratization processes in the economic and industrial spheres, respectively, are interdependent.

Debates in Sweden over "wage-earners' funds" (Meidner 1978) suggest a policy whereby economic democracy can be extended to not only small and inconsequential organizations but also large and important ones. The proposals for wage-earners' funds grew out of the need to reinforce the solidarity wage policy against the economic instability at the end of the long boom (Higgins 1980; Öhman 1983). But as we have seen, the concept goes back to Wigforss, who saw a legislated collective capital formation as an element of transitional strategy (Higgins 1985b). It would progressively outflank private capital formation in advanced capitalism, thereby extending wage-earner influence to strategic decision making in the enterprise and to the allocation of resources. A percentage of profits in the form of share issues would be diverted to a wage-earners' fund for all enterprises over a given size (Meidner 1978) suggested 50–100 employees). The effected voting rights would be exercised in the interests of wage-earners, and in accordance with the social priorities of their organizations. Capital would gradually be democratized as majority ownership passes to the collective. A number of regionally based funds, subject to some central influence, would control the placement of collectivized capital. This was the theory.

8. Organizational Relations/Organizational Democracy

Let us now look at the second question raised by "organicist" democrats, internal organizational relations. The chances of decision making being directly democratic varies with the heterogeneity and number of members of the organization, according to the research into "alternative organizations" cited previously. We may also add that the degree of democracy varies inversely with the degree of task diversity (Clegg 1983: 25–31).

In any fairly large or complex organization direct democracy will be unachievable. More representative forms of democracy would have to operate. As a consequence of these considerations Horvat (1983: 280) argues that the basis of organizational democracy would have to be a "work unit" which, in line with organicist arguments for direct democracy, "ought to be sufficiently small and homogeneous so as to make possible face-to-face interactions, informal communications and interpersonal contacts among members." Several of these could co-exist at the same horizontal level, but at the next level a "workers' council" should be established to decide on issues which emerge as a result of the decision of one work-unit impinging on another.

Work units would conform to principles of immediacy, both in terms of numbers of members and also in terms of relative homogeneity of members' interests. Works councils would conform to principles of democratic mediation of heteronomous work units and their interests. These two moments of democracy, Horvat (1983) suggests, have to be combined with principles which serve to guarantee that both democracy *and* efficiency are achieved simultaneously. Because some members may prove recalcitrant, "rights must be matched by sanctions' by ensuring that decision-making actors have to bear responsibility for the decisions made" (Horvat 1983: 281). Task discontinuity can be recognized in the principle that the "implementation of decisions – executive work and administration – is a matter of professional competence, not of democracy" (Horvat 1983: 281).

Clearly, there is a whole tradition from Marcuse (e.g. 1964) to Habermas (e.g. 1973) as well as that centered on Castoriadis (e.g. 1984) which argues that "professional-technical competence" and the "division of labour" are the source of all original sin in organizations, inasmuch as domination, masquerading as technical rationality, can enter, shape and distort social relations. It is from this tradition, in part, that arguments which oppose the division of labour derive much of their force. While not ignorant of this tradition, which is, indeed, one to which we have contributed (cf. Clegg 1975, 1979; Clegg and Dunkerley 1980), there is reason to think it over-drawn.

Writers in this tradition such as Castoriadis (1984) identify capitalism or state socialism, understood as forms of domination, with modern industry; to reject domination is thus to reject modern industry. In effect, this is what both Castoriadis' (1984) ecological socialism and Marcuse's (1964) critique of rationality amount to. Against this one must insist that some division of labour is functionally efficient and that a complex, organizationally based society can not abolish it and maintain the same quality and quantity of *per capita* outputs. What is critical is the realization that the existing distribution of skills do not create inviolable rights, power and monopoly as a basis for occupational and personal aggrandizement. A considerable body of empirical research, particularly in Sweden (e.g. Dahlström et al. 1966; Dahlström 1978; Gardell 1971), points to the technical superiority of some divisions of labour over others, building on the work of earlier socio-technical researchers, but emphasizing the work-reform potential of local, shopfloor expertise rather than outside consultants (Dahlström 1978: 81–82). Thus local initiatives can produce professional-technical competence *in* the division of labour so that it is not *imposed* upon the latter (Dahlström 1977) and skills can be regenerated and redistributed by the worker collectivity itself (Mathews 1985).

Administration and legislation are not the only functional requirements of a democratic organization: adjudication and control must also be built in: Adjudication is a two-way process between individuals and collectivities. Each, on occasion, may require protection from the actions of the other. A grievance commission might be formed to adjudicate any individual-initiated sense of injustice, while a work responsibility commission would adjudicate collectivity-initiated complaints of individual irresponsibility. The commissions would be legal-rational juridical subjects whose chairpersons would sit on the organization's supervisory committee, along with elected representatives of the work units. It is here that the function of control would be vested. As Horvat (1983: 286) puts it, this supervisory committee has an overall control function: it scrutinizes all decisions and their documentary basis; it subjects the organization to a detailed multifaceted audit. "However, the committee is not only an instrument of control and an unpleasant critic of management, it can also serve as a powerful instrument to an energetic and enterprising management" (Horvat 1983: 286).

Conflict can arise not only in the application of rules but also in their interpretation. Horvat proposes a council of reference as an external arbitration authority which will clarify legal rights and obligations. Further conflict may arise not only within the democratic organization but also between its decisions and those of other elements of a democratic economy and society. How can intra-organizational democratic rights be reconciled with inter-individual, inter-organizational and inter-societal equity?

Perhaps the most important aspect of economic democracy concerns those constituencies which it does not enfranchise, above all the unemployed and non-waged workers (particularly those with domestic responsibilities) of whom the greatest number presently are women. Beyond the single organization's internal democratic procedures the other organizations within a given "region" should be represented, together with proportional representation for the unemployed in a regional political assembly, which in turn will elect representatives to the central legislative assembly (as well as delegates also being nominated directly). Each of these three distinct levels – the society; the region, the organization, – will have inputs into the overarching developmental questions of future capital formation and investment, through the regional funds.

Organizations, although continuing some of their inter-relations through markets, should not be subject wholly to market dictates. Organizational revenues earned through markets will consist of three parts: a wages fund; an investment fund and a collective fund. Central, indicative planning would allocate resources between them. The central planning mechanism would be something like an Economic Planning and Advisory Council organized on both a central and an industry basis, as a body reporting to the central legislative assembly. It would formulate the framework for the whole exercise of indicative planning.

9. Conclusion

We put forward this constitutional sketch as a "provisional utopia" in the Wigforsian sense. It would clearly have to be adapted to the various structures of national financial markets, and the economic and organizational linkages characteristic of given state formations, reinforced against the potential for subversion of such a reconstruction that existing markets and linkages possess. We acknowledge these obstacles; we are aware that others regard them as insuperable (Block 1977). Elsewhere, it has been argued that such obstacles, under particular propitious political circumstances, can be challenged (Clegg et al. 1986: 285–390; Korpi 1983) where a counter-hegemonic labour movement has developed. This suggests a different strategy of organizational design to one premised purely on the organization level of analysis. Accepting the "political" critique concerning the determination of organization structure from authors such as Child (1972), we would propose that the politics of organizations be purposively linked to the political level. This is not to commit an "ecological fallacy" but to suggest that the interpenetration of organizational analysis and political theory in their focus on an organizational level is more often than not lost in the division between politics and economics.

The "provisional utopia" will neither eliminate rules or the division of labour; in this sense, it will not eradicate "bureaucracy" at all. To presume to do so would be chimerical. What it will achieve is a form of bureaucracy – administration by office and rules – which is not premised on hierarchy but on collectivity; not on authoritarianism but on democracy: a new ideal type of a bureaucratic, democratic and collectivist organization with in-built safeguards for the integrity of the individual – an organizational type which is rather more conspicuous by its absence than its presence in either contemporary critical theory or routine practice.

In conclusion, the argument presented here has several fundamental aspects. First, any adequate political strategy has to be one which is rooted in a conception of how economy and society should be re-organized and their organizations redesigned to meet the twin criteria of efficiency and democracy. Second, the development of new organizational structures is not a mere rationalistic search for new functionalist forms but is instead fundamentally political. It cannot be argued that the search is in vain because of the functionalist predetermination of any possible organization structure. Third, both the conception of, and the struggle for, new organizational forms must challenge the political and managerial defence of capitalism. As Weber (1948, p. 152) noted "the ultimately possible attitudes towards life are irreconcilable [...]. Thus it is necessary to make a decisive choice". The basic objection to critical perspectives on organization analysis as they have developed thus far is that they fail to prepare the struggle their choices propose.

References

Abell, P., The Viability of Industrial Producer Co-Operation, in: C. Crouch and F. Heller (eds.), *International Year Book of Organizational Democracy*. Volume 1. London: Wiley, pp. 73–103. 1983

Abrahamsson, B., *Bureaucracy or Participation: The Logic of Organisation*. London: Sage. 1977

Abrahamsson, B. and A. Broström, *The Rights of Labour*. London: Sage. 1980

Anderson, P., *In the Tracks of Historical Materialism*. London: Verso. 1983

Andors, S., Revolution and Modernization: Man and Machine in Industrializing Society, the Chinese Case, in: E. Friedland and M. Selden (eds.), *America's Asia*. New York: Pantheon, pp. 393–444. 1971

Benson, J. K., Paradigm and Praxis in Organizational Analysis, *Research in Organizational Behaviour* 5: 33–56. 1983

Berner, B., *Teknikens värld. Teknisk förändring och ingenjörsarbete i svensk industri*. Lund: Arkiv. 1981

Bernstein, E., *Evolutionary Socialism*. New York: Schocken. 1961

Block, F., The Ruling Class, Does not Rule: Notes on the Marxist Theory of the State, *Socialist Revolution* May–June: 6–28. 1977

Bradley, K. and A. Gelb, *Cooperative Industrial Relations: The Mondragon Experience*. London: Heinemann. 1983

Braverman, H., *Labor and Monopoly Capital*. New York: Monthly Review Press. 1974

Bricaner, S., *Pannekoek and the Workers' Councils*. St. Louis, Mo.: Telos Press. 1978

Broström, A., *MBL:s Gränser*. Stockholm: Arbetslivscentrum. 1982

Burawoy, M., *Manufacturing Consent*, Chicago: University of Chicago Press. 1979

Burrell, G. and G. Morgan, *Sociological Paradigms and Organisational Analysis*. London: Heinemann. 1979

Carchedi, G., *Class Analysis and Social Research*. Oxford: Basil Blackwell. 1987

Castoriadis, C., Marx Today: An Interview, *Thesis Eleven* 8: 124–32. 1984

Child, J., Organization Structure, Environment and Performance: The Role of Strategic Choice, *Sociology* 6: 1–22. 1972

Clegg, S., *Power, Rule and Domination*. London: Routledge & Kegan Paul. 1975

Clegg, S., *The Theory of Power and Organisation*. London: Routledge & Kegan Paul. 1979

Clegg, S., Organizational Democracy, Power and Participation, in: C. Crouch and F. Heller (eds.), *International Yearbook of Organizational Democracy*. London: Wiley, pp. 3–34. 1983

Clegg, S., P. Boreham and G. Dow, *Class, Politics and the Economy*. London: Routledge and Kegan Paul. 1986

Clegg, S. and D. Dunkerley (eds.), *Critical Issues in Organizations*. London: Routlege and Kegan Paul. 1977

Clegg, S. and D. Dunkerley, *Organization, Class and Control*, London: Routledge and Kegan Paul. 1980

Corrigan, P., H. Ramsay and D. Sayer, Bolshevism and the USSR, *New Left Review* 125: 45–60. 1981

Cutler, A., The Romance of Labour, *Economy and Society* 7, 1: 74–95. 1978

Dahlström, E., Efficiency, Satisfaction and Democracy in Work: Conceptions of Industrial Relations in Post-War Sweden, *Acta Sociologica* 20, 1: 25–53. 1977

Dahlström, E., The Role of Social Science in Working Life Policy: The Case of Post-War Sweden, in: H. Berglind, T. Hamish & E. Haayio-Mannila (eds.), *Sociology of Work in Nordic Countries: Themes and Perspectives*. Stockholm: The Scandinavian Sociological Association. 1978

Dahlström, E., B. Gardell, B. Rundblad and B. Windgard, Technical Change and Pleasure in Work, Mimeo. 1966

de Geer, H., *Rationaliseringsrörelsen i Sverige.* Stockholm: SAIS. 1978

Dickson, D., Technology and the Construction of Social Reality, *Radical Science Journal* 1: 29–50. 1984

Donaldson, L., *In Defence of Organization Sociology: A Response to the Critics.* Cambridge: Cambridge University Press. 1985

Dow, G., S. Clegg and P. Boreham, From the Politics of Production to the Production of Politics, *Thesis Eleven* 9: 16–32. 1984

Eco, U., *The Name of the Rose.* New York: Martin Secker and Warburg. 1983

Etzioni, A., Two Approaches to Organizational Analysis, *Administrative Science Quarterly* 5: 257–78. 1960

Eyerman, R., Rationalizing Intellectuals: Sweden in the 1930s and 1960s, *Theory and Society*, 14, 6: 777–808. 1985

Feher, F., The French Revolution as Models for Marx's Conception of Politics, *Thesis Eleven* 8: 59–76. 1984

Fox, A., *Beyond Contact: Work, Power and Trust Relations.* London: Faben and Faben. 1974

Gardell, B., Production Techniques and Job Satisfaction, Mimeo. 1971

Gramsci, A., *Selection from the Prison Notebooks.* Edited and translated by Q. Hoare and G. N. Smith. London: Lawrence and Wishart. 1971

Habermas, J., *Knowledge and Human Interests.* Translated by J. J. Shapiro. London: Heinemann. 1971

Habermas, J., *Toward a Rational Society.* London: Heinemann. 1973

Hadenius, A., *Facklig organisationsutveckling. En studie av Landsorganisationen i Sverige.* Stockholm: Rabén och Sjögren. 1976

Hayes, R. and S. Wheelwright, *Restoring Our Competitive Edge: Competing Through Manufacturing.* New York: Wiley. 1984

Hayes, R. and W. Abernathy, Managing Our Way to Economic Decline, *Harvard Business Review* 58; 4 (May–June): 67–77. 1980

Hearn, F., Rationality and Bureaucracy: Maoist Contributions to a Marxist Theory of Bureaucracy, *Sociological Quarterly* 19: 37–54. 1978

Heller, J., *Catch 22.* London: Corgi. 1962

Henley, J. and M.-K. Nyaw, Developments in Managerial Decision Making in Chinese Industrial Enterprises, in: S. Clegg, D. Dunphy and G. Redding (eds.), *Organization and Management in East Asia.* Hong Kong: University of Hong Kong Press. 1986

Higgins, W., Class Mobilisation and Socialism in Sweden: Lessons from Afar, in: G. Dow and P. Boreham (ed.), *Work and Inequality.* Melbourne: Macmillan. 1980

Higgins, W., Unemployment and the Labour Movement's Breakthrough in Sweden, in: J. Roe (ed.), *Unemployment – Are there Lessons in History?* Sydney: Hale and Iremonger. 1985a

Higgins, W., Ernst Wigforss: The Renewal of Social Democratic Theory and Practice, *Political Power and Social Theory* 5: 207–250. 1985b

Higgins, W., Industrial Democracy and the Control Issue in Sweden, in: E. Davis and R. Lansbury (eds.), *Democracy and Control at the Workplace.* Melbourne: Longman Cheshire. 1986

Higgins, W. and S. R. Clegg, Enterprise Calculation and Manufacturing Decline, *Organization Studies* 9, 1: 69–89. 1988

Hirszowicz, M., *The Bureaucratic Leviathan*. London: Martin Robertson. 1980

Horvat, B., The Organizational Theory of Workers Management, in: C. Crouch and F. Heller (eds.), *International Yearbook of Organizational Democracy*, 1: pp. 279–302. 1983

King, A. Y.-C., A Voluntaristic Model of Organization: The Maoist Version and Its Critique, *BJS* 28: 363–74. 1977

Korpi, W., *The Democratic Class Struggle*. London: Routledge & Kegan Paul. 1983

Krauss, R. and R. Vanneman, Bureaucrats Versus the State in Capitalist and Socialist Regimes, *Comparative Studies in Society and History* 27: 111–22. 1985

Lockett, M., Organizational Democracy and Politcs in China, in: C. Crouch and F. Heller (eds.), *International Yearbook of Organizational Democracy*, 1. London: Wiley, pp. 539–636. 1983

Marcues, H., *One Dimensional Man*. London: Routledge and Kegan Paul. 1964

Marglin, S., What Do Bosses Do? – The Origins and Functions of Hierarchy in Capitalist Production, *Review of Radical Political Economy* 6: 60–112. 1974

Marx, K., *Marx and Engels' Selected Works*. London: Lawrence and Wishart. 1968

Marx, K., *On the Paris Commune, the Civil War in France*. Moscow: Progress. 1971

Marx, K. and F. Engels, *The German Ideology*. London: Lawrence & Wishart. 1965

Mathews, J., Technology, Trade Unions and the Labour Process, *Working Papers in the Social Studies of Science*. Melbourne: Deakin University. 1985

Meidner, R., *Collective Capital Formation Through Wage-Earner Funds*. London: Allen & Unwin. 1978

Myrdal, A. and G. Myrdal, *Kris i befolkningsfragan*. Stockholm: Rabén & Sjögren. 1934

Öhman, B., The Debate on Wage-Earners Funds in Scandinavia, in: C. Crouch and F. Heller (eds.), *International Yearbook of Organizational Democracy*, 1. London: Wiley, pp. 35–52. 1983

Perry, N., Catch, Class and Bureaucracy: The Meaning of Joseph Heller's *Catch 22*, *Sociological Review* 32, 4: 719–714. 1984

Ramsay, H., Cycles of Control: Worker Participation in Sociological and Historical Perspective, *Sociology* 11: 481–506. 1977

Ramsay, H., An International Participation Cycle: Variations on a Recurring Theme, in: S. Clegg; G. Dow and P. Boreham (eds.), *The State, Class and the Recession*. New York: St. Martins, pp. 257–317. 1983a

Ramsay, H., Evolution or Cycle? Worker Participation in the 1970's and 1980's, in: C. Crouch and F. Heller (eds.), *International Yearbook of Organizational Democracy*, 1. London: Wiley, pp. 203–26. 1983b

Ramsay, H. and N. Haworth, Worker Capitalists? Profitsharing, Capital Sharing and Juridical Forms of Socialism. *Economic and Industrial Democracy: an International Journal*, 5/3: 295–324. 1984

Rothschild-Whitt, J., The Collectivist Organization: An Alternative to Rational-Bureaucratic Models, *American Sociological Review* 44: 509–27. 1979

Rothschild-Whitt, J., Worker Ownership in Relation to Control: A Typology of Work Reform, in: C. Crouch and F. Heller (eds.), *International Yearbook of Organizational Democracy*. 1, London: Wiley, pp. 389–406. 1983

Salaman, G., *Work Organizations: Resistance and Control*. London: Longman. 1979
Salvadori, M., *Karl Kautsky and the Proletarian Revolution 1880–1938*. London: New Left Books. 1979
Sandkull, B., Managing the Democratization Process in Work Cooperatives, *Economic and Industrial Democracy* 5, 3: 359–390. 1984
Shenkar, O., Is Bureaucracy Inevitable? The Chinese Experience, *Organizational Studies* 5, 4: 289–306. 1984
Smart, D. A., *Pannekoek and Gorter's Marxism*. London: Pluto Press. 1978
Tilton, T. A., Utopia, Incrementalism & Ernest Wigforss' Conception of a Provisional Utopia, *Scandinavian Studies* 56, 1: 36–54. 1984
Tomlinson, J., *The Unequal Struggle? British Socialism and the Capitalist Enterprise*. London: Methuen. 1982
Weber, M., Science as a Vocation, in: H. Gerth and C. W. Mill (eds.), *From Max Weber: Essays in Sociology*. London: Routledge and Kegan Paul, pp. 129–56. 1948
Weber, M., *Economy and Society: An Outline of Interpretive Sociology*. 2 vols., G. Roth and C. Wiltich (eds.), Berkeley: University of California Press. 1978
Wigforss, E., *Skrifter i urval*. Stockholm: Tiden. 1981
Williams, K., C. Haslam, T. Cutler, A. Wardlow and J. Williams, Accounting Failure in the Nationalized Enterprises – Coal, Steel, and Cars Since 1970, Mimeo, Department of Economic History, University of Wales, Aberystwyth. 1985
Winch, D., *Economics and Policy*. New York: Walker & Co. 1969

Political Domination and Reproduction of Classless Organizations

Amir Ben-Porat

I

This article deals with the reproduction of classless organization, within a society which is dominated by a capitalist mode of production. It deals with the conditions which enable the coexistence of two or more modes of production. The problem of coexistence of two or more modes of production within the same society is known in the literature as "the problem of articulation of modes of production" (Foster-Carter 1978; Wolpe 1980; Wright 1983). This paper is particularly concerned with the conditions which make the emergence of articulation possible, and the mechanisms which maintained articulation in the Jewish community in Palestine before and after the establishment of the state of Israel in 1948. It also discusses the articulation between the Kibbutz – treated as a socialist formation – and the capitalist modes of production which dominated the economy of the pre-state formation as well as the subsequent state formation.

Following the debate in the relevant literature (e. g. Albert and Hahnel 1978; Cohen 1978; Wright 1983), "mode of production" is here equated to the notion of a social formation integrating economic, political and ideological levels (Hindess and Hirst 1977; Poulantzas 1973). It is suggested firstly, that regarding mode of production or its extended version (Wolpe 1980) as a social formation is far more productive than other interpretations. Secondly, articulation between modes applies not only to the economic level, but also to the relatively autonomous levels and effects of politics and ideology (Poulantzas 1973).

Since this case study explanation is based on the concepts of mode of production and articulation, in regard to their concretization in an historical conjuncture, it is worthwhile discussing them at some length. Mode of production, then, is specified and distinguished by two prime elements: a) the manner by which surplus value is extracted, and b) the corresponding political and ideological arrangements which support and reproduce such extraction. This refers to the particular institutions which are functional to the reproduction of the mode of production, i. e. to the concrete organization which ensures the continuity of the process of extraction.

The relevant literature provides two opposing perspective on the plausibility of articulation between different modes of production (Cutler et al. 1977; Holton

1981; Wolpe 1980). The first views it as implausible (Radar 1979). The opposing view is that the social structure or formation can contain more than one mode of production, and that this is not merely a temporary juncture. Thus the important question is, what conditions and mechanisms make articulation between modes of production possible? In particular regard to the present case, what are the mechanisms of reproduction of the non-dominant mode which maintain the conditions of its continuity?

The point of departure of this paper is that articulation should be conceived of as a structural relation between two or more coexisting modes of production (Taylor 1979; Wolpe 1980; Wright 1983). They are interrelated because of their assumed mutual contribution to the reproduction of each other. Hence the coexistence of capitalist and non-capitalist modes is contingent on the reproductive requirements of each. Reproduction refers to the ability to maintain conditions of survival, whether this is accomplished autonomously, or by some dependency on the other mode of production. Articulation therefore, implies, *inter alia*, the possibility that reproduction of one existing mode of reproduction is contingent, at least in part, on the presence and support of other mode(s).

Since in practice the end result of articulation on the economic level is the convergence or elimination of one mode by the other, it is possible that articulation occurs on the political or ideological levels; each participating mode maintains its own principles and institutions while cooperating with, and placing constraints on, the other(s). Domination via the political level, as it occurs in capitalist democratic societies, is one way to maintain a multi-mode social formation. Nonetheless, political domination is related to, but not necessarily totally dependent on, control at the economic level. Socialist regimes in Western Europe are one example of "relatively autonomous relations" between politics and the economy, and the problems associated with partial, or minor political control of the economy.

Thus the study of actual historical instances of articulation, as well as that of conditions of social reproduction, must be concerned with the compelling structural relations between modes of production. Alternatively, when we deal with the coexistence of two or more modes of production in one concrete social formation (society), the study should centre on the structural relations between the levels of politics, ideology and economics.

The rest of this paper discusses the conditions of reproduction of the Kibbutz – a classless organization, describing the coexistence of this mode of production with a capitalist mode in the pre-state Jewish community in Palestine and then, Israel. By assigning these modes to historical capitalist and non-capitalist types, it is possible to treat the present casee in terms of a more general phenomenon of articulation of modes of production and their reproduction. Since the present case is a historical one, it is delineated by means of a narrative of the process of Jewish colonization and nation/state building.

II

The criteria here used to mark the main characteristics of each mode of production and to compare them are:
(a) The principle and mechanism of appropriation of surplus labour or value;
(b) The allocation of resources and disposition of surplus labour or value;
(c) The political and ideological arrangements/institutions and their correspondence on the economic level;
(d) The nature of classes as determined by the social relations of production.
These criteria, which centre on the extraction of surplus labour/value, have been suggested by Wright (1983), and are slightly modified here, mainly to specify the uniqueness of the Kibbutz vis-à-vis the others in the Israeli society[1].

The Kibbutz: the basic characteristic of this mode of production is its being a collective wherein the politics, ideology and entire process of production and consumption are controlled by the collective. The direct producers – who are also the real owners of the means of production – together determine their political and ideological practices. It follows that:
(a) The mechanism of appropriation of surplus labour is a collective process operating through the elected institutions of the Kibbutz.
(b) This process is the exlusive legitimate mechanism for the allocation and disposition of resources, surplus labour or any imported capital.
(c) Although political activities are organized through particular institutions, they are not separated from other levels, and the economy is, within limits, subjugated to political and ideological considerations. Following Wright (1983), the politics and ideology of the Kibbutz can be defined as "privatization within the social formation". It is impossible for members to follow political practices such as liberal pro-market economics within the Kibbutz in opposition to the basic principles of this social formation. Nonetheless, at the present time members are permitted to refrain from participation in the global politics of the country, and may even participate in political organizations which differ from those of the majority of the membership, provided these organizations do not oppose the very existence of the Kibbutz formation.
(d) By the Marxist definition of class, the Kibbutz is a classless organization. The necessary conditions for class structure – appropriation of surplus labour/value and exploitation of one category by the other – is absent.
As these criteria imply, it is the contention here that the Kibbutz collective mode of production is a socialist formation. In fact, it is close to a communist formation

---

[1] A lucid and more complete presentation of this issue requires an extension of this article to include the Arabs sector (Israelis and non-citizens). This is not possible considering the limits which are imposed on this article.

in most of its elements (Wright 1983). As will be shown later, the continuity of this formation was and still is dependent in part on its close association with the socio-economic organization and the political parties of the working class.

The other modes of production: Capitalist, the Histadrut (General Federation of Labour) and to a certain extent, the state, are not described in this paper. In regard to its primary rules the capitalist mode of production is basically the same as in other capitalist societies. The Histadrut is treated here as a "Mixed Mode" (Ben-Porat 1986). It is a public management socio-economic and also political organization. Allocation and disposition of resources and surplus labour – extracted from the direct producers in the Histadrut enterprises – are decided upon by political institutions elected by all the Histadrut members, many of whom are also the direct producers. In the present context it suffices that the nature of this organization and its connections with the working class parties and the Kibbutz formation are comprehended.

III

The Pre-Statehood Period: Colonization by Jews of Palestine with the concrete intention of establishing agricultural Moshavot (settlements) began in 1882. Palestine at this time was ruled by the Ottoman regime, and was primarily a feudalistic (pribanded) society (Porat 1974). While the basic forms of capitalist (proto-capitalist) and Kibbutz modes were established before the Great War of 1914–1918, the end of that war marked their effective point of departure.

The years immediately following the end of the Great War saw an acceleration of the transition from (pribanded) feudalism to capitalism in Palestine. The latter was imported by the British, who were granted a mandate to govern Palestine in 1920. The British administration allowed both Arabs and Jews to manage their own internal community affairs (Gross 1982). The Jewish sector (hereafter referred to as the "Yishuv") was much the most qualified to utilize the "realm of opportunities" afforded by the British.

Two and a half modes of production developed in this sector, a capitalist one, a socialist/Kibbutz one (which was organized into two or three federations according to their political affiliation), and the Histadrut – a politico-economic organization of the Jewish working class, in which the economy was "owned" by the political regime and indirectly, through election, by the Histadrut members themselves. However, the Histadrut's economy was based on wage labour and operated directly in the country's market, which was becoming predominantly by a capitalist mode.

As already mentioned, the development of the Jewish capitalist sector was accelerated after World War I, and made rapid progress from then till 1930. The centre of the Jewish community shifted from the rural areas to the cities and from agriculture to industry. Thus at the beginning of the 1930s, industry employed about 30% of the entire, mainly Jewish, workforce, and there were some 2,400, mostly small-scale enterprises in the Yishuv which contained about two hundred thousand people at that time.

Except for that established by the Histadrut and other public organizations, the development of industry and of other sectors of the economy (except public services) was almost entirely made possible by private capital. Through extended capital flux and the growth of the local market, the capitalist sector became the dominant mode in the economy of the Yishuv in the 1920s and 1930s. That is, capitalist rules of exchange, profit and accumulation determined or constrained the degree of opportunities of other modes in the economy. Yet this domination was limited by the fact that public capital (Ulitzur 1939) and non-profit organizations were also involved in the developing economy – and most importantly in the creation of the Yishuv's political institutions. What the capitalist sector of the Yishuv lacked was a unified supportive political organization. This limited its dominance over the socio-economy of the Yishuv. The fragmented bourgeois political organizations which did exist, could not gain sufficient effective autonomous power in order to ensure political domination. This was prevented in part by Zionist organizations in Europe and the USA and in part by the political regime in the Yishuv which was dominated by working class political parties. But most importantly, the economic domination of capitalist rules in the Yishuv, and also in Palestine at large, derived from the fact that most of the capital which was imported to the Yishuv was private. Even that which was imported by the Zionist organizations was recruited from the Jewish bourgeoisie outside Palestine. The British mandate – the capitalist state at that time – was also supportive.

After World War I the Jewish working class in Palestine succeeded in establishing political and economic organizations which constituted the most highly organized power-collective at that time. Through the Histadrut, the political parties of the working class gained much influence in the labour market vis-à-vis the Jewish bourgeoisie (Braslaveski 1963). At the end of the 1920s the Histadrut owned a wide variety of enterprises, such as a building company, a cooperative wholesale company, a Bank and so forth. At the beginning of the 1930s the working class, through its political organizations, became the dominant power in the political institutions of the Yishuv (the elected General Assembly and the National Committees) and the major power in the World Zionist Organization – the most important organization at that time with regard to the development of the Jewish community in Palestine. By achieving domination over this organization – although they actually had to form a coalition with non-working class parties – the working class parties established control over the allocation of imported public capital, and gained effective influence on other economic and political ventures (Ben-Porat 1986).

The first Kibbutz formation was established in 1909 as an experimental cooperative which was based on self-management and labour, motivated by the need to provide employment for unemployed Jewish workers, and by Zionist-socialist ideology. By 1922 there were 9 Kibbutzim with between 600 and 800 members. By 1930 the numbers were 30 and 4,291, and in 1947, on the eve of the establishment of the state of Israel, the number of Kibbutzim was 97 with 32,300 members, constituting about 7% of the Jewish population in Palestine of that year.

The Kibbutz economy was almost totally based on agriculture (Drin-Drabkin 1961; Shatil 1955; Vitales 1966). The members of a particular Kibbutz ranged in numbers from a few dozen to hundreds and were recruited from immigration and politically related organizations, following the division of the Kibbutzim into a small number of federations. Capital was channelled to the Kibbutzim by the Histradrut or from the Zionist organizations, the Histadrut assuming a mediatory role in both instances. Almost no individual Kibbutz was yet economically sound. On the contrary, by economic criteria, the Kibbutz was "effective", being dependent upon the support of other organizations, in particular those mentioned above. Once the working class parties had gained a relative majority in the community institutions and Zionist organizations, they were able to consolidate financial support. This is a major factor in explaining the capability of the Kibbutz to reproduce itself in a socio-economic conjuncture in which the capitalist mode dominated the economic level.

The emergence of a non-capitalist mode at about the same time as that of the proto-capitalist one was a direct result of the inability of the latter to provide socio-economic solutions, such as employment, for the many immigrants who constituted a working class proletariat. Many of the immigrants who came to Palestine in the second wave of Jewish immigration (1904–1914) were aware of the meager opportunities in Palestine. It is apparent that their Zionist and socialist persuasions determined their range of possible emigration-immigration alternatives, that is, acted as a "selector mechanism" regarding the limits of the country's economy, and thus chose the cooperative formation as the desirable form of settlement.

Until about 1930, when the working class parties gained a majority in the political institutions of the Zionist organizations, the continuing reproduction of the Kibbutz within a capitalist environment was dependent upon the organizations of the working class, and in concrete terms, on their ability to provide the Kibbutz with capital and human resources. Yet this was limited because the means of these organizations (essentially those of the Histadrut) were scarce. At the start of the 1930s the support of the above organizations increased; first, because the predominant position of the working class parties in the Zionist institutions and in those of the Yishuv enabled them to control the allocation of imported public capital; second, because the Kibbutz, although it was affiliated to the working class organizations, was considered to be an important participant in the process of (Jewish) nation building. This lessened the opposition of the bourgeoisie in Europe and the USA, who constituted the essential source of private and public capital to the Yishuv at that time.

Thus the reproduction of the Kibbutz formation was accomplished through its articulation with the Histadrut, which mediated between the Kibbutz and the (capitalist) economic level, and with the working class parties which assumed the same mediating agency on the political level. In practice, the Histadrut and the working class parties ensured the reproduction of the socialist formation of the Kibbutz. However, since these agencies were inadequate on the economic level, the reproduction of the Kibbutz was also contingent on its ability to relate itself to certain other political organizations and to be articulated within the nationalistic aims of the Zionist organizations.

All in all the main reason for reproduction derived from the historical situation constituting the "realm of opportunities" during the pre-state period. Nation/state building, particularly after 1930, became the dominant process. The domination of a capitalist mode of production in the economy was accompanied by the effective influence of the working class parties in the politics of the Jewish institutions inside and outside Palestine. Thus the limits which the economy usually imposes upon politics – and in this respect the relative autonomy of the latter – were transcended by the dependency of the economy upon external resources and the effective mediatory position of the political level in this conjuncture. Because of this particular situation, the socialist formation of the Kibbutz was able to reproduce itself without being dependent on its real economic capabilities.

IV

The establishment of the state of Israel in 1948 made the state the sole mechanism of articulation; it "constituted the factor of cohesion between levels of social formation" (Jessop 1977; Poulantzas 1978), and in a conscious and deliberate manner took over the function of coordinator of the modes of production which continued to coexist, the capitalist, the socialist and the Histadrut.

The working class political parties formed the government from 1948 to 1977, with "MAPAI" the major party, constituting the dominant power in the coalitions during that period. The capitalist sector remains the major one in the economy, employing about 60% of the workforce and producing about the same percentage of the net total product. The Histadrut employed about 23% of the workforce and produced about 20% of the net product. The rest was employed and produced respectively by the state economy (Barkai 1968). The state now provided direct support of the Kibbutz formation, following the critical influence of the working class parties and organizations on the government.

At the end of the 1940s there were 97 Kibbutzim with 32,000 members, at the end of the 1980s, there were 275 Kibbutzim with 120,000 members. The Kibbutz sector increased, yet its proportion of the entire population fell from 6.7% in 1945 to 3.6% in 1985. The change in the articulation between the Kibbutz and the other modes of production was gradual but concrete. The process of reproduction was still dependent upon state assistance, but began to shift to the economic capacity of the Kibbutz formation itself (Barkai 1986).

At the end of the 1950s the economic structure of the Kibbutz began to change and industry was introduced as an increasingly major economic sector. While few Kibbutzim had any kind of industrial enterprise prior to 1948, by 1962 they operated 143 such enterprises employing some 6,000 people. In 1970 these figures had risen to 235 in 186 Kibbutzim employing 10,500 people, and in 1987, 420 enterprises with 17,500 people. This meant that a high percentage of the total Kibbutz workforce engaged in industrial production, which was and remains much more profitable than agriculture. The mid 1970s marked a peak in industrialization, and almost every Kibbutz had a factory or possessed shares in industry, in other Kibbutzim or even cooperating with the private sector. In effect, in the 1980s, industry rather than agriculture now became the main source of Kibbutz income.

The economic expansion of the Kibbutz formation and in particular its industrialization, had some structural effects on the internal relations of this socialist mode of production. First, the expansion of industry increased the use of wage labour (hired, outside labour of nonmembers). In 1963 an average of 19% of the employees in Kibbutz economy was hired wage labour. Although this average decreased to some 14% in 1965 (Barkai 1968, 1986), it remains high in industry, about 25% in 1987. Thus at least part of the surplus value of this industry was gained by at least partial exploitation – that is, from surplus value of nonmember employees. Second, the expansion of the Kibbutz economy and the increased share of industry in it, forced the Kibbutz to became more involved in the capitalist rules of the game, hence in the exchange market. Actually the Kibbutz was involved in the economy of the Yishuv even before statehood, although this was limited and mediated by the Histadrut or other external organizations. Now the Kibbutz established its own organizations to deal with purchasing means of production and of consumption in the capitalist market, marketing its industrial products and recruiting capital, even through the stock market. Hence the reproduction of the Kibbutz formation within a capitalist economy made it impossible for the former to ignore the rules of the latter.

Indeed the most important change was the increasing power of the Kibbutz economy within that of the state (Barkai 1986). Nevertheless, all modes of production remained dependent on the state. The capitalist mode continued its economic dominance although it was still dependent on the state institutions which controlled directly or indirectly (by legislation) the allocation of capital, the import of capital and goods and so forth. It was a state which was ruled by "social democratic" parties which protected the capitalist sector and encouraged its development. This protection decreased from the 1960s on, but the state remained a major factor in maintaining the expansion of the capitalist sector and, *inter alia*, of every other sector (i. e. mode of production).

It is apparent that from the establishment of the state of Israel to the 1980s, the state has played a critical role in every instance of society, most importantly, the economic instance. There have been a number of objective constraints forcing the state to intervene in the economy, such as the torrent of immigration, particularily in the early 1950s, the meagre economy and correlatively, the country's dependence on the support of world Jewry and other external sources of capital and goods, such as German reparations to the state of Israel or USA grants and loans. No less important has been the need of the state to establish and reaffirm its legitimacy, and the constant need of the regime to maintain its constituency, that is, its actual and potential supporters. Among these is the Kibbutz which, although it constitutes only a small minority in the electorate, has assumed an effective ideological and political influence. The noncapitalist modes, Histadrut and Kibbutz and related organizations such as the Moshav (quasi cooperative settlement), have constituted the concrete economic power of the Labour Party in government. Therefore their continuing integration in the country's economy has been, among other factors, instrumental in their influence on the state.

Thus the reproduction of the socialist mode of production – the Kibbutz – after the establishment of the state was enacted by roughly the same mechanism as before, by the mediation of the political organizations of the working class. However, because of the dominant position of these organizations in the state institutions (parliament, government), the state apparatus and the Histadrut, their support is now almost a direct one. Articulation between modes has been adopted by the state as the best way of maintaining the balance of class power. The fact that state revenues have not been dependent on any single mode has enabled the government to restrain the modes and to support the reproduction of each one separately. Nonetheless, when the "Likud" (a federation of right-wing and liberal parties) took over power from Labour in 1977, the Kibbutz, because of its economic expansion during the previous years (Barkai 1986), was able to reproduce its formation mainly on its own resources. Yet because of it being articulated within the capitalist economy, it had to adjust to the policies of the new regime which was far less sympathetic to the Kibbutz formation than previous governments. It had therefore to ensure its continued reproduction without the protection of the state (although the political support of the Labour Party and its related organizations remained). The Kibbutz was able now to encounter the capitalist sector in the economy.

V

According to Balibar (1971) the principal issue is that of the law of coexistence of different modes of production and, *inter alia*, the explanation of their reproduction. The simple answer in the literature is that coexistence is a temporary conjuncture and that there are always structural contradicitions between two or more different modes. They coexist until the contradiction can no longer be consolidated. It is therefore anticipated that the more effective mode is historically bound to replace the lesser. It is possible to suggest another general explanation which is not totally different from the above and to argue that for certain functional reasons which concern the relationships between a major and a minor mode (e. g. capitalist and petty bourgeois), the historically "obsolete" mode continues to be reproduced. The literature, however, provides ample evidence that coexistence is not merely temporary, nor based on functional relationships alone. The explanation of the reproduction of the Kibbutz before and after the establishment of the State of Israel leans on structural terms and, practically, on the conjunctures characteristic of these periods.

The reasons that can be placed in the epitomized explanation of the continuing reproduction of the socialist formation since 1909, when the first Kibbutz was established, are embodied in the understanding of the correspondance between the politics and the economy in the Yishuv before (and after) 1948. After World War I the political instance became dominant in the Yishuv because of the particular socio-historical situation which facilitated the ascendence of politics (Ben-Porat 1986). In essence, the political institutions of the Yishuv and those of the Zionist organizations, exercised effective control over the economy, mainly by control of the import of public capital (although the major import of capital was private), but also by means of effective influence over other levels of the community. This remained true after the establishment of the state, but with different form and content, considering the mere fact that the state now became the "factor of cohesion," and the working class parties remained a major force in any coalition and in the state apparatus. Hence support for the Kibbutz was direct, through the state organizations, as was the support for the capitalist sector – a phenomenon which occurs in post-colonialist countries where the national formation is weak and the state form is approximately that of "state capitalism," functioning in practice as the major entrepreneur.

The explanation suggested here for the continued reproduction of a socialist formation within (or beside) a dominant capitalist mode is based on the contention of the existence of the "relative autonomy" of politics and ideology vis-à-vis the econommy. Through political mediation, i. e. the working class organizations, the Kibbutz was able to reproduce its form without being totally dependent on its economic capabilities. However, by 1977, when the Likud became the major force in the government, the Kibbutz had become economically competent to reproduce itself. Hence the support of the past was utilized for the creation of a solid economy ensuring the present continuing reproduction of the Kibbutz formation.

References

Albert, Michael and Robin Hahnel, *Unorthodox Marxism*. Boston: South End Press. 1978

Althusser, Louis and Etienne Balibar. *Reading Capital*. London: New Left Books. 1970

Balibar, E., The Basic Concepts of Historical Materialism, in: *Reading Capital*, L. Althusser and E. Balibar (eds.). London: New Left Books, pp. 273–308. 1970

Barkai, Haim, *Public Sector, Histadrut Sector, and Private Sector in Israel*. Jerusalem: Falk Institute (Hebrew). 1968

Barkai, Haim, Kibbutz Efficiency and the Incentive Conundrum. Jerusalem: Falk Institute. 1986

Ben-Porat, Amir, *Between Class and Nation*. Westpoint, Connecticut: Greenwood Press. 1986

Braslaveski, M., *The Labor Movement in Eretz Israel*. Tel Aviv: Hakibbutz Hamehuchad. 1963

Chase-Dunn, Christopher, Socialist States in Capitalist World Economy, *Social Problems* 27: 505–525. 1980.

Cohen, G. A., *Karl Marx's Theory of History: A Defense*. Princeton: Princeton University Press. 1978

Cutler, Anthony, Barry Hindess, Paul Hirst and Athar Hussain, *Marx's Capital and Capitalism Today*. Vol. I. London: Routledge and Kegan Paul. 1977

Drin-Drabkin, H., *The Other Society*. Merchavia, Israel: Sifriat Poalim. 1961

Foster-Carter, Aidan, The Mode of Production Controversy, *New Left Review* 107: 47–78. 1978

Gramsci, Antonio, *Selections from the Prison Notebooks*. Q. Hoare and B. N. Smith (eds.). New York: International Publishers. 1971

Gross, N., The Economic Policy of the British Mandatory Government in Eretz Israel, *Katedra* 24: 153–180 (Hebrew). 1982.

Hindess, Barry and Paul Hirst, *Modes of Production and Social Formation*. London: Routledge and Kegan Paul. 1977

Holton, J. Robert, Marxist Theories of Social Change and Transition from Feudalism to Capitalism, *Theory and Society* 6: 833–867. 1981

Jessop, Bob, Recent Theories of the Capitalist State, *Cambridge Journal of Economics* 1: 353–373. 1977

Porat, Yehoshua, *The Emergence of the Palestine-Arab National Movement, 1918–1929*. London: F. Cass. 1974

Poulantzas, Nicos, *Political Power and Social Classes*. London: New Left Books. 1973

Radar, Melvin, *Marx's Interpretation of History*. New York: Oxford University Press. 1979

Shatil, Y., *The Economy of the Communal Settlement in Israel*. Merchavia, Israel: Sefriyat Poalim. 1955

Taylor, C. John. *From Modernization to Modes of Production*. London: Macmillan Press. 1979

Ulitzur, A., *A National Capital and the Building of Israel*. Jerusalem: The Central Bureau of Keren Haysod (Hebrew). 1939

Viteles, Harry, *A History of the Cooperative Movement. Vol. I*. London: Valentine, Mitchell. 1968

Wolpe, Harold (ed.), *The Articulation of Modes of Production*. London: Routledge and Kegan Paul. 1980

Wright, Erik Olin, Capitalism's Future: A Provisional Reconceptualization of Alternatives to Capitalist Society, *Socialist Review* 68: 77–126. 1983

Appendix

This article is presented in categorical terms. Evidence is not presented in any detail to support the arguments and explanations, because of the necessity of keeping this presentation within limits. Furthermore, the concept and the form of the Kibbutz is not explicated here. It is assumed that the reader is familiar with this notion, but it is also recognized that more information is needed to convince the reader who is not highly familiar with the Kibbutz formation, particularly the contention that this is a "mode of production" and a socialist or even a communist one, if we consider the effects of the communist elements in this formation.

This presentation also suffers from the lack of explication of the political institutions of the Yishuv before statehood. This is also the case for the contention that the state after 1948 was "state capitalist," a concept which deserves some elaboration. Considering the scope of the present paper, this has not been possible. This appendix is therefore intended to provide some information about the Kibbutz formation in Israel at the present time, particularily its economy:

(1) The number of plants in the Kibbutzim in 1987 was 420. This constituted 7.4% of Israeli industry overall, excluding the diamond industry.

(2) Exports from the Kibbutz industries amounted to US 450 million in 1987, over 6% of the total exports for that year.

(3) The number of workers in Kibbutz industry in 1987 was 17,500. About 4,500 were wage labourers, that is, non-Kibbutz members.

(4) The Kibbutz industrial product amounted to between 6.4% and 7.4% of the total product of industry in Israel between 1980 and 1984.

(5) The following are two tables which present the Kibbutz industry in the years 1980–1984 (Tables 1 and 2).

Table 1. Sales, Export, Investment and Workers in Kibbutz Industry, 1980–1984

Year	Sale million IS Sheqels	Export million US dollars	Investment million IS Sheqels	No. of Workers
1980	139.402	215	14.658	13.014
1981	145.200	210	14.336	13.280
1982	149.286	196	9.817	13.537
1983	165.655	187	16.459	14.160
1984	191.347	244	24.192	15.490

Source: The Association of The Kibbutz Industry Annual Report, October 1985.

Table 2. Index of Sales; Kibbutz Industry and Israeli Industry, 1980–1984

Year	Kibbutz Ind.	Israeli Ind.
1980	100	100
1981	109	104
1982	110	107
1983	119	112
1984	137	122

Source: as above.

Socialised Industry: Social Ownership or Shareholding Democracy?

Tom Clarke

Privatisation may be one of the most lasting social revolutions of the twentieth century. It is also a movement in which Britain has led the world. (Nigel Lawson, *Observer*, 25 October 1987).

One of the most visible signs of the triumph of the New Right in the 1980s has been the sale of large parts of the public sector of industry. The concept of natural monopoly and the need for public service have been undermined, and replaced by a reinvigorated faith in the capacity of the market to resolve fundamental problems of economic production and social allocation. Privatisation barely featured in the orginal plans of the Thatcher Government in 1979, but it has become a relentless policy, a physical manifestation of Conservative ideology concerning economic freedom, self-help, and entrepreneurship, amounting to a renaissance of capitalism in Britain. As the policy has unfolded, it has seemed to possess increasing popular appeal, holding out the promise of a new shareholding democracy.

1. Introduction

The Conservative Party has never believed that the business of Government is the Government of business. (Nigel Lawson, *Hansard*, Vol. 1, 8th Series, col 440).

Three consecutive Conservative Governments between 1979–1988 deliberately shattered the consensus regarding the mixed economy and the appropriate balance of public and private industries all post-war governments in Britain had formerly upheld. A new determination to visibly "roll back the frontiers of the state" was based on the firm assumption that the public sector was too large, unproductive, inefficient, and wasteful. (As far as the first criticism was concerned, OECD *Annual National Accounts* which consistently indicated public expenditure in the UK was considerably *lower* than comparable European industrial countries in the early 1980s were disregarded, what Conservative politicians wanted the public to believe to be the case was what mattered.) As Chancellor of the Exchequer presiding over the de-nationalisation programme from 1983, Nigel

Lawson repeatedly emphasised the £ 33 billion per annum losses and borrowings of the nationalised industries, their poor return on investment and productivity, and inefficient service to customers typified by long delays. Yet in 1979 the nationalised industries accounted for one tenth of national output, one sixth of total fixed investment, and employed 1.75 million people.

Whatever efforts were made by the nationalised industries, with a government hostile to their very existence, they could not win: if they made a loss they were caricatured as chronically inefficient, if they made large profits they were condemned as consumer-exploiting monopolies. Successive governments in the 1960s and 1970s had issued White Papers enabling the Treasury to lay down a profusion of operating rules for the nationalised industries to act as "surrogates for the market" (Posner 1984). These included medium-term plans which set firm guidelines for activities, profit, subsidy and investment. From 1979 further restrictions were applied with the clear intention of preparing public enterprises for the market.

In theory the government regarded de-nationalisation as serving a multiplicity of self-reinforcing objectives:

Economic Freedom

Management of the privatised companies would be free to invest in market opportunities, and consumers free to choose. "The New Right come close to treating private ownership as an article of faith, in which it is axiomatic that the state coerces and that private markets liberate" (Parker 1987: 353).

Efficiency

The disciplines of the capital and product markets, and the profit incentive would enhance the pursuit of enterprise efficiency.

Public Sector Borrowing Requirement (PSBR)

Instead of being a "continual drain" on PSBR, sale of the nationalised industry assets would provide considerable revenue for the Treasury.

Public Sector Pay Bargaining

Privatisation would discipline the public sector unions, by making it more difficult to pass on excessive wage increases to consumers, and posing the threat of bankruptcy without the government to sustain losses.

Wider Share Ownership

Privatisation would promote popular capitalism through considerably widening share ownership.

Further unstated intentions of the privatisation policy were to reward the Conservative Party supporters in the private sector with enhanced profit opportunities; while undermining the workers, unions, and communities with a close identification with the nationalised industries, who were also associated with the Labour Party (Kay and Thompson 1986; Steel and Heald 1982).

Different ways to achieve privatisation were developed and applied including:
- De-nationalisation of public corporations and the sale of public assets (eg. British Telecom);

- Liberalisation involving the removal of statutory prohibitions on the private sector competing against the public sector (e. g. Transport Act 1985, enforcing the deregulation of public passenger road transport);
- Contracting-out of work (e. g. competitive tendering in the NHS and local government);
- Charging – introducing the (partial) substitution of user charges for tax finance (e. g. repeated increases in NHS prescription charges).

From modest beginnings in the early years of the first administration, successive Conservative Governments have dramatically escalated the scale and pace of the privatisation process, as confidence among Ministers and their City advisers has grown. Receipts from public asset sales initially arrived at the Treasury in hundreds of millions, but with the privatisation of British Telecom in 1984 they became billions of pounds. In total, the 8 year privatisation programme has raised £ 25 billion, and increased the number of shareholders in Britain from 2 million to 9.4 million. The government is now committed to £ 5 billion per year of public asset sales, and in preparing the Water Authorities valued at £ 8 billion and the Electricity Supply Industry valued at £ 18 billion for sale, seems certain to achieve its target. The Treasury has pencilled in receipts of over 340 billion from the programme as a whole. (In addition sales of council houses, public buildings and land since 1979 have brought in a further £ 12.2 billion.)

Meanwhile the policy of privatisation is sweeping the world. In France the short-lived government of Jacques Chirac lasted long enough to privatise more than 20 public companies with a market capitalisation of £ 10.26 billion, including the *Crédit Commercial de France*, and the *Compagnie Générale d'Électricité*. In Italy there is a major divestiture programme with £ 5.3 billion of assets sold since 1983, including Alitalia for $ 355 million. In Japan Nippon Telephone and Telegraph (a company with a market capitalisation potentially greater than the whole West Germany equity market) is to be established as a self-standing corporation by the sale of successive tranches of shares. Japan Airlines and Japan National Railways are also planned for sale. In New Zealand under David Lange's Labour administration "corporatisation" of forestry, land, coal, and other industries into free-standing corporations has occurred, in which the state retains 100 per cent of the voting shares, but loans and equity bonds will be raised in the private market. The Finance Minister, Roger Douglas, in an Economic Policy Statement of December 1987 introduced a further measure of free market "Rogernomics" with the sale of 14 billion NZ dollars of public assets, including Telecom and 25% of Air New Zealand (Freikhert 1988).

Nor has privatisation been confined to developed industrial countries with extensive public sectors. In the less developed economies of the Third World, where public enterprise has been regarded as the central component of economic development in the absence of sufficient activity in the market sector, the nostrums of privatisation are being canvassed widely. "State owned enterprises were looked upon as the pillars on which the economic infrastructure for the country would be built, but the pillars were found to be hollow" (Pendse 1985: 6). The IMF, World Bank, and Asian Development Bank are sponsoring privatisations as one way to resolve the mounting debt crisis of the developing countries. Privatisations have now occurred in South America, Africa, and the Far East, as recounted with considerable pleasure (and perhaps some profit) in *Privatising the World* (1988) by Oliver Letwin, the head of the International Privatisation Unit of N. M. Rothschild (and a former member of Mrs Thatchers Policy Unit). USAID officials were recently given a directive for the orientation of their policy discussions with aid recipients:

Policy dialogue should be used to encourage LDSs to follow free market principles for sustained economic growth and to move away from government intervention in the economy. This allows the market to determine how economic resources are most productively allocated and how benefits should be distributed (Commander and Killick 1988; Kirkpatrick 1988).

In the face of such an ambitious and apparently unstoppable programme, the Left has been hopelessly wrong-footed. In the early 1980s the labour movement was caught in a lingering debate concerning the viability of the Alternative Economic Strategy (AES) which proposed an industrial policy of extending public ownership and planning agreements. The problem with such a transitional strategy was that the economy was being rapidly transported in the opposite direction. While the supporters of the AES set their sights on the nationalisation of the "commanding heights of the economy" including banks, and leading companies from every industrial sector, the ideological ground of the existing public sector was being eroded away.

The Labour Party has singularly failed to articulate a coherent defence of the principle of public ownership or to mount an effective campaign against the gradual but systematic dismantling of an important part of the legacy of 1945 (Steel and Heald 1984: 16).

Each wave of privatisations has seen the Labour Party scramble to develop new policies to appeal to the general public, abandon the old image, and accommodate to industrial changes that would be difficult and expensive to reverse. Talk of "renationalisation without compensation," quickly gave way to "renationalisation with no speculative gain" as the size of the new shareholding constituency was realised. By the time of the Party Conference of 1986, a new industrial policy of Social Ownership had been formulated, which stressed that public ownership did not mean simply state ownership, and looked for a new positive role in industrial development for workers, consumers, and local councils. In the General Election of 1987, the Party's Manifesto declared that private shares would be converted into special marketable securities, carrying either a guaranteed return, or dividends linked to the company's growth. (As socialist slogans go, "Convert The Shares Into Marketable Securities" does not quite have the ring about it of "All Power To The Soviets" for example).

The industrial policy of the Labour Party is being further refined in the wake of the third election defeat, along with the other central planks of party policy. Some have condemned the new industrial policy as a revisionist reversal to Gaitskell's opposition to Clause IV of the Party Constitution that promised

To secure for the workers by hand and by brain the full fruits of their industry and the most equitable distribution thereof that may be possible upon the basis of common ownership of the means of production, distribution and exchange and the best obtainable system of popular administration and control of each industry and service.

Others have recognised in the new proposals a potential participative transformation of the economy in which planning and development could occur from below instead of being imposed from above. There are strong elements of both approaches in the policy that is emerging, and it is as yet unclear which will prove dominant either in theory or in practice. However, what is important is that there is a strong commitment to re-thinking the organisation and functioning of the public sector, to discard useless shibboleths, and fashion a policy for the future that can reverse the process of privatisation in an imaginative way. As Steel and Heald indicate,

In recent years, the critics of public ownership have begun to articulate their case more effectively. Their opponents should not only scrutinise these arguments carefully but also build an equivalent case in favour of public ownership in which attention is focused upon its objectives and the means of putting them into practice. Thirty years of consensus have tended to produce complacency among those who advocate a positive role for the public sector in industry. No longer, however, can they rely upon the status quo to defend their beliefs (1982: 346).

2. Privatisation Strategy

The origins of the public sector of industry in Britain lay not in the ambitions of a malign state, but in the recurrent recognition at local level of the inadequacies of market provision. From the early 19th century, local commissions were established to deal with cleaning, street lighting, road building, sewers, water supply and public health. Local councils in 1890 began to build low cost houses, and in 1902 local education authorities were given the responsibility to provide schools. "Public utilities were also established by local authorities, including public transport, water, gas and electricity supply" (IPM/IDS 1986). The post-war expansion of the nationalised industries was pursued by a Labour Government that emphasised the irresponsibility of private capital, the failure of the market system to provide the investment necessary to promote economic development, or to produce even essentials for those who could not afford to pay. In establishing the Welfare State, it was thought the rights of individuals without wealth and property could be protected. Cross-subsidy could ensure a comprehensive service to all. Rather than the goal of profit maximisation, the creation of a stable economic infrastructure for general economic growth was the aim.

Such beliefs came under increasing siege from the mid-1970s onwards following the spectacular fall of the Heath Government during the miners strike. Repeated public expenditure cuts, prompted by the IMF loan restriction, provoked increasing discontent in the public sector as wages were held down and services came under increasing strain in the face of escalating demands for them. In the absence of the profit motive and profit criterion, sophisticated management techniques were applied to ensure efficiency and value for money in the public sector including:
- cash limits
- manpower limits
- staff assessment
- periodic reviews of functions and organisation
- internal and external audits
- comparative studies of costs and outputs
- contracting-out ancillary services to competitive tender
- performance indicators and performance measurement (Pliatzky 1988).

A belief the public sector was synonymous with inefficiency was therefore a little unfair, and most of the evidence suggests the private sector is not inherently more efficient (Millward and Parker 1983). The public sector in fact had to repeatedly rescue and resuscitate at great expense parts of the private sector which had collapsed. "British Leyland in the 1970s was not unprofitable because it was nationalized, it was nationalized because it was unprofitable" (Kay and Silberston 1984: 10). (As with Rolls-Royce, nationalised by the Heath Conservative Government to avert bankruptcy and break-up.)

The first significant act of privatisation by the Thatcher administration was the sale of a 5% share in BP. On paper this passed control to the private sector of one of the largest British corporations, as the government share fell below 50% of the total. Other privatisations of British Airways, British Shipbuilders, and the National Freight Corporation were postponed because of the recession and the poor financial state of the companies. Instead, the best prospects in the public sector were offered on the market. British Aerospace in 1981 was oversubscribed 3.5 times and attracted 155,000 new investors, almost as many as in ICI or GEC, the flagships of British industry. The privatisation of Amersham International in February 1982 caused a scandal since the shares were set so low they were oversubscribed 24 times. The sight of the undignified scrum of stockbrokers eager to grab as much Amersham stock as possible, encouraged the government in the launch of Britoil to offer a loyalty bonus to small investors who held shares for three years or more; to distribute prospectuses and application forms to an unprecedented level; and to launch a major advertising campaign extolling the irresistibility of the offer, with special incentives to encourage employees to buy shares.

By 1983–84 privatisation revenue topped £ 1 billion for the first time, but with the sale of British Telecom in 1984 more than £ 2.5 billion had to be found. The government looked to two new markets for investors: the majority of the adult population who had never owned shares; and overseas investors. Glossy packaging was freely distributed around the regions of Britain, in Europe, America, and the Far East. Shares were acquired by 2.3 million UK investors and 230,000 BT employees. However, when trading opened, the shares attracted an immediate premium of 90%, and overseas investors who had acquired 13.8% of the issue rushed to take a quick profit.

Fixed price share launches had provided a speculator's dream rather than an encouragement to long-term investment by small shareholders. The British Airports Authority sale was designed therefore as a combination of tender and fixed price, encouraging public participation whilst maximising the proceeds from institutions. However, the attempt to shift the remaining 31.5% government stake in BP valued at a minimum of £ 5.7 billion, the world's biggest-ever stock market sale, brought a moment of truth. The whole privatisation euphoria was founded upon a bull market that had developed over almost a decade. Investors were accustomed to believe an automatic premium would arrive with the opening of stock market dealings in privatisation issues.

The BP sale at the end of October 1987 fatally coincided with the biggest global stock market crash since 1929. The Financial Times Share Index dropped 249 points on 19 October and 250 the next day, a cumulative total of 21.7% wiping £ 94 billion off share prices. Wall Street, Tokyo, and Hong Kong, as well as London were all seized with panic. The BP share offer priced at 330p was faced with a stock market share price of 266p, which meant most of the 2.2 billion shares would go the underwriters. They urged the government to cancel the sale, not because of their own potentially enormous losses they claimed, since they had laid much of the risk upon overseas underwriters, but because of the permanent damage that would occur to the reputation of the City of London; and the chaos that would be caused by foreign underwriters attempting to recoup their losses with the sale of unwanted shares, leading to the risk of another market crash. Nonetheless, Lawson continued with the sale, throwing a lifeline by indicating the Bank of England would buy back some of the unwanted shares. This case of reverse-privatisation, designed to protect the major City institutions, brought the jibe from Neil Kinnock that underwriting would become defined as "an activity undertaken to cover against risk, unless there is a risk" (*Guardian*, 30 October 1987).

A lot of the gloss had come off the government's privatisation strategy, as shares plummeted, and ministers explained blandly that markets go down as well as up to privatised industry shareholders who were facing losses rather than windfall gains. Rather than attempt full-scale privatisation of water and electricity as he had earlier intended, Lawson now delayed the decision until the end of 1988, and considered the sale of only 51% of the two utilities. For the first time, serious structural weaknesses in the government's privatisation programme had become apparent, but it is interesting that the market itself had exposed the reckless aspect of the policy, whereas more direct opposition remained muted. The lack of effective resistance to the government's ambitious proposals was a constant source of encouragement to extend them further. Unions that attempted to mount defences of the public sector were regarded sceptically as being self-interested. The heroic rearguard action of the miners in 1984/85, when finally defeated, allowed Thatcher to triumphantly tour the Far East claiming she had "seen off the unions."

Management opposition was worn down, where it existed, by Treasury imposed tight external financing limits upon the nationalised industries.

These were at odds with corporate plans and investment requirements and had been set with the PSBR, not the need of the business formally in mind. When they complained, they were told that such "public sector constraints" were an inevitable consequence of their nationalized status and the only way to relax them would be to set the industries "free in the market-place." Making life unnecessarily unpleasant for the nationalised industries thus became a convenient spur to a change in management attitude towards denationalisation (Steel and Heald 1984: 17).

Executives who refused to bow to the inevitable as at British National Oil Corporation (BNOC) were dispensed with. The government brought in obedient new chairpersons at British Airways, British Steel and BNOC to ease their passage towards privatisation. They were encouraged to cut back their industries to a level that would be attractive to the market. Most spectacularly, at British Steel this process of pre-privatisation restructuring between 1979–1987 involved a cut in workers from 166,000 to 52,000, a reduction in government external financing from £ 1,119 million to £ 24 million, achieving a net profit of £ 178 million instead of a loss £ 1,784 million on a similar £ 3,000 million turnover.

Most nationalised industries directors, it appeared, were prepared to do anything the government wanted as long as their corporations retained their monopoly position. As Sir Leo Pliatzky, who was a senior civil servant at both the Treasury and the Department of Industry during this time, reflected:

At top management level, the industries were mainly concerned to keep their enterprises intact on privatisation and to resist fragmentation into competitive elements, once that had been secured, the Boards looked forward to escaping from government control and joining the ranks of the self-perpetuating corporate oligarchies which dominate the modern industrial scene. Public versus private ownership (as distinct from public expenditure versus tax reliefs) has ceased, for good or ill, to be a live issue in British politics for the foreseeable future, though acute problems remain about the accountability and regulation of privatised monopolies (1988: 44).

It was not just to placate the existing management that the British government failed to introduce competition as a central component of its privatisation policy. If competitive efficiency had been the key objective then restructuring the nationalised industries into competing corporations and divisions would have been essential, but this would have greatly reduced the attractiveness of the offer to the stock market, and the government would have received considerably less in revenue from the sales: "where a successful disposal at a good price conflicts with liberalization, it is liberalization that loses out" (Prosser 1986: 81). Transforming public monopolies into private monopolies was a quicker, easier, and safer option, though it vitiated the government's claims concerning efficiency, contradicting the economic theory it had propounded: "allocative efficiency is a function of market structure rather than ownership. Thus, in the absence of competition, denationalization is unlikely to result in major gains in efficiency performance" (Kirkpatrick 1988: 240). As Kay and Silberston put it, "If privatisation is to be an effective policy rather than a slogan [. . .], it should be an element of a competitive industrial policy rather than, as at present, a substitute for it" (1984: 16).

The contortions of the Government and the Central Electricity Generating Board (CEGB) concerning the future of nuclear power stations after privatisation reveal that neither the privatisation of electricity, nor the nuclear industry itself, are primarily based on grounds of competitive efficiency, and that political considerations still take precedence over the market. In the consideration of how to privatise the electricity industry the attempt was made to exclude the nuclear industry entirely from the privatisation, or to provide it with a privileged pricing structure for the electricity it generated (Helm 1987; Pryke 1988). Reasons for this are that nuclear power stations are far too expensive to operate, and, for obvious reasons, impossible to insure on the insurance market. Consumers do not wish to become irradiated. But the CEGB presently is bound anyway by statute to generate electricity from the cheapest source. Unable any longer to sustain the fiction that nuclear power is cheaper than coal, the Department of Energy and the CEGB, in order to "increase the diversity of supply," have elaborated the fascinating device that nuclear power as a non-fossil fuel should be included in a new category, and compared with the costs of large-scale wind, wave, and tidal power (since there has not been any significant investment by the Department of Energy in any of these alternatives, the relative costs have had to be invented!) (*Private Eye*, 8 July 1988).

The advantages of a private monopoly compared to a public monopoly are difficult to imagine. The vision of leaner, more responsive organisations is unlikely to be achieved without any incentive or constraint to become so (Woodward 1988). Large-scale, complex, and remote bureaucracies exist in the private as well as in the public sector, as most organisation theorists from Max Weber onwards have emphasised (Clegg and Dunkerley 1980). Schumpeter (1950) stressed the inevitability of bureaucracy in private firms, and many economists since have acknowledged the problem. Periods of restructuring can cause significant changes, and the experience of privatisation would have a sharp effect. But to assume this invariably leads to a greater attention to performance and quality is unfounded, when monopoly allows the pursuit of very different inclinations. Kaletsky stated bluntly in the *Financial Times*:

The new system will tend to settle down and the natural lassitude of any huge monopolistic enterprise is likely to reassert itself [...] the natural frictions between any monopoly and its customers will come to the fore again (13 February 1986).

If corporate bureaucracies have survived virtually intact with privatisation, the direction in which they are driven has altered, with the substitution of the goal of profit maximisation and growth for the government definition of the public good. The problematic nature of this change in orientation has occurred even to the proponents of privatisation, including Beesley and Littlechild who advised the Department of Industry concerning BT privatisation:

Privatisation is intended to change motivations of management towards profit-making. A privately owned company will have greater incentive to exploit monopoly power commercially. To the extent that this is not limited, consumer benefits from privatisation will be less than they might be. Second, a privatised company will be less willing to proviede uneconomic services. The resources so released will be used more productively, but particular sets of consumers will lose by the change. This raises the question of how such losses, often thought of as social obligations, should be handled (1983: 4).

As the implications of releasing huge private monopolies in essential industries upon an unsuspecting public began to dawn, the critical importance of regulation became apparent. In the absence of competition, the creation of regulatory agencies was the only means to rescue the consumer from naked exploitation. The problem with regulatory agencies is that they are either subject to "capture" by the very industries they are supposed to regulate, or, if they are effective, become part of the political process, therefore exposing the necessary limitations upon the freedom of monopolies in essential industries. Inevitably, governments are drawn into discussions concerning the cost base, pricing policy, and investment programme of the industries concerned.

Ministers and MPs will continue to be the recipients of complaints about performance – and rightly so, since if competitive markets do not provide an opportunity for consumers to register dissatisfaction the political process is all that is left (Kay and Silberston 1984: 15).

The regulatory agencies established in privatised utilities (such as Oftel and Ofgas) have yet to prove they are more effective than the consumer councils of the former public industries. In addition, ingenious methods have been devised to restrain any tendencies to excessive abuse of monopoly position, including BT being restricted to overall price increases set several points below the retail price index, and proposals of Cecil Parkinson, the Energy Minister, to compensate for the natural monopoly in electricity distribution by imposing financial penalties on failure to deliver or install equipment or services on time, with the provision of automatic discounts or vouchers. These are fine ideas, it will be interesting to see if they survive in practice, and one wonders why Ministers are reluctant to introduce them for the industries remaining under their responsibility in the public sector. However, management are opposed to any form of regulation in the privatised industries, and now they have been reinforced by the self-interest of shareholders. The impatience of the Stock market with BT and British Gas is clear already, as one broker put it "The market has been looking at the regulatory side of the two business and realizing you must write in the growth rates and the p/es associated with regulated business. Both may now settle down to become low beat utility stocks" (*Observer*, 21 June 1987).

Among the ways it is certain the privatised companies will seek to enhance their profitability is by developing further domination of their market sector, regardless of what the government promises. One way this will be achieved is through increasing horizontal and vertical integration takeover of the existing independent companies in the sector. The Monopolies Commission is likely to prove an unsatisfactory safeguard against this process of concentration. The Commission examines only large mergers involving companies valued at £ 15 million or more, or where mergers will create or enhance a 25%+ share of the relevant market. In fact, only about 3% of eligible mergers are referred to the Commission, and only half of these are deemed to be against the public interest. Thus in 1988 the newly privatised British Airways quickly swallowed up its only serious national competitor, British Caledonian, resulting in there being significantly less competition in the air passenger market after privatisation than before.

A final form of regulation concerning the privatised industries, is the government retention of a "Golden Share". In Enterprise Oil and Britoil this device empowers the government to outvote any other shareholders if a single holder acquires 50% or more of the company's equity. In other companies the "Golden Share" may be used in the case of the disposal of 25% of the assets, winding up, or the issue of new shares without voting rights. This is designed to protect the strategic industries of British Airways and Rolls Royce, and to prevent BT, Cable and Wireless, and British Gas falling into overseas ownership, which is considered to be against the national interest. Similarly, to suppose that the Thatcher government's belief in the infallibility of the free market is sufficiently strong to allow essential public utilities such as water, gas, and electricity to go bankrupt and collapse, if that unlikely event were ever to threaten, is to strain credibility a little far: "de-coupling the state and the economy" is not as simple as it might at first appear.

3. Privatisation in Practice: A Shareholding Democracy?

Greed is all right. Greed is healthy. You can be greedy and still feel good about yourself (Ivan Boesky, Wall Street arbitrageur convicted for insider dealing).

What are the long-term benefits of the privatisation process in practice? The appearance of a booming shareholder democracy is deceptive. If the over-riding purpose of the Treasury was simply to raise cash, as some critics have argued, then its success in selling off state industries has not been as spectacular as is often claimed in terms of the real worth of the assets disposed of. Table 1 reveals that the major privatisation sales during 1979–1987 raised £ 21,725 million, yet the market capitalisation of these industries at 19/10/1987 implies an ultimate "loss" of £ 11,270 million on the sale in terms of the medium-term worth of the companies concerned. The advocates of privatisation would claim this is nonsense, that on the contrary, the present market capitalisation of the privatised companies reveals how successfully they have been turned around, offering dramatic proof of the commercial sense of the privatisation strategy. This view conveniently ignores a number of critical considerations.

Firstly, much of the work of restructuring these corporations was done as preparation for privatisation, a material prerequisite for a successful sale. As part of the restructuring and preparatory process, often enormous amounts of public funds were injected into the soon to be privatised companies. For example, in the proposed sale of the Rover Cars Group to British Aerospace in July 1988, the government wanted to inject £ 800 million, including the write-off of £ 560 million in debts, and £ 168 million for restructuring (BAe were to pay only £ 150 million for the whole group). The EEC commissioners for competition insisted upon a reduction of £ 200–300 million in state aid, which they perceived to be state subsidy (though BAe would be partly compensated by further British Government support for its Airbus business). Previously, the EEC had agreed in the privatisation of the French Renault Car Company to overlook a total of FFr 20,000 million ($ 3,400 million) in past subsidies and government-guaranteed debts (*Economist* 9 July 1988).

Secondly, privatisation shares were consistently seriously undervalued, partly deliberately as a premium to attract shareholders, mainly mistakenly due to poor advice concerning the real market value of the public companies (advice given by merchant banks and stockbroking firms that stood to make a fortune out of the general privatisation process, both in adviser fees and, more importantly, as players, if not on the privatisations they advised upon, then certainly in all of the others). Thus approximately £ 3,500 million of the government loss was recorded the moment dealings in the privatised shares opened in the market, including an immediate loss of £ 1,300 million on the day of the British Telecom sale (TUC 1987). In addition, the government paid a figure estimated at £ 600 million by the House of Commons Public Accounts Committee to City merchant banks, accounting firms, stockbrokers and advertising agencies to organise and promote the privatisation sales in a lavish manner. The firms handling the BT sale alone charged the government £ 128 million (Kay et al. 1986: 328). (Really the advertisers deserve a special mention: it was quite remarkable how nationalised industries, condemned for years by government ministers as being sluggish monsters,

Table 1. British Government Privatisation Programme 1979–87

Company	Date of issue	Govt. proceeds £ m	% of Equity	19/10/87 Market capital. £ m	"Loss" to govt £ m
BP	Nov 79	290	5	17.435	581
B. Aerospace	Feb 81	50	50	1.062	481
BP	Jun 81	15	5.6	17.435	961
Cable & Wire.	Oct 81	189	49	2.961	1.261
Amersham I.	Feb 82	65	100	272	207
Britoil	Nov 82	549	51	1.261	94
A. B. Ports	Feb 83	−34[1]	51.5	537	311
BP	Sep 83	566	7	17.435	654
Cable & Wire.	Dec 83	275	22	2.961	376
A. B. Ports	Apr 84	52	48.5	537	208
Enterprise Oil	Jun 84	392	100	747	355
Jaguar	Jul 84	294	100	915	621
B. Telecom	Nov 84	2.626	50.2	12.900	3.849
B. Aerospace	May 85	363	59[2]	1.062	264
Britoil	Aug 85	449	48*	1.261	156
Cable & Wire.	Dec 85	602	31[3]	2.961	223
B. Gas	Dec 86	7.720	100*	7.802	82
B. Airways	Feb 87	900	100*	1.188	288
Rolls Royce	May 87	1.080	100	1.473	393
B. Airports A.	Jul 87	1.275	100*	1.415	140
B. P.	Oct 87	5.727	31.5*	17.435	(+235)

Total government proceeds	£ 21.725m	Total government "Loss" £ 11.270m

Sources: Price Waterhouse; H. M. Treasury; Datastream; Observer 25/10/87.
[1] After cancelling debt.
[2] Including new share issue.
[3] Including rights issue.
* Other than shares retained to pay loyalty bonuses.

were suddenly projected in exciting, colourful, and extremely expensive advertisements as dynamic corporations, at the leading-edge of industrial progress, in the months prior to privatisation.)

Finally, to the extent that the public corporations have been turned around in terms of their profitability since privatisation, and therefore have earned their higher market capitalisation, it has not been primarily through the hard work of reducing costs, improving quality, and expanding activity, it has been through the far cruder, but effective, devices of increasing prices, selling off assets, reducing manpower, and cutting services. At any time, if they had abandoned their commitments to social responsibility (which many of the public corporations were urged to do towards their end), the former public corporations could have recorded higher profits in this manner, though whether their contribution to the wider economy and public good would have been as great as a result is open to question.

A thorough cost/benefit analysis of the government privatisation programme remains to be conducted, but elements would include the high cost of redundancy payments and unemployment benefits to the workers who lost their jobs as a result of pre-privatisation restructuring; the loss of revenue from the profitable public industries (in 1983/1984 public industries generated £ 4,600 million in funds and paid £ 2,700 million in interest, tax, and dividends to the Exchequer (Labour Party 1986: 1)); the loss of the capacity to meet social and economic priorities through cross-subsidisation; the increases in the retail price index and resulting inflationary pressures caused by those privatised industries that increased their profitability largely by increasing prices; and, paradoxically for a government convinced of the notion that public expenditure had crowded out private investment in Britain in the post-war years, the cost would have to be measured of the huge diversion of funds on the stock market to the privatised companies, and to the extent that this was not new money, away from the existing quoted companies. On the benefit side the government could record the substantial amounts of cash raised used to lower taxes, defer public expenditure cuts (and pay dole), and the revenue raised in tax from company profits.

The privatisation policy has created a huge and unprecedented expansion in the number of shareholders. Melvyn Marckus, City Editor of the *Observer* has insisted that

Table 2. Share Prices of British Privatised Companies 1979–88

Company	Date of issue	Offer price	Share price since High	Low	Price 1/7/88
BP	Nov 79	363p	410p	85p	254p
B. Aerospace	Feb 81	150p	688p	170p	408p
BP	Jun 81	290p	410p	85p	254p
Cable & Wire.	Oct 81	168p	503p	64p	363p
Amersham I.	Feb 82	142p	647p	142p	463p
Britoil	Nov 82	215p	359p	101p	–
A. B. Ports	Feb 83	112p	673p	69p	543p
BP	Sep 83	435p	410p	129p	254p
Cable & Wire.	Dec 83	275p	503p	135p	363p
A. B. Ports	Apr 84	270p	673p	81.5p	543p
Enterprise Oil	Jun 84	185p	496p	94p	489p
Jaguar	Jul 84	165p	628p	171p	281p
B. Telecom	Nov 84	130p	334p	168p	259p
B. Aerospace	May 85	375p	688p	295p	408p
Britoil	Aug 85	185p	359p	101p	–
Cable & Wire.	Dec 85	587p	503p	277p	363p
B. Gas	Dec 86	135p	200p	106p	186p
B. Airways	Feb 87	125p	239p	139p	149p
Rolls Royce	May 87	170p	232p	108p	129p
B. Airports A.	Jul 87	245p	290p	130p	275p
BP	Oct 87	330p	286p	243p	254p

Sources: Datastream; Financial Times Share Index.

[...] The Government [...] had, through the marketing of one counter, British Telecom, captured the imagination (and savings) of more members of the public than had previously been drawn into the entire 2,000 strong spectrum of UK registered companies quoted on the London Stock Exchange (25 October 1987).

But the question is posed whether the temporary acquisition of small shareholdings amounts to a fundamental break in the consciousness of working people and an immersion within the risks and opportunities of the market system, as if what was happening was almost "metamorphosing capitalism or class relations by making workers part-capitalists" (Ramsay and Haworth 1984: 295). Any suggestion that investors in privatisation shares were learning to take risks seems somewhat fatuous, as Table 2 shows. All the privatisation shares were intended to offer an immediate substantial gain to investors, and millions of small shareholders disposed of their shares long before any fluctuations in price occurred. (Profit per share at the end of the first day of trading in privatised stocks, as a percentage of the partly paid price, ranged from British Gas 25%, British Airways 68%, Rolls Royce 73%, BT 86% (Grout 1988: 70).) Buying Gas or Telecom shares, with the enticement of a discount on services in addition, was much less of an indication of a subordination of the working class to the imperatives of the market system than an occasional flutter on the races. The injunction of Ivan Boesky (echoed by the awesomely slick Gordon Gekko in Oliver Stone's film *Wall Street* (1987)) may have a particular resonance in the late 1980s, but not with the people who are used to paying for other peoples' greed. The level of real commitment of the mass of small shareholders induced by the privatisation issues is revealed in Table 3. The massive inflation in the number of shareholders appears to be a very ephemeral phenomenon.

Table 3. The Declining Number of Shareholders in Privatisation Stocks 1981–87

Company	1st Issue	2nd Issue	3rd Issue	Current number of shareholders	Date
Amersham I.	65.000	n/a	n/a	5.940	Oct 87
A. British Ports	45.500	8.000	n/a	9.666	Oct 87
B. Airports A.	2.187.500	n/a	n/a	1.500.000*	Oct 87
British Aerospace	155.000	260.000	n/a	102.788	Oct 87
British Airways	1.100.000	n/a	n/a	404.000	Oct 87
British Gas	4.407.079	n/a	n/a	3.000.000	Oct 87
British Telecom	2.300.000	n/a	n/a	1.417.905	Mar 87
Britoil	35.000	450.000	n/a	178.600	Jul 87
Cable & Wireless	26.000	35.137	218.588	174.758	Oct 87
Enterprise Oil	13.695	n/a	n/a	11.100	Jul 87
Jaguar	125.000	n/a	n/a	34.918	Oct 87
Rolls Royce	2.000.000	n/a	n/a	1.250.000*	Oct 87
TSB	3.000.000	n/a	n/a	1.970.000	Feb 87

Source: Observer Privatisation Survey 25 October 1987.
* Approximate

The extraordinary increase in shareholders is only sustained, as the government has realised, by repeated issues of enormous amounts of shares. The rate of sale of shareholdings in 1986–1987 indicates the British government will have to find about 5 million new shareholders each year if the present number of shareholders is to be maintained. This rate of share issues the government may be able to sustain until the early 1990s, when all the readily saleable public assets, including all the nationalised industries, and much of the public sector, will become exhausted.

The claim that soon the number of shareholders will exceed the number of trade unionists is interesting to speculate upon. Government ministers have gleefully insisted this suggests a fundamental (and by implication irreversible) shift in the class balance of society. As Table 4 indicates, trade union membership in Britain, after declining steeply during the recession of the early 1980s, began to stabilise at around 10 million members in the mid-1980s, as the level of unemployment began to fall. (The figure of 10 million is close to the average trade union membership in the whole post-war period.) During the privatisation programme there was a momentous growth in the number of shareholders from 2 million up to 9.4 million. The vast majority of new shareholders had brought shares as a direct result of government policy, either from privatisations or employee share schemes. More than 3.5 million shareholders had shares only in the privatised companies, 1.5 million workers held shares in the company that employed them, and 500,000 only held employee shares (NOP 1987). However, the number of shareholders peaked in 1987 after the British Gas, British Telecom, and BP privatisations, before falling rapidly away to 7 million during 1988 in the time spent preparing the next major privatisation. If the present rate of loss of shareholders is sustained, and the government does not resort to selling off the streets, then it is unlikely there will be more than 5 million shareholders in Britain by the mid-1990s.

Table 4. Number of Shareholders and Trade Union Members Compared 1983–87

Year	Total share ownership		Total trade union membership	
	% of adult pop.	approx. number	membership	as a % of working pop.
1983 (pre-BT)	5%	2m	11.2m	41.6%*
1984 (post-BT)	8%	3.2m	11.0m	39.9%*
1986 (post-TSB)	17%	7m	10.5m	37.6%*
1987 (post B. Gas)	23%	9.4m	10.7m	–
1988	17%	7m[1]	10.6m[1]	–

Sources: Dewe Rogerson Marketing Consultans 1986; Industrial Relations Review and Report 417, 1 June 1988.
* Includes the self-employed and unemployed. If these excluded, the figures of union membership as a percentage of the working population rise to over 50% in these years.
[1] Estimates.

Behind the expensively erected facade of privatisation, there has been little change in the distribution of ownership of property, as indicated by Tables 5 and 6. The 20% of shareholders with investments in 3 or more companies are the ones who are likely to have a real stake in the system. The other 80% of shareholders are just passing through. In fact, as Table 6 reveals, 53% of present shareholders have investments of less than £ 1,000 in the UK, and 70% have investments of less than £ 3,000 (Grout 1987). (At a time when the typical family car costs £ 6,000, the investment in shares remains quite a modest commitment.) Despite all the brouhaha surrounding privatisation, the concentration of ownership of property has continued unabated. As Howard Hyman of Price Waterhouse, seconded to the Treasury, put it:

Although the percentage of adults owning shares was dramatically increased the proportion of the total equity market controlled by individuals rather than institutions continues to decline. Between 1963 and 1981 the proportion of the stock market directly owned by individuals fell from 54% to 28%. Statistics available for 1986 indicate that out of a total equity market valued at £ 368 billion, some £ 88 billion was owned by individuals or 24 per cent (*Observer* 25 October 1987).

The new army of small shareholders is therefore a minority of a minority in investment terms, which the City of London neither particularly wants or needs, though is often too polite to say. Some stockbrokers did close their offices to "mickey mouse" shareholders during privatisation issues, and others demanded a minimum portfolio of £ 100,000 from investors. Attending to millions of minute transactions is hardly a profitable affair for the brokers, and back-offices remain buried in paperwork until the introduction of a fully computerised dealing system.

Table 5. The Number of Companies Invested in by Individual Shareholders in 1987

Shares in:	% of Shareholders	Approximate number
1 Company	56%	5.4 million
2 Companies	22%	2.1 million
3 Companies	9%	0.8 million
4 to 9 Companies	8%	0.8 million
10 plus Companies	3%	0.3 million

Source: Dewe Rogerson Marketing Consultants 1986.

Table 6. Value of Shareholdings (for Positive Respondents) 1986

Value of Shareholdings	Percentage of Shareholders
Less Than £ 500	34%
£ 501–£ 1000	19.4%
£ 1001–£ 3000	18%
£ 3001+	30%

Source: Grout 1987; Stock Exchange Survey 1986.

Therefore doubts must be entertained when Nigel Lawson states so confidently, "The Government has no plans to abandon its previous policies of offering state assets at a material discount to the private sector to encourage its dreams of an ever-widening share-owning democracy" (*Observer* 21 June 1987). The government must be aware by now of the almost universal quick sale of shares by the mass of new shareholders. The government is in fact achieving two rather different results from its privatisation policy:

(a) Introducing people to some of the mechanics of capitalism with which they were unacquainted, while giving them a very small financial stake in the dismemberment of the public sector, and an interest in electing future Conservative governments;

(b) Concealing the enormous transfer of assets from the public sector to large financial, multinational, and overseas corporations under the camouflage of "popular capitalism."

Already large blocks of shares in British privatised industries have been acquired in Japan and the USA, and the prospect of major British utilities being owned by overseas corporations is in sight as ways around the restrictions on overseas ownership are found. In 1988 the Kuwait Investment Office purchased 22 per cent of BP. With government pressure it is likely that the Monopolies Commission will rule this holding "against the public interest," though as *Private Eye* records, "It should then take the KIO roughly five minutes to buy itself a collection of nominee shareholders in Zürich who will continue the situation by another name" (8 July 1988). BP had insisted upon the shares being offered to overseas investors to reflect the groups overseas earnings base, which appears to have left the company open to re-nationalisation by the Kuwaiti Government!

Table 7. British Telecom Performance 1985–1987

	Profits	Complaints
1985 Pre-privatisation	£ 1.480	10.000
1986 Post-privatisation	£ 1.810	16.000
1987	£ 2.067	24.000

Sources: *Which?* May 1987; *BBC TV News* 6 June 1988.

If a shareholder democracy has proved somewhat elusive, how has the consumer democracy fared? Regrettably, behind the explosion of profits in the recently privatised industries there is not a host of newly delighted customers. Some economists who support the governments policies applaud the enhanced profitability of the privatised companies, without inquiring too closely where the profits came from (Mathews and Minford 1987). For example, the sale of British Telecom was accompanied by promises of higher standards of service as well as better profit performance. The latter has certainly been achieved, but hardly the former, as Table 7 indicates. It should be appreciated those who take the trouble to register an official consumer complaint are only a tiny fraction of those who are aggrieved but feel incapable of doing anything about it, or that if they attempted to, nothing constructive would result. As one visitor from Africa put it, "I can understand these profit figures for BT. When in London I put my money in the phone box, it took it, but nothing happened. I tried again, but still couldn't get through. I rang the operator and she said, "I will credit your account." But I have no account! This happened to me three times during my stay!" Surveys by Oftel (the telecommunications regulatory agency) discovered 23% of call boxes were out of order in 1987 (17% in 1986). BT did make hurried efforts to repair call boxes in 1987–1988 when Mercury Communications, a subsidiary of Cable and Wireless, were offered entry into the phone box network, though Mercury are only interested in the prime city centre sites. In July 1987 the National Consumer Council published a *Mori Report* which revealed 52% of consumers considered BT prices were unreasonable, compared to 40% in 1980 prior to privatisation. The same poll recorded much less dissatisfaction with gas (23%) and water (28%) prices, while these utilities were still in the public sector. A *Which Report* in May 1988 revealed serious public disillusion with the standard of service on offer from BT. One reason for the increase in consumer complaint was the fact BT increased domestic tariffs where the likelihood of future competition was slight due to the extent of sunk investment, in order to reduce business tariffs, a market Mercury were interested in. One BT worker put the situation bluntly, "The management are not interested in the consumer. We were a monopoly and we still are."

The promise of privatisation was a dramatic improvement in consumer choice, as corporations were set free to respond to market demands rather than political constraints. The worry concerning privatisation was the effect upon the quality and range of provision, and the access to it, as the elimination of cross-subsidisation undermined a comprehensive service: "freedom in markets requires freedom to participate and [...] this depends upon the distribution of income and wealth" (Parker 1987: 357). The fear of consumer bodies is that privatisation of the vital utilities gas, water, and electricity will seriously threaten the most vulnerable consumers in society as the interests of shareholders take precedence over service, with falling standards, higher prices, and mounting disconnections. As the National Association of Citizens Advice Bureaux' evidence regarding disconnections stated to the Department of the Environment, "If financial interest takes precendence over social considerations now, how much greater will the pressures be when the Water Authorities must account to their shareholders?" (1987).

Finally, the position of workers in the privatised corporations deserves consideration. Any impression that they are worker-owners should be dispelled. Though facilities for employee shareholding were made available in every privatisation, and in most were taken up by the great majority of the workers concerned, the value of the total worker shareholdings remains at a derisory level. As with earlier employee-share ownership schemes, the object seems to have been to promote a sense of loyalty to the firm, without conceding, even to the slightest extent, any real powers of ownership. Worker shareholders may have the right to attend the AGMs of their companies, and to receive Annual Reports, but the prospect of influencing the directors of the company with the tiny percentage of shares the workers collectively possess is remote. For example, British Aerospace sold 3 million shares to its workforce, which amounted to 1.3% of the total. In the privatisation of British Steel, workers with twenty years of service would receive a few hundred pounds worth of shares. Any hope these minuscule holdings could be gradually built into majority stakes in the companies concerned is unfounded. The tendency has been for workers conscious of the enormity of the problem to lose interest in their shares and to sell them off. The case of the National Freight Corporation (NFC) is instructive. The privatisation was achieved by a management buy-out in which the ordinary employees held a significant percentage of the shares. Yet in 1988 the workers were persuaded to launch NFC as a public company on the market, therefore opening up the prospect of a large company taking over NFC. The commodity status of labour does not seem to have changed all that much.

Nonetheless the image of cheerful, profit-hungry corporate Stakhanovites is that preferred by the advertising agencies. There is one group of privatised employees who are pretty cheerful, and Table 8 explains why. Salary increases of up to 350% for chief executives in the three years following privatisation are quite an incentive. But the wages, job security, and morale of ordinary workers in these industries have not fared quite so well. For example, Sir Dennis Rooke, Chair of British Gas, awarded himself a rise of £ 74,000 to £ 184,000 p. a. in 1987, a 68% pay increase, whilst the average pay rise for British Gas employees for 1987 was 6%, raising the average salary to £ 11,900 (*Financial Times* 14 July 1988).

Trade union recognition, bargaining, and consultation rights have been lost in a range of privatised companies. At British Telecom, the management quote the Stock Exchange rules against "insider trading" in denial of access to information, on the grounds most union members are now BT shareholders! Wage improvements have been modest, not remotely reflecting the increase in profits or dividends. Minimum wages have been abandoned, allowances eroded, and benefits removed, particularly index-linked pensions (TUC 1986a). Even in some areas as important as health and safety, where the nationalised industries had a good record in recent years due to the cumulative pressure of the unions and successive governments, neglect and the urge to cut corners are creeping into the privatised concerns. At BT the competition introduced into working methods as part of the privatisation strategy has been accompanied by a steady rise in the rate of accidents; meanwhile the number of safety officers has been reduced (*Labour Research* November 1987). In the British coal industry the safety laws, "legislation written in blood," are among the best in the world, but British Coal regard these regulations as an obstacle to privatisation and profit making. Already 140,000

Table 8. Increase in Directors' Salaries after Privatisation

Company	Before	After Privatisation				%
		Year 2	Year 3	Year 4	Year 5	Inc
Amersham I.	£ 30.360 (1981–2)	£ 88.983 (1983–4)	£ 130.178 (1984–5)			328%
A. British Ports	£ 35.196 (1982)	£ 58.749 (1984)				66%
B. Aerospace	£ 44.467 (1980)	£ 73.378 (1982)	£ 87.260 (1983)	£ 100.790 (1984)	£ 125.000 (1985)	181%
BP	£ 120.385 (1979)	£ 158.151 (1981)	£ 172.770 (1982)	£ 183.134 (1983)	£ 241.547 (1984)	100%
B. Telecom	£ 67.900 (1983)	£ 111.399 (1985)	£ 160.000 (1986)			135%
Britoil	£ 72.000 (1982)	£ 98.000 (1984)				36%
Cable & Wireless	£ 30.277 (1981)	£ 111.952 (1985)	£ 136.881 (1986)			352%
Enterprise Oil	£ 28.560 (1983)	£ 90.000 (1985)				215%
National Freight Consortium	£ 51.046 (1982)	£ 98.292 (1984)				92%
British Airways	£ 52.000 (1987)	£ 178.000 (1988)				225%
British Gas		£ 184.000 (1988)				68%

Source: TUC 1985e; British Institute of Management Survey on Top Salaries, 1988; Financial Times, 14 July 1988.
Note: The average increase in earnings during the period 1980–1986 in the UK was 7.5% per annum.

colliery jobs have gone since 1979, less than half the 1979 workforce surviving, and the pressures upon the miners remaining in the pits have increased considerably with much higher accident rates resulting. Yet British Coal are still looking for "radical changes in legislation" (*Labour Research* June 1988).

A dramatic reduction in manpower in some of the other privatised industries has occurred also, primarily in preparation for privatisation as at British Steel, though often with further reductions later. Table 9 indicates that in total 1 million jobs have disappeared from the nationalised industries since 1979. Many of these workers will have transferred with their companies to the private sector, but hundreds of thousands of jobs were casualties of the process of transition. (At British Steel 13,000 jobs were lost directly in the course of transfer of subsidiaries to private owners, at BT 16,500 jobs were cut, at British Airways 23,000 (TUC 1986a).). The official government explanation of this is that such a shake-out was essential in reducing the unit costs and restoring the efficiency of the companies concerned, and most of the redundant workers are now profitably employed in the expanding sectors of the economy, particularly the service industries. However, this answer is unsatisfactory to workers who face long-term unemployment, or life in the new low paid, flexible workforce, when what they produced formerly is still needed in the economy and society.

Table 9. Number of Employees in Nationalised Industries

Year	Number (000)	Fall From Previous Year (000)	%
1979	1.849		
1980	1.816	33	2%
1981	1.657	159	9%
1982	1.554	103	6%
1983	1.465	89	6%
1984	1.416	49	3%
1985	1.137	279	20%
1986	1.065	72	6%
1987	870	195	18%

Source: CSO *Economic Trends* December 1987; *Labour Research* June 1988.

That *control* is a critical dimension behind the privatisation process is revealed by those who suffer the worst fate of all and become involved in contracting-out procedures. As with privatisation, the process of contracting-out began in a relatively small way but eventually threatened to engulf much of the work of the Civil Service, National Health Service, and Local Authorities. In the civil service the aim has been to cut 100,000 jobs by hiving off parts of the service to the private sector and contracting out work such as cleaning, laundry, and maintenance to private contractors. In the NHS, competitive tendering for catering and laundry services was introduced, with the rescinding of the Fair Wages Resolution of 1946 to obviate the need for contractors to observe NHS rates of pay and conditions in September 1983. In the local authorities the Local Government Act (1988) established compulsory competitive tendering for refuse collection and street sweeping; building cleaning; school catering; leisure centre management; ground maintenance; and other catering. (The Secretary of State is enabled to add to the list, and one Conservative MP has suggested 33 additional services should be contracted-out including social services, day centres, burials, and art galleries.) There are presently 350,000 low paid workers (almost entirely women) currently employed in the school cleaning and meals service, "Thus, the government's proposals are on a vast scale, likely to affect 1 in 20 of the country's *total* workforce directly" (Thomas 1988: 158).

Private companies (and part of the public sector) have always used external contractors to provide services: in order to reduce operating costs; minimise the use of capital; meet peak workloads; and provide a specialist capacity not available inhouse. However contracting-out as now imposed in the public services is rather different as one guide to competitive tendering in the NHS coyly states, "The particular services being considered are for the most part already being provided by existing in-house departments" (IPM 1986: 6). In the CBI report *Efficiency in the Public Services*, it is contended, "Competitive tendering brings market forces to bear in the provision of services normally provided in-house. It provides an opportunity to minimise costs either by contracting out services or acting as a spur to in-house efficiency" (1984).

In a government review, *Using Private Enterprise in Government* published by the Cabinet Office Efficiency Unit (1986), five main reasons are given for promoting contracting-out of services: to save money; to save management time; to obtain expertise not available in-house; to retain flexibility; and to re-establish management control (from the unions). Such arguments either ignore, or have no regard for, the contrary views that in-house services provide better quality; are more reliable and flexible (in doing the job rather than being hired and fired); private contractors cut corners to provide profit; private employees usually have little training or loyalty to the job; contracting-out closes off options if it is desired to bring the service back in-house; finally, contracting-out undermines pay and conditions, manning levels, and reduces trade union rights (IPM 1986).

With reference to NHS competitive tendering; the House of Commons Social Services Committee report in June 1985 stated:

The whole exercise, which has now been underway for around four years, has involved a considerable amount of management time and effort; has caused disruption and discontent, not exclusively among NHS staff directly employed in these services, and to date has not brought home the bacon (IPM 1986: 16).

Contradicting the extravagant claims of government regarding cost-savings is mounting evidence of contractors inflicting lower standards in the public services. In Wokingham Hospital the private cleaning contractors, Exclusive, were discovered employing children; in Cambridge the private contractors, having secured the cleaning contract, added £ 257,504 to the bill, £ 177,099 more than the in-house tender; more seriously there are widespread reports of stained lavatories, dirty surgeries, and potentially dangerous lapses. In Oxford District Health Authority the contractors Hospital Hygiene Services Ltd were discovered to have left piles of filthy laundry, dirty nappies were left uncollected in childrens wards, and floors in wards and corridors were uncleaned. The extensive catalogue of wilful neglect masquerading under the pretence of "efficiency" would make anyone angry (Hastings and Levie 1983; TUC 1985d; TUC 1986b). The standard procedure of the private contractors upon winning a contract is to attempt (often unsuccessfully) to recruit the workers previously employed, though on much lower rates of pay, and expecting them to do the same amount of work in a fraction of the time it previously took. If local authorities or hospitals hope to win tenders, it is only by adopting similar tactics:

For local authorities their traditional aims to be "good employers" and to place "equity" alongside economy, efficiency and effectiveness as organizational watchwords were beginning to look increasingly distant goals or expensive luxuries to be jettisoned (Thomas 1988: 170).

"Getting the state off our backs", as far as local authority and NHS contracting-out is concerned, translates into forcing low paid workers, who have poor conditions of work, to accept even lower pay and worse conditions. One outraged union official described contracting-out thus:

I believe the process of compulsory tendering decided by the government is immoral in all its aspects. It does things to people which should never be done by any employer, by any government. First, it entirely deprives ancillary workers of job security – that is a terrible thing to do, particularly for people who joined the service because of that one thing it offered them – it did not offer them good pay, nor good conditions and offered them a pretty horrible job in many instances – but it did offer job security. So the government has taken away the one aspect that people valued. It puts people in the position of having to bargain for their existing job – its a demoralising and alienating experience – which is not fully appreciated by people until it's applied to them or people who are important to them (Thomas 1988: 165).

4. Conclusions

The study of privatisation reveals how changes in ownership and control, in competition and regulation, associated with the transfer of industries from the public to the private sector, alters the objectives, priorities, constraints, and incentives of industrial organisation. In turn, this leads to the reproduction of different patterns of class relations and class inequalities, both within the organisation, and within wider society. Undoubtedly, behind the veneer of a shareholding democracy, the lasting effect of the privatisation process has been to reassert the commodity status of labour, to worsen income differentials, and to re-introduce the authority relations of unregulated capitalism.

However, it is simplistic, naive, delusory, and dangerous to suggest that public ownership is invariably good, and private ownership invariably bad in results (or the converse). This form of what is called "ideologicisation" in Eastern Europe, denies the most dreadful experiences in reality in preference for the deceit of elegant theory. If recognition of this in the East has resulted in the dramatic attempt at perestroika of the command economies, it is a curious historical irony that in the West we have become seduced by the ideology of the market.

Some evocations of the market achieve an almost lyrical quality in which it stands revealed as a thing of terrible beauty and awesome symmetry, and no myth has proved more persistent than the belief in a lost Golden Age in which true competition existed (*New Statesman* 12 February 1988).

An assumption in some quarters is that Thatcher has engendered an *Economic Renaissance in Britain* (Walters 1985), when it is capitalism that has ben restored, not the economy. The belief that monetarist policy and privatisation have transformed the economy conceals an unspectacular performance relative to industrial growth in Europe, the enormous economic advantage of North Sea Oil, and the fact that higher productivity and profits have been recorded in the public sector as well as the private. As Kirkpatrick has observed, the privatisation process is a "confluence of ideology and pragmatism" (1988: 237). Despite profuse protestations to the contrary, neither is particularly concerned with either economic democracy or efficiency.

Privatisation is a contradictory policy, and the resulting industrial structure is highly unstable. The private monopolies have a built-in tendency to become both less commercially efficient and less socially responsible than was tolerated until recently when they were part of the public sector. John Smith, the Shadow Chancellor, has distilled the essential irresponsibility of privatisation thus:

Privatisation has represented an unrepeatable sale of state assets at knock-down prices. It has transferred rights to profits from state enterprises for present and future generations to private shareholders. It has redistributed wealth from the nation as a whole to those in a position to provide "up-front cash" in order to stage issues. It has elevated the pursuit of private profit above the imperatives of public service in our once public utilities. It has created private sector monopolies and thereby exposed the whole nation to the danger of monopolistic exploitation (*Observer* 25 October 1987).

Untrammelled privatisation has caused the loss of a legacy of fifty years of patient social democratic construction of the public sector of industry in Britain. It is no intellectual satisfaction to suggest the perennial deficiencies of the public sector both in terms of economic democracy and efficiency made the loss inevitable. However, we are beginning with a clean slate in reconstructing economic and industrial democracy, and the substantial amount of pioneering work on forms of democratic organisation conducted around the world is a stimulus and example that was not available to those who earlier in the century regarded the command economy of the Soviet Union as the only relevant model. A policy of social ownership comprehends that public ownership is not simply state ownership, but represents a multiplicity of potential forms. If these diverse forms are to have any cutting edge at all in severing the attractions of privatisation, the right of workers and consumers to participate at every level of industrial decision making will be central.

References

Bosanquet, N., The "Social Market Economy": Principles Behind the Policies, *Political Quarterly* 55: 245–256. 1984

Cabinet Office Efficiency Unit, *Using Private Enterprise in Government*. London: HMSO. 1986

CBI, *Efficiency in the Public Services*. London: CBI. 1984

Clegg, S. and D. Dunkerley, *Organization, Class and Control*. London: RKP. 1980

Commander, S. and T. Killick, Privatisation in Developing Countries, in: P. Cook and C. Kirkpatrick (eds.), *Privatisation in Less Developed Countries*. Brighton: Wheatsheaf Books. 1988

Dewe Rogerson, *Survey Conducted for Trustee Savings Bank*. London: Dewe Rogerson Consultants. 1986

Freikhert, D., The Kiwi Tendency, *New Socialist* 55, May/June: 19–21. 1988

Grout, P., The Wider Share Ownership Programme, *Fiscal Studies* 8,3: 59–74. 1987

Grout, P., Employee Share Ownership and Privatisation: Some Theoretical Issues, *Economic Journal* 98: 97–104. 1988

Hastings, S. and H. Levie, *Privatisation?* Nottingham: Spokesman. 1983

Helm, D., Nuclear Power and the Privatisation of Electricity Generation, *Fiscal Studies*, 8,4: 69–73. 1987

Hepworth, N., Measuring Performance in Non-Market Organizations, *International Journal of Public Sector Management* 1,1: 16–26. 1988

House of Commons Services Committee, *Public Expenditure on the Social Services*. London: HMSO. 1985

Institute of Personnel Management and Incomes Data Services Public Sector Unit, *Competitive Tendering in the Public Sector*. London: IPM/IDS. 1986

Kay, J. A. and Z. A. Silberston, The New Industrial Policy-Privatisation and Competition, *Midland Bank Review* Spring: 8–16. 1984

Kay, J. A. and D. Thompson, Privatisation: A Policy in Search of a Rationale, *Economic Journal* 96: 18–32. 1986.

Kay, J., C. Mayer, and D. Thompson, *Privatisation and Regulation*. London: Institute of Fiscal Studies. 1986

Kirkpatrick, C., The UK Privatisation Model: Is it Transferable to Developing Countries? in: Ramanadham, pp. 235–243. 1988

Labour Party, *Social Ownership*, Statement by the NEC to the 85th Annual Conference, Blackpool. 1986

Labour Research Department (LRD), *Public or Private: The Case Against Privatisation*. London: LRD. 1982

LRD, *Privatisation – The Great Sell-Out*. London: LRD. 1985

Labour Research, Big Fish Grab Sell-Off Shares, 76, 9, September: 7–8. 1987

Labour Research, Public Assets Going For A Song, 77, 6, June: 14–16. 1988

Letwin, O., *Privatising the World*. London: Cassell. 1988

Mathews, K. and P. Minford, Mrs Thatcher's Economic Policies 1979–1987, *Economic Policy* October: 57–102. 1987

McCarthy, W., Privatisation and the Employee, in: Ramanadham, pp. 73–84. 1988

Millward, R. and D. Parker, Public and Private Enterprise: Comparative Behaviour and Relative Efficiency, in: R. Milward et al., *Public Sector Economic*. London: Longman. 1983

NOP, *Shareholder Survey*, London: Stock Exchange. 1987

Observer, *Privatisation Survey*, 25 October 1987. 1987

Parker, D., The New Right, State Ownership and Privatisation: A Critique, *Economic and Industrial Democracy* 8, 349–378. 1987

Pendse, D. R., Some Reflections on the Role of Donor Agencies in the Privatisation Process, *National Westminster Bank Quarterly Review*, November: 2–18. 1985

Perotin, V. and S. Estrin, Does Ownership Matter? Typescript, London School of Economics. 1987

Pliatzky, L., Optimising the Role of the Public Sector: Constraints and Remedial Policies, *Public Policy and Administration* 3, 1: 35–44. 1988

Posner, M., Privatisation: The Frontier Between Public and Private, *Policy Studies* 5,1 (July): 22–32. 1984

Prosser, T., *Nationalised Industries and Public Control*. Oxford: Basil Blackwell. 1986

Pryke, R., Privatising Electricity Generation, *Fiscal Studies* 8,3: 75–88. 1987

Ramanadham, V., *Privatisation in the UK*. London: Routledge. 1988

Ramsay, H. and N. Haworth, Worker Capitalists? Profit Sharing, Capital Sharing and Juridical Forms of Socialism, *Economic and Industrial Democracy* 5: 295–324. 1984

RIPA, *Contracting-Out in the Public Sector*. London: Royal Institute of Public Administration. 1984

Shackleton, J., Privatisation: The Case Examined, *National Westminster Bank Quarterly Review* (May): 59–73. 1984

Schumpeter, J., *Capitalism, Socialism and Democracy*. 3rd Edition, London: Allen and Unwin. 1950

Steel, D. and D. Heald, Privatising Public Enterprise: An Analysis of the Government's Case, *Political Quarterly* 53: 333–349. 1982

Steel, D. and D. Heald, *Privatising Public Enterprises*. London: Royal Institute of Public Administration. 1984

Stock Exchange, *The Changing Face of Share Ownership*. London: London Stock Exchange. 1986

Thomas, C., Contracting-Out: Managerial Strategy or Political Dogma? in: Ramanadham, pp. 153–172. 1988

Thomas, D., The Union Response to Denationalisation, in: D. Steel and D. Heald, pp. 59–76. 1984

Thomas, D., In the Pipeline, *New Socialist* January: 34–36. 1986

TUC, *Privatisation By Order: The Government Plan For Local Services*. London: TUC, May. 1985a

TUC, *Stripping Our Assets: The City's Privatisation Killing*. London: TUC, May. 1985b

TUC, *The £ 16 Billion Gas Bill: The Real Costs of Privatisation*. London: TUC, November. 1985c

TUC, *Contractors Failures The Privatisation Experience*. London: TUC, February. 1985d

TUC, *Privatisation and Top Pay*. London: TUC, December. 1985e

TUC, *Bargaining in the Privatised Companies*. London: TUC, February. 1986a

TUC, *More Contractors Failures*. London: TUC, November. 1986b

TUC, *The UK Privatisation Programme*. London: TUC, June. 1987

Walters, A., *Britain's Economic Renaissance – Margaret Thatchers Reforms 1979–1984*, Oxford: Oxford University Press, for the American Enterprise Institute. 1985

Woodward, N., "Managing" Cultural Change on Privatisation, in: Ramanadham, pp. 85–104. 1988

Whitfield, D., *Making it Public – Evidence and Action Against Privatisation*. London: Pluto. 1983

Notes on Contributors

Amir Ben-Porat works at the Humphrey Centre. Ben Gurion University of the Negev in Israel. During 1987–1988 he spent the year at James Madison University in the United States of America. He is the author of a substantial study of class formation entitled *Between Class and Nation: The Formation of the Jewish Working Class in the Period Before Israel's Statehood* (1986).

Raimo Blom is an associate professor, University of Tampere, Finland (Doctor of Administrative Sciences, University of Tampere). He has published on state theory, sociology of law and class analysis. He is author of *Confidence in the Court of Justice* (1970), *Yhteiskuntateoria ja valtio* (Social Theory and the State 1981) and co-author of *Suomalaiset Luokkahuvassa* (The Finns in a Class Photo 1984). He has headed the Finnish research group in Erik Olin Wright's "Comparative Project on Class Structure and Class Consciousness" since 1980. Editor of *Acta Sociologica* 1985–1987.

Val Burris received his Ph.D. in sociology from Princeton University in 1976 and is currently Associate Professor of Sociology at the University of Oregon. He has written extensively on the middle classes in advanced capitalist society and on other topics in Marxist and neo-Marxist theory. His current research focuses on the power structure of American corporations, business support for right-wing political movements, and the politics of the American ruling class.

Guigelmo Carchedi was born in Italy, educated in the United States and works in the Netherlands. He is the author of three books in the area of class analysis, of which the most recent is *Class Analysis and Social Research* (Blackwell 1987). He holds a position at the University of Amsterdam in the Economics Faculty.

Tom Clarke is a senior lecturer in Industrial Sociology, Trent-Polytechnic, Nottingham, England. He has developed research interests in producer co-operatives; the political economy of the mass media; and the international division of labour. With Laurie Clements he is the editor of *Trade Unions Under Capitalism* (Fontana 1977; Harvester/Humanities Press 1978).

Stewart Clegg was born in Bradford, and educated at Aston and Bradford Universities, and, after a period of post-doctoral study as the EGOS Research Fellow, has spent most of his subsequent career in Australia where he is currently Professor and Head of the Department of Sociology at the University of New England in Armidale, NSW, from where he will shortly move to the University of St. Andrews, Scotland. He is an editor of *Organization Studies* and has contributed many books and articles to the areas of organization and class analysis. Recently he was a member of the Australian project on "Class Structure and Class Consciousness," and for a number of years he was co-editor of the *Australian and New Zealand Journal of Sociology*. In 1990 he takes up a Chair of Organization Studies at the University of St. Andrews, Scotland.

Rosemary Crompton was a researcher at the Department of Applied Economics, University of Cambridge in the 1960s, a researcher then teacher at the University of East Anglia, 1967 to 1989. Currently she is at the University of Canterbury in Kent. Major publications include: "Technology and Workers" Attitudes," 1970, (with Dorothy Wedderburn), *Economy and Class Structure*, 1978 (with Jon Gubbay), *White-Collar Proletariat*, 1984 (with Gareth Jones) and *Gender and Stratification*, 1986 (ed. with Michael Mann). Currently she is working on research on Occupational Segregation, which is linked to the ESRC Social Change and Economic Life Initiative.

Nigel Haworth is Senior Lecturer in Labour Relations in the Department of Management and Labour Studies at Auckland University. He has written extensively on labour-capital relations and politics in Latin America, and also on the topic of multinational corporations and international labour. He is an active member of the International Labour Reports collective, and has worked in particular on the nature of and response to closure decisions at Massey Ferguson and Caterpillar Tractor plants in Scotland. Since his recent move to New Zealand he has been developing his international work in the Pacific Basin context.

Ulrich Heisig is a Research Fellow at the University of Bremen. He is a graduate of the Universities of Marburg and Frankfurt. Currently he is engaged on a research project on the change of the work of engineers in research and development.

Winton Higgins is Senior Lecturer in Politics at Macquarie University, Sydney. He has published extensively on Sweden and social democracy in journals such as *Theory and Society* and *Political Power and Social Theory*, and has recently co-authored a major work on *The Unions and the Future of Australian Manufacturing* (Allen and Unwin 1987). He holds degrees from the Universities of Sydney, London and Stockholm.

Barry Hindess is Professor of Sociology at the Australian National University. He is the author of several books including *Parliamentary Democracy and Socialist Politics*, 1983, *Freedom, Equality and the Market*, 1986, *Politics and Class Analysis*, 1987, and *Choice and Rationality in Social Theory*, 1988. He previously held a chair at the University of Liverpool in England.

Notes on Contributors

Frans The. S. Kerstholt graduated from the University of Groningen in 1970. He teaches at the Sociology Department of the University of Tilburg (The Netherlands). He is at the moment engaged in a theoretical and methodological critique of the mainstream of current stratification research which in his view fails to provide proper micro-macro linkages.

Markku Kivinen, is a research fellow, Academy of Finland (Licentiate of Political Sciences, University of Helsinki). He has published on the theory of the state and on class analysis. He is author of *Parempien piirien ihmisiä* (People who move in better circles), 1987 and co-author of *Suomalaiset luokkakuvassa* (The Finns in a Class Photo), 1984. He has participated in Erik Olin Wright's project on Class Structure and Class Consciousness since 1981. Editor of *Acta Sociologica*, 1985–1987.

David Knights is a Senior Lecturer in the Department of Management Sciences, UMIST. He has undertaken research in the areas of equal opportunity and management control. He is joint organizer of the UMIST/ASTON Labour Process Conferences and is editor, with Hugh Willmott, of *Job Redesign, Gender and the Labour Process, Managing the Labour Process* and *New Technology and the Labour Process*.

Reinhard Kreckel is Professor of Sociology in the University of Erlangen – Nuremburg (F. R. G.). His latest books are *Soziologisches Denken* (3rd ed., 1982), *Soziale Ungleichheiten* 1983 and *Regionalistische Bewegungen in Westeuropa* 1985. Currently, he is writing a book on *The Political Sociology of Social Inequality*.

Hakon Leiulfsrud is a Research Associate in the Department of Sociology, University of Uppsala. His work has focused on recent developments in the class structure in the Scandinavian and British context. He is presently conducting a comparative study of Sweden, Finland, the United States and the United Kingdom analyzing "Female Wage Employment in the Post-War Period."

Wolfgang Littek is a Professor of Industrial Sociology, Sociology of Work and Organizations at the University of Bremen, West Germany. He has taught formerly at the University of Munich, and was educated in Economics and Sociology at both Munich and Northwestern Universities. He has completed a number of research projects and published extensively on theory and methodology, white-collar workers and their class position, technology and skill formation and the rationalization of work. He is an active member of the International Sociological Association's Research Committee on the "Sociology of Work."

Jane Marceau is currently Professor of Public Policy at the Australian National University. Previously Professor of Sociology, University of Liverpool, U.K., she has also taught at diverse academic institutions, including the University of Paris X (Nanterre), INSEAD and Manchester Business School, and spent three years full-time in the OECD. Major interests include class and all manifestations of social and economic inequality. Major publications include *Class and Status in France*, Oxford University Press 1977, *Masters of Business?* (with R. Whitley and A. Thomas), Tavistock 1981, *Education, Urban Development and Local Initiatives*, OECD 1983 and *A Family Business? The Creation of an International Business Elite*, Cambridge University Press 1989. She is currently working on three projects: the organizational impact of the introduction of new technology in large firms on their clients and suppliers; the relation between training and career structures in private industry and the industry-education interface; and the impact of organizational arrangements on public compliance with government policies.

Harri Melin is a Professor of Sociology at the University of Tampere in the Department of Sociology and Social Psychology and has been extensively involved on research on social class in Scandinavia, currently as a member of the Finnish Class Project.

Glenn Morgan M. A. (Cantab.), M. A. (Essex) was a Senior Lecturer in Sociology at Bradford and Ilkley Community College and a Visiting Fellow at the Management Centre, University of Bradford. Currently he is employed in the Financial Services Research Centre at UMIST. He has published various articless on the textile and tobacco industries and is currently completing a book on *Organizations in Society*.

Harvie Ramsay is Lecturer in Industrial Relations at Strathclyde University. He has worked on a number of areas related to the industrial democracy question, and also on the implications of new technology, particularly office computerization, and on financial participation schemes. He has also written numerous items on the issues raised by transnational corporations for labour responses and rights, including a report for the Australian government.

Dennis Smith studied modern history at Cambridge and sociology at the London School of Economics. Following a period as a lecturer in sociology at Leicester University he moved to Aston University where he is currently a Senior Lecturer in the Management Centre. His previous publications include: *Conflict and Compromise: Class Formation in English Society 1830–1914*, Routledge 1982, *Barrington Moore: Violence, Morality and Political Change*, Macmillan 1983 and *The Chicago School: A Liberal Critique of Capitalism*, Macmillan 1988 as well as several papers on aspects of history, sociology and management. Recent major projects have included a study of industrial, residential and political development in South West Birmingham, as part of the ESRC Initiative on Changing Urban and Regional Systems.

Chris Smith is Associate Fellow, Work Organization Research Centre, and Lecturer in Industrial Relations, Aston University. He studied sociology at North East London Polytechnic and Briston University, and has worked at Aston since 1982. He has researched and written on social class and white-collar unions, as well as completed studies on managerial strategies towards restructuring the labour process. He is author of *Technical Workers: Class, Labour and Trade Unionism*, and co-author of *White-Collar Workers, Trade Unions and Class* (with Pete Armstrong, Bob Carter and Theo Nichols). He is also co-author of a forthcoming book *Innovations in Work Organization: The Cadbury Experience* (with John Child and Michael Rowlinson).

Timo Toivonen is Associate Professor of Sociology at Turku School of Economics and the author of several publications on classes and strata, more recently also on classes and consumption. He will soon publish a book on classes and strata in Finland 1930–1985.

John Urry M. A., Ph. D. (Cambridge). Currently Professor of Sociology and Head of Department, University of Lancaster, U. K., and the author/joint author of *Reference Groups and the Theory of Revolution* 1973, *Social Theory as Science* 1975, 1982, *The Anatomy of Capitalist Societies* 1981, *Capital, Labour and the Middle Classes* 1983, *Localities, Class and Gender* 1985, *The End of Organized Capitalism* 1987, *Contemporary British Society* 1988, *Restructuring, Class and Gender* 1989.

Hugh Willmott is a Lecturer in the Management Centre, University of Aston. His research activity has been in the areas of managerial work, management control and accounting regulation. He is a joint organizer of the UMIST/ASTON Labour Process Conferences and has published in various management, sociology, psychology and accounting journals.

Alison E. Woodward is a Professor in Sociology and Anthropology at the University of Antwerp and the Free University in Brussels (Vesalius College). Her work has focused on issues in urban bureaucracies and the position of women in the family. She is presently working on a book about cross-class families and beginning research on bureaucratic cultures within the EEC.

Index